THE TWO HORIZONS OLD TES

J. GORDON McCONVILLE and CRAIG BARTHOLOMEW, *General Editors*

Two features distinguish THE TWO HORIZONS OLD TESTAMENT COMMENTARY series: theological exegesis and theological reflection.

Exegesis since the Reformation era and especially in the past two hundred years emphasized careful attention to philology, grammar, syntax, and concerns of a historical nature. More recently, commentary has expanded to include social-scientific, political, or canonical questions and more.

Without slighting the significance of those sorts of questions, scholars in THE TWO HORIZONS OLD TESTAMENT COMMENTARY locate their primary interests on theological readings of texts, past and present. The result is a paragraph-by-paragraph engagement with the text that is deliberately theological in focus.

Theological reflection in THE TWO HORIZONS OLD TESTAMENT COMMENTARY takes many forms, including locating each Old Testament book in relation to the whole of Scripture — asking what the biblical book contributes to biblical theology — and in conversation with constructive theology of today. How commentators engage in the work of theological reflection will differ from book to book, depending on their particular theological tradition and how they perceive the work of biblical theology and theological hermeneutics. This heterogeneity derives as well from the relative infancy of the project of theological interpretation of Scripture in modern times and from the challenge of grappling with a book's message in Greco-Roman antiquity, in the canon of Scripture and history of interpretation, and for life in the admittedly diverse Western world at the beginning of the twenty-first century.

THE TWO HORIZONS OLD TESTAMENT COMMENTARY is written primarily for students, pastors, and other Christian leaders seeking to engage in theological interpretation of Scripture.

Psalms

Geoffrey W. Grogan

WILLIAM B. EERDMANS PUBLISHING COMPANY
GRAND RAPIDS, MICHIGAN / CAMBRIDGE, U.K.

© 2008 Geoffrey W. Grogan
All rights reserved

Published 2008 by
Wm. B. Eerdmans Publishing Co.
2140 Oak Industrial Drive N.E., Grand Rapids, Michigan 49505 /
P.O. Box 163, Cambridge CB3 9PU U.K.
www.eerdmans.com

Printed in the United States of America

14 13 12 11 10 09 08   7 6 5 4 3 2 1

Library of Congress Cataloging-in-Publication Data

Grogan, Geoffrey.
    Psalms / Geoffrey W. Grogan.
        p.   cm.   — (The two horizons Old Testament commentary)
    Includes bibliographical references and index.
    ISBN 978-0-8028-2706-7 (pbk.: alk. paper)
    1. Bible. O.T. Psalms — Commentaries.   I. Title.

    BS1430.53.G76   2008
    223'.207 — dc22

                                                    2007051594

Contents

Preface

It has been a privilege to write this commentary and I am thankful to the Lord for all the new insight, encouragement, and challenge that have come to me through intensive study of this important part of Holy Scripture. I am grateful to the publishers for their invitation to me to write this volume. I owe a quite special debt to my editor, Professor Gordon McConville, for the many helpful comments and suggestions he has made to me in connection with this enterprise. The work would have been much poorer without his help.

I have benefited much from discussions, either face-to-face or by correspondence, with various friends, many but not all of them former or present colleagues on the teaching staff of the International Christian College, Glasgow, who have made suggestions about content and bibliography. Among these friends should be mentioned Darrel Cosden, Roy Kearsley, Tony Lane, Michael Lefebvre, Fergus Macdonald, Eryl Rowlands, David Smith, and Howard Taylor. Special thanks are due to my niece, Joy, and her husband, the Reverend Derek Guest, who kindly checked the manuscript for readability and pastoral relevance, and also to a friend, the Reverend Malcolm Maclean, who did the same. I am grateful also to Christian Focus Publications, who accepted and published my volume *Prayer, Praise and Prophecy: A Theology of the Book of Psalms*, which, after many years of loving and studying the Psalms, set me on the track of writing about them. As always, the patience and support of my wife, Eva, have been indispensable.

What I owe to my students, both at the International Christian College (and its predecessors) and at the Scottish Baptist College, is beyond calculation. Their enthusiasm for the study of the Psalms has been most inspiring, and classroom interaction has always been stimulating. I well recall one young lady asking an apparently very simple question, which I had to confess I could not answer (always good for a teacher, so long as it does not happen all the time). I searched the literature in vain and then telephoned a friend, an acknowledged international expert on the book of Psalms, and was almost relieved to hear him say, "I don't know, and in fact nobody knows!"

I have benefited greatly from the research and writings of others and especially, because this is a theological commentary, from those who have made substantial theological comments on particular psalms. Many could be mentioned, but I am aware of a special debt to the writings of Derek Kidner and Michael Wilcock.

The commentary is based on the text of the New International Version, and I am grateful to its publishers for permission to quote extensively from it. I make clear where I have used some other version. The paragraphing system used in a particular English version should never be treated as sacrosanct, but that employed in the NIV has strong merits and is often, though not always, reflected in the way the commentary on particular psalms is organized.

Nobody knows whether the process of putting the Psalter together into its ultimate shape was the work of one or more redactors, and so I have normally employed the singular to avoid the frequent repetition of the clumsy "redactor or redactors" or else "redactor(s)," which raises questions as to whether a singular or plural verb should be used.

In accordance with the policy of the series, inclusive rather than gender-specific language has been employed where appropriate. I have followed the example of Leslie Allen, who uses inclusive language except where it would misrepresent the culture of the text, and he is probably correct in holding that cultural factors suggest that all the psalms were authored by men.[1] Not to adopt this practice would mean the use of either "he or she" or "she or he" many hundreds of times in the exegetical section of the commentary, as Konrad Schaefer does in his. I hope this will not cause offense to female readers.

---

1. Allen, *Psalms 101–150*, viii. Sheppard ("Theology," 148) is, however, unsure if this widely held assumption is correct.

Important Advice to the Reader

Readers rarely read a substantial commentary on a particular biblical book right through unless they are engaged on some major project that requires them to do so. Because this commentary contains much more than exegesis, readers are advised to treat all the material apart from the exegesis as a volume for consecutive reading. On the assumption that readers are going to follow this advice, I have not given many cross-references, except in the exegesis.

I have tried to follow a logical pattern in the arrangement of the volume, and the appendix is an example of how the earlier material may be employed in preparation for preaching. It is my fervent hope and prayer that readers who are also preachers or teachers will be stimulated to introduce their listeners to more and more of the riches of this wonderful part of Holy Scripture.

Abbreviations

ANET	J. B. Pritchard, ed., *Ancient Near Eastern Texts Relating to the Old Testament*, 3rd ed. Princeton: Princeton University Press, 1969
BZAW	Beihefte zur Zeitschrift für die alttestamentliche Wissenschaft
ESV	English Standard Version
ET(s)	English translation(s)
FOTL	Forms of Old Testament Literature
IBD	*Illustrated Bible Dictionary*, ed. J. D. Douglas, et al. 3 vols. Wheaton, IL: Tyndale, 1980
Int	*Interpretation*
JBL	*Journal of Biblical Literature*
JETS	*Journal of the Evangelical Theological Society*
JSOT	*Journal for the Study of the Old Testament*
JSOTSup	Journal for the Study of the Old Testament Supplements
JTS	*Journal of Theological Studies*
KJV	King James (Authorized) Version
LXX	Septuagint
mg.	margin
MS(S)	manuscript(s)
MT	Masoretic text
NASB	New American Standard Bible
NBC	*New Bible Commentary: 21st Century Edition*, ed. D. A. Carson et al. Downers Grove, IL: InterVarsity Press, 1994
NDBT	*New Dictionary of Biblical Theology*, ed. T. D. Alexander and B. S. Rosner. Downers Grove, IL: InterVarsity Press, 2000
NEB	New English Bible
NIV	New International Version
NRSV	New Revised Standard Version

NT	New Testament
OT	Old Testament
OTL	Old Testament Library
REB	Revised English Bible
RSV	Revised Standard Version
SBET	*Scottish Bulletin of Evangelical Theology*
SBL	Society of Biblical Literature
SBLDS	Society of Biblical Literature Dissertation Series
SJT	*Scottish Journal of Theology*
TB	*Tyndale Bulletin*
VT	*Vetus Testamentum*
WBC	Word Biblical Commentary

N.B. *Kethib* ("read") and *Qere* ("written") are Masoretic terms, indicating respectively the Hebrew consonantal text and the alternative reading recommended by the Masoretes.

In transliterating the Hebrew consonants בּ, גּ, דּ, כּ, פּ, תּ *(b, g, d, k, p, t)*, no distinction has been made between the hard and soft forms.

Introduction

This commentary series is aimed primarily at students and pastors, so this introduction is intended to provide general information to aid the exegesis of the text. I will therefore deal mostly with scholarly views now generally regarded as valuable for this purpose.

The Familiar and Yet Unfamiliar World of the Psalms

Biblical introduction helps us to live imaginatively in the biblical world so that we can read Scripture from the standpoint of its original readers. We shall never do this perfectly, and many modern writers are deeply skeptical about the possibility of our doing it at all. Some go further still, denying that there is any value in the attempt. These questions will be addressed later, but meantime we will assume it to be both desirable and, at least to some extent, possible.

If we accept the NT approach to the OT, we will see that Christians worship the same God as the OT believers. Our understanding is greatly enriched by his supreme revelation in Christ, but this revelation builds on the earlier disclosures of his character and purposes recorded in the OT.

Ancient writers and modern readers share many common emotions. This is why we can still read ancient literature and find it engaging with our feelings and many of our human concerns. This is true of Scripture and nowhere more so than in the book of Psalms, which touches the full range of human emotion in all its heights and depths, its joys and sorrows. This is not only because it is poetry and as such has an important emotional quality, but also because all these feelings are poured out in prayer and praise to the God of the psalmists, who is also our God.

Yet although Christians have a real sense of spiritual kinship with David and other writers of the psalms, and so feel somewhat at home in the Psalter, we are also conscious of real differences. We need always to bear in mind the difference between the two horizons, the psalm author's and our own. The matter is even more complex, for, as we shall see, we should not only read each psalm as a distinct piece of literature but also in terms of its place within the whole Psalter.

The psalms make reference to historical events in which God reveals, saves, and judges. Because these poems belong to different periods of history, they reflect this feature in their historical references. If there are psalms either by or about David, there is real value too in studying his story as told in 1 and 2 Samuel and in 1 Chronicles. The complete Psalter was not put together until a late period, certainly after the exile, so that those who first read it as a whole knew they were heirs to a long history and to many acts of God in his dealings with them.

There are also geographical references, especially to Jerusalem, but also to other places in the land and to the nations round about. Some passages reflect the type of land, especially the rocky terrain of Judah. For instance, 65:9-13, with its promise of large harvests, begins with the streams being filled up with water. After months of complete dryness, southern Israel's wadis flow once more. We encounter the farming methods of the day when the psalmist writes of the irrigation streams (1:3) and of water from a fountain (36:9). The weapons of war belong to that time and place, for instance, the bow, the spear, the shield (46:9).

The most important aspects of the background, however, are religio-cultural. The Psalter is the worship book of a theocratic nation that had religious institutions on a national scale, and these had a marked physical dimension. There was a sanctuary, there were priests, sacrifices, and special regulations governing them, regulations too for vows.

It is good to get to know the Psalter's background as fully as possible. George Adam Smith's *Historical Geography of the Holy Land* is about a hundred years old but it has never been bettered.

Scholars have taken many different approaches to understanding the Psalms. This introduction will attempt to define, illustrate, and estimate the value of these types of study or "criticism."[1]

---

1. For an introduction to the various approaches of contemporary scholarship to the OT, including the Psalms, see Baker and Arnold, eds., *Face of OT Studies.*

Textual Criticism

The accuracy of the text is vitally important for literature considered inspired and authoritative. The main textual sources for the Psalms are the Masoretic Text (MT), the Dead Sea Scrolls, and the Septuagint (LXX).

Oral traditions of pronunciation and meaning are more basic than written, for the latter depend on the former. Moreover, even if general rules of pronunciation and meaning in a language are known, exceptions in pronunciation (e.g., in English between "through" and "tough") and developments in meaning ("let" meant the opposite of "permit" in Elizabethan English) need to be taught to avoid mispronunciation and misunderstanding.

The need for attention to oral tradition was particularly great in Hebrew, for its written text consisted mostly of consonants. The vowel sounds were known to the reader but were not part of the text. How important then for that vocalic tradition to be preserved! The rabbis strongly emphasized memorization, so promoting accurate oral transmission.

The Masoretes were Jewish scholars who devised a sign system for vowels and who suggested occasional alternatives (the *Qere*) where they questioned traditional pronunciations (the *Kethib*). They produced major editions of the Psalms during the ninth and tenth centuries AD. It is uncertain when they started work, but the Talmud, compiled about AD 500, shows no knowledge of them.

Scholars now generally agree that the MT, our main Hebrew authority, although not without problems, should be taken very seriously. Its chief contender for centuries was the LXX. More recent manuscript discoveries, especially the Dead Sea Scrolls, have tended to increase rather than diminish confidence in the MT, although occasionally they support LXX readings diverging from it.

The LXX is the Greek translation normally employed in the NT because it was used in the Dispersion synagogues. It is even quoted occasionally when it differs significantly from the MT, but the essential point is usually little affected. It was translated at Alexandria, the chief intellectual center of Dispersion Judaism, over several generations. The Psalter appears to have been one of the last books translated, and most textual critics place it in the second century BC at the latest, but some have recently argued for a first century AD date. The earlier date has, however, been well supported by T. F. Williams among others.[2] The LXX is strongly literal and unidiomatic, often quite woodenly so, but this is helpful as testimony to the wording of the Hebrew manuscripts the translators used.

---

2. Williams, "Towards a Date."

The LXX psalm numbers differ from the MT, as the former unites 9 and 10 in book 1 and Psalms 114 and 115 in book 5; it also divides Psalms 116 and 147 into two. Accordingly the LXX numbers differ by one from 10 onward and then coincide with the MT for the final three psalms. Also it has an extra item, Psalm 151, although it declares this to be "outside the number."

The Dead Sea Scrolls include many psalm fragments, large and small. One manuscript of major importance contains all or parts of thirty-nine psalms, although, apart from book 1, these differ in their order from the MT and the LXX. There are also some noncanonical psalms. All the psalms in book 5 from 118 onward, except 120 (which was probably in a damaged section of this scroll), are included, plus a few from book 4. Psalms 121–132 follow the normal order. Taking all the evidence from Qumran together, however, it tends to support the Masoretic order as the major one, and the superscriptions vary little from the traditional text.

Some passages are difficult to translate, occasionally almost impossible, so commentators may suggest textual emendation. Some Hebrew letters are very similar in appearance, and even the most meticulous scribe may make an occasional mistake. Conjectural emendation should, however, be a last resort, to be suggested tentatively and modestly. All translators and commentators need to respect the manuscripts, for "the task is still to comment on the . . . text, not to remake it."[3]

Sense Rhythms of the Psalms

The poetic nature of the psalms is given visual expression in the way modern translations set out the text.[4] Their aesthetic character can hardly be missed as we see the symmetry of Psalm 8, the vigor of 18, the pounding waves in 93, the wonderful descriptiveness of 104, and the combined comprehensiveness and succinctness of 148.

Some reader may say, "But what matters to me is truth. Beauty may be a bonus but it is hardly relevant." But the beauty is no mere package for the truth, for in the aesthetic features the feelings of the psalmists are expressed, and these aid our awareness of their response to God's revelation. W. P.

---

3. Eaton, *Psalms of the Way*, 47.

4. For more information on psalmic poetry, see Miller, *Interpreting Psalms*, 29-47; Seybold, *Introducing Psalms*, 59-79; Wilson, *Psalms*, 1:31-57; Longman, *How to Read Psalms*, 95-110. For fuller studies of biblical poetry, see Alter, *Art of Biblical Poetry*; Kugel, *Idea of Biblical Poetry*; Fokkelman, *Reading Biblical Poetry*. Fokkelman gives helpful poetical analyses of several psalms.

Brown is right in affirming that biblical poetry is poetry with a purpose and that the psalms not only express but also impart and teach. He goes on to say, "To read the psalms is to *hear* their rhythms; to hear them is to *behold* the rich imagery they convey; to behold the psalms is to *feel* them in all their pain and promise; and to feel them is, ultimately, to 'taste and see that the LORD is good' (Ps 34:8a)."[5] Here then the Word of God comes to us through the many avenues of communication with which he has endowed us. We might add of course that this happens when the hearing, beholding and feeling are accompanied by or lead to believing engagement with all that is being conveyed. Many examples of the value of aesthetic appreciation for interpretation may be found in such commentaries as those by Derek Kidner, Robert Davidson, Michael Wilcock, and Konrad Schaefer.[6]

The characteristic rhythms of the Psalter are more of sense than of sound. Two or more poetic lines form an idea unit, presenting similar or contrasting thoughts or mutually enriching development. In this way the reader is slowed down somewhat and given time to meditate on the thought presented. This parallelism is also a feature of other ancient Semitic poetry, as found, for instance, at Ugarit.[7]

This feature was first identified for modern readers by Robert Lowth in 1753. He distinguished three types, calling them synonymous, antithetical, and synthetic parallelism, with the third taking several forms. Examples of synonymous parallelism are in 9:1-5, antithetical in 37:21-22, and synthetic in 4:2-3. Antithetical parallelism is the easiest to recognize. It is very common in the book of Proverbs and in Ps 1:6 it summarizes a whole psalm.

The value of the third category has long been disputed, largely because of its miscellaneous nature, but more recently the first has also come under fire. In this poetry exact synonyms are comparatively rare, and apparently synonymous lines often approximate to the synthetic, with line b subtly modifying line a, so that together they present a fuller truth. In 104:33, for instance, the psalmist says, "I will sing to the LORD all my life; I will sing praise to my God as long as I live." The phrases "all my life" and "as long as I live" are exactly parallel, but line b indicates both the nature of the song and the psalmist's sense of relationship to God; yet we cannot dispense with line a, which shows the psalmist's God to be the LORD, Yahweh, God of Israel, the only true God.

---

5. Brown, *Seeing the Psalms*, 2. His book is a valuable exploration of the use of poetic metaphor in the Psalter.

6. Kidner, *Psalms 1–72; Psalms 73–150;* Davidson, *Vitality of Worship;* Wilcock, *Psalms 1–72; Psalms 73–150;* Schaefer, *Psalms.*

7. See Craigie, *Ugarit,* for a balanced assessment of the relationship between Ugaritic and OT forms of poetry and of thought.

In the Psalms the uniting of beauty and truth at once stimulates the mind and moves the heart. Truth presented in parallelism demands not just acceptance but reflection.[8] Tremper Longman III expresses this kind of poetic pattern as "A, what's more, B," and he makes the good point that the view held before Lowth, which interpreted two parallel lines as if they always say different things, and Lowth's view need to be used to modify each other, for there is truth in each.[9]

So-called synonymous and synthetic parallelism are not, however, identical types. Gerald Wilson, who favors "affirming," "opposing," and "advancing" for the three types, shows that in the second and any later lines of the affirming type, continuity is maintained with both the structure and meaning of the first line while at the same time the thought progresses. In advancing parallelism, however, the thought continues, "but without any obvious concern to maintain grammatical, structural, or thematic similarity to the initial line."[10] In 37, for instance, verses 1 and 2 are synonymous or affirming parallelism, while 3 and 4 are synthetic or advancing.

Such poetry gives great freedom to the poet, who has many different ways of expressing his mind and heart. Wilson points out how in three psalms line 1 is differently developed in line 2, so that "Sing to the LORD a new song," is followed by "sing to the LORD, all the earth" in 96:1, by "for he has done marvelous things" in 98:1, and by "his praise in the assembly of the saints" in 149:1.[11]

It is important to read the Psalms imaginatively and with sensitivity to this stylistic phenomenon as no other literary feature is more important for their appreciation and understanding.[12] I will deal with other features under "Rhetorical or Literary Criticism."

Historical and Source Criticism

The first thing I look for in any book is its publication date. Why? Because every writer reflects her or his historical background, so that we need historical imagination as much when entering an old book as when entering an old building. This makes social history very important. Historical criticism is about the historical background to literature. To see a book's relevance to the

---

8. Clines, "Parallelism of Greater Precision," 95.

9. Longman, *How to Read Psalms,* 97. See also Kugel, *Idea of Biblical Poetry,* 52.

10. Wilson, *Psalms,* 1:33. See his whole discussion, 39-48.

11. Wilson, *Psalms,* 1:45. He then gives further examples, 45-46.

12. Mays, *Psalms,* 5.

writer's day is at least to start on the road to seeing its relevance now. The related discipline of source criticism seeks to discover any earlier documents behind the books we have.

Many psalms cannot be dated even approximately, but all we can glean about their background has real value, and the scholar should never give up asking historical questions. Such questions are crucial for the Gospels and important for the OT historical and prophetical books, but less important for largely devotional literature like the Psalms. Like the book of Job, many psalms are timeless, reflecting fundamental difficulties, agonies, and spiritual problems that godly people meet in every age. The same applies to many causes for thanksgiving. Even so, historical information is useful. Also knowledge of the general OT cultural background will aid interpretation.

The Hebrew Psalter has no general heading. "Psalms" comes from the Latin title *Liber Psalmorum,* itself from ψαλμός, *psalmos* ("playing strings"), the LXX rendering of מִזְמוֹר, *mizmôr* ("stringed instruments"), which heads many psalms. "Psalter" is from ψαλτήριον, *psaltērion* ("stringed instrument"). Codex Vaticanus uses ψαλμός, and Alexandrinus ψαλτήριον. Often "book" was added. The rabbis called it תְּהִלִּים, *tĕhillîm,* "Songs of Praise," and this is apt because, despite its many laments, praise becomes more and more dominant as the book's climax approaches.[13]

Without addressing the wider issues of historical criticism, we can agree with Bullock that the psalms do reflect an accurate picture of OT history. He points out that the order of events and their descriptions are the same as in the historical books, that additional details may be attributed to oral tradition, and that the importance of the period from the book of Exodus to that of Joshua is reflected in the Psalter's historical comments.[14]

Some psalms read like prophetic oracles (e.g., 50 and 110), and the openings of 36 and 45 remind us of the prophetic sense of divine inspiration. In some laments the psalmist knows God has heard him (e.g., 6:8-10; 28:6-8), and he is perhaps responding to a prophetic word given at the temple.

The relationship between psalmists and prophets, however, goes well beyond such features, exhibiting countless links of vocabulary and theme. For instance, the stand of the eighth-century prophets and Jeremiah against excessive ritualism is clearly seen in Psalm 50. Scholarship widely recognizes a close relationship between the two groups, but this has not always been viewed in the same way. Reversing earlier critical views, many scholars now give general

---

13. Wilson, *Psalms,* 1:22.
14. Bullock, *Encountering Psalms,* 102.

chronological priority to the psalmists.[15] R. J. Tournay, however, holds that after the demise of prophecy the Levitical singers revived the prophets' vocabulary and themes, so bringing prophetic theology with its emphasis on the covenant and the messianic promises into the temple worship.[16] There is certainly broad theological harmony between the two groups, so that the themes of the one literary corpus may often be illustrated from the other.

Superscriptions

The superscriptions belong to the biblical text and are in both the MT and the LXX, so predating the NT. They were therefore in our Lord's Bible. The New English Bible should not have omitted them. They represent the earliest material we possess for interpreting the psalms. They are of various kinds, associating them with particular people, giving their composition circumstances, literary types, occasions for use (e.g., "songs of ascents" and "Sabbath"), plus some notes about instruments and tunes. These musical notes underscore the antiquity of the superscriptions, because many are untranslated, showing their meaning had been forgotten. This is particularly impressive when we remember that Hebrew culture tended to stress the importance of memorization. The superscriptions are not unique, for Isaiah 38, Habakkuk 3, and certain sections of the book of Proverbs (Prov 1:1; 10:1; 24:23; 25:1; 30:1; 31:1) also have them. Most were editorial, but it is possible that some were added by the authors.[17]

The LXX Psalter gives some headings not in the MT, for example, ascribing still more to David. Sometimes this is difficult to understand as, for instance, David could not have written 137. These LXX headings can hardly be by the same editors as those in the MT. There are also some variations in the superscriptions to the Targums (Aramaic paraphrases) of the psalms.

Particular superscriptions often make reference to some person or group, preceded by ל, *lĕ*. These are David (3–9, 11–32, 34–41, 51–65, 68–70, 86, 101, 103, 108–10, 122, 124, 131, 133, 138–145), Moses (90), Solomon (72, 127), Jeduthun (39, 62, 77), Heman (88), Ethan (89), Asaph (50, 73–83), and the sons of Korah (42, 44–49, 84, 85, 87, 88). All except David, Moses, and Solomon appear as Levites in the historical books (1 Kgs 4:31; 1 Chr 6:31-44; 15:19; 16:5; 2 Chr 5:12; 29:30).

15. Bellinger traces the development of scholarly thinking on the subject in *Psalmody and Prophecy*, 11.

16. Tournay, *Seeing and Hearing*, vii.

17. A survey of the various theories concerning the superscriptions may be found in Bullock, *Encountering Psalms*, 25-34.

Is לְדָוִד, *lĕdāwid* (lit. "to/for David"), a claim to authorship? See the excursus for a discussion of this. Were Levitical psalms authored by the named persons? Some of them were probably written by later members of the choirs established by Asaph and others named. Psalm 74, for example, unmistakably refers to the destruction of Jerusalem's temple by the Babylonians. This is a different issue from the question of Davidic authorship, as many Davidic psalms make reference to events in David's life, a feature unparalleled in the Levitical psalms.

The term אֱלֹהִים, *'ĕlōhîm* (Elohim), dominates Psalms 42–83 (the "Elohistic Psalter"), instead of יהוה, *yhwh* (Yahweh), which is more common elsewhere. Why? Perhaps these psalms were used where "Yahweh" was already thought too sacred for ordinary use.[18] M. D. Goulder, following John Peters, thinks such psalms originated at the northern shrine of Dan, but it is more likely that northern Levites who felt unable to function at the apostate northern shrines wrote psalms later used at Jerusalem on such occasions as those mentioned in 2 Chronicles 30 and Jer 41:4-5.[19]

What about Psalm 90, headed "a prayer of Moses the man of God"? Its uniqueness in this respect is an impressive witness to the redactor's concern for truth, for the considerable postexilic emphasis on the Mosaic law could well have tempted him to employ Moses' name more often. Not even Psalm 119 has his name attached to it. Beth Tanner's study of Psalm 90, though not concerned with authorship, shows many links of idea and vocabulary between the psalm and pentateuchal passages featuring Moses, especially Exodus 15, 32–34, and Deuteronomy 32 and 33.[20]

Psalms lacking author ascriptions are known as "orphan psalms." The highest concentration, twenty-eight in all, is in book 5, probably the last of the five to be put together. C. Hassell Bullock suggests that by then psalm writing had become commoner among ordinary folk and that names were attached only when the authors were well known.[21] This seems very likely.

Some superscriptions include biographical notes. All but 102 and 142 are in books 1 or 2, and only 102 is not explicitly associated with David. They are discussed in the excursus to this chapter.

Attempts to assign other psalms to specific historical occasions have met with varying success. One psalm's background is crystal clear, for 137 must have been written in the exile or shortly afterward by a returned exile.

18. So Wilcock, *Psalms 1–72*, 152.

19. Goulder, *Psalms of Korah*, 16-22, 35-37; on the latter point see Rendsburg, *Linguistic Evidence*, 103.

20. Tanner, *Psalms*, 85-107.

21. Bullock, *Encountering Psalms*, 25.

Some headings mention the director of music, musical terms such as *maskil* and *miktam*, the songs of ascents, the psalm for the Sabbath, and so on. These will be dealt with under "Psalm Genres and Form Criticism."

Psalm Genres and Form Criticism

The desire for helpful interpretation has been a factor in the emergence of some major theories.[22] Much eighteenth- and nineteenth-century historical and source criticism appeared somewhat meager and uncertain in its results, so it is no surprise to find psalm study taking a new turn early in the twentieth century. Historians were now giving some emphasis to social history, and this new "form criticism" focused attention on the social setting of the psalms.

Literary genre obviously affects interpretation.[23] It does matter whether a psalm is a prayer, hymn, meditation on history, or exhortation. Form criticism, however, goes beyond genre identification in its concern with a psalm's social context, its life setting *(Sitz im Leben),* the purpose of its writing or later adaptation, and the extent to which this purpose determined formal standardization. A nonspecialist can often identify a psalm's genre, but discerning its form *(Gattung)* requires study of its religio-cultural background.

The Psalter's Hebrew title, *Tehillim* ("Praises"), shows it was viewed as a worship manual. This is evident in many psalms, particularly in headings that have instructions for the director of music, references to tunes and instruments, and terms like *miktam* and *maskil*, which are of uncertain meaning but which probably have a worship connection.[24] There are occasionally allusions to a psalm's intended worship setting, for the Sabbath (92), the thank offering (100), the memorial offering (38 and 70). The reference to the dedication of the house (30) is rather obscure.[25] Psalm 136 was probably sung antiphonally (cf. also 24:7-10). We note also David's association with sung worship in Chronicles and the linking of many psalms with the Levites. The Jews had three pilgrim feasts: Passover, associated with the exodus (and the barley harvest); Pentecost, linked in NT times with Sinai (and the wheat harvest); and Tabernacles, associated with the wilderness wanderings (and the fruit

---

22. Mays, *Psalms*, 9.
23. Longman writes helpfully on this, *How to Read Psalms*, 19-36.
24. For all these terms see Kidner, *Psalms 1–72*, 36-43.
25. See the comments on this psalm.

harvest). Two large collections were sung at the pilgrim feasts: the Songs of Ascents (120–134), enlarged as the Great Hallel (120–136), and the Egyptian Hallel (113–118), which was sung especially at the Passover.

Even though "song of ascents" is variously interpreted, these certainly appear to have been sung by pilgrims traveling to Jerusalem's annual feasts. They vary in literary type,[26] but seem appropriate for people anticipating corporate worship. The Mishnah says the Levites sang them on the fifteen temple steps, but we cannot be sure if this was taking place prior to the final redaction of the Psalter.

References to other aspects of worship occur, and some scholars stress their importance while others note their paucity. J. H. Hayes, for instance, suggests reading the Leviticus chapters on sacrificial ritual alongside the prayers in the Psalms because ritual and spoken word go together.[27] Nahum Sarna goes too far in the opposite direction, seeing prayer and sacrifice as kept in discrete domains to distinguish Israel's worship from contemporary pagan patterns.[28] In fact, 2 Chr 23:18 clearly links them.

The word תּוֹדָה, *tôdâ,* in the heading of Psalm 100, means either "for thanksgiving" or "for the thank offering," which the worshiper may have viewed as one. There are several references to thank offerings (e.g., 54:6; 107:22; 116:17; cf. 27:6), and one to a votive offering (66:13-15), which often expressed gratitude. It seems strange that the ark is explicitly mentioned only once in the Psalter (132:8), but 68:1 quotes Num 10:35, which relates to its movement. Psalm 40 was apparently written and offered in place of a sacrifice, and then could become available to other worshipers. Klaus Seybold detects here a clue to the collecting of lament psalms and those that combine lament and praise.[29]

The comparative paucity of ritual references may reflect the theology the psalmists shared with the prophets, who, facing exaggerated ritualism, stressed instead the worshiper's attitude. Right sacrifice is required, but is second to obedience (40:6-8; cf. 1 Sam 15:22-23) and must not be offered in a pagan spirit (Ps 50:5, 8-15, 23). Psalm 141:2 anticipates later Judaism in spiritualizing sacrifice as prayer. Psalm 51 strikes a balance, for it emphasizes the heart without setting aside sacrifice altogether (vv. 16-19), although some consider its ending to have been written later.

Wilson reminds us to distinguish the occasion *from* which a psalm

---

26. Wilson, *Psalms,* 1:58.
27. Hayes, *Understanding Psalms,* 57.
28. Sarna, *On Psalms,* 9-10.
29. Seybold, *Introducing Psalms,* 39-43.

was produced and that *for* which it was written; the latter has tended to dominate form-critical discussion.[30] God's personal dealings with the psalmist are one thing; the use of his psalm in corporate worship is often something else.

Form criticism takes much interest in public worship occasions like festivals, which tend to be somewhat stylized. Biblical form criticism was founded by Hermann Gunkel (1862-1932), and has had a considerable influence on all subsequent discussion of the Psalms. What distinguished his work from normal genre classification was the way he sought to link particular types of psalms to their life setting, especially in Israel's worship. Like Julius Wellhausen, a major figure in nineteenth-century source criticism, he viewed most psalms as personal poetry but as adapted for ritual ends by the religious community. Explicitly communal psalms, however, were linked to worship from the first. He identified five major psalm forms (hymns, laments of the people, laments of the individual, individual songs of thanksgiving, and "spiritual poems"), plus minor ones. He knew that traditional folk stories and children's tales often assume a set shape after centuries of repetition, and he considered something similar had happened with the psalms.[31]

Sigmund Mowinckel (1884-1965) developed Gunkel's views in a new direction. He had been trained in social anthropology as well as biblical criticism. Since Babylon's seasonal nature cult centered in an annual festival when the king, representing the god Marduk, was ritually humiliated and reenthroned in a drama thought to ensure the coming of spring, Mowinckel believed something similar took place in Israel at the Feast of Tabernacles, with the Davidic king as the chief actor, and that many psalms took their origin and significance from this. So most psalms were never private prayers but were written specifically for ritual use. For him 93–99 constituted this liturgy's core, and he concluded that all but about ten, the wisdom group, had cultic connections. The exile ended the Davidic monarchy, and so the royal psalms were now viewed as messianic.

Many scholars accepted his views, some even developing them further, while others modified or rejected them. The importance of Tabernacles is still widely recognized, but Artur Weiser, for instance, sees it as the setting for a renewal (perhaps a covenant renewal) ceremony, while H.-J. Kraus thinks it a festival celebrating Jerusalem's connection with David's royal dynasty.

There is, however, scant OT evidence for Mowinckel's view, or even for

---

30. Wilson, *Psalms*, 1:146.

31. Gunkel's major work on the psalms is *The Psalms: A Form-Critical Introduction.*

a regular as distinct from an occasional ceremony of covenant renewal or royal Zion celebration. Many agree with Claus Westermann, who thinks Gunkel's work had real value; but, against Mowinckel, he is unprepared to consider most psalms to have a cultic origin.[32] Erhard Gerstenberger viewed the psalms as originating in family and small-group rituals, although they were later used in worship.

M. R. Hauge's title for his study of the "I" psalms, *Between Sheol and Temple,* is thought-provoking, for these represent the two poles of the world of the Psalms. The psalmists' lives often seem under threat, with the pull of death very great, yet they always have an orientation toward God. In this respect the Psalms, Job, and Jeremiah are at one. We might even compare Ecclesiastes, where an orientation toward God so often modifies the writer's apparent skepticism and stands out clearly at the end. In the Psalter, the strength of this orientation is underlined by the increasing predominance of praise psalms in the last two books.

Westermann identified two main psalm types, laments and praise psalms, with two kinds of the latter, "declarative," proclaiming the divine acts, and "descriptive," focusing on the attributes those acts revealed. Wilson's view is similar, but he puts thanksgiving psalms between lament and praise. They have deep roots in pain, but this is now past and divine deliverance evokes thanksgiving.[33] Bullock draws attention to psalms of trust, which lie between laments and thanksgivings.[34] Here the threat is still present, but the psalmist knows Yahweh will answer his call, because his theology and his experience based on it anchor him in his God. Surprisingly only two of the Songs of Ascents are really thanksgivings (124) or hymns (134), for most are psalms of trust. So then going up to Jerusalem was an expression of faith as well as an opportunity for praise. Employing terms used in the thought of Paul Ricoeur, Walter Brueggemann distinguishes between psalms of orientation, disorientation, and reorientation, and this distinction provides the structure for one of his many books on the Psalms.[35]

So in terms of Sheol and temple we find an ascending scale of overlapping features in the Psalms, from lament through petition, trust, and thanksgiving to hymns in which the Lord is extolled as his people's gracious and faithful Savior.[36] Some of these psalm types seem more like genres than

32. Westermann, *Praise and Lament,* 15-35.

33. Wilson, *Psalms,* 1:65-66.

34. Bullock, *Encountering Psalms,* 165. He identifies those of the individual as 4, 16, 23, 27, 62, and 73, and of the community as 90, 115, 123, 124, 125, and 126.

35. Brueggemann, *Message of Psalms.*

36. Hymns occur, however, as early in the OT as Exod 15 and Judg 5.

forms in the technical sense, and in many psalms several of these elements come together. If they were used in worship by people with varied concerns, however, this brings them into the sphere of form criticism.

At the lament pole, we find complaint against God, against enemies, against oneself, although rarely all in one psalm. Bullock gives a helpful table analyzing the elements in fifteen individual psalms of lament, and he points out that both the psalms of praise and of lament give reasons for their praise or lamenting.[37]

Some of the problems occasioning the laments were self-caused, while some were induced by others, but many were both, because Absalom's rebellion, for instance, had its ultimate cause in David's sin.[38] Where the cause is personal, we expect to find repentance and forgiveness and are surprised at the rarity of its occurrence in the Psalter. Possibly this is because his sin is now past, the psalmist has gratefully accepted forgiveness, and will have already given heartfelt thanks.

Nineteen of the twenty-nine individual psalms of lament occur in book 1 with its Davidic orientation, but there are no communal laments here although there are in books 2-5.[39] In communal laments the enemies are normally foreign nations, which is sometimes true in the individual ones, while in others they are clearly Israelites. At times the latter seem to be manipulating Israel's legal system for their own ends, and Wilson compares the way Jezebel used false testimony to secure Naboth's death.[40]

How were the laments used in worship? The Pentateuch provides for one communal fast, the Day of Atonement (Lev 16), and some of the penitential psalms would be sung then and also perhaps laments like 44, 60, 74, 79, 80, 83, 85, 89, 90, and 137. These could also be used on some of the fast days referred to in Zechariah 7, fasts that were associated with Jerusalem's destruction by the Babylonians. Some individual penitential psalms would be very suitable in association with sin and guilt offerings.

Gerstenberger connects the lament psalms not to the cult but to healing ceremonies within the family circle, a kind of group therapy.[41] Patrick Miller says that his work at least poses a challenge to others to assess theologically the significance of small social groups.[42]

How did the laments come to be written down? Seybold maintains that

37. Bullock, *Encountering Psalms*, 136; for the table see 141-42.
38. See heading to Ps 3.
39. Bullock, *Encountering Psalms*, 139.
40. Wilson, *Psalms*, 1:147-48.
41. Gerstenberger, *Psalms*, 1:5-22.
42. Miller, *Interpreting Psalms*, 7.

writing them down testified to the fact that they had been answered.[43] If so, then, even the darkest laments, such as 88, were really utterances of faith that found a divine response.

In some psalms of faith an assurance of divine help appears quite suddenly, even unexpectedly. What was its cause? W. H. Bellinger Jr. has explored the prophetic oracles in the Psalms, and he sees in many of them the certainty of a hearing. Perhaps this comes through faith operating within the prayer, but, following Joachim Begrich, he thinks the intervention of a cult prophet or priest more likely, because the change of mood is so sudden.[44] Psalm 60:6-8 certainly seems to be an oracle of salvation.[45]

Most thanksgiving psalms are individual while most hymns are communal, but their essential difference is that the thanksgivings normally relate to one divine act of deliverance,[46] while the hymns focus more generally on God himself and his qualities. Westermann's distinction of these as declarative and descriptive psalms of praise, respectively, is widely accepted.[47]

How do the thanksgiving psalms relate to the temple worship? Sometimes the psalmist says he will offer public praise because of what God has done for him (e.g., 22:22-24; 40:9-10; 52:9; 71:15-16). There are also references to thank offerings and vows (e.g., 54:6; 56:12; 66:13-15; 116:12-14, 17-19). The material offering and the thanksgiving song were probably united in one heartfelt act of worship.

Westermann sees an intimate connection between the psalms of declarative and descriptive praise. He writes of the descriptive language in the hymns:

> It is speech directed toward God in the sense that it looks away from the unique occurrence of a specific deliverance and speaks of God's majesty and grace in a summarizing, recapitulating, and descriptive manner. But in Israel this recapitulating praise which brings together descriptions never lost its connection with the unique, concrete intervention which was experienced in the history of the people or of the individual.[48]

So then praise never took its rise from speculation about God's being and nature, but rather the psalmist was deeply moved by God's acts for his

---

43. Seybold, *Introducing Psalms*, 42.

44. Bellinger, *Psalmody and Prophecy*, 78-81.

45. Seybold, *Introducing Psalms*, 115.

46. Even Ps 18, which, in terms of its superscription, might seem an exception, gives a graphic description of a particular divine intervention.

47. Westermann, *Praise and Lament*, 22.

48. Westermann, *Praise and Lament*, 118.

people.[49] In Psalm 145, for instance, he is praised for his greatness, goodness, faithfulness, righteousness, and much else. These are not simply abstract qualities, for the psalmist, writing of God's greatness, immediately refers to his wonderful and awesome works, evidence of that greatness. No doubt he could have done the same with the other divine attributes he extols. An important group of hymns are the יהוה מָלָךְ, *yhwh mālāk*, psalms (93, 96, 97, 99). They commence with or contain this affirmation, meaning "The LORD reigns!" and they celebrate his supreme sovereignty. Others contiguous with them (94, 95, 98) have thematic links with them even if these words are absent.[50]

We cannot read the Psalms without becoming aware of the deep feelings stirred whenever the people thought of God's house and the worship there. Several classes of psalms call for special attention in this connection.

In some the psalmist cannot get to worship, and he expresses great longing for God's house (42, 43, 63, 84). Psalms 42 and 84 are ascribed to Levites, and 43 appears to be a continuation of 42; but 63 is not Levitical but is ascribed to David, so that this longing was not confined to those most professionally involved in regular worship.

Then there are entrance psalms like 15 and 24, which specify the moral and spiritual conditions for worship there. Here we see the prophetic emphasis on the heart in contrast with a ritualism that may lack true spiritual commitment. Psalms 100:4 and 118:20 also relate to entering the temple precincts.

Psalms 42 and 84 express the delights of pilgrimage, and the same emotions can be discerned in the Zion psalms like 46, 48, 76, 87, and 125. The people loved to visit Jerusalem, not simply as their capital, but to worship their God in his temple. Such psalms were probably sung when Jerusalem was thronged with worshipers during festivals. The Songs of Ascents (120–134) were certainly sung on such occasions, and the Egyptian Hallel (113–118) at least at Passover and Tabernacles, while at Pentecost 29 and 68 were employed.

The distinction between genre and form comes out clearly in connection with the royal psalms, which relate to human kings appointed by God, for there are real differences of genre between them, some being laments and others thanksgivings, while form critics often see them all as used in acts of worship where the king had a special role. We have already encountered the views about this of Mowinckel and those influenced by him.

How many royal psalms are there? Gunkel listed 2, 18, 20, 21, 45, 72, 89 (tentatively), 101, 110, 132, 144:1-11, and this list has become somewhat standard. Psalm 101 is included because its author appears to have considerable

---

49. Longman, *How to Read Psalms*, 25-26.
50. See comment on 93:1.

power in the land. J. H. Eaton, however, sees more than fifty as royal psalms, but many psalms scholars remain unconvinced. Bellinger, for instance, attacks Eaton's view that the "I" lament psalms are royal, seeing them simply as a class of laments.[51] Miller is more positive: "The connection of the psalms to the Messiah and the christological use of them by the early church would be even more direct should such an interpretation be on the right track."[52] If the Davidic references in the superscriptions relate to authorship and are reliable, there could be even more, although we should remember that when pursued by Saul David was simply king-elect. Some scholars have even included 119 because of the connection of the king and the תּוֹרָה, *tôrâ*.[53]

Much recent psalm research has been stimulated by Wilson's studies in the royal psalms found at special points, the "seams" between books 1-3 of the Psalter.[54] He sees their presence there as indicating the importance of this theme for the final redactor. He maintains too that book 4 was put together to move the reader's attention from the human to the divine kingship, hence the presence of *yhwh mālāk* and similar psalms in it. Some writers have noted that book 5 takes up the kingship theme again, especially in 110 and 132, thus giving the Psalter as a whole a messianic focus. The importance of the Davidic messianic kingship theme in the whole Psalter has been expounded and defended by David Mitchell.[55]

As we shall soon see, a didactic motive appears in the Psalter's final arrangement, and teaching on God's ways with his people is often an important byproduct of the experiences of the psalmists. There are some psalms, however, where a didactic purpose is particularly apparent, and these are of several different types.

The historical psalms draw lessons from God's dealings with his people. Psalm 78 is explicitly didactic, opening with the words, "O my people, hear my teaching." After an important general reference to God's deeds and law, Israel's history from the exodus to David is surveyed, highlighting both his goodness and the rebelliousness of his people. This is the general thrust of 106, while 105 focuses entirely on God's great deeds, with a reference to the law toward the close.

Psalms 1 and 19 give considerable prominence to the Torah, and the Torah completely dominates 119. It is referred to in other psalms (18, 25, 33, 68, 78, 81, 89, 93, 94, 99, 103, 105, 111, 112, 147, 148), not always necessarily in refer-

---

51. Bellinger, *Psalmody and Prophecy*, 29-31.
52. Miller, *Interpreting Psalms*, 8.
53. This is argued in detail by Soll, *Psalm 119*, 126-54.
54. See esp. Wilson, "Use of Royal Psalms."
55. D. C. Mitchell, *Message of Psalter*.

ence to the Decalogue or even the Pentateuch but sometimes perhaps to all Scripture then available.[56]

The placing of Psalm 1 at the start of the Psalter is now widely reckoned an encouragement to read the book as Holy Scripture. R. N. Whybray is uncertain about this, holding that although the book of Psalms was probably used in this way there is little evidence it was so designed by its editors.[57] Much depends, of course, on whether תּוֹרָה, *tôrâ,* is used narrowly or broadly here, and it is not easy to decide. Westermann suggested that the Psalter ended with 119 at one time.[58] If so, then two psalms of the *tôrâ* (1 and 119) constituted an inclusio, an envelope for the whole book, highlighting the importance of the Word of God, either with special reference to the Law or to the Psalter. He also points out that the theme of 119 is "not just the Torah in the wider sense . . . but, deliberately and specifically, the statutes and ordinances."[59] If then there was an earlier edition of the Psalter from 1 to 119, it is very doubtful if *tôrâ* in 1 would have had the wider sense at that stage.

Bullock says that in seeking to distill the essence of the Torah, the psalmists and prophets found this not in ritual but in doing God's will (Mic 6:8; Pss 40:6; 50:23; 51:16-17; 141:2), which came to be identified as the Torah.[60]

The wisdom psalm is the most difficult genre to identify or even to describe accurately, and there is no agreed list. Some even regard it as a pseudo-genre.[61] Much of Whybray's book is concerned with the wisdom category and attempts to define and identify wisdom psalms.[62] Among those reasonably happy with the category, such psalms as 1, 37, 49, and 73 would be included. Psalm 37 is the most like the book of Proverbs. Part of the problem is that Israel's wisdom literature was never simply philosophical speculation, for, whether explicitly or implicitly, certain "given" points were recognized, and these often occur in other types of psalms. The Law might not be mentioned specifically, but the OT wisdom writers never questioned it. The one apparent exception (Eccl 7:16) is probably either irony or a reference to self-righteousness. If Psalm 1 may be classified as a wisdom psalm, then here is a clear connection with the Law, or at least with written divine instruction in general.

---

56. Bullock, *Encountering Psalms,* 214. See comment on Ps 1.

57. Whybray, *Reading Psalms.*

58. Westermann, *Praise and Lament,* 252-53.

59. Westermann, *Living Psalms,* p. 296.

60. Bullock, *Encountering Psalms,* 214.

61. See Crenshaw's discussion, *Psalms,* 87-95. Wilson deals with the characteristic terminology of the wisdom literature in *Psalms,* 1:72-73.

62. Whybray, *Reading Psalms,* 37-87.

The form-critical approach dominated much psalm study in the twentieth century, but interest in it has recently diminished. The critical pendulum is swinging again, and there is a renewed interest in the psalms as products of personal piety.[63] Many scholars have come to question whether the work of a substantial number of form critics has yielded results for the interpreter commensurate with the time spent on it,[64] especially if, as many now think, the great influence of Mowinckel has led to some scholarly dead ends. Nevertheless, Gunkel's work is of lasting value, and form criticism has underlined for us the place of the psalms in Israel's worship.

Redaction Criticism

Redaction and canonical criticism are distinguishable and yet have become closely related. I will deal with the redaction of individual psalms here, but will treat the redaction of the Psalter in its totality under canonical criticism.

Today, largely through the writings of Brevard Childs, there is much emphasis on the final form of the biblical text, the form authoritative for the Christian church. This does not, however, rule out redactional criticism. Indeed, the hand of redactors has probably been alleged more in connection with the Psalter than any OT book outside the Pentateuch. The Psalter's very existence presupposes redaction, for somebody must have given it shape. Many superscriptions could hardly have been added by the authors, for instance, "Song of Ascents," which heads fifteen psalms of several different types. Probably too the praise conclusions of books 1-4[65] were added editorially, anticipating the five praise psalms with stylized introductions and conclusions at the end of the Psalter. Discerning such features opens the door to other possibilities. Several editors were probably involved, with an ultimate redactor or redactors giving the book its final structure.[66]

That psalms sometimes were divided is fairly evident, for 9 and 10 present an acrostic pattern that runs through them both, and 42 and 43 have a common theme, phraseology, and refrain. Some scholars think the reverse has also happened, so that some psalms consist of two or more earlier psalms or psalm fragments. This is now less confidently affirmed, particularly where

63. Brueggemann, "Psalms and Life of Faith," 26 n. 39; idem, "Costly Loss of Lament," 67 n. 8. See also Broyles, *Conflict of Faith,* 20.

64. Miller, *Interpreting Psalms,* 51.

65. Pss 41:13; 72:18-19 (or 72:17-19); 89:25; and 106:48.

66. From now on the singular "redactor" will be used, but more than one person may have been involved.

there is a change of mood, as this is feasible psychologically. We cannot, however, discount it totally. Miller recognizes this feature and writes of the obvious use of some psalms in other psalms. He sees 18 and 144 to be related, also 115 and 135, 70 and 40:13-17, but warns us to be cautious in identifying this feature because of the stereotyping of worship language.[67]

So far so good; but to go further is to enter a highly subjective field. For instance, Seybold comments on the literary diversity in 19: "Surely the only possible conclusion is that we are dealing here with a textual entity made up of component parts (1-6; 7-10) each of which had its own separate life before they were brought together and provided with a closing prayer (11-13 + 14)." Yet, strangely, he also writes of the psalm's obvious thematic unity.[68] C. S. Lewis, a major literary specialist, on the other hand, was convinced of this psalm's authorial unity.[69] A versatile author is often a master of several styles, and distinguishing sources on the basis of stylistic criteria can be hazardous. In this psalm the expansive heavens are described in an expansive style, but the peremptory dictates of the law in somewhat staccato phrases, both styles well adapted to the subject matter. By way of comparison, consider the various styles present in 2 Cor 2:14–6:13, a section of this epistle not normally divided between authors or even regarded as two letters.

Then there is the updating of psalms to indicate their appropriateness to a changed situation. An example often quoted is Psalm 51, where verses 18 and 19 look beyond the individual penitent. Yet not all scholars view it in this way. For instance, W. L. Holladay considers it a unity and its composition to have been during the exile.[70] Accepting the Davidic authorship, J. A. Motyer comments, "David, as king, could not sin simply as a private individual: his sin threatened the fabric of public life. Consequently, he would be as anxious for the building up of Jerusalem (18) as for his own restoration."[71]

Wilson refers to "the long history of collection, reuse, preservation, and adaptation of earlier psalms for the needs and purposes of the exilic community," and he instances 9 and 10, "where apparently original references to more localized Israelite enemies of the psalmist are reinterpreted as 'the nations' who oppose the people of God."[72]

But can we be sure of this? Is there anything unnatural for a king, appointed by God and promised divine support, to relate his present danger

---

67. Miller, *Interpreting Psalms*, 11-12.
68. Seybold, *Introducing Psalms*, 51. See his whole section, "Traces of Reworking," 49-56.
69. Lewis, *Reflections*, 56.
70. Holladay, *Psalms*, 58.
71. Motyer, "Psalms," 518. See also the excursus to this introduction.
72. Wilson, *Psalms*, 1:148.

from local enemies to a more general threat? I am not advocating a negative reaction to such suggestions, for there is plenty of evidence of editorial activity, and 14 and 53, for instance, give us different versions of what is basically the same psalm. In some ways, the issue is like that of conjectural emendation. We should exercise caution and respect the text we have, assuming its unity unless there are compelling reasons for doubting this.

Canonical Criticism

Students of the Psalter have often noted the way words or phrases found in one psalm are often to be found also in the psalm that follows it, but we cannot always be sure to what extent this was viewed as significant in the mind of the redactor or redactors. In his commentary Konrad Schaefer is particularly sensitive to this feature and to other signs of deliberate arrangement.

Psalms study took an important new turn in the 1980s, largely due to the influence of Brevard Childs. He argued that while earlier forms of the biblical text are not without interest, closer attention should be given to the final text because it is this that forms the authoritative canon of the Christian church.[73] Canonical criticism of the Psalter builds on redaction criticism but goes well beyond it.

It is difficult to believe that the Psalter was put together without any principles of selection or of order, so, in addition to the intentions of the individual authors, consideration should be given to the ultimate redactor's intention. As Christopher R. Seitz says, "This intentionality is reflected in the fact that the final text also has its own special integrity as it participates in but also brings to consummation earlier levels of intentionality."[74]

Childs's suggestion was taken up by his student, Gerald Wilson, who argued that study of the Psalter's five sections shows the final editor's concern that in the face of the loss of their country, their temple and especially their monarchy, his readers might be focusing too much on a human Davidic king when their hope should be in Yahweh, the divine King.[75]

Wilson's work led to a flood of articles and monographs exploring the Psalter's overall structure. Particularly valuable are the contributions of James Mays, J. C. McCann, Patrick Miller, Walter Brueggemann, and David Mitchell, all developing the idea of significant structure. Somewhat distinctive have

---

73. Childs, *Introduction to OT,* 69-83.
74. Seitz, *Word without End,* 80.
75. See Wilson, "Evidence"; and *Editing.*

been the writings of Goulder (some predating Wilson's work) and Whybray. Goulder takes the psalm superscriptions seriously as the earliest interpretive hints we have and focuses on particular psalm groups, such as the Asaphite and Korahite groups. Whybray introduced a healthy skepticism into the debate, questioning some widely agreed views, especially the idea that the main purpose of the ultimate redactor was to encourage consecutive reading and meditation. Sound theories can only benefit from such questioning.

Modern translations normally indicate the division into five books, clearly referred to in the Mishnah and recognized at Qumran. Each closes with a doxology, except book 5, which concludes with a special group of five psalms, each beginning and ending with "Hallelujah." This structure, clearly influenced by the Pentateuch, does not appear to follow it thematically, although some writers have endeavored to show this. The number may symbolize the fact that, like the Pentateuch, this book is Scripture.[76]

Wilson highlighted the significance of the "seams" of the Psalter. In the first three books these clearly reflect a royal concern. Psalm 1 has been widely viewed for a long time as introducing the whole Psalter. For instance, Calvin says that the person who collected the psalms into one book "appears to have placed this psalm at the beginning, by way of preface, in which he inculcates upon the godly the duty of meditating upon the law of God."[77] Many now believe that Psalm 2 shares the function of introducing, focusing on the promise of God that undergirded the Davidic dynasty. The royal theme of Psalm 2 is picked up again at the end of book 1, for Psalm 41 shows a man who seems to be a king, concerned for the weak, knowing God's blessing "in the land" and deliverance from his enemies. Ending books 2 and 3, Psalms 72 and 89 are manifestly royal, although 89 has a distinctly negative note.

There is no royal psalm at the end of book 4, so Wilson sees the five books as falling into two groups, divided after book 3. Book 1 concentrates on Davidic psalms, and this concentration continues, less fully, in book 2; but in book 3 only 86 has a Davidic ascription. This "Psalter within the Psalter," beginning with such an emphatic divine promise to the king, ends with 89, which concludes it by bemoaning the apparent failure of the promise.

Wilson regards book 4 as the Psalter's theological center, focusing on the divine King, not the human one, an emphasis that continues into book 5, where the main psalm of a human king (110) is clearly, Wilson says, not about

---

76. Could it be significant also that the Jews called a group of small OT books (Ruth, Esther, Lamentations, Ecclesiastes, and Song of Songs) the Five Rolls, and that Matthew's Gospel presents much of the teaching of Jesus in five major passages?

77. Calvin, *Psalms*, 1.

a Davidic king at all, but somebody somewhat like the priest-kings of the Hasmonean/Maccabean line. Here too the promise of a future powerful horn (in 132, which looks like an answer to 89) appears to promise "kingly" power to the people as such, not to a monarch.[78] Here then is the message of the final redactor to readers discouraged by the demise of the Davidic dynasty: "Focus on Yahweh, your Sovereign God, rather than on the human monarchy."

There is much to be said for Wilson's thesis, at least in relation to the first four books. An NT analogy might be the Epistle to the Hebrews, where the writer encourages his readers, whose faith too was being tried, to concentrate their attention not on Judaism's forms and ceremonies but on the Christ to whom these pointed.

If Wilson is right, the Psalter follows a pattern we can find in other biblical books where the second half interprets or develops the first. So in Isaiah the conquering king becomes the Suffering Servant, while in Mark likewise the Son of Man fulfills the Servant's role. In the Gospel of John, Christ's "own" are first of all Israel as such (John 1:11) and then his disciples (13:1). In Romans forensic salvation is developed in terms of union with Christ, and in Ephesians the purpose of being seated with Christ in the heavenlies is seen to be to walk worthily on earth. In this biblical literature the end does not contradict but rather interprets or balances the beginning.

Sometimes this happens in two successive books by the same author. Luke clearly wrote the Acts of the Apostles as a sequel to his Gospel. In the first there is movement toward Jerusalem and then, in the second out from it into all the world. As F. D. Bruner has shown, 1 Corinthians with its picture of a church richly endowed with many gifts of the Spirit is succeeded by the teaching of 2 Corinthians that power comes through recognition of weakness.[79] Supremely, of course, the NT interprets the OT.

There are other examples of this kind of pattern in the Psalter. Psalm 1 could be misunderstood as promising a problem-free life for the righteous, but this idea is countered by many later psalms, most of all by 73. The Davidic psalms with their pictures of affliction for the king serve to interpret Psalm 2 in the light of 2 Samuel 7.

The division between books 1-3 and books 4-5 comes out clearly when one compares Psalms 89 and 90. Psalm 89 first of all emphatically affirms the Davidic covenant, but concludes with a most poignant passage bemoaning its apparent demise. How significant then is the placing of 90 after this! It is Mo-

---

78. But see comment on this psalm.
79. Bruner, *Theology of Holy Spirit.*

saic, as if to say, "God's purpose is far older than the Davidic covenant"; it reminds the reader of Yahweh's eternity and his close relationship with his people, as if to say, "His eternal purpose for his covenanted people will be worked out in due course"; it emphasizes his wrath, as if to say, "A time of chastisement is most fitting, because Israel and its kings have been so sinful"; and it encourages prayer for a revelation of God's unfailing love to his people. What a marvelous means of grace!

Wilson points out that in books 4 and 5 מֶלֶךְ, *melek* ("king"), describes both human kings and Yahweh but never Israel's king, but that "servant" and "anointed" apply to him in all five books, a feature directing attention more to Yahweh than to the king, and that this prepared the way for Jesus in his understanding of himself as the Suffering Servant.[80]

Indeed, as Mays seeks to show, Yahweh's kingship is the Psalter's dominant motif, just as John Bright regarded this as the OT's overriding theme.[81] To Mays, "The LORD reigns!" in 93, 97, and 99 is the key statement of the whole Psalter, and it occurs in the context of worship.[82] The redactor evidently wants the people to recognize Yahweh's kingship effectively in their prayers and praise. McCann makes the important point that 2 introduces the essential implication of the divine instruction commended in 1, that is, that Yahweh reigns, and that this psalm is more about his reign than that of the Davidic monarch.[83] Book 4 is simply emphasizing what is true even for the first three.

So then Wilson, McCann, and Mays all underline the divine kingship. Mitchell does not overlook this but argues that the whole thrust of the Psalter is toward the future, and that the placing of the royal psalms was meant not only to focus on the actual Davidic kings, but to encourage hope in a great Davidic king of the future, the Messiah. Book 3 does not show the discrediting of the Davidic covenant, but simply raises questions as to its interpretation, and the "horn" expected in 132 and 148 is in fact the Messiah. So the Psalter, as ultimately arranged, was intended to encourage, not to downplay, the messianic hope.

Book 5 contains three psalms of special kingly significance: 110, 132, and 148. Psalm 132 seems messianic, apparently promising a future Davidic king (v. 17), while 148 is in tune with this if the perfect tense of verse 14 is prophetic. Both employ קֶרֶן, *qeren* ("horn"), a symbol of power, which, very significantly, is used of the Davidic king in 89:17.

80. Wilson, *Psalms*, 1:116-17.
81. Bright, *Kingdom of God*.
82. Mays, *Lord Reigns*, 12-22.
83. McCann, *Theological Introduction*, 41.

What of 110? McCann thinks the ultimate editors meant to show that the hope centered on the Davidic dynasty was misplaced, but as Whybray says, the placing of 110 makes this difficult to accept.[84] This psalm used to be regarded as very late, its concept of a priest-king being influenced by the priestly nature of the Hasmonean dynasty. Now, however, it is widely viewed as early and as reflecting the fact that the Davidic line ruled in the city of the Jebusite priest-kings, such as Melchizedek. Here then the kingly role of the Messiah is enriched by a high priestly one, a foretaste of the combination of many roles fulfilled in the work of Jesus as the Christ.

What then about the royal psalms in books 1-3? Some scholars consider they were originally intended to be understood as related to a Davidic monarch and later were adapted to the messianic theme. But could they not have been viewed from the beginning as foreshadowing the future ideal king, as suggested by Roland de Vaux?[85] Genesis 49, "The Blessing of Jacob," is widely regarded as very ancient. The NIV renders verse 10 as "the scepter will not depart from Judah, nor the ruler's staff from between his feet, until he comes to whom it belongs and the obedience of the nations is his." If this reading is correct, it provides an early prophecy that there would be a kingly line in Judah that would find its consummation in a special monarch with wide-ranging authority.[86] This would support de Vaux's view.

If this is correct, the prophecies of a future Davidic messianic figure in book 5 (i.e., in 110; 132:17-18; and 148:14) would be pointing in the same direction as the types of books 1-3, that is, to a special kingly figure of the future.[87]

If Psalm 2 introduces the Davidic kingship/messianic theme, what is the function of 1? Like 2, it has no author ascription. Because it precedes 2 we might expect its purpose to be more comprehensive, and many have seen this as an encouragement to read the Psalter, on the assumption that תּוֹרָה, *tôrâ*, there has its broad sense as "instruction."[88] Could the narrower Mosaic sense have been that of the author and the broader that of the redactor? This is not problematic, because the broader sense does not deny but rather includes the narrower. This would mean that for the redactor the Psalter, like the Pentateuch, was the Word of God, to be read and pondered as such.[89] We note that Jesus said of 82, "as it is written in your law" (John 10:34).

---

84. Whybray, *Reading Psalms*, 94.

85. De Vaux, *Ancient Israel*, 1:110.

86. See Sailhamer, "Genesis," 179-80, for discussion of this translation.

87. I have tried to show elsewhere (in "Prophecy and Typology") the close connection between prophecy and typology.

88. See comment on Ps 1.

89. McCann, *Theological Introduction*, 27.

Whybray recognizes the real value of reading the psalms consecutively: "in doing this, readers find themselves caught up in worship not merely into moods that they find most congenial at the moment of reading, but successively into a variety of different moods, and in an order that they have not chosen for themselves, but that has already been laid down for them."[90] He does, however, query the comparatively recent idea that the ultimate editor arranged the psalms with the encouragement of this mainly in view.

He points out that the idea that Psalm 1 was written to introduce the Psalter, which goes back at least to Jerome, cannot be clearly demonstrated.[91] He also thinks the imposition of a reinterpretation would have required more than a few newly incorporated psalms, although he agrees that reinterpretation could often have taken place in the reader's mind, so that 72, for example, would probably be viewed eschatologically. If, however, de Vaux's view mentioned above is correct, the possibility of an eschatological interpretation was already present within these psalms, so that this is more an unfolding of their meaning than a reinterpretation.[92] Moreover, a substantial number of psalms highlight the importance of teaching (e.g., 25:4; 27:11; 32:8; 86:11; 94:12; 143:10).

McCann has stressed the importance of the positioning of the three major *tôrâ* psalms, 1, 19, and 119, with 19 and 119 acting as reminders of the theme as introduced by 1.[93] Westermann thought 1 and 119 were added at some fairly late stage to make the Psalter a book for meditation based on consecutive reading.

The Psalter is concerned both with the two ways of Psalm 1 but also with the divine sovereignty that, in 2, is more important than the human sovereignty it undergirds. Yahweh is the great King, and doing his will is of supreme importance. Mays sees 1 as a wisdom psalm, with its main subject matter relating to texts in Joshua and Deuteronomy, particularly to Josh 1:7-8 and Deut 17:18-20.[94] This could be highly significant for a book with a strong kingly theme, as these two passages show the importance of divine instruction for those in leadership under God.

Dennis Olson notes that Deuteronomy is the only book in the Pentateuch that calls itself *tôrâ*, which it does over and over again (Deut 1:5; 4:8; 17:18-19; etc.), and even as "this Book of the *tôrâ*" in 29:21; 30:10; and 31:26. In

---

90. Whybray, *Reading Psalms*, 11.

91. Whybray, *Reading Psalms*, 41. But he also makes similar inferences, for example, in relation to Torah interpolations in psalms that did not originally have Torah reference, e.g., 78 (*Reading Psalms*, 48).

92. Whybray, *Reading Psalms*, 40.

93. See also Mays, "Place of Torah-Psalms."

94. Mays, *Lord Reigns*, 129.

his judgment, Deuteronomy as torah is best understood as a catechetical program, "the process of education in faith from one generation to another based on a distillation of essential tradition."[95]

Despite genre differences there is a clear parallel here, for the Psalter too is a "process of education in faith," and Josh 1:8 was probably in the mind of Psalm 1's author, so linking Deuteronomy and the Psalter, two great books of divine instruction. Moreover, the king was commanded to read the book of the Law every day (Deut 17:18-19; cf. Ps 1:2), and the Psalter includes many psalms of David the king. Joshua was not a king, but in terms of his overall authority he was not unlike one. If a "distillation of essential tradition," the material for an OT theology in miniature, is to be found in any OT literary corpus, it is best sought either in Deuteronomy (especially in chs. 1–11) or the Psalter.

After quoting Deut 5:3, Olson says, "The contemporary reader is invited to join Deuteronomy in a transformative journey that leads from past to present and on to a future yet to be revealed."[96] If the Psalter in its final form was intended to foster hope in a coming Messiah, then it too has an eschatological goal and a transformative purpose.

What lessons would the consecutive reader learn from the Psalter? Certainly the importance of God's rule, but also that he does not always explain his ways, so that the reader must learn to trust and hope in him as well as to obey him. This shows the pivotal nature of 73, where verse 1 is not unlike 1:6, but which shows God's goodness to his people will be fully seen only eschatologicalically. This confidence is given notable repetition, just before the concluding Hallel psalms, in 145:20, "the LORD watches over all who love him, but all the wicked he will destroy." Here is a kind of theodicy.

Are there any other important purposes in the book's final arrangement? Placing the five Hallel psalms at its end strongly emphasizes praise in their form and content. Their fivefoldness perhaps means that the great and gracious acts of God, recorded in the Pentateuch from creation to the entry into Canaan, should become themes for praise by the Lord's people. Bullock considers the movement from lament to praise an intended emphasis of the compilers, finding confirmation of this in the doxologies that conclude each book.[97]

On the interesting but unproved assumption that the Psalter once ended at 119, what was the main function of 120–150? These are predomi-

95. Olson, *Deuteronomy and Death of Moses*, 10-11.
96. Ibid., 17.
97. Bullock, *Encountering Psalms*, 124; cf. Mays, *Lord Reigns*, 62.

nantly psalms of festival and praise, so that the ultimate redactor would surely be telling us to focus on God in praise.

To what extent was the apparently studied nature of the Psalter's structure understood by the people? We cannot say. To see its significance depends on a generally fixed order, and the LXX shows that this existed some time before Christ. The Qumran sect, however, varied the order somewhat, although it is uncertain why.

Research on the canonical shape of the Psalter continues apace. This type of scholarship must establish clear and widely accepted principles and guidelines. Whybray has a good summary of findings that were agreed and matters still disputed at the time of his book.[98]

In terms of an authoritative Christian canon, not only is the completed Psalter authoritative but each psalm is itself the Word of God. This was certainly the view of Jesus (e.g., in Matt 21:16; Luke 20:17) and of the NT writers (e.g., in Acts 1:20; Rom 3:4). So, if *tôrâ* in Psalm 1 originally meant "the Mosaic law," the psalm must be true in this sense as well as in the wider sense of "divine instruction." Also, if 2 originally referred to the historical Davidic monarchy, it must be true in this sense as well as in the messianic sense given by its important place in the whole Psalter.

The canonical status of the psalms has led to their extensive use, first in the synagogue, then in the Christian church, and in the lives of individual believers. Bullock points out how freely Calvin moves between the experiences of the psalmist and the Christian, and the way Christians find personal meaning in them despite differences of time and culture. Bullock says that the work of the redactors, in so far as it involved reapplication, gives some canonical authority to this kind of transference.[99] Yes, but it is important normally to see some real parallel lest application becomes completely uncontrolled and we claim canonical authority for unbiblical ideas and actions of our own.

The canonical approach may well have vast potential for further profitable scholarly research. For this reason, therefore, it is important that it be subjected to searching critical scrutiny. The Psalter is not unlike a great symphony in five movements, the last concluded with a mighty coda. Just as a music critic's detailed analysis of a symphony may raise questions as to whether some of the details were actually in the composer's mind, so it is with scholarly research of this kind. It also of course raises the further question as to whether there may be more beauty in the symphony or Psalter than their human authors realized.

---

98. Whybray, *Reading Psalms*, 29-31.
99. Bullock, *Encountering Psalms*, 45-46; cf. Mays, *Lord Reigns*, 49-50.

Rhetorical or Literary Criticism

The term "literary criticism," at one time an alternative to "source criticism," is now used for the study of the Bible's literary features, now also called "rhetorical criticism," a term coined in 1968 by James Muilenburg. Form criticism classifies psalms, rhetorical criticism treats every psalm as unique.[100] In fact, this type of criticism has always been applied to literature, and, though less formally, has been used in all responsible Bible study. For instance, in his seven-volume work, *The Treasury of David*, which shows considerable appreciation of earlier writers such as the Puritans, but makes little reference to critical theories current in his day, C. H. Spurgeon spent much time in showing the progress of thought in particular psalms.

Mays well sums up the approach of rhetorical critics:

> They look for features that mark smaller units, search for foreshadowing that spans such indications of demarcation, and specify the signs of reiteration and summation. Critics also look for suasive techniques, metaphorical speech, editorial additions, changes in speakers, direct address to readers, play on words . . . and other literary features. This approach, still in its infancy, has enormous potential despite some excesses by its practitioners.[101]

Such scholars also look for inclusio and chiasm, plus acrostics. Inclusio occurs when a psalm begins and ends with the same word, phrase, or clause, the author's thought returning to base, its mission accomplished, as in 8 and 103. The psalmist is indicating his major theme, coloring our understanding of what lies between these points. Chiasm is a pattern of reversal, an ABBA pattern, and it normally, though not exclusively, applies in a small unit, as in 90:5-6. Wilson appropriately warns us that because chiasm belongs to the original language, we must be sure we are not taking from the English what is not present in the Hebrew.[102] In the Hebrew Bible acrostics generally use alphabetical order to structure a psalm.

Scholars interested in this kind of criticism are also concerned to define the general intention of the author, whether it be to inform, to persuade, to warn, to chastise, or to inspire the reader.

All this applies to individual psalms but is also applicable to the way they function in their location in the Psalter. This brings rhetorical criticism

---

100. Muilenburg, "Form Criticism and Beyond," 88.
101. Mays, *Lord Reigns*, 97.
102. Wilson, *Psalms*, 1:51.

close to canonical criticism, and the two developed around the same time. Of course, the literary factor is not irrelevant in identifying the forms of some psalms. For example, a wisdom psalm's promotion of its message is by way of its rhetorical features, and so an accumulation of argumentative and persuasive elements may well indicate such a psalm.

Inevitably, subjective factors surface when we examine the poetry and structures of particular psalms. We may contrast Brueggemann's statement that 145 gives us "a not very interesting collection of clichés" with Jonathan Magonet's characterization of it as "subtle and complex."[103]

Repetition of words, phrases, or ideas usually indicates emphasis, as in the repetition of "heart" in 73. A refrain is a stylized form of repetition found in such psalms as 49, 42–43, and, most fully of all, 136. Wilson notes that most psalms with refrains are in book 2 (42, 43, 46, 49, 56, 57, 59, 62, 67) with only one each in 3 (80) and 4 (99) and two in 5 (107, 136).[104]

There are six complete acrostics, in which all 22 Hebrew letters are represented (25, 37, 111, 112, 119, 145), and also some that are slightly incomplete or irregular, such as 9–10, almost certainly one psalm originally, and 34. Magonet notes some small irregularity in them all, except 119.[105] Their form was probably an aide-mémoire, particularly necessary if 119 was to be memorized, where the acrostic pattern is monumental, the same initial letter occurring in each eight-verse sequence. The probable purpose is expressed in verse 11, "I have hidden your word in my heart that I might not sin against you."

There is no general consensus as to the meaning of *Selah*. It may be a musical term, suggesting a change of melody or of voices or a raising of the musical pitch. Alternatively, it may give emphasis, suggesting a pause for thought. It could be a point where the author or redactor is suggesting the reading of an appropriate passage of Scripture. In the case of the "Davidic" psalms this may be from the books of Samuel or of Chronicles.

What rhetorical features are to be found in the Psalter viewed as a complete book? Some psalms seem to have been placed together for comparison or contrast, for instance, 105 and 106, also 103 and 104. Important but less obvious examples are 89 and 90.[106] When the final five psalms are read consecutively, "Hallelujah" becomes like a punctuating refrain binding the whole together and making a most impressive emphasis.

Then there is the arrangement by books, with a consecutive thread of

---

103. Brueggemann, "Psalms and Life of Faith," 7; Magonet, *Rabbi*, 44.
104. Wilson, *Psalms*, 1:55.
105. Magonet, *Rabbi*, 73.
106. See the comments on each of these psalms.

meaning running through the series. Book 1 reveals how God supported the king in affliction, book 2 shows other divine appointees afflicted and supported, book 3 gives some focus (especially in 74 and 79) to the exile as the ultimate affliction, raising problems of theodicy but also showing the people's sin and their need for repentance. Book 4 directs their minds to God the great King, and book 5 builds on this, calling for celebration of his great deeds and encouraging hope in the king to come.

Intertextuality is about the way texts function when they influence other texts. This is a major feature of Scripture, particularly in the NT's use of OT passages. It also occurs quite extensively in the OT and particularly in the book of Psalms. B. L. Tanner says, "The psalms are a sponge for the ideas, emotions, and historical events of the period in which they were written. It is this connection to a greater reality that enables us, as readers, to connect these images with our own ideas and emotions and to become one with the emotional world of ancient worshippers."[107]

In her philosophical approach to intertextuality, Julia Kristeva, a feminist writer, broke new ground in a controversial fashion. Tanner outlines the history of its modern study, including the work of Kristeva, and then applies it, but in a much less extreme way than Kristeva, to the Psalter. She has chapters on Psalms 88, 90, 112, and the *yhwh mālāk* psalms. Her study of 90 is particularly valuable, as she takes both its superscription and its location into account as well as pointing out textual links with other OT passages. In her treatment of 88 and 112, she seeks to show how they minister to the distinctive needs of female readers.

Reader-Oriented Criticism

In considering the relationship between author, text, and reader, modern philosophers of language have increasingly focused attention on the reader. Speech-act theory identifies different functions texts are designed by their authors to perform, whether informing the mind, affecting the emotions, or moving the will. Of course the author's intention and the text's actual effect may not be the same, for individual readers may react differently, and the same reader may react differently at different times and in different moods.

This kind of approach is still in its infancy as a method for use in biblical studies, and has not been much applied to psalm study. The two most likely reasons for this are an understandable caution about an approach that

---

107. Tanner, *Psalms,* 49.

questions the objectivity of the text and its increasingly complex technical vocabulary.

D. K. Berry has provided such an approach in his study of Psalm 18. Having outlined the form-critical and rhetorical-critical approaches to it, he then employs reader-response methods. He shows what this psalm was likely to do when used in an OT worship setting and then how a modern reader, approaching it as a lyric poem, might be affected by it if she or he identifies with the writer. "The newer approaches exchange manageability of texts for increasing awareness of the reading process, and although the objectivity of the text fades into the background, increased understanding of the reader's role more than compensates for its diminution."[108]

We certainly should consider reader response, because Scripture is revelation intended to evoke godly response, but Berry's judgment on the matter is questionable. Better understanding of what reading may effect is obviously desirable, but the text itself is of great importance because it is Holy Scripture. K. J. Vanhoozer's study, *Is There a Meaning in This Text?* provides a balanced approach in which author, text, and reader are all seen to be important.

Appraisal of the Various Types of Criticism

A certain logic runs through the succession of types of criticism applied to the book of Psalms since the nineteenth century. Source criticism has a strongly historical interest, with its concerns about authorship, occasion, date, and so on. Continuing research into the historical background of the psalms should be welcomed, although confident assertions should be avoided unless the evidence is clear-cut. Form criticism's interest in socioreligious background can be useful, but attempts to place psalms in hard-and-fast formal categories can be counterproductive. Some psalms seem to show signs of adaptation to new purposes by redactional work.

Discovering redactional principles running right through the book or a substantial part of it then raises questions about its canonical shape, which then moves discussion to questions of purpose, both the purpose of individual psalms and the book as a whole, so that the rhetorical development of thought becomes a focus. It is then appropriate to ask what kind of responses may and do result from the reading of the book by a modern reader, so long as we do not surrender to a completely subjective approach.

Basic to all, of course, are questions about the authenticity of the text

108. Berry, *Psalm 18*, 148.

and also about the nature of its poetry. Such matters have interested scholars throughout the whole period.

These forms of criticism should be regarded as complementary. John Eaton demonstrates how different approaches affect the interpretation of particular psalms, taking examples from about twenty commentators representing different critical positions.[109] Some scholars are too inclined to put all their eggs in one basket. Helmer Ringgren criticizes many scholars for their too easy rejection of some aspects of form-critical thought, but himself rejects views of other scholars too quickly and easily, and it is doubtful if he always appreciates the positive points made by others.[110]

There have been gains from all these forms of criticism, but several, particularly source and form criticism, have a history littered with discredited theories. Although none of the main approaches should be abandoned, Mays is surely right in saying, "Form-critical and historical questions are subordinate rather than primary agenda."[111]

Miller correctly emphasizes that no part of Scripture bridges the past and the present better than the Psalms, as they are not time-bound historically or in terms of content.[112] Because so many once widely held views are now discredited, we should be both cautious and humble. The expression "assured results" has been used too much in this field of study, and a blushing Bible scholar is not a pretty sight! Moreover, the higher our view of biblical authority is, the more tentative we should be, lest we elevate some particular system of literary study to a position above the biblical text itself.

Use of the Psalms Today

Over the ages the Psalms have been used in many ways, but mostly for prayer, both private and public, in worship, both public and private, and to learn more about the ways of God with his people. In *The Psalms through Three Thousand Years*, Holladay provides a valuable survey of their use through the ages.

All three main uses of the psalms are relevant to those called to the proclamation of the Word of God, for this is normally done in the context of a service of worship and prayer. Terry Muck has well said that the use we

---

109. Eaton, *Psalms of the Way.*
110. Ringgren, *Faith of Psalmists.*
111. Mays, *Psalms,* ix.
112. Miller, *Interpreting Psalms,* 20-26.

make of them should not contradict their message, which he sums up as the greatness and goodness of God, remarking that our use should glorify God and not ourselves,[113] important guidance for Christian preachers.

Excursus: The Davidic Psalms

The authorship of the Davidic psalms is a complex issue, involving several kinds of criticism that are best considered together.

Seventy-three psalms are superscribed לְדָוִד, *lĕdāwid.* The preposition *l* means they were related in some way to him without specifying this more fully, although authorship is a most natural way of understanding this. Even the medieval Jewish scholar Ibn Ezra, however, thought it might not always imply authorship, although the Jews normally took it this way. The Talmud went so far as to assert David's authorship of every psalm (even 137!), probably because, according to 1 Chr 23:1-5 and 2 Chr 23:18, the musical guilds responsible for so many other psalms were established by him.[114] This talmudic tradition is not entirely misguided, for in some ways the relationship of the Levitical writers to David is not unlike that of the prophets to Moses and the apostles to Christ — in other words, the sharing of a theology and the relating of its principles to new situations.[115]

Most nineteenth-century critics rejected Davidic authorship of the psalms superscribed *lĕdāwid,* and they regarded most psalms as postexilic, very often even Maccabean. Since then, however, there has been a gradual but definite tendency to move them earlier. The impact of form criticism, especially the work of Mowinckel, which gave the king an important ritual function, was to bring many into the preexilic period. Psalm 110 was at one time widely regarded as Maccabean, because it is about a priest-king, like the Maccabean monarchs. Now many think it early because they consider that the priestly functions of the Jebusite kings, like Melchizedek, passed to the Davidic monarchs whose capital was Jerusalem, formerly a Jebusite city. Many scholars now accept that some psalms may be by David, but others deny this.[116]

---

113. T. C. Muck, "General Editor's Preface," in Wilson, *Psalms,* 1:11-12.

114. Goulder's in-depth studies of the Korahite and the Asaphite psalms (*Psalms of Korah* and *Psalms of Asaph*) have shown each group to have distinctive features binding them together.

115. Probably the same was true of the relationship to Paul of "apostolic legates" like Timothy and Titus, although this can hardly be explored as we possess only letters to them, not from them.

116. E.g., Cooper, "Life and Times," 129.

Mays uses 2 Sam 1:17-27 and 2 Samuel 22 to build a good case against extreme anti-Davidic dismissiveness. The former shows that the narrator knew that a song attributed to David was part of a written collection. The latter, which interprets David's story theologically, culminates in a prophecy that David's dynasty would experience God's "unfailing kindness," his covenant faithfulness, suggesting that David's story was to be read as a pattern for the future.[117]

In the books of Samuel, David is a musician and psalmist (1 Sam 16:15-23; 2 Sam 1:17-27; 22:1; 23:1-7; cf. Amos 6:5). Some psalms give information about him (18:50; 78:70-72; 89:3-4, 20-37, 49; 132:1-5, 10-12, 17-18; 144:10).[118] Two of these (18 and 144) have Davidic superscriptions. 2 Samuel 23:1 refers to "the oracles of David," implying he was a prophet. Tournay says, "If David is a prophet, it is natural that psalms containing theophanies and oracles should be attributed to him by tradition. Psalm 18 contains a magnificent theophany." He points out too that other "Davidic" psalms contain oracles.[119] But could not this tradition, taken seriously in the NT (Acts 2:30), be accurate?

The wording of the superscription to Psalm 18 (cf. 2 Sam 22:1) indicates that the redactor believed David gave voice to this psalm, whether or not he was responsible for committing it to writing. Psalm 72:20, "This concludes the prayers of David son of Jesse," also redactional, comes at the end of book 2. It probably applies to the Davidic psalms in the first two books, not just in book 2; otherwise we would have expected it to precede that psalm's doxology, for the doxologies concluding books 1-4 are probably all editorial. A large percentage of the psalms with a Davidic superscription are in books 1 and 2, in other words before 72, and the designation "prayers" would certainly apply to most of them.[120]

It is true that some NT references to traditional authors of OT books may simply be means of locating these passages for the readers, but others are clearly meant to point to their authors. The Davidic authorship of 110 is basic and essential to the argument of Jesus himself in Mark 12:36-40, and his argument is important not only for its substance but also for its location, for in Mark it closes the record of his public teaching ministry. In Acts 2:25-36 Peter's argument from Psalm 16, which he links with 110, also depends on Davidic authorship (cf. Acts 13:35-37). In Rom 4:6-8 Paul quotes Ps 32:1-2 as

---

117. Mays, *Lord Reigns,* 91.

118. The list given by Bullock, *Encountering Psalms,* 72.

119. Tournay, *Seeing and Hearing,* 44.

120. For comment on the superscription to Ps 72, see the exegesis of this psalm.

from David. In Acts 4:25-26 the church at prayer quotes Psalm 2 (which does not even have a Davidic superscription) as the words of David.

Some superscriptions contain biographical references, mostly attached to the Davidic psalms of books 1 and 2.[121] Most are linked to events during Saul's persecution or Absalom's rebellion. Most are similar in grammatical structure, perhaps suggesting a common redactor. They are often regarded as still less reliable than the author ascriptions, and certainly in some cases there are real difficulties, but we should not hastily discard them.[122] Motyer reminds us of the important fact that they should be read not as descriptions but as reflections.[123] After all, nobody in imminent danger would pause to write a psalm! Wilcock shows considerable skill and insight in indicating their appropriateness.[124] It is not impossible that in some cases they were added when or shortly after these psalms were written, although this is not the view of most scholars.[125]

Wilson notes that the last four psalms in book 1, whether or not written by David, "reflect the uncertainty, confusion, and plotting that characterize the transition between kings,"[126] and that two of them (38 and 41) ask for deliverance from sickness, which may suggest they were written by an old man, although we cannot be certain of this.

What about the apparently anachronistic use of terms like "temple" and "house of God" in the Davidic psalms? These terms also occur in 1 and 2 Samuel, where they are used appropriately of the shrines at Shiloh (1 Sam 1:7, 9; 3:3), and presumably at Gibeon (2 Sam 12:20; cf. 1 Chr 16:39-40). On Zion's hill, however, there was in David's day only the tent with the ark in it, so that, as the contrasting use of terms in 2 Sam 7:5-6 clearly shows, the terms "temple" and "house of God" would not be appropriate. Why then are they used in the Davidic psalms?

The deep concern David had for the construction of the temple is seen not only in 2 Samuel 7, but in 1 Chronicles 16 and 17, where he makes extensive preparation for it in terms of building materials and personnel. This preparation included the provision of choirs and their leaders. In 1 Chr 16:7-36 he commits a psalm to Asaph and his associates.[127] As he was a musician and an

---

121. The exception is Ps 102, also exceptional in being in book 4.

122. Longman, *How to Read Psalms,* 41-42.

123. Motyer, "Psalms," 486.

124. Wilcock, *Psalms 1–72; Psalms 73–150.*

125. See Holladay, *Psalms,* 67-91.

126. Wilson, *Psalms,* 1:90.

127. This psalm consists of portions of 96, 105, and 106. See the exegetical comments on these.

inspired poet, it seems highly likely he would have made quite extensive preparation in terms of actual songs, so that to find many psalms of his (plus others by the choirs he established) is just what we might have expected.

His psalms could well have originated in his personal experience and then have their language updated by him for use in the temple that was for long in his heart and that God promised that his son would build. It seems highly likely that Psalm 68 was used on a regular basis to commemorate the arrival of the ark in Jerusalem, but this does not of itself rule out Davidic authorship. The term "sanctuary" in 68:24 is not inappropriate, as David's tent contained the ark, and 2 Sam 7:6 clearly implies that God dwelt in David's tent just as much as he did in the wilderness tabernacle. This means that a theology of the divine presence in relation to this tent was quite appropriate. The only significant alteration (as distinct from omission) from the part of Psalm 96 quoted in 1 Chronicles 16 is the alteration from "sanctuary" to "place of my habitation." This suggests that some flexibility in the use of terms for the place of worship was familiar both to the author and to his readers. Psalm 68:29 with its reference to the coming of kings to the temple clearly refers to the future rather than to the present.

The quotation of Psalm 68 in Paul's *pesher* use of it in Eph 4:8 shows an NT writer making small changes to the text, not to alter its teaching but to indicate, without the need for lengthy explanation, its fulfillment in Jesus (cf. also the use of Isa 40:3 in Mark 1:3). Could not David have done something similar to relate his psalms to the planned and promised temple worship, which, like the coming of Jesus, was also the fulfillment of divine promise?

The playing down of sacrifice and the emphasis on obedience in Ps 40:6-8 might seem to reflect the outlook of the prophets, especially the eighth-century prophets and Jeremiah. In fact, however, its nearest comparison is with the words of Samuel (himself, like David, a prophet, according to Acts 3:24) in 1 Sam 15:22-23.

Of course, the principle of the canonical importance of the text's final form, emphasized by Childs, means that the work of redactors in giving the Psalter its final shape is of considerable importance.[128] If the apparent anachronisms were not due to updating by David himself, they could have been done, with the same motive, by later redactors, who may in any case have added such verses as 51:18-19. To alter teaching and to give further application that is consistent with that teaching are two quite different things, and ethically are poles apart. The latter occurs in countless Christian pulpits every Sunday.

---

128. Childs, *Introduction to OT,* 69-83, 504-25.

An alternative to the view that David authored the psalms to which his name is attached has become increasingly popular, largely through its promotion by Childs, and it is probably now the majority view among scholars. This takes the references to David in the superscriptions seriously, but sees many of them not as indicating authorship but rather as pointing to David as a model of piety and as representing in his life the values to be seen in these psalms. On this view, the biographical superscriptions are usually regarded not so much as indicating the circumstances of their composition but as giving suggestions for profitable reading from 1 and 2 Samuel as a background to these psalms. This reading would be particularly helpful for worshipers facing various afflictions and problems in some way comparable to those of David. The suggestion that *Selah* could indicate the value of reading appropriate passages at the points where it occurs is in line with this.[129]

The aptness of this general approach may be seen in that what strikes us in many of the Davidic psalms is not so much David's kingly office as his evident humanity.[130] Miller rightly says he was as much a representative human being as any OT character, and he refers, for instance, to David's sin and weakness concerning Bathsheba and Uriah and also to his anguish and despair in relation to Absalom. He then says, "It is that sort of ambiguous mixture of good and bad, joy and despair, obedience and disobedience, that is what we all are."[131]

A further point needs to be made. The books of Samuel in their patent honesty present the character of David "warts and all."[132] The Davidic psalms show David as a good example because we see his commitment to the one true God, to whom he took all his concerns. His failings too are clearly presented, so that there is here also a "model" of divine grace to a sinner, grace based on God's promise to David and his dynasty, highlighted in Psalm 2 and with a reminder to the discerning reader in the superscription to 3.

The "model of piety" view has the advantage of removing all possible anachronisms at one stroke, and of avoiding the necessity for finding close correspondence between these psalms and the history of David in the books of Samuel and Chronicles. It is true too, as C. C. Broyles says, that "even if a psalm had been composed by David for a particular historical moment, it was preserved not to give us information about David's biography but to give us

---

129. See p. 30.
130. Childs, *Introduction to OT,* 521.
131. Miller, *Interpreting Psalms,* 26-27.
132. See, e.g., the catalogue of his faults detailed by Gordon, *1 and 2 Samuel,* 48-49.

verbal models for prayer and worship."[133] Significant problems with this view would not arise if some of the superscriptions (especially those to 16 and 110 but also at least 18 plus the conclusion to 72) do relate to authorship. This would mean, though, that the same kind of superscription would have two different purposes in the Psalter, thus introducing a strange untidiness into the redactional work.

These two views need not be regarded as mutually exclusive. If Davidic authorship is maintained for the Davidic psalms as a whole (and this is my own point of view), the redactor's motive in mentioning his name so often may have been partly to point to him as an example, for despite his many faults, he reveals the covenanted grace of God to sinners and models the importance of a God-centered devotional life. Moreover, the frequent references to God's חֶסֶד, ḥesed (love within a covenant relationship),[134] would deepen the conviction of the readers that in due course the ultimate messianic "David" would come as evidence of God's faithfulness to his people. After all, the people not only shared David's faults, but, for all their unworthiness, were heirs of the covenant promises of God.

Certainly there is much about the history of the shaping of the Psalter that we do not know. Sufficient is known, however, for us to see the Davidic psalms as, first of all, examples of utterances arising out of actual life situations, then as shaped for use in the temple worship, and finally as examples of hope in the God of the covenant and commitment to devotional God-centeredness for emulation by the godly reader of the whole book. Features of each stage will be represented at various points in the exegetical section of this commentary, but with some prominence given to the final stage, because, in the guidance of God, it gave rise to the book as we now have it.

133. Broyles, *Psalms*, 29. His whole treatment of the issue (26-31) is an argument for the "model of piety" view that shows sensitivity to the problems it raises for those accustomed to regard these psalms as written by David.

134. See pp. 279-80.

Exegesis

Exegesis, or grammatico-historical interpretation, is the primary task of a commentator. It seeks to show the meaning of the biblical text for its first readers. One hopes that the contemporary reader's main concern (i.e., *your* main concern) is to read the text to understand its message and to adjust his or her personal outlook and practical life in its light, but this requires first of all standing where the first readers stood. Only in this way can we avoid making the text mean what we want it to mean, perhaps even pursuing disobedience while using the language of obedience ("'I will, sir,' but he did not go," Matt 21:30). To identify with the original readers our approach to the text should involve our whole person.

In prose, the words need to be understood in their sentences, the sentences in their paragraphs, and so on. In psalmic poetry too the part must be understood in terms of the whole, not only the whole psalm but, as is increasingly being realized, also the whole Psalter, so that literary context is all-important. Furthermore, we need knowledge of the OT world, its geography, its history, its culture, and especially its religious ethos.

It is not, however, just a matter of the understanding, although this is very important. Other dimensions to this task are often overlooked. God has given us an imaginative faculty, and our knowledge of the biblical world and careful study of each psalm will enable us, at least in part, to "inhabit" that world, to see it from within. Ideally, the biblical world should become as familiar to us as our own. Even time spent with a map, learning the locations of biblical towns, hills, and valleys, pays dividends. For the Psalms, however, what is even more important is its culture and especially all that concerns its religion.

Most of all, though, we need spiritual sympathy with the authors of the psalms. If proper understanding of literature requires the love of a story well told, and if proper understanding of music requires delight in beautiful sounds, so for the proper understanding of the psalms we need to love the God of the psalmists who is also our God. If the psalmist's words, "my heart and my flesh cry out for the living God," find no echo in our own hearts, our approach to his psalm is bound to lack an essential, indeed, *the* essential, ingredient. Scholarship and spirituality should not be viewed as enemies, but as friends.

Two recurring topics are discussed in the introduction: for interpretation of the headings see "Superscriptions"; and for *Selah* see "Rhetorical or Literary Criticism."

BOOK 1

For the Psalter's division into five books, see pp. 21-28.

Psalm 1

This anonymous psalm, whenever composed, was perhaps placed here to commend the Psalter as Holy Scripture, a book for divine instruction in practical godliness.[1] "Law" translates תּוֹרָה, *tôrâ*, which can have the wider sense of "instruction," divine truth for daily life.[2] If this is so, the narrower and wider senses may represent the thought of the psalmist and of the Psalter's ultimate redactor, respectively, for these senses are not mutually exclusive. The law is God's Word and so is the Psalter. Deuteronomy also calls itself *tôrâ* and "this Book of the Law" (Deut 29:21; 31:26), and the similarity of verses 2 and 3 to Josh 1:8, which appears to refer to Deuteronomy, suggests a clear and important relationship between Deuteronomy and the Psalter. In the Psalter, themes from the Pentateuch are taken up in a book of sung praise that itself becomes also the inspired vehicle for a clear message from God. We recall too Deuteronomy's strong emphasis on the two ways (Deut 28–31).

1:1-3 The psalm starts positively, warmly encouraging a godly lifestyle,

1. For the history of this psalm's interpretation, see Eaton, *Psalms of the Way,* 14-52.

2. Many scholars now understand תּוֹרָה, *tôrâ,* here, at least in the mind of the ultimate redactor, to refer to the Psalter (e.g., Childs, *Introduction to OT,* 513-14; McCann, *Theological Introduction,* 27; Broyles, *Psalms,* 41-42). Whybray argues against this (*Reading Psalms,* 38-42), and his comments should warn us against assuming too easily what, despite having good support, has yet to be proved.

for its opening word, אַשְׁרֵי, 'ašrê (NIV "blessed"), simply means "happy."
The NIV ends verse 1 with a full stop, but the NRSV with a semicolon, which
is more appropriate, as the major cause of the happiness is surely found in
verse 2. This passage is rather like Jer 17:5-8, but that uses the more "religious"
word בָּרוּךְ, bārûk. This positive note continues as the tree illustration presents a most attractive, deeply satisfying lifestyle. Before that, however, 'ašrê is
followed by three negative clauses. So, taken together, verses 1-3 present godliness as a positive joy but with clear negative implications. Like Proverbs (e.g.,
1:10-19; 14:14-19), these verses warn against intimate association with the ungodly. Perhaps the writer intended verse 1 to suggest development, from listening to bad counsel through commitment to the advised lifestyle to eventual identification with mockers, even perhaps sitting down to teach others.

Meditation "day and night," followed by the illustration of the deeply
rooted tree, suggests growth's dependence on constant nourishment from
God's truth.[3] The "streams of water" are irrigation canals, common in the
Near East. Planted thus, the tree fulfills its intended potential, just like someone refreshed and nourished by God's Word. Someone so planted is prosper-
ous. If this psalm is indeed introductory, this implies that, despite all the trials
and afflictions of the godly reflected in later psalms, true prosperity is their
portion.

1:4-5 With studied abruptness the psalm introduces the contrasting
lifestyle of the wicked, already mentioned in verse 1. Community language
("the assembly of the righteous") is used of the godly, modifying the apparent
individualism of verses 1-3. The terse "not so the wicked!" negates the whole
thrust of verses 1-3, not just the tree/chaff contrast, although this gives the
contrast illustrative concreteness.[4] "Judgment," followed by reference to "the
assembly of the righteous," may imply facing and not prevailing in an Israelite
court. Alternatively these expressions may suggest loneliness in judgment and
fellowship in blessing, respectively. In verse 6 "judgment" is described as per-
ishing, strongly suggesting that this is divine eschatological judgment.[5]

1:6 This summary binds the whole psalm together and concerns not
just the persons but their lifestyles. Hence the psalm is well fitted as a practical
introduction to the Psalter. "Watches over" is literally "knows," in a pregnant
sense, not simply factual knowledge but also, as in the NIV rendering, personal relationship and loving concern. If verse 5 does refer to an Israelite

---

3. The tree is a standard OT metaphor for the godly life; cf. Prov 11:30; 15:4; Jer 17:7-8, and
also the exploration of its suggestiveness in Brown, *Seeing the Psalms*, ch. 3.

4. For chaff driven by the wind as a metaphor of judgment, cf. 35:5.

5. See further comment on judgment on pp. 258-59.

court, the thought now moves on to divine eschatological judgment. The first and last words of the psalm, "happy" and "perish," are in marked contrast.

Psalm 2

If Psalm 1 is about personal commitment to God's instruction, the interest here is more corporate, focusing on the nation and its king. Here ungodliness is not simply an unacceptable alternative but active antagonism to God's purposes and those representing it. Here happiness involves taking refuge in God (2:12) as well as walking in his ways (1:1-2). This psalm shows the Psalter's consecutive reader that Psalm 1 should not be read as promising a problem-free life.

This orphan psalm is identified, without explanation, by author ("David") in Acts 4:25 and as "the second Psalm" in Acts 13:33, the sole biblical reference to the Psalter's order.[6] It was probably used at successive enthronements. In the king's "adoption" by God and the kiss of fealty, the language of Near Eastern enthronement rituals appears. The enthronement is God's act, so the psalm defiantly addresses his enemies. Because Psalm 1 begins and 2 ends with a beatitude, it is highly likely they were placed here to introduce the Psalter, to stress practical commitment to God's Word, and to focus attention on God's support for David's kingly dynasty and also on the messianic hope.[7] Psalm 2 is dramatic in character; we hear various voices, each referring to sin and each amplifying some important feature of the previous stanza. Synonymous parallelism appears in almost every verse.

2:1-3 The psalmist speaks about sin as irrational and introduces the voices of the rebels. Here is the first of the Psalter's many questions, almost as characteristic as its hallelujahs.[8] The divine King and his anointed human king are dual targets of the revolt of nations and their rulers, who view their rule as bondage. This revolt was premeditated, and the verb הָגָה, *hāgâ*, translated as "meditates" in 1:2, is here rendered "plot," so different are the concerns of the righteous and of the wicked. Such a revolt fits David's time, for he did dominate other kingdoms (see 2 Sam 8 and 10).

2:4-6 These verses exegete verse 1's phrase, "in vain." As Motyer says, "The Lord neither negotiates with rebels, nor adjusts himself to suit their demands, but simply reaffirms his royal plan."[9] The divine King speaks, treating

---

6. For NT use of this psalm see pp. 301, 350, 356-57.

7. For canonical criticism see pp. 21-28.

8. See Davidson, *Wisdom and Worship,* 120.

9. Motyer, "Psalms," 489.

sin as derisory, for it is so irrational. The reference to God's heavenly enthronement underlines this, and his support of the king on Jerusalem's hill, made holy by revelation and worship there (2 Sam 24:15-25), is both emphatic and moral, for his derision expresses his wrath against sin.[10] Perhaps the redactor saw a contrast between sinful human mockery in Ps 1:1 and wholly appropriate divine mockery here (cf. 59:8).

2:7-9 The anointed king speaks, telling of God's decree, perhaps an actual document presented to him (cf. 2 Kgs 11:12). At his enthronement ("today") he has been adopted as God's son (cf. 2 Sam 7:14), for his rule is God's gift and he accords him fatherly protection (cf. "watches over" in 1:6). The promise of a worldwide inheritance involved subduing the rebellious nations, and was always an unrealized ideal in the history of the monarchy, but would have particular significance for the messianic perspective of the Psalter's final redactor.[11] This stanza confirms verse 6's strong affirmation, showing sin to be useless.

2:10-12 The psalmist speaks again, addressing the kings with a "wisdom" admonition based on verse 9, exhorting them to serve Yahweh and his son (here brought together for a second time), with a subject's kiss of obedience (cf. 1 Sam 10:1). "Son" here, although not in verse 7, is an Aramaic word. After discussing various interpretations, Peter Craigie says,

> Aramaic is known to have been used in Syria-Palestine from at least the ninth century B.C. . . . The words are addressed (in the mouth of the poet) to *foreign* nations and kings (Aramaic speaking?), whereas בֵּן, 'son,' in v 7, is used by God in speaking to his king. It is possible that the poet deliberately uses a foreign word (loan-word) to dramatize his poetic intent at this point.[12]

If so, this accords well with other evidence of this psalmist's high poetic gift. Need rebellion be final? No, for there is a choice (as in Ps 1), either to know God's anger or to trust him and find refuge. This starts the Psalter's important "refuge" theme.[13] There is a way of blessedness (cf. 1:1) and of rejoicing even for erstwhile rebels — through repentance.

---

10. "I" (v. 6) is emphatic.
11. For canonical criticism see pp. 21-28.
12. Craigie, *Psalms 1–50*, 64.
13. See Creach, *Yahweh as Refuge*. His whole book explores this theme.

Psalm 3[14]

This is most appropriately placed after Psalm 2 when one considers it in the light of 2 Sam 7:11-16 and 12:10-14.[15] There David experiences his sin's consequences, but he has been pardoned (cf. Ps 2:10-12) and, under the Davidic covenant, can look to the Lord for protection. The uprising of nations (2:1-3) is replaced in the superscription by one led by his own son. He takes refuge in God (cf. 2:12). Mays regards the location of this psalm as especially important, because it is the first with a Davidic superscription. It shows an attitude to God that will be repeated time and again.[16]

3:1-2 The numerous enemies are confident of victory, either because they doubt the power of the psalmist's God or, more likely, because they think God is on their side. Perhaps they consider themselves God's punitive instruments and wrongly conclude from this that God has forsaken him. He is evidently aware of what they are saying among themselves. Mays says, "This devastating appraisal organizes the whole prayer. It discloses the true significance of the hostility. The assertions of trust deny its validity. The petitions are an appeal to God to disprove it. The conviction, 'Salvation belongs to the Lord,' contradicts it."[17]

3:3-4 The statements of trust begin not with "I" but with "you." "Trust has its foundation in Yahweh, not in the believing human being."[18] In verse 3 the initial personal pronoun is "an emphatic way of expressing the inner quietness of the psalmist."[19] The shield metaphor (v. 3; cf. 7:10; 18:2; etc.) is apt, but the psalmist's thought breaks its bounds, for no shield can surround someone completely, just as no earthly protection can be as comprehensive as God's. Glory and the lifting up of the head show here a king's confidence of restoration to kingly power,[20] for both suggest his shame's removal. He is away from the Jerusalem shrine (cf. v. 4 with 2:6), but still calls on the God worshiped there. His geographical remoteness does not restrict God's power to answer.

---

14. Mays effectively employs Ps 3 to show how the "anatomy" of a psalm may be found (*Psalms*, 4-7).

15. Craigie points out the many parallels between the historical record of David's flight from Absalom and this psalm's language (*Psalms 1–50*, 72-73).

16. Mays, *Lord Reigns*, 123.

17. Mays, *Psalms*, 52; Sheppard, "Theology," 149-52.

18. Kraus, *Psalms 1–59*, 139.

19. VanGemeren, "Psalms," 76.

20. But NIV mg. views "glory" as a name for God in its alternative rendering, "Lord, my Glorious One, who lifts . . ." (cf. 106:20; 1 Sam 4:22).

3:5-6   Now we see how meaningful verse 3a's imagery is, as the outer encirclement of enemies is more than offset by God's inner-protecting encirclement.

3:7   This articulates his cry, and "my God" shows his assured relationship.[21] The enemies are like wild animals, for the jaw with its aggressive teeth is the chief organ of animal attack, so the plea is not necessarily for vengeance but for release. "Arise, O LORD," is reminiscent of Num 10:35, spoken when the ark advanced against enemies. As Wilcock says, "It is words already ancient in his day that the psalmist finds to be a living basis for his assurance."[22] Craigie points out how extensive is military language in this psalm.[23]

3:8   Appropriately, the disclosure of his very personal experience concludes with a general affirmation of faith in the God of salvation, and, showing his shepherd heart, he asks for blessing on God's people, who are also his own people. So three psalms in succession promise or pray for a blessing (cf. 1:1; 2:12), although here the more "religious" word בְּרָכָה, *běrākâ*, is used, as in Num 6:22-27.[24]

Comparison of 3:5 and 4:8 suggests that the redactor intended 3 and 4 for regular morning and evening use, respectively, and this perhaps accounts for their early position in the Psalter. The reader would probably recall that meditation on God's Word is also to be by day and night (1:2).

Psalm 4

Although clearly an individual's work, this psalm is assigned to the music director, so was obviously deemed suitable for communal worship. It has been variously interpreted, chiefly as a prayer for protection from verbal and physical assault or of commitment to the true God in contrast to enemies who have turned to worship false gods.[25] The latter may not appear to fit the canonical context so well, but perhaps the psalm was placed here partly to illustrate the concluding clause of Psalm 2; true refuge is only in the Lord. I will take it this way, but note important points where it is understood differently.[26]

---

21. Eaton lists systematically the king's designations for God as his personal savior in the Psalms (*Kingship*, 170-72).

22. Wilcock, *Psalms 1–72*, 28.

23. Craigie, *Psalms 1–50*, 71.

24. The abstract noun connected with בָּרוּךְ, *bārûk*. See comment on 1:1.

25. See Broyles, *Psalms*, 52-53.

26. For the NT use of this psalm see p. 331.

4:1   The psalmist's address to God (אֱלֹהֵי צִדְקִי, *'ĕlōhê ṣidqî*), rendered as "my righteous God" (NIV), is unique and could mean "God of my right" (NRSV), presumably "my kingly right," a probable reminder of the Davidic covenant. He shows his conviction that Israel's God, his God, is righteous, setting right what is plainly wrong. In terms of 2:12, he is taking refuge in the true God.

4:2-3   "My glory" may be a name for Yahweh here.[27] If so, the verse is entirely about forsaking the true God for pagan deities. Others apply the phrase to David's kingship and the desire of his enemies to dethrone him (cf. 3:3b). If so, they are telling lies about him rather than turning to false gods.[28] The term's use in 3:3 suggests that the redactor, by putting these psalms together, showed he understood it here in the former sense. The psalmist's confident assertion (v. 3) reminds us of the king's security in Psalm 2 and his address to the rebels there. This verse shows the significance of "my" (v. 1). The word "godly" is singular and is connected with חֶסֶד, *ḥesed*, implying faithfulness or love within a covenant relationship, though not necessarily sinlessness. He and the Lord are mutually committed, so he is sure of an answer to his prayers.

4:4-5   If these words address the psalmist's enemies, he is counseling them against continuing in sin (cf. 2:10-12), to offer sacrifices to the Lord and trust in him. The Hebrew emphasizes "the LORD," as if to distinguish him from pagan deities. Some, however, think these verses are addressed to his friends, suggesting they are favoring precipitate action, possibly causing a sinful massacre, whereas he counsels sleep and examination of motives, but also trust in the Lord expressed in the offering of right sacrifices (cf. 51:19; Deut 33:19), showing their allegiance to Yahweh.

4:6-8   Others may despair of a good outcome to the present distress, but the psalmist asks a sign of God's favor (cf. "light of your face" with Num 6:24-26), with the implication of divine blessing. His joy in his God is so much greater than that of pagan revelers, who praise their agricultural deity at harvest time (cf. Hos 2:8). Because he is faithful to the Lord and has not turned to false gods (cf. "you alone, O Yahweh," with Exod 20:3), his sleep is peaceful and secure. On 4:8 see 3:5 above.

---

27. See comment in n. 20 on 3:3.
28. This follows NIV mg. for v. 2b.

Psalm 5

A morning followed by an evening prayer, then by another for the morning (Pss 3, 4, 5), was probably to teach the importance of regular prayer.[29] Comparing the contents and headings of 4 and 5 may suggest gentle strings were reckoned more fitting to accompany an evening prayer, and flutes a morning prayer. The term *sheminith* (Ps 6) may mean "on an eight-stringed instrument." This psalm is somewhat chiastic, starting with prayer for help and ending with assertions about God as protector, while in verses 4-6 and 9-10 the wicked are in view, perhaps implying they are a threat to the psalmist. In the central stanza (vv. 7-8), the psalmist's resort is to God's character.

5:1-3 The psalmist earnestly prays, conscious of the Lord's kingly supremacy and of their personal relationship. He is a subject laying his complaint before a powerful monarch, praying in faith, confident that the Lord hears him. The God who answers prayer is the one certain factor as the day begins.[30]

5:4-6 Both Psalms 1 and 2 may find illustration here, for, in line with 1:4-6, he asserts God's hatred of evil. Expressions like "arrogant," "lies,"[31] and "bloodthirsty and deceitful men" remind us of the conspiracy against God's appointed king in 2. The God who hears the psalmist (v. 3) bans the arrogant from his presence. The moral principles of access to God in worship are given in two other Davidic psalms, 15 and 24.

5:7-8 The moral qualities of the psalmist's God are in view here. The psalmist does not assert his own moral qualities, but instead sees his access to God's house in reverent worship as due to God's merciful love,[32] and his protection and guidance on God's path as the product of God's righteousness.

5:9-10 The thought of verse 6 is now expanded, with emphasis on the sins of deceitful tongues, whose words show they are gripped by the impulse to destroy. "Their throat is an open grave," symbolizing death, but more forcefully (in a hot climate) "an abominable stench; in the pure air of morality, their words create an abominable smell."[33] The succession of singular

---

29. For NT use of this psalm see pp. 301, 331.

30. The verb אֶעֱרָךְ, *'e'ĕrāk*, translated "lay . . . before" (v. 3 [MT 4]), means "prepare" and lacks grammatical object. Some commentators argue for "sacrifice" rather than "requests," and this might seem appropriate after 4:5. This finds some support in the word's use in sacrificial contexts for arranging the sacrificial material (e.g., in Lev 1:8), and also in v. 7's reference to the temple. On the other hand, the NIV reading works well as identical parallelism with v. 3a. The overall message of the psalm is unaffected whichever is correct.

31. For further comment on lying see pp. 328-30.

32. For the use of "house" and "temple" here and elsewhere, see pp. 36-37.

33. Craigie, *Psalms 1–50*, 88.

49

nouns ("mouth," "heart," "throat," "tongue") suggests a consortium of enemies. As in 2:1-2 they are rebels against God, and the psalmist implicitly appeals to God's righteousness in judgment. It would be fitting for the enemies to be hoist with their own petard.

5:11-12 The psalmist now seeks for others who are right with God the blessings of protection, joy, and divine favor. Here then, as in 2:12 and 3:8, it is clear that God's loving concern is not only with the king of Psalm 2 but with the wider company of the righteous in Psalm 1.

Psalm 6

Although traditionally reckoned a penitential psalm, personal sin is less in view than in most, although verse 1 appears to imply it. The unity of the lament (vv. 1-7) with the later expression of confidence (vv. 8-9) is seen in several verbal links, including the references to mercy (vv. 2, 9) and turning (vv. 4, 10). The NRSV highlights another by translating verses 2b-3a, "My bones are shaking with terror. My soul also is struck with terror," and verse 10 as "all my enemies shall be . . . struck with terror."[34]

6:1-3 The psalmist is apparently experiencing an agonizing illness, not clearly specified, for both "bones" and "soul" probably refer to the whole person, although they could be metaphors for deep distress. He recognizes he is (or at least might be) under God's judgment, and appeals to his mercy for quick relief.[35] His doubled "how long?" (cf. 13:1-2) intensifies the impression of agony.

6:4-5 The illness seems to him potentially lethal, so he prays for a change in God's dealings with him ("turn") and so for physical salvation. His assertion about שְׁאוֹל, *šĕ'ôl* (v. 5, NIV mg.),[36] may reflect his awareness that death would cut him off from worship in God's house rather than a theological comment on life after death.[37]

6:6-7 He reverts to the theme of verses 2 and 3 with a simple yet vivid picture of a night in agony. The foes that appear so often in Davidic psalms give his sufferings another dimension but also perhaps remind him of the promises of God's faithfulness ("unfailing love," v. 4) to his covenant with

---

34. For the NT use of this psalm see p. 300.

35. Craigie suggests that his concern about God's wrath is because he is lamenting rather than simply trusting God's providence (*Psalms 1–50*, 92-93).

36. See pp. 290-91.

37. D. W. Pao emphasizes the connection between remembering and giving thanks, with special reference to 6:5 (*Thanksgiving*, 68). For further comment on life after death, see pp. 423-24.

him.[38] The translation "foes" assumes that the Hebrew noun is connected with a verb meaning "to show hostility to." This is much more likely than theories based on possible Ugaritic and Akkadian parallels.

6:8-10 The vigorous, dramatic change from appeal to assurance suggests to some scholars that a divine word has come to him through a prophet.[39] This is not certain, but it is clear he is now sure of God's answer, so he calls on his foes to depart. The phrases "ashamed and dismayed" and "sudden disgrace" may imply defeat in battle or worsting by God in some other way. In the final verse the soft consonant, ב, *b*, is repeated several times, eloquently displaying a spirit of calm assurance.

Psalm 7

Cush a Benjaminite is otherwise unknown. Saul was a Benjaminite, so the redactor's intended setting is perhaps when David was persecuted by Saul, or during the reign of Ishbosheth, Saul's son, in much of the kingdom. Yet this lament would certainly not be out of place if the reference is to an event during Absalom's rebellion.[40]

7:1-2 Verse 2 shows the king under attack but supported by the heavenly King. Verse 1 says the Lord is a refuge for his people, and verses 3-7 all show the psalmist seeking refuge from his foes in God. Here from his divine refuge he prays for defense from enemies that seem like ravenous beasts (cf. 22:12-21).

7:3-5 His foes have apparently justified their enmity by false accusations. He invokes a virtual curse on himself if their charges are true, which recalls the tender conscience David showed in refusing to harm "the LORD's anointed" (1 Sam 24 and 26).

7:6-9 Words like "arise" and "awake," as elsewhere, suggest divine aid that is not automatic but comes in response to prayer.[41] God comes to his help when he calls, like a human judge responding to pleas for justice.[42] He pictures justice being dispensed in a great international assembly, so the issue in view seems a national one. He seeks justice from a righteous God because

---

38. Cf. Ps 2 and 2 Sam 7.

39. E.g., Craigie, *Psalms 1–50*, 94-95; Kraus, *Psalms 1–59*, 163.

40. Note the incidents connected with Shimei (2 Sam 16:5-14) and Sheba (2 Sam 20:1-22), both Benjaminites. See Wilcock's treatment of each of these psalms (*Psalms 1–72*, 26-45) in the context of his argument that Pss 3–10 are a group originating from this time.

41. E.g., the former in 3:7; Isa 33:10; the latter in Ps 44:23; Isa 51:9.

42. See further comment on judgment on pp. 258-59.

his cause is righteous and he knows that God sees his heart. The phrase "minds and hearts" is physical, literally "hearts and kidneys," the former often associated with thought and the latter with emotion.

7:10-13 He moves from prayer to meditation on the power and righteousness of God the Judge.[43] God's wrath here rather consoles than scares him, assuring him that God is righteous, and he knows his own cause is just. The first "he" of verse 12 could, like the others, be God or it could be his enemy. The latter is the more likely in this context.

7:14-16 The psalmist's familiarity with warfare is shown by his plentiful use of battle imagery. The more general word "refuge" (v. 1) is replaced by "shield" (v. 10), and God's use of sword, bow, and fiery arrows (vv. 12 and 13) is now replaced by the enemy's use of the booby trap. This snares his own feet, and God causes the stone to return on its thrower's head like a boomerang. Verse 14 presents a different figure, a pregnant woman whose offspring is anything but to her liking.

7:17 Here the heading, which calls this psalm a song, is vindicated, for it ends with heartfelt praise to God, the universal, righteous, and supreme judge.

Psalm 8

Here is a sudden major change of theme and emotional tone, with a praise psalm following a series (Pss 3–7) in which the psalmist faces with God the attacks of his enemies.[44] Yahweh's praise as the Supreme One is, however, the climax of Psalm 7 (i.e., in 7:17), so there is a thematic link. Wilcock mentions many features this psalm has in common with Psalms 3–7,[45] but it also takes us back to the two introductory psalms. Like 1, it distinguishes the godly and the ungodly (v. 2); like 2 it focuses on kingship, divine and human, although now the human king is not Israel's monarch but humanity as such. The individual stance of Pss 1–7, with the frequent first person singular, is also found in 8:3, but now in the context of corporate praise ("our Lord," vv. 1, 9), addressed to Yahweh as God of the whole universe. It exhibits both inclusio (vv. 1a and 9) and chiasm (vv. 1b-2 and 5-8), where God's glory and the divinely given human status are in view.

43. Verse 10a reads lit. "my shield is upon God." Craigie (*Psalms 1–50*, 98-99) gives various translations that have been suggested. He sees it as implying that God holds a shield to protect his servant. He also says that, following the Syriac, the word "upon" could be omitted and the line translated, "My shield is God." See also Kraus, *Psalms 1–59*, 168.

44. For NT use of this psalm see p. 350.

45. E.g., the "glory" of 3:3; 4:2 (Wilcock, *Psalms 1–72*, 38).

8:1a, 9 This exclamation of praise identifies Yahweh ("Lord") as "our *Adonai* ("Lord" or "Master"), rightful governor of his people Israel.[46] This term with the possessive is very rare. His kingly majesty is, however, revealed (implied in "your name"), not just to Israel but throughout the earth (cf. Isa 6:3).

8:1b-2 All creation testifies to its glorious Creator. "The language distinguishes between creator and creation while marveling at the majesty of the one discernible in the other."[47] His transcendence is even above the heavens (cf. 1 Kgs 8:27),[48] yet he has decreed praise from the smallest human creatures specifically to silence his enemies (cf. Matt 21:15-16). "Decreed praise" follows the LXX, for the Hebrew translates as "founded a bulwark." The LXX wording here is "probably a paraphrase to show the meaning of the unusual metaphor of an audible bulwark."[49] Verse 2 may be meant as a reminder of "the seed of the woman" bruising the serpent's head in Gen 3:15, especially in view of the links of later verses with Genesis 1.

8:3-5 Although manifestly a hymn, this is one person's contemplation,[50] seeing all as the work of God, not as objects to be worshiped (cf. Deut 4:19). "Set in place" is a reminder of the same verb in Gen 1:17, and the act of creation is vividly presented in the anthropomorphic reference to God's "fingers." In verse 4 מָה, *mâ* ("what?"), rather than מִי, *mî* ("who?"), implies deprecation (cf. 1 Cor 3:5), so intensifying the psalmist's awe at the greatness of apparently insignificant humanity. Moreover, "man" translates אֱנוֹשׁ, *ʾĕnôš*, and "son of man" בֶּן־אָדָם, *ben-ʾādām*, both terms often implying human lowliness or frailty.

This is complemented by reference to our transience in 144:3, which should remind the consecutive reader that even here the great theme is not humanity but God. The mindful care is not expounded but should be compared with 1:6. The glorious divine King now gives glory to humanity, his human king, so that verses 1b-2 and 3-5 are complementary. "Heavenly beings" (v. 5) translates אֱלֹהִים, *ʾĕlōhîm*, which could also mean "God." The NIV fol-

---

46. Later Judaism combined the two words, with the consonants *yhwh* associated with the vowels of *Adonai* (yielding the mistaken rendering "Jehovah"), because it was thought irreverent to pronounce the great Tetragrammaton.

47. Mays, *Psalms*, 65.

48. There are translation difficulties in v. 1b. Dahood (*Psalms*, 1:49) emends the text slightly on the basis of Ugaritic parallels and translates, "I will adore your majesty above the heavens." This is a possible alternative to the NIV translation.

49. Kidner, *Psalms 1–72*, 67 n. 1.

50. This almost childlike sense of wonder fitly follows the reference to children in v. 2. See Davidson, *Vitality of Worship*, 38.

lows the LXX, which may reflect later Judaism's tendency to overemphasize God's transcendence, but could still be correct, especially as elsewhere in the psalm the author never simply refers to God but always addresses him. "Crowned him with glory and honor" must refer to humanity's vicegerency, made explicit in verses 6-8 (cf. Gen 1:26-28). Nowhere is human dignity more strongly affirmed than here.

8:6-8 Here is kingship as God's gift to humanity as such, perhaps indicating this is meant to be an earthly revelation of the divine kingship. The three realms of sentient creatures, the land, the air, and the sea, are all included in the scope of human sovereignty. Nowhere is human dignity more strongly affirmed than here.

Psalms 9 and 10

These are treated as one in some Hebrew manuscripts, the LXX, and the Vulgate.[51] They have some word and thought links, as a comparison of 9:19-20 with both 10:1 and 10:18 reveals. Whether or not originally one, they are, like 32 and 33 and also 105 and 106, feasible companions. Psalm 9, like 1:4-6, gives assurance of the judgment of the wicked,[52] and 10 expresses puzzlement because they apparently sin with impunity (cf. 73:3-14). Psalm 10 has no heading, most unusual in book 1. Together they form an acrostic, which virtually settles the issue.[53] I will assume they belong together.

Although a lament, like Psalms 3–7, Psalm 9 differs from them in starting not with an appeal to God but with praise, and this is very apt after 8. Its theme is God's sovereign judgment, and it moves between the third person of doctrinal affirmation (9:7-9, 11-12, 15-18) and the second of personal worship (vv. 1-6, 10, 13, 19-20). Psalm 10:1-13 appears to question 9's affirmations about God,[54] but faith then reasserts itself (vv. 14-18). So this is not a contradiction, but "a tension to which an honest faith can hardly fail to bear witness."[55] Psalm 9 focuses on God's judgment on nations, while in 10:2-15 it is the judg-

---

51. For NT use of Ps 10 see p. 301.

52. For general discussions of righteousness and judgment see pp. 249-50 and 258-59, respectively.

53. See pp. 29-30. This acrostic is slightly incomplete; Wilcock (*Psalms 1–72*, 42 n. 73) gives the details. Many scholars think it arbitrary, with diverse elements made to fit an artificial scheme; see Mays, *Psalms*, 71, for a contrary view. Wilcock calls the acrostic "a great help in seeing the point of this fascinating two-part poem" (*Psalms 1–72*, 41).

54. Cf. Ps 89, where vv. 38-51 question the affirmations of vv. 1-37.

55. Davidson, *Vitality of Worship*, 41.

ment of the wicked individual that is in view, the assumption being that all wickedness merits punishment.

9:1-6 Wholehearted praise (v. 1; cf. 103:1) is focused on God's revealed wonders, perhaps in nature (cf. Ps 8) or in supporting his servant (cf. Pss 1–7).[56] Certainly the latter becomes the focus of verses 3-6, where the psalmist affirms God's righteous support of his cause against his enemies. The historical and the eschatological appear to be linked, for the perfect tenses of verses 3 and 4 are historical and those of verses 5 and 6 prophetic.

9:7-10 Here the divine King's eternal, universal, and righteous judgment is declared. It is both the guarantee of ultimate justice (v. 8) and the ground of confidence that those experiencing oppression can trust him with full assurance.

9:11-12 Yahweh's judgment throne is localized in Zion, but his praise there is to be heard by all nations, an implication of his right to judge the whole world (cf. v. 8). Israel, afflicted by their enemies, knows him as their avenger.

9:13-16 Because that is the kind of God he is, the psalmist cries to him in his situation of persecution, asking that for him the gates of death[57] may be replaced by the gates of Zion, where he will praise God in his temple. Again verses 15 and 16 contain prophetic perfects (variously rendered as past and present tenses in NIV), in which he envisages God in justice making the punishment fit the crime (cf. 7:14-16). The meaning of *Higgaion* is uncertain but probably has musical significance.

9:17-18 He looks from the present to the future for complete fulfillment of God's righteous judgment both on the wicked and on those they afflict.

9:19-20 In view of this he can call on the Lord to arise as judge of all the nations, asserting his deity against the wicked schemes of puny humans.

10:1 These questions follow well after 9:19-20, for the cry to God to arise suggests he seems inactive at present. Sometimes God can seem too transcendent.

10:2-11 These verses focus on the wicked person, whose chief characteristic is pride, clearly in view in verses 2-5 and probably shown in complacent self-assurance in v. 6. Here is a devious bully (2), blasphemously reversing values to make possible approval of greed and reviling of God (3; cf. Isa 5:20). Unlike those who know God's name (Ps 9:10), this person does not seek him (10:4) and indeed is anxious to exclude God and his laws from personal

---

56. Ps 7 ends, as this begins, with praise, and the intervening Ps 8 is a praise psalm, revealing editorial design.

57. Presumably to enter Sheol. See also 9:17 and pp. 290-91.

life and thought (4-5), with a complacency that knows no bounds (6). As verse 2 shows and as verses 7-11 amplify, the wicked person is also aggressive and cruel, murderously scheming and, like the hungry lion and the fisherman, employing secret stratagems to accomplish wicked ends. The complacency of verse 6 reappears (v. 11), but now more blatantly irreverent.

10:12-15 The psalmist calls on God for help, using in verse 15 the language of the law court. Verse 13 probably asks the reason not for human sin but for divine inaction in the face of it. This is immediately followed by statements of confidence in him, based on experience. This oscillation of complaint and conviction is somewhat characteristic of the book of Job.

10:16-18 The psalm ends, as Psalm 9 began, with strong confidence in the Lord's sovereignty and his care for the weak, now specified as the fatherless and the oppressed. The psalmist apparently has in view some national emergency, so that the wicked person here will be a personification representative of the aggressive invading nations. The links of thought and language between 9:18-20 and these verses serve to underline how impossible it is for the wicked to oppress the defenseless with impunity. Arrogant humans, whether as nations or individuals, cannot stand before God's judgment. That God hears their prayers is an encouragement to the afflicted godly.

Psalm 11

This anticipates 73 in raising questions about the oppression of the righteous by the wicked.[58] What is its setting? Much here would fit Absalom's rebellion when the foundations of David's kingdom seemed to be destroyed, so it is surprising that it lacks biographical superscription. Moreover, Wilcock is able to relate it to an earlier period in David's life.[59] In view of this, it might be wise, and be in line with the redactor's intention, to see its appropriateness as encouraging trust in God whenever the kingdom was under threat.

11:1a Putting "in the LORD" in the emphatic first place in the sentence follows the Hebrew, countering from the beginning the pessimistic counsel that follows. The theme of a divine place of refuge first occurs at the close of the king's enthronement psalm (2:12).

11:1b-3 How much of this is the advice of the pessimists? Just verse 1b, or 1b-2, or even 1b-3? The last would make good sense, but we cannot be cer-

---

58. For general discussions of righteousness and judgment in the Psalter, see pp. 249-50 and 258-59.

59. Wilcock, *Psalms 1–72,* 45-48.

tain, and verse 3, for instance, could be the psalmist's own reflection on the situation. We will assume, with NIV, that the whole section records their words. Echoes of Absalom's rebellion are at their strongest here if the mountain suggests where the cave of Adullam was ("*your* mountain"), if the plural "flee" includes David's faithful followers (cf. 1 Sam 22:1-2), and if the reference to a bird called to mind God's protection recorded in 1 Sam 26:20. "The foundations" probably relates to something specific, like the kingship. "The upright in heart" and "the righteous" do not imply sinlessness but a right relationship with God.[60]

11:4-6 In the face of the pessimism of others, the psalmist asserts his confidence in God. Yahweh is both the one true object of worship and the sole universal sovereign. Moreover, unlike earthly monarchs he is not only supreme but all-knowing, with detailed understanding clearly distinguishing the righteous and the wicked. If verse 4a, like 4b, is in synonymous parallelism, then the temple would appear to be heavenly, not earthly; but if it is in fact earthly,[61] the psalmist's understanding that the Lord discriminates between the righteous and the wicked accords with the new perspective the author of 73 received when he entered God's temple (73:17). The word "examine" suggests a refiner's testing of metals and so a positive purpose in the sufferings of the righteous, in contrast to the destructive fire of judgment, devouring the wicked, reminiscent of Sodom's judgment (Gen 19:24), with the scorching desert wind providing a further illustration.[62]

11:7 The psalm that opened with confidence in Yahweh's protection concludes by affirming his justice and its ultimate evidence. "See his face" suggests divine favor (cf. 4:6; 16:8-11; Num 6:24-26).

Psalm 12

Many of the sins mentioned here, such as lying, flattering, deceiving, boasting, and maligning, are sins of the tongue (cf. Jer 9:1-9), and the main emphasis of the psalm is on the contrast between human falseness and divine veracity, serving the ends of oppression and justice, respectively. Verse 5 may suggest a law court, with a strong, boastful oppressor and his weak, needy vic-

---

60. See discussion of "righteous" in pp. 249-50.

61. For the use of "temple" here and elsewhere, see pp. 36-37.

62. Here "their lot" is lit. "the portion of their cup," reflecting the way the family head distributed drinks at table. It is used at times somewhat ironically of divine punishments, e.g., in 75:8; Isa 51:17; Hab 2:16.

tim. The former flatters and deceives the judge and, although vile, is honored by him, while the latter groans under continued oppression.

12:1-2 Allan Harman points out that this is a cry of desperation, not even completed by the word "me."[63] The hyperbole in the author's words is understandable. The help for which he asks becomes clear later (vv. 5, 7). "Lies" (v. 2) is שָׁוְא, *šāw'*, used in the third commandment (Exod 20:7) of speech empty of truth.

12:3-4 Here is blatant godlessness, because for a godly person the question (v. 4) can have only one answer — the Lord. Several psalms refer to God as "arising" in connection with acts of judgment (cf. 3:7; 7:6; 44:26; 68:1). Broyles notes that the description of the wicked in verses 2-4 is similar to the description of what disqualifies a person from temple entry in Psalms 15 and 24.[64]

12:5-6 Verse 5 is a divine oracle, possibly uttered through a prophet or priest, or alternatively given directly to the psalmist. Verse 6 is probably meant to be both specific (the oracle will certainly be fulfilled) and general (this is what the Lord's words are always like).

12:7-8 The psalmist sums up by asserting his strong conviction of God's protection of his people from falseness and its arrogant triumphalism, and this is based on the veracity of his word of promise. The reiterated "us" shows his community concern. With its graphic picture of rampant evil, verse 8 does not deny divine action but rather reaffirms its need.

Psalm 13

This, the Psalter's shortest prayer for deliverance, exhibits a striking change of tone. It starts with urgent, agitated complaint (vv. 1-2), moves through prayers that, although still urgent, are in a quieter spirit (vv. 3-4), and climaxes in joyful trust (vv. 5-6). What has caused this change? Reflecting on God's covenant with his people and the acts of salvation that resulted from it (v. 5).

13:1-2 The Psalter's longest series of consecutive questions, although showing the psalmist's deep, intensifying concern, also reveals his faith, for it queries not the fact of the Lord's intervention in his situation but its delay. Schaefer points out that even the sound of the Hebrew phrase, עַד־אָנָה, *'ad-*

---

63. "Here, and also in the Hebrew text of Psalm 118:25, the shout is never finished. It is like a drowning person calling out 'Help'" (Harman, *Psalms*, 94-95).

64. Especially 15:2-3; 24:4 (Broyles, *Psalms*, 82-83).

ʾānâ ("How long"), is "a plaintive moan over the loss of God's nearness."[65] "Hide your face" shows he is missing the tokens of divine acceptance, for the Lord's face no longer appears to shine on him (cf. Num 6:24-26 and Ps 4:6). Verse 3 shows this causes him agonized theological questionings. The nature of the situation emerges clearly in the final question.

13:3-4 "Look on me" contrasts with "hide your face from me" (v. 1). Perhaps he has suffered a potentially lethal wound. If so, "light to my eyes" contrasts sharply with "sleep in death." Sleep is an apt metaphor for death, for a sleeping body could at times be mistaken for a dead one. His demise would seal the enemy's triumph. Some have even suggested that death itself is the enemy here, while "my foes" would be human.[66] This is possible, but verse 4's parallelism makes it more likely both the enemy and the foes are human, perhaps Saul or Absalom along with their supporters.

13:5-6 At this point of "remarkable transition,"[67] his faith, never in eclipse but lacking joy, becomes articulate in song. Has he been reassured by a divine word or act on his behalf? Perhaps, but the text does not say so. The basis of his faith is the covenant,[68] and "salvation" here is either the saving acts of the God of the covenant in past days, his own anticipated deliverance, or, most likely, the expectation of the latter, encouraged by recalling the former. Verse 6 summarizes his ultimate verdict on the situation, viewed retrospectively.

Psalm 14

Psalm 10 gives an extended description of the wicked person (10:1-11); now we see how widespread is that wickedness and its basis in godlessness.[69] Verses 4 and 7 suggest that the psalm is to be viewed as a lament that closes with the psalmist's deep longing for a better day through divine action. Psalms 14 and 53 are similar, but there are some significant differences between 14:5b-6 and 53:5. See the commentary on 53.

14:1 This is, if not theoretical, at least practical atheism, deeply ingrained in a person's heart. This ungodliness is associated here with bad character and bad deeds, as in Rom 1:18ff., and the final statement is repeated in verse 3.

---

65. Schaefer, *Psalms*, 32.

66. Cf. Craigie, *Psalms 1–50*, 142.

67. McCann, *Theological Introduction*, 90-98, in a most helpful interpretation of this psalm.

68. "Unfailing love" is חֶסֶד, *ḥesed*, love within a covenant relationship.

69. For NT use of this psalm see p. 301.

14:2-3 At Babel God came down to see (Gen 11:5); here he looks down. The parallelism of verse 2b and its context suggest that the lack of understanding is the practical atheism of verse 1. The strong statements here, with the psalmist's emphatic reiteration, may in this context relate particularly to the evildoers he has in view in verse 4, but Paul's use of these verses in Rom 3:11-12 in his catena of OT quotations shows that he saw their language to be appropriate to express sin's universality. The word translated "corrupt," though different from that in verse 1, has a similar force.

14:4-6 These verses suggest qualification of the strong statements of verses 1-3. Broyles in particular shows how the psalm's context helps our understanding,[70] for Psalm 11 shows God, as here, examining "the sons of men" (11:4-5) and finding both righteous and wicked, while Psalm 12 starts with strong statements about sin's universality but also shows God protecting the weak and the needy, presumed to be godly. Broyles sees the apparent contradiction as evidence of justifying grace in an OT context, possibly why in Romans Paul's mind turned to this passage.[71]

So then God has his people (v. 4), in whose company he is present (v. 5) and who are often poor (v. 6). The failure of evildoers to learn forms a link with verse 2, although their dread strongly suggests practical rather than theoretical atheism. The particular sin in view looks like the oppression or exploitation of the poor by the powerful rich, so often condemned by the prophets, most significantly by Nathan in 2 Sam 12:1-7. In verse 6 the psalmist addresses the evildoers. The refuge theme is a major feature of the Davidic psalms.

14:7 The thought connection with the rest of the psalm is not obvious. Perhaps it indicates the extension of folly to international relations and so to the persecution of Israel by foreign nations. Here, as often, Zion (probably the house of God there; cf., e.g., 3:4) is the source of divine help.[72] Restoring the fortunes of God's people is often taken as a reference to the return from exile, added by the redactor, but it could relate to an earlier deliverance.

Psalm 15

This entrance liturgy's contrast with Psalm 14 suggests deliberate editorial juxtapositioning. The introductory Psalm 1 set out the two ways, that of the

---

70. Broyles, *Psalms*, 88-90.

71. Mays (*Psalms*, 82-83) is of much the same mind. Broyles saw evidence of justifying grace in an OT context in another Davidic psalm (32:1-2), quoted in Rom 4:7-8.

72. This might appear to introduce an anachronism, but see comment on pp. 36-37.

righteous and that of the wicked. Here they have a psalm each, but in reverse order. Note also a negative expression of the same theme in 5:4-5, and that Psalm 24 is another entrance psalm. Wim VanGemeren has well said that it should be seen as more than an entrance psalm, for "its purpose is to guide God's people into a life of holiness, justice, and righteousness so that they may live in the presence of God, wherever they may reside."[73] It could be significant that there are no penitential psalms between 15 and 24 and that the emphasis in this section of the Psalter is on godliness.

15:1 In a pentateuchal context, the question would expect an answer in ceremonial, Levitical terms. The word "sanctuary" (v. 1) is literally "tent," suggesting both the place of worship and the home. "If God, in the words of Ps. 14:5, is 'with the company of the righteous,' then who may rightly belong to this company and thus be welcomed as a guest, the LORD's guest, in his tent (i.e., temple)?"[74] This psalm tells us.

15:2-5b Here fitness is shown by conduct, an emphasis in line with the teaching of the prophets.[75] "Blameless" translates תָּמִים, *tāmîm*, meaning "wholehearted" and therefore completely faithful to Yahweh.[76] Mowinckel thought the qualities of the accepted person here were modeled on the Decalogue, not by exact correspondence but simply because there are ten of them, this feature providing an aide-mémoire.[77] There is some alternation of positive and negative groups in the list. The godly lifestyle is expounded largely in terms of the tongue's use, as so often in the Psalms. The fool of 14:1 has a godless heart, the perfect worshiper here a truthful one. Slander breaches the ninth commandment (Exod 20:16) and is serious enough to dominate verse 3.[78]

Verse 4, while not explicitly imprecatory, rejects particular qualities and admires others, not considered abstractly but focused on their possessors. Those honored are not just moral but truly godly, for "fear of the LORD" is basic to OT Yahwism.[79] Oath keeping is a function of such fear, for oaths were made in God's presence. Usury was permissible in dealing with foreigners but not Israelites.[80]

This challenging picture of a righteous person is of obvious general ap-

---

73. VanGemeren, "Psalms," 149.
74. Davidson, *Vitality of Worship*, 56.
75. E.g., in Isa 1:10-17; Mic 6:6-8.
76. Note how in Deut 18:13 it sums up vv. 9-12.
77. Mowinckel, *Psalms in Israel's Worship*, 1:179.
78. See comment on sins of the tongue on pp. 328-29.
79. E.g., Deut. 6:2, 13; Josh 24:24; Ps 22:23; Prov 3:7.
80. Deut 23:19-20; cf. "neighbor" here (v. 3).

plication, but the superscription reminds us that to bestow honor (v. 4) and to administer justice (v. 5), while not exclusively regal functions, were major prerogatives of the king, of David and his royal successors. Moreover, worship in the sanctuary (v. 1) was not to be viewed as mere ritual in which moral considerations played no part.

15:5c Perhaps this closing comment suggests such a person will be as unshakable as the sanctuary where he may dwell (cf. 125:1).

Psalm 16

Although it starts like many laments, with a prayer for safety, this psalm breathes joy, and it is a fit sequel to Psalm 15, for here is a profoundly God-centered person.[81]

16:1 This is both a prayer and a demonstration of confident faith, for David is sure God will protect him (cf. 2:12c).

16:2-4 There are textual difficulties and two completely different interpretations of these verses. Some, including the NIV translators,[82] see in them a decisive, unqualified commitment to Yahweh as master reminiscent of Joshua (Josh 24:15) and Elijah (1 Kgs 18:21, 36), with recognition too that all good comes from him. David delights in the saints (קְדוֹשִׁים, *qĕdôšîm*), the glorious ones, with perhaps the suggestion that as king he supports them (cf. 15:4 and the comment there).

Others, noting that "I said," is in the MT "you said,"[83] and that both קְדוֹשִׁים, *qĕdôšîm*, and אַדִּירֵי, *'addîrê*, translated "glorious ones," can be used of pagan deities,[84] consider verses 2 and 3 a hypocritical profession of faithfulness to Yahweh by a paganizing syncretist, presumably an acquaintance of the psalmist, and see verse 4 as the psalmist's comment.[85] This is now the majority view and has the merit of following the Hebrew the more closely.

The psalmist's conviction in verse 4a is in tune with 1:4-6, but, if verses 10 and 11 contrast with this, it may be understood eschatologically. His assertion of personal religious separation perhaps suggests he is thinking of paganism in the land rather than elsewhere.[86]

16:5-6 "Portion" and "inheritance" may have been suggested by "land"

81. For NT use of this psalm see p. 358.
82. See also Kidner, *Psalms 1–72*, 83-84; Weiser, *Psalms*, 173-74.
83. But often read as "I said" in the LXX, many Hebrew MSS, and other ancient versions.
84. See Dahood, *Psalms*, 1:87-88.
85. See Anderson, *Psalms*, 1:141-42; Craigie, *Psalms 1–50*, 153-56; Harman, *Psalms*, 102.
86. Note "who are in the land" (v. 3).

(v. 3), for they are territorial terms reminiscent of the division of the land executed by lot (cf. Josh 17:5). They are better viewed as spiritual rather than literal, and their link with "cup," with its connotations of refreshment and celebration, tends to confirm this. The portion analogy is developed to the end of verse 6, which has an aesthetic reference, while that of the cup is not spelled out but remains suggestive.

16:7-11   The joyful praise becomes more explicit. אֲבָרֵךְ, *'ăbārēk*, rendered "I will praise" in NIV, is literally "I will bless" (so NRSV), suggesting a desire to give to the Lord. God gives him practical counsel, even at night (v. 7, perhaps suggesting light in the darkness), showing him the way of life instead of death (vv. 10-11). Verse 8a affirms again his earlier commitment to Yahweh. His divine counselor also stands alongside him to keep him stable and secure (cf. v. 1). He is convinced he will be brought to the eternal pleasures of God's presence. Verse 10 may refer to preservation from (premature) death, but clear contextual support for this is lacking as the psalm does not suggest imminent peril of death, and the petition of verse 1 in no way dominates it. It can therefore be read, quite naturally but startlingly, as rescue after death. This is the way the NT applies it (Acts 2:25-31; 13:35-37), presumably typologically, with the antitype (Christ's resurrection) going, as always, beyond the type (the psalmist's simple conviction of life beyond death). Verse 11bc certainly appears to relate to life beyond death.[87]

Psalm 17

Here is assurance based on the covenant. חֶסֶד, *ḥesed* ("love," v. 7), love faithful to a covenant, is therefore a key word here. Davidson remarks on the way literary craftsmanship is here put to theological service.[88] Like Psalm 16, it is fitting in a sequence that follows 15, which is an entrance psalm.

17:1-5   This prayer is urgent, as the threefold parallelism of verse 1 shows, and is based, throughout these verses, on the psalmist's righteousness (cf. also v. 15), and righteousness in the OT never implies total sinlessness but rather commitment to Yahweh.[89] He is without deceit (v. 1; cf. v. 3), his heart fixed on God, and the all-seeing one knows he does not follow the ways of the violent (cf.

---

87. V. 11c is not easy to explain if the psalmist is writing of deliverance from going into death, although it could simply mean that now his thought has moved beyond his immediate situation and he is thinking about life after death. Some, however, view "eternal" here as meaning "as long as life shall last" (e.g., Anderson, *Psalms*, 1:146).

88. Davidson, *Vitality of Worship*, 61.

89. See the discussion of righteousness on pp. 249-50.

perhaps 1:1), but rather God's paths. His concern for vindication suggests his integrity has been impugned, which would account for his strong moral statements. As in 16:1-4, 8, his commitment to his God is total. There he was counseled during the night (16:7), which is when God tests him here. Verse 4 suggests the sanctifying function of God's Word, so much extolled in Psalm 119.

17:6-12 Verse 6 virtually repeats the prayer of verse 1, plus the assurance of an answer. Verse 7 pleads the covenant as well as extolling it and the security it gives those it protects. The "right hand" underlines God's power to save, signally revealed at the exodus.[90] Verse 8 illuminates the thought of verse 7 by two vivid images: the eye's pupil and the bird's young, both so vulnerable and needing protection (cf. Deut 32:10-11). Both this and the previous psalm seem to echo the thought and even the language of Deut 10:12-14. Verses 9-12 memorably portray the psalmist's enemies, so aggressive, so near, so all-encircling, so cruel and proud, as brutal, as resourceful and as eager for blood as a great lion. The arrogance of their lips (v. 10) contrasts with the sincerity of his prayer (v. 1).

17:13-15 Here again prayer (vv. 13-14a) moves into assurance (cf. v. 6). God is like a warrior roused from slumber to protect others from their foes (cf. 3:7; 9:19-20). Verse 14a and verses 14b and 15 are in strong contrast.[91] It might seem as if both the wicked and the righteous have material benefits, but the psalmist looks beyond this life to an awakening. A reference to resurrection here seems more likely than just the dawning of a new day, making a fitting contrast with "this life" (v. 15).[92] Resurrection is pictured as awakening also in Isa 26:19 and Dan 12:2. In a psalm with Mosaic echoes, seeing God's likeness reminds us of Exod 33:18-23; Num 12:8; and Deut 34:10.

Psalm 18[93]

Most scholars now see this psalm as very old, and the possibility that all or much of it is by David is quite widely (but not universally) accepted, even by

---

90. V. 7 and Exod. 15:11-13 have a number of linguistic links.

91. Translation of v. 14 is particularly difficult; see Craigie, *Psalms 1–50*, 161. Some, including NRSV, take v. 14b quite differently. Weiser, for instance, views v. 14b as "gruesome irony," with the psalmist picturing God destroying the enemies by "a mysterious food secretly stored up by God for future retribution, whereby they as well as their children and grandchildren shall 'be satiated'" (*Psalms*, 182).

92. Cf. 16:10-11 and comment there.

93. For NT use of this psalm see p. 356. For a reader-response approach to it see D. K. Berry, *Psalm 18*.

some denying most other psalms to him.[94] It is sometimes used as a yardstick for measuring whether others headed לְדָוִד, *lĕdāwid*, are by him. This can hardly produce assured results, for consistency of style, *Sitz im Leben*, and so on, are unlikely in a long life's literary output. The psalm also occurs with some variations in 2 Samuel 22. It may have been used regularly at festival time to celebrate God's support of the king.[95]

18:1 A rare expression of the psalmist's love as distinct from his faith or joy, the word used being normally employed not of human love but of divine.[96] In the Psalter's order it is apt after 17:7[97] and points to a close, warm relationship between the Lord and David before, in "Yahweh my strength," he sounds the psalm's keynote.

18:2-3 The oft-repeated possessive demonstrates David's exclusive devotion and trust in Yahweh. Among the largely inanimate images, we note the personal "deliverer." The repetition of "Rock" (vv. 31, 46) is reminiscent of Deuteronomy 32, with its roots in the exodus–wilderness wandering tradition. His faith (v. 2) prompts his prayer (v. 3), recalling for the consecutive reader Yahweh's promises to the king in Psalm 2.

18:4-6 Two analogies are employed, with that of the hunter's snares repeated, perhaps because the threat came from human sources.[98] שְׁאוֹל, *šĕ'ôl*, is clearly a synonym for death. Verse 6 intensifies the impression that, after verses 1-3, the psalmist is focusing on one personal crisis. The temple here is almost certainly heavenly, not earthly.

18:7-15 These verses are outstanding for their vivid, dynamic imagery. This indicates not only that God "pulled out all the stops" to help him, but that he had already shown his power in nature and in history. Kraus says, "The entire event is sketched to form an archetypal happening in whose vast realm the petitioner 'finds a place' for himself and his specific distress."[99] Here is the imagery of the earthquake (v. 7), the thunderstorm (vv. 11-14), and perhaps the volcanic eruption on sea and land (v. 15). It is often thought to draw on language employed of the storm god in Near Eastern mythology, to show that Yahweh is the true author and controller of all such phenom-

---

94. For evidence of its early preexilic dating, see Cross and Freedman, "Royal Song," 72. Broyles (*Psalms*, 102) sees it as an edited composition, and some scholars view it as two or more separate works.

95. See Eaton, *Kingship*, 113-16.

96. An interesting anticipation of the NT use of ἀγαπάω, *agapaō*, for the love both of God and of Christians.

97. Davidson (*Vitality of Worship*, 65) argues for its appropriateness here.

98. Cf. the portion and cup in 16:5-6 and the comment there.

99. Kraus, *Psalms 1–59*, 259.

ena,[100] but it also recalls Yahweh's historical acts for his people, especially the exodus, the giving of the law at Sinai, and, in verse 14, the dramatic events of Joshua 10.[101] God's wrath (vv. 7 and 15) was manifested in his routing of David's enemies (v. 14) and so in his rescue. The term "Most High" (v. 13) is ancient (cf. Gen 14:18), suggesting his universal kingly power exhibited in victory over foreign foes.

18:16-19   This is if anything even more strongly anthropomorphic. Verse 16 develops the watery imagery of verse 4, and in this verse, as Schaefer says, "the divine descent spans the cosmos."[102] The plural and singular of the psalm's heading perhaps reflect verse 17, with Saul as the "powerful enemy." The day of disaster is unidentified, but the superior strength of David's enemies may suggest Saul's persecution. Perhaps too verse 19 relates to David's emergence from the cave of Adullam when danger from Saul was past.

18:20-24   These verses show why God delighted in him (v. 19). The whole passage is emphatic, using both repetition and variation within the same general idea. The repeated reference to not turning away (expressed by different verbs in vv. 21 and 22) may be the key to this section, emphasizing his faithfulness to God's laws and therefore to the way of life he has prescribed. In the Psalter and in the OT generally "righteousness" is not so much sinlessness as integrity.[103] For "blameless" (v. 23; cf. v. 25), see the comment on 15:2. Davidson says that in verses 20-31 what we find is not self-congratulation but recognition of God's favorable acceptance of the obedient.[104] In this respect it is fitting after the entrance psalm (15), which is followed by 16 and 17, both illustrating godliness.

18:25-29   Not surprisingly, after verses 20-24, this passage gives priority to faithfulness. God requites the faithful with faithfulness (cf. 21:7), dealing with both the righteous and the wicked as their characters require (cf. 1:6). Verse 27 shows verses 20-24 to be compatible with humility. Keeping his lamp burning is used in 132:17 with reference to the messianic king[105] but has a different nuance here, suggesting also a change of fortunes under God's hand. Verse 29 now shows David going from defense to attack (cf. vv. 16-19).

18:30-36   Verse 31 demonstrates David's monotheism, the basis of his

---

100. See pp. 240-41.

101. The cherubim appear also as attending on Yahweh (v. 10), again in connection with a storm, in Ezek 1.

102. Schaefer, *Psalms*, 42.

103. See p. 339.

104. Davidson, *Vitality of Worship*, 67.

105. See also 2 Sam 21:17, where David is "the lamp of Israel," and 2 Sam 22:29, where he says, "You are my lamp, O LORD."

faithfulness. The double perfection (vv. 30, 32) probably sums up verses 25 and 26a, but the psalmist attributes perfection not to his character but to his way, ordered by God's flawless Word (cf. 17:4), itself testimony to God's own perfection. Verses 31 and 32 recall verses 1 and 2, but emphasizing now victory rather than rescue. In hand-to-hand fighting the stability of the feet is as important as the skill of the hands. He attributes all this to God's powerful right hand. He had reached down to rescue him (v. 16); now he stoops to make him great (v. 35). The terrain here (vv. 33 and 36) is certainly consistent with David's movement around rocky Judah when pursued by Saul.

18:37-42 The focus is now on David's enemies. His victory over them had been overwhelming, for they were utterly destroyed, fleeing headlong from him (v. 40). Bowing at his feet (v. 39) was either before their destruction or else is a figure for their total vanquishing. That they called on Yahweh might fit the time of strife between the men of David and Ish-bosheth (2 Sam 2–4), as the latter too were Israelites, although Jon 1:14 shows us pagans calling on the God of Israel.

18:43-45 עַם, 'ām ("people"), is used twice in verse 43, both in the singular. Comparison with 2 Sam 22:44 suggests that the first refers to his own people, but the second is used, unusually, of Gentiles. David's headship of the nations (cf. 89:27), shown historically in 2 Samuel 8, made him almost like an emperor, foreshadowing the fulfillment of 2:8. Verses 44 and 45 were also historically true (2 Sam 8:9-10).

18:46-50 This coda's high emotion is almost as unmistakable as that of Romans 8. The psalm's implicit note of praise becomes explicit. David avenged, saved, exalted, rescued, now overflows with praise. The opening affirmation, "Yahweh lives!"[106] recalls his words to Goliath (1 Sam 17:26). The psalm ends (v. 50) with supreme confidence in the abiding character of the Davidic covenant, reminding us of Psalm 2 and even more of 2 Samuel 7. Some reckon that verse 50 cannot be Davidic because of its third person form, but this form occurs on David's lips in the basic covenant passage (2 Sam 7:20, 26).[107]

Psalm 19

In the opinion of C. S. Lewis, this is the greatest poem in the Psalter.[108] There is a deep undercurrent of joy here, which disappears only briefly in verses 12

---

106. Mays calls this the "theological climax" of the psalm (*Psalms*, 90).
107. There is a fine, fuller exegesis of this psalm in Davidson, *Vitality of Worship*, 64-69.
108. See his whole comment, *Reflections*, 56-57.

and 13. If Psalm 15 shows the conditions of fellowship with God and 16 to 18 reveal godliness in action, this reveals its basis in deep commitment to the Word of God and dependence on his power.[109]

19:1-4   The controlling idea here is that the skies, both day and night, communicate knowledge about God, his glory, and his creative activity, either universally (as in NIV of v. 3) or, following NRSV ("There is no speech, nor are there words; their voice is not heard"), voicelessly.[110] Compare and contrast this with Psalm 29, where God's voice is audible in the storm. The communication is universal (vv. 3-4), for the sky is visible everywhere, and it is unceasing. This is not natural theology. "The psalmist is not arguing from the world to God. He is looking at the world through the eyes of a faith born of Israel's encounter with and response to God, the faith which he confesses in verses 7-14."[111]

19:5-6   Building on the foregoing, these verses move from the general to one particular, the sun and its regular motion, the sky's most impressive regular feature. The language is phenomenal, as in Genesis 1, without scientific motive or intention, and, like that great chapter, appears to be antipagan. Here the sun is no deity, as so many in the Near East believed, but is controlled by the one true God. The two illustrations indicate both motion and joy, for the bridegroom goes to claim his bride and the champion attains his intended goal. Like the voice of the heavens, the sun's heat is felt everywhere.

19:7-10   Now the divine name, Yahweh, is introduced, with, most appropriately, a perfectly structured series of synonymously parallel statements about the תּוֹרָה, *tôrâ* ("law").[112] C. S. Lewis noted how easily the psalmist passes from the sun to the law, which "hardly seems to him something else because it is so like the all-piercing, all-detecting sunshine."[113] Nothing is hidden from the heat, whether of God's sun or his Word.

Many terms used of the law in Psalm 119 are employed, suggesting their technical character. The statements ascribe particular qualities to it, with some emphasis on its reliability, capacity to enlighten, and attractiveness. Its consequences in imparting life, wisdom (which goes beyond the knowledge

---

109. For NT use of this psalm see pp. 301, 311, 349.

110. Either is possible, depending on whether v. 3 is viewed as anticipating the thought of v. 4. See Wilson, *Psalms*, 1:433. קָו *qāw*, normally meaning "line" (v. 4), is here translated "voice." It is used in Isa 28:11 for unintelligible language and is employed here for the kindred idea of communication without articulated speech. See Kraus, *Psalms 1–59*, 271-72; and for other suggestions, Anderson, *Psalms*, 1:169.

111. Davidson, *Vitality of Worship*, 70.

112. See Magonet, *Rabbi*, 92-94.

113. Lewis, *Reflections*, 56.

displayed through the skies), joy (like the sun's "joy"), and light (an intended comparison with the sun?) are uniformly blessings. In the Psalter's final arrangement, this passage may have functioned to recall the basic Psalm 1 with its commendation of meditation on the divine revelation, *tôrâ*, in the sense of instruction, including the whole Psalter, although the sense "law" is clearly that intended by the psalmist himself.[114]

19:11-14   The psalmist's thought moves from the objective spheres of the universe and the law to his own heart. In verse 11 he sees the law's value both to warn and to encourage (cf. 1:1-3), and he develops the former in verses 12 and 13a. He is anything but self-righteous, for he sees that even his unrealized sins need forgiveness and that there are sins that are paradoxically both willful and yet, unless God intervenes in keeping power, evidence of moral incapacity. It is God's action that will preserve him from such willfulness, so he ends with prayer that both his articulated and unarticulated thought may please him.[115] He is his Rock and Redeemer, both echoing the exodus complex of events, for God redeemed the people from Egypt and was their Rock in the desert experiences that followed (cf. Deut 32:4, 15, 18, 30-31).

Significantly the psalm ends as it began with reference to communication. Was the psalmist here aware of the inspiring Spirit at work in his mind and on his tongue? Comparisons of language and thought with 2 Sam 23:1-4 might suggest so.

Psalm 20

Psalms 20 and 21 are clearly companions, for 20 intercedes for the king before battle (see vv. 5-8), and 21 expresses thanks for the help that came to him from God and declares confidence in him for the future. For the consecutive reader they recall Psalm 2, which promises the heavenly King's support of the earthly king and encourages him to pray. The king's plans and their success (20:4; 21:2) contrast with those of the rebels in 2:1-3. If Psalm 15 shows the conditions of fellowship with God *at* his sanctuary, and if Psalms 16–19 explore the godly character, these psalms show God sending help *from* the sanctuary to a godly king.

The king is referred to in the third person in 20:6, 9, and 21:1-7 (as he is in the whole of 72) and in the second person (which is singular throughout both psalms) elsewhere. There seems little doubt that these psalms were used

---

114. See comments on Ps 1.
115. Possibly recalling the articulate and the inaudible communications in vv. 1-4.

liturgically in times of war.[116] The king is never named, suggesting these psalms were viewed dynastically so that the protection of the present king would symbolize God's support of the Davidic line. In this respect they may be likened to 72 if there a prayer for Solomon became also a regular prayer for the reigning monarch and so for the Davidic line as such.

This psalm's poetic beauty has often been noted.[117]

20:1 The prayer opens with a general appeal to Yahweh as "God of Jacob," the God of the patriarchal covenant, so grounding it in a relationship long predating the Davidic covenant.[118] It presupposes the faithfulness not only of the Lord but also of the king, for it is to Yahweh and none other he calls, and Yahweh's name is again the focus of faith in verses 5 and 7.

20:2-3 These verses center on Zion and its sanctuary offerings. For "help from the sanctuary" cf. 3:4. The support God gives the king in the battle will show his acceptance of the sacrifices offered.

20:4-5 His heart's desire may be a limited one, success in the battle, but it has a wider context, perhaps a long-term military strategy. The sudden change to the first person plural shows that earlier a representative of the people, probably a priest or prophet, has been praying on their behalf. The banner was a rallying standard in a battle.

20:6-8 Verses 1-5 record what the king heard of the people's prayer. Now he speaks personally. Sacrifices (vv. 2-3), prayers (vv. 4-5), and God's promises to the anointed king (vv. 6-8; cf. 2 Sam 7) all show God as the one author of his people's victory. The reference to "his anointed" may suggest he is thinking not only personally but dynastically. Now the answer comes from Yahweh's heavenly dwelling rather than from the earthly sanctuary, which was its symbol. "His right hand" is a reminder of his power, shown supremely at the exodus (cf. Exod 15:12). Both NIV "trust" and NRSV "take pride in" (v. 7) are possible ways of taking the Hebrew,[119] which literally means "remember" or "acknowledge." Verse 7a reflects the divine constitution for the king in Deut 17:14-20. Verse 8 suggests comparison with the general promise to the righteous in 1:6. The "name" is all-powerful (cf. vv. 1 and 5).

20:9 This sums up the theme and also shows that the good of the whole people was bound up with that of the king.

---

116. But Eaton, Weiser, and some others consider it a festival psalm; see Eaton, *Kingship*, 116-17.

117. See, e.g., VanGemeren, "Psalms," 187-88.

118. See comments on Pss 89 and 90.

119. The verb occurs just once, at the close of the verse, but must be intended to relate to both clauses.

Psalm 21

This psalm's many links with 20[120] plus their contiguity suggest they were meant to be understood together, probably as a prayer before (20) and after (21) battle[121] and in the consciousness of the Davidic covenant of 2 Samuel 7 and Psalm 2. They probably became liturgies for regular dynastic use, and I will treat this as the psalm's *Sitz im Leben*.[122] The covenant name Yahweh is used throughout.

21:1-7 The king's victories come from God,[123] bringing him overflowing joy as they show Yahweh's covenant faithfulness. In the canonical arrangement, verse 2 looks like the answer to the prayer of 20:4, but the differences in the Hebrew show the correspondence has not been artificially contrived. Verse 3 recalls the coronation as a symbol of the covenant blessings. The redactor perhaps saw the hyperbole of verses 4 and 6 as literally true of the ultimate Davidic king, the Messiah. The divine qualities in verse 5 show the king to be God's vicegerent.[124] Verse 6 too looks beyond earthly blessings, of which the gladness of verse 1 is an earnest (cf. 16:11). Verse 7 is strongly covenantal, with the divine חֶסֶד, *ḥesed* ("unfailing love"), being met by the king's responsive trust. Davidson says, "The opening word of verse 7 is best taken as an emphatic statement," and he suggests the translation "Yes, indeed," instead of "for."[125]

21:8-12 The king is addressed, either by the people or, in a liturgical setting, by a word from Yahweh coming through a prophet or priest.[126] A major Hebrew tense change takes place, for before this most verbs were perfects, related to past acts, they are now all imperfects, quite properly translated here as futures.[127] What God had done already encouraged the psalmist in his forward look. Verse 10 spells out the implications of the destruction of the king's enemies,[128] and verse 11 is strongly reminiscent of 2:1-3, the Psalter's basic Davidic covenant passage.

21:13 Most fittingly, the psalm ends with the kingship of the Lord himself, for "be exalted" clearly implies this. The king attributes all his strength to the Lord, as in Psalm 2.

120. Succinctly itemized in Wilson, *Psalms*, 1:397.

121. Some, e.g., Mowinckel, *Psalms in Israel's Worship*, 2:62, think both precede battle.

122. See comments introducing Ps 20.

123. Note the plural, so appropriate if the psalm has dynastic bearing.

124. Cf. 8:5, where humanity's delegated kingship is in view.

125. Davidson, *Vitality of Worship*, 77. The word is כִּי, *kî*.

126. See pp. 7-8, 15.

127. The tense system in Hebrew is quite different from European languages.

128. Cf. comment on 137:8-9.

Psalm 22

Because of Christ's use of its opening line on the cross (Matt 27:46; Mark 15:34), some Christian expositors assume that this deep lament followed by thanksgiving is purely prophetic, with no reference to the trials of its author, while others, including Calvin, see it arising initially out of the psalmist's experience, but using language peculiarly appropriate to Christ's sufferings and vindication.[129] In this exegesis I will proceed on the latter assumption, concentrating at this point on the meaning for the psalmist. There is a marked contrast with the six preceding psalms, in which the godliness described in 15 finds personal illustration. Here there is real trust in God, who comes to the rescue of his devotee, but only after at first apparently abandoning him. Predominantly first singular and second singular sections alternate throughout it (except for its last ten verses), highlighting the sufferer's sense of isolation from God, although he never ceases to cry out to him. Wilson notes many links between 22 and 69–71.[130]

22:1, 2 The impassioned urgency of the doubled imperative is unmistakable.[131] "The words of my groaning" presumably refers to this opening cry. "O" is not represented in the Hebrew; a second verse starts with "My God," intensifying still further the opening cry's passion. The phrases "by day" and "by night" show the experience to have been prolonged, and the lack of answer contrasts strongly with 3:5; 4:8; and 5:3.

22:3-5 He turns from his sufferings to think about God. He is the holy ruler of all, worshiped by Israel, so that the apologetic problem of a holy and all-powerful God's permission of evil, although not made explicit, may be in his mind. Like another sufferer (77:10-20), he recalls the history of God's saving activity for his people, but, unlike the other, this does not relieve his despondency.

22:6-8 The contrast with his own situation causes further reflection. The worm illustration may reveal his own self-estimate; it certainly shows the people's.[132] These are presumably Israelites who see his sufferings and despise him, perhaps because of a theology like that of Job's comforters. The key to verses 7 and 8 is the final line, its undoubted sarcasm implying his trust must be ill-founded, for God has no delight in him.[133]

129. For NT use of this psalm see pp. 338, 357.

130. Wilson, *Psalms*, 1:412.

131. Cf. the same feature, e.g., in Isa 51:9; Luke 22:31. This initial doubling finds an echo in the frequent twofold synonymous parallelism that provides this psalm with a unifying factor. See also Mays, *Psalms*, 107.

132. Cf. Isa 41:14; 53:3.

133. See Ps 18:19, where similar phraseology occurs in a strikingly different context.

22:9-11 Again his focus is on God. By adding "breast," "birth," and "womb" to the first "womb," he emphasizes that the one he addresses had always been his God and he had always trusted him.[134] On this twofold basis he cries again for help, stressing that God is his sole hope (cf. 62:1, 2, 5-8).

22:12-18 This detailed presentation of social and physical suffering is without OT parallel, not even in Isa 52:13–53:12, where, terrible as it is, it mostly takes second place to comments on the *significance* of the servant's sufferings. God is far away (vv. 1, 11) but the enemies are near, surrounding him (vv. 12, 16) like animals, with a bull's strength,[135] a hungry lion's capacity to satisfy its voracious appetite, and a wild dog's aggressive demeanor. Verse 15 seems to echo Gen 3:19. The enemies inflict physical suffering (v. 16) and shame (v. 17; cf. vv. 7-8). Staring may be understandable, gloating despicable.[136] Verse 18 suggests his death and shows his enemies cynically despoiling him. The pictures of poured-out water and a bone-dry potsherd are mutually exclusive, probably designedly to show how indescribable his physical sufferings were, defying consistent analogy. His bones stick out (vv. 14-15), no longer disciplined by their covering flesh. Verse 15c shows awareness of death's imminence and is unique in this section as describing an activity not simply of the enemies but of God. How Job-like the psalmist appears here!

22:19-21 Again he turns to God, for the first time (except in quoting others in v. 8) using the covenant name, Yahweh. God as his strength recalls Psalm 18, which, with its dramatic rescue from foes, sharply contrasts with this psalm, at least to this point. Again, with just a little variation (wild oxen instead of bulls of Bashan), the foes are pictured as animals (cf. vv. 12-13, 16).

22:22-24 The prayer has been answered, for the whole tone changes, so much that some scholars consider that this was originally a different psalm. This suggestion is unnecessary, for often psalms beginning in agonized prayer end in gratitude for divine intervention (cf., e.g., 4, 13). The change in the social scene is striking, for there is no antagonism. The parallelism of "my brothers" with "the congregation" shows that the former phrase is unlikely to designate simply his own family but the worshiping people, like him descendants of Jacob/Israel. He calls them to join him in praise, for God's attitude

---

134. Mays (*Psalms,* 109) thinks God is here portrayed in the role of a human father.

135. Bashan, east of the Jordan, was renowned for its cattle; cf. Ezek 39:18; Amos 4:1.

136. Verse 16c contains major translation difficulties: see the NIV mg. Most Hebrew MSS read כָּאֲרִי, *kā'ărî* ("like a lion"), instead of "they have pierced" (which follows LXX). The NT never quotes this verse of Christ, but for detailed, judicious comment on its difficulties and strong support of the translation "pierced," see Kidner, *Psalms 1–72,* 107-8. Craigie (*Psalms 1–50,* 196) gives a full technical summary of different proposed solutions, and translates, "my hands and my feet were exhausted."

contrasts totally with that of his enemies (cf. vv. 24 and 26), and God has eventually answered his prayer.

22:25-28 The theme of his praise came from God because it was his saving act. His public vows are prompted by gratitude. Verse 26 may have a fellowship offering in view, for this was always shared with others. His love for them shows clearly in the last clause of verse 26, so that his evident love for God includes God's people (cf. 16:2-3). His sufferings and vindication are of more than national significance, will be known to the whole world, causing its peoples to turn to Yahweh in submissive worship. Verse 27 shows the world as a community of national families, as often in the OT. His throne is not only over Israel (v. 3) but over all (v. 28).

22:29-31 All human life is here, for both the rich and those impoverished to the point of imminent death[137] enjoy the feast in an atmosphere of worship, again suggesting a fellowship offering. Such striking vindication would be recounted to future generations, becoming virtually part of Israel's ongoing proclamation of God's great acts. It will proclaim God's righteousness, for he had put right the psalmist's situation, rescuing him from evil foes. Most appropriately the psalm, which started with a cry of dereliction, complaining of the divine absence, ends with a triumphant cry, proclaiming a work effected, accomplished, by the Lord himself (cf. John 19:30).

Psalm 23

Psalms 23 and 21 contrast sharply with much of 22, which they enclose, yet 23 also has points of comparison with 22:25-31 and would figure as Davidic because of David's experience as a shepherd, although this does not in itself settle the authorship.

The covenant name Yahweh resonates with the personal character of the psalmist's relationship with him. Craigie indicates detailed comparisons with the account of Israel's wilderness years, too many to be accidental,[138] and in verses 2-4 and 6 there is movement, suggesting a comparison of general theme as well as detail.[139] So the individual found his personal experience within and patterned by God's relationship with Israel, made even more sig-

---

137. V. 29 could be about the living and the dead; see Kraus, *Psalms 1–59*, 300. Anderson (*Psalms*, 1:194-95) discusses various interpretations.

138. Craigie, *Psalms 1–50*, 206-8.

139. Note that the shepherd analogy is used in 77:20; 80:1; 95:7, each time in an exodus or wilderness wandering context.

nificant if, as the king, David is viewed as personally summing up the nation's experience.

23:1-4   The psalmist's conviction of a general divine supply of his needs (v. 1; cf. Deut 2:7) is followed by a number of specifics.[140] Verse 2 shows the shepherd's care for the sheep, including virtual restoration of life or at least of vitality (v. 3) by rescue from danger or the healing of serious wounds.[141] He guides them in right paths and protects them from predators in the dark, threatening ravine by using his cudgel (rod) and the staff he uses to round up and keep them together.[142] All this has its spiritual analogies, and "for his name's sake" and "you are with me" recall Yahweh's grace and the personal nature of the relationship.

23:5-6   Most commentators, probably rightly, see here a change of analogy, from the shepherd and flock to the host and guest, the second reinforcing the sense of security and provision found in the first. The scene could be a temple thanksgiving offering, but the reference to enemies does not fit this well. Perhaps verse 5 is a victory celebration with the enemies present as captives, causing the victor to recall (in v. 6) that God will welcome him to feast in his presence in the very temple itself. If so, this is a kind of realized (v. 5) and futurist (v. 6) eschatology, for in view of the eschatological implications of 16:10, 11, and 17:15, it seems unnecessary to set limits to verse 6b.[143] "Love" here is חֶסֶד, *ḥesed* ("covenant love"), so that the psalm closes on a covenant note.

Psalm 24

This entrance psalm is a complete change from Psalm 23, from the intimately personal to the universal, but they are united in interest in the house (23:6) or holy place (24:3) of the Lord. This psalm may be connected with the ark's installation there (1 Chr 13:7-8),[144] and may have been used in later celebrations

---

140. Cf. 103:2-5; Eph 1:3-14.

141. The Hebrew is נַפְשִׁי יְשׁוֹבֵב, *napšî yĕšôbēb*.

142. In the immediate context צֶדֶק, *ṣedeq*, probably means "right" rather than "righteousness," but there may well be a play on its double meaning because the pastoral imagery serves in the psalm to illustrate spiritual truth. See Wilson, *Psalms*, 1:433. How often this theme of protection occurs in book 1!

143. See comments on each. For the apparent anachronism of "house of the LORD," see pp. 36-37.

144. Cf. also comments on Pss 68 and 132. We cannot, however, be certain; see Cooper, "Life," 122. For the psalm's links of idea with Ps 15 and their dual function in the structure of Pss 15–24, see p. 273.

of this event. It forms an inclusio with Psalm 15, and the psalms in between focus on the life of godliness commended in these two psalms. Most scholars now accept the unity of this psalm.

24:1-2 Paganism often divides creation into spheres of influence between different deities, but, the psalmist says, the earth is the Lord's by foundation, including all it contains, not forgetting its human inhabitants. The use of תֵּבֵל, *tēbēl* ("world"), shows, by parallelism, that אֶרֶץ, *'ereṣ*, has its wider ("earth") rather than its narrower ("land") meaning. The sea too is his, not the possession of any chaos monster, as the Babylonians and Canaanites thought.[145] Derek Kidner says that the poetic image in verse 2 pictures the solid earth rising out of the waters, an allusion to Gen 1:9-10, as in 2 Pet 3:5.[146]

24:3-6 The psalmist moves from the world to a comparatively tiny location within it, Jerusalem, where God will meet his own people. Verse 3's questions are answered not in terms of ceremonial qualifications but rather by echoing the second and ninth commandments of the Decalogue.[147] All idol worship must be excluded. Blessing or righteousness (צְדָקָה, *ṣĕdāqâ*, NIV "vindication") comes to those qualified ("clean hands, . . . pure heart"), for they seek the Lord, not pagan deities. Some dislocation is apparent in the text of verse 6, for "Jacob" is surely "God of Jacob" (see NIV mg.), a phrase occurring elsewhere in the Psalter (e.g., 46:7, 11). דּוֹר, *dôr* (NIV "generation"), can indicate a type of person (e.g., in 112:2), and this must be its sense here.

24:7-10 This has a military atmosphere. In dramatic apostrophe, the psalmist calls on the gates[148] to give access to God, who, unlike humans, needs no entry qualifications, for the holy place is his own. Moreover, he has confirmed his right by great victories, perhaps with the thought that all false deities have been overcome by him, all potential rivals worsted. The dialogue could be purely poetic dramatization or it could represent two groups, one at the sanctuary and asking the question, the other approaching it and giving the answer.

145. VanGemeren says, "We are not to assume that the Israelites knew the Canaanite cosmogony, but they may have become familiar with words and phrases that were adapted to Israelite purposes without giving credence to the whole pagan association" ("Psalms," 221). See also Craigie, *Psalms 1–50*, 209-15.

146. Kidner, *Psalms 1–72*, 114. Cf. also Job 38:8-11.

147. Cf. Ps 15 and comments.

148. "Ancient" may indicate that the gates are not the temple's but rather those of the city on the route to it. They were ancient because this was an old Jebusite city.

Psalm 25

This is a slightly irregular acrostic and is somewhat chiastic.[149] It presents wisdom teaching similar to the book of Proverbs, emphasizing the fear of the Lord and the need to be taught the right path, but it does so in a context of prayer. "It points to the way such teaching could find a natural home in worship and be part of a deeply spiritual experience."[150] Much in it would recall Psalm 1 for the consecutive reader, and it shows divine help is needed to follow the right way, the way illustrated in Psalms 15–24, and so to know God's blessing, especially in view of the psalmist's reference here to his sins. His request for guidance, therefore, is primarily about knowing how to live a godly life rather than about a detailed shaping of his particular circumstances. Its language suggests that the author was elderly (vv. 7, 16-17; cf. 31:10; 71:5-6, 9, 17-18).

25:1-3   The NIV follows MT by putting "To you" in the emphatic initial position. The psalmist puts his trust in God into a prayer that his enemies will not shame him, a major concern in Middle Eastern cultures.[151] This faith is based on his convictions about God's moral nature. "Treacherous without excuse" probably implies that those concerned might have tried to plead extenuating circumstances.

25:4-7   Read in the light of Psalm 1, this is a prayer for illumination of God's truth in his Word for practical purposes, the word דֶּרֶךְ, *derek* ("way"), occurring frequently (vv. 4, 7, 8-10, 12). Verse 7 is the first explicit mention of the psalmist's personal sin in the Psalter (but see 6:1), reminding us that Psalm 1's blessing is for the righteous, hence this frank admission and prayer for mercy. He also casts himself on Yahweh as God of the covenant, for "love" in verses 6 and 7 is חֶסֶד, *ḥesed,* love within a covenant relationship. "From of old" may include the Abrahamic and Mosaic covenants as well as the dynastic covenant of 2 Samuel 7. Magonet has explored in detail the extensive links with Exod 34:5-7, a passage affirming the Mosaic covenant.[152]

25:8-14   He now shows confidence that God instructs even sinners in his ways. His reference to humility shows that recognition of moral frailty induces a desire for God's moral instruction. The covenant theme continues, and the word itself, בְּרִית, *bĕrît,* now occurs for the first time in the Psalter (vv. 10, 14). Verses 10 and 12-14 remind us again of Psalm 1, while verse 11 under-

149. See p. 30.
150. Davidson, *Vitality of Worship,* 89.
151. Cf. 34:5 and comments there.
152. Magonet, *Rabbi,* 75-82.

lines the plea of verse 7, grounding it in what God is, not in what the psalmist is. טוֹב, *tôb* ("prosperity," v. 13), literally means "good,"[153] and can include all kinds of good, spiritual, social, and material. A. A. Anderson compares its use in 34:10.[154] Verse 14 implies a relationship that, like a good marriage, has both the warmth of informality ("confides") and deep assurance based on a formal structure ("his covenant").

25:15-21   The enemies, out of sight since verses 2 and 3, reappear. They have set a snare for him, are multiplying and are filled with hatred, seeking his life and his shame. He asks for salvation, not just from them but also from his sins, for he is now penitent and upright.

25:22   This verse is possibly an editorial addition, applying the psalmist's sentiments to the community,[155] but alternatively reflecting his conviction that God's gracious covenant embraces all Israel, not just himself. After all, other psalms move from singular to plural forms quite naturally and with no suggestion of an authorship change (e.g., 89:1-2, 17-20). Do the troubles include sin? We cannot tell, but this verse, with its redemptive language, may anticipate 130:7-8.

Psalm 26

This seems strange after 25, with that psalm's references to personal sin, so the Psalter's redactor must have been clear that the noun תֹּם, *tōm* (vv. 1, 11), did not claim sinlessness but exclusive commitment to the Lord.[156] Some consider this an entrance psalm, like 15 and 24, offered before entering God's house, while others reckon it a prayer for vindication in the face of specific accusations from some human source.[157] We cannot be sure. This and the next three psalms all express the psalmist's trust in the Lord.

26:1-3   The psalmist calls Yahweh to be his judge, for "vindicate" translates שָׁפַט, *šāpaṭ*, "to judge," and he asserts his integrity, his single-minded trust in him. Verses 2 and 3 have the same thought, but his call to God to

153. In v. 8 it describes God.

154. Anderson, *Psalms*, 1:211.

155. This verse stands outside the acrostic pattern, but this is inconclusive, as there are other irregularities in this pattern.

156. Thus NRSV and NASB have "integrity," rather than NIV "blameless." This is why David, despite his faults, can be treated in the books of Kings as a standard by which other kings are judged (1 Kgs 3:6; 9:4; 11:33, etc.).

157. For the former see Craigie, *Psalms 1–50*, 223-28; for the latter see Anderson, *Psalms*, 1:213-19.

judge him becomes more specific (cf. 17:3 and, more generally, 7:9). He always keeps God's חֶסֶד, *ḥesed* ("love," i.e., covenant love), in mind, implying continued commitment to the covenant, and he makes practical response to God's revelation.

26:4-8   Broyles sums up these verses thus: "in contrast to entering their assemblies I choose to enter Yahweh's."[158] Verses 4 and 5 recall 1:1 and could refer to a definite accusation faced by the psalmist. Verse 6 is ceremonial in tone and is associated with the laver used by those who officiate in God's house, although the emphasis is not on sacrifice but on sung praise,[159] especially associated with David in the OT historical literature (e.g., in 2 Sam 23:1). To engage in this makes Yahweh's house very precious to him (cf. Pss 42–43, 63, 84).[160]

26:9-11   He is still thinking in legal terms, but now more in relation to penalties than to charges. As so often, it is deceitful men of violence he has in view, once more pleading his integrity (cf. v. 1); but now, with contextual justification, the NIV translates by a present rather than a past tense. "Redemption" here is not necessarily deliverance from sin, but probably just a richer synonym for physical salvation; however, "be merciful" perhaps has such a meaning, although this often simply means to have compassion.

26:12   The psalmist ends confidently, his words suggesting moral stability and the praise he will offer in a corporate gathering for worship.

Psalm 27

27:1-3   Intimately personal, this psalm challenges and encourages the reader, for it is a psalm of confidence showing David finding every indispensable blessing in God.[161] The Lord is his light, the source of all good, and his salvation, giving physical safety, with "stronghold" perhaps suggestive of the cave of Adullam (1 Sam 22:1-2). Verses 2 and 3 suggest enemies attacking in ever-increasing numbers but without reducing his confidence in God.

27:4-6   The change of motif is more apparent than real, for verses 5 and 6a clearly continue the first theme, while the remainder locate the divinely provided place of safety as God's sanctuary, variously described here.[162]

---

158. Broyles, *Psalms,* 137.

159. Both the laver and altar here are literal, for the psalmist is coming to worship.

160. For this apparent anachronism, see pp. 36-37.

161. Some, e.g., Anderson, *Psalms,* 1:217, divide it into two psalms, but Broyles argues persuasively for its unity (*Psalms,* 141-42).

162. For apparent anachronisms see pp. 36-37.

These two conceptions of places of safety are remarkably interwoven. The sanctuary provides safety (cf. 1 Kgs 1:49-51) but also true worship ("to seek him"), for he recognizes the Lord's supreme worth ("the beauty of the LORD"). He will offer him a sacrifice and instrumental and vocal music. The exalted rock perhaps suggests Saul's pursuit of David among Judah's hills (e.g., 1 Sam 23:26) and some occasion when, from a high and hidden vantage point, he could see his enemies searching in vain below.

27:7-12   He turns to prayer. Verse 8 may be rendered in two ways, the NIV margin emphasizing the divine initiative, the NIV text the psalmist's past experience of prayer. His plea may reflect times when he sensed a barrier between God and himself. There is, however, an abiding relationship, for he is God's adopted son (v. 10) and is confident of God's help. At verse 11 his opening statement, "The LORD is my light" (v. 1), comes into its own. During Saul's persecution, God guided David's steps so that he was kept safe (e.g., 1 Sam 23:26); hence God was both then his light and his salvation. The "straight path" is perhaps the road with no physical snags or traps for the unwary (cf. Ps 18:29-36). Again, if David's experiences are in view, the false witnesses may be seen as gaining Saul's ear.

27:13-14   His experience has encouraged continued confidence in God, and he appears sure God has more work for him to do. He ends by encouraging others to wait for the Lord and be strong.

Psalm 28

This psalm has many points in common with 26 and 27, although also distinctive features.

28:1-2   These verses are an urgent cry for mercy and help. If God does not hear him, he will die.[163] He is at worship and is making his petition toward the inner sanctuary, representing God's very presence.[164]

28:3-5   Dragging away (v. 3) and tearing down (v. 5; cf. Jer 24:6) are graphic images of God's judgment. The psalmist cries out for a divine judgment that will discriminate between the wicked and himself as God's servant. As so often in the Psalms, the wicked are presented as devious and hypocritical (cf. 2:1-3). Both verses 4 and 5 refer to value judgments, God's on the wicked and the wicked's on God.

28:6-7   There is a dramatic change here. Has a prophet brought him an

---

163. בּוֹר, *bôr*, here translated "pit," is a synonym for שְׁאוֹל, *šĕ'ôl*, in 30:3; 88:4; 143:7.
164. For the apparent anachronism see pp. 36-37.

oracle or has God spoken to him directly? Either is possible. His gratitude employs the language of his plea in verse 2, and "my strength" and "my shield" recall the sheltering Rock in verse 1. His faith and his joyous praise for God's answer are intensely personal.

28:8-9   The personal is replaced by the communal, as the declarative has already given way to the descriptive in verses 6 and 7.[165] The psalmist now writes of God's people and prays for them, for both the king and the people he represents may know God as Savior. He moves on from a plea for salvation (i.e., physical deliverance) to one for blessing, in which they are pictured as the Lord's territory,[166] and also as his sheep, not to be led as in Psalm 23, but carried as in Isa 40:11.

Psalm 29

Psalm 28 shows the psalmist extolling and trusting in the power of God, while 29 graphically exhibits a revelation of that power in a great storm. It puts vivid description to the service of praise. There are clear links of language between 28:8-9 and 29:11. Like 19, this psalm reveals the conviction that Yahweh, Lord of redemption, is also the God of nature.

29:1-2   Verses 1 and 2a are in a poetic form known as staircase parallelism, where each line takes the thought further. The psalmist calls heavenly beings, the sons of God or of the gods (אֵלִים, *'ēlîm*), to praise Yahweh. If the former, they are angels (cf. 89:5-7; Job 1:6); if the latter, pagan deities called to submit (cf. Ps 97:7). The latter is likely, for some of the language has parallels in Canaanite Baalism, and the exceptionally frequent use of Yahweh ("LORD" — eight verses use it twice) is probably to assert that Yahweh, not Baal, rules the storms and alone deserves worship, making this an anti-Baalism polemic.[167] To "ascribe" is literally to give, here rendering praise fitting for Yahweh's glory and strength (cf. Rev 4:11; 5:12-13). Verse 2b is either heavenly or earthly worship, for "the splendor of his holiness" is literally "in holy garments," appropriate for either angelic or priestly worship. "Holiness" here is a virtual synonym for "majesty."

29:3-9   This magnificent poetic description of a thunderstorm defined as God's voice (v. 3) from the heavens recalls Sinai's thunders, so linking God's revelations in nature and history. Schaefer aptly comments that the

---

165. See pp. 13, 15-16.
166. "Inheritance" is normally land in the OT.
167. See Craigie, *Ugarit*, 68-71.

phrase "voice of the Lord" "thunders seven times at irregular intervals, like lightning."[168] The repeated "over" is apt, for, in a thunderstorm, the rain descends beneath the thunder's sound. Verse 5 suggests thunderbolts and 6 an earthquake, again reminiscent of Sinai. The storm starting out at sea comes from the north, where the great mountain ranges of Lebanon (with its cedars) and Sirion are. If verse 7 means that the thunder and lightning come together, the storm is just overhead, perhaps locating the psalmist in Israel's heartland. It then moves south into the desert lands through which Israel came to Canaan, shaking again indicating an earthquake (for this is rift-valley country) or else poetically the thunder itself. Verse 9a takes up verse 4's theme of power, showing its effect on the trees. Worshipers in the temple[169] hear the thunder, discern God's voice in it, and respond with "Glory!" which says everything.

29:10-11 Verse 10 may be meteorological (Yahweh is Lord of all nature) or historical (Yahweh sovereignly presided at the Genesis flood), probably the latter, for the word rendered "flood" occurs elsewhere only in Genesis 6–11. So here natural and historical revelation come together. After the storm, the psalmist reflects on God's blessings, including "peace," so apt after the storm's noise with its suggestions of judgment.[170]

Psalm 30

This is "a prayer that is wholly praise; it is also praise that comes out of prayer."[171] It reveals similarities to Hezekiah's prayer in Isa 38:10-20. For reasons not clearly understood, it was used at the Feast of Hanukkah, celebrating the cleansing of the temple.[172]

30:1-3 The psalmist will reciprocate Yahweh's lifting up of him by in turn exalting him. Verses 2 and 3 reveal he has experienced disease and faced death; therefore "the depths" (v. 1) means the same as "the grave" and "the pit" (v. 3).[173] So his enemies would gloat over him, not because of their own actions but because of his death through illness. So he exalts the Lord, recog-

---

168. Schaefer, *Psalms*, 71.

169. For the apparent anachronism see pp. 36-37.

170. Glancing at the theory that this psalm was originally Ugaritic, Sheriffs aptly characterizes the prayer of v. 11 as thoroughly Israelite (*Friendship of the Lord*, 131).

171. Mays, *Psalms*, 141.

172. See its heading, although "temple" is interpretive, for it is lit. "house." Wilcock discusses various possible ways of understanding this (*Psalms 1–72*, 105).

173. "Grave" is שְׁאוֹל, *šĕ'ôl*. See pp. 290-91. "Pit" is בּוֹר, *bôr*.

nizing his supremacy but also his personal relationship to him ("my God"), for he has answered his prayer for healing.

30:4-5 To "exalt him" (v. 1) and to "praise his holy name" (v. 4) are virtual synonyms, so he now calls God's saints[174] to add their voices in praise. He has experienced God's anger,[175] weeping in consequence, but this now seems but a moment as he basks in God's favor.

30:6-7 He reflects on the past, perhaps seeing his illness as punishment (cf. "anger" in v. 5) for his self-confidence. Psalm 15:5 and particularly 16:8 show confidence, but more in God and his righteous dealings than in himself. "My mountain" is probably Jerusalem's location.

30:8-10 Verses 9 and 3 are probably about the same experience. His plea for mercy is based on what his death would mean to God rather than to himself. The questions of verse 9b may suggest a negative answer but could equally indicate his incomplete knowledge.

30:11-12 Verse 11b combines the symbolic (removing sackcloth) with the metaphorical ("clothed me with joy"; cf. Isa 61:3). The personal note recurs (cf. v. 2).

Psalm 31

The theme is familiar, especially in book 1, where prayer for deliverance from enemies occurs frequently.[176]

31:1-5 Verses 1 and 2 are similar in thought to 28:1-2,[177] but include an appeal to the Lord's righteousness, suggesting false accusations or malicious gossip (cf. vv. 17 and 20). Verses 2 and 3 recall 18:1-2. "For the sake of your name" and "God of truth" imply that the Lord's reputation was at stake. A trap has been set (cf. 18:4-5) and he asks both for deliverance from it and for guidance, suggesting divinely led avoidance of further traps. The strong confidence of verse 5 (quoted in extremis by Jesus in Luke 23:46; cf. Acts 7:59) anticipates the trust expressed in verses 6 and 14. "Redeem" here is simply a richer synonym for "deliver."

31:6-8 His hatred stems from his commitment to Yahweh and his hor-

---

174. חֲסִידִים, *ḥăsîdîm*, those bound to him by חֶסֶד, *ḥesed*, "steadfast love." See pp. 279-80. Possibly the redactor placed Ps 30 after 29, with the latter's call to heavenly beings to praise Yahweh, to highlight the distinctive nature of human praise as prompted by gratitude, not just awe at superior power.

175. Several events in the books of Samuel would fit this, e.g., 2 Sam 12:1-12; 24:1-17.

176. For NT use of this psalm see pp. 357-58.

177. See comments there.

ror that people should resort to any other supposed source of supernatural help.[178] His prayer has been answered, and God's covenant love[179] gives him joy. The "spacious place" reminds us of 18:19.

31:9-13 Is he facing one crisis or experiencing a continued history of trouble? These verses may suggest the latter, but could be simply an expanded, deeper version of the original prayer. His considerable distress manifests itself psychosomatically, and "my years" shows he feels old. The accusations of his enemies are taken seriously by his neighbors and friends, who ostracize him. Broken pottery was apparently a familiar image for something once useful but now valueless (cf. Jer 2:13). Verse 13 reminds the consecutive reader of 2:1-3.

31:14-18 Here, as in verses 6-8, the psalmist expresses confidence in the Lord, calling him "my God." David's experience in 1 Sam 23:26-28 shows the guidance of God in timing. God's shining face implies his favor (Num 6:22-27), based on the covenant. In verse 17 the psalmist's prayer is for God to show discrimination (cf. 1:6). The shaming and death of his enemies are linked, perhaps because death alone guaranteed their silence. He clearly includes himself among the righteous (v. 18), because on this matter he is sure he is in the right.

31:19-22 This psalm is both a lament and an expression of confidence in God, which some think may have come through a prophetic oracle, and which now blossoms into praise. David expresses the blessedness of those who fear the Lord and take refuge in him (cf. 2:12). God's goodness is his bountiful beneficence, and verse 20 shows that the hiding place God provided from the devious, false accusations of enemies is not simply prepared by him but is actually himself. Verse 21 could be reminiscent of David's uncomfortable sojourn in Keilah (1 Sam 23:9-14). Verse 22 seems illogical, combining fear that God had forsaken him (cf. 22:1) and fervent prayer to him, but this is psychologically authentic.

31:23-24 He passes on what he has discovered in God. Aware of God's great covenant love for him (vv. 7, 16), he now calls "his saints," those faithful to the covenant, to love the Lord (cf. 18:1). We recall that 30:4 exhorts "you saints of his" to sing the Lord's praises. He is convinced that God discriminates between the righteous and the wicked (cf. 1:6). Verse 24 reminds us of Josh 1:6-9.

---

178. See comments on the imprecations of the psalms on pp. 19-21.
179. חֶסֶד, *hesed*, as again in v. 16; cf. 2 Sam 7. It means love within a covenant relationship.

Psalm 32

Few psalms focus on the theme of forgiveness (e.g., 38 and 51), although 103:3 also sees forgiveness as the primary blessing springing from God's gracious relationship with his people. Here it is not only celebrated but its conditions are made clear.[180]

32:1-2 These beatitudes differ from those earlier in the Psalter (1:1; 2:12) in promising happiness (אַשְׁרֵי, *'ašrê*) not to the righteous but to the forgiven sinner, on condition that there is no deceit, probably meaning no hiding of sin but rather full and frank confession (compare and contrast Saul and David in 1 Sam 15 and 2 Sam 12). The experience of divine grace is presented in picture language, with removal of a burden ("forgiven") followed by covering and then probably by debt remission.[181]

32:3-5 He describes how God brought him, after a time of silent refusal to admit his guilt, to repentance and forgiveness. His language recalls 31:10, but his weakness here has a different cause: not his enemies but his sins. He saw this constant experience ("day and night") as due to divine chastisement, and it is evident that he was in agony. Verse 5 shows his silence giving place to full confession, the direct speech form suggesting explicit articulation. God, but not the sinner, may cover his sins (cf. vv. 5 and 1). Verse 5 shows the experiential basis of verses 1 and 2.

32:6-7 Addressing God, he now underscores lessons for others from his experience.[182] In this moral context, "while you may be found" is strongly reminiscent of the call to repentance in Isa 55:6-7, and "everyone who is godly" suggests the sensitivity to sin that accompanies true piety. "Mighty waters" may recall the historical flood as a symbol of judgment or, as in Isa 8:6-8, God's use of historical enemies to punish his people, with particular comparison between the grace expressed in "reaching up to the neck" in the Isaiah passage and the promise "they will not reach him" here. The picture of God furnishing a hiding place is common in the Psalms (see esp. 18:1ff.). Perhaps the songs of deliverance are sung by worshipers he has told of his deliverance.

32:8-10 The change to the first person singular and comparison with 25:4-7, which also refers to sins, strongly suggests the Teacher here is God.[183] Because forgiven, the psalmist is now among the righteous who, as in 1, re-

---

180. For NT use of this psalm see p. 301.

181. Anderson helpfully discusses the terminology of vv. 1-2 (*Psalms*, 1:255-56).

182. McCann notes that now, forgiven, the psalmist focuses attention not on himself but on God and others (*Theological Introduction*, 109).

183. Not all commentators agree, e.g., McCann, *Theological Introduction*, 110.

ceive God's instruction. Verse 10 unites both sides of the covenant: God's unfailing love and his people's trust in him.

32:11 The godly are now addressed, and the psalmist calls them to rejoice and sing God's praises. In its context this verse suggests too that the penitent transgressor is now reckoned righteous, as Paul clearly saw in his comment on this psalm (Rom 4:5-8).

Psalm 33

This psalm has no heading, most unusual for book 1, possibly because it was regarded as a companion to Psalm 32, to which it has a number of resemblances including benedictions (32:1-2; 33:12) and the description of God as teacher (explicitly in 32:8 and by clear implication in 33:4). There is also the call to sing praise to the Lord, which ends 32 and opens 33. This last may even suggest that the two psalms were originally one, but this is uncertain, and moreover is unlikely as this twenty-two-verse psalm, although not an acrostic, has a structure imitative of acrostics.

33:1-3 The praise call is addressed to the righteous or upright, for it is fitting for their right relationship to God to find such expression. It is to be both instrumental and vocal, the former presumably accompanying the latter, which makes specific articulation possible. The song is new, for the Lord is always doing new things for his people.[184] After Psalm 32's message of full forgiveness, it is not unlike the joy of Isaiah 54 after Isaiah 53.

33:4-11 The subject of praise is God's word, which is true because he is faithful. His moral qualities are emphasized, as is, in an unusual expression, the fact that his unfailing love fills the earth. This either refers to the Noachian covenant or could view the act of creation as in some sense covenantal.[185] If the latter, this would explain why the psalmist moves on from the (presumably) written word (vv. 4-5) to God's word in creation (vv. 6-7), then to a call to all the world to praise him. Verses 6-9 recall Gen 1:1–2:4, with its reiterated "God said," its use of the word צְבָאָם, *ṣĕbā'ām* ("multitude," Gen 2:1 NRSV), its reference to the gathering together of the waters (Gen 1:10). Here there are vivid imagery (v. 7) and emphasis on the firmness of what God did, recalling the "firmament" (KJV; NIV "expanse") of Gen 1:6-8.

---

184. The expression "new song" occurs also in 40:3; 96:1; 98:1; 144:9; 149:1; Isa 42:10 plus Rev 5:9 and 14:3. Longman argues that it always occur in the context of a holy war ("Psalm 98," 269).

185. "Unfailing love" is חֶסֶד, *ḥesed*, love within a covenant relationship.

Verses 10 and 11 remind us of Psalm 2 with its foiled conspiracy, but also, because of the many allusions to Genesis 1, the tower of Babel story (Gen 11).

33:12-19   This is the first Psalter beatitude referring explicitly to the chosen nation, although 2:12 closes a psalm where God the King affirms support for Israel's king. Verses 13-15 may have the story of the tower of Babel (Gen 11) in view. Verse 15 shows the Lord's knowledge encompassing human thoughts, and verse 17 may allude to Deut 17:16, where the king is instructed not to accumulate horses for war but to trust the Lord, as here in verses 18 and 19. Verse 19 extends God's care beyond war to famine. Could this too be a Genesis allusion, to Abraham or to Jacob's family?

33:20-22   Here trust takes the form of hope, with the future safe in the hands of the covenant God, his people's help and shield.

Psalm 34

This acrostic psalm consists of praise and godly advice, both arising from his testimony to God's deliverance.[186] Its reference to divine instruction links it to 32 and 33, and would remind the consecutive reader of the introductory Psalm 1.[187]

34:1-3   His praise embraces all occasions, and he calls the afflicted to join in, perhaps assuming their experience tallies with his, which is detailed from verse 4.

34:4-7   Book 1 is largely a book of testimonies,[188] and these verses are very personal. "Seeking the Lord" and "looking to him" are synonyms for prayer. Salvation was not simply from troubles, as often in the Psalms, but also from fear, which tunes in with the many exhortations not to be afraid found elsewhere in the OT.[189] The radiance perhaps recalls the shining of Moses' face as he descended Mount Sinai (Exod 34:29-35). As Kidner says, "radiance is delight but also glory: a transformation of the whole person." It is the very opposite of shame. David was poor if he had abandoned his possessions on going to Gath, or else he is to be seen here simply as someone to be pitied.[190] "The angel

---

186. For acrostics see pp. 29-30. The historical event referred to is recorded in 1 Sam 21:10-15. Achish, king of Gath, is here called Abimelech, meaning "my father is king," apparently a title rather than a name.

187. For NT use of this psalm see p. 331.

188. See p. 413.

189. E.g., in Deut 1:17; Josh 11:6; Prov 3:24.

190. VanGemeren, however, thinks the psalmist may have been pointing to somebody in the audience as "this poor man" ("Psalms," 283).

of the LORD" often appears in the OT for the blessing of God's people. He went before Israel into the promised land (Exod 23:20-23), and the view of him here as a protector fits this well.

34:8-10   The exhortations are based on his testimony. The unusual analogy reminds us that prophets are sometimes said to "eat" the words God gives them,[191] but here the grammatical object is the Lord himself, experienced as good because he provides safety. Verse 9 builds on verse 7, with the righteous described as saints, who are assured of provision, not just protection. The lions are powerful carnivores normally well able to provide for themselves.

34:11-14   This is like Proverbs 1–9, with its direct address to "my children," its call for attention and its subject, "the fear of the LORD," which according to Prov 1:7 is the beginning of knowledge. If we see David as the psalm's author, we wonder if Solomon learned this style from his father. The precepts have long life as their reward, and truth and peaceableness as features.

34:15-22   The words "eyes," "ears," and "face" suggest the Lord's concentration on the needs of the righteous, reminding the reader of his goodness (v. 8). His face that shone on the righteous (v. 5 implies) is set against evildoers, who will be denied the long life promised in verse 12. The troubles of the righteous are heartbreaking and crushing, but the God who is close to them hears their prayer. Their troubles are real but limited (vv. 19-20), and it is significant that John 19:36 applies verse 20 to the crucified Christ. Verses 21 and 22 virtually summarize Psalms 1 and 2.

Psalm 35

This lament is "an outpouring rather than a coherent, organized poem,"[192] and it contains varied imagery, especially from the law court (as in vv. 1a, 11, 20, and 27, where the contention is verbal rather than military), warfare (notably vv. 1b and 2, but also 15, 17, 23), and hunting (vv. 7-8). Is all this metaphorical or is some of it literal?[193] Wilcock argues that David's flight from Saul is in view here, understanding the language of the chase and the battlefield literally and the law court language metaphorically.[194] Even though met-

---

191. E.g., in Jer 15:16; Ezek 2:8-9.

192. Motyer, "Psalms," 507.

193. For NT use of this psalm see p. 337. See also the introduction to Ps 36.

194. Wilcock, *Psalms 1–72*, 118-24, but Eaton thinks the military language suggests the period of David's kingship (*Kingship*, 41-42).

aphor, this would be particularly appropriate if corrupt legal officials were employed by the powerful against the weak. The theme of slander and divine vindication becomes dominant from verse 11 onward.

35:1-3 The scene is set. David faces accusation from those who have the means to harm him, and God appears both as his vindicator (cf. vv. 23 and 24) and combative savior. He appeals to him to intervene and seeks a word of assurance, perhaps with memories of Josh 5:13–6:5 (cf. also Isa 63:1-6).

35:4-10 In verses 4-8 he asks God to ensnare his adversaries in their own trap, and in 9 and 10 praises him in anticipation. They seek his life by plotting, which certainly fits Saul's diverse attempts on David's life, and the reiterated expression, "without cause" too is apt, for he was innocent of designs on Saul's own life (see 1 Sam 24 and 26), and he sought not their deaths but their disgrace. In verses 5 and 6 the angel of the Lord effects judgment, while in 34:7 salvation, but the two are complementary, for deliverance from enemies implies judgment on them. Just as verse 4 reminds us of Psalm 2, so verse 5 is reminiscent of Psalm 1. For verses 9 and 10 compare 103:1-2, where the psalmist's whole being goes out in praise of all God gives. His exclamation (v. 10) is like Isaiah 40's rhetorical questions. Verse 10b resembles Hannah's song (1 Sam 2), and perhaps even more the Magnificat (Luke 1:46-55).

35:11-18 Once again law court language appears (cf. v. 1). Saul's persecution could have been litigious as well as physical. The reference to illness fits David's help to Saul when the latter experienced illness as a judgment.[195] His enemies had now put all gratitude aside. "Like the ungodly" is appropriate, for Saul was a worshiper of the true God, yet his actions were ungodly. How like the situation at Christ's trial! Indeed, verse 17, with its lion imagery,[196] is much like the prayer of 22:19-21, a psalm the NT applies to the suffering Christ.

35:19-28 This too is highly reminiscent of Christ's trials and of the mockery he encountered on the cross, and he quoted part of verse 19 in John 15:25. "Without cause," "without reason," are reiterated from verse 7. Harman suggests that "narrow the eyes" (in hostility) better conveys the thought of verse 19 than "wink the eye."[197] The false witnesses tell what they claim to have seen, but David appeals to the all-seeing God (vv. 21-22). Verses 23 and 24 employ the language both of legal and military defense, and he again requests

---

195. See 1 Sam 16:14-23. Sackcloth was worn in times of great sorrow, especially in mourning (e.g., 2 Sam 3:31; Amos 8:10). Janzen argues that the psalmist's feelings are likened to a mother bereaved of her young ("Psalm 35," 55-69).

196. Broyles suggests the lion imagery is still in view in vv. 21a and 25 (*Psalms,* 171).

197. Harman, *Psalms,* 157.

the shaming of his enemies. He wants his faithful supporters to know of his vindication, sharing his joy and praise, so there is an element of testimony here, which is transferred from wish to assertion in verse 28. His enemies seek to exalt themselves over him, but instead of exalting himself he prays for the Lord's exaltation. This suggests that even the imprecation factor in this psalm is more for the Lord's sake than for his.

Psalm 36

"The collection so far comes to something of a climax with Psalm 35, which envisages in the most real and personal terms, and asks God for, a fulfilling of Psalm 1:6. . . . The order of the first psalm is reversed in the thirty-sixth, which deals with the wicked man first; and where 1 spoke of the end to which his way would take him, 36 speaks of the way itself."[198] Note also a link between its heading and 35:27, as in both David is called God's servant.[199]

36:1-4 This section may be a prophetic oracle, but in general terms rather than against a particular group or individual. Some, however, view it as a solemn but sinful utterance of a wicked man or even of personified Wickedness, directed to the psalmist's heart (see NIV mg.); but such a use of the oracle form would be most unusual, so I view it as normal prophecy. "The fear of the LORD" is characteristic of wisdom literature, so here prophecy and wisdom are closely linked, and there is also a link with Psalms 14 and 53. Sin has blinded the sinner both to God and to his own sin, characterized especially as pride and malicious, deceitful plotting, much as in Psalm 2. Verse 4 clearly shows sin's volitional nature, and it contrasts with 1:2 and compares with the plotting of 2:1.[200]

36:5-9 What a contrast between the wicked in verses 1-4 and the God revealed here! The Lord is lovingly faithful to his covenant,[201] and his justice is absolute. The psalmist expresses the superlative nature of these sublime qualities by likening them to the world's dimensions and its greatest features, much as another psalmist does in 89:1-8. Harman suggests that verse 6c alludes to the ancient covenant with Noah (Gen 8:15-22), especially as this follows a reference to the great deep.[202] This love is beyond price, embracing all, providing protection. "Refuge" is a note often sounded since 2:12. The psalm-

---

198. Wilcock, *Psalms 1–72*, 124-25.
199. For NT use of this psalm see p. 301.
200. But of course this is in individual, not communal, terms, as in Ps 2.
201. "Love" here, as in v. 10, is חֶסֶד, *ḥesed*, love within a covenant relationship.
202. Harman, *Psalms*, 159.

ist's thought moves from analogy to analogy, from the bird's protecting wings to the overwhelmingly generous host who provides both food and drink, then to God, the source of both life and light, as in John 1:4-5.

36:10-12   Romans 1:18 suggests that unrighteousness is grounded in ungodliness, while here the opposite is in view, as "the upright in heart" parallels "those who know you." This is unsurprising, since verses 5 and 6 link God's covenant love with his justice. Covenant love is, by definition, unfailing, so verse 10 asks God to demonstrate his abiding character. The foot and hand are the chief organs of individual combat, and "proud" and "wicked" recall the unpleasant picture in verses 1-4. Verse 12, like so many prophetic oracles, depicts God's coming judgment, the eye of the psalmist's faith clearly seeing the downfall of the enemies.

Psalm 37

Psalm 36 contains a wisdom element, but 37 could have come straight out of the book of Proverbs. It addresses not God but people. Its pattern is acrostic, with the double verse as the unit, although the versification of our versions does not follow this exactly.[203] It is the Psalter's most direct affirmation of God's justice in spite of wickedness; Psalm 73 does this too, but there the writer takes an autobiographical approach.[204]

37:1-11   The same basic idea is expressed in varied ways, reinforcing its impact. Verses 1, 3, 5, and 7 exhort the reader to trust God in the face of the wicked's apparent prosperity, expressed negatively and then positively (cf. Ps 73). Verse 4 goes further with its exhortation to delight in the Lord, while verse 8 counsels against the anger the righteous may feel. There is the promise of judgment on the wicked (vv. 2, 9-10) and an inheritance in the land for the righteous (vv. 3, 9, 11), an emphasis on the future that recurs frequently later in the psalm. Thus God will clearly show the cause of the righteous to be just (v. 6). Jesus quotes verse 11 in Matt 5:5.

37:12-17   Because the psalm addresses the apparent prosperity of the wicked, it is no surprise to find references to poverty and wealth (vv. 14, 16). The Lord's laughter at the wicked recalls 2:4, for his commitment to retributive justice, making the punishment fit the sin (v. 15), makes their wickedness ridiculous (cf. 35:8). Verses 16 and 17 remind the righteous poor that he will both judge the wicked and uphold them, his people.

203. See pp. 29-30.
204. For NT use of this psalm see p. 300.

37:18-26 The thought of verses 12-17 continues, except that the contrasting destinies are now viewed without reference to the antagonism of the wicked against the righteous. They are "the Lord's enemies," and as in 1:4 are lightweight and ephemeral (v. 20). As in verses 1-11, the righteous are promised inheritance in the land and material blessing, and their generosity contrasts with the financial unfaithfulness of the wicked. The psalmist's personal testimony to what he has seen (vv. 25-26), including blessing both of the righteous and of their children, rounds off this section, and it harmonizes with verses 16 and 17. Broyles says verse 25 should be understood in the light of verse 26: "It is the generosity of the righteous community (note also v. 21) that precludes righteous children from begging bread."[205]

37:27-29 The psalmist's pastoral concern now includes the wicked, for he exhorts them to repent, reminding them of the consequences of conduct.

37:30-40 He again deals with the right attitude of the righteous to the wicked, beginning by describing a righteous person (vv. 30-31), whose wisdom is linked to observing God's law from the heart (cf. Jer 31:31-34). The wicked's designs of ambush and litigation will be unsuccessful.[206] Faith now takes the form of sure hope (v. 34; cf. v. 9), and once more the blessings are land inheritance. The psalmist again gives testimony (cf. vv. 35-36 with 25-26), this time to the judgment of the wicked. There is a call for reflection, with the righteous one described as a peaceful person, perhaps in contrast to the antagonistic designs of the wicked. The psalm concludes in a way common in book 1, with reference to God as his people's savior and refuge, a link with 2:12.

Psalm 38

This is a penitential psalm (cf. 32 and 51), and its inclusio form[207] (vv. 1, 21-22) vindicates the heading, "a petition." Its focus is on the psalmist's health problems, apparently connected with his bodily frame (vv. 3 and 7), while festering wounds (v. 5) suggest he has been attacked, perhaps by his enemies (vv. 12, 16, 19-20). His pounding heart, inability to muster strength or even to see clearly (v. 10), may mean he fears their continued threat.

The ultimate source of all this is God's punitive arrows and disciplining hand (cf. Isa 1:4-9). The psalmist traces the cause of his illness to God's wrath

---

205. Broyles, *Psalms*, 182.
206. Cf. v. 33 with the references to litigation in Ps 35 and comments there.
207. See p. 29.

(vv. 1-3), and this in turn to his sin (vv. 4-5), which burdens (v. 4) and troubles him (v. 18), so that his downcast demeanor is like that of a mourner (v. 6).[208]

There are social consequences too, for his friends and neighbors avoid him because of his wounds, perhaps because of his appearance or smell, or, more likely, if they thought at all like Job's friends, because of the witness of his wounds to his sin, or a combination of these. His enemies deceitfully plan his death ("harm" is thus interpreted in v. 12's parallelism) with vigor (v. 19), gloating over his fate (v. 16), slandering him, misrepresenting his intended good to them (v. 20). Although God is justly angry with him because of his sin (vv. 3-4), his enemies have no cause to hate him (v. 19).

He cries to God for mercy (v. 1), for which he longs and sighs (v. 9). It is very evident that he is in agony. He asks God to save him from the gloating of enemies over his impending fall (vv. 16-17), imploring God to draw near again speedily, for he is Yahweh his Savior. Perhaps the picture of the deaf and dumb man (vv. 13-14) is literal, with all his faculties seizing up in the presence of his enemies, although it could pictorially depict quiet trust in God. The former seems the more likely, for the rest of the psalm is certainly not quiet.

Psalm 39

This is the second of four psalms in which personal sin is confessed. These psalms close book 1, which opens (if Pss 1 and 2 are a general introduction to the Psalter) with a superscription to Psalm 3 reminding the sensitive reader of David's sin and its consequences (2 Sam 12:7-12). So every answer to prayer and all other divine blessings in book 1 were the product of God's grace.

39:1-3 The psalmist, puzzled by life's brevity, says nothing, not wanting the wicked to think him disloyal to his God. Sometimes the best way to avoid verbal sin is complete silence. So, when his thoughts become overheated and silence unbearable, it is to God he speaks (cf. 73:15-20).

39:4-6 He confronts the problem fairly and squarely, using various analogies. "Breath" (vv. 5, 11) is הֶבֶל, *hebel*, translated "in vain" in verse 6, and highly characteristic of Ecclesiastes,[209] while the emphasis on life's brevity anticipates 90:3-10. Verse 5 uses the body's limbs as rough indicators of

208. There is, of course, no suggestion here that illness is always linked to specific sin, but a worshiper aware of a personal connection could use it in prayer. See the excursus on "Sickness and Sin in the Psalms" in Mays, *Psalms*, 163-65.

209. Where NIV renders the word as "meaningless," Eccl. 1:2, 14; 2:1, etc., Wilcock comments that if the use of *Selah* after *hebel* in vv. 5 and 11 indicates a break for a Scripture reading, Eccl 2:17-26 and 5:10-15 would be very suitable (*Psalms 1–72*, 138).

length.[210] Life is busy but evanescent, with even the constant pursuit of wealth ultimately valueless.

39:7-11 This is a model of the right approach to God when conscious of sin. First of all, his hope is only in God. Then he asks for salvation from his transgressions (v. 8), not just their penalty (which comes in v. 10), and, with a new motive now for silence, accepts his punishment as divinely inflicted without complaint. He then generalizes, recognizing that God does not take human sin lightly, and that his punitive acts may affect prosperity.

39:12-13 With the threefold petition of verse 12 his prayer intensifies. Leviticus 25:23 calls Israelites aliens and tenants in God's land, but God commanded Israel to care for the alien,[211] so he is probably requesting this kind of care from God. Verse 13 means "do not look at me to punish me." The final verse shows he has well learned life's fleeting nature.

Psalm 40

40:1-4 This psalm provides an apt contrast to the preceding 39, for it is a striking testimony to a great, unspecified act of the Lord's personal deliverance.[212] "Waited patiently" is literally "waited, waited," revealing a sense of urgency. The slimy pit, mud, and mire suggest danger and perhaps defilement, while the rock indicates firmness and suggests safety, possibly also that this is to be found in God himself (cf. 18:2). In consequence the psalmist sings, expecting this will bring others to trust in Yahweh instead of in paganizing human beings (cf. 118:8-9). So here the exhortation in 2:12, early in book 1, finds virtual repetition toward its close.

40:5-10 He widens the scope of his praise and sees this event as just one of God's many wonders (cf. 77:11-15) done for him ("my God," v. 5a), but also for his people ("for us," v. 5b). Probably "the things you planned to do for us" refers to past wonders but could also include God's future gracious purposes. Neither speech (v. 5) nor sacrifice (v. 6),[213] but only total surrender (vv. 7-8) is adequate response. Verses 6-8 may echo Samuel's stern words to Saul (1 Sam 15:21-23). The pierced ears are not those of Exod 21:5-6 (where the singular is used), but ears opened for obedience as in Isa 50:4-5.[214] The "scroll" is

---

210. Cf. our own use of "foot" for twelve inches.

211. I.e., the רֵג, *gēr*, "resident alien," not simply the casual visitor (cf. Deut 24:17-18).

212. See also the introduction to Ps 39; for NT use of this psalm see pp. 350, 358.

213. Cf. 50:7-15 and comment there.

214. V. 6 is lit. "you have dug two ears for me." Craigie says, "The safest approach is a literal translation, based on the assumption of ancient idiomatic usage of which the precise sense

best understood as Deut 17:14-20, where the king's duty was obedience to God's law, which, of course, included sacrifice. This he embraces with all his heart. His dedication produces more adequate speech,[215] and he publicly praises the Lord's great acts and the moral attributes they reveal. As king, opportunities for this would have been his at national times of worship.

40:11-17   He has further troubles, but views his present and future with faith, encouraged by this recent experience, for "Do not withhold" (v. 11) should read, "You will not withhold."[216] His solemn dedication has not robbed him of a sense of sin (could it even have deepened it?), and he recognizes how deep and how prone to moral blindness he is (cf. Ps 51). Surrounded by many troubles, some at least caused by enemies bent on his destruction, he urgently calls God to save him. He prays not for their destruction but for their shaming. "Aha, aha" seems a cry of triumph, which events will show to be most inappropriate. Again there is testimony, for he asks that the godly should say, with him, "the LORD be exalted." There is no thought of self-exaltation.[217] His poverty can hardly be literal but rather expresses his sense of weakness, so that he ends by asking God for speedy help.

Psalm 41

This is a psalm (like 35) in which the psalmist seeks vindication when slandered by enemies.[218]

41:1-3   If book 1 is organized on a kingly pattern,[219] we might expect a psalm of the king at its close, and a godly king would have a special concern for the weak, which is certainly revealed here. Moreover, the Psalter starts by showing the type of person God blesses, and Psalm 2 promises God's support of his appointed king. Here these two themes coalesce. Blessing in the land was promised if the nation was obedient (Deut 28), and this clearly involved deliverance from the king's enemies. Verse 3, however, shows one particular trouble, illness, is afflicting him. Wordplay is a feature of this psalm.[220]

41:4-9   He frankly confesses he is not sinless (cf. 40:12). His enemies

---

is no longer clear" (*Psalms 1–50*, 315). It seems likely, however, that it means to be given acute hearing. See NIV mg. for the LXX reading.

215. Cf. vv. 9-10 and v. 5.

216. Kidner calls this translation "unquestionably right" (*Psalms 1–72*, 160).

217. Cf. 35:22-28, a passage with many similarities to this.

218. See the introduction to Ps 39; for NT use of this psalm see pp. 328, 358.

219. See pp. 21-28.

220. See Schaefer, *Psalms*, 102-3.

feign concern for a sick man, while secretly hoping for a fatality. The reference to his close friend strongly suggests Ahithophel, who joined David's enemies in his time of need (2 Sam 15:10-12, 31), and whose attitude Jesus saw reflected in the treachery of Judas (John 13:18). To commit treachery after sharing food was, in Near Eastern thinking, deeply shocking.[221]

41:10-12 His opening confidence now returns as he looks to God, not at his foes. Now clearly penitent, he knows this pleases the Lord, to whom he can now look for protection, confident his relationship with God will never cease. The theme of slander and vindication in this psalm reminds us of 35. Verse 12 is widely recognized as the conclusion not of this psalm but of book 1, but even so it is most apt at the close of this particular psalm.[222]

There are some parallels between this psalm and Isaiah 38 and 39, but also differences. If this psalm is indeed David's, it may have encouraged Hezekiah, possibly even providing inspiration for his own psalm recorded in Isaiah 38.

BOOK 2[1]

Psalms 42–43

At the start of a new book of the Psalter, we have a new author.[2] It is virtually certain that 42 and 43 were originally one, because of their similarity of theme, identity of refrain (42:5, 11; 43:5), and the absence of a separate heading, unique in book 2 (apart from Ps 71, q.v.). This psalm has great poetic beauty, fostered perhaps by the beauty of architecture and priestly garments the psalmist saw every day in his Levitical work. There is great emotional depth too in this lament, somewhat as in the book of Job, where complaints to God alternate with assertions of confidence in him. It is no surprise that so many of the Levitical psalms (which now begin) have a focus on the temple or on Jerusalem, its location.

42:1-5 His geographical remoteness from God's house (vv. 2, 4) is agonizing, comparable to an animal's desperate thirst for water. Weeping, he recalls joyous festivals when the temple was thronged with worshipers, some

---

221. The Hebrew phrase of v. 9c, lit. "he has made his heel great," is unique. Craigie discusses various possibilities, and says, "though the idiom is rare, the sense is clear enough" (*Psalms 1–50*, 319). It must relate to an act of treachery or of violence.

222. See p. 19.

1. For the Psalter's division into five books see pp. 21-28.

2. See p. 31.

perhaps having traveled from his present location. God to him is the living God, as he was to Joshua (Josh 3:10), David (1 Sam 17:26, 36), and Elijah (1 Kgs 18:15), but unbelievers taunt him with his apparent absence.[3] In a refrain, an important indicator of the psalm's main point, he rebukes himself for his melancholy and puts his hope in God to give him "a garment of praise instead of a spirit of despair" (Isa 61:3).

42:6-11   He follows his own advice, with "therefore" (v. 6) an important word. He is at the furthest remove in Israel from Jerusalem, at Jordan's headwaters on mighty Mount Hermon.[4] Its tumultuous, dangerous cataracts, linked in his imagination with even greater dangers at sea, are frightening, yet the repeated "your" (v. 7) perhaps shows hope, for even nature's most threatening manifestations are under God's control. Jonah apparently quotes verse 7b in his own prayer for help (Jon 2:3). The daily tears and taunts (v. 3) are countered by God's reminder of his covenant love (חֶסֶד, *ḥesed*, v. 8), so prayer becomes God-given song. "The God of my life" may be "the living God."[5] In verses 9 and 10 depression takes over again, but not entirely as he refers to "God my Rock." The taunters now appear as enemies and his very body feels his pain, but most of all he asks God why he is not being helped (cf. 22:1-2). Once again the refrain shows him putting his hope in that same God.

43:1-5   The taunters of 42:3, seen as his enemies in 42:9-10, now appear as "an ungodly nation" (unspecified) in 43:1. He uses law-court language here, as he knows his enemies to be wicked. The Rock of 42:9 becomes a "stronghold" in 43:2 (cf. 18:2), in verses of similar despondency. Now he looks to God's Word ("your light and your truth") to build his faith. "The holy mountain," "the altar," even the harp may not be literal but symbolize nearness of access to God even in his present location. So in his despondency he finds joy in God himself. The reiterated use of God's name and of the possessive pronoun gives emotional depth to this verse. The refrain, because it ends the psalm, remains in the mind as its abiding message.

Psalm 44

This psalm of lament oscillates between plural and singular, unlike 42–43, which is uniformly singular. A Levitical worship leader here takes the people's

---

3. For "meet with God," NRSV has "behold the face of God." See technical note in Broyles, *Psalms*, 97.

4. *Mizar* cannot be identified.

5. Following the reading of many MSS, the Syriac, and v. 2; the difference is only in one Hebrew letter, חַיֵּי, *ḥayyî*, and חַי, *ḥay*, respectively.

burden on his heart, speaking to God occasionally as an individual but more often as representing the whole people.[6] So then book 2 begins with an individual lament followed by a corporate lament, just as book 3 does.

44:1-8   This passage concerns God's past victories for and through Israel. Its reference to oral learning reflects Deuteronomy's emphasis on training children, especially as the psalmist's problem relates to the Deuteronomic theology that national obedience secured blessing and disobedience led to punishment (e.g., in Deut 28). The main focus is on the entry into the land[7] and the subsequent victories, attributed, much in Deuteronomic fashion and with considerable emphasis, to God's strong arm (cf. Deut 4:34; 5:15; 7:8; 26:8; Josh 24:1-13). God's love for them also recalls Deut 7:7-8, while the light of his face, showing affectionate approval, recalls Num 6:25, which, as a priestly blessing, would be well known to a Levite. Verses 4-8 show the oscillation of number, and stress trust not in weapons but in God (cf. 118:8-9, 15-16). Significantly, in view of what follows, the psalmist says his praise of God will never terminate (v. 8).

44:9-16   This resembles Psalm 89's *cri de coeur*. "The word *but* beginning verse 9 wrenches the psalm violently out of the 'feel-good' atmosphere of verses 1-8."[8] The nation's armies have been defeated and the psalmist sees this as rejection by God. Employing familiar pastoral imagery,[9] he likens them to sheep reared only for slaughter. They have also been scattered. The exiling of Israel and Judah was attributed to their sin by the OT writers,[10] but the psalm later protests the people's faithfulness, so this must be some lesser event. Defeat brought shame and derision, which in that culture was particularly hard to bear.

44:17-22   This is the heart of the problem. God apparently forsook them when they had kept his covenant, walked in his ways, and been true to his sole worship, all true also of Job, so this was a Job-like experience.[11] Verse 22 is the psalm's key. It employs the sheep imagery again (cf. v. 11), and is quoted in Rom 8:36, although there with a sense of divine purpose probably not felt by the psalmist's troubled mind. The phrase "for your sake" shows that, especially in OT times, a heavy price had sometimes to be paid for loyalty to God. Here then the OT anticipates Christ's teaching about bearing the cross for his sake (Luke 9:23).

---

6. For NT use of this psalm see pp. 337-38.

7. The analogy of planting (v. 2) appears also in 80:8-15; cf. also Isa 5:1-7.

8. Wilcock, *Psalms 1–72*, 159.

9. E.g., in Ps 23; Jer 23:1-4.

10. E.g., in Deut 28; 2 Kgs 17:1-23; Jer 32:26-35.

11. For further comment on apparently undeserved suffering see pp. 339-41.

44:23-26   The author makes an impassioned plea for God to intervene, not only appealing to his covenant (the implication of "your unfailing love") but showing confidence in it, perhaps realizing this was a temporary, if severe, trial of Israel's faith, another parallel with Job. The word קוּם, *qûm* ("rise up"), has military associations with the ark of God (Num 10:35).[12]

Psalm 45

This is a wedding ode, unique in the Psalter in addressing the king, greatly contrasting in mood with 44, and showing by its presence here in a book of religious poetry that OT religion touched life's every aspect. Pointing out the frequency of reference to the king, J. S. M. Mulder also notes that the word "God" appears three times, always in key verses (vv. 2, 6-7), and says, "the king's relation with God must be one of the central items of this poem."[13] Although obviously composed for a particular royal wedding, it was probably used often on such occasions. A royal wedding was important because of its relevance to the continuity of the Davidic dynasty, which was underwritten by the divine promise (2 Sam 7:12-16).[14]

45:1   This unusual and impressive introduction stresses the theme's nobility. All the poet's resources of speech and writing would be given to this deeply heart-stirring task. It effectively concentrates the reader's attention.

45:2-9   The combination of moral qualities with kingly dignity synthesizes the concerns of Psalms 1 and 2, suggesting that an ideal is being pictured here, perhaps with a touch of the conventional compliments paid to a monarch on such occasions. The king, a military figure, is clothed in garments befitting the dignity of his office, but, as in 72, his power is for promoting moral ends (v. 4), including even humility (cf. Zech 9:9). God's blessing too reminds us of 1:1. The references to anointing (vv. 2, 7) are figurative but apt for an anointed king. Luke 4:22 may allude to verse 2. His enemies are foreign nations (v. 5), and "beneath your feet" may echo Gen 3:15, for he is God's agent against evil. Verse 6b explains 6a, for the king, God's vicegerent, exercises judicial functions properly divine,[15] and "for ever and ever" finds its aptness in dynastic terms (2 Sam 7:11-16).[16] This is balanced by "God, your God" (v. 7),

12. See comment on 3:7.

13. Mulder, *Psalm 45*. The introductory Ps 2 also stresses the relation of the king to God.

14. For NT use of this psalm see p. 358.

15. Cf. Ps 82 and comments there.

16. For the NT it is fulfilled ultimately in Christ in a way that goes beyond its application to a king of Judah, for the quotation of it in Heb 1:8 is part of a catena of OT passages giving OT

which clearly shows the king is human. He has virtually imperial, not simply royal, status, for there are royal women, presumably foreign, in his household. The location of Ophir is uncertain. Now the bride is introduced.

45:10-15 The queen is addressed (vv. 10-12), then she and her companions are described (vv. 13-15). There is a threefold call for her attention (cf., e.g., Isa 55:2-3). Her commitment to the king should be total (cf. Gen 2:24). He brings her admiration; she should respond with respect. Verse 12 may refer not to Tyre's queen but to the Tyrian people,[17] for their merchant city was a byword for wealth (cf. Isa 23:3). She therefore shares the king's honor, and his glorious array is complemented by hers. Verses 14-15 suggest an imminent wedding.

45:16-17 These verses address the king, as the gender shows in Hebrew. He finds his place within a continuing dynasty. His memory is perpetuated by the psalm itself, and he is to be universally and eternally praised, a hint both of the continuing promise of 2 Samuel 7 and also the ideal nature of the king here portrayed, addressed, and extolled.

Psalm 46

Much in this psalm of Zion recalls Psalm 2, for the protection there promised to the king is here given to his capital city.[18] Either 2 Chr 20:1-30 or 2 Kgs 18:13–19:36 could be its setting, but there are other possibilities and certainty seems unattainable, especially, as VanGemeren points out, because it combines the hymnic and oracular genres.[19]

46:1-3 In 18:1-2 God is both David's internal strength and external refuge, and this psalmist echoes these convictions. So fear is removed, fear even of the most extreme physical disasters, affecting symbols of stability like the earth and mountains and of instability such as surging seas and volcanic earthquakes.[20] All this could be literal or could represent powerful, aggressive enemies (cf. v. 6).

---

support to the assertion of his divine glory (Heb 1:1-14). All major commentators discuss this verse, with various interpretive suggestions. See particularly Harris, "Translation," who, after a full and helpful discussion, accepts the KJV and NIV rendering and the kingly and messianic interpretation; also D. C. Mitchell, *Message of Psalter*, 246-48.

17. Cf. "daughter of Zion," e.g., in 9:14; Isa 1:8.

18. For further comment on the Zion psalms see p. 16.

19. VanGemeren, "Psalms," 350.

20. McCann says these verses seem to involve something worse than "a combination of a class-five hurricane and an earthquake measuring a ten on the Richter scale" (*Theological Introduction*, 137).

46:4-7   The focus changes from the cosmos to the microcosmic "city of God." "Surrounded by a world aflame, God's people are 'the city of God.'"[21] Jerusalem's water supply was through the brook Siloam, a symbol in Isa 8:6-8 of divine protection against Assyria's mighty power, itself symbolized by the Euphrates,[22] and a symbol here of all-round divine provision. "Most High" is a term connected with Jerusalem and used of the true God from at least Abraham's time (Gen 14:18, 22). "Break of day" may suggest Isaiah's period as the psalm's date, for Jerusalem's people then saw visible evidence of his protection (Isa 37:36; cf. also Exod 14:27). Jerusalem's internal peace and safety contrast with the fall of external national foes (v. 6). Verse 6b, with its reference to the earth, points to the psalm's unity (cf. vv. 2, 8, 10). The voice that effected its creation can also destroy it. Verse 7 reinforces the opening conviction, for "God of Jacob" suggests God's grace to the unworthy.

46:8-11   The call to view the present desolations (perhaps the judgment on Assyria) is because they are an earnest of the day God will end all warfare (cf. Isa 2:1-5). Both Israel and God's enemies come to know God, although differently, in his self-revelation (cf., e.g., Exod 6:7; 7:5), so that "be still" may call God's people to remain calm or else warring nations to halt their aggression, as he will ultimately be exalted (cf. Isa 2:10-22). By its repetition in verse 11, verse 7's affirmation becomes a refrain, staying in the reader's mind as the psalm's keynote and clear message: God is with his people as their refuge.[23]

Psalm 47

This exceptionally joyous hymn of praise is well placed after 46, which, apart from its refrain, climaxes in God's assertion of his supreme exaltation, which is where this present psalm begins. Some verbal links with 2 Samuel 6 suggest that it was perhaps written to commemorate the bringing up of the ark to Jerusalem under David.[24]

47:1-4   "Yahweh Most High" is unmistakably Israel's God,[25] yet it is the

---

21. VanGemeren, "Psalms," 352.

22. Some commentators, including Broyles, have argued for a kind of double symbolism, the river symbolizing the temple, which itself symbolizes the presence of God with his people (*Psalms*, 209).

23. This psalm's superb poetic quality is explored particularly well in Weiser, *Psalms*, 365-74.

24. Although, following Mowinckel, many exegetes link it to an assumed annual enthronement festival. See pp. 12-13.

25. This title finds an echo in "God has ascended" (v. 5) and "he is greatly exalted" (v. 9).

nations who are called to rejoice. The reason becomes clear in verse 9. The Assyrian monarchs were called "the great king," but here this is the Lord's title. Their joy's physical expression is comparable to that of the trees in Isa 55:12. Verse 3 probably refers to the nations subdued when Israel entered the land, an earnest of David's empire, and "our inheritance" is a phrase reminiscent of Deuteronomy (e.g., Deut 4:21) and Joshua (e.g., Josh 1:6). "Under our feet" (cf. Ps 45:5) recalls Gen 3:15 with its picture of conquered evil. "Jacob, whom he loved" (cf. Mal 1:2-3), goes beyond "the God of Jacob" (46:7, 11) in suggesting amazing grace (cf. John 13:23; Gal 2:20).

47:5-6   Parts of verse 5 occur verbatim in 2 Sam 6:15, and "ascended" probably refers to the movement of the ark, symbolizing God's presence, to the temple. The great joy of that special event is reflected in the fourfold call to praise in verse 6, with a fifth in verse 7.

47:7-9   The universalistic note of the first three verses returns. "Psalm" here is מַשְׂכִּיל, *maśkîl*.[26] The ideas of verses 7 and 8 are familiar in the Psalter, but verse 9 is surprising and amazing. The nations and their rulers belong to God in the same special sense as does Israel! The word גּוֹי, *gôy*, "nation," is often used of foreign powers, but עַם, *'am*, "people,"[27] is usually reserved for Israel. Here the special relationship Abraham and his descendants had with God belongs also to foreign nations, fulfilling Gen 12:1-3, and anticipating Psalm 87, Isaiah 19, and the missionary universalism of the NT.

Psalm 48

The case for some kind of ritual drama in Israelite festival worship is at its strongest in this psalm of Zion,[28] although it reads perfectly well without such a background; and, as Kidner says, evidence for such drama in Israel's worship is "indirect and ambiguous."[29]

48:1-3   The psalm begins, where its predecessor ends, with God's greatness, praised in his city (i.e., in the temple), the focus of this psalm. Is "loftiness" poetic hyperbole? Jerusalem is certainly lower than its surrounding hills, but the eschatological perspective of Isa 2:1-5 may provide an interpretive clue. "Zaphon" means "north," hardly appropriate for Jerusalem, but was

---

26. See p. 10.

27. This is the MT reading, but the LXX evidently read עִם, *'im* ("with"), assuming different pointing, and perhaps suggesting forced submission. In favor of the MT is its very unexpectedness, in view of the OT's theology of Israel's election.

28. For further comment on the Zion psalms see p. 16. For festival worship see pp. 10-17.

29. Kidner, *Psalms 1–72*, 180.

also the name of a mountain sacred to the Canaanites, so the psalmist is apparently saying that because of Yahweh's victory over hostile forces, Zion is clearly the rightful place of worship for all. The "Great King" is not David but God, as we see from verse 1. Verse 3a is reassuring, 3b even more so and reminds us of 18:1-2.

48:4-8   We cannot identify the occasion referred to with certainty, but it could be the event recorded in Isa 37:36,[30] if we interpret the reference to "the kings" (v. 4) through Isa 10:8 as a reference to vassal monarchs of Assyria. If so, this departure was not, strictly speaking, caused by the sight of Zion, but it is probably poetic hyperbole. Verse 7 recalls Isa 2:16 (NIV mg.).[31] The divine word, perhaps in Isa 37:33-35, promising the city security, is now confirmed by sight.

48:9-11   The foreign threat over, the people meditate on God's covenant love and see his revelation ("name") and praise spreading widely, whether through the territories of the beaten foes or, in eschatological vision, literally throughout the earth. "Righteousness" and "judgments" here are parallel concepts, denoting God's activity in putting things right.[32] Here, as in verse 2, there is joy, shared by the villages because in a siege their people would come within the city's walls.

48:12-14   These verses move from the statement "we have seen" (v. 8) into exhortation, as if the psalmist is saying, "Come and see for yourself what we have seen." All has been preserved by divine action, so the event now enters into the people's recital of God's deeds to the next generation. This great event confirms his abiding relationship with his people.

Psalm 49

This psalm contains more problems of translation and interpretation than most, and some are quite complex, but its general meaning is clear.[33]

49:1-4   This wisdom psalm is addressed to the whole world and notably to rich and poor alike, for it is a meditation on the serious limitations of riches, "a persuasive reflection on the abrupt, bleak end of the wealthy."[34]

---

30. See comment on v. 2.

31. Ships of Tarshish may have been built at Tarsessus, a Phoenician colony in Spain or Sardinia, but could equally be large ships suitable for the long journey there. See J. A. Thompson, "Tarshish," *IBD* 3:1517-19.

32. See also pp. 249-50, 258-59. and comment on 52:5-7.

33. For detailed discussion see VanGemeren, "Psalms," 368-72.

34. Schaefer, *Psalms*, 123. For further comment on the wisdom psalms, see p. 18.

"Low and high" are literally "sons of man and sons of man," but the first phrase uses the generic אָדָם, *'ādām,* and the second the individual אִישׁ, *'îš.* In verse 4 the proverb may be the whole psalm, the refrain, or the parts of it common to both instances (vv. 12, 20), while the riddle is probably the question of verse 5.[35] The psalm was evidently meant to be sung (v. 4).

49:5-9   The psalmist's focus is on wicked deceivers whose trust is in their wealth (vv. 5-6). They should not be feared, for their money will never buy a reprieve from death for others or for themselves (5-9). The NASB (and KJV), "no man can by any means redeem his brother" (v. 7), is more literal than the NIV and makes good sense, probably alluding both to the redemptive function of the near kinsman (Lev 25:47-49) and to the temporary nature of the firstborn's redemption from death (Exod 13:11-16).

49:10-12   Somewhat after the fashion of Ecclesiastes, he now appeals to experience. Verse 11 does not deny an afterlife but simply a return to ordinary sentient life. The name, viewed as human life's most permanent aspect, will be without lasting value. Death claims humans as well as animals.

49:13-15   These verses introduce a contrast. Those who trust in wealth are destined like animals for Sheol, with predatory Death feeding on them, and with decay instead of earthly splendor.[36] Verse 14b reads literally, "the upright shall have dominion over them in the morning," possibly suggesting that the psalmist's "night" of affliction by evildoers (v. 5) will not last forever.[37] The psalmist expresses confidence that what human riches cannot do, God will do, redeeming him from Sheol and taking him into his personal presence, the verb translated "take" being used also of Enoch and Elijah (Gen 5:24; 2 Kgs 2:5).

49:16-20   Riches and splendor should not overawe the reader, for the rich man's self-assessed blessing and high reputation with others will come to nothing; he will be possessionless and in darkness, like his ancestors. The refrain of verses 12 and 20 reads like a proverb, the variation being due to the need to stress first the temporary character of riches and then, by implication, the permanent nature of wisdom ("understanding"), which endures because its possessor endures.

---

35. The two also occur together in 78:2 and in Prov 1:6; Ezek 17:2. The NIV phrase "wicked deceivers" is based on different pointing from the MT and may be right; MT "the guilt of my heels" is difficult.

36. For Sheol see pp. 290-91. Cf. Death's personification in Rom 5:14. "This passage ranks for sinister effect with Jeremiah 9:21, where death climbs in at the windows to carry off the living. Now he is no intruder; he is on his home pastures" (Kidner, *Psalms 1–72,* 184).

37. This assumes that wealth and rule are normally linked, as is often true. See the note on this verse in Davidson, *Vitality of Worship,* 161.

Psalm 50

This is a prophetic psalm, and the call for attention in verse 7 links it to Psalm 49, which begins similarly, although here the call is to God's people alone.[38]

50:1-6 An awesome accumulation of great divine names and titles, as here in verse 1, often introduces the threat of judgment (cf., e.g., Isa 1:24). A source of light and of heat can be identical, so both God's light shining from beautiful Zion (cf. 27:1 and 48:2) and the fire of judgment going before him reveal the same holy God. God speaks to summon the heavens and the whole earth as assessors (cf. Isa 1:2) when, accompanied by fearsome natural phenomena (cf. Exod 19:16-19),[39] he comes to judge his own people. "My consecrated ones" (v. 5a) translates חֲסִידָי, *ḥĕsîdāy,* meaning "those faithful to me in covenant," and verse 5b emphasizes their responsive entry into this covenant with him, a possible reminder of Israel's reiterated promise of obedience in connection with its covenant sacrifice (Exod 24:2, 7).

50:7-15 God speaks again, now to his people and now as witness for the prosecution. "I am God, your God," alludes to the covenant (Lev 26:9-12). That their sacrifices and offerings are ever before him suggests excess, so we may date the psalm to the eighth or seventh century, for, in the face of external threats, especially from Assyria and Babylon, this was a feature of Israel's religion then (see esp. Mic 6:6-8). Their fault is not in offering sacrifice, but in their theological understanding and motivation, for verses 9-13 suggest a baalized concept of Yahweh as needing sacrifice to survive, an idea in Babylonian religion, which had close connections with Canaanite religion. "They thought that religion is man reaching out to God, serving him and ministering to him, the deepest of all religious errors."[40] Verse 14 calls for the union of ritual ("thank offerings") and sincerity ("fulfill your vows") if prayers for deliverance, probably from some external foe, are to be answered.

50:16-21 God now speaks to the blatantly wicked, who do not simply have a wrong theology but are rebels under a religious cloak. Outwardly they conform (v. 16), but they refuse God's teaching. They break the eighth, seventh, and ninth commandments, referred to in that order, the last to an ex-

---

38. Goulder suggests that an Asaph psalm was placed here, between a Korahite and a Davidic sequence, because its theme was close to that of Ps 51, "obedience rather than sacrifice" (*Prayers of David,* 250). For further comment on the prophetic psalms, see pp. 7-8.

39. Anderson appropriately comments, "the Sinai story may have coloured all subsequent descriptions of other theophanies" (*Psalms,* 1:382), for, of course, they were all manifestations of the same awesome God.

40. Motyer, "Psalms," 518.

treme degree.[41] Verse 21 alludes to verse 3. They treat God as if he is amoral, and he now comes out against them. These verses challenge all whose religion and life are at variance.

50:22-23 The psalmist now deals with the blatantly wicked and the religious formalist in summary form. The former are in imminent danger of judgment and must repent (surely implied in "Consider this . . . or . . ."), and verse 23, with its reference to honoring God, clearly assumes the new attitude outlined in verses 14 and 15. Davidson points out that, like Psalm 2, this psalm ends with a warning and a promise.[42]

Psalm 51

This is the first of a series of psalms with Davidic superscriptions (66, 67, and 71 are exceptions) that brings book 2 to a close. Many of these superscriptions have biographical notes, so the redactor evidently meant us to keep the events referred to in mind. We will do this, bearing in mind too that, as Davidic psalms, they are reminders of the overall messianic message of the Psalter.[43]

The first Davidic collection (Pss 3–41) began with a psalm whose superscription reminds the reader of David's sin, and the superscription of the first of this further group focuses directly on it. The divine promise that established the Davidic covenant and that forms the basis of the introductory Psalm 2 threatened punishment but not removal of the covenant for the sins of David's successors (2 Sam 7:14-16). Here we see that same divine grace extended to David himself.[44]

51:1-2 In this penitential lament, we hear David crying to God for mercy,[45] pleading both God's covenant faithfulness ("your unfailing love") and his compassion, asking, by varied metaphors, for the removal of his sin.

51:3-6 His sin confronts him as Israel's burnt offerings confront God in 50:8, for the phrase is the same in both verses. The words "transgressions" and "sin" (along with "iniquity," v. 2) probably do not introduce distinctions but rather place strong emphasis on sin, although "transgressions" implies deliberateness. In 2 Samuel 11 and 12 David's sin has harmed others, but here

---

41. For misuse of the tongue see also pp. 328-30.

42. Davidson, *Vitality of Worship,* 165.

43. For NT use of this psalm see p. 310. For canonical criticism see pp. 21-28.

44. See also the excursus to the introduction, pp. 34-39. Broyles points out its strong links of terminology with prophetic passages related to Judah's exile, but agrees that nothing rules out the possibility of Davidic authorship (*Psalms,* 226-27).

45. The same verb is used in 2 Sam 12:22.

he sees it to be fundamentally against God, accepting his judgment as utterly right. His sin is congenital, but this aggravates rather than mitigates it.[46] As Mays expresses it, he is saying, "My problem is not just the need of pardon for a particular wrong but deliverance from the predicament of myself."[47] Truth should be inward and deep, and there is contrast here with the hypocrisy attacked in Psalm 50. Moreover, such practical wisdom needs to be taught, and by God himself.

51:7-12   He pleads for divine cleansing, using various analogies, including the use of hyssop for the leper in Mosaic ritual cleansing (cf. Num 19:6, 18). The crushing of his bones clearly represents punishment of some kind. He looks to God for moral regeneration, and creation and renewal suggest something radical and constant.[48] Eaton argues well that נְדִיבָה, *nĕdîbâ* (v. 12), should be translated "princely" rather than "willing," in relation to David's endowment with the Spirit for his royal work (1 Sam 16:13).[49] He also looks to God for the joy that accompanies renewed fellowship and asks him not to reject him, perhaps with Saul's experience in mind (cf. 1 Sam 16:13-14).

51:13-17   His experience of God's mercy will equip him to instruct others, and so this psalm joins 49 and 50 as psalms of instruction. In a further plea for that mercy, he highlights a specific sin. David committed a series of sins on that occasion, but here the most serious is underlined (v. 14). He brings oral worship that is deeply felt and contrite rather than sacrificial worship (cf. 50:8-15); no sacrifice was prescribed for such "sins with a high hand." He interprets sacrifice as penitence, because, of course, the two were never meant to be divorced.

51:18-19   Many scholars hold that these verses were added during the exile, when they would be particularly appropriate, for the remainder of the psalm could then feature as the penitence of the individual worshiper because of his or her participation in the sins that had brought this judgment on the nation. Nevertheless, an origin in David's period is not impossible, for having recently captured Jerusalem, he would be concerned for its prosperity and defense and the acceptance of godly sacrifice within the house of God to be built

---

46. He here acknowledges in relation to himself what another Davidic psalm applies to the wicked (58:3)! Neither psalm is used as evidence for original sin in the NT and both could be hyperbole, but not necessarily, for a deepened sense of sin could have been accompanied by a deepened theology of sin.

47. Mays, *Psalms*, 201.

48. Cf. Jer 31:31-34; Ezek 36:25-27. The psalmist's word, בָּרָא, *bārā'* ("create"), is used in the OT only of divine activity, and, as McCann points out, the occurrences of רוּחַ, *rûaḥ* ("spirit") are another reminder of Gen 1:1-2 (*Theological Introduction*, 105).

49. See Eaton, *Kingship*, 71 and 205 n. 41.

there. Perhaps the editors meant to contrast this with the baalized view of sacrifice attacked in Psalm 50.

Psalm 52

This psalm is unusual because it is directed specifically against one person, who is identified as Doeg in its superscription. See 1 Sam 21:7; 22:9-23.[50]

52:1-4   Great in his own sight, this man is disgraceful in God's,[51] for behind his action was the intent to destroy (cf. 2:1ff.). There is here a piling up of words for deceit (cf. Jer 9:3-9). His tongue was both deceitful and harmful, suggesting that there was not only malice in his actions but also some other factor, such as misrepresentation of David's motives. His sense of values was perverse (vv. 3-4).

52:5-7   The threefold parallelism in verse 5 is progressive, from ruin through forcible removal from home to death, with "everlasting" probably governing the thought in all three clauses. The righteous will be filled with awe-struck reverence as they see God's righteous act of judgment.[52] Their ironic laughter is in tune with God's in Psalm 2,[53] and the stronghold reminds us of 2:12. In a largely pastoral country, the keeper of the monarch's flocks could become rich, and verse 7b implies perhaps that his destructiveness brought him ample financial rewards.

52:8-9   When David was a fugitive, he could not attend God's house, yet, through trust in God's covenant love ("unfailing love" is סֶחֶד, *ḥesed*), he is like an olive tree flourishing there, an analogy recalling Ps 1:3. "For ever and ever" may be suggested by the olive tree's longevity. Olive oil was used for sacred purposes in God's house. There he will engage in communal praise with the covenant people (חָסִידִים, *ḥāsîdîm*, "saints," v. 9), and worshipers using this psalm at the temple would share these sentiments.

---

50. See the introduction to Ps 51. Wilcock recognizes the difficulty of equating the all-too-frank shepherd of the story with the deceitful rich man of the psalm, but deals helpfully with the problem (*Psalms 1–72*, 191).

51. הַגִּבּוֹר, *haggibbôr* ("mighty man," v. 1), and הַגֶּבֶר, *haggeber* ("man," v. 7), are almost certainly sarcastic, so that in v. 1 we might render, "you hero, you!"

52. For righteousness see pp. 249-50; and for judgment see pp. 258-59.

53. The interpretation of vv. 1 and 7 given in n. 51 strengthened by the obvious irony here.

Psalm 53

This is largely identical with Psalm 14, but it calls God Elohim, not Yahweh, a general tendency in book 2.[54] The reason for the repetition may be sought in each psalm's position in its collection. Psalm 14 brings to a climax 9–13, featuring enemies and their antagonism, so suggesting a reason: their practical atheism. Psalm 53 occurs between two psalms with their enmity as the theme but now linked by their superscriptions to specific events in 1 Samuel 21–26. This section in 1 Samuel contains the story of Nabal, whose name means "fool" (1 Sam 25:25), the word used here, so that the reader of this psalm, turning to 1 Samuel, finds there an appropriate illustration of what the psalm says, underlining the psalm's lesson.

Most of the differences are small, do not affect the overall message, and so will receive no comment. Verse 5, however, differs significantly from 14:5b and 6. There the focus is on the righteous, but here on the wicked, "those who attacked you." Some suggest this psalm was modified to fit a specific historical event, such as 2 Kings 19 (Wilcock), although it could have referred to some victory of David.[55]

Psalm 54

The occasion the heading mentions is recorded in 1 Sam 23:19-24, and, except for its shorter length, the question of the Ziphites here is identical with that in 1 Sam 23:19.[56]

54:1-2 In the Hebrew text, אֱלֹהִים, *ʾĕlōhîm*, "God," opens these two verses, suggesting urgency. The psalmist's prayer is not simply for physical deliverance from his enemies but for divine vindication, so he invokes God's name, not just his might. The divine name is associated particularly with worship at the temple as the house of Yahweh, for there he placed his name (1 Kgs 8:29; cf. Deut 12:5).[57]

54:3-5 He brings together his enemies (v. 3), his God (v. 4), and the inevitable enemy downfall through God's action. Description of his enemies (v. 3) moves from the fact that they are strangers through their character to their

---

54. For detailed comment on their common features, see the commentary on Ps 14. On the divine names see p. 9.

55. See the introduction to Ps 51. For NT use of this psalm see p. 301.

56. See the introduction to Ps 51.

57. For the apparent anachronism of this see pp. 36-37.

practical atheism,[58] which reminds one of Psalm 53. He is confident in God to help and sustain him, the second verb suggesting perhaps that he will be upheld in God's great purpose of kingship (cf. 2:6). He pleads God's faithfulness.

54:6-7 Here sacrifice and vocal praise, OT worship's two main features, come together in the psalmist's promise. God's goodness is revealed in his acts, on this occasion in his deliverance. The trouble of verses 1-5 may now be past, although it is much more likely that these verses reveal his certainty of a hearing and of consequent divine action on his behalf. He is filled with praise.

Psalm 55

This psalm of lament and trust shows familiarity with some pentateuchal narratives. Its concern with the psalmist's enemies links it with many others in this part of book 2. Its lack of a biographical superscription is strange, given its place in a series most of which have such, especially if it concerns David's relations with Absalom or Ahithophel.[59] Perhaps, like Psalm 53 with its obvious link with Nabal,[60] the redactor wanted to leave the reader to make the connection.

55:1-3 Here is an impassioned threefold cry to God. The psalmist's trouble is inward, and its cause is both the voiced abuse and the silent antipathy of his enemy.[61]

55:4-8 Overwhelmed by horrific fears, including that of death itself, he longs to have wings for escape to the desert with its freedom from ferocious storms and perhaps (v. 8) with a rock as a refuge.[62]

55:9-11 He focuses on the city, but it is unclear whether he is inside or outside it. The enemies are vocal in their abuse, and their constant prowling on the walls suggests they were eager either that he should not escape the city or else be excluded from it. Confusing them and confounding their speech (v. 9) suggests an analogy with the story of Babel (Gen 11:1ff.).

55:12-14 Now the focus is on the leading enemy, and the psalmist's

---

58. Wilcock, following Kirkpatrick, points out that the Ziphites were from Judah, David's homeland (Josh 15:55), so that the reference to them as "strangers" pillories them for behavior inconsistent with neighborliness (*Psalms 1–72*, 196-97).

59. See the comment on vv. 12-14. It is possible, of course, that the redactor, like the modern commentator, could not identify the enemy with certainty.

60. See the comments on Ps 53.

61. עָקַת, *'āqat,* translated "stare" in NIV, is a hapax legomenon in the MT. NIV follows Dahood in deriving its meaning from Ugaritic. See Tate, *Psalms 51–100,* 51.

62. "Like a dove," not "of a dove," contra NIV.

emotional hurt is evident. Which enemy is in view? If the psalm is by David, there is tragic irony in that he himself acted treacherously against Uriah, one of his closest associates (2 Sam 23:39), so that the treachery alluded to here would certainly be a punishment fitting the crime.[63] In many ways Ahithophel would figure as the treacherous friend, as would Absalom, except that we would expect some indication of a blood relationship in his case. Certain identification seems unobtainable.

55:15-19 Again the focus is on the enemies as a group. Verse 15 is strongly reminiscent of the story of Korah and his company, and this is apt, for that too was a rebellion against divinely appointed men, therefore against the Lord himself.[64] Like Daniel later (Dan 6:10), the psalmist prayed three times a day. The God who ransoms him is the supreme king, pledged, as in Psalm 2, to support his anointed human king.[65]

55:20-21 Here is the leading opponent again. The picture of a hypocritical friend is nauseating.

55:22-23 Verse 22 is a wisdom element in this psalm, a word of assurance to the righteous in general (cf. Ps 1).[66] Premature death is God's punishment for the wicked here, and of course this was true of both Ahithophel (2 Sam 17:23) and Absalom (2 Sam 18:14-15). The psalmist sums up his whole trusting attitude as the psalm closes, and later worshipers, if facing similar treachery, could identify not only with his complaint but with his faith.

Psalm 56

This psalm moves from lamentation through expression of confidence in God to praise for his deliverance.[67] With its word "escaped," 1 Sam 22:1 strongly suggests that David was taken captive by the Philistines while in their land, as the superscription here also indicates.[68]

56:1-2 The hot pursuit all day implies constant imminent danger, while "slanderers" and "in their pride" may point to Saul's men rather than to

---

63. Harman, *Psalms*, 210.

64. Num 16:23-40; here also "the grave" is Sheol; see pp. 290-91. Cf. also Ps 2.

65. Here ransom is simply a vivid metaphor for deliverance.

66. For comment on wisdom psalms see p. 18.

67. See the introduction to Ps 51, and the comments on 34, which is given a similar setting.

68. In line with his theory that Pss 51–72 follow events in the life of David from the death of Uriah to the accession of Solomon, Goulder (*Prayers of David*, esp. 24-30) relates this psalm to David's flight from Absalom. It could fit that situation, but reference to the earlier occasion indicated in the heading is equally plausible.

the Philistines, although the reference to the nations (v. 7) looks in the opposite direction.[69] David was caught between a Scylla and a Charybdis.

56:3-4   In his fear he trusts in God and praises his word, which strikingly contrasts with the misuse of words by "slanderers" in verse 2. The word here may be God's promise that established his covenant with David (2 Sam 7). The adjective "mortal" underlines his conviction of human inability to harm him when he trusts in God.

56:5-6   Once again the slanderers are in view. "Plotting" suggests Saul and his men, but, for the consecutive reader of the Psalter, it also recalls 2:1-3. David is in constant mortal danger.

56:7-8   The psalmist's deliverance from present foreign foes is an earnest of the ultimate downfall of the nations.[70] Movingly and with vivid metaphors, he pleads with God to record this lament, listing his tears as liquid goes into a bottle, drop by drop,[71] writing them down meticulously.

56:8-11   God's answer will assure him that he is committed to him. Verses 10 and 11 are almost identical to verse 4, each forming a refrain, underlining the main theme of his psalm.

56:12-13   The trouble now appears to be past, either as a biographical fact or, more likely, in the psalmist's faith that God had heard and would act on his behalf. He will now pay his vows with thank offerings. Verse 13 sums up his causes for praise as deliverance from death and as being kept in the right way so that he may walk in the light of life (cf. 1:1-3). Many an Israelite worshiper would find both encouragement and challenge in the psalmist's faith and praise here.

Psalm 57

Here is a prayer for help uttered in strong faith, showing sustained confidence in God. If, as the superscription indicates, we are to think here of David in the cave of Adullam, it is clear that his trust was not in its walls but in his God.[72]

57:1   The opening plea is identical with that of 56,[73] but doubled, reflecting even greater urgency. Psalms 55:6 and 56 (superscription) refer to a dove; now we find the psalmist likening God to a bird protecting its young (cf. 61:4).

---

69. See the discussion in Tate, *Psalms 51–100*, 70.
70. For the imprecatory element here see pp. 257-58.
71. Following NIV mg., which takes נֹאד, *nō'd,* as "wineskin," its most frequent sense.
72. See the introduction to Ps 51.
73. Despite slightly different wording in NIV.

57:2-4   Once more he cries out, describing his God and his enemies in sharply contrasting terms. The Lord (cf. v. 9) is God Most High, exalted in heaven, while they are on earth, surrounding him like predatory beasts. God is faithful to his covenant purpose ("love" is חֶסֶד, *ḥesed,* love within a covenant relationship), perhaps an allusion to David's anointing for kingship, and so intervenes from heaven to save him.[74] Thus God rebukes his pursuer, now disqualified as king through rebelliousness. There is contrast too between this rebuke and the tongues of the enemies (cf. 56:2, "slanderers").

57:5   Prayer now becomes praise to the God of heaven and earth, who had acted from the former to set right a situation in the latter.[75]

57:6   Here is the immediate threat, portrayed with an analogy from hunting reminiscent of 1 Sam 24:14 (cf. 1 Sam 26:20), where (as also in 1 Sam 26), the tables were turned, with Saul at David's mercy.

57:7-10   He utters praise again, affirming his definite commitment to his God, for "steadfast" here means "set firm." He pictures himself using instruments[76] to "awaken the dawn," suggesting that, like Paul and Silas (Acts 16:25), he was singing God's praises during the night. Hidden in a severely limited space, a cave, he wants to praise God to all the world. This was apt, for, as Psalm 2 shows, his kingship in Zion had international significance. God's faithful love, displayed on earth (v. 3), is great enough to encompass the universe, as verse 10 implies (cf. 89:1-8).

57:11   The refrain's second occurrence (cf. v. 5) intensifies the psalmist's desire to point beyond the immediate situation to the greatness of the God who has intervened for him.

Psalm 58

This psalm shows, in a particularly marked way, its author's flair for graphic analogies, invariably the gift of great poets. Schaefer, whose commentary shows sensitivity to poetic features, calls its imagery "masterful."[77] It contains a number of textual problems.[78]

74. Eaton refers to 18:16 (he says 18:7, but this must be a misprint) and 144:7 as saying the same thing and showing God's support for the king (*Kingship,* 46). The consecutive reader recalls also the promises of Ps 2.

75. Note how often the word "heaven" occurs in the psalm, suggesting faith that God can well deal with mere earth-bound mortals.

76. This is surely figurative when he was a fugitive.

77. Schaefer, *Psalms,* 143.

78. Only those with important bearing on interpretation will be mentioned. See Anderson, *Psalms,* 1:429-34; or Tate, *Psalms 51–100,* 82-84, for fuller discussion.

58:1-2   Here there is a challenge to unjust rulers, which could call to mind either Saul or Absalom, for both combined injustice and violence.[79] The plural may suggest that both are in mind, or else that the psalmist's thought widens to embrace unjust rulers generally.

58:3-5   It now widens still more to the wicked generally (cf. Ps 1). In 51:5 he applies to himself the insight of verse 3. In the psalms, speaking lies is often linked, as here, with violence. The analogy with the cobra, which is deaf and responds not to the sounds but to the movement of the charmer, illustrates both the capacity for evil of the wicked and their refusal to hear God's Word.

58:6-8   He now calls God to act against them. The teeth of predators are of course used on their victims. A dramatic change of illustration occurs in verse 7, implying perhaps that, through God's action, these savage predators can become as harmless as disappearing water. Harman says, "The connection between the slug and the stillborn child is that neither sees the light of the sun *(verse 8)*. The slug leaves its trail behind, but that is gone when the sun rises. The stillborn child never sees the light of the sun. So the psalmist wishes his wicked enemies to become as if they had never existed."[80]

58:9-11   The text of verse 9 is extremely difficult to interpret, but whatever analogy is intended, the main thought is clear: God's quick dispatch of the wicked. Verse 10 is exceptionally strong, its language very vivid, almost too vivid for many readers, but it shows confidence in the God whose justice, though perhaps long awaited, is nevertheless sure. In a psalm so full of metaphors, it should not be taken literally.[81] Verse 11 may remind us that the statements of Psalm 1 are true, despite all appearances to the contrary.

Psalm 59

Most unusually, this psalm has two different sets of refrains answering to its two main features, one stressing the constant menace of David's enemies and the other his confidence in God's protection, a demonstration therefore of both realism and faith.[82]

---

79. The MT has אֵלֶם, *'ēlem,* "in silence," but this hardly makes sense. Most translators and commentators assume different vocalization, reading the text as אֵלִים, *'ēlîm,* "gods" or "rulers" (e.g., NIV); cf. 82:1-2 (a psalm of Asaph), which, however, employs אֱלֹהִים, *'ĕlōhîm.* The persons addressed here must be human in the light of the way they are described, especially in v. 3. See Tate, *Psalms 51–100,* 82-83, and my comments on 82:1.

80. Harman, *Psalms,* 218. See Anderson, *Psalms,* 1:433, for a different interpretation.

81. As Harman says, "bathing feet in blood is a biblical image for victory (cf. Isa 63:1-6; Rev 14:19-20; 19:13-14)" (*Psalms,* 219).

82. See the introduction to Ps 51.

59:1-2   This plea to God describes the enemies in terms first of their antagonism and then of their general character. The verb "protect" is from the same root as "fortress" in verses 9, 16, and 17, and implies elevation beyond reach, so that "rise up" belongs to the same picture language.

59:3-5   Here we can picture David looking at these men from his window. His moral assertions do not claim sinlessness but only innocence of any offense against them or presumably against Saul. Twice he calls God to see, twice to arise for his help, and he accumulates titles of God that combine covenant faithfulness ("Lord," i.e., Yahweh, and "God of Israel") with power ("God Almighty"; cf., e.g., Isa 1:24). He calls on God to punish all the nations, because he knows that judgment within Israel is part of universal judgment.[83] The last clause of verse 5 returns to the local situation.

59:6-8   The enemies are particularly active in the evening, perhaps hoping to catch him asleep and vulnerable. They are like dogs, often sleeping during the day but marauding at night, and their murderous talk (probably with each other) is like wild dogs salivating. Their practical atheism (cf. Pss 14 and 53) makes them imagine they have no listener. Verse 8 reminds one of 2:1-5, 8, and suggests that the psalmist saw their antagonism as a microcosm of universal rebellion against God.

59:9-10a   The language here is reminiscent of 18:1-3. He watches for God to act because of his intimate covenant relationship ("my loving God").

59:10b-13   The description of God as a shield continues the reminder of Psalm 18 (18:2). Malice is suggested by "gloat," but this verb means only "to see." He asks for a gradual fall for the enemies, so that, in Deuteronomic style, his people may learn a lesson, and not Israel only but the world's nations. If this seems to be meeting cursing with cursing, we should note that the purpose is divine revelation.[84]

59:14-16   Verse 14 is repeated from verse 6 as a kind of refrain, giving emphasis. Now, however, the frustrating of their desire for food (i.e., the psalmist!) is implied.[85] He now brings God praise, taking up earlier language from the psalm, such as "strength" (v. 9), "your love" (cf. "my loving God," v. 10), "my fortress" (v. 9). The final clause of verse 16 is reminiscent of 2:12.

59:17   Verse 9's refrain returns but now as praise rather than prayer, for the prayer has been answered.

---

83. See further comment on judgment on pp. 258-59.

84. For comment on imprecation in the Psalms see pp. 257-58.

85. In v. 15b NIV follows the early versions, assuming the verb לִין, *lîn*, "to murmur," rather than MT לוּן, *lûn*, "to spend the night." As Tate says, "Either reading is adequate — and unpleasant enough" (*Psalms 51–100*, 94).

Psalm 60

For the geographical references in the heading see NIV mg., and for their historical background see 2 Sam 8:13.[86] This attributes the victory against the Edomites not to Joab but to David, while 1 Chr 18:12 credits it to Abishai. The three are not necessarily inconsistent, for David-Joab-Abishai looks like a chain of command. The numbers slain are also different, perhaps reflecting a division of the army into two sections, one under Joab and Abishai, the other directly under David.[87] There are three sections, with dramatic changes of mood. The retrospective reference in 1 Kgs 11:15-16 to burying the dead probably implies an Israelite defeat prior to Joab's victory, according with the contents of the lament here. Verses 5-12, with minor differences, are found also in 108:7-13.

60:1-4   This is not simply a lament but a complaint that levels accusations against God. Verses 1-3 have a whole sequence of verbs attributing acts against Israel to him, with his rejection of his people governing them all (cf. 44:9ff.; 89:38ff.).[88] The shaking (v. 2) reminds us of the universal judgment in Isaiah 24. The figure of drunkenness (cf. Ps 75:8) also occurs in Isaiah (Isa 29:9; 51:17; 63:6). Verse 4 is difficult to interpret because of varied word meanings, and Wilcock opts for such a rendering as: "You raise a banner over a place of refuge, to which they may run from the battle," arguing that it leads well into the next few verses.[89] The prayers in verses 1 and 2 are somewhat peremptory, revealing desperation rather than irreverence.

60:5-8   The plea emphasizes both God's power ("your right hand"; cf., e.g., Exod 15:6) and his love for his people ("those who fear you," Ps 60:4). The words, "God has spoken from his sanctuary," may suggest a prophetic oracle during a festival, or else an inspired word coming to the psalmist himself while at worship.[90] Kidner makes helpful comments on the geographical locations, and then says, "in a few bold strokes the early history and distinctive areas of Israel are called to mind, and the chief agents of defence and rule (*helmet* and *sceptre*) are named."[91] Verses 6 and 7, referring to the apportionment of land and the fact that the land is God's, are strongly reminiscent of the book of Joshua. Israel's neighbors too are his possessions, but are

---

86. See the introduction to Ps 51.

87. See the helpful comment in Broyles, *Psalms*, 252.

88. For judgment see comment on pp. 258-59.

89. Wilcock, *Psalms 1–72*, 216. For detailed comment on this difficult verse see Kidner, *Psalms 1–72*, 216-17; Tate, *Psalms 51–100*, 101-2.

90. See the discussion on prophetic psalms on pp. 7-8.

91. Kidner, *Psalms 1–72*, 217.

described more menially. Tossing the sandal probably implies Edom's slave status.

60:9-12   Another abrupt change occurs here. Edom, though just a slave, will be difficult to overcome, as anybody visiting Petra even today will acknowledge, especially if its natural defensive advantages were supplemented by humanly engineered fortifications.[92] The God who has rejected them is the only one who can lead the people against Edom, so the psalmist prays for this, confessing human powerlessness. Verse 12 sums up the thought of this stanza.

Psalm 61

"If the psalmist is praying for himself in verses 1-4 and for the king in verses 5-8, the train of thought is disjointed, and the division is then so marked that the two halves seem unrelated. If the psalmist is himself the king, and in verses 6-7 is praying for himself in the third person, everything falls into place."[93]

61:1-4   This prayer is for security in God, describing him, as the Davidic psalms often do, as his refuge, and he has already experienced him as such. Certainly during Absalom's revolt, exclusion from the Zion he loved must have seemed to David like being at "the ends of the earth," and he must often have thought of the way God protected him during his flight from Saul. God is graphically pictured as an elevated rock (as in 62:2), a strongly constructed defensive tower, as providing a tent (suggesting at least the protection of a family and perhaps of God's house),[94] and the intimate shelter of a bird's wings (cf. 57:1).

61:5-8   He pleads his loyalty to God, perhaps expressed in votive offerings. "Fearing God" and "inheritance" appear together in 25:12-14. Here the concept is probably spiritual rather than physical. Verses 6 and 7 are often seen as a prayer, not by the king himself but by others. If the psalm is basically Davidic, these verses would reveal its later adaptation for this purpose, although David could be making his own security in God the basis of a prayer for protection for each king of his dynasty.[95] This would explain "for many generations" and "forever," and would look back not only to Psalm 2 but to

---

92. Petra is the biblical Sela, a major Edomite city.

93. Wilcock, *Psalms 1–72*, 217-18. Cf. the frequent use of "your servant" and "the house of your servant" in 2 Sam 7:18-29.

94. Cf. 15:1 and comments there.

95. See comments on the superscription to Ps 72.

the covenant promises of 2 Samuel 7. Love and faithfulness too suggest a covenant, for this is "covenant love" (חֶסֶד, *ḥesed*). The psalm fitly closes with a commitment to praise and to the fulfillment of vows.

Psalm 62

In this psalm of great confidence in God we see some of the ways Hebrew has of placing emphasis.

62:1-2 The word אַךְ, *'ak,* occurring seven times in this psalm, is an emphatic particle that here indicates exclusiveness, and NIV translates it as "alone" in verses 1, 2, 5, and 6, as "fully" in verse 4, and twice as "but a" in verse 9. The emphasis thus secured is intensified by the fact that each time it is the first word in the sentence. The word translated "rest" suggests quiet serenity, and "my salvation," "my rock," and "my fortress,"[96] in which emphasis now comes through a sequence of nouns each with a possessive pronoun, remind us of these words in 18:1 and 2, following a heading about God's deliverance of David from all his enemies.

62:3-4 The peace of the first stanza is in the midst of storm, for the psalmist faces a sustained attempt to topple him from his lofty place, probably his kingship. This, especially with the references to lies and hypocrisy, recalls Absalom's rebellion. The leaning wall and tottering fence represent either his enemies' estimate of him or his estimate of himself without God, more likely the former.

62:5-8 Verses 1 and 6 state his settled attitude, while verse 5 is self-exhortation to continue in this in the present circumstances.[97] Because of his conviction that God is his salvation, he finds hope in the present assault. Moreover, "never" in verse 2 is, both logically and in experience, the basis of "not" in verse 6. The reference to his honor tends to confirm that this is an assault on his kingship. Verse 8 is a "wisdom" reflection reminding us of 2:12, which closes another psalm about kingship under attack.[98]

62:9-10 "Lowborn men" and "the highborn" translate "sons of men," the first using the generic אָדָם, *'ādām,* and the second the specific אִישׁ, *'îš,* together suggesting people of all kinds and conditions. Verse 9a reminds us of Ecclesiastes and its use of "vanity," the same word as is translated "nothing" here. Instead of trusting God, as David is doing, the wicked are governed by

---

96. Note the similarity of the strong refuge theme here to that in Ps 61.

97. Cf. 42:5, 11; 43:5.

98. For wisdom in the psalms see p. 18.

their avaricious hearts, the opposite attitude to that required of the king (Deut 17:17).

62:11-12   Trust in God depends on the great revealed facts about him. God has spoken to him more than once.[99] The books of Samuel show his frequent experience of God's power and covenant love, often illustrated in the Davidic psalms. Verse 12b concludes a psalm that emphasizes the different objects of trust of the righteous and of the wicked. Here, in an OT context, is the same insight as we see in Jas 2:14-26: true faith is shown in works.

Psalm 63

The word "king" in verse 11 suggests this is related to David's exile from Jerusalem in Absalom's rebellion (2 Sam 15:23), rather than to his flight from Saul.

63:1   Adversity has deepened his sense of personal relationship with God ("my God"). "Everything else in the psalm hinges on this certainty,"[100] and it also shows his deep desire to worship God (cf. 42:1-2). The verb שָׁחַר, *šāḥar*,[101] well translated "earnestly seek," is apparently connected with a root meaning "morning." Its passionate nature is confirmed in its use in Isa 26:9. This thirst for God is reflected in the barren land through which he is passing. "My soul" and "my body" each stand for the whole man, viewed now internally, now externally.

63:2-5   Moving farther and farther from Jerusalem with its sanctuary, he recalls how God revealed himself to him there, but his separation from it will not stop him from praising God. "Your love is better than life," with its use of חֶסֶד, *ḥesed* (love within a covenant relationship), may suggest a sense of eternity. He expresses his worship both vocally and physically, and his deep satisfaction in God's love is articulated in the analogy of a feast.

63:6-8   Deep longings continue into the night,[102] divided into watches for the city guards, suggesting he has been thinking much about the city he has left behind. A vivid image expresses his realization that, though away

---

99. Cf. Amos 1:3, 6. In our psalm "one" and "two" could easily be literal or they could simply suggest repetition.

100. See Davidson, *Vitality of Worship*, 198, where he also comments, "It is striking how Old Testament authors have the ability to convey the most profound theology in the simplest of language."

101. It is not the cultic word בָּקַשׁ, *bāqqaš*, which is used in v. 9. See Tate, *Psalms 51–100*, 127; Davidson, *Vitality of Worship*, 198-99.

102. Wilcock's exposition helpfully develops the morning/evening motif in this psalm (*Psalms 1–72*, 63).

from the sanctuary, God is still with him to protect him (cf. 61:4). Verse 6 shows his confidence in God's power, presumably to uphold him as king (cf. 2 Sam 7:16; Ps 2:6).

63:9-10 In verse 1 he seeks God to praise him, but here his enemies seek him to destroy him,[103] quite unavailingly, for God his refuge will destroy them. Jackals eat what other predators have left, so he is saying the destruction of his enemies will be complete.

63:11 Here is a sense of an abiding kingship, secure despite the endeavors of his adversaries, and this finds expression in praise, in which he encourages other faithful believers to join. The word "liars" recalls the deceitfulness of Absalom.

Psalm 64

There are an unusually large number of translation problems here, especially in verse 6, but the overall message of this lament is clear.[104]

64:1-2 The psalmist voices his "troubled thoughts"[105] and prays for protection. The word פַּחַד, *paḥad,* translated as "threat" in NIV, is rendered "dread" in NRSV and NASB. Tate well translates it as "dreadful threats."[106] Certainly the plots of conspirators are hidden at first, so he is really saying, "hide me from those who are trying to hide their designs from me." The designs find expression, of course, in the threatening noise of the mob they enlist.

64:3-6 The conspirators are like hunters, hiding as in an ambush or in the secret placing of a trap, confident none will see them.[107] Their plan includes the evil use of the tongue, perhaps in lying deceit. The psalmist's general comment (v. 6c) has a "wisdom" flavor.[108]

64:7-8 Their sudden attack (v. 4) finds its reply in God's sudden counterattack, in which their downfall is caused by their own words. Their ruin will be public.

---

103. This time בָּקַשׁ, *bāqqaš* ("seek"), is used. See n. 101 above. His passion was for God; theirs, pursued with quasi-religious fervor, was for his destruction.

104. For fuller comment on the problems, see Tate, *Psalms 51–100,* 130-35; Anderson, *Psalms,* 1:460-64.

105. Kidner's suggestion instead of "complaint" (*Psalms 1–72,* 227).

106. Tate, *Psalms 51–100,* 130-31.

107. Perhaps not even God. NIV "we have devised" (v. 6), which is in general agreement with NRSV and NASB, assumes the correctness of a minority of MT MSS as against the majority, which read, "we are complete."

108. See p. 18.

64:9-10 As so often, the psalmist looks beyond his immediate situation, seeing that his salvation will ultimately spread the fear of God far and wide and bring him deeply thoughtful praise. The righteous are to learn a lesson and, themselves finding refuge in God (cf. 2:12), are to bring him praise.

Psalm 65

Psalms 65–68 are all called "songs," and, as many commentators note, their atmosphere is very different from those with biographical notes, which dominate Psalms 51–64. Apart from 66:13-20, they are communal rather than individual. Each seems to take its starting point from some pentateuchal passage, 65 perhaps from Genesis 1, 66 from Exodus 12, 67 from Num 6:22-27 (with Gen 12:1-3), and 68 from Num 10:35, but in each case their abiding relevance for the people is clear.[109] Psalm 64:9 introduced a universal element into this part of book 2, and the universal note is a key feature of Psalm 65.

This psalm uses the plural, so that the psalmist is expressing the people's praise. It was probably composed for a festival, but which one is uncertain, as its closing verses survey much of the farming year.[110] It has three sections, "each focusing on a different locale and each placing Yahweh in a distinctive role. He is the atoner at the temple (vv. 1-4), the warrior establishing order in all creation (vv. 5-8), and the dispenser of water and fertility in the land (vv. 9-13)."[111]

65:1-4 The word דֻּמִיָּה, *dumîyyâ,* translated "awaits," implies silence, here silence before God in his house (cf. Hab 2:20). The reference to vows is a promise of obedience, for there has been forgiveness for communal sin of which the people are now well aware ("overwhelmed," v. 3).[112] God's renewed acceptance of them is betokened especially as the Levites continue to live in the courts of the Lord (the apparent meaning of v. 4a), and all the people experience the blessings of worship. Verse 4b reflects the fact that many of the

---

109. An interesting parallel to the use of Pss 8, 95, 110, and 40 in Heb 2–4, 7, and 10, respectively, where in each case the writer of the epistle makes a further christological comment on each.

110. Many commentators relate it to the provision of harvest after God delivered Jerusalem from the Assyrians, while Motyer ("Psalms," 525-26) suggests 2 Sam 21:1-14 as an equally apt background. For the relationship of the festivals to farming, see pp. 10-11.

111. Broyles, *Psalms,* 266.

112. NRSV translates דִּבְרֵי עֲוֺנֺת, *dibrê 'ăwônōt* (NIV "sins"), as "deeds of iniquity"; cf. Tate ("sinful deeds"), and his note for other possibilities (*Psalms 51–100,* 136-37).

sacrifices provided for corporate feasting.[113] The universalism of the next stanza is anticipated in verse 2, where "all men" is literally "all flesh."

65:5-8 The "awesome deeds of righteousness" are probably national victories (cf. 45:4),[114] implying perhaps earlier defeats through sin. The psalmist foresees the whole world coming in prayer to Israel's God,[115] and his universalism embraces the creation of the mountains and the disciplining of the waters (cf. Gen 1:6-9), symbolizing God's control of the nations. In prophetic style, he envisages people everywhere joyfully singing God's praise.

65:9-13 The NRSV "earth" is preferable to the NIV "land"[116] in verse 9, as it is more appropriate to the universalism of this psalm. Here again is water controlled and used for blessing, under God's purpose that nature should supply human need (cf. Gen 1:29-30). Verses 9 and 10 view the growing and verses 11-13 the harvest season and picture God as the great farmer with overflowing crop-filled carts. Even the desert oases are thus blessed. Hills, meadows, and valleys wear the clothing of vegetation and sheep God has given them, and finally, in a bold anthropomorphism, their voices join in God's praise.

Psalm 66

The universal note sounded in Psalm 65 is also heard here.[117] This orphan psalm unites the nation's praise for the exodus and an individual's gratitude for his own experience of God's intervention. This makes it like 18, where it is the God of the exodus who intervenes in David's life.[118] Some have thought its author Hezekiah, others reckon it postexilic, although this seems unlikely in book 2.[119] Kidner thinks it is probably designed to give a private worshiper a public setting for his votive offering.[120]

66:1-4 These verses are a call to the whole world to raise a joyous shout, its cause and content being God's acts of power that cause his enemies to cringe.

---

113. Especially the fellowship offerings of Lev 3.

114. However, Goulder argues that a thunderstorm is in view as an answer to prayer (v. 2) and that this pledges the renewed fruitfulness of the land (*Prayers of David*, 172-73). Although somewhat speculative, this is possible. For comments on righteousness see pp. 249-50.

115. For prophetic universalism in the Psalter see comment on Pss 65–67.

116. Heb. הָאָרֶץ, *hā'āreṣ*, has both senses.

117. See the introduction to Ps 65.

118. See comments on Ps 18.

119. For canonical criticism see pp. 21-28.

120. Kidner, *Psalms 1–72*, 233 n. 1.

66:5-7   The divine deeds for mortals[121] are specified, and verse 6 shows the crossing of the Red Sea is in view, also perhaps that of the Jordan. Coming after Psalm 65, this may show the redactor's conviction that God controlled the waters equally at creation and in Israel's early history. These victories over Egypt and the nations of the land, and the revelation these acts give of Israel's God's omnipotence and omniscience, are a warning not to rebel (cf. 2:10-12).

66:8-12   These words could possibly apply to the exodus–wilderness wanderings–entry to the land group of experiences or to later events, even possibly to the exile. The consistency of God and the paradigmatic nature of the exodus events mean that later generations could easily relate such psalms to their own experiences of God's gracious intervention.[122] The passage contains a remarkable amount of illustrative language. Ultimately, the trials were past and they were in a place of abundance, suggesting either the initial or the postexilic experience of the promised land.

66:13-15   Here an unspecified individual affirms his intention to offer sacrifices, in fulfillment of vows made when he was in trouble.[123]

66:16-20   Like verses 5-7, these verses invite appreciation of God's deeds, verse 5 appealing to the sense of sight, while verse 16 to that of hearing,[124] although now the deeds are personal to the individual who addresses the readers. Here the "trouble" of verse 14 is specified and God's deliverance extolled. There is a realization that sin erects a barrier against divine rescue, but the psalmist rejoices that God has accepted his prayer, seeing this as evidence of his covenant love (חֶסֶד, ḥesed).

Psalm 67

The universal note struck in 64:9 and continued in 65 and 66 comes to a climax here.[125] This orphan psalm is a meditation in chiastic form on two OT passages taken together, somewhat after the manner of the Epistle to the Hebrews.[126] These are the promise to Abraham in Gen 12:1ff. and the Aaronic blessing in Num 6:24-27. Its reference both to salvation and to crops makes it

---

121. NRSV "mortals" is preferable to NIV "man" for בְּנֵי אָדָם, běnê 'ādām.

122. See the comments on Ps 107.

123. The particular animals suggest a person of some wealth.

124. Both commence with לְכוּ, lĕkû, "Come!" So Davidson aptly heads this psalm, "A Shared Faith" (*Vitality of Worship*, 205).

125. See the introduction to Ps 65.

126. See, e.g., Gen 14 and Ps 110 in Heb 7. On chiasm see p. 18.

highly likely that it was composed for one of the pilgrim feasts.[127] There are problems concerning the mood and tense of the psalm's verbs, so that many of the petitions could be read instead as credal statements. Tate outlines the arguments and decides, probably rightly, for a translation along similar lines to NIV, NASB, and NRSV.[128]

67:1-2   Like Num 6:24-27, this passage seeks God's blessing on Israel, but, like the promise to Abraham, it looks to its effect on the whole world. God's favor, shown in the shining of his face, and his saving ways with Israel, are to be widely known.[129]

67:3-5   Here "nations" and "peoples" occur together but with five occurrences of the latter to three of the former in NIV.[130] עַם, *'am*, "people," which has more of a social than a political connotation, is largely restricted to Israel in the OT.[131] Its wider use here strongly implies a widening of the people of God beyond Israel.[132] The peoples are to unite in praise of Israel's God because as king and judge he rules well, and as shepherd he also guides them, for "guide" is often used in a pastoral context.

67:6-7   Verse 6a should be rendered, with NRSV, "the land has yielded its increase." This is evidence of God's blessing, which will continue into the future, so that the whole world will come to fear him, and therefore, it is perhaps implied, worship him, not pagan deities.

Psalm 68

This "rushing cataract of a psalm — one of the most boisterous and exhilarating in the Psalter," characterized by "almost uncontainable enthusiasm," presents more exegetical difficulties than most.[133] The number of translation problems is exceptionally large, and only those importantly affecting its interpretation will be noted here. What I offer assumes many decisions that would

---

127. See Lev 23 and Deut 26:1-11.

128. Tate, *Psalms 51–100*, 154-55.

129. For universalism in the psalms see comment on Pss 65–67.

130. V. 2 (MT 3) uses the common term גּוֹי, *gôy*, vv. 3 and 5 (MT 4, 6) use the common עַם, *'am*, four times, while v. 4 (MT 5) twice uses the much less common לְאֹם, *lĕ'ōm*.

131. See Tate, *Psalms 51–100*, 154; VanGemeren, "Psalms," 443-54.

132. Cf. Ps 87 and Isa 19:23-25.

133. Quotations from Kidner, *Psalms 1–72*, 238, 245. More difficulties are noted and discussed in Kidner, *Psalms 1–72*, 238-45; and all significant ones in Tate, *Psalms 51–100*, 159-86, who notes (170) that it has at least 15 words not used elsewhere in Scripture and a number of other rare words.

have to be discussed at length in a fuller critical commentary.[134] Its general structure is clear, however, when it is seen to be about God's triumphant journey, represented by the movement of the ark of the covenant, from Sinai to the Jerusalem sanctuary, at the head of his people.[135] It is not impossible that the actual installation of the ark is in view, but most commentators take it that the psalm was composed for regular festival celebrations of this fact.[136]

68:1-3 Psalm 67:1 alludes to Num 6:24-26, God's blessing on his people through the Aaronic priests. In contrast, there is now a free quotation from Num 10:35, expressing God's purpose of judgment on his enemies. Psalm 1 likens the wicked to chaff driven away by the wind, while here the analogies are smoke and wind along with wax and fire. Verse 3, in contrast, calls for the glad praise of the righteous and recalls the joyousness of Psalm 67.[137] Most translations treat verses 1-3 as prayers, although this requires different Hebrew vocalization for the verbs in verse 1, but it brings it into line with Num 10:35 and is probably correct.[138]

68:4-6 These verses are a call to praise and rejoice before God (cf. 18:9-10). The word translated "clouds," עֲרָבָה, *ʿărābâ*, normally relates to a semidesert with few plants (loosely, a wilderness), but the Ugaritic word for "clouds" is very similar. At Ugarit Baal was "rider of the clouds" and, in a combative psalm like this, the thought could be that Yahweh's victories show that he alone has the right to this title. Comparison with verse 33, also in a praise context, might tend to confirm this, but the psalmist perhaps chose this word for its ambiguity, for God rides both in the heavens and, ahead of his people, through the desert. After all, this is poetry! The covenant love implicit in the name Yahweh finds expression in his care for all the socially marginalized, the fatherless, the widow, the lonely, with perhaps a glance at the exodus in the mention of the prisoners. This would be most appropriate, for the exodus is the supreme OT evidence of this care and concern. Is "his holy dwelling" heaven, Sinai, or the Jerusalem sanctuary? Perhaps it joins them all, for they are all in the psalm, so that wherever God is, he is all this to his people, showing that his holiness is not remoteness. Let the rebellious beware, for he has proved in history that rebels stay in the desert!

68:7-10 Verses 7 and 8 appear to allude to the Song of Deborah in Judg

---

134. Davidson, *Vitality of Worship*, 210.

135. Most commentators now take it this way.

136. See the introduction to Ps 65. For NT use of this psalm see p. 358.

137. The verbs in vv. 1-3 may be read as futures, although most translators and commentators take them to be jussives.

138. NEB retains the MT pointing and translates each verb in vv. 1-3 as indicative. See also Kidner, *Psalms 1–72*, 238-39.

5:4-5, a passage generally reckoned very ancient. The downpour (v. 8)[139] in time of war was succeeded by refreshing showers during the settlement (v. 9). These verses emphasize divine provision. God's "inheritance" is Canaan, which he distributed in Joshua's day so that the people could settle in it. Its weariness may recall its former pagan occupation. Verse 10b is reminiscent of the book of Ruth, which illustrates the compassionate laws of gleaning so well.[140]

68:11-14 "The Song of Deborah still echoes here, in this tumble of swift images and excited snatches of description."[141] The Hebrew shows those who proclaimed the word here to be women. 1 Samuel 18:6-7, showing women singing about the victories of Saul and David, is a possible comparison. If so, they proclaim victory simply on the basis of the divine word, implying faith in its fulfillment, which is then shown in verses 12-14.[142] The emphasis on kings underlines God's supreme kingship. Verse 13 is obscure, possibly a reference to jewelry taken in war. Zalmon too is unknown, and the snow may refer to the distant appearance of many dead on the hilly slopes.[143]

68:15-18 Bashan, a large area in northern Transjordan, would include mighty Mount Hermon. In vivid apostrophe, David pictures its envy of Mount Zion. The chariots represent martial angelic forces (cf. Deut 33:3). Verse 17b virtually sums up the whole psalm, and makes plausible the view that it was sung at the ark's entry into the Zion sanctuary in David's day or else at a regular feast, possibly the Feast of Tabernacles, over many years.[144] The ascension here is the climb up Mount Zion with the ark. The captives are perhaps Jebusites, taken prisoners during Jerusalem's capture (2 Sam 5:6-9), representing those captured over the years since Sinai. The gifts are victory tributes.

68:19-20 Statement gives way to praise. God is physical savior of his people, an experience they had known right from the exodus, and a constant resource for them with their heavy loads.[145]

---

139. The verb, as in Judg 5:4, is נָטַף, *nāṭap,* normally meaning "drop" or "drip," which seems inappropriate here. Tate argues cogently for the sense "pour" (*Psalms 51–100,* 163).

140. Lev 19:9-10; and cf. also v. 5 here.

141. Kidner, *Psalms 1–72,* 240. These verses are remarkable, even in this psalm, for their difficulties. See Tate, *Psalms 51–100,* 164-65, 178-80; or, more selectively, VanGemeren, "Psalms," 448.

142. NRSV translates v. 12b as "the women at home divide the spoil" and should probably be accepted; cf. also NASB. The NIV rendering requires a slight emendation, unnecessary in the light of Judg 5:29-30.

143. VanGemeren has a full and helpful note on the difficulties of vv. 13-14 ("Psalms," 448).

144. See pp. 12-13.

145. Most scholars consider that "God daily carries" (or "loads") us, the literal sense, means that God carries our burdens, which fits the context well, but loading us with benefits is also a possible way of taking the words.

68:21-23 Certainty of God's victory over remaining enemies rests on his past victories, for he had brought Israel across the Jordan (Bashan is on the east) and through the Red Sea, so that he now repeats in judgment on his enemies what he had earlier done in salvation for his people. Verse 23 is strongly worded and its pictures horrify the imagination, but clearly God's antagonism is based on their continuance in sin (v. 21).[146]

68:24-27 This is a particularly graphic section of a vivid psalm. The procession has reached the sanctuary, and the musicians and various tribes (Benjamin and Judah represent the south and Zebulun and Naphtali the north) come together in worship, the two words "congregation" and "assembly" both designating a religious gathering. The expression translated "great throng" is most obscure and could be rendered "a shouting crowd."[147]

68:28-31 "As the procession marched toward and then ascended Zion's hill it recapitulated for marchers and watchers alike the whole long cavalcade of Israel's history and of the Lord's grace and power."[148] The call to God to act as before is also found, differently expressed, in Isa 51:9-11. Kings will join those who have already brought gifts (v. 18). The beast among the reeds is clearly Egypt, the old enemy, vanquished at the exodus, and the bulls and calves other nations. Silver here is tribute,[149] while in verse 13 it is apparently the spoils of war. Egypt is now referred to explicitly, and Cush (roughly Ethiopia) represents remoter nations, so leading us into the next verse.

68:32-35 A call, somewhat like other psalms, to all the earth to praise God,[150] specifically because of his great acts for Israel. The last verse focuses on the sanctuary where the ark now is and on God, the source of power for Israel. All is rounded off with praise.

Psalm 69

If there was a change of atmosphere between Psalms 64 and 65,[151] this is far more marked between 68 and 69. Here is a deep lament, although like 22, one that ultimately issues in thanksgiving.[152]

---

146. See pp. 257-58.

147. See Tate, *Psalms 51–100*, 168.

148. Motyer, "Psalms," 528.

149. Although there are other possibilities. See brief but helpful comment in Kidner, *Psalms 1–72*, 244.

150. Coming after the universalism of Pss 65–67, it is notable that even this particularistic psalm contains such a note.

151. See the introduction to Ps 65.

152. For NT use of this psalm see pp. 301, 331, 337, 357.

69:1-5 Here is a cry of desperation, vividly presented as coming from a man drowning in deep, fast-flowing water with a miry bottom, shrieking for help to one for whom he looks in vain until he is so hoarse he is hardly heard. At verse 4 more literal statements take over. A host of enemies are wrongly accusing him of stealing something unspecified, which they force him to restore.[153] Their antipathy is causeless as lacking adequate grounds, but this does not mean he is sinless.

69:6-12 He addresses God as all-powerful and as Israel's God, therefore as able and, by covenanted promise, willing to aid his people. He is concerned lest the accusations against him should put other godly people in a bad light, perhaps because to others he represents them. His family has turned against him. Could the zeal for God's house be understood as David's desire to build a temple?[154] Possibly, but we cannot be sure. If it is, the insults against God here may emanate from those with no time for a project designed to honor God. He is in mourning (vv. 10-11), either through bereavement or in repentance, but his enemies, seated at the city gate, the place of social converse, business deals, and, ironically, the dispensing of justice, simply mock him.[155]

69:13-18 There is a slight but discernible change of tone here. Compared with verses 1-3, the cry is just as urgent, but less complaining. Harman is probably right in seeing an echo of Exod 34:6 in these verses with their appeal to the LORD's revealed character.[156] The imagery of the unstable place and floodwaters returns, supplemented by that of a gaping pit (vv. 14-15), but the implication of the phrase "God of Israel" (v. 6) now becomes explicit in an appeal to God's covenant love (חֶסֶד, *ḥesed*, in both vv. 13 and 16), and in the psalmist's confidence that his salvation is sure and that in God's own time,[157] he will answer him. The urgency is still present (vv. 16-18) but is expressed with deeper assurance.

69:19-29 God's knowledge of the psalmist's sin (v. 5) is paralleled by

---

153. However, v. 4c could be a question, as in NRSV, "What I did not steal must I now restore?"

154. Broyles thinks "the time of your favor" here "may refer to the morning (5:3; 46:5; 143:8; cf. 32:6) and to the time of the morning sacrifice in particular (Num 28:1-8)" (*Psalms*, 287-88).

155. In general agreement with NASB and NRSV, Tate argues for "complain" or "talk about" as the sense of יָשִׂיחוּ, *yāśîḥû*, rendered "mock" in NIV, but this does not affect the general thrust of this part of the psalm. See Tate's discussion of various translation possibilities (*Psalms 51–100*, 189).

156. Harman, *Psalms*, 245; cf. also VanGemeren, "Psalms," 458.

157. Cf. "looking for my God" (v. 3).

knowledge also of the sins of his persecutors (v. 19).[158] The theme of disgrace returns. His enemies are implacable and give him bitter-tasting food and drink, either literally or figuratively. The sufferer does not take action against them but calls on God to do so,[159] to demonstrate his wrath, making the punishment fit the sin ("an element of poetic justice"[160]), because it would begin with their own food and drink (v. 22).[161] Clearly he is calling for their death (v. 25). When God was bringing affliction, perhaps because of the sins alluded to in verse 5, they aggravated this by their own antagonism. He calls for them to be divinely blacklisted,[162] then utters another urgent cry (v. 29).

69:30-36 The psalmist's vindication is more implied than stated here. His song will be more significant than a large and valuable sacrificial animal, for the poor will see they too can praise God. Verse 33 generalizes from the psalmist's own experience and sees God's intervention reaching even those held captive. The psalm has apparently been given an ending appropriate to the Babylonian captives and the restoration of Zion promised by Jeremiah (e.g., Jer 30:18–31:14; cf. Ps 51:18). Here then the vindication of the individual finds an echo in the rehabilitation of the nation, which may well have sung this psalm to celebrate that divine act of grace.

Psalm 70

"What Psalm 69 says at length, Psalm 70 expresses as a sharp, urgent cry."[163] It is almost identical with 40:13-17. There is some variation in the terms used for God and other small alterations not requiring detailed comments, but tending to tighten the thought, giving still more urgency to the prayer. We cannot be certain whether the longer or shorter form came first, although the presence of Psalm 40 in book 1 may suggest its priority. Both are near the end of their respective books and express in brief compass the cries for help recorded, often at greater length, earlier in each book. Perhaps the redactor saw

---

158. The two expressions are identical in Hebrew.

159. For comment on the imprecations of the psalms see pp. 257-58.

160. Davidson, *Vitality of Worship,* 220.

161. Accepting the MT pointing of שְׁלוֹמִים, *šĕlômîm,* as the plural of שָׁלוֹם, *šālôm,* "peace," NRSV translates v. 22 as "Let their table be a trap for them, a snare for their allies" (i.e., those at peace with them), while NIV accepts the pointing assumed in LXX, שִׁלּוּם, *šillûm,* which evidently read the noun as connected to a root meaning "trap." Certainly *šālôm* in the plural is very rare. See Tate, *Psalms 51–100,* 190.

162. For the book of the righteous see Exod 32:32-33.

163. Motyer, "Psalms," 530.

them too as related to the divine promise to support the Davidic king, which is the theme of Psalm 2.

Psalm 71

This psalm lacks a heading. The editor may have intended it as a virtual continuation of Psalm 70, for its opening verses have the same general theme and they are combined in some manuscripts. It is the work of an aging man.[164] He knows other psalms and quotes them, suggesting personal devotional use.[165] Here then is the fruit of reflection on God's Word, such as Psalm 1 encourages, placed near the close of book 2, perhaps as a reminder. Broyles draws attention to the frequent references to "your righteousness" (vv. 2, 15, 16, 19, 24) and the parallel expressions "your salvation" (v. 15) and "your mighty acts" (v. 16), and says, "key to the understanding of the spirituality of this psalm is that while it makes reference to the speaker's lifelong devotion to God, its ultimate appeal is to 'your righteousness.'"[166] He is the God who is committed to putting everything right, often a concern of old age.

71:1-4　Most cries for rescue in the Psalms are urgent, arising from immediate need. This seems less true here. He is asking God always to be what he has constantly been, although verses 3b and 4a could possibly be cries for immediate help. God is his permanent refuge, to whom he can always have recourse (cf. perhaps 2:12).

71:5-8　He testifies to God's help over many years, for he has trusted him ever since his birth. He is like a portent to many, probably because his sufferings have made them view him as divinely rejected (v. 11), somewhat like Job's comforters. Verses 1-4 were prayer but this is now praise, which will be as long-term as his trust (cf. v. 8 with v. 3).

71:9-13　He wants to know God as his refuge still, despite the onset of old age. Enemies conspire against him (cf. 2:1ff.), and they think God has withdrawn his protection. The note of urgency is sounded now (v. 12), and his

---

164. Vv. 9, 18, and the backward glances at birth and youth (vv. 5, 6, 17) need not mean that old age has been reached but that it is anticipated by a middle-aged man; however, Wilcock points out: "it is hard to find a clear shape to Psalm 71. . . . But greater use of familiar words, and less concern with a disciplined structure, are for writers and speakers one of the privileges of age" (*Psalms 1–72*, 246).

165. Cf. esp. vv. 1-3 with 31:1-3a and several echoes of Ps 22, e.g., in vv. 4-6 (cf. 22:9-10), 12 (cf. 22:11), and 18 (cf. 22:22).

166. Broyles, *Psalms,* 290. For comment on righteousness see pp. 249-50.

prayer stresses more his accusers' shaming than their death, for shame is sometimes dreaded as much as death.

71:14-18   He promises to tell of God's righteous saving acts, probably not just for him but for his people down the ages, the full compass of which he cannot take in (v. 15).[167] These acts were part of his teaching by God, perhaps initially in the family circle, and his concern for God's continued aid in his later days is to enable him to pass on what has been taught to him.

71:19-21   He reflects again on the greatness of God's righteous acts, which give him confidence that God will bring him through life's bitter experiences. "The depths of the earth" may be a metaphor for deep trouble, especially in view of the reference to increased honor, or it could indicate confidence in resurrection.

71:22-24   The musical references here remind us both of David and of the Levites. Now "faithfulness" and "Holy One of Israel"[168] bring a covenant note into the psalm, previously only implied in the use of "Yahweh" in verses 5 and 16. Verse 24a virtually repeats verse 15a, perhaps with the intention of a refrain, and he shows the cause of his praise in the shaming of his enemies. His God has indeed put things right.

Psalm 72

This and 127 are headed "of Solomon," yet the editor appended "this concludes the prayers of David son of Jesse" to this one, evidently seeing no contradiction in this, and suggesting he viewed it as written by David for his son and successor.[169] 1 Kings 2 records the closing address of David to his son, and verse 3 promises him prosperity if he keeps the law of Moses (cf. Ps 1:3). As a prayer for a monarch, Psalm 72 was probably used also for succeeding Davidic kings, for its elevated language suggests special occasions like coronations.

Is it a prayer or a prediction? Many of its verbs could be either imperfects, properly translatable here as futures, so functioning as predictions, or imperatives, and so prayers. Distinguishing some that are necessarily either

---

167. סְפֹרוֹת, *sĕpōrôt*, rendered "measure" in NIV, occurs only here in MT and is from a root normally referring to writing, numbering, or recounting. Tate suggests a possible alternative to NIV, "though I do not know the scribal art" (*Psalms 51–100*, 208-10).

168. This phrase is of rare occurrence outside the book of Isaiah and suggests both God's distinction from and his commitment to his people.

169. See comments on the preposition לְ, *lĕ*, on pp. 8-9. The phrases "the king" and "the royal son," although functioning as synonymous parallelism, also may suggest a continuing dynasty, and the second was appropriate for Solomon, but not for David.

one or the other, Wilcock sees verses 2-7 and 12-14 as prophecies and 10 and 15-17a as prayers, with verses 11 and 17b two slightly different versions of a refrain.[170] So the prophecies chiefly concern the king's moral qualities and the prayers his universal dominion. I will follow this pattern. It seems significant that both Psalms 41 and 72 (closing books 1 and 2) emphasize the moral qualities of the king.

72:1-7 The link between the divine and human rulers means the human king should show divine moral qualities.[171] The prayer of verse 1 governs verses 2-7, so that the king's moral qualities are the result of divine action. Here he rules "your people" (i.e., Israel), but with special reference to the needy, to be rescued from oppressors. Verse 3 probably means the normally untillable mountain areas will grow food, verse 6 attributing this to the king's qualities. His righteous reign will encourage righteousness in others (v. 7). He will endure forever, as will prosperity, which perhaps should be interpreted dynastically rather than individually (cf. 2 Sam 7:15-16, 29).

72:8-11 These verses are a prayer for the king's universal dominion, adapted and greatly extended from Exod 23:31.[172] This will include the distant places, the extreme south,[173] the desert tribes, and all his enemies. It is all summed up in the grand universalism of verse 11.[174]

72:12-14 Again moral qualities are in view, but "for" (v. 12) suggests that the prayer for universal dominion deserves a positive answer because of the qualities God shows.[175] These verses are similar in theme to verses 2 and 4, with a conclusion showing why he acts for such people. Like Abel, persecuted and killed by Cain in Genesis 4, their blood is precious to him.[176]

170. Wilcock, *Psalms 1–72*, 250.

171. This link is seen also in Ps 2.

172. This connection with Exod 23:31 makes Tate's view that "the river" may be the stream issuing from the temple as in Ps 46:4 and Ezek 47 very unlikely.

173. Regarding the distant places, Tarshish always appears to be in the far west. See note on 48:7. As for the south, Sheba and Seba may be the same place or neighboring areas in South Arabia.

174. Is the universal rule of the king intended literally or is this as much conventional hyperbole in relation to space as the words, "O king, live forever!" (Dan 2:4), are in relation to time? Comparison with the similar passage in Isa 11, esp. vv. 9-10, tends to support a literal interpretation. For universalism in the Psalter see comment on Pss 65–67.

175. Following Dahood, Tate points out that כִּי, *kî*, translated "for" (NIV), can also mean "if," and that the conditional clauses thus introduced may extend through vv. 12-14, so that the earlier promises of national and universal peace all depend on his work for the poor. This is certainly possible. See Tate, *Psalms 51–100*, 221.

176. Broyles points out how remarkable these criteria are, in the context of Near Eastern concepts of a good reign as estimated in military and/or architectural terms, and that here they are not so much an expression of compassion as simply of justice (*Psalms*, 297).

72:15-17 The psalm becomes a prayer again, and one that people will continue to pray for him. There is a call for blessing on him, so that he may be remembered (a major concern in OT times) and for physical blessing in the fruitfulness of the land (cf. vv. 3, 6),[177] even the normally less fruitful hilly areas. In verse 16c the NASB reads, "may those from the city flourish like vegetation of the earth,"[178] which, although unusual, probably refers to increasing population. The NIV and NRSV require emendation of the Hebrew, without real necessity. The prayer is unusual as asking that the promises to Abraham (cf. Gen 12:1-3) will be fulfilled in blessing to all nations specifically through the king.

72:18-20 Clearly editorial, these verses extol Israel's God, not inappropriate in such a psalm. As there are Davidic psalms later in the Psalter, verse 20 identifies the end of the present Davidic collection.[179]

BOOK 3[1]

Psalm 73

This psalm is often reckoned specially important, not only as linking books 1 and 2 with 3-5, but even as summing up the whole Psalter, for what might appear to be complacency in Psalm 1 (and also in 37) is here tested by experience and found true at a deep, not a superficial, level,[2] so preparing the way for the unqualified praise with which the Psalter ends. McCann observes that it sums up the lesson of Psalms 1–72 that blessedness is more about being assured of God's presence in the midst of peril than about material prosperity.[3] The psalm is characterized by repetition of key words such as "surely," "good," and "heart."[4]

73:1-3 אַךְ, *'ak* ("Surely"), is a word of emphatic assertion, occurring also in verses 13 and 18. It introduces a fundamental, almost credal, statement of God's goodness to Israel, which is then qualified in moral terms.[5] This is

---

177. Cf. 65:9-13 and 67:6-7.
178. The LXX assumes the MT reading.
179. See p. 19.
1. For the Psalter's division into five books see pp. 21-28.
2. But see comments on Ps 1.
3. McCann, *Theological Introduction*, 143.
4. See Allen, "Psalm 73," 93-106, for useful comments on this feature.
5. MT reads לְיִשְׂרָאֵל, *lĕyiśrā'ēl* ("to Israel"), and should be retained. NRSV, with many

then virtually negated (vv. 2 and 3), because the psalmist sees it is the wicked who prosper (contra 1:3). He becomes envious,[6] almost losing his moral and theological foundations.

73:4-12 He now complainingly describes his observations. The wicked lack health problems; their clothing, metaphorical, as often, for lifestyle (e.g., in Rom 13:14; Eph 4:22, 24), is pride and violence. Their hearts are hard (cf. Ezek 36:26) and sources of all kinds of evil (cf. Gen 6:5; Eph 4:18). They scoff.[7] Their limitless conceit claims the whole universe for themselves (vv. 7, 9). Verse 10 in NIV implies they are therefore attractive to their friends, but the Hebrew reads not "their people" but "his people," indicating that their prosperity is a temptation to God's people.[8] Verse 11 can hardly deny God's omniscience, but rather means they act as if he lacks knowledge.[9] Verse 12 is a summary.

73:13-17 He makes a second strong affirmation directly contradicting verse 1, in a tone not unlike parts of Job (e.g., Job 9:29-31; 21:15), and also, as in Job, proving to be somewhat tentative. Verses 15-17 represent an important change. As a Levite, he has a teaching responsibility, giving theological and moral guidance. Articulating these thoughts would undermine the confidence of others, remarkably described as "your children," very unusual for the OT.[10] Reason is unavailing but worship gives him light, revealing God's perspective. His entry to the sanctuary and his consequent enlightenment provide the psalm with its key thought and turning point. He sees clearly that God's judgment on the wicked is sure, even if delayed.[11]

73:18-20 A third confident affirmation (cf. vv. 1 and 13) introduces verses expounding verse 17b. It is they, not he (cf. v. 2), who, lacking adequate foundation, are destined for terrifying judgment. To God, arising from the "slumber" of apparent inaction (cf., e.g., 7:6), they will be of no more weight than figures in a dream (cf. the chaff, 1:4).

73:21-26 He reflects on his earlier sorry state, feeling he had no more spiritual understanding than an animal, but now counting his very consider-

---

modern commentators, emends to לְיָשָׁר אֵל, *lĕyāšār 'ēl*, "God . . . to the upright," which is good parallelism but lacks textual warrant. Brueggemann sees more at stake here than grammar. "The change from 'Israel' to 'upright' changes the religious world in which we do our interpretation" (*Message of Psalms*, 116).

6. Transgressing the tenth commandment.

7. Or mock; cf. 1:1; Prov 1:22, although the Hebrew word is different.

8. See Tate, *Psalms 51–100*, 228-29.

9. Cf. the practical atheism of Pss 14 and 53.

10. Cf. Deut 14:1; Isa 1:2, 4.

11. For divine revelation as the key to moral insight, cf. Job 42:5-6; Isa 6:5. For judgment see pp. 258-59.

able blessings. These include God's presence and his support, guidance, and strength in weakness. In this context, the promise of "glory" and a portion forever seem eschatological, especially if he intends a contrast with the wicked's destiny, strongly suggested because "afterward" here and "end" in verse 17 have the same Hebrew root.[12] As in Psalm 16, the psalmist finds all he needs in the God who encompasses heaven and earth and who is, far more than his territory in Canaan, his portion forever. So the psalmist's outlook has now greatly changed.

73:27-28 These verses round off the psalm, in effect interpreting Psalm 1's convictions in explicitly eschatological terms. How different is the lot of those "far from" God and those "near God." In verse 28 טוֹב, *ṭôb* ("good"), and כִּי, *kî* ("but"), seem deliberate echoes of vv. 1 and 2.[13] Refuge recalls 2:12, and the closing clause is a promise to praise the Lord.

Tate sees verses 17-28 revealing three reorientations for the psalmist: new views of the outcome of the actions of the wicked, new understanding of his own heart, and a renewed sense of God's presence.[14]

Psalm 74

This Asaphite psalm, a communal lament, was almost certainly written in the exile, for it reflects the same situation and emotions as the book of Lamentations, and it might have been used at one of the fasts mentioned in Zech 7:1-7.

74:1-3 The psalmist asks an agonized question,[15] given poignancy by the phrase, "the sheep of your pasture." Then, using various terms reflecting God's special relationship with his people[16] and the place of his worship on Mount Zion, he calls on God to remember his people by acting for them.

74:4-9 The people's praise has been replaced by the enemy's ugly roar, the temple's divine symbols by military standards, the reverence of the wor-

---

12. See the discussions in Tate, *Psalms 51–100*, 230, 236-37; Kidner, *Psalms 73–150*, 262-63; Davidson, *Vitality of Worship*, 234-36; Crenshaw, *Psalms*, 254-56.

13. See comment on vv. 1-3.

14. Tate, *Psalms 51–100*, 238-39.

15. Following W. A. Young, Tate uses "unrelenting" to translate לָנֶצַח, *lāneṣaḥ*, which NIV renders "forever." לָנֶצַח, *lāneṣaḥ* or נֶצַח, *neṣaḥ*, occurs also in vv. 3, 10, and 19. The two main senses of these words are "forever" and "totally." See Tate, *Psalms 51–100*, 241.

16. The expression "tribe [singular] of your inheritance" occurs elsewhere only in Jer 10:16 and 51:19 and reflects something of the fluidity of kinship terms in the OT. See Grogan, "Concept of Solidarity," 161.

shipers for the fabric of God's house by the sound of destructive tools.[17] The enemies are equally antagonistic to Yahweh and his worship and to his people. Worst of all, no end is in sight, with neither special acts of God nor prophets to speak his word in evidence.

74:10-11 The questioning of verse 1 returns, with emphasis on God's delay and a vivid anthropomorphic image in verse 11.[18]

74:12-17 This intense stanza, made more so by the change from the plural ("us" and "we") to the singular (v. 12), argues powerfully for divine intervention. God is king, so is all-powerful, and he has acted in salvation before, in three great acts in particular. At the exodus the Red Sea was split and the monster, Egypt, with its multiple heads at the Nile Delta and its dead soldiers feeding the desert scavengers, was vanquished.[19] Before this God had both created and regulated the waters of the earth and created day and night, while after the flood his promise undergirded the seasonal regularity. The repeated "it was you" is like a challenge to the apparent divine inactivity.[20]

74:18-21 Again he calls God to remember (cf. v. 2), not his people now but the enemy, characterized as doves and wild beasts, respectively. The enemy are godless fools, and they not only attack but mock Yahweh's sacred name. The appeal to the God of past action (vv. 12-17) is now reinforced by reference to the covenant, in which he has pledged salvation to his poor and needy people.

74:22-23 The final verses specially stress that it is God himself who is under attack and whose enemies mock him with ever-increasing noise. So, in final entreaty, he calls God to arise and no longer to restrain his punitive action.

17. V. 5 contains major translation problems (dealt with at length in Tate, *Psalms 51–100*, 242), but the general sense is clear: "It is a picture of furious destructive energy" (Kidner, *Psalms 73–150*, 266).

18. In v. 11 too, despite translation problems, the general sense is clear if חֵיקְךָ, *ḥêqĕkā* ("your bosom," the *Qere,* followed by LXX) is read rather than the *Kethib* חוֹקֶךָ, *ḥôqĕkâ* ("your decree"). See Tate, *Psalms 51–100*, 243.

19. Vv. 13 and 14 use language from Canaanite mythology, applied there to Baal's victory over the dragon and the seven-headed serpent, Leviathan, but now to Yahweh and to redemptive history, not myth. See Kidner's comment, *Psalms 73–150*, 268-69, including his reference to the translation of v. 14b. The implications of this in the Babylonian setting of the exile, where Marduk was king of the gods, would not be lost on the Judean exiles. The wording here perhaps alludes both to creation and to the exodus, with the implication that both were executed by the same divine power, which also divided the waters both at creation and at the Red Sea.

20. The emphatic pronoun "your" (אַתָּה, *'attâ*) occurs no less than 7 times in vv. 13-17, well expressed as "it was you" (and so perhaps, by implication, not Baal) in 4 of these instances in NIV, and by simple "you" in vv. 15b, 16, 17b.

Psalm 75

How much in this psalm, which opens with thanksgiving, is direct divine speech? The NIV inserts, "You say" (v. 2), to show God is speaking at that point, but does his speech continue as far as verse 8 or does the psalmist himself speak in verses 5 or 6-8? We cannot be sure. Also God probably speaks again in verse 10. In fact, all is spoken either by God or about him, so the psalm's main message is clear.

75:1 What a contrast with Psalm 74! Here is victory, not defeat, much needed as encouragement for the consecutive reader. The psalmist commences fitly with praise. God's "Name" (i.e., Yahweh), symbol of his solemn covenant, is near, as his works for his people reveal.

75:2-8 God's sovereignty in judgment is stated (v. 2) and empha-sized,[21] then illustrated in vivid metaphors: the great earthquake (v. 3), the amputated horns (vv. 4-5, an illustration completed in v. 10),[22] the bitter cup drunk to its dregs (v. 8). These are clearly the actions of a sovereign and righteous God, for he holds the main structure firm during the quake, he acts against the arrogant who think they can challenge him,[23] and the cup, made bitter by adding spices, is poured out from his hand for all the wicked to drink.[24] Verses 6 and 7 assert God's sole control of the ups and downs of history in his judgments (cf. 1 Sam 2:7-8).

75:9-10 The psalmist resumes his declaration (cf. v. 1c) of praise to Israel's God, the God of Jacob. "As for me, I" is emphatic. God acts sovereignly, but the psalmist has his part to play in uttering praise. The last word is God's, for the psalmist asserts, using one of his illustrations, God's destruction of the wicked's power, with power transferred instead to the righteous.

Psalm 76

The LXX adds "according to the Assyrian" to the heading, confirming the impression gained from the psalm that God's judgment on Sennacherib's army (2 Kgs 19:35-36) is its setting.[25] Its position near Psalm 74 with the latter's al-

---

21. "It is I" translates the emphatic personal pronoun. For judgment see pp. 258-59.

22. The animal imagery of the horn symbolized power (e.g., 1 Sam 2:1) and consequent glory (e.g., 89:17, 24).

23. For NIV "outstretched neck," NRSV has "insolent neck," which is less literal but brings out well the allusive force of the words.

24. Cf., e.g., Isa 51:17, 21-22; Ezek 23:31-34.

25. Contra VanGemeren, "Psalms," 494. For judgment see pp. 258-59.

most certain reference to Jerusalem's fall to the Babylonians would convey a message about the way God dealt with his people in judgment on their sin but also in grace when they cast themselves on him, for he now appears as Zion's protector (vv. 2 and 3).

76:1-3 The place names indicate God's special relationship to a small locality. Salem is Jerusalem (Gen 14:18) and is where God reveals himself (v. 1), where he dwells (v. 2), where he acts decisively against his people's foes (v. 3). The words translated "tent" and "dwelling place" (v. 2) are also used for the den of a fierce animal,[26] such as a lion, and the context suggests this sense here.

76:4-10 This great warrior God is now seen in blazing light (cf. 104:2), suggestive of revelation (cf. v. 1), and "mountains rich with game" is literally "mountains of prey," picturing the Assyrian army on Judah's mountains as prey for the divine predator, so that verses 5 and 6 are self-explanatory. The suggestion of admiration implicit in "valiant" (lit. "men of heart") is unusual, but should not modify for us the force of "rebuke," implying divine judgment, made explicit in verse 8. "You alone" is emphatic,[27] denying deity to Assyria's gods. אֶרֶץ, *'ereṣ*, "earth" or "land" (vv. 8 and 9), may be "land," so that the quietness after the invasion's demise may reflect the meaning of "Salem" (i.e., "peace"). If it means "earth," however (and heaven and earth often appear together in the OT), then a local event has become a microcosm of universal judgment, and the past tenses will be prophetic perfects.

Verse 10 makes explicit the praise that seems implicit throughout.[28] If the NIV understands this verse correctly, the psalmist is saying that God's wrath results in judgment, but a saving judgment that puts things right for the afflicted, and those enemies not slain are restrained. The NASB, however, renders it more literally: "For the wrath of man shall praise You; With a remnant of wrath You will gird Yourself." So human evil may rage and rage, but "its defiance and perversity simply throw into splendid relief his power and glory and therefore redound to his praise,"[29] and, as Kidner says, the second part of the verse may be paralleled in Isa 59:17.[30]

76:11-12 God's people are called to express their thanks by vows made and fulfilled, then other lands are summoned to bring him gifts, because this signal judgment shows he is Lord of all, not just of his people.

---

26. סֹךְ, *sōk* (10:9; Jer 25:38) and מְעוֹנָה, *mĕ'ônâ* (Ps 104:22; Amos 3:4).

27. Tate vigorously translates v. 7a as "O You! You are the Awesome One!" (*Psalms 51–100*, 261).

28. This verse is exceptionally difficult to interpret. Tate discusses its problems at length (*Psalms 51–100*, 262).

29. Davidson, *Vitality of Worship*, 246.

30. Kidner, *Psalms 73–150*, 276.

Psalm 77

This psalm, which starts as a lament, takes a dramatic turn in the middle and becomes an expression of full-hearted praise.

77:1-6   A problem, unspecified, causes the psalmist to utter impassioned prayers throughout sleepless nights when he will not let go (cf. v. 2c with Gen 37:35). Thinking about God leads to groaning and faintness of spirit as it prompts the thought that it is God who is keeping him awake. Former blessings recalled simply intensify the sense of present trouble, because, unlike earlier times, he cannot sing God's praises.

77:7-9   The problem plus the apparently unavailing prayer raises deep questions about God, focusing on his character toward his people, guaranteed by his covenant ("unfailing love" is חֶסֶד, *ḥesed*) and normally expressed in favor, mercy, compassion, and faithfulness. Could he, perhaps, be angry (v. 9)? Yet the psalmist confesses no sin.[31] Verse 8a contains an inner contradiction reflected later in verse 10's major change. The questions may represent his depression's deepest point, but they may prompt in the psalmist an unexpressed "No!" and show the resurgence of strong faith. The former interpretation is perhaps the more likely.

77:10-12   Translations of verse 10 differ.[32] The NRSV translates it, "And I say, 'It is my grief that the right hand of the Most High has changed'" (cf. also NASB), but the NIV fits the context well, and its supply of "I will remember" to complete the sense seems warranted, as this verb occurs twice in verse 11. "The years of the Most High" suggests the exodus, the supreme act of God's power and grace for his people. He considers these great acts. The word "meditate" suggests pondering the record of these acts in Scripture.[33] At last he turns his mind away from himself, and paradoxically, this gives a greater sense of intimacy with God shown in the frequent use of "your," right through to the psalm's end.

77:13-20   Here phraseology and ideas from Exodus 15, especially verses 6 and 11-13, suggest that this is the passage he meditates on. The Lord showed his uniqueness in the exodus, defeating Egypt's gods; his miracles (including opening the Red Sea and the Jordan) effected redemption. "The psalmist is in a dark night . . . but by remembering the Exodus the night is illumined, just as the pillar of fire accompanied the people through the desert."[34] The names of

---

31. Harman points out the similarity of tone in these questions to those of 85:5-6 (*Psalms,* 266), although that psalm is communal and there is reference in it at least to past sins.

32. Broyles deals with these succinctly, *Psalms,* 318.

33. The same word as in 1:2.

34. Schaefer, *Psalms,* 190. His whole treatment of this psalm is excellent.

Jacob and Joseph (v. 15) suggest entry into the promised land as fulfillment of their trust in God's promises (cf. Gen 47:29-31 and 50:24-26). God acted upon the waters at the Red Sea and the Jordan just as at the creation, and Sinai, with its storms, its thunder and lightning, also revealed his might. God took the people through the sea, but although they saw Moses and Aaron, the undershepherds, they never saw God, the chief shepherd, yet all the mighty works they did see were in fact his (cf. Deut 4:34).

So the psalmist has been lifted from his despondency by meditating on God's works for his people, probably as celebrated in earlier Scripture. As Kidner notes, "By the end of the psalm the pervasive 'I' has disappeared, and the objective facts of the faith have captured all his attention and all of ours."[35]

Psalm 78

78:1-8 This psalm, the Psalter's second longest, has a didactic wisdom style like Proverbs 1–9, but is addressed to "my people" instead of "my son" or "my sons."[36] It is תּוֹרָה, *tôrâ*,[37] rendered "teaching" in verse 1. It reminds them of God's commands, but the reminder is as much *tôrâ* as the Law itself. Its form is parabolic (v. 2), meaning simply instruction by comparison,[38] which can be as much from historical fact, as here, as from edifying fiction, for instance in the parables of Jesus. It is helpful to read it through first at a sitting before considering it section by section.

It concerns passing instruction from one generation to another (cf. Exod 10:1-2; 12:26-27; Deut 4:9; 6:20-25; 32:7-9; Pss 44:1-3; 71:14-18). The purposes are to teach trust in God, remembering what he has done, and obedience to his law (v. 7). He utters hidden things, suggesting, in this context, "the paradox of Israel's inability to trust God's great acts of deliverance, despite the long-continued and repeated nature of those acts."[39] He criticizes the forefathers for their rebellion and disloyalty (v. 8), then moves into a historical review and, as in Psalm 68, follows the story from Egypt to Judah and the Jerusalem sanctuary.

---

35. Kidner, *Psalms 73–150*, 277.

36. Its opening is somewhat like that of Ps 49, except that this is addressed to "my people," whereas Ps 49 is to "you peoples."

37. See pp. 17-18, 25-27.

38. Cf. the use of מָשָׁל, *māšāl*, variously translated "proverb" (e.g., Prov 1:1, 6; Ezek 12:22-23), "oracle" (e.g., Num 23:7, 18), and "discourse" (e.g., Job 27:1; 29:1).

39. Tate, *Psalms 51–100*, 281.

78:9-16 The event referred to in verses 9-11 is not easy to identify, but may be that mentioned in verses 56-64, for Shiloh was in Ephraim's tribal area. The name "Ephraim" was also used of the northern tribes generally, particularly in Hosea, so it could refer to some defeat of the northern armies, verse 10 then relating to the apostasy of the northern tribes. The incidents specified are recorded in Exodus 17 and Numbers 20. Zoan (v. 12) was a major Egyptian city. Their unfaithfulness was highly culpable in view of all God had done for them.

78:17-31 He emphasizes the sustained nature of the people's rebellion and unbelief despite continued divine acts of miraculous provision, both of food and drink, combining material from Exodus 16 and Numbers 11, and recalling the judgments associated with these events. Despite everything, however, God still provided for them. The manna is called "the grain of heaven," "the bread of angels" (vv. 24-25), not literally but emphasizing its heavenly origin. The function of the winds (v. 26) is shown in Num 11:31. In verse 28 the MT reads "his camp," while the LXX has "their camp." The MT should be followed, as "your tents" would be an implied and very apt reference to the tabernacle, marking the camp as Yahweh's.[40]

78:32-39 Even these judgments failed to have the desired effect, for their penitence was temporary, lacking full sincerity. This reminds one of Judges 2, which sets out a general theme illustrated many times in Judges. "He did not stir up his full wrath" perhaps means he did not impose the ultimate penalty: expulsion from the land (Deut 28). Verse 39 suggests this was due to God's pity.

78:40-55 Here the psalmist adopts a cyclic approach, returning to the exodus events and marveling at Israel's rebellion and unbelief in view of these things. It was Egypt then that felt the force of God's anger,[41] executed by "a band of destroying angels" (v. 49), suggesting that the "destroyer" of Exod 12:23 was an angel and that all the plagues were executed through angels. The Egyptians are called "Ham."[42] The flock imagery is used also in 77:20 and 80:1. This section concludes with the conquest of Canaan.

78:56-64 Even in the land God gave them their rebellion continued in their idolatry, which characterized the period of the judges (and beyond). This was the reason for Shiloh's judgment (1 Sam 4; cf. Jer 7:9-15). "He rejected Israel completely" contrasts with verse 38 and sees the capture of the

---

40. See Johnson, *Cultic Prophet*, 52.

41. The word חֲנָמַל, *ḥănāmal*, in v. 47 is a hapax legomenon, and so "sleet" is an educated guess by the translators, but this or something similar is suggested by the parallelism.

42. Cf. 105:23, 27; 106:22; and Gen 10:6, where Mizraim is Egypt.

ark, obviously of great significance for a Levitical writer, as evidence.[43] Verses 62-64 take up details of 1 Samuel 4.

78:65-72   The dramatic image of verse 65 introduces a highly positive section, with verse 66 embracing at least David's victories and possibly also those of Samuel and Saul. Verse 67 recalls the earlier references to Ephraim (v. 9) and Shiloh (v. 60), now replaced by Judah and Zion.[44] Perhaps the writer considered Ephraim, the leading tribe, particularly culpable and thus appropriately set aside. The Jerusalem temple was built securely on a mountain, symbolizing perhaps God's settled purpose for it. David was chosen as monarch and his conduct (in general, at least) justified this choice.

Broyles rightly points out that the teaching of this psalm takes place on two levels: "One has to do with the *personal* decision the current generation of listeners faces, the other has to do with corporate tribes and God's elected program for Jacob-Israel."[45] Davidson memorably dubs its revelation of God's character "stubborn compassion."[46]

Psalm 79

Wilcock points out that the compilers of the Asaph psalm group must have seen the irony of placing Psalms 78 and 79 together:

> In 78 David has come to the throne, and his rule as shepherd king promises an end to centuries of folly and evil. In 79 four more centuries have gone by, and the Davidic monarchy has itself come to an end, mired in the selfsame folly and evil it was supposed to remedy. At the close of 78 God's sanctuary has been "established forever" on Mount Zion; at the start of 79 the holy temple is defiled and the holy city is in ruins.[47]

This psalm could have been used at one of the fasts mentioned in Zech 7:1-7.

79:1-4   The psalmist's horror is unmistakable and, as in Psalm 74 and Lamentations, suggests an eyewitness. The temple was "defiled" by the presence or actions (or both) of the invading nations. The birds and beasts were to

---

43. In v. 61 the words "the ark of" have been added by the translators as it is clear that the reference is to 1 Sam 4:3-8, 21-22.

44. Wilcock comments on "the masterly chiasmus of verses 67-68" (*Psalms 73–150*, 25) and sees this as a hint of the psalm's careful composition. His whole comment on the structure of this "ramble with landmarks" is well worth reading (*Psalms 73–150*, 24-30).

45. Broyles, *Psalms*, 319.

46. Davidson, *Vitality of Worship*, 260.

47. Wilcock, *Psalms 73–150*, 30.

be governed by humanity (Gen 1:26-28; Ps 8) but here they actually eat the dead. Harman suggests verse 3 may echo Jeremiah's description of the death of the covenant breakers (Jer 34:17-20).[48] Blood was meant to be sacred, but like Abel's, it was poured out on the earth (Gen 4:10-11). Possibly verse 4 is about the predatory Edomites (Obad 10-14), but it could have wider reference.

79:5-8 The nation's situation is desperate, so the psalmist calls urgently for speedy revelation of God's mercy (vv. 5, 8). He acknowledges the sins of the fathers (cf. Ps 78),[49] but asks that the present generation be not judged for them. "Jealousy" suggests the sin of idolatry, while verse 6 virtually pleads the covenant, for it implies Israel's distinction from pagan nations.

79:9-11 Verse 9 (cf. 25:11) suggests that not only deliverance but forgiveness reveals God's character. Verse 10 implies that saving them will reveal his faithfulness to his covenant. "The prisoners" are probably those already taken into exile, and those condemned to die may be eminent captives.

79:12-13 "Seven times" suggests fullness of judgment. Like many Asaphite psalms, this views God's people as his sheep (cf. 77:20; 78:71-72; 80:1; and perhaps 83:12). The reference to praise contrasts with the shame and reproach his people, and by implication the Lord himself, are bearing just now.

Psalm 80

Much in this lament suggests the time of Samaria's capture and the exile of the northern tribes. The first plural could suggest it was written by a northerner, but verse 1c has the Jerusalem temple in view, very apt after Psalm 79, and verse 17 may be about the Davidic king, so it is best viewed as southern but written by a Levite with a deep sense of the oneness of the fractured kingdom.

80:1-3 The shepherd is a familiar figure in the Asaph psalms (cf., e.g., 74:1; 78:52: God; 77:20: God through Moses and Aaron; 78:70-72: David). Samaria's fall confirmed the rejection of the Joseph tribes, Ephraim and Manasseh, the chief northern tribes (78:67), but here there is concern for God to save them and Benjamin, like them a descendant of Rachel (Gen 30:24) and in practice a buffer between north and south. Verse 1b perhaps reminded the psalmist of guidance in the desert (cf. 77:20) and so of the pillar of fire, which in turn recalled the Shekinah glory in the temple and finally (v. 3) the Aaronic

---

48. Harman, *Psalms*, 277.

49. רִאשֹׁנִים, *ri'šōnîm*, rendered "the fathers" in NIV, can also mean "former." This would then bring it into line with v. 9, but Goulder argues from the stress on the sins of the forefathers in 78 and also from 81:12 (both Asaphite psalms) that a reference to the sins of the ancestors is appropriate here (*Psalms of Asaph*, 135).

blessing (Num 6:25). Verse 3 introduces a refrain (cf. vv. 14, 19) emphasizing the psalm's main concern. The verb translated "restore," a favorite of Isaiah (probably contemporary with the psalm's author), can combine physical and spiritual return.[50] While much of the psalm suggests the former, verse 18 implies the latter also. In a situation of exile, restoration and salvation are equivalents.

80:4-7 The change from the first to the third person here may suggest prayers in Judah for God to be merciful to the northern kingdom, and the resumed first person in verse 6 would then show a sense of the solidarity of the two kingdoms in God's purpose. Perhaps the two analogies of verse 5 recall the manna and the water from the rock during the wilderness period (cf. 78:15, 24), now replaced by tears. As both Israel and Judah worshiped Yahweh, they would share the mockery directed by antagonistic neighboring states against his apparent inability to save.

80:8-15 The analogy changes, with the vine image developed rather as in Isaiah 5. Verses 10 and 11 suggest territory including Lebanon, symbolized by the cedar, and stretching to the Mediterranean and the Euphrates (the Sea and the River), so that the days of David and Solomon are in view. "Why" (v. 12) finds an answer in Isaiah 5 in terms of the people's sin, and the boars suggest unclean foreign foes. Verse 14 begins like the refrain (vv. 3, 7, 19), but ends differently. Its reference to looking from heaven, instead of the shining of God's face, suggests that God now seems remote. Verse 15 uses a further analogy, perhaps developed from the vine, with a branch of it as its "son,"[51] a term used of Israel in Exod 4:22-23 and Hos 11:1.

80:16-19 The vine is not simply ravaged but is apparently destroyed,[52] and this is the act of God. "Man" and "son of man" are synonyms (cf. 8:4), appearing in the context to refer to Israel or Judah. The Targum on it, however, representing later Jewish interpretation, renders "son of man" here as "King Messiah." Could this understanding have been current at the time of the Psalter's final editing? We cannot be sure. Verses 17 and 18 show that the source of spiritual renewal is God himself, who will restore the people to life. This therefore gives extra meaning to the final occurrence of the refrain in verse 19.

---

50. שׁוּב, *šûb*, "turn, return"; e.g., it is incorporated in the name of Isaiah's son (Isa 7:3).

51. וְכַנָּה, *wĕkannâ*, translated "root" in NIV, is a hapax legomenon, but most translations assume, from the context, that it has a plant reference.

52. "Your vine" (v. 16, NIV) is not in the text but its addition finds warrant from the context. "Your people," too, is also a translators' addition, but the clause could refer to the enemies of the people, and it is not easy to decide as either fits the context.

Psalm 81

This psalm begins as a hymn but becomes a prophetic oracle,[53] suggesting that the prophetic word was given while the people were at worship.

81:1-5 The readers are to use both voice and instrument to praise God, who is described by two phrases reminiscent of 46:7 and 11, divine titles suggesting strength available for the weak and failing who are also God's chosen people. The setting is a festival, with the customary ram's horn (Exod 19:13; Num 29:1) signaling the start of the festival month, culminating two weeks later in the feast itself, which is probably Tabernacles, for this began at a full moon.[54] Israel's major festivals were established by divine decree. Psalms referring to the Law, in this case the festival regulations, often multiply synonyms, as this one does (cf. Pss 19 and 119).

Other Asaphite psalms associate Jacob and Joseph (e.g., 77:15; 78:67, 71). "He" in verse 5b is probably God rather than Joseph (see Exod 11:4), and the last clause has been variously understood. Tate translates it fairly literally as "I hear speech I have not understood."[55] This could refer to Israel's time in Egypt, but NRSV, by its paragraphing, sees it as introducing the divine oracle in verses 6-10, and this is probably right, making it "a statement of wonder at the LORD's words which are to come."[56]

81:6-10 Here is God's word, clearly related to the freedom secured by the exodus. In verse 6 the Hebrew reads "his shoulders" and "his hands," but NIV uses the plural pronoun, as the reference is obviously to the captive nation. The change to second plural (v. 7) puts this beyond reasonable doubt. This verse appears to relate successively to Exod 2:23ff.; 19:16; and 17:1-7.

Verses 8-10 recall Exodus 19 and 20, especially 19:23 and 20:1-3, because of the restatement of the first commandment, and the reader might expect the rest of the Decalogue to follow. Instead there is the command and promise of verse 10c. Does this refer to the reception of God's word with a view to uttering it,[57] or to the gift of food? In the light of verse 16, it appears to be the latter, meaning, of course, the manna, although it is not impossible, in view of verse 5c, that the writer's words are deliberately ambiguous.

81:11-12 These verses are general enough to cover several incidents in Exodus and Numbers, and probably relate to the wanderings as such.

81:13-16 Here the lessons of the past are applied to the present, showing

53. For comment on prophetic psalms see pp. 7-8.
54. I.e., 15 days after the New Moon (Lev 23:34).
55. Tate also deals with other possibilities (*Psalms 51–100*, 317-20).
56. Harman, *Psalms*, 282-83.
57. Cf., e.g., Exod 4:15; Jer 1:9.

obedience as the key to blessing (cf. Ps 1), a Deuteronomic theme (e.g., Deut 28). It is doubtful if verse 15b threatens eternal punishment in the NT sense, for it probably refers to groups rather than individuals. In contrast, Israel would be well provided for, again in terms reminding us of Deuteronomy, which, of course, points to the lessons of the exodus. Broyles compares these verses with Isa 1:19-20.[58]

Psalm 82

Much of this psalm, like Psalm 81, consists of a prophetic oracle,[59] given perhaps at a feast, with verse 1 giving its setting and verse 8 closing it with prayer. An important and most complex issue of interpretation, central to the understanding of the whole psalm, confronts us. Who are the gods in verses 1, 6, and 7? Four possibilities have been canvassed:

1. Canaanite deities — but they seem to be real beings with real spheres of authority, so how do we square this with OT monotheism? Unless, of course, they are simply treated as real initially because their worshipers and worship were real, then shown to be worse than valueless, and finally theologically negated ("you will die," v. 7).
2. Angels, elsewhere called "sons of God"[60] — but death (v. 7) certainly suggests humans.
3. The judges of Israel, called "gods" because they are given, under God, one of God's prerogatives — judgment.
4. The people of Israel as "the great assembly" (v. 1) and as "all sons of the Most High" (cf. Deut 14:1), but with a focus on their rulers as charged with exercising judgment within Israel. "Assembly" here is עֵדָה, *'ēdâ*, applied with great frequency in the OT to the assembly of Israel.

Does the position of the psalm in book 3 indicate how its compilers understood this? Psalm 81 highlights the giving of the law, which was on the great "day of the assembly" (Deut 10:4; 18:16), but it also refers to the ban on the worship of other gods, so supporting either views 1 or 4 above. Psalm 86:8 may be too far away from 82 to be significant, but 80:15 calls Israel God's son, so that the contextual argument slightly favors view 4. John 10:34-36 presum-

---

58. Broyles, *Psalms,* 334.
59. For comment on prophetic psalms see pp. 7-8.
60. Cf. Job 1:6; 38:7 (both NIV mg.), and probably Gen 6:2, 4.

ably relates to a (or, more probably, the) standard Jewish interpretation in NT times, and the use of verses 6 and 7 by Jesus there[61] certainly indicates application to human beings. I will assume view 4.[62]

82:1-4 In this prophetic oracle, God rises up, a frequent idea in the Psalms for God righting things that are wrong. As at Sinai he shows his supremacy over the whole nation[63] and now addresses its judges. As often in the prophets (e.g., Isa 1), he accuses Israel, and most of all its judges, of failing in judgment, a major purpose of which is to protect those who, without it, would be vulnerable to oppression (mentioned in vv. 3 and 4), for, as in Amos 5:7-13, they are being wickedly exploited.

82:5-7 Judges need light, for they must assess evidence. The moral foundations are shaken, which is viewed so seriously that it is depicted as shaking the foundations of the earth. Judgment is the only option, and those who gloried in their status will find they are "mere men," simply human beings, for this is probably what אָדָם, *'ādām*, in verse 7 means, unless this is intended to be a personal name here and an allusion to Genesis 3.

82:8 The prophetic oracle now receives a response from the psalmist, who calls God to judge the whole earth, not simply Israel, because all belongs to him.[64] "Your inheritance" is the language of accommodation, vividly saying that all rightly belongs to him.[65]

Psalm 83

This Asaphite anthem ("song") is a cry to the God of Israel in national crisis and is replete with historical references and vivid imagery.

83:1-4 The setting is a conspiracy of Israel's enemies to destroy it decisively and finally. The three verbs of verse 1 form an intense plea for divine action, and, as these are "your enemies," this plea is then reinforced by an appeal to God to see and hear, for he is omniscient. As in Psalm 2, the cunning, plotting, and scheming of the enemies is featured.

---

61. Note particularly his words, "to whom the word of God came."

62. Wilcock argues for this most persuasively (*Psalms 73–150*, 40-43); cf. also Kidner, *Psalms 73–150*, 296-99. The NIV rendering seems to favor either view 3 or 4. Davidson argues for view 1 (*Vitality of Worship*, 270-73), as does Tate, with much technical detail (*Psalms 51–100*, 328-42).

63. עֲדַת־אֵל, *'ădat-'ēl*, rendered "great assembly" in NIV, is lit. "assembly of God."

64. For judgment see pp. 258-59.

65. Tate has a long note on the interpretation of this verse, understanding v. 8b as the basis for the petition in 8a, which comes out clearly in NIV (*Psalms 51–100*, 331-32).

83:5-8 The alliance is multinational, virtually surrounding Israel, with Edom and the nomadic Ishmaelites and Amalekites to the south; Moab, Ammon, and the Hagrites to the east;[66] Philistia to the southwest; and Tyre to the northwest; the identity and location of Gebal are disputed.[67] Lurking behind this association of small states is mighty and aggressive Assyria, which eventually devoured them all. "The descendants of Lot" are Moab and Ammon (see Gen 19:36-38), probably the group's leaders (v. 8), but the phrase also recalls that many (Edomites and the Ishmaelites as well) had a blood relationship to Israel. Family hatred is often particularly bitter and sad.[68]

83:9-12 The psalmist cites God's action against historical enemies, the Midianites (Judg 7) and the northern Canaanites (Judg 4) against whom God used Gideon's reduced force and the woman Jael, to offset the frightening accumulation of names in verses 5-8.[69] The words "of God" (v. 12) remind God that these are *his* enemies (cf. v. 2), and the people of Israel his sheep (cf. 79:13).

83:13-16 The vivid imagery of verses 13-15 (cf. 1:4) presents the thought that God's power is like a mighty wind. "What begins with plant images . . . and a brush fire, mounts to hurricane proportions (vv. 13-15; cf. Is 17:13; 40:24)."[70] The psalmist calls for the enemies to perish, is especially concerned for them to be shamed, to "lose face," but his great desire is that the God of Israel should be acknowledged as "Most High," and so, by implication, superior to the gods of all these nations. Perhaps the men who are to seek him (v. 16) include even the defeated foes.

Psalm 84

The Asaphite psalms are now replaced by other Levitical ones associated with the sons of Korah. This one is clearly a pilgrim song for use at the pilgrim feasts.[71]

---

66. For the Hagrites see 1 Chr 5:10.

67. If it is the same Gebal as in Ezek 27:9 it would appear to be Byblos in Lebanon (cf. Josh 13:5).

68. Wilcock suggests that "the psalmist is looking back over the centuries and presenting a poetic picture of the many enemies that have arisen against Israel at various times, from the earliest (Amalek, Exod. 17:8) to the latest (Assyria, 2 Kgs. 15:19)" (*Psalms 73–150*, 44-45). This is possible but "alliance" seems to imply a contemporary grouping.

69. For Endor see its link with Taanach in Josh 17:11 and the reference to the latter in Judg 5:19.

70. Schaefer, *Psalms*, 205.

71. See p. 16.

This psalm uses wordplay, typical of Jewish wit. This perhaps explains some of its enigmas. Its main structural features may be the occurrences of blessing (אַשְׁרֵי, 'ašrê, "happy"), or of "LORD Almighty," or the alternation of sections addressing and describing God (in vv. 2, 7, 11, 12). But these descriptive sections may be simply to foster praise or prayer to God. That it starts with an exclamation of love for God's house, and, apart from verses 2, 8, and 9, has an atmosphere of joy, would support the "blessing" structure, but the "LORD Almighty" structure is even more pervasive, for every stanza (according to NIV paragraphing) contains it, except verses 5-7, where it is replaced by "Blessed are those whose strength is in you," which makes a similar point. I will therefore adopt this structure.

84:1-2 יְדִיד, *yādîd*, "lovely" (NIV), means "beloved," and "dwelling place" is מִשְׁכָּן, *miškān* ("tabernacle"), clearly referring to God's house at Jerusalem (cf. v. 4). יהוה צְבָאוֹת, *yhwh ṣĕbā'ôt* (lit. "Yahweh of hosts"; NIV "LORD Almighty") clearly suggests strength (cf. vv. 5 and 7). That the pilgrims needed physical strength, with the implied contrast with those already in God's house (v. 4), may have determined the term's frequency here.

84:3-4 He is obviously away from the temple, but he imagines it, with its bird life (the courts were open to the sky) and its priests and Levites (he was a Levite himself) constantly engaged in God's praise. The combination of great terms for God with tiny birds building their nests suggests that God's strength is employed in tender care for his people.

84:5-7 The pilgrim party is pictured. Translating with the hyphenated "pilgrim-ways," Tate thinks verse 5 may have a double meaning, the ways being both the pilgrimage roads and God's "ways." "They are both in the heart of the pilgrim."[72] Baca cannot be located, but occurs in the plural in 2 Sam 5:23, where it is rendered "balsam trees," which grow in arid places.[73] Its consonants (בכא, *bk'*) are similar, though not identical, with those of the verb בכה, *bkh* ("to weep"), so this may be a play on words. Its transformation to a place of plentiful water is ascribed to them, but is caused by God's strength. They gather strength as the journey proceeds,[74] and this carries them to Zion,

72. Tate, *Psalms 51–100*, 353.

73. The exact identification intended by references to flora and fauna in the OT is not always easy.

74. Slight emendation would give "from rampart to rampart" instead of "from strength to strength," suggesting perhaps REB "from outer wall to inner," but the unemended text makes good contextual sense and should be retained. "Conceivably, by a word-play, the psalmist has substituted 'strength' for 'stronghold' ('rampart') in making the pilgrimage a figurative rather than a literal journey" (Kidner, *Psalms 73–150*, 305 n. 4). This would harmonize with the general tendency to wordplay in this psalm.

where the temple is. Appearing before God signifies appearing at the sanctuary (Exod 34:23; Deut 16:16).

84:8-11   The prayer resumes from verses 1 and 2, and asks God to look favorably on the king (v. 9), for "shield" and "anointed one" must be identical in their reference.[75] God the ultimate king is also the ultimate shield (v. 11) and, as light bringer, the ultimate sun (cf. Ps 27:1), and source not only of favor (cf. v. 9) but, like the sun, of glory.[76] Verse 11b is strongly reminiscent of Psalms 1 and 73:1. "God of Jacob," combined with "Lord God Almighty" or "Lord Almighty," is found elsewhere in psalms focusing on Zion (e.g., 46:7, 11).

84:12   This sums up the two main thoughts of the psalm: both joy and strength are to be found in God.

Psalm 85

Psalm 84 makes much use of wordplay, on various words. So does this lament, but with only one word. This is שׁוּב, *šûb*, meaning "turn," "return," or "restore," which occurs in verses 1, 3, 4, and 8, and, as Kidner notes, is the basis of the "again" in verse 6,[77] for there a literal rendering would be, as Tate translates it, "will you not turn (and) give us life?"[78] Whenever written, this psalm's appropriateness for use in the exile is evident.

85:1-3   This historical reference would fit many events, from the entry under Joshua to the reentry after the exile. Restoring Jacob's fortunes could refer to the coming of Jacob's descendants into the land he left when he moved to Egypt. The reference to forgiveness could equally well apply to their sins in the wilderness or to those that caused the exile. Supporting a reference to the original entry, Wilcock notes at several points that the psalm's wording recalls Exodus 32–34.[79] The divine expiation of their sin (v. 2) was also God's own self-propitiation (v. 3).

85:4-7   Like 80, this psalm calls for God's restoration of his people, which here must mean "restore us to your favor," although it could include a return to the land. Verse 6 asks God to "restore and revive." They call him "God our Savior" because they are apparently suffering from the activities of their enemies, although this is not explicit. The psalmist asks God to repeat

---

75. For the divine King supporting the human one, cf. Ps 2.

76. "Honor" is כָּבוֹד, *kābôd*, otherwise translated "glory."

77. Kidner, *Psalms 73–150*, 308.

78. Tate, *Psalms 51–100*, 364.

79. Wilcock, *Psalms 73–150*, 84. Note, e.g., v. 3 and Exod 32:11-14, v. 10 and Exod 34:6.

his forgiveness referred to in verses 1-3, and his call for his "unfailing love" to be shown is an appeal to God's covenant with Israel, "that bedrock upon which the nation's very existence depended."[80]

85:8-9 Verse 8 looks like the anticipation and delivering of a prophecy, especially as the singular is now used. The message is both promise and warning, rather as in Isa 1:18-20. Verse 9b recalls the departure of God's glory symbolized in the name Ichabod (1 Sam 4:21-22), so that the psalmist's concern in verse 8 may be that the people's constant backsliding in the era of the judges (cf. Judg 2:10-19), which included the opening chapters of 1 Samuel, should not be repeated.

85:10-13 This is highly poetical not only in form but in tone, and clearly assumes that the restoration prayed for has taken place. God's attributes, especially those connected with his covenant promises, are personified in verse 10. This is not a resolution of conflict between attributes, but rather members of the same "family" glad in their meeting and mutual expression. Verse 11 too personifies them as expressing the harmony of heaven and earth, presumably because God's grace has found an answering response in his people. In verse 12 the renewing of God's favor toward the land (cf. v. 1) is shown in a good harvest, and verse 13 pictures righteousness as Yahweh's herald, probably suggesting his eventual coming will be a judgment putting everything right.[81]

Psalm 86

It is not clear why the psalm breaks up the "sons of Korah" sequence at this point. This is the only Davidic psalm in book 3 and was perhaps incorporated in it as a reminder of the special place of David in psalmody. It consists mostly of echoes of Davidic psalms from books 1 and 2. Possibly it was put together by book 3's compiler, and appropriately called "a prayer of David," to reflect the earlier history of its parts.[82] The word "prayer" is certainly apt, for in few psalms are petitions so frequent. Space does not permit noting in detail the unique way material from other psalms is used and the way stock psalmic phrases bind the whole psalm together, but the former are well identified by Tate and the latter by Broyles.[83] Notice especially the frequency of כִּי, *kî*, "for"

80. Davidson, *Vitality of Worship*, 281.
81. For righteousness see pp. 249-50, and for judgment see pp. 258-59.
82. See Wilcock, *Psalms 73-150*, 54-55.
83. Tate, *Psalms 51-100*, 380-83; Broyles, *Psalms*, 347-49.

(causal; vv. 1, 2, 3, 4, 7, 10, 13, 17), which also occurs at the start of verse 5 (not translated by NIV; cf. NRSV).

86:1-4   The psalmist calls to God, grounding his appeal in his need, for God especially cares for the poor and needy.[84] His need here, as verse 16 shows, is for resources of strength. His devotion to God is covenant love (חֶסֶד, *ḥesed*), and he now addresses God as אֲדֹנָי, *ʾădōnāy* ("Lord" or "Master"), characteristic of this psalm and answering to his own role as God's servant (cf. 2 Sam 7:5). The problem is ongoing (v. 3 "all day long"), and joy will come to him when he receives his answer.

86:5-7   Now his grounds of appeal move to God's character, with clear echoes of the great divine disclosure in Exod 34:6-7. The Davidic psalms 32 and 51 speak of God's forgiveness and his faithful love, not only to the Davidic covenant but, as "to all who call to you" indicates, to the wider ones with Israel. Contemplation of God's character makes him sure of an answer to his prayers.

86:8-10   Now he asserts first the divine uniqueness of the Lord and then his sole deity, especially as shown in his deeds, and he predicts the ultimate conversion of the nations to his worship, so seeing his own problem in the context of a large divine purpose.[85] The use of the emphatic "you" in verse 10, anticipated in "you are my God" (v. 2) and "you are forgiving" (v. 5), has already shown a total focus on Israel's God.

86:11-13   For all nations to worship God requires a massive change of heart, and he now sees that he too needs not only God's teaching but divine action in his inner life to secure godly fear. Then his praise will be wholehearted and fitting for the God of covenant love who has delivered him from death.

86:14-17   Appropriately, after verse 13b, his trouble is for the first time spelled out. Several periods of David's life could be in view here, and God's covenant qualities are appealed to again in words reminiscent of a basic covenant passage in Exod 34:6-7. He needs strength (cf. Ps 18:32), and the sign he asks for is presumably an act of God's deliverance. His past experience (v. 17) is a further ground for his confidence that God will do this. Twice more[86] (vv. 15, 17) the psalm uses the emphatic "you."

---

84. Cf. 35:10; 37:14.
85. For the Psalter's universalism see comments on Pss 65–67.
86. See comment on vv. 8-10 above.

Psalm 87

This psalm of Zion[87] is highly staccato in its language, punching its sentences out in a breathless sequence. For the compilers of book 3, perhaps, it is an exposition of 86:9.[88]

87:1-4   Verse 1 is somewhat like 2:6, but the focus is the city, rather than the king, on Zion's hill. "Mountain" is plural, perhaps referring to the range to which Zion belongs. God has chosen it beyond all other towns in Jacob/Israel. The "glorious things" may be in prospect in this psalm or may have been said in other psalms, especially other Korahite psalms (e.g., 46 and 48), and "city of God" is found also in 46:4.

Verse 4 is extraordinary, its nearest parallel in the OT being Isa 19:23-25, and this is one of many links between this psalm and Isaiah.[89] Recording names for genealogical purposes was important in Israel,[90] but here other nations are recorded as acknowledging Yahweh. There are major enemies: Egypt, represented by the mythical Rahab (cf. 89:10 and Isa 30:7),[91] and Babylon; then Philistia, a smaller nation often a thorn in Israel's side; Tyre, a friendlier nation (at least in the days of David and Solomon); and Cush (roughly equivalent to Ethiopia), probably representing the fringe of Israel's world.

87:5-7   Nations are now replaced by individuals, and "born there" may symbolize becoming proselytes. This will not threaten Zion's establishment by "the Most High," a divine term often associated with Zion (cf. Gen 14:18-20; Ps 46:4), because it is God who will effect this. These foreigners join the musical praise and sing of Zion, the source of their refreshment. The alternative view that the psalmist is writing instead about Jews born elsewhere who will be reckoned citizens of Zion, rather like "Roman" citizens born in various parts of the Roman Empire, hardly fits a straightforward reading of the text.[92]

---

87. See p. 16.

88. For universalism in the Psalter see comment on Pss 65–67.

89. But see also the comment on 47:9 and also Isa 56:5-6. These links are explored by Broyles, *Psalms*, 351.

90. It is also used of the righteous in passages like Exod 32:32-33; Ps 40:7; Isa 56:5.

91. See pp. 240-41.

92. See the comments in Tate, *Psalms 51–100*, 389.

Psalm 88

Psalms 88 and 89 close book 3 with an individual and then a communal lament, just as the individual 73 and the communal 74 open it, although the closing laments reach new depths. This one is very dark, an exercise in spiritual realism, revealing deep spiritual depression. No definite background can be assigned, although there are many suggestions, including a time of severe illness: "In eloquent, impressionistic strokes the poet intermingles the psychological and physical symptoms."[93] Despite its plentiful use of singular verbal forms and two emphatic first person singulars in verses 13 and 15a, the Targum treats it as a communal lament relating to the exile, presumably expressing the group's cry through an individual voice, although this is by no means the only possibility. VanGemeren suggests that its tendency to repetitiveness is due to the psalmist's preoccupation with his suffering.[94]

88:1-2 This opening is like many other psalms of lament. The psalmist constantly calls on God, invoking him as "the God who saves me," strongly suggesting faith based on past experience, even if combined with disappointment at a lack of present divine saving action.

88:3-5 Here is the cause of his cry. His sense of death's nearness may be realistic or simply due to extreme depression. He is convinced too that, once dead, God will no longer care for him.[95]

88:6-9a He develops his lament, ascribing his predicament to God's wrath, pictured as an overwhelming flood. Friendless, shunned, and lonely, he weeps bitterly.

88:9b-12 Again he calls out to God (cf. "every day" with v. 1). He asks many questions about the realm of the dead, to which he is sure he will soon go (v. 3). It is in life that God is praised, for it is in life that he shows his wonders and his sublime qualities of love and faithfulness. The reiterated "dead"[96] and the sequence of "the grave," "Destruction," "the place of darkness," and "the land of oblivion" all show a horror of death, each anticipating the answer "No!" which is never actually spelled out, so this is the language of emotional questions, not of divine answers.

---

93. Schaefer, *Psalms*, 215.

94. VanGemeren, "Psalms," 564.

95. חָפְשִׁי, *ḥopšî*, rendered "set apart" in NIV, "forsaken" in NASB and NRSV, is lit. "freed." Tate, after full discussion, may be right to understand this in an ironic sense, as implying "relieved of duties among the dead!" (*Psalms 51–100*, 396).

96. In v. 10b "those who are dead" translates רְפָאִים, *rĕpā'îm*, which clearly relates to the dead and, in this context at least, to their total inability. See Tate's full note, *Psalms 51–100*, 397-98.

88:13-14 Here is another cry, the agony intensified by unanswered questions as to the reason for God's apparent rejection of him.

88:15-18 He sees the whole of life as an existence near death, viewing his troubles as manifestations of divine wrath, again using drowning imagery (cf. v. 7). Verse 18 echoes verse 8, and the psalm's final word is "darkness." As Davidson says, the three friendship phrases of verse 18 may all be taken together, God removing every human comfort, so that "darkness" is "the psalmist's final exclamation, a protest or a sigh that sums up his whole experience in one dramatic word, 'darkness'!"[97]

Psalm 89

The occasion here is unstated, but verses 44 and 45 have suggested to many commentators that its lament relates to the time when the Babylonians took the young king Jehoiachin into exile in 597 BC (2 Kgs 24:8-17), after which the Davidic dynasty's rule soon ended. Deep concerns are expressed in verses 38-51, and, instead of moving from questions to affirmations of God's faithfulness and then to prayer as in 74, this begins with emphatic affirmations of God's faithfulness to the Davidic covenant and closes with questions. Some have suggested that the psalm may have had two authors (the work of the first ending at v. 37) four hundred years or so apart.[98] Whether this is the case or not, it is notable that the earlier verses were allowed to remain. A rebellious unbeliever like Jehoiakim tried to destroy God's word (Jer 36), but our psalmist, crying out in bewildered anguish, still accepted the promise and, presumably, expected its fulfillment.[99]

89:1-4 חֶסֶד, *ḥesed* ("love"), is the first word, setting the psalm's theme, the subject both of the psalmist's praise and his instruction to others, with special emphasis on its enduring quality. Verses 3 and 4 refer to Nathan's oracle in 2 Sam 7:7-17, God's promise of an abiding covenant with David's house.

89:5-8 These verses develop the thought of verse 2b, where the holy ones, the heavenly beings,[100] join the psalmist's praise of God's covenant-keeping faithfulness. His unique power and faithfulness are joined in their worship.

---

97. Davidson, *Vitality of Worship*, 292.

98. See Wilcock, *Psalms 73–150*, 65-72.

99. For NT use of this psalm see p. 301.

100. "Heavenly beings" translates בְּנֵי אֵלִים, *běnê ʾēlîm*, beings endowed with some godlike qualities; cf. the same expression in 29:1. These angels form Yahweh's court, but he is incomparably great, so that they are there not to advise him but to execute his will.

89:9-13 This section develops verse 8's reference to his power. Rahab, the Canaanite chaos monster,[101] symbolizes all Yahweh's enemies, as verse 10b makes clear. Tabor and Hermon are impressive mountains, the first so isolated, the second so high.

89:14-18 These verses now develop the theme of God's faithfulness, for it is his consistent character, not just his power, that guarantees the covenant. Verses 15 and 16 remind us of Psalm 1, verses 17 and 18 of Psalm 2. "The light of your presence" (v. 15) recalls Num 6:24-27. The animal horn symbolizes strength (cf. 1 Sam 2:10), and the shield is the king as protector of his people (84:9). The king too has a protector, the Holy One of Israel.[102]

89:19-29 The Nathan prophecy is again referred to. "Once you spoke" stresses the message's divine authority, and "in a vision" its oracular character. "From among the people" (v. 19)[103] probably alludes to Deut 17:15, although the wording is different, and verse 22 to 2 Sam 7:10. Verse 25 may take up the thought of 72:8, especially if that psalm was used at the coronation of each successive Davidic monarch.[104] Verses 26 and 27 allude to 2 Sam 7:14, along with Ps 18:2 and perhaps also 2 Sam 7:9. Verses 28 and 29 revert to the theme of verses 3 and 4, which theme has never been completely out of sight.

89:30-37 The psalmist now acknowledges the warning of chastening incorporated in the covenant promise of 2 Samuel 7, and the consecutive reader of the Psalter sees that the righteous conduct extolled in Psalm 1 should characterize the king of Psalm 2. The stress on divine covenant faithfulness is very strong, affirmed as constant despite the king's sin and undergirded by a most solemn divine oath, and it will be as unchanging as the heavenly bodies God has established.[105]

89:38-45 The emphatic "you" heralds a most dramatic change. Events have raised questions about Yahweh's faithfulness. What is now most evident is his wrath. The covenant seems to be over, for the king has been deposed,[106] and the defensive city walls are all broken, enabling simple looting, perhaps a

---

101. See pp. 240-41.

102. כִּי, *kî*, rendered "indeed" in v. 18, is emphatic, underlining the relationship between Yahweh and the king, so important for the psalm.

103. In v. 19 NIV "young man" follows a Ugaritic cognate, which may be correct.

104. See comments on Ps 72.

105. Note the contrasting uses of "violate" (the same Hebrew verb is employed) in vv. 31, 34. For "the faithful witness in the sky" (v. 37, NIV), NASB translates, "And the witness in the sky is faithful," which is more likely in view of the word order of the Hebrew. See Tate, *Psalms 51–100*, 411.

106. מִטְּהָרוֹ, *miṭṭĕhārô*, rendered "splendor" in NIV (v. 44), is a hapax legomenon, which many scholars take as a noun, though others regard it as a verbal form. See Tate, *Psalms 51–100*, 412.

reference to the Edomite incursion (cf. Obad 11-14). So much here clearly reverses what is affirmed in verses 19-29. Moreover, all is seen to be God's work. VanGemeren points to the verbs used here as revealing the depth of the psalmist's emotions.[107] Davidson points out that the word translated "renounced" in verse 39 occurs only once elsewhere in the OT, where it concerns God's renunciation of his temple in Lam 2:7.[108] Verse 45 could suggest death, but more probably refers to the deposing of the young king Jehoiachin.[109]

89:46-51 The psalm's whole burden is concentrated into a cry of bewildered agony. "How long?" is often asked in the Psalms (see esp. 13:1). Life is short, but God's promises are long-lasting. How is it then that this covenant promise has apparently failed? The shame of defeat and the king's exile have involved others, the psalmist included,[110] and he concludes with the word translated "anointed one," a poignant reminder of the Davidic covenant.[111] Where, though, is the promise undergirding it now?

89:52 This is the praise ending to book 3.[112] Knut Heim has argued that the editors of the Psalter would have felt this quite incongruous at this point unless they believed that the prayers that preceded it would be answered.[113]

BOOK 4[1]

Psalm 90

This is most appropriately placed to open book 4, and also after Psalm 89, which expresses concern at the apparent demise of the Davidic dynasty, raising problems for the psalmist about the Davidic covenant. Schaefer notes that the plaintive question, "How long?" in 89:46 and 90:13 provides a link be-

---

107. VanGemeren, "Psalms," 383.

108. Davidson, *Vitality of Worship*, 294.

109. See esp. the reference to his prison clothing in 2 Kgs 25:29.

110. The singular "servant" in NIV follows 24 Hebrew MSS and clearly intends the king, while the standard MT and LXX have the plural. See Tate, *Psalms 51–100*, 412.

111. For the compilers of the Psalter this is perhaps also a reminder of the messianic hope. See pp. 44-46.

112. See p. 19.

113. Heim, "(God-)Forsaken King," 304-5. For comment on this psalm's position in the Psalter see pp. 23-24.

1. For the Psalter's division into five books see pp. 21-28.

tween books 3 and 4.[2] Ascribed to Moses, this psalm's placement here encourages the reader's reflection on God's dealings with Israel, both in mercy and judgment, from its earliest days, underlining for him or her the abiding relevance of God's Word. If this psalm is indeed Mosaic, its view of time may well reflect a sense of the oneness of the generation of the exodus with the patriarchs, all set against the ultimate background of the creation. Many scholars have thought it was composed in or after the exile,[3] but a number of recent scholars, although not necessarily accepting Mosaic authorship, have seen the aptness of a reference to Moses in its superscription. Gerald Sheppard highlights the significance of its placement here: "Moses intercedes on behalf of Israel who has been given a divine promise that now seems to be in jeopardy."[4] A most helpful exegesis of this psalm, exploring particularly its links with Exodus 32–34 and Deuteronomy 32 and 33 in the light of its superscription, is given by Beth Tanner.[5] Walter Brueggemann, who does not accept the attribution to Moses, nevertheless suggests that the psalm be heard as if Moses was now at Pisgah (Deut 34).[6] If book 4 was put together during or shortly after the exile, this opening psalm would deepen the people's sense of sin but at the same time encourage them to trust in the eternal God of the covenant.

90:1-2 These verses appear to echo the words of Moses in Deut 33:27, especially as both use מָעוֹן, *mā'ôn*, "dwelling place" or "refuge."[7] From 2:12 onward, many psalms call God his people's refuge. This asserts that he, and he alone ("you" is emphatic), has been their home through their whole history, for he is everlasting, which would later bring great comfort to those now lacking their original home, Jerusalem. "Born" and "brought forth" are bold imagery, which, in an OT context, certainly cannot mean that the world is a kind of generated deity.[8]

90:3-6 This contrasting stanza views humans not as eternal but as very temporal, with a clear allusion to Genesis 2 and 3 and perhaps (in v. 4) to Genesis 5. The NIV supplies the second "to dust," whereas the NRSV and NASB see God's words as a call to repentance. Perhaps a play on two meanings of שׁוּב, *šûb* ("turn"), is intended. Verse 4, incorporating the thought of

---

2. Schaefer, *Psalms,* 225.

3. E.g., Broyles, *Psalms,* 90.

4. Sheppard, "Theology," 150-51.

5. Tanner, *Psalms,* 85-107.

6. Brueggemann, *Message of Psalms,* 110-15.

7. The proposal to emend מָעוֹן, *mā'ôn,* to מָעוֹז, *mā'ôz,* "refuge," following LXX, is unnecessary, as the former, used as it is of the dens of animals, may have "refuge" as a secondary sense, and conveys more intimacy then the latter.

8. The OT uses a wealth of analogies for God's creative work.

verse 2, is as near the abstract concept of eternity as anything in the OT. The analogies of a flood[9] and of grass quickly withered in the hot summer sun (cf. Isa 40:6-7)[10] emphasize that life is brief, an idea developed later. Death as sleep (cf. Dan 12:2) is probably suggested by the body's appearance in death.[11] As Kidner says, "The swift changes of metaphor add to the sense of insecurity and flux."[12]

90:7-10 Not only is life brief but shadowed by God's wrath against human sin, both overt and secret, all seen clearly in the divine light. Old age with its decline and its final sigh is vividly portrayed in verse 9, followed by reference to its shortness, in contrast with God's eternity in verses 2 and 4, perhaps also with the longevity of Genesis 5. Moses too lived beyond this (Deut 34:7). Its somber character is also emphasized in language reminiscent of Ecclesiastes. If the Babylonian exiles had read this psalm, "seventy years" spent under God's wrath may have reminded them of Jer 25:8-14.

90:11-12 Verse 11 apparently means that as the reverential fear of God should be absolute, so is God's wrath. A proper perspective on time becomes a road to wisdom. Verse 12 is "a lesson not in elementary arithmetic but in life-changing theology."[13] Here the poem reveals itself clearly as a wisdom psalm.[14]

90:13-17 The psalm becomes a prayer, and verse 13 uses "Yahweh" (otherwise absent from the psalm) very aptly in a plea based on the covenant.[15] Again (cf. v. 3) *šûb* ("turn") occurs ("relent" in one edition of NIV) and is used of God by Moses in Exod 32:12, 14, and Deut 32:36, where it is rendered "have compassion on." Verse 13 would suit both the wilderness wanderings and the long years of Egyptian bondage.[16] "In the morning" probably means "in the days of our youth" (cf. Eccl 12:1). He invokes God's covenant love (equally apt whether this is the Abrahamic or the Mosaic covenant), and verse 14 contrasts sharply with verse 10b, with its echo in verse 15. The characteristic pentateuchal emphasis on teaching later generations is seen in verse 16. Verse 17 asks for wrath to be replaced by favor and work that, because of this, will last.

---

9. NASB "You have swept them away like a flood" is a more literal rendering than NIV.

10. Tate disputes the sense "new" (or "renewed") for חָלַף, *ḥālap*, in vv. 5 and 6, adopted by the main English versions, and suggests "nonlasting" (*Psalms 51–100*, 431, 434).

11. NIV "in the sleep of death" is an interpretive rendering, for "death" is absent from the Hebrew, but some such sense seems likely. See discussion of this difficult verse in Tate, *Psalms 51–100*, 433-34.

12. Kidner, *Psalms 73–150*, 329.

13. Wilcock, *Psalms 73–150*, 77.

14. For wisdom psalms see p. 18.

15. In v. 14 "unfailing love" is חֶסֶד, *ḥesed*, love within a covenant relationship.

16. Wilcock makes out a strong case for the latter (*Psalms 73–150*, 78). If the psalm was so understood by readers in Babylonian exile, it could well echo their own feelings.

Psalm 91

This psalm of confidence in God ends with a brief divine oracle.[17] Sheppard sees the psalm, in terms of its placing after 89 and 90 and the link of idea between 91:1 and 90:1, as insisting that God's promises will be honored in the protection of his people.[18]

91:1-2 Here a general statement is followed by a personal affirmation based on it. If verse 1 seems tautological, it is the tautology of emphasis. Verse 2 is somewhat like 18:1-2, and the concept of God as refuge is so frequent in Davidic psalms that it is not surprising the LXX attributes this psalm to David. The shadow is a stock OT metaphor for protection (cf. 17:8; Isa 30:2-3; Lam 4:20). A name (Yahweh), three titles, and several metaphors build a strong objective basis for the psalmist's trust.

91:3-8 The individual reader is now addressed ("you" is singular throughout the psalm), so this psalm is a good companion to the entirely communal Psalm 90. The emphatic "surely" finds its justification in what verses 1 and 2 say of God. Many illustrations of danger and protection occur (vv. 3-6),[19] with one repetition ("pestilence" in vv. 3, 6). Verse 6 graphically personifies the dangers. The strong promise of verse 7 is not qualified, except in terms of verses 9, 14, and 15. Retribution against the wicked (cf. 1:4-6) is sure, and the godly will see justice being done. Broyles suggests that verse 8 implies that the protection promised in the psalm is from divine judgment, not general disasters.[20]

91:9-13 Verse 9 clearly alludes to verses 1 and 2, while "you" and "my" instruct the reader, for the psalmist is encouraging him to follow his example of trust.[21] Verse 10 repeats the promise of verse 7 in other words, and verses 11 to 13 indicate the means of divine protection. Just as God's angel protected Israel when they approached Canaan (Exod 23:20), so God's angels protect the individual believer, whether the danger is inanimate or animate. Verses 12 and 13 also present contrast, for the foot that does not strike against the stone treads on the wild beasts, suggesting dominion as well as conquest, perhaps even reminiscent of Gen 3:15, particularly in view of the serpent reference.

---

17. For NT use of this psalm see p. 328.

18. Sheppard, "Theology," 151.

19. וְסֹחֵרָה, *wĕsōḥērâ*, rendered "rampart" in NIV, following Syriac. It is a hapax legomenon from a root meaning "circle," and so is often translated "buckler," as in NRSV.

20. Broyles, *Psalms*, 362.

21. The interpretation of v. 9 has been much debated; see Tate, *Psalms 51–100*, 448-49. But the NIV rendering makes good sense if the psalmist is linking his teaching to his testimony. "You" here is emphatic.

91:14-16 The verb translated "loves" implies decision to love, and is employed of God's love in Deut 7:7, "set his affection on" (NIV). To acknowledge God's name is to accept his self-revelation. Verse 15 shows that such a committed believer will find God answering his prayers. Verses 14 and 15 lend credence to the suggestion by Broyles given earlier, for they show that there are situations of trouble where the believer will need God's deliverance, so that she or he may know the promised blessing of long life.

Psalm 92

Wilcock, taking the heading seriously, suggests this psalm was sung on the opening Sabbath of the Feast of Tabernacles.[22] The LXX attributes it to David. The lack of such an attribution in the MT supports the idea that the superscriptions were based on tradition, not guesswork, as such an attribution would seem most natural in view of the musical references in verses 1-3.

92:1-3 Worship proclaims God's qualities (cf. Acts 2:11), particularly his covenant love and faithfulness. Perhaps the morning and evening are specified as the times when the two daily sacrifices were offered (Exod 29:38-46). "Good" (v. 1) may be from either a divine or a human perspective or even both. The word translated "melody" may refer either to the sound of the harp or a melody sung to harp accompaniment.

92:4-7 Here is the "good" (v. 1) of worship on its human side. The memory of God's deeds brings the worshipers gladness. Verse 5 relates both to God's outward works and to the thought lying behind them, almost anticipating the Logos concept of John 1:1-18, at least as interpreted by the Greek patristic church. Verse 6 shows similar godlessness to that in Psalms 14 and 53. The transitoriness of evildoers (expressed as "chaff" in 1:4) is something the godless do not discern (cf. 90:12).[23]

92:8 This central affirmation of a somewhat chiastic psalm focuses on God, forever exalted. "You" is emphatic, implying "you alone."

92:9-11 "With a true biblical emphasis *the wicked* (7) become *your enemies.*"[24] This is a most "Davidic" stanza, as the defeat of enemies is a frequent theme in the Davidic psalms. God exalting his horn, employing the same verb

22. Wilcock, *Psalms 73–150,* 85.

23. The word "that" (v. 7) is not represented in the Hebrew and has been inserted in the interest of good sense. The verse makes good sense without it, however, and its omission would mean that v. 6 now becomes a comment on v. 5. Either way of taking these verses can be well argued. See Wilcock, *Psalms 73–150,* 84.

24. Motyer, "Psalms," 547.

as in verse 8, recalls the two kings, divine and human, of Psalm 2. The horn symbolizes strength, and the fine oils may suggest renewal of anointing, not literally but implying God's active reaffirmation of David's kingship.[25] For the visual reference of verse 11, compare 91:8.

92:12-15 This is strongly reminiscent of Psalm 1, but the trees are specified: the stately palm and the huge and strong cedar. In Psalm 1 the righteous are planted by streams of water, here in the house of God, both suggesting refreshment or sustenance from divine sources. The parallel with 1:3 becomes particularly striking in verse 14. Verse 15 clearly suggests their great occupation in old age is God's praise in terms both of his character and his strength.

Psalm 93

93:1-2 Psalms 93, 97, and 99 all begin, "The LORD [Yahweh] reigns!"[26] Grammatically, this can mean "Yahweh has become king," and Sigmund Mowinckel viewed this as the people's acclamation of Yahweh's reenthronement at the Feast of Tabernacles, assuming that this feast was modeled on the Babylonian reenthronement festival; but this is controversial and has been heavily criticized.[27] The more usual translation "Yahweh is King" has been well defended by H.-J. Kraus,[28] who sees it as an exclamation, as in NIV, not just a simple statement. Verse 2 is clearly an affirmation about the past, not the present; Yahweh's reign is firmly grounded. The picture of verse 1b-c is of a military ruler. The throne's stability is due to Yahweh's everlasting reign. Broyles sees the psalm's liturgical use reflected in the third person affirmations of verses 1 and 4 and the hymnic ascriptions of praise.[29]

93:3-4 Here is the (theoretical) threat from water, literally "the rivers,"[30] rendered "the floods" in NASB and NRSV. The emphatic repetition, a marked feature of this psalm, is here at its most intense. NIV's "the seas" is suggested by "the pounding waves," but this phrase could envisage waves at

---

25. See comment in Harman, *Psalms*, 314.

26. Cf. Isa 52:7 (which, however, uses "Elohim" rather than "Yahweh"), one of many points of similarity between book 4 and Isa 40–55.

27. See pp. 12-13 and Kitchen, *Ancient Orient*, 102-6.

28. Kraus, *Theology of Psalms*, 87.

29. Broyles, *Psalms*, 367. There are some parallels with what is said about Baal at Ugarit, so that this psalm could have been written with an anti-Baalism motive. It is Yahweh, not Baal, who reigns.

30. Although "sea" in v. 4 is an exact translation.

the mouths of the rivers. The reiteration suggests relentless pounding, but all to no avail against Yahweh's supreme might. The Lord is exalted (cf. 92:8), so is not threatened by any unruly element.[31]

93:5 This verse is not a complete change of subject, for the overall theme is of divinely ordered stability, here in the law, earlier in the world (cf. Ps 19). The holiness regulations concerning worship were grounded in the law's abiding firmness.

Psalm 94

This psalm faces the puzzle of the arrogance and power of the wicked in a world ruled over by the God who is the fount of justice.[32] It might seem misplaced here, separating 93 from other divine kingship psalms (95–100),[33] yet as supreme judge, putting things right, Yahweh is demonstrating his kingship. Whose wicked reign (v. 20) is in view — a king of Judah like Manasseh? Perhaps, but it could relate to Israel's oppression under Pharaoh. Either is feasible, but the latter fits in well with Wilcock's view that the whole of book 4 is connected with the exodus theme and the Feast of Tabernacles, possibly to prepare the people in Babylon for return from exile.[34]

94:1-3 This call to the divine avenging judge is aptly compared by Wilcock with Deut 32:35 and 33:2,[35] and shining forth here and in Deut 33:2 suggests the revelation of God's majestic glory (Pss 50:2; 80:1). His vengeance is not arbitrary but truly moral (v. 2). The impatient cry of verse 3 is like many in the psalms (e.g., 13:1).

94:4-7 Now four related charges are leveled against the wicked. They are arrogant; it is God's people they oppress; they kill the socially vulnerable, including the alien;[36] and they insult Yahweh by declaring that he sees none of this.

94:8-11 There had been godless fools among Israel in Egypt,[37] and there were still, so verse 8 would fit either view. Verse 10a reasserts that Yahweh is a God of judgment, based on his perfect knowledge, making it truly retribu-

---

31. Cf. Gen 1:6-10, with its emphasis on God's control of the waters.

32. For NT use of this psalm see p. 297.

33. Tate explores and justifies its position in book 4 (*Psalms 51–100*, 488-90).

34. Wilcock, *Psalms 73–150*, 73-74, 90-91.

35. Wilcock, *Psalms 73–150*, 90.

36. This is the גֵּר, *gēr*, the resident alien, specially protected by the law (e.g., Deut 24:14-15).

37. The people's rebelliousness in the wilderness demonstrates this.

tive.[38] Verse 11 is somewhat like Ecclesiastes in asserting the futility of human thinking (cf., e.g., Eccl 1:12-18).

94:12-15   This beatitude gives discipline a positive sense.[39] Verse 12 is a powerful reminder of Psalm 1 for the consecutive reader.[40] Trouble will pass, the wicked judged, God's commitment to his people vindicated, and both judgment and the way the righteous are to follow will be based on the divine righteousness.[41]

94:16-19   Here the psalmist quotes his own thoughts before God rose in judgment (cf. v. 2). The Lord, his covenant love and his consolation, all became his experience, saving his life, supporting him (cf. 73:2), renewing his joy.

94:20-23   Here the reference to the wicked in verse 16 is spelled out more fully. The chief oppressor is a powerful but evil authority figure ("a corrupt throne"), the conspiracy of verse 21 recalls Psalm 2 and verse 22 recalls 18:1. The final verse reasserts the divine retributive justice.

Psalm 95

This is in two contrasting parts; therefore many earlier scholars considered it two psalms brought together. Now, however, it is widely regarded as one psalm composed for the Feast of Tabernacles, because of its comment on the wilderness wanderings.[42]

95:1-2   It begins with joy. The reference to God as Rock recalls its frequent use in Deuteronomy 32, at the close of the wanderings. The congregation now praise the Rock of their salvation instead of rejecting him (cf. Deut 32:15).

95:3-5   Here is the reason for praise. Like many others in book 4, this psalm celebrates Yahweh's kingship, emphasizing both his supremacy over all regarded as gods, and his creation and ownership of the world in all its depths and heights,[43] its seas and land. The four statements of verses 4 and 5 convey comprehensive lordship.

---

38. For comments on righteousness see pp. 249-50; and for judgment see pp. 258-59.

39. The verb used in v. 12 is the same as that in v. 10.

40. For תּוֹרָה, *tôrâ*, here rendered "law," see comment on 1:2.

41. V. 15a is lit. "for justice will return to righteousness," but NIV probably expresses the sense intended by this.

42. For NT use of this psalm see pp. 328, 350.

43. The word translated "depths" is a hapax legomenon, and that rendered "peaks" is rare, but NIV is apt in both cases, especially in view of the reference to הָרִים, *hārîm*, "mountains." See Tate, *Psalms 51–100*, 497.

95:6-7c   The joy of verses 1 and 2 is now complemented by abasement, bowing and kneeling both symbolizing subjection. God is now seen not just as the maker of the inanimate creation but of human life too and especially of Israel. The shepherd/sheep analogy occurs in other psalms in relation to the journey from Egypt to Canaan (74:1; 77:20; 79:13; 100:3).

95:7d-11   Submission is shown in obedience, so God now speaks, perhaps through a prophet.[44] The people are warned to learn from their history. The rock incidents in Exodus 17 and Numbers 20,[45] early and late in the wanderings, showed not only Israel's unbelief but their persistence in it. Putting God to the test suggests cynical refusal to believe unless he should act beyond the great exodus redemptive deliverance. Verse 10 suggests the wanderings were not just physical but spiritual, perhaps continuing the sheep analogy. For verse 10c compare 103:7 and comment there. The oath meant exclusion from Canaan, often pictured as rest (e.g., in Deut 3:20; Josh 1:15).

Psalm 96

This is a great descriptive praise psalm.[46] The precise occasion of its composition is unknown, but most of it is quoted in 1 Chr 16:23-33, where it is linked with David and Asaph, and it was sung when the ark was brought up to Jerusalem. Although that event was local, the psalm's perspective is universal.

96:1-3   These verses are a threefold call to all the earth to sing Yahweh's praise,[47] followed by a threefold call to declare his glory among the nations, so that he may be praised, for knowledge must precede worship. His salvation and marvelous deeds are almost certainly those respecting Israel, but all are called to worship him because of them. As Broyles says, "what is new here is not necessarily its contents, but its singers, 'all the earth.'"[48]

96:4-6   The doubled "for" is important because it introduces reasons. He is to be praised because he is great,[49] and also because he made the heavens. The gods of the nations are not worthy for they are simply idols, the works of human hands in contrast to the Creator of the heavens. His divine qualities are manifested in the sanctuary, for, of course, his ark is there.

---

44. See pp. 7-8.

45. The meanings of the place names are given in NIV mg.

46. See p. 13.

47. For "a new song," see n. 184 on 33:3. For the universalism of the Psalter see comments on Pss 65–67.

48. Broyles, *Psalms,* 374.

49. For "great is the LORD" cf. also 48:1; 145:3.

96:7-9 The opening call to the nations to praise Yahweh is reiterated, with reference now to his qualities extolled in verses 4-6.[50] "Most worthy of praise" (v. 4) now becomes "due his name" (v. 8). The "families of nations" probably relates to the characteristic OT designations, "children of Edom," "children of Ammon," and so on. The nations are to bring their offerings to the Jerusalem sanctuary (vv. 8-9). The phrase rendered "in the splendor of his holiness" could also be understood as "in holy attire" (NASB),[51] but the idea that the nations can wear priestly garments when most of Israel cannot is very startling and was probably meant to be interpreted morally. For "tremble before him," compare verse 4b.

96:10-13 The affirmation, "The LORD reigns,"[52] may relate to some specific event, perhaps the bringing up of the ark, as evidence of God's reign, but it is to go to all the nations. There is evidence of it in the stability both of the physical and the moral orders. The world in its various aspects is to rejoice in anticipation of the establishment of his moral order. Judgment is a cause of praise, for it puts things right and is based on his truth, therefore, by implication, is much superior to human judgment.[53]

Psalm 97

This is a praise psalm, but it includes a moral exhortation in verse 10.

97:1 For the opening statement, cf. 93:1; 96:10; 99:1.[54] The exhortations to rejoice are given because it is the guarantee of universal stability. The "distant shores" אִיִּים, *'iyyîm*, are really the islands, a term often used in Isaiah 40ff. for the Mediterranean coastlands as representing the world's nations.[55]

97:2-6 The natural phenomena remind us of Sinai, and the law-giving there was a major revelation of Yahweh's nature and character. His reign is based on his moral qualities, his righteousness and justice, and so his foes cannot stand against him. Even the apparently everlasting mountains melt before his coming. The very heavens testify to his righteousness, for his character is the basis of all that is.

97:7 Many rightly see this verse as central to the psalm. The revelation

---

50. Cf. the almost identical 29:1-2, which is linked with David in its superscription.

51. בְּהַדְרַת־קֹדֶשׁ, *běhadrat-qōdeš*, found also in 29:2 (see comment there); 1 Chr 16:29; 2 Chr 20:21. See Tate, *Psalms 51–100*, 511.

52. See comment on 93:1.

53. For comment on judgment see pp. 258-59.

54. See comments on 93:1-2.

55. E.g., Isa 40:15; 41:5; 49:1; cf. Jer 31:10.

of Yahweh as the righteous guarantor of the world's stability means that idols are utterly inappropriate, and, in dramatic apostrophe, the psalmist tells the gods to worship Yahweh.[56]

97:8-9 Verse 8 is reminiscent of Isa 40:9, where Zion shares good news about God with its surrounding towns. Here, but not in Isaiah 40, the word translated "villages" is literally "daughters." Here again (cf. 96:13) it is God's judgments that bring rejoicing, because he puts things right. His exaltation above the gods is absolute, and "Most High" is characteristic of the Zion psalms.

97:10-12 The NRSV renders verse 10a, "The LORD loves those who hate evil," but this requires minor textual changes. The MT is supported by the LXX and makes good sense, so should be retained. To hate evil courts trouble from evildoers, but God gives his protection, adding to this his light and joy.

Psalm 98

"There is no mention of defeated enemies and no mention of the gods of other peoples, as in Psalms 96 and 97. They have faded into the background. The LORD alone holds center stage."[57]

98:1-3 This song of joy was evoked by the saving acts of God.[58] The references to his hand and arm strongly suggest that the exodus (e.g., cf. Deut 4:34), or some exodus-like event like the return from exile or even all the exodus-like divine acts of which the psalmist knew, were in view. As Schaefer comments, there is nothing to prevent it from referring to a divine eschatological intervention.[59] Here is his saving righteousness in which he puts things right by delivering his people.[60] This shows his covenant love to Israel but is revealed to all nations.[61] If the exodus is in view, the revelation was first to the Egyptians.

98:4-6 These verses anticipate Psalm 150 with its reference to singing and various musical instruments. The blast of the ram's horn was heard at Sinai, signaling God's presence (Exod 19:13).

---

56. כָּל־אֱלֹהִים, *kol-'ĕlōhîm*, rendered "all you gods" (cf. 96:5), could refer to angels (as in LXX and Heb 1:6) or, possibly, to all supernatural beings, whether real (angels) or unreal (gods), so stressing Yahweh's sole worthiness of worship. Also the verb could be imperfect rather than imperative.

57. Davidson, *Vitality of Worship*, 323.

58. For "a new song" see n. 184 on 33:3.

59. Schaefer, *Psalms*, 252.

60. For righteousness see pp. 249-50.

61. For the universalism of the Psalter see comments on Pss 65–67.

98:7-9   The reference to "everything in the sea" implies the fish, so that all creation is to join in praise. In magnificent apostrophe, the rivers are to clap and the mountains to sing. That this cannot be visualized is irrelevant;[62] it is simply a vivid assertion of the all-embracing character of the universe's praise. Again, as in Psalm 97, the joyous theme is God's judgment,[63] which is to put things right and to be administered with "equity" or "uprightness."

Psalm 99

Jerome Creach and others have explored a possible relationship between book 4 and Isaiah 40–55.[64] If there is such, there could be links with other parts of Isaiah. In this psalm the reiterated "he is holy" (vv. 3, 5, 9), occurring in progressively longer verses (in the Hebrew) as a refrain, plus emphasis on Yahweh's kingship and his forgiveness, suggest connections with Isaiah 6, although with reference to cherubim instead of seraphim, but cherubim occur in pentateuchal references to the tabernacle.

99:1-3   Once again the assertion comes, "The LORD [Yahweh] reigns" (cf. 93:1; 96:10; 97:1).[65] He is universal king, but also specially resident in his greatness in Zion and its sanctuary, enthroned between the cherubim, winged creatures portrayed above the mercy seat (2 Sam 6:2). All nations therefore should praise him as great and holy, the latter term suggested by the worship and sacrificial system of Israel in its concern about sin.

99:4-5   His holiness has both power and moral content.[66] His own actions for his people are just and upright. So the call is to exalt him at the temple (where he dwells and so where he has placed his feet), remembering his holy character.

99:6-7   Although so great and holy, he answers his people's prayers. Both Moses, who acted as priest before the system bearing his name was set

---

62. Attempts to rationalize this, for instance as the clash of waters at the confluence of two streams, are almost certainly mistaken. This is poetry, not prose.

63. For judgment see pp. 258-59.

64. Kraus argues somewhat unpersuasively against a link between this particular psalm and Isa 40–55 (*Psalms 60–150*, 851).

65. See comment on 93:1.

66. It may suggest a pilgrim feast, perhaps Tabernacles, as the occasion of this psalm.

Verse 4a has been variously translated and interpreted, sometimes with slight changes to vocalization or word order. See Kidner, *Psalms 73–150*, 354 n. 1; and Tate, *Psalms 51–100*, 526-27. But NIV's understanding that it contains two brief statements and that the king is divine (so "King") is more likely to be correct than most other renderings.

up,[67] and Samuel called God to forgive his people (Exod 32:11-13; 1 Sam 12:18), and Aaron perhaps is a reminder of his sin (Exod 32), thus stressing the amazing character of God's responsiveness to prayer in view of the people's sin. In verse 7 the pillar of cloud underlines the exodus reference, followed by a clear Sinai allusion.

99:8-9 Verse 8 sees God's answering as manifestation of his forgiving grace, but its closing sentence shows this should not be presumed on and suggests some modification of the statement of verse 7b.[68] Verse 9 is the refrain in its longest form. The holy mountain now is not Sinai but Zion.

Psalm 100

In this processional psalm (v. 4), Broyles points out that, unusually, calls to praise heavily outnumber references to causes for praise.[69] This is true, but those who first sang it had minds well stocked with such reasons, especially from their history.

100:1-3 Verses 1 and 2 address the whole earth,[70] calling for joyful worship to Yahweh. Verse 3a continues this, asserting that Yahweh and, it is implied,[71] he alone is God. "Know" here may mean "confess to knowing" and so "acknowledge." Then the special relationship he has with Israel is asserted, for the sheep imagery is applied in the Psalms only to Israel (74:1; 77:20; 79:13; 95:7), so that the assertion that God is their maker will include making them as a nation but perhaps will also embrace their creation as human beings. For "and we are his," the NIV margin reads, "and not we ourselves," but the former is widely, although not universally, accepted as correct.[72]

100:4-5 These verses are probably addressed simply to Israel, for the

---

67. Tate is sympathetic to Johnson's view that this should be rendered, "Moses, and Aaron His priest, and Samuel as one who calls on His Name," but this requires that the plural כֹּהֲנָיו, *kōhĕnāyw* ("priests"), should be understood as a plural of majesty, which seems unnecessary (Tate, *Psalms 51–100*, 527).

68. Tate, following Brueggemann, suggests that "the juxtaposition of the God who forgives and the God who punishes may reflect Exod 34:6-7" (*Psalms 51–100*, 530).

69. Broyles, *Psalms*, 386.

70. V. 1 is identical with 98:4a.

71. By the use of the personal pronoun, הוּא, *hû'*, so giving "Yahweh, he is God."

72. The text follows MT *Qere*, supported by some Heb. MSS, Targum, Aquila, and Jerome, while LXX, Symmachus, and Syriac support the alternative, which is the *Kethib*. The difference arises from the sounded similarity of לֹא, *lō'*, "not," and לוֹ, *lô*, "his." Little depends on resolving this, but the *Qere* is usually favored because it reads more smoothly than the *Kethib*. See Kidner, *Psalms 73–150*, 356-57; and more fully Tate, *Psalms 51–100*, 533-34.

gates and courts apply to the temple, and the nations could enter only its outer court. Also verse 5 relates to the covenant in which Yahweh's enduring love and faithfulness are expressed.

Psalm 101

In book 4 only this and Psalm 103 are ascribed to David. It has the personal character that marks most Davidic psalms, is a personal commitment to high moral standards, apparently for kingly rule, is introduced by praise to the Lord, and could relate to his enthronement in Jerusalem (see v. 8) as king of all Israel. Most commentators recognize its kingly character, because the person concerned has considerable power and authority (vv. 5-6).

101:1-3a   The opening commitment to sing Yahweh's praises saves the psalm from being simply moralistic, even if the love and justice in view are the king's.[73] The occurrence of "sing" in both lines of verse 1, however, suggests Yahweh is in view in both. God's virtues are, in any case, the standard for the king's and also their source. Allen sees the hymnic nature of verse 1 as decisive evidence that the king's justice here is "a human response to Yahweh's own qualities."[74] The question, "When will you come to me?" may confess his need for divine grace to keep this commitment or it may express his desire for the ark, the symbol of God's presence, to come to Jerusalem. Verses 2b-c and 3,[75] set alongside 2 Samuel 11, make sober reading, as it was precisely in his house and by misusing his eyes that David sinned so grievously.

101:3b-8   Here we see an administrator with powers of choice and judgment. He traces evil to the heart (vv. 4-5; cf. v. 2). "Far from me" perhaps implies he will apply moral tests to workers in his household. Verse 5 indicates that a royal palace can be a center of whispered intrigue and that workers there may be puffed up with pride, while verses 6 and 7 show the moral criteria for service there. "Every morning" probably refers to times he set aside for judging legal cases (cf. 2 Sam 15:2-4; Jer 21:12). The "city of the LORD" was, of course, Jerusalem, where Yahweh reigned as king.

---

73. Here "love" is חֶסֶד, *ḥesed*, covenant love, and so implies this. In v. 1 "your" is not in MT; see NASB and NRSV.

74. Allen, *Psalms 101–150*, 2.

75. תָּמִים, *tāmîm* (vv. 2a and 6), and תָּם, *tām* (v. 2c), relate to integrity rather than blamelessness. See comment on Ps 26, n. 156. In v. 3 the words "vile thing" translate בְּלִיָּעַל, *bĕlîyāʿal*, probably meaning "worthlessness." See VanGemeren, "Psalms," 642. The phrase "faithless men" translates סֵטִים, *sēṭîm*, which is a hapax legomenon, but is probably from שׂוּט, *śûṭ*, "to fall away," as in NASB, NRSV.

Psalm 102

The heading is unique in giving the psalmist's circumstances in general terms but with no Davidic reference. It is perhaps an editorial suggestion as to the reader's use of it.[76] It twice changes from lament (vv. 1-11 and 23-24) to hymn (vv. 12-22 and 25-28), so some scholars think two separate psalms have become joined, yet they make sense when interpreted as one poem in which the psalmist compares his own situation to that of Jerusalem.

102:1-11 An urgent call for help, typically Davidic, for, as E. J. Kissane points out, verses 1 and 2 are composed of phrases from other psalms, all of them Davidic.[77] It is full of similes, suggesting transience ("smoke," v. 3; "the evening shadow," v. 11), illness ("withered like grass," vv. 4, 11), and loneliness (vv. 6-7), for the owl was shunned as an unclean bird. He is gripped by fever (v. 3b), and cannot sleep (v. 7). Is his illness literal? If drinking tears is figurative, then eating ashes probably is also (v. 9). His condition produces constant enemy taunts (v. 8). All is attributed to the divine wrath (v. 10), although no specific sins are mentioned. He seems a Job-like figure.

102:12-22 Here is a dramatic turn, contrasting the weak, transient psalmist, reviled by his enemies, in verses 1-11, and the great eternal divine King with a renowned name revered worldwide.[78] Is this a complaint to a God exalted and eternal and therefore unaffected by the psalmist's problems? Surely not, for verses 12-17 show that this view of God has inspired the psalmist's confidence, emboldening him to pray not just for himself but for Zion (vv. 13, 21). The time seems to be the exile. The psalmist is sure God will rebuild Jerusalem and do it soon. He writes of the Lord's compassion (v. 13), that he will appear in his glory (cf. Isa 40:5), and will hear "the prayer of the destitute," so that verse 17 connects this section with verses 1-11. The psalmist calls for God's actions for his people to be recorded for posterity, in line with the emphasis of Deuteronomy and Proverbs on training future generations, and he looks forward to great worldwide gatherings of praise to Yahweh.[79] As Kidner says, "the theme of *prisoners* released and of *peoples* and *kingdoms* flocking to *Zion* is radiantly presented in Isaiah 60–62."[80]

102:23-28 Commentators differ greatly in interpreting this section. The NIV follows the MT, in which verses 24-28 are the psalmist's words addressed to God, declaring first his eternal nature over against the psalmist's

76. For NT use of this psalm see pp. 350, 358.

77. Kissane, *Psalms*, 2:144.

78. "But you" in v. 12 is emphatic.

79. For the universalism of the Psalter see comment on Pss 65–67.

80. Kidner, *Psalms 73–150*, 362.

own transience (very much like v. 12 after v. 11) and then the amazing fact that the godly will live and be established in his presence — eternally (v. 28).[81] The contrast in verses 26 and 27 is intensified by the fact that "but you" in verse 27 is most emphatic (וְאַתָּה־הוּא, *wĕ'attâ-hû'*). The LXX, however, following the same consonantal text but a different vocalic tradition,[82] and adding the vocative κύριε, *kyrie* ("Lord"), sees verse 24a as the psalmist's plea to God and verses 24b-28 as God's answer. This LXX rendering is astonishing as implying the translator's belief not only in the messianic nature of this psalm but in the lordship of the Messiah, represented by the psalmist, over creation. This formed the basis of the psalm's use messianically in Hebrews 1.[83]

Psalm 103

This is explicitly a psalm of praise in verses 1-5 and 20-22, but is implicitly so throughout, as we see from its inclusio form plus its exposition of God's loving faithfulness to his people.

103:1-5 Like the Davidic psalms generally, this starts on a personal note, and disavows any merely formal worship, for the psalmist's inmost being is engaged in praise. His call to himself not to forget the Lord's benefits is reminiscent of Deuteronomy.[84] In specifying these, he starts with forgiveness, suggesting that we are to think of a time subsequent to David's sin in relation to Bathsheba and Uriah. Now come healing and safety,[85] so that, even without reference to deliverance from enemies, he has summed up his experience of God's saving activities. The assertion, he "crowns you with love [חֶסֶד, *ḥesed*] and compassion," where "crowns" has royal implications, suggests the continuance of the Davidic covenant. The "good things" that satisfy his desires may be physical, spiritual, or both,[86] and the renewal of the eagle's youth relates to its ability to rise swiftly well into old age (cf. Isa 40:31).

103:6-7 A praise psalm without reference to God's acts is extremely rare. Here the general statement of verse 6 is illustrated from the exodus, which revealed strikingly God's righteous concern for the oppressed. It is doubtful if a sharp distinction between outward acts ("deeds") and inner

---

81. For the afterlife in the Psalter, see pp. 423-24.

82. See p. 2.

83. For the messianic theme in the Psalter see pp. 21-28.

84. See, e.g., Deut 4:9, 23; 6:12; 8:11; 32:18.

85. שַׁחַת, *šaḥat*, "pit," is often a synonym for שְׁאוֹל, *šĕ'ôl*.

86. עֶדְיֵךְ, *'edyēk*, is lit. "your ornament," which is puzzling. Anderson indicates the varied renderings of the versions (*Psalms*, 2:13-14). NIV follows LXX in rendering "your desires."

meaning ("ways") is intended, although "ways" is reminiscent of Exod 33:13, a request from Moses that God answered with the great revelation of Exod 34:6-7, echoed here in verse, but God's deeds too were revelatory.

103:8-18   Like David, Israel had experienced the Lord's forgiveness, and the psalmist illustrates this from cosmology, geography, and family relations, with decreasing spatial spheres but increasing intimacy. Verse 12 perhaps suggests both comparison and contrast with the Day of Atonement scapegoat, which went only into the desert, not to the ends of the earth (Lev 16). The emphasis on the transience of human life over against God's eternity compares with Psalms 90 and 102, but here stresses that his love is sustained throughout the generations. In verse 14 "he" is emphatic, suggesting perhaps that a father's compassion is related to his understanding of the child's frailty, and "dust" echoes Gen 2:7; 3:19. The repeated "those who fear him" (vv. 11, 13), followed by reference to keeping his covenant (18), shows the importance of reverential, obedient response on Israel's part. This, along with the reference to grandchildren (v. 17), is particularly significant if book 4 was put together to encourage the exiles to prepare for their return,[87] because two generations had now passed since the exile began. "His righteousness" (v. 17) looks like an implicit promise to continue expressing his love in putting things right by renewed saving deeds for his people.

103:19-22   Now explicit praise returns, but it is the heavenly beings who are exhorted to engage in it. The term translated "mighty ones," occurring only here in the OT, is a synonym for angels in the Dead Sea Scrolls.[88] The "heavenly hosts" too may be the angels or the starry hosts (cf. Isa 40:26). His people's obedience will now resonate with that of the worlds beyond human life. Verse 22 extends the praise call to the entire universe before closing with the personal exhortation with which the psalm began.[89]

Psalm 104

This magnificent poem, aptly described as "Genesis 1 set to music," follows the order of the Genesis days but not woodenly, for it is a meditation (v. 34), set within a beginning and ending that constitute it a psalm of praise.[90] The psalmist ponders both creation and its providential extension in God's pres-

---

87. See pp. 21-28.
88. See Anderson, *Psalms*, 2:717.
89. For the universalism of the Psalter see comment on Pss 65–67.
90. For NT use of this psalm see p. 350.

ent work in his created handiwork. It begins and ends just like 103 and was probably deliberately written as its complement, to show Yahweh as creator as well as redeemer, to be praised in both roles. It is therefore implicitly antipagan, just as Genesis 1 is, with the sun and moon (great deities in Egyptian and Babylonian religion) simply as season markers and as lamps designed by God to give the earth light (vv. 19-23; cf. Gen 1:16-18). "Its words would create a sense of recognition in the ears of Egyptians and Canaanites, but its message focused firmly on the one true God."[91]

104:1-4   This section covers days 1 and 2. It illustrates God's greatness from his clothing (light), his dwelling (tent and house, implied in the laying of the beams),[92] means of transport, and servants, all distinctive in a royal being. The movement of thought from tent to house perhaps reflects the tabernacle's replacement by the temple, although it is his dwelling in the universe rather than in Jerusalem that is in view.[93] Laying beams on waters may seem incongruous, but we should remember that this is poetry. In verse 4 the NIV margin mentions that "messengers" may be rendered "angels." The LXX, quoted in Heb 1:7, is perfectly valid. Some think it does not fit the context,[94] but if we consider the wider context in book 4, not just in Psalm 104 itself, it harmonizes well with 103:20-21, particularly significant if it was written to complement this other psalm.

104:5-18   This section covers day 3 but moves beyond Genesis 1 (represented by vv. 5-9) to the present operation of God's world, so inevitably mentioning creatures from later stages of the Genesis 1 pattern, especially those related to day 5. The psalmist concentrates largely on the role of water in both creation and providence. Verses 5-9 do not simply state but picture the ordering of the waters, and the reference to "the deep" in verse 6 makes clear that this too is God's creation.[95] "Rebuke" does not here imply judgment, but simply makes vivid the portrayal of a Creator in absolute control of the elements. It is possible verse 9 not only echoes Gen 1:9-10, but also the postdiluvian promise of Gen 8:21-22; 9:8-17.[96] Verse 10 both contrasts and compares with

---

91. Craigie, *Ugarit*, 79. See his whole discussion of this psalm (76-79).

92. The tent analogy is much used in Isa 40–55; cf., e.g., 40:22; 42:5; 44:24; 45:12; 51:13.

93. MT v. 4 follows the way the quotation is worded in Heb 1:7 rather than that of NIV.

94. E.g., Davidson, *Vitality of Worship*, 341.

95. At this point therefore, if the psalmist is consciously commenting on Gen 1, he is making clear that 1:2, which, as here, uses תְּהוֹם, *tĕhôm*, "deep," is not about conditions existing prior to God's creative work (which would suggest comparisons with Babylonian creation mythology), but rather those resulting from its initial phase.

96. See comment on 29:10, itself in a psalm chiefly about God's activity in the physical world.

verse 8, for water flowing between the mountains replaces water flowing over them. The psalmist recognizes the fundamental nature of water as provision for wild animals, birds, grass, and trees. The work of human beings (not yet created in the Genesis order) is celebrated in verses 14[97] and 15, and the provision of homes for the creatures in verses 17 and 18 (cf. v. 12).

104:19-26 Now come days 4 and 5. Much of the language here is similar to the Egyptian Hymn to the Sun by Akhenaton,[98] who promoted the restriction of worship to the sun god Aton, so placing the moon before the sun here may be meant to show that the sun has no necessary precedence. These bodies exist to mark off the seasons (cf. Gen 1:14) by divine decree, for it is God who brings the darkness (v. 20). There is a sense of nature's rhythm, shown also in the beasts prowling at night, while human beings work during the day. In verse 24 the psalmist bursts forth into praise of God's power and wisdom and the sheer variety of his creatures. The author returns to his interest in water, contemplating the creatures and ships of the sea. Leviathan is used in the OT both of great beasts (cf. Job 41) and also of the dragon of Babylonian and Canaanite mythology used as a symbol for evil powers (Job 3:8). Here he is probably the great whale, with perhaps a hint that all existence is divinely created, so that no uncontrollable powers exist.

104:27-30 These verses celebrate the dependence of all creatures on God the Creator-Provider. The phrase "at the proper time" (v. 27) continues the emphasis on seasons and times in verses 19-23, and "gather" continues the emphasis on the fact that work is needed to make use of what God has given (cf. vv. 14 and 15). Verses 29 and 30 relate to the initial and constant dependence of all creatures on God's Spirit (cf. Gen 1:2).

104:31-35 Verse 31 probably alludes to "very good" in Gen 1:31,[99] but verse 32, with its reminder of Sinai, anticipates verse 35's moral realism. The psalmist wants to sing God's praise throughout his life and to rejoice in him,[100] just as God rejoiced in his own works. His meditation is the psalm itself. Verse 35 strikes a realistic note, recognizing that sin has entered this perfect world and longing to see it banished. The psalm ends as it began (cf. Ps 103) if, with the LXX and many modern scholars, we see the final "Praise the LORD" as opening Psalm 105.

---

97. The verb עָבַד, 'ābad, "cultivate," occurs also in Gen 2:15.

98. See the text of it in *ANET*, 369-71. Acquaintance with it, which is clear, need not imply literary dependence, which is most unlikely as there are considerable differences.

99. Note also the link between "glory" and creation in 19:1. Another link between these two psalms is to be found in 104:34 and 19:14.

100. Perhaps remembering that he is made in God's image: Gen 1:26-27.

Psalm 105

As Schaefer remarks, the relationship of Psalm 104 to 105 and 106 is like that of the opening of Genesis to the rest of the Torah.[101] This historical psalm and the next are "non-identical twins,"[102] interpreting the events that made Israel a nation but from quite different angles. Verses 1-15 plus Psalm 96 and 106:1, 47-48, occur in 1 Chr 16:8-22 in connection with the arrival of the ark in Jerusalem. Psalm 105:45b may be the beginning of 106, which would mean that both 105 and 106 start and finish with "Praise the LORD."

105:1-7 Brueggemann says the Psalter as a whole moves "from obedience to praise,"[103] but this psalm reverses the order. It recites God's wonderful acts to the nations, with singing and joy. To praise is to seek the Lord (cf. Amos 5:4-6) and his face, perhaps a reference to Num 6:22-27. God will give strength for doing his will. Comparison with Psalm 84 suggests pilgrimage to Jerusalem may be in view. There is an implied reference to the covenant with the patriarchs,[104] and the miracles in Egypt were in fact judgments on the Egyptians.

105:8-11 The call to remember (v. 5) is now followed by an affirmation that the Lord himself remembers his covenant. For "a thousand generations," see Deut 5:10. The covenant is specifically called "the word he commanded," emphasizing God's initiating promise, and "oath" underlines its solemnity,[105] while "decree" points to its authoritative nature. In verse 10 "Jacob" is the patriarch, but "Israel" probably embraces both him and his descendants who inherit the covenant. The land of Canaan is frequently viewed as an inheritance in Deuteronomy and Joshua. In verse 11a "you" is plural, but in 11b is singular, suggesting first the patriarch's descendants, then the patriarch himself.

105:12-22 This surveys the patriarchal period, first of all generally and with reference to the movement of the patriarchs and the protection of their line from Pharaoh and Abimelech (Gen 12:17-20; 20:2-5; 26:6-11). The word translated "strangers" (v. 12) is the plural of גֵּר, *gēr*, the resident alien, with recognized status under the law (e.g., Deut 24:14-15),[106] so perhaps it already suggests divine protection. For verse 15 see Gen 20:6-7, and for the somewhat unusual concept of the anointing of prophets, compare 1 Kgs 19:16. This is not meant literally but indicates their divine appointment and equipment for

---

101. Schaefer, *Psalms*, 259.
102. Wilcock, *Psalms 73–150*, 128.
103. Brueggemann, "Bounded by Obedience."
104. Only in this psalm (vv. 6, 9, 42) and in 47:9 does the Psalter refer to Abraham.
105. Cf. Gen 22:16; 26:3-5.
106. Translated "alien" in 94:6.

their distinctive work. Verses 16-22 feature Joseph, probably because the concept of God's prophetic word occurs in his story too. The phrase "all their supplies of food" (v. 16) is literally "every staff of bread"; and Isa 3:1, which uses this sort of expression for both food and water, suggests that "staff" implies support. Verse 19a probably has Joseph in view, but if instead it is God, the general lesson is the same. The NASB renders verse 22a as "to imprison his princes at will," which follows MT, while NIV follows LXX, which may be correct here in seeing identical parallelism in the verse.[107]

105:23-36 This section concerns Israel's time in Egypt, the plagues, and the destruction of the Egyptian firstborn.[108] It stresses God's actions, even in turning the Egyptians against them (v. 25), a reminder of the hardening of Pharaoh's heart (Exod 4:21). So the psalmist strongly emphasizes God's sovereignty in his acts. As the patriarchs were chosen, so were Moses and Aaron. The many references to God's acts are complemented by reference to his words (vv. 28, 31, 34). Eight of the ten plagues are mentioned. The psalmist was apparently not concerned about comprehensiveness or chronological sequence. The supernatural darkness is placed first, perhaps as an evident judgment on the sun god worshiped in Egypt, while the death of the firstborn, as the most horrific, is placed last.

105:37-45 The psalmist picks out certain events from the exodus narrative. For verse 37, see Exod 3:21-22; for 38, Exod 15:16; for 39, Exod 13:21; for 40, Exod 16:13 and 16:4; and for 41, Num 20:11. The basis of the selection is God's provision of his people's needs. All was done to fulfill his promise to Abraham, and the joy and sheer gift of the land certainly suggest divine grace, while the Israelite reader was challenged to observing God's laws, with the implication that such a bountiful God deserves nothing less. The closing exhortation rounds off the psalm with praise.

Psalm 106

This and Psalm 105 are "non-identical twins" (Wilcock) interpreting the events that made Israel a nation but from quite different angles. This psalm's emphasis is like that of Psalm 78, although that is purely didactic whereas this places historical reflections in a worship context.

106:1-5 This psalm, which documents so much rebelliousness, never-

---

107. MT reads לֶאְסֹר, *le'sōr*, while LXX apparently read לְיַסֵּר, *lĕyassēr*. Scribes would easily confuse the two words.

108. "The land of Ham" is Egypt (cf. Gen 10:6).

theless starts with praise. Extolling Yahweh's goodness, his enduring love, his mighty acts, serves to show up the people's rebellion as sheer ingratitude. The beatitude of verse 3 reminds us of Psalm 1,[109] as does "prosperity" in verse 5, and verses 4 and 5 are a poignant, somewhat unusual plea for personal involvement in the forthcoming gracious divine saving act.

106:6-12   This confession of the people's solidarity with their fathers in sin characterizes many great OT prayers, for instance, Daniel's prayer in Dan 9:4-20.[110] The psalmist begins his recital in Egypt. Verse 7 refers to Exod 14:10-12[111] and says it was for his own name's sake that God saved.[112] They believed the promises after their fulfillment rather than before (v. 12)! Here he refers to Exodus 15.

106:13-18   Verses 13-15 summarize Num 11:18-20, 31-34, while 16-18 move on to Numbers 16. Reference to Nathan and Abiram but not to Korah by name may reflect sensitivity to the Levitical sons of Korah, who, despite their ancestry, served the Lord faithfully.

106:19-33   Verses 19 and 20 are full of irony in the words "cast from metal" and "which eats grass"; cf. also "offered to lifeless gods" in verse 28. There is here a touch of the deep sarcasm used of idolatry in 135 and Isaiah 40–48. The NIV helpfully capitalizes "Glory," showing it as a reference to God.[113] Verses 24-27 relate to Numbers 14 and Israel's refusal to enter the land of promise. This provoked God's solemn vow to exclude that generation.[114] Verse 27 apparently relates to the exile, probably because it was the same sin of idolatry that caused both their initial and this later exclusion from the land and that had characterized much of their history. There was further idolatry in the wilderness, recorded in Numbers 25 and commented on here in verses 28-31. In verse 28 "to lifeless gods" is literally "to the dead," but the NIV's interpretation is probably correct.[115] As in 95, there is reference now to Num 20:1-13. Verses 23 and 30 point to intercession's importance and the significance of one man standing for God in the midst of apostasy. Verse 31, with its

109. See comment on 1:1, which uses the same word.

110. Anderson notes that all three verbs here are also found in 1 Kgs 8:47 and Dan 9:5 and suggests they may form part of a formula of confession (*Psalms*, 2:738).

111. NRSV "against the Most High" instead of "at the sea" involves a change in MT and is unnecessary.

112. The verb "rebuked" (v. 9) is from the same root as "your rebuke" in 104:7. See comment there.

113. Cf. 1 Sam 4:21; Jer 2:11. There may be an echo of this verse in Rom 1:23.

114. Raising the hand was a gesture often accompanying an oath. Cf. Gen 14:22; Num 14:34; and by contrast Ps 144:8.

115. See Anderson, *Psalms*, 2:744, for other suggestions. He supports the addition of "the Lord" in ETs of vv. 29 and 32.

similar phrasing to Gen 15:6, underlines the reward to Phinehas for his stand for God in his becoming the ancestor of all later Aaronic priests. Verses 32 and 33 document the sin of Moses.

106:34-39   The story moves on to Canaan and Israel's failure to exterminate the Canaanites. The author accepted the categorization of paganism as demon worship in Deut 32:15-18. He shows they not only disobeyed God in this but were themselves defiled by what they did.

106:40-46   Their constant relapses into sin and their consequent cries and deliverances by God, summarized in Judges 2 and detailed later in that book, link verses 40-43 and 44-46. Verse 46 is difficult to document but may suggest the psalmist knew facts not recorded elsewhere.

106:47   This impassioned plea looks like a reference to a return from exile, and the psalmist resumes praise that, although implicit throughout, has not been expressed since the opening verses. Psalm 107:3 asserts what the present verse asks for, so providing a link not only between two psalms but between books 4 and 5.

106:48   This is the praise conclusion to book 4 and calls for a response from the people.[116]

BOOK 5[1]

Psalm 107

This great thanksgiving hymn has apparent simplicity but actual subtlety. Moreover, as in John's Gospel, its depths belong to exegesis, not simply to further application. Wilcock has exhibited some of these.[2] Space constraints necessitate concentration on the way the message emerges from the overall structure, but I will suggest some allusions the psalmist may have intended.

107:1-3   After the opening "Hallelujah," verse 1 is identical with 106:1, bridging books 4 and 5. Both then rehearse God's mighty acts. The reference to Yahweh's covenant love shows that the following pictures or short stories illustrate the covenant structure of God's faithfulness.[3] They are "open para-

---

116. See p. 19.

1. For the Psalter's division into five books see pp. 21-28.

2. Wilcock, *Psalms 73–150*, 146-53.

3. The word is חֶסֶד, *ḥesed*, love within a covenant, as is "unfailing love" in vv. 8, 15, 21, and 31.

digms of deliverance into which any and all who have benefited from God's saving work can enter."[4] Verses 2 and 3, however, view them as picturing liberation from an enemy and gathering, presumably in the Holy Land. It therefore seems unlikely that, with the probable exception of the first, they are meant simply to be taken literally, but rather to symbolize either the Egypt/Canaan exodus events or those of the Babylon/Canaan return, most likely the latter, as the compass points suggest groups in different parts of the Babylonian Empire.[5] Possibly they are even meant to recall both, as together they show the same gracious purpose of God, even perhaps embracing possible future gatherings, as "west" does not easily fit either deliverance. Verse 3 asserts what 106:47 requests, so further linking the two psalms and also books 4 and 5.

107:4-9 The word "some" is not in the text,[6] so all four main pictures apparently concern the same people. "Wandering" clearly recalls the wilderness wanderings (cf. 106:14, 24-27), while "a city where they could settle" (vv. 4 and 7) suggests rather the return to Jerusalem, although it could link the earlier events with David's ultimate capture of Jerusalem, somewhat as in Psalm 68. The psalmist is probably indicating that the two events together show an ongoing divine redemptive purpose.[7] A "straight way" suggests the later rather than the earlier events, although of course this was God's purpose in the exodus-entry situation also. Their cry in Egypt is recorded in Exod 2:23-25, and in Isa 51:9-11 the prophet cries for God to repeat the exodus in a new deliverance. Verses 8 and 9 introduce a continuing refrain that has varied conclusions.

107:10-16 If meant literally, this is difficult to link in detail with any OT narrative. The reference to rebellion suggests Babylonian exile rather than Egyptian slavery, but the reverse is true of the bitter labor. An allusion to King Jehoiachin's imprisonment is not impossible, and verse 16 clearly alludes to the work of Cyrus, through whom Babylon's captives received their freedom to return (Isa 45:2). This combined allusion to two major events suggests that

---

4. Mays, *Psalms*, 346.

5. In v. 3 the Hebrew reads מִיָּם, *mîyyām* ("from the sea"), which NIV and most commentators reckon a scribal error for מִיָּמִין, *mîyyāmîn*, ("from the south"), probably correctly. Motyer, however, suggests that "from the sea" may signify "from overseas" ("Psalms," 557).

6. This applies also to vv. 10 and 17 and to "others" in v. 23. This casts doubt on Mowinckel's view that this psalm accompanied a communal thank offering featuring the praise and offerings of different groups (*Psalms in Israel's Worship*, 2:42).

7. The apparent ambiguity here may show a deliberate typological intent, somewhat after the fashion of Isa 40–55, the two events being the gracious activities of the one God for the same people.

both manifested the same unfailing love of God. The reference to rebellion placed near the beginning underlines the cause of the exile.

107:17-22 Again rebellion points to the exile, and "fools" suggests a set godless character, the usual OT sense of this word (e.g., in Pss 14 and 53). A life-threatening illness is pictured. Verse 20 and Isaiah 38 are strikingly similar, and Isaiah 39 identifies Hezekiah's actions as a cause of the eventual Babylonian captivity. Thank offerings (v. 22) were highly appropriate after recovery from illness.

107:23-32 This, the longest picture section, is somewhat surprising, as ships at sea feature little in the OT. Allusion to Jonah is unlikely as the differences considerably outweigh any similarities. This reminds us that the stories are basically illustrations of God's covenant faithfulness and his responsiveness to urgent prayer. Verse 32 shows that acknowledgment of God's gracious actions should be public, not just private.

107:33-38 Here the pattern changes, but the emphasis on God's actions in relation to his people continues. His hand can be seen in their whole history, the bad times as well as the good. Significantly, as this psalm has major reference to the return from exile,[8] it is the land that features here, both its desolating, echoing Sodom and Gomorrah's destruction, and its subsequent blessing, with echoes both of the land's settling after the entry under Joshua and of the promises of Isaiah 35 and of Isa 41:18 (v. 35).

107:39-42 Here, with the same stress on God's acts, the psalm moves to more recent history, with reminders of the devastation caused by the Assyrians and Babylonians and the fact that the judgment of the exile had special relevance to the "nobles," the people's false shepherds. Now, though, the exile is over and the people are growing in numbers again.[9]

107:43 This conclusion shows this is not only a hymn but a wisdom psalm,[10] with historical lessons spelled out for practical instruction. Both this and the previous verse recall Hos 14:9, which comes at the close of a passage offering divine blessing in response to true penitence. The consecutive reader of the Psalter who recalled Psalm 1 when reading verse 42 would also think of 2:10 when reading this.

---

8. Compare particularly the repetition of ideas and language from vv. 4-9 in v. 36.

9. Some scholars reverse vv. 39 and 40; see Allen, *Psalms 101–150*, 84. Certainly v. 39 would read well as referring to the consequences of v. 40, but it is not impossible for a cause to be referred to after its effects.

10. For wisdom psalms see p. 18.

Psalm 108

Here begins a short Davidic group (Pss 108–110), the first such since book 2, although there are isolated Davidic psalms in books 3 and 4. This psalm combines praise, petition, complaint, and confidence, and is a combination of 57:7-11 and 60:5-12, with some minor variations. Both those psalms have superscriptions relating them to different periods in David's life, a time of danger and one of defeat. For details see comments on each.

It differs from either Psalm 57 or 60, giving a more positive emphasis by omitting the earlier part of each, although verse 11, with its perplexity, is retained. The first half (from Ps 57) is an address to God in the first person singular, which changes to the plural when the Psalm 60 section begins, returning briefly to the singular (v. 10) before resuming the plural. Thus are combined the king's roles as individual Israelite and as royal representative of the people, in whom the whole nation speaks in prayer and praise.

Psalm 109

Taken as a whole, this is the fiercest of the imprecatory psalms.[11] It has been understood in two quite different ways.

Some reckon verses 6-19 an imprecation against the psalmist rather than by him, pointing out that the enemies of verses 1-5 become one man in verses 6-19, while the plural is resumed in verse 20. They therefore view 6-19 as a lengthy quotation of his accusers, as in NRSV.

This is possible, but why did not the psalmist simply insert, "They say," at the start of verse 6? Moreover, verses 16 and 22 are somewhat similar, suggesting they emanate from the same person. If our problem is that they appear to have been uttered by a godly man, we should note that Jer 18:19-23, although briefer, is almost as fiercely imprecatory and is likewise from a man of God. Verse 8b is quoted of Judas in Acts 1:20, and attributed to the Holy Spirit through David in Acts 1:16.[12] The attribution to David accords with the reference to a sin against friendship in verses 4 and 5.

For all its difficulties, therefore, it seems best to see this psalm as a plea for God to make the punishment fit the crime, the very thing recognition of God as supreme judge implies.[13] Kidner comments, "David's curse, however

---

11. See pp. 19-21.

12. For NT use of this psalm see p. 334.

13. See Anderson, *Psalms*, 2:758-59; and also the full, clear discussion in Allen, *Psalms 101–150*, 72-73, although his conclusion differs from mine.

ugly its motivation, could still have been the vehicle of God's judgement, like the curse of Jotham (Jdg. 9:57)."[14]

109:1-5　It starts with praise and a call to God to answer those whose mouths speak lies, possibly in the context of a law court, and who reveal hatred against him.[15] Verses 4 and 5 can find illustration in Ahithophel's defection to Absalom. Verse 4b probably implies he has prayed for them.

109:6-15　The singular probably refers to the group's leader. The reference to an "evil man" may seem difficult, but God used evil nations in his judicial punishment of his people and even an evil spirit against Saul (1 Sam 16:14). Apparently the accuser stood at the right hand of an accused man in court (Zech 3:1). His prayers could be pleas for clemency, described by Davidson as "pseudopious."[16] The NASB renders verse 10b, "And let them seek *sustenance* far from their ruined homes" (the italics indicate the word is supplied). The NIV assumes a small element of textual corruption. Either is possible.[17] The references to his children, his wife, and his descendants show family solidarity (Exod 20:5) extending his personal punishment. Verse 12 seems exceptionally harsh, but in this context it will mean nobody should seek to turn aside the punitive implications of the divine verdict against him. Verses 14 and 15 imply that the man belongs to an ongoing evil family line. There is no suggestion of penitence, so we cannot know what the psalmist would have said if there had been.

109:16-20　The imprecatory note continues, fully based on quid pro quo. His lack of kindness is to be aptly requited (v. 16; cf. v. 12), and the unusual reference to "the brokenhearted" might point to bereavement, so that to be robbed of his children would again be payment in kind. The whole principle is summed up in verse 17. Verses 18 and 19, with their vivid imagery, suggest sin contains at least something of its punishment within itself. The plural resumes in verse 20, and the psalmist asks for personal vindication against those who wrongly speak evil of him.

109:21-25　There is now an emphatic appeal to the God of the covenant for deliverance.[18] He identifies himself as one of the victims described in

---

14. Kidner, *Psalms 73–150*, 390; see also Motyer's thought-provoking treatment of the issue ("Psalms," 559-60).

15. See the passage on false witnesses in Deut 19:15-21, and the comment on lying on pp. 328-30.

16. Davidson, *Vitality of Worship*, 361. Cf. Isa 1:15, which in its historical context may refer to prayers for clemency in the face of divine judgment through the Assyrians.

17. MT reads וְדָרְשׁוּ, *wĕdārĕšû*, while NIV assumes יְגֹרְשׁוּ, *yĕgōrĕšû*.

18. "You" in v. 20 is emphatic, meaning, "You, as over against my false accuser," and would fit the view that vv. 6-19 are the words of the accuser himself, although not necessarily.

verse 16, is treated as somebody of no account (v. 23), and even feels it himself (v. 24) when so scorned by his accusers (v. 25).

109:26-29   Once more he appeals to the Lord's covenant love (cf. v. 21), asking for an unambiguously divine vindication, using again the vivid language of clothing (v. 29; cf. vv. 18-19).

109:30-31   The imprecations over, he now gives God public praise. He had asked that his opponent would find an accuser standing at his right hand (v. 6); now he is assured that the God of the covenant will so stand by him.

Psalm 110

This royal psalm is attributed to David by Jesus, and the way he used it (Mark 12:35-37) makes it difficult to consider it less than fully messianic, not simply foreshadowing but predicting the Messiah.[19] If, as David Mitchell has argued, the redactor's ultimate purpose was to promote messianic anticipation,[20] this psalm's many links with Psalm 2 must be highly significant. Verses 1 and 4 record two related divine oracles, while verses 2 and 3 spell out the implications of the first and verses 5 and 6 those of the second.

110:1   Here, as in Psalm 2, two kings are introduced, the one Yahweh, the other David's *Adonai* ("lord" or "master"). So David writes not about himself nor, it would seem, about any normal dynastic successor, for he recognizes the superiority of the one about whom he writes. Yahweh's support for this king is total (cf. Ps 2), giving him power and honor (cf. 45:9; 1 Kgs 2:19) and promising that he will totally subdue all his enemies (cf. Josh 10:24; Isa 51:23). There is a possible link between verse 1b and Gen 3:15. Psalm 8 is another with two kings, Yahweh the majestic one and humanity as crowned and ruling over all God's works.

110:2-3   God's king reigns from Zion (cf. 2:6), but his rule extends beyond this to control his enemies (cf. 2:8; Isa 9:7, "increase"). In verse 3a there are possible allusions to the Gideon story (Judg 7:1-7), significant if, as seems likely, "the day of Midian" became shorthand for a great and surprising victory accomplished by God's power (Isa 9:4; 10:26). Like Gideon's three hundred, the Messiah's troops would be fully willing for battle (cf. also Judg 5:2).[21] "Holy majesty" may already suggest the combination of regal and

---

19. For NT use of this psalm see pp. 350, 357. For the messianism of the Psalter see pp. 348-49.

20. This is the thesis of his whole book, *Message of Psalter*.

21. The expression בְּהַדְרֵי־קֹדֶשׁ, *běhadrê-qōdeš*, rendered "holy majesty" in NIV, follows MT, but NRSV follows a minority of Hebrew MSS (supported by Symmachus and Jerome) that

priestly roles, and the remainder of verse 3 implies the king's constant freshness for the battle. Verse 3b is difficult, and is highly figurative, mixing metaphors. The king's arrival on the battlefield resembles the coming of God's light at dawn (perhaps because the enemies were in pagan darkness), and he will have all the vigor of youth, like vegetation refreshed and renewed by the dew. Wilcock puts it thus: "As the morning mysteriously brings forth the dew, so the king is miraculously refreshed and renewed."[22]

110:4 This alludes to Genesis 14. Just as Melchizedek, a pre-Davidic king in Jerusalem and a worshiper of the Most High God, was also a priest, so will the messianic king combine these offices, doing so not just by the promise but by the oath of God. The latter is associated with the Davidic covenant in 2 Sam 3:9 and Pss 89:3, 34-35; 132:11, and "forever" recalls 2 Sam 7:13-16.

110:5-7 "The Lord" here is probably Yahweh,[23] although the use of *Adonai* raises the possibility that he is the king of verse 1. The latter finds some support in the reference to the right hand in both verses 1 and 5, but of course such references are metaphorical. As Kidner says, "The scene has changed from throne to battlefield, to present this new aspect of the partnership."[24] In any case the king, being at God's right hand (v. 1), exercises the prerogatives of divine kingship, so that all here would be appropriate either of the divine or of the human king. His crushing victory of kingly foes is echoed in 2:9-12, and the nations they rule will share this crushing defeat (cf. 2:1ff.). There is a repetition of the promise that he would be constantly refreshed.

Psalm 111

This is the first of three praise psalms opening with "Hallelujah" ("Praise the LORD!"). It is a well-constructed acrostic,[25] as is Psalm 112.

111:1-6 The psalmist speaks his personal praise, not in isolation but when the people are assembled, probably for a festival. He places great stress on the Lord's works.[26] Are these his creative or his redemptive acts? Pon-

---

read בְּהַרְרֵי־קֹדֶשׁ, *běharěr-qōdeš*, "on the holy mountains." The priestly suggestiveness of the MT, however, is not out of tune with v. 4 and should probably be retained.

22. Wilcock, *Psalms 73–150*, 165. For other interpretations of v. 3 see Anderson, *Psalms,* 2:769-70; and Allen, *Psalms 101–150*, 117.

23. This is the most common interpretation. For others see Allen, *Psalms 101–150*, 117.

24. Kidner, *Psalms 73–150*, 396.

25. See p. 30. The acrostic commences after the opening "Hallelujah!"

26. Davidson points out how frequently the verb עָשָׂה, *'āśâ*, "do" or "make," occurs in this psalm (*Vitality of Worship*, 368).

dering (v. 2) may suggest either, for both are deep, but both the later context and "his righteousness" suggest the latter.[27] This phrase probably means that his deeds right what is wrong, which certainly would apply to the exodus.[28] "Verses 3-6 give a terse, allusive rehearsal of Israel's foundation story from Egypt to the promised land, drawing on the story as it is told from Genesis through Joshua."[29] Verse 4 takes up the Deuteronomic theme of remembrance,[30] and sees the gentler divine qualities of grace and compassion unfolded in his works. "He provides food" may be translated with a past tense, which would fit the context as a reference to the manna and quails in the wilderness (Exod 16; Num 11; cf. Ps 78:23-25). Verse 6 recalls that the entry to Canaan too was a mighty deed of God, fulfilling his promises.

111:7-10   Verse 7 is transitional, highlighting first the divine moral attributes revealed in his historical acts, then moving to the Law, the product of the same faithful divine character, probably implying the blessedness of such a benign legal regime. The NIV, NASB, and NRSV all appear to see verse 8 as continuing the reference to God's character, but it could indicate his people's responsibilities.[31] Either suits the context, although, if Psalms 111 and 112 are complementary, the first focusing on God and the second on the man of God, this would support the NIV. Verse 9's reference to redemption recalls the exodus, while the rest of the verse alludes to the Sinai covenant and its revelation of God's utter holiness. There is a linguistic link between "awesome" (v. 9) and "fear" (v. 10). This closing verse presents a key thought for all the wisdom literature,[32] and shows the connection between wisdom and the Law, for the former is not speculative but rooted in divine revelation. The psalm ends as it began, with praise.

Psalm 112

This is a praise psalm (though with a strong wisdom element in it) and the second of three that begin, "Praise the LORD!" ("Hallelujah!").[33] A close com-

---

27. For righteousness see pp. 249-50.

28. Broyles provides a detailed comparison with other OT passages, especially in Exodus (*Psalms,* 419).

29. Mays, *Psalms,* 356.

30. Cf. also Exod 12:14. The term זֵכֶר, *zēker,* translated "remembrance," is rendered "gained renown" in NRSV, as it can also indicate proclamation.

31. Allen translates v. 8b: "to be performed with faithfulness and uprightness" (*Psalms 101–150,* 89).

32. See, e.g., Job 28:28; Prov 1:7; 9:10; Eccl 12:13. On the wisdom psalms see p. 18.

33. For NT use of this psalm see p. 349. For wisdom psalms see p. 18.

panion of Psalm 111, it has a similar acrostic structure,[34] and it develops the thought of 111:10. One was clearly composed with the other in view. Psalm 111 concerns God, and 112 godliness, the one the product and, because God is concerned to conform his people to his character, the counterpart of the other. Wilcock traces out the main points of comparison particularly well.[35]

112:1   Here the thought of 111:10 is expressed in different words, with God's praise introducing the verse instead of closing it, both appropriate in view of the position of these verses in their respective psalms. Comparing the two verses shows a virtual identification of wisdom and blessing, with the Law featuring positively in each. "Blessed" is אַשְׁרֵי, *'ašrê,* ("happy"), as in Psalm 1, and the whole verse reminds us of that psalm.

112:2-9   The blessing is not simply individual but family-related. Here power and riches are linked to blessing, perhaps on the analogy of the wealth of the patriarchs (cf. also Prov 3:9-10). This person is both righteous and gracious, with unshakable uprightness and overflowing generosity. Verse 4 has been differently translated. The NIV glances realistically at possible problems for this person but asserts that even in dark days there will be light (cf. Isa 58:8, 10), presumably sufficient to walk righteously and graciously. Kidner translates the verse, "He rises in the darkness, a light to the upright; he is gracious, merciful and righteous," thus continuing the portrait of the righteous person.[36] Either is possible, the former continuing the thought of verses 1-3 and the latter providing a transition to verses 5 and 6. Broyles, surely rightly, rejects Brueggemann's description of this person as probably well off, economically secure and politically significant, and says, "Order needs to be affirmed most strongly in times of disorder."[37] Here character is clearly based on trust in the Lord (v. 7). Verse 8, where "secure" means "supported" (i.e., by the Lord), implies that life will have its troubles and the righteous person will have foes, but that vindication will ultimately come from God. "His horn" implies power and honor, and verse 9c expounds its meaning, apparently tautologically but intending emphasis.

112:10   This also recalls Psalm 1 for us, although here the wicked person is dismissed in one verse.

---

34. See p. 18 and comments on Ps 111.

35. Wilcock, *Psalms 73–150,* 171-75. See also Davidson, *Vitality of Worship,* 369-71; Mays, *Psalms,* 359-61.

36. Kidner, *Psalms 73–150,* 399; cf. also Weiser, *Psalms,* 703-4.

37. Broyles, *Psalms,* 421.

Psalm 113

This is both the last of a trio starting, "Praise the LORD!" (Hallelujah!), and also the first in the Egyptian Hallel.[38] It is an exquisite and quite complex piece of Hebrew poetry, presenting "a theology of wonder which speaks of a God whose greatness goes hand in hand with his compassion for those most at risk in life."[39]

113:1-3   Praise dominates these verses to an exceptional degree, הָלַל, *hallal* ("praise!"), coming four times in verses 1 and 2a, followed by יָהּ, *yāh*, "Yah," once, then יהוה, *yhwh*, "Yahweh," three times. NASB and NRSV show that verse 2 commences with בָּרַךְ, *bārak* ("bless"), which the NIV translators clearly saw as simply stylistic variation. The word "servants" for worshipers anticipates the reference to Yahweh's exaltation in verses 4 and 5. They praise his name, so their submissive response as servants is to his self-revelation, "the loving homage of the committed to the Revealed."[40] Verses 2b and 3 move beyond local worship to show a God who is to be worshiped in all time and space.

113:4-6   These verses extol Yahweh's greatness to a degree exceptional even for the Psalter. Verse 4 sees him exalted not only above the earth, but even above the heavens (cf. 57:11; 148:13; cf. 8:1), verses 5 and 6 confirming this with the unusual affirmation that he looks down on both (cf. 1 Kgs 8:27). His exaltation is kingly, and the adoring rhetorical question of verse 5 recalls exultant questions in Exod 15:11; Isa 40:18, 21-22, 25; and Mic 7:18-20.

113:7-9   The thought moves from God's greatness to his care of the needy, remarkably anticipated at the human level in 112:3-9. In verses 7 and 8 the language of exaltation is now applied not to God but to the objects of his grace. Verses 7 and 8 employ, almost exactly, Hannah's words in 1 Sam 2:8. Moreover, verse 9 fits this context perfectly, finding illustration in Hannah's experience. Those singing the psalm after the exile would probably recall Isa 54:1, for what God promises here to do for the individual he also did for the nation. The psalm ends, as it began, with "Praise the LORD" (cf. Pss 105 and 106).[41]

---

38. For general comment on Pss 113–118 see pp. 11, 16.

39. Davidson, *Vitality of Worship*, 373. Its poetic features do not much affect interpretation, but are noted in Allen, *Psalms 101–150*, 135-36. See also Wilcock, *Psalms 73–150*, 113-14.

40. Kidner, *Psalms 73–150*, 401.

41. But see comment on 114:1.

Psalm 114

An unmistakable atmosphere of joy here turns to awe in verses 7 and 8.[42]

114:1-2   Psalm 113, the first Egyptian Hallel psalm, does not mention the exodus, but shows the kind of God, exalted above the nations yet concerned to raise the needy, revealed in that event. The present psalm, however, is most explicit. The LXX treats 113's closing Hallelujah as opening this psalm, making it the last of four in sequence starting thus. This is quite feasible, especially as in the Hebrew verse 2 has simply "his sanctuary," implying rather than expressing a reference to God. The phrase "a people of a foreign tongue" recalls Israel's sense of alienation in Egypt. Is "Israel" (v. 2) the whole people or the northern kingdom? It probably designates the same people as "Judah" (the southern kingdom), Israel's sole representative after the northern kingdom's fall.[43] Kidner remarks on the dramatic change of status between the first verse and the second, where the people are settled in the land.[44] Many commentators point out the parallel between Exod 19:6 and verse 2.

114:3-4   The joyful lyricism here embraces the Red Sea and Jordan crossings and probably (in v. 4) the dramatic accompaniments of the Sinai revelation (Exod 19:16-19), but as yet without explicit reference to their divine cause.

114:5-6   These verses, with their rhetorical questions, take up the language of the previous stanza, again without express reference to God, to prepare the way for verses 7 and 8.

114:7-8   Here, following "this majestic whimsicality,"[45] the psalmist makes clear that all this agitated movement is due to God. The word אֶרֶץ, *ereṣ*, can mean either "earth" or "land," implying that Sinai's trembling should be reproduced either in Canaan or in the whole world. Then, as in Psalm 113, the thought moves from God as great to God as compassionate, providing by miraculous power for his people's bodily needs (Exod 17:6).

Psalm 115

The LXX and some Hebrew manuscripts unite this psalm of praise and confidence to Psalm 114, probably mistakenly as their styles are utterly different.

---

42. For general comment on Pss 113–118 see pp. 11, 16.

43. Allen, *Psalms 101–150*, 103.

44. Kidner, *Psalms 73–150*, 403.

45. Allen, *Psalms 101–150*, 105. Mays too comments on the almost playful atmosphere of this psalm (*Psalms*, 364).

This psalm does not mention the exodus, but its theme of trust in Israel's ever-active God, not in false gods, is appropriate in celebration of God's liberating acts for Israel.[46]

115:1-2 The negation is doubled for emphasis. "Glory" is anarthrous (contra NIV), so the disclaimer may be general, or else it could relate to an event provoking the question of verse 2, in which case it is, in effect, "an urgent plea that God should act decisively to defend himself, his own power and his own authority, which are now under attack."[47] The question of the nations may be due to the Babylonian captivity, and, in the verses that follow, "the psalm, in effect, mocks their mockery."[48] But first the psalmist extols God's covenant faithfulness, manifest in every generation.

115:3-8 The question is answered, possibly at the festival by a priest or prophet,[49] in terms of God's active sovereignty. "Where is he? Why, in heaven, sovereignly controlling everything!" The contrast of Israel's God with idols made by human hands, and so impotent, is a special theme of Isaiah 40–48 (cf. Jer 10:1-16),[50] and verses 4-8 here recur in Ps 135:15-18. Their bodily parts are detailed, but their inability to speak is specially stressed, for the speech organs are referred to twice. In contrast, of course (though not stated here), Israel has the great privilege of God's Word. Verse 8 recalls Psalms 111 and 112, where a comparison of the two shows the godly being conformed to their God's character. People become like the objects of their worship.

115:9-11 Here is obvious contrast with the useless trust of verse 8. The verbal form used three times in verses 9-11 is treated by NIV, NASB, and NRSV as imperative, on the analogy of 118:2-4 and 135:19-20, but it could be indicative, yielding the sense, "the house of Israel trusts in Yahweh," which seems more natural in view of the threefold "their" (rather than "your") help and shield. The first two groups are the people and the priests, while the third probably includes Gentile worshipers of Israel's God. Perhaps it is the origin of "God-fearer," a technical term in the NT for such worshipers.

115:12-13 The assertion that God remembers them recalls Exod 2:24-25, perhaps making a parallel between Israel's Egyptian and Babylonian captivities, so inspiring confidence. A general affirmation of God's intention to bless is then applied to each group.

115:14-15 The theme of blessing continues. The family allusion recalls the blessing of the righteous man in Psalm 112 (cf. also Gen. 22:17; Deut 1:11).

---

46. For general comment on Pss 113–118 see pp. 11, 16.
47. Davidson, *Vitality of Worship*, 376; cf. Ezek 36:22-23; 39:7, etc.
48. Broyles, *Psalms*, 433.
49. See pp. 7, 15.
50. See esp. Isa 44:9-20.

The reference to God as Creator recalls that it is the nations who raise questions about God (v. 2), and "those who fear the LORD" may include Gentiles.

115:16-18 Verse 16 looks back to verse 3, but goes on to acknowledge God's gift of life to be used to praise him. Verse 17 perhaps operates within the OT horizon of a godly life in this world, and its "not" could form a kind of inclusio with the "not" of verse 1.[51] On the other hand, verse 18 may go further if "for evermore" means more than simply "in every Israelite generation," perhaps showing verse 17 to be only a tentative statement, reversed in this final verse.[52]

Psalm 116

This thanksgiving psalm contains some Aramaisms, suggesting a postexilic date. It has a similar flavor to many of the Davidic psalms, so its author had probably nourished his devotional life on them.[53] The LXX, followed by the Vulgate, divides it after verse 9, but it has both good form and good sense as a unity.[54] For instance, the verb "call" (vv. 2 and 4) later becomes part of a virtual refrain in verses 13-14 and 17-18, and these, possibly with verse 7, provide natural structure markers.[55] Mays's comment that verse 7 is "probably a rhetorical statement of an intention to visit the temple as the sphere where God's presence provides relief and security," so that each of the three parts "concludes with a performance statement,"[56] is somewhat conjectural, but possible.

116:1-7 This begins simply "I love," without any expressed object,[57] although he is clearly thinking of Yahweh.[58] He will always call on him, for God's answer (mentioned three times in vv. 1 and 2) betokens constant willingness to hear him. Verses 3 and 4 are reminiscent of the hunting imagery in 18:4-6. He was clearly near death.[59] "On the name of the LORD" begins the Hebrew sentence, giving it emphasis (v. 4). Verse 5 recalls the godly person's description in 112:4, showing how such a person reflected God's character. "Simplehearted" is too flattering a translation, as the Hebrew word normally

51. See Wilcock, *Psalms 73–150*, 181-82.
52. Kidner's comment moves in this direction (*Psalms 73–150*, 406-7).
53. For NT use of this psalm see p. 307; and for general comment on Pss 113–118 see pp. 11, 16.
54. Allen makes extended reference to its structure (*Psalms 101–150*, 153-54).
55. See Mays, *Psalms*, 369. On the refrain see Kidner, *Psalms 73–150*, 408.
56. Mays, *Psalms*, 369.
57. This applies also to "call" in v. 2.
58. This is spelled out in 18:1, although the verb there is different. Here it is אָהַב, 'āhab.
59. "The grave" here is שְׁאוֹל, šĕ'ôl. See p. 44.

implies naive stupidity (e.g., in Prov 8:5; 9:4; 14:15). Verse 6b simply sums up verses 3 and 4. Self-address (v. 7) is somewhat unusual in the psalms, and here, unlike Psalms 42–43, apparently needs no repetition.

116:8-14 The address to God resumes, with reference not only to deliverance from death and sorrow but from stumbling, which, because of the link between verses 8 and 9, suggests going astray from God. His life was now to be lived for God, the verb "walk" reminding one of 1:1. The parallel between "I love" (v. 1) and "I believed" (v. 10), both without grammatical object, is inadequate warrant for the LXX's division into two psalms. Indeed, it may reveal deep feeling,[60] so providing evidence of unity. Because he believed and could trust God completely, he could tell him his troubles and his concern about human unreliability.

Rescue calls for response and verses 12-14, together with 17-19, seem to imply thanksgiving in public, perhaps (as this is part of the Egyptian Hallel), at Passover. The cup is probably a drink offering (cf. the thank offering in v. 17) and the vows a public expression of gratitude.

116:15-19 He reflects on his salvation as evidence of the Lord's concern for him when he was at the point of death and the paradoxical fact that he has been set free (with "chains" now the equivalent of "cords" in v. 3) for God's service, which he sees, without explanation, as continuing his mother's service. The master was expected to have concern for his servant, so that NIV "truly," which takes account of an emphatic particle, means God's actions have given the psalmist assurance.[61] The thank offering was a festal meal, shared with others in the Lord's presence (Lev 7:11-21). Verse 18 confirms and underlines the commitment of verse 14, and verse 19 makes clear its public setting. The ending "Praise the Lord!" ("Hallelujah!") is certainly appropriate, although the LXX may be right in transferring it to the start of Psalm 117.

Psalm 117

No psalm is shorter in length or larger in its theme. It is addressed to all nations (cf. Pss 96, 97, and 100), implicitly rebuking their paganism, for Yahweh is, of course, the God of Israel. Not only so, but it is his covenant love for Israel for which the nations are to praise him![62] This extends into the future, an

---

60. So Harman, *Psalms*, 372.

61. Cf. Allen, *Psalms 101–150*, 112; Anderson, *Psalms*, 2:795.

62. For NT use of this psalm see p. 301; and for general comment on Pss 113–118 see pp. 11, 16.

idea already implicit in "faithfulness," but spelled out in "endures forever."[63] This harmonizes well with the general thrust of OT teaching and narrative, in which Yahweh's purpose for non-Israelites is that they should acknowledge Israel's God as theirs also. So at Passover this psalm was sung, looking forward to universal worship, just as Zechariah 14 predicts in connection with Tabernacles. The psalm ends, like several other Egyptian Hallel psalms, with "Praise the LORD!" *(Hallelujah!).* "Its cosmic applicability makes this psalm a little jewel."[64]

Psalm 118

This psalm of thanksgiving and confidence presents some difficulties, but its main thrust is clear, and it fitly closes the Egyptian Hallel.[65] There are sections in the first singular (vv. 5-7, 10-12, 17-21, 28), but one employs the plural (vv. 23-27), so most commentators think the individual speaker is the king or a national leader like Nehemiah, coming to the temple with his people, for whom he speaks as their representative. The occasion is a festival (v. 27), probably the Passover, but the historical setting cannot be clearly identified. It has marked links with Exodus 15. After showing links between verses 14 and 28 and Exod 15:2, and verses 15 and 16 and Exod 15:6, Mitchell Dahood says that these plus the psalm's economy of language indicate an early date,[66] although many commentators view it as postexilic.

118:1-4 Verse 1 is identical with 106:1 and 107:1, suggesting a standard ascription of praise to the God of covenant love. There is a call, perhaps by a priest, for this affirmation to be uttered by three groups, probably the same as in 115:9-11.[67]

118:5-9 The speaker's record of his experience may be Israel's put into individual terms by the king, for freedom suggests the exodus and the anguished cry of Exod 2:23-25, and his confidence before his foes may be national faith in God engendered by the redemption from Egypt. If the psalm is postexilic, however, it could be freedom from Babylon put in language recalling the earlier liberation. Verses 8 and 9 may be spoken by either leader or

63. For the universalism of the psalms see comment on Pss 65–67.

64. VanGemeren, "Psalms," 729.

65. For NT use of this psalm see pp. 319, 358; and for general comment on Pss 113–118 see pp. 11, 16.

66. Dahood, *Psalms,* 3:156.

67. See comment on 115:9-11.

people, expressing lessons learned in experience. Princes, of course, represent rulers with considerable human resources.

118:10-16   If the speaker is the ruler, it seems ironic that this follows the reference to princes, but he does not achieve victory in his own power but only in the name of the Lord, as David did when facing Goliath (1 Sam 17:45-48). The reference may not be to one event, but to continuous victory given by God when the nation trusted in him, not in itself. The threefoldness of verses 10-12 is probably again liturgical, following the pattern of verses 2-4. The verb אֲמִילַם, *'ămîlam*, translated "cut off," most often means "to circumcise,"[68] but here the similes of bees and fire suggest the alternative sense "to ward off," as in the LXX. A recent deliverance perhaps (v. 15) was not easy,[69] but the king proved to be God's help, so that he could sing the Song of Moses, for verse 14 exactly reproduces Exod 15:2 (cf. also v. 21), and the threefold reference to the Lord's right hand, probably liturgical, recalls Exod 15:6. The tents may be Israel's army's dwellings or the temporary homes of Passover pilgrims.

118:17-21   Rescue from death after severe chastening (a possible reference to the exile) prompts thankful proclamation of God's act, taking place within the city gates or, more likely, those of the temple, for "righteousness" and "righteous" recall Psalms 15 and 24 and their entrance liturgies.

118:22-24   The procession nears the temple. Perhaps a discarded stone prompts the thought that Israel, little regarded by others, has been greatly used by God. The capstone is a keystone tying others together or, if it is the final one, showing the architectural plan's perfect execution (cf. Isa. 28:16). So the people rejoice on this special festival day.

118:25-27   The prayer is for God to continue his saving activity. Verse 26 suggests that the people already in the temple were blessing those now advancing, first the leader, then those accompanying him ("you" is plural). "Light" recalls Num 6:25, suggesting that the blessing (v. 26) was pronounced by priests. Verse 27 is difficult to translate and interpret. The NIV text and margin represent different renderings, but it is clear that the procession is reaching its goal at the altar.[70] The marginal reading makes good sense and may be correct.

118:28-29   In verse 28 the solo voice is probably the leader's, expressing his personal gratitude, then taken up as the people repeat the words of verse 1.

---

68. Dahood compares this with the event mentioned in 1 Sam 18:25-29 (*Psalms*, 3:157-58).

69. "Deliverance" or "salvation" (NASB) is to be preferred to "victory," in view of the verbal link with v. 14.

70. Davidson, *Vitality of Worship*, 387; Anderson, *Psalms*, 2:804-5; Allen, *Psalms 101–150*, 163.

Psalm 119

This is the supreme acrostic psalm, arranged according to the twenty-two Hebrew letters, with eight verses given to each, each verse commencing with the governing Hebrew letter of the section.[71] It employs eight different terms for the "word" of God, which, with their regular NIV equivalents, are as follows: תּוֹרָה, *tôrâ* ("law");[72] דָּבָר, *dābār* ("word"), מִשְׁפָּטִים, *mišpāṭîm* ("laws"), עֵדוֹת, *'ēdōt* ("statutes"), מִצְוֹת, *miṣwōt* ("commands"); חֻקִּים, *ḥuqqîm* ("decrees"), פִּקּוּדִים, *piqqûdîm* ("precepts"), and אִמְרָה, *'imrâ* ("promise," but occasionally "word"). The psalm treats them as virtual synonyms. Kidner gives helpful comments on each.[73] The Qumran scroll of this psalm has six verses differing from the MT as to the synonym employed.

It stands between two groups associated with pilgrim feasts, the Egyptian Hallel (113–118), linked with Passover, and the Songs of Ascents (120–134), linked with Tabernacles. Between these two feasts stood Pentecost, and between the two psalm groups stands this psalm with its emphasis on the law. It is no surprise therefore that the Jews came to link it with Pentecost. Certainly its placing strongly suggests that the Psalter's ultimate compiler saw its special appropriateness to Sinai. The law here is no abstraction, but is *God's* law. We should recall too that Sinai, like the pilgrim feasts, was a worship occasion (Exod 3:18; 24:1-11).

There are traces in it of the influence of other OT books, especially (and most markedly) Deuteronomy but also Proverbs, Isaiah, and Jeremiah.[74]

The arrangement looks haphazard, and there have been various attempts to "correct" it, but close study shows careful design. Apart from verses 1-3 and 115, every verse is addressed to God, so it is really an extended prayer constituted as a wisdom psalm by its introduction.[75] Many expressions in it are characteristic of laments (e.g., in vv. 25, 50, and 146),[76] and some writers classify it accordingly.[77]

119:1-8 (Aleph) This section is an appropriate opening. Verses 1-3 are highly reminiscent of Psalm 1. Then verses 4-6 express the psalmist's concern

---

71. On acrostic psalms, see pp. 29-30.

72. See pp. 263-64.

73. Kidner, *Psalms 73–150*, 417-19. His commentary is on the RSV, but the NIV equivalents can easily be found from the forms transliterated from the Hebrew.

74. These cannot be explored here, but see Allen, *Psalms 101–150*, 180-92.

75. For wisdom psalms see p. 18. Freedman et al. (*Psalm 119*) is a valuable study of the form and theology of this psalm.

76. See Sheriffs, *Friendship of the Lord,* 120.

77. E.g., Soll, *Psalm 119*, 59-86.

to obey (cf. Deut 5:29), followed by praise for God's laws (v. 7) and personal commitment to them. Verse 8 makes clear that divine aid is needed to undergird this commitment.

119:9-16 (Beth) Proverbs 1–7 show a man instructing his son. The verses here focus on the young man, for verse 8 may govern the whole section. The psalmist recognizes his proneness to sin (vv. 9-11) and is committed to living according to the Word wholeheartedly, learning it, thinking about it, and delighting in it, all with a view to practical living.

119:17-24 (Gimel) His deep commitment to God's instruction is reiterated; he asks God to teach him, aware of his morally alien environment. The word "stranger" may recall not only the Egyptian and Babylonian captivities, but also that the promised land was God's (cf. Lev 25:23).

119:25-32 (Daleth) In some way his life is threatened (v. 25), sorrow has drained all his energy (v. 28), and others seek to shame him (v. 31). Moreover, he is aware of his own sinful tendencies (v. 29), but is committed to follow God's instruction, so looks to him for strength and grace. The word דֶּרֶךְ, *derek* ("way"), occurs in verses 26, 29, and 30, and is rendered "path" in verse 32. This verse views commitment to God's law not as bondage but as exhilarating liberty.

119:33-40 (He) Wilcock points out that this letter is the characteristic initial letter of causative verbs,[78] so it is not surprising to find here strong emphasis on God's activity in teaching, directing, and redirecting. Clearly the psalmist's own obedience depends on God's prior grace.

119:41-48 (Waw) This letter is the simple conjunction "and," tying all the verses together, and, occurring in verse 41, it unites the section to all that precedes it. This section is like a brief summary of God's law in itself, touching so many of the great themes of the rest of the psalm. The psalmist begins by looking to the Lord as God of the covenant, for "unfailing love" is covenant faithfulness. He loves God's Word, is committed to it, meditates on it, finds freedom in it, answers his enemies out of it, declares it even in the presence of kings, and lifts up his hands in prayer.

119:49-56 (Zayin) He calls on the Lord to remember his word to him, for in God he has found hope and comfort, much needed for his life has been in danger, presumably from the attacks of the wicked, who feature greatly here. His commitment to God's law is firm, for he will recall God's laws and his name (vv. 52, 55) wherever he stays, by night or day, and as shown in his constant practice.

119:57-64 (Heth) Behind the revealed Word stands the God who has re-

---

78. Wilcock, *Psalms 73–150*, 198.

vealed it, and both are in view here. God is his portion (this is the language of inheritance),[79] he has sought God's face and seeks his grace, singing at midnight to thank him, finding friends among those who fear him, and discovering the earth to be full of his love. No wonder the words of such a God are precious to him! He seeks to obey.

119:65-72 (Teth) Four verses here begin with טוֹב, *ṭôb* ("good"), for "precious" in verse 72 is this same word and it begins the verse, so the idea of the divine goodness dominates this section. Verse 65's opening verb should probably be seen as imperfect, not imperative, and be rendered, "You did good," so that the verse means God has kept his promise of blessing (cf. Ps 1). Affliction has actually gladdened him, teaching him to respect and value God's laws, an outlook not shared by those hardened in their wickedness.

119:73-80 (Yodh) The psalmist recognizes the Lord as both his creator and revealer. Here God's moral attributes are much to the fore, his righteousness, faithfulness (seen in the psalmist's afflictions, presumably with vv. 67 and 71 still in mind), his unfailing love, sure promise, and compassion. He wants to understand God's Word, so meditates on it. Verse 80 shows his sense of dependence on God if he is to keep his decrees from his heart.

119:81-88 (Kaph) He has a distinct sense of threat from enemies, and no part of this anonymous psalm is more like the Davidic laments. There is even an imprecatory verse (v. 84), and he puts a number of passionate questions to God.[80] Despite all his troubles, however, he is still set on doing God's will. The analogy of verse 83 relates to the wineskin's ruined state. "His afflictions have left their mark on him."[81]

119:89-96 (Lamedh) How fitting this section is after its predecessor! Verses 89-91 are full of confidence: in God's Word, which is eternal; in his faithfulness, which never ends; and in his laws, which are as enduring as the earth itself. The next two verses affirm how much he owes to God's law, and verses 94 and 95 reaffirm his commitment to it. On verse 96 Kidner remarks that it could easily serve as a summary of Ecclesiastes.[82]

119:97-104 (Mem) Here we see how greatly he values God's law, loving it (cf. vv. 47, 48, 113, 119, 127, 159, 163), meditating on it, finding that it gives him wisdom, insight, and understanding beyond anything human teachers can impart, so that he keeps God's commands, finding his Word a constant delight.

---

79. See comment on 16:5-6.
80. For the imprecations of the Psalter see pp. 19-21.
81. Harman, *Psalms*, 390.
82. Kidner, *Psalms 73–150*, 426-27.

119:105-112 (Nun)   The thought of the blessedness of God's Word continues here in verses 105 and 111, but the main theme now is the psalmist's commitment to it, despite his sufferings and the snares set for him by the wicked. Verse 112 sums this up.

119:113-120 (Samekh)   The psalmist has shown great decisiveness, so his opening sentiment here is understandable. He trusts God as his refuge, with the assumption that evildoers are bent on harm. Verse 115 is the only one (apart from vv. 1-3) not addressed to God, but is just as God-centered. The psalmist knows that God shares his attitude to the wicked (v. 119). Because his confidence is in God, he does not fear them, but stands in awe of God and his laws.

119:121-128 (Ayin)   Verses 121-124 consist of appeals to God to come to his aid (cf. v. 126). He then requests teaching, reaffirming his delight in the law and his commitment to it. Verses 121 and 122 are unusual in not mentioning God or his word, but they are nevertheless God-centered because they are prayers.

119:129-136 (Pe)   Again we see his delight in God's statutes, which are wonderful, enlightening and giving guidance. He loves God's name, wanting to live in the light of his pleasure (cf. Num 6:22-27) and to understand his will. Verse 136 is unique in the Psalter in showing how deeply the psalmist's emotions were affected by disobedience to God, rather like Paul's feelings when encountering Athenian idolatry in Acts 17:16.

119:137-144 (Tsadhe)   Righteousness dominates these verses, the righteousness of God's character and his laws,[83] righteousness that guarantees the truth of his promises and law. Despite the trouble caused by his enemies, his commitment to God's Word never wavers.

119:145-152 (Qoph)   Wholeheartedness is the key here. Both in his prayers and his meditation on God's Word there is a commitment constantly controlling him. He calls on God in the conviction of his love, his nearness, and the eternity of his Word.

119:153-160 (Resh)   His troubles from his enemies almost dominate this section rather as in some Davidic psalms, but he is not overwhelmed, for he looks confidently to God to deliver him, assured of his compassion and the truth of his Word, which he loves.

119:161-168 (Sin/Shin)   Verse 161 shows that the psalmist lives under a godless, lawless regime, but despite persecution he has great peace from God. Isaiah 66:2 shows the blessing of those who tremble at God's word, and our present verses are paradoxical for he both trembles and rejoices in what God

---

83. For righteousness see pp. 249-50.

says. Of course, the two sides of the paradox meet in godly experience. He loves the law so much and is so concerned to obey it that he is constantly praising God for it.

119:169-176 (Taw)   This sums up much said earlier. He is concerned for practical understanding, for deliverance from his enemies; he sees the laws of God as righteous and delights in them, expressing this delight in praise. The final verse, like the ending of Psalm 19 (vv. 12-14), shows his awareness of failure, but affirms his concern to serve God by keeping his law.

Psalm 120

Wilcock, following Goulder, argues persuasively that the Songs of Ascents (Pss 120–134) as a collection may have been first used at the Feast of Tabernacles in 445 BC, when Jerusalem's walls were rebuilt.[84] The names Jerusalem and Zion occur twelve times. This psalm was probably seen as appropriate for people who, though living in Judah in Nehemiah's time, felt the environment to be alien because of the antagonistic presence of the Samaritans.

120:1-2   Allen has well remarked that the psalm hovers between promise and fulfillment, like so much of the Bible.[85] It begins rather like a Davidic lament, but with implied gratitude also for God's anticipated answer. It is the deceit of his enemies (Sanballat's company?) that troubles the psalmist here.[86]

120:3-4   Verse 3 is apparently based on the self-imprecation formula found in passages like 1 Sam 14:44 and 2 Sam 3:9. He is sure God's punishment will fully fit the sin. The best charcoal was made from broom tree wood.

120:5-7   Meshech was on the shores of the Black Sea (Ezek 38:2), and Kedar designates Arab tribespeople (Ezek 27:21) living south of Israel. So a strictly literal interpretation is impossible, for the psalmist could hardly be in two places at once. Allen discusses this fully, then says, "the most common interpretation is to judge the ethnic references to be simply metaphorical: the psalmist's enemies are no better than hostile barbarians."[87] Their deceitful tongues, therefore, were apparently used to foment strife. Mays sees peace (שָׁלוֹם, *šālôm*) as the psalm's central issue and as determining its place at the head of this collection, for it figures much in the Songs of Ascents. It is a much richer idea than our English word expresses, for it embraces whole well-being.[88]

---

84. Wilcock, *Psalms 73–150*, 221, Goulder, *Psalms of the Return*, passim.
85. Allen, *Psalms 101–150*, 202.
86. Neh 4:1-5; 6:1-14, etc. For lying see pp. 328-30.
87. Allen, *Psalms 101–150*, 202.
88. Mays, *Psalms*, 389.

Psalm 121

This psalm of confidence is unique among its group as being not a song of ascents but rather "a song for ascents,"[89] underlining its obvious reference to pilgrimage.

121:1-2   The pilgrim passes through hills en route to or from Jerusalem. The former fits the psalm sequence better, as in Psalm 120 the psalmist is away from Jerusalem while in 122 he is in it. How does he view the hills? If positively, they will remind him of God's strength, perhaps as the Rock (cf., e.g., 18:2). If negatively, they will be places of danger from robbers or else be crowned with pagan shrines.[90] The last seems the more likely in view of verses 5 and 6, especially if this is postexilic and the land had been peopled by foreigners. There can be no help from them, but only from Yahweh, who made far more than the hills.

121:3-4   Here the pilgrim addresses himself (cf. Pss 42–43 and 103:3-5), although some consider this a dialogue with somebody else, probably a priest, but this would fit best if he was leaving rather than entering Jerusalem.[91] His journey would be over rocky ground, especially dangerous if undertaken partly at night. The emphatic הִנֵּה, *hinnēh*, translated "indeed," introduces a general statement of God's unsleeping concern for Israel, so his assurance is grounded in his protection of the whole people. This may be in contrast to Baal, who as a nature deity needed awakening from a seasonal sleep (cf. 1 Kgs 18:27).

121:5-6   Protection is now from the heavenly bodies, particularly apt if these are pagan deities worshiped at the hilltop shrines. If the fear of sunstroke and so-called moonstroke (cf. our "lunatic") are in view, they are "examples of the many vicissitudes that bring fears both rational and irrational."[92]

121:7-8   The psalmist returns from the particular to the general, closing with comprehensive assurance. The "coming and going," often referring to the journey to and from work (Deut 28:6), probably here represents the regular pilgrimage journeys to and from Jerusalem. No matter how long life is, the protection will be constant, "for evermore" even perhaps suggesting life beyond death.

---

89. לַמַּעֲלוֹת, *lammaʿălôt*, instead of הַמַּעֲלוֹת, *hammaʿălôt*.

90. Allen, after a full note on the interpretation, regards line B as an indirect question, and he translates it, "to see from where is to come my help," yet another possibility (*Psalms 101–150*, 206-7).

91. Anderson, *Psalms*, 2:851; Davidson, *Vitality of Worship*, 407-8.

92. Allen, *Psalms 101–150*, 208.

Psalm 122

This Davidic psalm of Zion,[93] apt throughout the people's history, becomes highly appropriate in this pilgrimage group. The Hebrew perfect tense of the verbs "to stand," "to go up," and "to sit," in verses 2, 4, and 5, probably has a present sense (as in NIV), for in verse 3 the psalmist is apparently surveying the city from inside its gates.

122:1-2 The proposal to "go up" is a technical term for worship at Jerusalem (Isa 2:3; Jer 31:6; cf. Ps 24:3). The psalmist may have started, with others, in some remote place. In verse 2 they are at the city but not necessarily yet at the house of God.

122:3-5 The psalmist's joy (v. 1) leads him to survey the city, lovingly reviewing its merits. Broyles refers to its "virtually sacramental significance, symbolizing God as protector," and he refers to 48:12-14.[94] The psalmist sees it as the well-ordered focus of the national unity (cf. 48:12-13). Its status as the worship center was established by divine statute (Deut 12:13-14; 16:1-17). The combination of joy (v. 1) and law (v. 4; cf. Exod 23:14-17) reminds us of the delight in the law often shown in Psalm 119. As the capital it recalled the dynasty, and perhaps therefore God's dynastic promise (2 Sam 7), and the need for just rule (cf. Ps 72). Both emphases would recall Psalms 1 and 2 for the consecutive reader.

122:6-9 Hebrews 7:2 links "Jerusalem" and "peace," for *Salem* is from the same root as שָׁלוֹם, *šālôm*, "peace," used three times in these verses. The psalmist seems to be praying that it will live up to its name. Peace within the walls implies security from external foes, but the threefold "within" suggests to some commentators that it is internal peace (perhaps between the tribes gathered for the feasts) that is chiefly in view. Verse 8 could refer equally to residents or pilgrims or both, revealing a strong sense of community fellowship akin to that of the NT. Verse 9 suggests that the Lord's house would benefit from the general prosperity of the city.[95]

Psalm 123

123:1-2 This psalm is one of humble dependence on God. It opens rather like Psalm 121, but moves straight to the divine object of the psalmist's trust. The

---

93. For the psalms of Zion, see p. 11. Allen notes that 2 Hebrew MSS, the oldest LXX text, and Targum all lack לְדָוִד, *lĕdāwid*, here, giving some reinforcement to his view that the psalm is not Davidic (*Psalms 100–50*, 213).

94. Broyles, *Psalms*, 450.

95. For the apparent anachronism of "house of God," if this psalm is by David, see pp. 36-37.

redactor placed it after Psalm 122, perhaps because, as in Psalm 2, the heavenly throne (so often in view in Pss 93–100), guarantees the Davidic one (122:5). In verse 2 the plural replaces the singular, and the twofold analogy, in an Eastern society where communication often employs gesture, may suggest guidance or discipline, protection or provision. Here the verse as a whole suggests either of the last two, perhaps even in combination.[96]

123:3-4 The psalmist, on behalf of his community, reiterates his cry for mercy, thus giving it emphasis. It is clear they are facing much ridicule. He twice uses שָׂבַע, *śābaʿ* ("endured"), which means "satisfied" or "sated," clearly here in the second sense. God gives good food, but this community is being fed with contempt. This is much like Nehemiah's situation and would fit very well the circumstances of his time and work.

Psalm 124

A general characteristic of this psalm of corporate thanksgiving is emphasis, first by repetition, then by multiple analogies. Perhaps its original context was the Philistine threat (2 Sam 5:17ff.), but it would be seen as applicable to many later threats. It contains a number of Aramaisms, leading scholars to argue for a late date,[97] but this is not conclusively against Davidic authorship.

124:1-5 Here, as in 129:1, a solo cantor calls the people to utter and so give emphasis to Yahweh's help against their foes (cf. v. 8), simply designated as "men" to stress the futility of their attacks against God's people. In their angry attack they intended Israel's complete obliteration, like some great monster intent on swallowing them, some overwhelming flood that would engulf them (perhaps in a dry wadi inundated with water when the rains came). The flood illustration is expressed in three different ways, evoking "the sense of a power before which one is helpless (18:16; 69:1-2; 144:7; Isa. 8:7-8)."[98]

124:6-8 At verse 6 he pauses in the midst of his illustrations to bless the Lord (NIV "Praise" translates בָּרוּךְ, *bārûk*, lit. "bless"). Now come two further analogies, the pursuing predator and the hunter's snare. As Wilcock says, the four illustrations diminish in scale but increase in torment.[99] Verse 8 closes the psalm with a similar sentiment to 121:2, but it is plural, for he writes for his people.

96. See Allen, *Psalms 101–150*, 217.
97. E.g., Allen, *Psalms 101–150*, 219, 221.
98. Mays, *Psalms*, 396.
99. Wilcock, *Psalms 73–150*, 229.

Psalm 125

125:1-2 In this psalm of Zion[100] two similes arise from contemplation of Mount Zion surrounded by other mountains. Although not particularly high, it becomes a symbol of the stability of those who trust Zion's God while the other mountains symbolize its protection.[101] The two pictures, with their complementary lessons, encourage great confidence in Yahweh. Davidson suggests reading Psalms 46 and 48 to catch the full flavor of the picture here.[102]

125:3 "The scepter of the wicked" clearly points to evil rulers. Are they evil preexilic kings of Judah, or Persian overlords, or Samaritan rulers like those Nehemiah encountered in Judah? It is difficult to be sure. The land is seen, after the fashion of Deuteronomy and Joshua, as allotted to Israel by God (cf., e.g., Deut 4:38; Josh 1:3). The psalmist fears its continued government by evil men may lead the righteous to use ungodly ways to secure its release or else to be tempted more generally to turn aside from God's way.

125:4-5 These verses recall the sharp distinctions of Psalm 1 and its promise of just retribution. Clearly the good, the upright in heart, are people faithful to Yahweh who in consequence walk in his ways. Harman points out that "good" has covenant overtones, "for it is used of the things which were promised under God's covenant," and he refers to 1 Sam 25:30, 2 Sam 7:28, and Ps 23:6.[103] Verse 5a seems an allusion to the possibility referred to in verse 3b, while the peace or well-being of verse 5b recalls 122:6-9.

Psalm 126

This appears to celebrate the return from exile and to pray for a physical renewing of the land. This may be correct, but the manuscripts do not all give the same verbal forms,[104] and "brought back the captives" (v. 1) and "restore our fortunes" (v. 4) could be viewed in both places either as return from captivity or restoration of fortunes. So verse 1 could refer either to the return or to relief from some other calamity. I will assume it is the return from exile.

100. For the psalms of Zion see p. 11.

101. Allen (*Psalms 101–15*, 225) quotes Othmar Keel for statistics showing that Zion is lower than the hills surrounding it.

102. Davidson, *Vitality of Worship*, 415.

103. Harman, *Psalms*, 409.

104. The matter is complex. For detailed comment see Anderson, *Psalms*, 2:864-65; Allen, *Psalms 101–150*, 170-72.

After full discussion and finding the psalm's center to be in verse 4, Allen declares, "The psalm as a whole is to be judged a communal complaint, the central petition of which is bordered by a reminder of Yahweh's past aid to motivate future intervention and by a strong affirmation of coming blessing."[105]

126:1-3 These verses express "an almost childlike delight in what the LORD has done."[106] A decree of Cyrus the Persian was the human cause of the return, but the exiles saw this as a great work of God. The psalmist refers to its startling suddenness, joyous nature, and international significance. The sentiment of the nations was more than reciprocated, and with great joy, by the returning exiles themselves.

126:4-6 It is evident from Haggai and Zechariah that life was difficult for the returned exiles; for example, there were poor harvests. The psalmist gives two illustrations of the blessing for which the people pray. The unpromising land of the Negev, in Judah's extreme south, is blessed during the rainy season when water fills the dry wadis;[107] also the farmer's hard toil in sowing is rewarded by abundant harvest.[108] Both the verbs for departure (הָלַךְ, *hālak*) and for return (בּוֹא, *bô'*) are doubled for emphasis, showing the psalmist's confidence that God will answer his prayer; we might translate "without doubt goes out" and "will certainly return." The prayer may be for physical fulfillment or for more general blessing.

Psalm 127

If "of Solomon" denotes authorship, there is something ironic about this psalm, especially if "the house" means not simply the physical structure but the family, for how do Solomon's many wives fit into such a picture? Yet there is another probable reference to him, for the word translated "those he loves" (v. 2) is closely related to his alternative name, Jedidiah, "loved by God" (2 Sam 12:25). The psalm has a wisdom flavor, not surprising in view of the ascription to Solomon.[109] Sadly a human channel of God's Word may deny God's teaching by his lifestyle.

127:1-2 Whether "house" is the edifice or the family, and whether the city is a walled group of buildings or a living community, the same lesson applies — only what God does stands firm. The ambiguity of the house recalls

---

105. Allen, *Psalms 101–150*, 172.
106. Davidson, *Vitality of Worship*, 417.
107. Cf. comment on 124:4-5.
108. Mays, *Psalms*, 400.
109. For wisdom psalms see p. 18.

God's foundation promise to the whole Davidic dynasty (2 Sam 7). The ineffectiveness referred to in verse 2 is not quite the same as the vanity often described in Ecclesiastes, but both lack lasting value. Work, never despised in the OT, can be excessive when, it is implied, God is left out of account, but rest from toil is his gift. Verse 2d is difficult to translate, but the NIV is probably correct.[110]

127:3-5 The words בּוֹנִים, *bônîm* ("builders," v. 1), and בָּנִים, *bānîm* ("sons," v. 3), are probably an intentional pun. Does verse 5 refer to a protective mini-army for an elderly man? Possibly, but it seems more likely his sons are viewed as his advocates in disputes at the place of justice "in the gate" (v. 5). This is a blessing from the Lord.

Psalm 128

This anonymous psalm clearly forms a companion to Psalm 127.

128:1-4 Verses 1-4 form something of an inclusio, although "blessed" is אַשְׁרֵי, *'ašrê* ("happy") in verses 1 and 2, but בָּרוּךְ, *bārûk,* in verses 4 and 5.[111] For the consecutive reader, verse 1 is somewhat reminiscent of 1:1 and verses 2 and 3 of 1:3. In both Psalms 127 and 128 food has to be worked for, but in 128:2 it results from fearing the Lord while in 127:2 from unremitting toil, which need not be mutually exclusive. Davidson points to the sharp contrast between the blessing of the wife "within your house" and what is said of the adulteress in Prov 7:11-12.[112] As in Psalm 127, sons are a blessing from God, "round your table" symbolizing family fellowship. Verses 2 and 3 could have started life as a priest's blessing before a family returned home from one of the feasts.

128:5-6 The psalm's "wisdom" tone now gives way to prayer, suggesting that the blessings of verses 1-4 are not automatic.[113] The emphasis on Zion/Jerusalem[114] and the reference to peace well fit a song of ascents and reflect that God in his sanctuary is his people's fount of blessing. Jerusalem's prosperity ensures the temple's security (cf. 122:6-9 and comments there). Long life is a characteristic OT blessing. In the closing prayer for peace, identical with the close of Psalm 125, we may again hear the voice of a priest, indicating that the blessing is intended for the whole community.

---

110. See the detailed note in Kidner, *Psalms 73–150,* 442; and the comments in Mays, *Psalms,* 401-2.

111. See comments on Ps 1.

112. Davidson, *Vitality of Worship,* 421.

113. See esp. the comment in Broyles, *Psalms,* 463-65. For wisdom psalms see p. 18.

114. For the psalms of Zion see p. 11.

Psalm 129

This psalm of thanksgiving and imprecation has some similarities to Psalm 124.[115] Verse 4 suggests its origin in a particular event, perhaps the return from exile, but the remainder is very general, emphasizing Yahweh's repeated aid in a history of repeated oppression,[116] somewhat like the book of Judges but unlimited as to historical period. Its agricultural imagery suggests use at one of the pilgrim feasts, which celebrated both God's historical deliverances and his provision at harvest times.

129:1-4 What seems at first an individual assertion, probably sung by a solo voice, becomes a congregational affirmation when the people are called to express the same (cf. 124:1). So "the individual's oppression is seen in the context of the corporate body, with national suffering understood on the level of the individual."[117] The assertion is emphasized by repetition, but is followed by an important affirmation expressed negatively. The original assertion is then put metaphorically (v. 3), and the action pictured may be that of scourging. Isaiah 51:23, often compared with this verse, employs a different metaphor but to the same effect. Verse 4 uses another, the cutting of cords, perhaps to free yoked oxen.[118] The affirmation, "But the LORD is righteous," means he has put things right. The freeing could apply to the exodus but more probably to the return from exile.

129:5-8 Because the verbs here are ambiguous, the passage could be either a prayer (as in NIV) or a series of statements about the future. Clearly the singers are in Zion, but there are still enemies who wish harm. Weiser's suggestion that these are Jews, perhaps from the northern kingdom, not enemy nations,[119] has found little support. The grass on the roof appears to be cereal seeds that have escaped during the normal sowing and been completely lost, unable to grow because of total exposure to the sun. Verse 8 has more agricultural overtones, reminding us of Ruth 2:4 and possibly a stock blessing used at reaping time. Now those who pass by Israel's enemies find there is nothing to reap. The psalm closes, however, on a positive note, the blessing now directed, perhaps by the temple priests, toward the congregation.

---

115. For the imprecations of the psalms see pp. 257-58.

116. See Allen, *Psalms 101–150*, 249.

117. Broyles, *Psalms*, 466.

118. However, Wilcock argues that it probably refers to the cutting of the cords binding one who is to be flogged (*Psalms 73–150*, 237).

119. Weiser, *Psalms*, 771-72.

Psalm 130

Kidner points out that this psalm climbs from the depths of despair to the height of assurance of God's redemption from sins, not only for the individual but for Israel.[120] Schaefer points out that both "forgiveness" (v. 4) and "unfailing love" represent nouns with the definite article.[121] This fact, together with the assurance of future redemption from all their sins for Israel (vv. 7-8), quite unique in the Psalter and moreover effected by the Lord himself, suggests a decisive future divine act, with inevitable suggestiveness for the Christian reader.

130:1-2   The psalmist's lament shows deep despair, and he uses language normally associated with the sea (Isa 51:10) and with drowning (cf. Ps 69:1-2; Ezek 27:34). He does not yet specify his trouble, but the context shows it is either his sins or some affliction he considers their consequence. His despair is not absolute, for out of it comes his threefold cry to God.

130:3-4   God is deeply aware of human iniquity (Ps 90:8), but forgiveness means the expunging of the record (Isa 1:18; 44:22; Mic 7:18-19), and the psalmist knows his sins will now never be raised against him (v. 3). Forgiveness induces fear, not craven fear but deep reverence for a profoundly moral God who nevertheless is willing to forgive. "It must be part of a continuing relationship, cradled in mystery, which requires a response of awe and reverence which will shape his life."[122]

130:5-6   The crying (vv. 1 and 2) gives place to waiting. He looks forward to unspecified blessings from God, promised in his word, which can either be Scripture or a prophet's contemporary word. He knows light will succeed the darkness, anticipating it more eagerly than those who watch on the city walls through a seemingly interminable night.

130:7-8   He now encourages the whole people to hope in Yahweh, their God whose unfailing love is his commitment to his covenant, and in his full redemption. This expression, which normally refers to physical deliverance, is astonishingly applied to redemption from sins, the one place where the OT links "redemption" and "sins." Moreover, that this is God's action is emphasized in the words "he himself."

---

120. Kidner, *Psalms 73–150*, 445-46.

121. Schaefer, *Psalms*, 311. "Unfailing love" here is חֶסֶד, *ḥesed*, love within a covenant.

122. Davidson, *Vitality of Worship*, 425.

Psalm 131

This Davidic psalm of trust is too general in its sentiments to relate to any specific period of David's life.

131:1-2   The pride here may be intellectual, defined in terms of verse 1b, where he recognizes the limitations of knowledge set by God (cf. Deut 29:29). Pointing out that בְּנִפְלָאוֹת, *běniplā'ôt,* translated "things too wonderful," is normally used of God's great deeds (71:17; 72:18), Harman suggests the author is saying that he refuses to elevate himself into a godlike position.[123] He rests content in God, like a weaned child no longer desperate to feed at the breast but content simply to be with its mother. Possibly too the child is pictured as often carried by his mother but now by his father (the psalmist) to the festival, for עַל, *'al,* used twice in verse 2 and rendered "with" and "within," most frequently means "upon." Allen therefore translates verse 2b, "like a weaned child carried by his mother, like the weaned child I carry, is my soul."[124]

131:3   Clearly his testimony (vv. 1-2) is penned to encourage his people to look to God for the future, presumably in the same spirit of quiet confidence.

Psalm 132

This is by far the longest song of ascents, and, as Davidson notes, it has generated much inconclusive discussion.[125] I will focus on the major issues. Clearly it was written after David's reign (v. 10), but perhaps not long after, for Dahood has demonstrated that its language is archaic.[126] It aptly follows a Davidic psalm, and may have been seen by the redactor as amplifying 131:3, but with an emphasis on Zion as the place where God's house was, to which the ark came, and where the Davidic dynasty was located. It therefore justifies theologically the pilgrimages for which this group of psalms was put together.[127]

Although it has points of similarity with Psalm 89, it ends not in perplexed distress but in triumphant expectation. Nothing could more clearly

---

123. Harman, *Psalms,* 416.

124. See his whole note and comment, *Psalms 101–150,* 259-61.

125. Davidson, *Vitality of Worship,* 428.

126. Dahood, *Psalms,* 3:240-49, although some view it as later but still preexilic (Davidson, *Vitality of Worship,* 428), while still others consider it postexilic (Mays, *Psalms,* 411-12). See also Broyles, *Psalms,* 471.

127. See Mays, *Psalms,* 411.

show the difference between the overall tone of books 3 and 5.[128] Wilcock sees a strong correspondence between verses 1-9, centering in David, and verses 10-16, centering in his descendants.[129] We might therefore compare it with Psalm 72, which appears to celebrate the dynastic promise passing from David through Solomon to his descendants.[130]

132:1-9 The phrase כָּל־עֻנּוֹתוֹ, *kol-'unnôtô* (NIV "all the hardships he endured," v. 1), is better rendered, "all the pains he took," and both Allen and Wilcock suggest 1 Chr 22:14 NRSV ("with great pains I have provided for the house of the LORD") as a parallel.[131] His sense of concern (vv. 2-5), although based on 2 Samuel 7, is even more strongly worded here. The phrase "Mighty One of Jacob" (v. 2) is an ancient designation of Israel's God found in Gen 49:24 (cf. also Isa 1:24).

Although not mentioned until verse 8, the focus is on the ark throughout verses 6-9. "Ephrathah" is normally the district around Bethlehem (Ruth 4:11; Mic 5:2), but many, viewing the verse as exhibiting identical parallelism, consider it must refer to the district of Kiriath Jearim (cf. 1 Chr 2:19, 24, 50), apparently intended by the phrase "the fields of Jaar."[132] It is best to see the verse as referring to a search made in several areas. The people encourage one another to worship at God's house, and to facilitate this David brings the ark to Jerusalem. Verse 8 recalls Num 10:35-36, and Ps 68:1. Priests and the people of the covenant (חֲסִידִים, *ḥăsîdîm*) worship together.[133] The priests wore special clothing, but are said here to be clothed with righteousness, underlining moral rather than ceremonial conditions (cf. v. 16 and Pss 15 and 24).

132:10-18 Here the post-Davidic nature of the psalm is clear, but its theology rests on the event recorded in 2 Samuel 7. God chose both David (vv. 10-12) and Zion (vv. 13-16), and the two are brought together in verses 17 and 18, for not only was Jerusalem David's political capital but he made it the religious capital by bringing the ark there. VanGemeren makes the point that although 2 Samuel 7 does not mention a divine oath, "here it is a poetic expression for the certainty of God's promise to David."[134] Also in verses 11-12 there are conditions not found in 2 Samuel 7 (but cf. 1 Kgs 2:4; 2 Chr 6:14-17), but the consequences of their nonfulfillment are not here spelled out. 2 Samuel 7

---

128. For canonical criticism see pp. 21-28.

129. Wilcock, *Psalms 73–150*, 241-42.

130. See comments on Ps 72. For NT use of this psalm see p. 355.

131. Allen, *Psalms 101–150*, 264; Wilcock, *Psalms 73–150*, 241.

132. Allen, *Psalms 101–150*, 271-72.

133. However, some commentators consider "saints" synonymous with "priests" here, as Allen notes (*Psalms 101–150*, 273).

134. VanGemeren, "Psalms," 807.

gives these as punishment, but not removal of the covenant. Both physical and spiritual blessings are promised (vv. 15-16), the former in line with the blessings of obedience in Deut 15:4-6.

The promise that God will make a horn (symbolizing power) grow and set up a lamp (symbolizing light) strongly implies the postexilic break in the succession of actually reigning Davidic kings, so that it seems to be messianic (cf. Jer 23:5; 33:15; Ezek 29:21).[135] The language of clothing employed in verses 9 and 16 is now differently applied to shame and honor.

Psalm 133

This psalm is difficult to classify, but, as teaching a lesson, it has something of a wisdom flavor.[136] Brotherly unity is to be treasured, and two analogies are used, both indicating its downward flow and so its divine origin. The first (v. 2) is from the high priest's anointing ceremony, especially apt as he represented the whole nation before God. The second is from dew, well known for falling abundantly on Mount Hermon and so contributing to the freshness of well-watered Galilee. It is as if this were also falling on dry Judah, represented by Mount Zion, the normal impossibility of this underlining the point, for the first was in northern Israel, the second in Judah, ultimately to be torn apart. There is a similar geographical analogy with the same deliberate straining of credence for effect in Isa 8:6-8. Schaefer sees the word "there" (v. 3) to be "polyvalent, referring to the assembled fraternity, the collar of Aaron's vestment, and Zion. In all three the divine benediction is present, communicated, and enjoyed."[137] "For evermore" perhaps sums up the Aaronic blessing of Num 6:22-27.

Several distinctive features give emphasis. The psalm starts with הִנֵּה, *hinnēh*, often rendered "behold," represented in NIV by an exclamation point; גַּם־יָחַד, *gam-yāhad*, "together in unity," means "in full harmony";[138] the same participle, יֹרֵד, *yōrēd*, is translated "running down" (v. 2) and "falling on" (v. 3), so stressing the divine origin of blessing; both "Zion" and "bestowed" commence with the letter tsadhe (צ, *ṣ*); and כִּי שָׁם, *kî šām*, ("for there") contrasts Zion with Hermon, which seems to have had pagan connections,[139] probably due to its impressive height.

135. For the messianism of the Psalter see pp. 44-46.
136. For wisdom psalms see p. 18.
137. Schaefer, *Psalms*, 316.
138. Dahood's suggested translation (*Psalms*, 3:251).
139. Judg 3:3, "Mount Baal Hermon."

Verse 1 can hardly be simply commendation of the extended family principle along lines indicated in Deut 25:5,[140] for Kidner, referring to Deut 15:3, 12, and 25:3, points out that all Israelites, no matter what their status, "were brothers in God's sight."[141] The linking of Hermon and Zion means that, for Israel, no limit was being set to the need for harmony.

Psalm 134

It is fitting that the final song of ascents is located in the temple, while the first is located far away (120:5). The demonstrative הִנֵּה, *hinnēh* (which also introduces Ps 133), untranslated here, is aptly rendered "come" in NRSV, for here it certainly seems a call to worship. The verb בָּרַךְ, *bārak* ("bless"), is translated thus in verse 3 but as "praise" in verses 1 and 2.

134:1-2   The "servants of the LORD" may be the priests or the priests and Levites together (Deut 10:8; 1 Chr 9:33; 23:26, 30), but is more probably the whole worshiping assembly,[142] which was meeting night by night,[143] perhaps during the Feast of Tabernacles.[144] Lifting up the hands was a gesture often accompanying prayer (28:2) or praise (63:4), symbolizing the direction from which aid was sought or toward which praise was offered. The "sanctuary" is the holy place, into which only the priests could go, but NASB and NRSV, over against NIV, render the accusative "to" rather than "in," and this would fit the whole assembly.

134:3   Here the universal and the local, the general and the particular, are linked. Yahweh is creator of all, but his blessing is to be found in a particular location, the temple at Zion.

Psalm 135

Here is a major example of biblical intertextuality, for, as Kidner points out, "every verse of this psalm either echoes, quotes or is quoted by some other part of Scripture,"[145] and yet it is a strongly integrated whole. The more im-

140. See discussion in Anderson, *Psalms*, 2:885.

141. Kidner, *Psalms 73–150*, 452.

142. Allen gives a useful bibliographical note on this point (*Psalms 101–150*, 283).

143. The word "night" is plural (לֵילוֹת, *lêlôt*). Another possible translation is "during the night hours." Communal worship at night is referred to in Isa 30:29.

144. See Davidson, *Vitality of Worship*, 433-34.

145. Kidner, *Psalms 73–150*, 455. For NT use of this psalm see p. 301.

portant of its many OT links are listed by Broyles.[146] This psalm of praise was viewed by the Jews as part of the Great Hallel, which added Psalms 135 and 136 to the Songs of Ascents (120–134).

135:1-2 A call to praise, having links with 113:1 and 134:1-2, but with the use of הַלֵּל, *hillēl,* as in 113, instead of בָּרֵךְ, *bārak,* employed by 134. The servants of the Lord include the priests (v. 2a), plus all who can enter the courts of the Lord, the temple precincts (v. 2b), which appear at first only to be Israelites, although verse 20 widens the call.

135:3-4 In verse 3 the first "Lord" is יָהּ *(yāh),* the rarer short form of the divine name, the second the more usual יהוה, *yhwh* (Yahweh).[147] A reason for praising him, a pleasant duty, is his goodness, then defined in terms of his election of Israel (Exod 19:5; Deut 7:6; Ps 47:3-4; Mal 3:17), probably called "Jacob" because divine election is seen especially in the choice of Jacob (Gen 25:23; Mal 1:2-3).

135:5-7 A further cause of praise is his greatness, contrasting him with all other gods, and shown in the general freedom of his will to act in the created universe, not simply in his choice of Israel. Verse 7 specifies some particular examples of this. "Storehouses" uses poetic metaphor, and the term often occurs in relation to the weather (Deut 28:12; Job 38:22-23; Jer 10:13).

135:8-12 Here is the familiar appeal to Israel's history, seen especially in terms of God's judgments: the destruction of the Egyptian firstborn, the signs and wonders (probably the plagues and the opening of the Red Sea), followed by Yahweh's vanquishing of the nations in the land, starting with the killing of the two Transjordanian kings. This made possible Israel's occupation of the land, seen, in Deuteronomic fashion, as an inheritance from God (cf., e.g., Deut 31:7). The address to Egypt (v. 9) is unusual but hardly warrants textual emendation. The exodus was so often celebrated that we need not doubt there was often a dramatic sense of personalized encounter. Wilcock's comment about the whole psalm, that everything here is as vivid to the psalmist as to those from whom he took his materials, is certainly true.[148]

135:13-14 Name perpetuation was important for the OT people. Yahweh's own name endures, not just for a time, but forever. "Your renown" is literally "your remembrance." Verse 14 suggests Yahweh will uphold Israel's name, not just his own, thus showing his compassion.

135:15-18 Here is the characteristic OT scorn of idols (cf. 115:5 and

---

146. Broyles, *Psalms,* 476.

147. Allen thinks the sixfold repetition of the divine name in vv. 1-4 may have been intended to match that in vv. 19-21 (*Psalms 101–150,* 289).

148. Wilcock, *Psalms 73–150,* 249.

many passages in Isa 40–48), humanly constructed from lifeless metal and with no living function to their bodily parts, quite unable to respond to the needs of their worshipers.

135:19-21   The various groups exhorted to praise the Lord conclude with "you who fear him," which, as in 115:13, probably includes Gentiles who worship Israel's God.[149] If so, then the particularism of verse 21 balances it and stresses, as does verse 4, that the only true God is Yahweh, God of Israel.

Psalm 136

This thanksgiving hymn concludes the Great Hallel, which starts with Psalm 120. It has many similarities to Psalm 135 but its structure is unique, for its theme is God's covenant love revealed both in creation and history. So it sees behind the stories of the universe and of Israel a special divine quality. Its liturgical and antiphonal structure is very evident, with the refrain forming a response, probably congregational, to each priestly or choral exhortation (vv. 1-3, 26) or description (vv. 4-25). This refrain, which is found also in 106:1; 107:1; and 118:1, 29, contains a virtual tautology, for הֶסֶד, *hesed*, "love within a covenant relationship" (simply "love" in NIV), is by definition totally enduring, especially in application to God, but Israel would have regarded this as blessed tautology indeed!

136:1-3   This sets the tone, not just of worship but of thanksgiving, so verse 26 becomes simply a reminder that the whole is intended as a corporate expression of gratitude. God is identified first of all as Yahweh, and so as Israel's covenant God, then as supreme God, indicating that he alone deserves praise, and supreme Lord, for he alone deserves human submission.[150] The phrases "of gods" and "of lords" (cf. Deut 10:17) do not imply the real existence of other divine beings but simply emphasize Yahweh's supremacy.

136:4-9   This clearly reflects Genesis 1, with "by his understanding" (v. 5) somewhat reminiscent of wisdom's role in creation in Proverbs 8 (cf. also Prov 3:19; Jer 10:12). NIV "spread out" is לְרוֹקַע, *lĕrôqaʿ*, from the same Hebrew root as רָקִיעַ, *rāqîaʿ*, translated "expanse" in Gen 1:6-8, 15-17. In the light of Gen 1:16, many commentators consider the reference to the stars a gloss incorporated in the text,[151] but the author may have felt their inclusion necessary in a psalm

---

149. It is noteworthy that Gentile believers in the God of Israel were called "God-fearers" in NT times (Acts 10:2; 13:26).

150. There is a possible adaptation of this pattern in 1 Cor 8:4-6.

151. Allen, *Psalms 101–150*, 294.

praising Yahweh because of their prominence in Near Eastern religions. This section shows that comprehensive thanksgiving was not restricted to Yahweh's redemptive actions but embraced also his acts of creation.[152]

136:10-15   The psalmist moves straight from Genesis 1 to the exodus events, so pivotal in Israel's faith and so worthy of extended coverage in a psalm of thanksgiving for covenant love. There is no reference to the plagues, but the judgment on the firstborn introduces the note of judgment (v. 10), which emerges again in verses 15 and 17-20. An act of covenant love for Israel was also a judgment on their enemies.

136:16-22   The wilderness wanderings are passed by without comment, in line with the emphasis of the whole psalm on God's deeds, not Israel's. The covenant love displayed in the exodus came to its climax in the gift of Canaan. This required the destruction of its inhabitants, and the spotlight turns especially on their kings. The inheritance language of Deuteronomy and Joshua appears here (cf., e.g., Deut 31:7; Josh 1:6).

136:23-25   Some relate these verses to the period of the judges, but they could be recapitulatory, referring to the exodus, as in the OT later generations are often identified with those who were in Egypt. For the first time the psalmist writes of "us," so this is probably about the return from exile, showing the thankful spirit of postexilic worshipers.[153] There is an unexpected shift from the particular to the universal in verse 25, where, in the spirit of Psalm 104, not only all humans but all living creatures are viewed as benefiting from God's covenant love, perhaps a reminder of the Noachian covenant (Gen 9:8-17).

136:26   This reminds the reader of the thanksgiving theme set in the opening verses. As Harman reminds us, "God of heaven" is a divine designation particularly associated with the postexilic period (Ezra 1:2; Neh 1:4; Dan 2:18).[154]

Psalm 137

This deep lament touches a wide range of human emotions, from the joy of verses 3b and 6c through the sadness and nostalgic love expressed in the whole psalm to the angry curses of verses 8 and 9. Anderson suggests it was written shortly after the return from exile, when the Jerusalem temple was

---

152. Cf. Pss 103 and 104, placed together by the redactor as companion psalms.
153. Allen discusses various interpretations (*Psalms 101–150*, 295).
154. Harman, *Psalms,* 427.

still in ruins while Babylon, although defeated, was still a major city in the new Persian Empire.[155]

137:1-3 The "rivers of Babylon" probably include the Tigris and Euphrates, their tributaries, and a network of irrigation canals. The extent of the settlement of the Jewish captives is not known. Rivers and poplars suggest a good land, but the people's sadness is almost palpable. This was not just nostalgia, because "Zion" symbolized so much in religious terms. The singers and players here were probably members of the Levitical choirs and orchestras. The parallel use of "songs of joy" and "songs of Zion" suggests songs of joyous praise sung when people now living near one another as captives had formerly met for joyous worship at the pilgrim feasts in the land. The word תּוֹלָלֵינוּ, *tôlālênû*, translated "tormentors," is a hapax legomenon that could also mean "captors."[156]

137:4-6 Joyous worship and Jerusalem were inextricably linked in the psalmist's mind, and deeply mournful reminiscence was a dominant mood among the captives. As indicated in NIV, "its skill" (v. 5) is not in the text, but was thought by the translators to be implied.[157]

137:7-9 Edom was an ancient enemy who took advantage of the Babylonian destruction of Jerusalem to pay off old scores (Obad 10-14). The psalmist asks God to remember and so to take action against the Edomites. Verses 8 and 9, so horrifying to modern Christian readers, show how the OT's concreteness, so often helpful, can sometimes become almost unbearable. The word אַשְׁרֵי, *'ašrê*, "happy" (NIV "blessed"), introduces many a beatitude in the Psalter and elsewhere but here is used with startling uniqueness. The writer's concern was for the ending of the evil Babylonian dynasty, which put more abstractly means something like, "may the evil Babylonian dynasty be brought to a complete end!" The destruction of the Babylonian children had been prophesied in Isa 13:16.[158]

Psalm 138

This thanksgiving psalm is the first of a final group of eight Davidic psalms that precede the Final Hallel (146–150).

---

155. Anderson, *Psalms,* 2:897. Motyer too argues for it as the reflections of a returned exile ("Psalms," 577).

156. Allen, *Psalms 101–150,* 302; Dahood, *Psalms,* 3:270-71.

157. See Davidson, *Vitality of Worship,* 440-41, who argues for a reference to the withering of the hand.

158. For more extended comment see pp. 257-58.

138:1-3   The praise here is much like some of the communal psalms, but is fully personal. The psalmist's wholeheartedness (v. 1) resembles that of another Davidic psalm (103:1). The word אֱלֹהִים (*'ĕlōhîm*), rendered "gods," has been variously understood,[159] but in this context is probably just a way of expressing Yahweh's supremacy against paganism. Bowing in the temple's direction (cf. Dan 6:10) may have become particularly meaningful in the exile, a symbolic gesture of loyalty to the God there worshiped. "Love" (חֶסֶד, *ḥesed*) and "faithfulness" have obvious links to "your name" and "your word," respectively. Allen understands verse 2's last clause to signify that "by fulfilling the promise Yahweh has surpassed all previous self-revelation."[160] His prayer was apparently in a situation where he needed boldness.

138:4-5   David was an international figure, an emperor ruling subject peoples, and what is envisaged here is the universal spread of the knowledge of God's ways (presumably his dealings with Israel; cf. 103:7), with consequences in equally wide worship, and with special focus on the submission of earthly kings.[161]

138:6-8   There is contrast between "all the kings of the earth" (v. 4) and "the lowly" (v. 6). The highest king of all has the greatest concern for the apparently insignificant. Verse 6 distinguishes knowing as fellowship from knowing as conceptual but not intimate. Verse 7 virtually sums up the Davidic psalms of lamentation and deliverance. Stretching out the right hand is a reminder that his God is the God of the exodus (cf. 136:12). Verse 8 shows his conviction that his life has been preserved for a purpose, God's purpose, and this preservation also reveals God's faithful love. This provides the basis for the touching plea that ends the psalm in the author's concern that God should carry his work (either for his people or for him as an individual) through to the end.

Psalm 139

This meditative psalm of prayer is very personal and at the same time includes many aspects of God's relationship with the writer, but especially God's knowledge of him.

139:1-4   Verbs of knowledge, important in the whole psalm and forming a link with Psalm 138 (v. 6), dominate this section. "Searching" suggests

---

159. Anderson, *Psalms*, 2:901-2.
160. Allen, *Psalms 101–150*, 311.
161. For the universalism of the Psalter see comment on Pss 65–67.

deep penetration. Sitting and rising may have been suggested to his mind as he sat composing his psalm. His work ("going out"; cf. 104:23) and rest are also familiar to God, but the idea that recurs is God's knowledge of his thoughts (vv. 2, 4) before ever he speaks them or, perhaps it is implied, pens them.

139:5-6   Is this divine knowledge threatening or comforting? The wording could be interpreted either way, and he may simply be stressing the fact of it and nothing more.[162] God is there, behind, before, above him. The word "wonderful" is פְּלִיאָה, *pĕlî'â (Qere)*, from a root normally employed in connection with God (e.g., in Judg 13:18; Isa 9:6), so this knowledge is distinctively divine (cf. also v. 14).

139:7-12   God's profound knowledge implies his omnipresence, not viewed abstractly but in terms of constant personal encounter. This too can be either a threat[163] or a comfort. The Spirit, experienced by David when Samuel anointed him as king (1 Sam 16:13), is how God's presence is known, and the parallelism of verse 7 could even suggest his deity. God is not only in the heavens but also in Sheol (see v. 8 NIV mg.), the place of the dead, an unusual thought for the OT.[164] If this going up and down recalls verse 3, rising and setting (v. 9) remind us of verse 2, so the author expands rather than radically changes his thought. Verse 10 certainly seems comforting, for being held by the right hand, the hand of power (cf. 118:15-16), confirms the comforting thought of guidance. Now the more threatening implication appears to come in verses 11 and 12, where he thinks not only of being hidden in darkness but of the whole twenty-four hours being dark. Verse 12c is a most apt expression of full monotheism: God sees all as light because he has total knowledge.

139:13-16   "For" (v. 13) links this section to the preceding. Can God work in darkness as well as light? Yes, it was God who formed the psalmist out of human sight in his mother's womb, represented figuratively as "the depths of the earth" (v. 15). The first "you" in verse 13 is emphatic. The cloth-making verbs, "knit together" and "woven together," suggest design. His awe and wonder at this fills him with praise (v. 14), and he realizes his whole life was foreordained ("written in your book") from conception to death.

139:17-18   The exclamations of verse 17 are praiseful, for not only are God's works wonderful (v. 14), but his thoughts concerning the psalmist, vast in their range, are precious (note v. 17, NIV mg.). The grains of sand were a standard illustration of numerical greatness (cf. Gen 22:17; Job 29:18). Verse

---

162. Dahood, *Psalms*, 3:288; Wilcock, *Psalms 73–150*, 258-59.

163. Note esp. the word "flee."

164. For Sheol see pp. 290-91.

18b perhaps develops "lying down" (v. 3). Sleep seems to transport us to another world, but on awaking we see that God has been with us all the time.

139:19-22 Here is a striking contrast both in subject and tone, suggesting that the psalmist's interest in God's constant presence with him even during sleep was because of danger from enemies (cf. 4:2, 8). He longs for the Lord to take retributive action, and his chief concern is for God's honor among humans.[165] He cannot tolerate those opposed to such a God. God's enemies are necessarily his too. Davidson sagely comments that the maliciousness displayed by his enemies may suggest a reason why the psalmist explored his own relationship with God, the deepest and most lasting he had.[166]

139:23-24 These verses echo the psalm's beginning. He has already stated God's perfect knowledge of him. Now he shows he welcomes it and wants his outlook to be tested. His anxious thoughts presumably arose out of his concern about his enemies shown in verses 19-22. Thought promotes action, so he ends on a practical note, showing he knows there are limits to his self-knowledge and that he desires to walk in God's ways (cf. Ps 1). Like verse 18b, "the way everlasting" may suggest a future life, the imperishable way (1:6), but we cannot be sure.

Psalm 140

This psalm of lamentation and trust seems typically Davidic in its references to enemies and to personal trouble.[167] The enemies are singular in verses 1, 5a, 9, and 12, and plural elsewhere. The singular could refer to a leader, but the NIV and most modern translations and commentators translate with plurals, viewing אָדָם, *'ādām* ("man"), as collective. The syntactical connection between verses 2 and 3 and between verses 5a and 5b suggests this is correct.

140:1-3 The psalm's occasion is uncertain, but shows likeness to Psalm 2. Here is no thoughtless violence but evil planning, with the lips too employed as weapons. The illustrations from snakes reflect the country's fauna, but specific identification is difficult.

140:4-5 The opening plea is reiterated, and the "evil plans" are seen as a plot to bring him down by tripping his feet. Verse 5 presents three similar situations from hunting.

140:6-8 He does not plead his character qualities but simply his com-

---

165. For the imprecations of the Psalter see pp. 257-58.
166. Davidson, *Vitality of Worship*, 449-50.
167. For NT use of this psalm see p. 301.

mitment to Yahweh, implying that because of this Yahweh will answer his prayer. Verse 7 recalls Psalm 18, especially its opening verses picturing God as mighty deliverer. Allen comments that in the Psalms, "I say," as in 31:14 and 142:5 as well as here, introduces a confession of contemporary faith, each time preceded by a description of lament and followed by a petition for deliverance.[168] Verse 8 shows his belief in God's overall sovereignty. The last line of verse 8 reads literally "they lift up," and has been variously understood,[169] but the NIV rendering is in line both with the verb and its context. Already his enemies are proud (v. 5) and success in their evil plans would confirm them in this.

140:9-11   These imprecations are based on the *lex talionis*, for "never to rise" (v. 10) answers to "trip my feet" (v. 4), just as "their lips" reminds us of verse 3, and "hunt" recalls verse 5.[170]

140:12-13   Verse 12, grounding retribution in God's justice, shows how the reader should view verses 9-11. The psalmist appears to cast himself in the role of the poor and needy, perhaps because, in his situation, his enemies had superior resources. Verse 13 makes the psalm one of trust.

Psalm 141

This petition shows the psalmist's concern not just about evildoers but about his own need to be kept from evil. Schaefer aptly heads it, "Lead us not into temptation."[171]

141:1-2   This prayer is urgent, and the psalmist asks that it may be as acceptable to God as the incense and sacrifices ordained by him. קְטֹרֶת, *qĕṭōret*, "incense" (cf. Lev 16:13), could also be understood as the smoke of the burnt offerings, as in Ps 66:15, with the former the more likely.[172] Verse 2 may suggest this is an evening prayer (cf. Exod 29:38-43).

141:3-4   He prays not just against his enemies (v. 5) but, unusually, for protection from personal involvement with them in evil, both of speech (v. 3) and of action (v. 4), from a heart seduced. "Their delicacies" could be either ill-gotten or have pagan associations, but it is more likely that he means eating with them would imply fellowship with evil.

141:5a-c   These are unusual but appropriate affirmations extolling the

---

168. Allen, *Psalms 101–150*, 336.

169. Dahood, *Psalms*, 3:303; Allen, *Psalms 101–150*, 333; Davidson, *Vitality of Worship*, 452.

170. For the imprecations of the Psalter see pp. 257-58.

171. Schaefer, *Psalms*, 330.

172. Anderson, *Psalms*, 2:918-19.

blessedness of genuinely concerned discipline (cf. Prov 9:8). The NIV mg. suggests "the Righteous One" instead of "righteous man." צַדִּיק, *ṣaddîq,* can be so understood here, although the context, with its references to evildoers, may suggest simple contrast between human ethical types.[173] "Oil on my head" soothes and heals (cf. 23:5).

141:5d-7 There are several translation problems here, but NIV is both faithful to the Hebrew and meaningful.[174] The rulers are mentioned, either as leaders in evil or for weakly acquiescing in it. Casting down from a cliff (cf. 2 Chr 25:12 and Luke 4:29) was a simple means of execution. Their scattered bones resembled Sheol's greedy mouth (cf. Isa 5:14).[175]

141:8-10 As in 140:6-8, the psalmist makes his commitment to God and seeks refuge in him, with his plea for protection. Verse 9 recalls 140:5, and verse 10, 140:9-11.

Psalm 142

This lament has a number of similarities to Psalm 16. A locational heading (cf. Ps 57) occurs only here in book 5.

142:1-2 His desperation, confessed in verse 6, reveals itself here in the loud cry and the verbs "lift up" and "pour out." The complaint is before God, although not against him but against his enemies. Because these verses are statements introducing a prayer, Broyles considers the psalm instruction on how to pray when in trouble.[176]

142:3-4 The phrase "It is you" is emphatic, so that, although utterly weak, he looks to God, who knows his way, presumably the way out of his situation. This comforts him, for he knows his enemies have snared his path (cf. 140:4-5; 141:9). The right hand is where the legal advocate stood (cf., e.g., 16:8), but he is without human friends to support or protect him.

142:5-7 Verse 1's cry is resumed and intensifies because his need is great. It is, however, an expression of strong faith, for he asserts that God is both refuge and portion to him, the second word suggesting territory, inheritance, blessing. He is like the Levites, with God as his inheritance (cf. Deut 10:9). His reference to his prison suggests a link with the cave of the heading, either the cave of Adullam (1 Sam 22:1ff.) or, more likely, that at En Gedi

---

173. For righteousness see pp. 249-50.
174. See Wilcock, *Psalms 73–150,* 265.
175. See pp. 290-91.
176. Broyles, *Psalms,* 494-95.

(1 Sam 24:3).[177] Some think the prison is meant to be taken literally but this is unlikely.[178] Mays thinks the ambiguity may be intentional,[179] so that the psalm could be used by people in various predicaments.

Deliverance will bring God praise and recognition of God's goodness by godly friends, who will then gather round the psalmist, dispelling his loneliness (cf. v. 4).

Psalm 143

Broyles comments, "This individual psalm is highly formulaic . . . yet it reflects an intimacy with God that is strikingly singular among the psalms." The word כִּי, *kî*, translated "for" in verses 2, 8 (twice), 9, and 12, and untranslated at the start of verse 3, gives emphasis to the petitions at these points.[180] The singular ("enemy") of verse 3, perhaps referring to the leader of his foes,[181] is replaced by the plural in verses 9 and 12.

143:1-2 These verses are a cry to God for help. Both this and the reference to divine attributes are familiar in the Davidic psalms, but the sentiment of verse 2 is most uncommon (though cf. 130:3). God's righteousness, his determination to put things right, contrasts with the psalmist's sense of sin, yet he is God's servant.[182]

143:3-4 He is pursued by an enemy, and both the singular and the reference to darkness would fit Saul's pursuit and David's resort to cave dwelling.[183] The dead were buried in caves and this is what he feels like, for he is utterly crushed in spirit.

143:5-6 These verses are much like 77:11-12. He recalls either God's works for him and for his people or for the world in general, probably his people, as these are what are most recalled in the Psalms. "Meditate," the same verb as in 1:2, here applies to God's works rather than his Word. Verse 6 shows prayer's outward symbol and inner reality (cf. 42:1-2; 63:1).

143:7-10 Wilcock aptly entitles verses 1-6, "The cry intensified," and verses 7-12, "The pleas multiplied."[184] As in 141:1, he requests a quick answer,

177. Allen, *Psalms 101–150*, 348.
178. Allen, *Psalms 101–150*, 347.
179. Mays, *Psalms*, 431.
180. Cf. Aejmelaeus, *Traditional Prayer*, 78.
181. But Anderson sees the singular here as collective (*Psalms*, 2:927).
182. For righteousness see pp. 249-50.
183. See the heading of Ps 142.
184. Wilcock, *Psalms 73–150*, 268.

needing God's favor (cf. v. 7c with Num 6:22-27). His life is in danger, for "pit" is a near synonym of Sheol (cf. Pss 30:3; 88:3-4).[185] Verse 8 may mean he seeks a prophetic oracle of blessing or simply that events in the morning will reveal God's covenant faithfulness in answering his prayers. If he can then emerge from his dark cave dwelling (cf. v. 3), he will need both physical and moral direction, and is confident of this because of his relationship with God.

143:11-12   Again he appeals to God's revealed character, calling for the silencing and destroying of his foes, asserting he is God's servant despite his awareness of sin (cf. v. 2).

Psalm 144

This psalm of thanksgiving is often regarded as a postexilic patchwork composed almost entirely from other psalms, both Davidic (material from Pss 8 and 18 is particularly influential) and non-Davidic. It certainly uses older material, but this is mostly from psalms and, as Kidner suggests, some of the language may have been stock psalmic phraseology. If so, the ultimate provenance of this phraseology is virtually impossible to trace. Here it seems that the king is facing foreign foes and encouraging himself from divinely given victories such as those celebrated in Psalm 18.[186]

144:1-2   These verses recall 18:1-3, 30-36. The unique expression translated "my loving God" (better, "my enduring love"),[187] may owe something to David's reference to his own love for God in 18:1, although the two words are different. Verse 2's final line may be rendered in two ways, with substantial manuscript evidence for each.[188] Contextually, the NIV reading seems the more likely, in view of the virtual refrain in verses 7-8, and 11.

144:3-4   Psalm 8, of which verse 3 is reminiscent, celebrates God's gift of kingship to humanity and the subjecting of the animals. He may be feeling amazement at his own privileges. Verse 4 moves in a different, but equally logical, direction from 8.

144:5-8   Here again is language from Psalm 18, although verse 5 links with the (apparently) non-Davidic 104:32. He calls on God to do what he thanks him for doing in Psalm 18, so this is prayer based on experienced deliverance. It is therefore unlikely that "part the heavens" refers to God's creative

---

185. See pp. 290-91.
186. See the comments on this psalm in Zenger, "Composition."
187. Cf. "my lovingkindness" (NASB).
188. See NIV mg. and Allen, *Psalms 101–150*, 359.

acts.[189] What are figuratively "mighty waters" are literally "the hands of foreigners," so it is from aliens that he needs to be rescued. Perhaps this prayer is also promoted by the affirmation of verse 2d (see the comments above).

144:9-10   The song is new perhaps in relation to the older song of Psalm 18.[190] Psalm 33:2 also mentions this type of lyre. Verse 10 moves from a general reference to God's sovereignty over history to his special providence toward David. The phrase "his servant David" invariably applies in the Psalter to David himself, not a descendant.[191]

144:11   This verse repeats verses 7 and 8 in shortened form, thus constituting a refrain and showing probably the psalm's occasion and why a previous song of praise for victory has been reused.

144:12-15   These verses offer a picture of a land at peace. "As the blessing progresses it moves through ever widening circles: first for the family, then for the agricultural produce of the land, and then for national security against foreign invasion. As such, the entire psalm opens and closes with the notion of blessings."[192] The word translated "blessing" here is אַשְׁרֵי, *'ašrê*.[193]

Psalm 145

This psalm is an acrostic, but with the nun section (v. 13b) absent from most Masoretic manuscripts, but present in one, in the Dead Sea Scrolls, and in some versions.[194] It is virtually inconceivable it was absent from the original, so I will include it. The psalm may once have concluded the Psalter, before the adding of the Final Hallel, and it summarizes its teaching about God, so the value of such a memorizing device is evident. The psalmist clearly found it no impediment to the development of his majestic theme. Here the distinction between teaching psalms and cultic praise breaks down, and it is noticeable that the word "praise" appears only here in the Psalter's headings. Davidson comments that this may be to prepare for Psalms 146–150.[195] "The psalmist's artistic skill, his breadth of vision, and the deceptive simplicity of his message are evident."[196] Mays, fol-

---

189. Allen, *Psalms 101–150*, 363-64.

190. For "new song" see n. 184 on 33:3.

191. Allen, *Psalms 101–150*, 364.

192. Broyles, *Psalms,* 503. He also deals there with some translation problems in v. 14; see also Davidson, *Vitality of Worship*, 465.

193. See comment on 1:1.

194. See pp. 3-4.

195. Davidson, *Vitality of Worship*, 466.

196. Wilcock, *Psalms 73–150*, 271.

lowing Gunkel, comments that statements of praise and attribute declarations alternate in the psalm's four panels (vv. 1-3, 4-9, 10-13, and 14-21), with the components reversed in the last panel, so that the psalm ends with praise.[197]

145:1-2 Exaltation aptly defines a king's praise of the supreme King. The repeated "for ever and ever" may, at the very least, reveal lifelong determination and even praise beyond death.

145:3-7 "Great is the LORD" governs this section. "Great" and "greatness" may seem abstract, and "the glorious splendor of your majesty" may appear to draw attention to his person rather than his works, but the main focus is the latter. In typical OT fashion, verses 4-6 show education of later generations in Yahweh's acts, which are mighty, wonderful, and awesome. The NIV of v. 5 follows the Dead Sea Scrolls and some versions, relegating the MT to the margin, but the latter is quite intelligible, so may be retained.[198] The exodus, although not explicitly mentioned, may be the main act in mind. For postexilic users of the psalm there was a long history of such acts.

145:8-13a This section does not lose sight of Yahweh's greatness but unites some of his gentler attributes with it. Verse 8's four descriptive nouns and phrases give much emphasis to Yahweh's covenant love, while verse 9 declares his general beneficence, repeated in verses 13 and 17. The wider beneficiaries and the "saints"[199] come together in praise, further declaring his glorious kingly rule. This will endure through all generations, those referred to in verse 4.

145:13b-16 Again he turns to the gentler virtues, declaring God's faithfulness to his word, his general love, his special concern for the needy, and his providential goodness in supplying the physical needs of all his creatures, a theme with many similarities to Psalm 104.

145:17-20 Yahweh's righteousness is referred to for the first time.[200] His concern both to do right and to show compassion to all is matched by willingness to hear sincere prayer, for he is not only great (as earlier verses show) but near (cf. Deut 4:7). Verse 19 takes up verse 16's theme but relates it, probably with special applications in mind, to God's own people. If this psalm did once conclude the Psalter, 1:6 and verse 20 would have formed an impressive inclusio, with verse 21 added to end all with praise.

145:21 Here is an inclusio within the psalm itself, as comparison with

197. Mays, *Psalms*, 438.
198. Contra Allen, *Psalms 101–150*, 367.
199. חֲסִידִים, *ḥăsîdîm*, "those faithful to the covenant."
200. For righteousness see pp. 249-50.

verses 1 and 2 makes clear. Appropriately the psalm ends with a commitment to personal praise and a call for this to be made by all creation.[201]

Psalm 146

This commences a series of five praise psalms all beginning and ending הַּֽ הַלְלוּ, *halĕlû yāh* ("Praise the LORD!") Motyer comments, "there is step-by-step progression in this praise. It begins with the individual (146:1), involves the community (147:1, 12), extends to heaven and earth (148:1, 7). If, however, the whole world is to offer praise for what the Lord has done for Israel (148:13-14) there is need for the praise of a people committed to mission (149), until everything that has breath praises the Lord (150:6)."[202]

146:1-2 Like Psalm 103, this begins on a personal note and becomes very wide-ranging.

146:3-4 This establishes trust as a leading motif. The linguistic connection between אָדָם, *'ādām* ("men"), and אֲדָמָה, *'ădāmâ* ("ground"), obviously alludes to Gen 3:19, underlined by the equally obvious indebtedness of verse 6 to Genesis 1. Human life is transitory and so also are human plans to help the needy.

146:5-9 This section, contrasting with verses 3-4, builds true faith, linking descriptions of God with a catalogue of the blessings he brings the needy. Verse 5 reminds the reader of Jacob's prayer in Gen 32:7-12, implying that his helpless descendants may find help in the same God. "Maker of heaven and earth" occurs in several psalms, and verse 6 recalls not only Genesis 1 but Psalm 8. His faithfulness is expressed in the situations mentioned and perhaps recalls the covenant with Jacob. Even if the Zion theology is its background (e.g., Ps 46:7, 11),[203] this will rest on the Genesis story. Isaiah 61:1-3 proclaims Yahweh's gracious acts somewhat similarly, although the list of beneficiaries is longer here. The Hebrew lacks "gives sight," but this must be implied. Why are "the righteous" in the midst of this catalogue instead of its start or finish? Perhaps to secure a link with the גֵּרִים (*gērîm*),[204] resident aliens personally committed to Israel and to Yahweh. Verse 9 too is reminiscent of Pss 1:6 and 145:20, although there are linguistic differences.

146:10 The reference to aliens perhaps suggests the utter supremacy of

---

201. For the universalism of the Psalter see comment on Pss 65–67.
202. Motyer, "Psalms," 581. For the universalism of the Psalter see comment on Pss 65–67.
203. Allen, *Psalms 101–150*, 376. For the psalms of Zion see p. 16.
204. Note that this is plural.

Zion's God. In contrast to human princes (vv. 3-4), "his tenure is not tempo-rary."[205] He is to be worshiped in all generations, for, of course, as 145:4-7 and 10-12 indicate, his mighty acts will be proclaimed from one generation to an-other.

Psalm 147

This praise psalm moves from God's concern for Jerusalem through his work in the heavens, his provision of food for his creatures, then for human beings, to thankfulness for his laws given to Israel.[206] As Allen points out, it appears to include literary references to Isaiah 40–66, Psalms 33 and 104, Job 37–39, and Deuteronomy 4, all "skillfully woven together with traditional psalm lan-guage into a new composition of praise."[207] Mays shows how the psalm re-veals a unified theology of the divine sovereignty by placing God's concern for his people and his control of the world side by side.[208] The LXX divides it into two after verse 11, but this is unnecessary.

147:1 This psalm has an atmosphere of joy, for praise is a glad duty. "How," used twice, represents the emphatic כִּי, *kî*, here regarded as exclama-tory.[209]

147:2-3 These verses would be most appropriate after the return from exile, with verse 3 showing the returning exiles' feelings on seeing Jerusalem's ruined condition.

147:4-6 The divine orderliness of the heavens and language reminis-cent of Isaiah 40 (cf. v. 5 and Isa 40:28) point to God's greatness, perhaps re-minding the writer of Isa 40:1-11, which heralds God's plan to restore the ex-iles. God's comprehensive knowledge of all the stars could be an implicit attack on stellar paganism (cf. Gen 1:16) as well as an implied assurance that he knows the returned exiles individually and even perhaps suggesting he will increase their number (cf. Gen 15:5). Verse 6 is like a summary of 146:7-9.

147:7-9 A renewed call to praise leads to further reference to creation, rather as in Psalm 104, for the rain's purpose is food supply. There is probably an implied a fortiori argument here: if he supplies food even to the ravens, how much more to his people!

147:10-11 The reference to the horse's strength means that military

---

205. Mays, *Psalms*, 441.

206. For the universalism of the Psalter see comment on Pss 65–67.

207. Allen, *Psalms 101–150*, 384. See also Kidner, *Psalms 73–150*, 485.

208. Mays, *Psalms*, 442-43.

209. See Allen, *Psalms 101–150*, 381-82.

might is in view here. The postexilic community was small and could not rely on help from great powers in the way preexilic parties had played off Egyptian and Mesopotamian military powers against each other. The exile had taught them that God's delight is in godliness. He had shown his unfailing covenant, for, despite their sin, they were now back in Jerusalem.

147:12-14   These verses develop verses 2-3, but now in terms of praise. There God was seen in the city's rebuilding, here in Nehemiah's work on the gates. The two basic civic concerns of peace and provision are both covered, with the first reference now to the food supply to meet the human need.

147:15-18   Now, developing the thought of God's provision of food, there is further reference to his control of the natural elements, in which winter is followed by spring and so, perhaps by implication, the development of crops. This is produced not by impersonal forces but by God's word of command, for the creation serves his purposes. The references to his word clearly imply he is constantly active in the universe and not simply its maker. The rhetorical question of verse 17 recalls those in Isaiah 40 and God's questions to Job in Job 38 and 39.

147:19-20   The people were taken to captivity because of disobedience, so the obedient universe of verses 15-18 provides a challenge. Possessing God's law is seen not just as a responsibility but a privilege (cf. Deut 4:5-8).

Psalm 148

148:1a   This psalm exhorts all creation to praise him and, guided probably by Gen 1:1, views first the heavenly, then the earthly sphere. "No other psalm witnesses more clearly to the breathtaking comprehensiveness of Israel's faith."[210]

148:1b-6   The general call of verse 1a now focuses first on those who can give God intelligent praise (v. 2), then (vv. 3 and 4) the heavenly bodies and reservoirs of rain, this last a reminder of Gen 1:6-7. Wilcock sees these three spheres reflecting the three heavens identified by the Jews.[211] Verse 5 focuses on God's creative word (cf. also 33:6, 9) and his setting of limits to the various elements (again Gen 1:6-7 and Ps 104:5-8).

148:7-12   Now praise from the earthly sphere is called for, in the opposite order to that of the heavens, the articulate praise of intelligent beings now

---

210. Davidson, *Vitality of Worship*, 474.

211. Wilcock, *Psalms 73–150*, 280; cf. 2 Cor 12:2. He makes many perceptive comments on the structure of this psalm.

coming last. Verse 8 recalls 147:15-18. The catalogue is not, of course, exhaustive, but suggests all God's earthly creation, both impersonal and personal, is called to praise him.[212]

148:13-14   Verse 13 calls all to worship Yahweh alone, perhaps glancing at the "kings of the earth and all nations" (v. 11), many then worshiping other gods. In a manner reminiscent of Solomon (1 Kgs 8:27), verse 13c sees God's glory not so much in as above the created universe, an astonishing declaration of his utter transcendence. Verse 14, with masterly contrast and yet climax, declares that God has raised up a horn for Israel (i.e., a king; see NIV mg. and 89:17-18), with a prophetic perfect probably alluding to the messianic hope of a powerful king (cf. 132:17), and so a great cause for praise.[213] Israel brings the ultimate in praise,[214] for Yahweh does not keep them at arm's length but embraces them.

Psalm 149

This psalm seems to develop the thought of 148:14, where the praise of the whole creation climaxes in God's people's praise. Kidner argues for this from verbal links between the two psalms.[215]

149:1   This is another "new song" of a corporate nature,[216] for קְהַל חֲסִידִים, *qĕhal ḥăsîdîm* ("assembly of the saints") relates to God's covenant people gathered for worship. *Ḥăsîdîm* is also rendered "saints" in verses 5 and 9.

149:2-5   Here is a strong atmosphere of joy (cf., e.g., 147:1). Israel and Zion are virtually identified, suggesting a postexilic situation. Yahweh is celebrated as maker of the nation (cf. 95:6; 100:3); praised with dancing and the tambourine, which Miriam used to praise Israel's maker after he had opened the Red Sea (Exod 15); and celebrated as king with the harp, the instrument of David, Israel's earthly king (1 Sam 16:23). All the people have a royal aspect, for he "crowns" them with salvation, giving them deliverance and kingly status. So night as well as day becomes a time for praising him.

149:6-9   Israel's deliverance from Egypt through the Red Sea was at the same time God's judgment on Egypt. The song of praise in Exodus 15 is

---

212. For the universalism of the psalms see comment on Pss 65–67.

213. For the messianism of the Psalter see pp. 348-59.

214. Allen (*Psalms 101–150*, 389-91) translates the second colon of v. 14 as "even the renown of all the recipients of his loyal love," and this is possible. Davidson, however, makes the point that this does not fit the overall theme of the psalm well (*Vitality of Worship*, 475).

215. Kidner, *Psalms 73–150*, 488-89.

216. For "a new song" see n. 184 on 33:3.

quickly followed by Israel's victory over the Amalekites in Exodus 17, when Moses said, "The LORD will be at war against the Amalekites from generation to generation" (Exod 17:16). This "sentence" (v. 9) is now generalized concerning all who will not submit to Yahweh, with Israel as the judgment's executors.[217] Broyles compares 148:14 and suggests that "rather than calling on God's people to take up the sword, our psalm calls on them to inflict vengeance via the realm of worship."[218] This requires the parallelism of verse 6 to be synonymous. We might have expected such a spiritualization of warfare to be more clearly and fully expressed. This psalm was perhaps placed here to balance realistically the many psalms that foresee all the nations worshiping Yahweh. This service for God, like praise, is a great honor (cf. vv. 9 and 5).

Psalm 150

Most appropriately, at the end of the Psalter, everything named is related to praising God, with nothing to divert the mind elsewhere. As Mays says, "It is, in fact, the liturgical cry, 'Hallelujah,' turned into an entire psalm."[219] It was probably intended as a praise conclusion to book 5 and the whole Psalter, somewhat comparable to the doxologies concluding the other books.

150:1-2 Verse 1 presents an immediate contrast, yet harmony, between local human worship in Israel's sanctuary and the worship of angels (and perhaps the heavenly bodies) in the heavens (cf. 148:2-4). It is less likely that the sanctuary is heavenly and the whole verse an exhortation to the heavenly beings, for verses 2-5 are clearly about human worship.[220] Verse 2 moves from God's acts of power, chiefly for Israel at the exodus and later, to the divine quality they reveal.

150:3-6 Chronicles refers to many of the instruments here as associated with worship and with David (e.g., 1 Chr 15:16, 28; 25:1, 6). The trumpet may have special significance as a symbol of God-given liberty, for it was used to signal the start of the Jubilee Year (Lev 25:9), and the tambourine and dance would remind the Israelites of the exodus, when Miriam used them in leading the people in grateful praise (Exod 15). Before the final *halĕlû yāh* the psalmist moves from the instrumental to the vocal, calling the whole world to give praise to Yahweh.

217. For judgment see pp. 258-59.
218. Broyles, *Psalms*, 510. His understanding of 148:14 is likewise somewhat controversial (*Psalms*, 516).
219. Mays, *Psalms*, 449.
220. The various possibilities are fully discussed in Allen, *Psalms 101–150*, 403.

Theological Horizons of Psalms

THE PSALTER'S KEY THEOLOGICAL THEMES

The term "theology" has wider and narrower uses. Meaning "thinking about God," it is used narrowly for theology proper, the Christian faith's teaching about God himself, but more widely for all the ideas contained within a Christian doctrinal system. It is wise, however, to keep the broader use in close contact with the narrower. The only real interest a theologian has in anything, qua theologian, is its relationship to God. We must always start with God. Without God there can be no theology, for theology is thinking about God, and every other theological topic owes its relevance to its relationship to him. This is why the thematic section here has been structured with this in view at every point.[1]

There is, however, another reason. If the book of Psalms teaches us anything, it is that the only proper outlook for the people of God is to focus constantly on God himself, on his character, his deeds, his purposes, and so on. Kraus rightly says, "It is not the pious human being and his religion that are the objects of a theology of the Psalms, but the testimony by which those who sing, pray, and speak point beyond themselves, the 'kerygmatic intention' of their praise and confession, their prayers and teachings."[2]

This focus on God becomes more and more intense as the Psalter proceeds, until it becomes totally overwhelming in the closing group of psalms. If we have read the book through and taken the lesson to heart, then our thematic treatment should reflect this God-centeredness.

---

1. Somewhat different approaches, but still with the focus on God, may be found in Gunn *(God in the Psalms)* and Grogan, *Prayer, Praise and Prophecy,* 65-169. Kraus *(Theology of Psalms)* adopts a different scheme.

2. Kraus, *Theology of Psalms,* 13.

The Basic Convictions of the Psalmists

The Nature and Importance of These Themes

Every person who has a coherent worldview has basic convictions from which all else emerges and to which all else returns, affecting especially their values and their motives. Even for the nonreligious, there is what Herman Dooyeweerd calls a "religious root." This is concerned with "what makes me tick," and it usually turns out to be a comparatively small number of non-negotiable convictions to which we cling tenaciously.

Paul shows something of his own religious root when he uses the expression μὴ γένοιτο *(mē genoito)* (KJV "God forbid!"), which could be rendered as "Perish the thought!" in modern parlance. There were thoughts that his mind, as a Christian, could not tolerate, and, as we find on examining the passages where this expression occurs, they were all ideas that denied or at least questioned his convictions about God.

The book of Job shows us how deep was the religious root in Job, for despite his agonizing trials he did not give up belief in God. Physical pain, social ostracism, and even the most agonizing questions about God himself — none of these could get him to abandon his fundamental convictions about God.

Because it consists of many separate poems, of different genres and with a variety of authors, the book of Psalms has often been regarded simply as a miscellany, and so its overall theology has been neglected. A close study of it, however, shows clearly that there is an important uniting feature. This consists of a series of convictions that the writers have in common. The more important of them are comparatively small in number but they serve to give unity to the book. They all concern the God of the psalmists, the God of Israel, their relationship with him, and his acts for them. These ideas represent the backbone of the faith of the psalmists, and they may be found at many different points and in various religious forms and literary genres.

Although the history of God's dealings with his people as such is the basis of a number of psalms, such as 68, 78, 105, 106, and 136, there is a focus in the Psalter on certain historical events as of quite special importance, as teaching lessons that various subsequent events would serve simply to confirm, reinforce, and further illustrate. For instance, the flood, important though this must have been, was not highlighted in the way that these primary acts of revelation were. Which were the most fundamental of the psalmists' convictions?

Gerhard von Rad thought chiefly in terms of two.[3] The first interven-

---

3. Von Rad, *OT Theology,* 1:355.

tion is associated with the exodus, Sinai, and the gift of the promised land, and the second is the choice of David. J. V. Taylor, thinking more in terms of revelatory experiences than simply of saving events, says, "In the Old and New Testaments four experiences are paramount — the Exodus, the Davidic Kingdom, the Babylonian Exile, and the event of Jesus Christ. It is hard to think of any element in the Bible that is not derived from reflection on one or other of these four revelation experiences." He points out that this feature is most marked in the book of Psalms.[4]

This too is a helpful insight, but there is good reason for adding the creation, at least for the Psalter. This was hardly a human experience in the way the others were (although it produced the human race), but the fact that God is creator is important in the Psalter, and although there are analogies between his creative work and the redemption from Egypt, as we shall see, the two are not tied together. Israel's meeting with God at Sinai too can be added. Despite the comparative paucity of references to Sinai in the book of Psalms, the moral convictions of the psalmists bear unmistakable marks of the divine revelation given there.

The psalmists are convinced that Yahweh, their God, is the only God who exists,[5] that he is the God of creation, of the exodus, of Sinai and of Zion, and that he is the God of the future, whose purposes will find ultimate fulfillment. These are the key theological themes we will address in the following pages.

Religious convictions may be expected to reveal themselves in various types of verbal utterance, whether spoken or written. Their formal expression is the creed or theological confession, and although the Psalms do not present us with any kind of itemized creed, many passages have forms approximating to the credal, where important statements are made about either the acts or the attributes of God, typically in the declarative and descriptive psalms of praise.[6]

They may also be found in the laments, where the psalmists either appeal to great basic qualities in God, qualities revealed in the great events of the past, or else make complaint that God does not seem to have acted toward them or their situations in accordance with those qualities.[7] What is particularly characteristic of the Psalms is that these convictions are here taken into

---

4. Taylor, *Christlike God*, 17.
5. But see comment on Ps 82.
6. E.g., in Ps 145.
7. E.g., see Ps 10, where the complaints of vv. 1-13 are followed by definite assertions about God.

the devotional lives of the people of God, finding mention in their prayers and forming so much of the substance of their praise.

The laments express the feelings of their writers, and Michael Widmer is surely right when he says, "They give voice to 'temporary' pain, while a divine revelation as for example found in Exodus 34:6-7 is by the standard of the canon of definite and enduring authority."[8] It is the kind of truth expressed in the Exodus passage that supports their faith when negative feelings bid fair to overwhelm them. These convictions are quite evidently based on history, and, although they are an important feature of the Psalter, the psalmists share them with other OT writers, who understand them in much the same way.

Commenting on one particular psalm (111), Allen highlights that the psalmist glories in God's great past deeds and their abiding significance. He then says, "Those events have a once-and-for-all value such as the NT in turn attaches to their christological counterparts (for instance at Rom 6:10; Heb 10:10; 1 Pet 3:18). . . . Such words and deeds were a window through which God's purposes for each generation of Israel could be clearly discerned or a signpost pointing to God's enduring care and claim."[9]

History and theology are of course distinguishable, but in the Bible they are intimately linked. Theology is based on history, and the book of Psalms is no exception. Despite H. A. L. Fisher's famous comment that he could not see a thread of purpose running through history, Lessing's equally famous statement that the necessary truths of reason cannot be derived from the contingent facts of history, and the nervousness many modern theologians have shown about making too firm a link between history and theology, we must assert that in the Bible, and so in the Psalms, theology is firmly based on history. The psalmists could see meaning in the past, a meaning in terms of God. Truly "history is his story."

There is something reassuring in the fact that biblical truths are grounded in historical events. For one thing, ideas can have a disconcerting fluidity that does not apply to history. David Wells says, "What we have in Scripture is a framework provided by God's redemptive acts whose meaning he himself provides. . . . God's self-disclosure was tied to specific acts, because those acts, being external, secured and preserved the objectivity of God's revelation."[10]

John Goldingay makes the point that this is as true of the NT as of the

---

8. Widmer, review of *God in the Dock*, 57.

9. Allen, *Psalms 101–150*, 126.

10. Wells, "Modernity and Theology," 135 n. 29.

OT. "Its gospel is not essentially or distinctively a statement that takes the form 'God is love,' but rather the form 'God so loved that he gave.'" He notes that the Apostles' and Nicene Creeds are much closer to this form than are the Reformation confessions.[11] He also says, "Nonnarrative books such as the Psalms, the Prophets, and the Epistles, abound in material that has taken the first step from narrative to discursive statement, while keeping its implicit and explicit links with the gospel, with the OT and NT story."[12]

Although these basic themes are distinct, they are closely related. This is due largely to the fact that they were all the deeds of the one true and living God, and, because his character is consistent, they are bound to show common features. The clear marks of the one true God who is at the same time the God of Israel are upon them all. For this reason it is not surprising that there is a degree of interpenetration, with particular words, phrases, and ideas being transferred from one event to another. So, for instance, when the God of creation establishes his people through the covenants, he is said to create them. When later events like the return from exile are described, it is often the language of the exodus that is used.

In Psalm 18 the language of verses 6-15 echoes that of the creation, the exodus, and the Sinai revelation, and it is particularly striking that it is not always possible to identify clearly which of these is in view, for much of the language could apply to more than one, giving these acts of God important elements of unity. We notice also the link between God's revelation in creation and his revelation in the Law in Psalm 19.[13]

The exile called a great deal into question. It was in some ways like a death for Israel, as Donald E. Gowan highlights in entitling his book *Theology of the Prophetic Books: The Death and Resurrection of Israel.* There was a "resurrection" after it, and there is much in Ezekiel's prophecy that relates to this. The book of Psalms in its present form represents that resurrection.

That the book has a postexilic perspective is shown by the presence of psalms like 137 and 107 in it and is also strongly suggested by its emphasis on the Torah, even though this appears to be conceived at times more broadly than the Mosaic law, on which there was increased emphasis after the exile. It is important to see in what form the convictions of the psalmists survived and the extent to which this prepares us for the NT.

These convictions, which were in the hearts of all godly Jews, were not abandoned by Jesus' disciples when they came to believe in him as the Son of

---

11. Goldingay, "Biblical Narrative," 130.
12. Goldingay, "Biblical Narrative," 134.
13. See Bullock, *Psalms,* 1:104, for other examples of this.

God. Rather, this faith became the crowning conviction that forever confirmed all the others (2 Cor. 1:20). Such convictions are implanted by God himself. As Jesus said to Simon Peter, "Blessed are you, Simon son of Jonah, for this was not revealed to you by man, but by my Father in heaven" (Matt 16:17).

We will look at the fulfillment of these themes in Christ in a later section, but meantime we note that, according to the NT, he effects a new creation in which dwells righteousness, so that the moral order is restored (2 Pet 3:13); he brings about a new exodus (Luke 9:31, "departure" renders ἔξοδος, *exodos*), for he is the Redeemer (Heb 9:12) bringing in the new covenant (Luke 22:20); he establishes the ultimate kingdom, God's kingdom (Luke 22:28-29); and he restores sinners from their exile from God through his propitiatory work (1 Pet 3:18).

Yahweh, Israel's God, Is the Only God There Is

This is the most basic conviction of the psalmists. Before considering those convictions that are linked to specific events, we will study the belief of the psalmists that Yahweh, the God of Israel, is the only God there is. It is important to note not only that this too is historically grounded, but that it is also the basis of all the others. He is the God who exists eternally (90:2; 102:24-27), before every event to which the people looked back, including the creation of the world. The God who created the world, intervened at the exodus, spoke at Sinai, established the Davidic dynasty, and ultimately revealed himself in Christ crucified and risen, is the God who has always existed, and each successive divine act bears witness to that existence.

The distinction between functional and ontological statements about God, between those that relate to what he does and those that tell us about his being and his nature, is an important one. For many years the biblical theology movement tended to keep itself within the bounds of functional statements, just as the Ritschlians, a generation or two earlier, had tried to do. For instance, Oscar Cullmann's *Christology of the New Testament*, valuable as it is, did not advance much beyond a functional to an ontological Christology. He saw the NT titles of Christ as related to what Christ did rather than to who he was. This almost meant making the person of Christ a subset of his work.

We must remember that the acts of God are acts of a person and that it is the same person who is at work in all the events we have identified as central to the convictions of the psalmists. He is the creator and he is the redeemer, the lawgiver, the guarantor of the Davidic dynasty, and he is also the sure and certain hope of the future. Ever since the publication of Eichrodt's *Theology of the OT* (German original, 1933), there has been discussion as to what is the central theological theme of the OT. Not surprisingly, many have concluded that it is simply "God." In saying this, we are making confession of an ontological reality behind all the wonderful functions that we see God performing in the OT and that so inspired the trust and evoked the praise of his people.

Yet of course this is the central conviction of other religious writings, for example the Koran. This means then that we need to go further and say that the God of the psalmists is the God who creates, who redeems, who instructs, and so on, and that these great facts are all revealed through a quite special series of acts for his people. In other words, we cannot reduce all these convictions to one without losing the essence of the OT revelation.

At one time, Herbert Spencer's ideas concerning the evolution of religion were applied by many scholars to the OT, and they saw OT religion as passing through a number of stages on its way from more primitive forms to full monotheism. This view has long been questioned, but it was always difficult to apply to the Psalter. This is because this book is dominated by a theology in which the God of Israel is at least utterly supreme and unchallengeable, and in many psalms clearly the sole deity. If the material in the book is all late, as many of the early source critics maintained, then this is at least understandable. If it spans many centuries, however, we would expect to find clear evidence for it. Of course, one might argue that this is due to redactional work, but if so, this would have to be extensive, and the onus of proof must be on those who maintain this.[14]

He is the universal sovereign Lord.

Perhaps we can go beyond the bare statement that the great theme of the OT is simply "God," for in every part of the book, the God who is described, prayed to, and praised is seen in various relationships and activities. These in turn demonstrate his sovereignty. John Bright identified the central motif of the OT as the kingdom of God. It is certainly an important theme in the OT, and in the NT also. Whatever may be said in its favor as a general theme for the OT, a particularly strong case can be made out for it in the book of Psalms. In this respect it has been promoted particularly by Mays.[15]

Just as Eichrodt's championship of the covenant theme has sometimes

---

14. See Smith, *Early History of God,* and the reply by Bauckham, "Biblical Theology."
15. E.g., in his *Lord Reigns.*

been thought to reflect his background in a Reformed Church with its federal theology, so the fact that Mays was reared in the Reformed Presbyterian Church, with its strong Calvinistic theology, may have inclined him toward divine sovereignty as a general theme. This does not invalidate his position at all, but it does mean that it has to be carefully scrutinized. In fact there is considerable evidence for his position.

Mays proposes that the organizing center of the Psalms be found in the affirmation of Yahweh's kingship, יהוה מָלָךְ, *yhwh mālāk* (i.e., "Yahweh reigns," 9:7; 93:1; 97:1; 99:1; 146:10; cf. 47:8). While recognizing the varied nature of thought about God in the psalms, he sees Yahweh's kingship as the key metaphor. He points out that warrior, judge, benefactor, and shepherd, among other designations of God, are all kingship ideas,[16] that the king/servant relationship dominates the Psalter and that all other ways of expressing the relationship between God and his people may be viewed as subsets of this. Also the use of military, political, and legal metaphors and the constant use of the language of salvation and deliverance support this. He says too that "the theological setting-in-life in which all the prayers for help can be read is the relation of an *'ebed* to an *'adon*,"[17] that is, the relation of a servant to a master.

His greatness and supremacy are beyond doubt and clearly imply that he is the only true God. This supremacy is indicated in Exod 15:18 and Deut 33:5, two passages that have close links with the Psalms. In Exodus 15 (i.e., in v. 11) he is also holy (cf. Pss 22:3; 99:3, 5, 9), and, especially in these contexts where the idea is associated with his kingship, this means his utter transcendence and awesomeness.

In many passages he is called king or is said to reign, such as 9:7; 10:16; 11:4; 18:13, 16, 46-50; 22:28; 83:18; 95:3; and 148:13. He is called "Yahweh of hosts," "Yahweh Elohim of hosts," or "Elohim of hosts," and NIV renders these "LORD Almighty," "LORD God Almighty," and "God Almighty," respectively. They indicate his power and his command of unlimited resources. He is called the "Most High" (עֶלְיוֹן, *'elyôn*, 91:1; 97:9) and "God Most High" (78:35), pointing to his total supremacy. His rule over the universe is unchallengeable, as Psalm 2 makes plain. Even though his judgment throne is sometimes said to be in Zion, his people are to praise him and proclaim his deeds to the whole world (9:7-12).

This supreme kingship is celebrated again and again in book 4. This book was probably compiled either just before or just after the return from exile, and this makes its Yahwistic universalism very impressive, for the na-

---

16. Mays, *Lord Reigns*, 13.
17. Mays, *Lord Reigns*, 29.

tion, Yahweh's own people, was at that time a small group whose liberty had been extinguished by the mighty Babylonians. There are interesting links between book 4 and Isaiah 40–55, very significant if both were intended to minister specifically to the people of Israel in exile.

Psalm 145 is structurally important as bringing the Psalter to its close, apart from the Final Hallel group, and Jonathan Magonet points out that the kingship theme governs this psalm because its opening is matched by the strong emphasis of verses 11-13.[18] Exodus 15, the Song of the Sea, appears to have had much influence on the psalmic tradition (it might even be described as the first psalm), and it ends with the affirmation, "The LORD will reign for ever and ever" (Exod 15:18), and this comes just after a reference to the sanctuary.

His greatness is, if anything, accentuated rather than negated by his evident love and concern for the apparently insignificant. The one whose name is majestic in all the earth, whose glory is set above the heavens, their luminaries put in their place by him, receives praise from the lips of infants (8:1-2) and is also the God of the poor and needy (35:10; 40:17). Here is not only the kind of sovereignty that embraces small details as well as large, but greatness of character as well as of power, most reassuring for his people. This reminds us that Jesus, in fulfilling his loving and powerful ministry toward the needy, showed that he was infinitely greater than Tiberius, who sat on the imperial throne.

As already noted, book 2 and part of book 3 (usually known together as the Elohistic Psalter) are characterized by the much greater frequency of the title Elohim than the name Yahweh. Mays suggests this may have been a monotheizing procedure to emphasize that Yahweh, Israel's God, rules over all.[19] He also emphasizes, however, that Yahweh did not become the world's God by becoming the God of Israel, but vice versa.[20] In the final arrangement of the book, the introductory Psalm 2 describes him as "the one enthroned in the heavens," implying absolute overlordship, again underlined by his ability to promise universal rule to the Davidic monarch. At the close of the book, too, there is a call to praise him "in his mighty heavens" (150:1).

The assertion *yhwh mālāk* ("Yahweh is king!" or lit. "Yahweh reigns!"; 93:1; 96:10; 97:1; 99:1) is slightly unusual in that in Hebrew the verb usually precedes the noun, suggesting that the proclamation (for this is what it is) means "Yahweh, and no one else, reigns!" In the context of the ancient Near

---

18. Magonet, *Rabbi*, 39.
19. Mays, *Psalms*, 12-13.
20. Mays, *Lord Reigns*, 69.

East, this has more than a touch of antimythology about it, and will not simply mean that he is supreme over the earth with all its nations but also over the heavens. None can challenge his universal sovereignty.

No other truly divine being exists.

In 86:6-10 the psalmist moves from asserting Yahweh's uniqueness ("among the gods there is none like you") to an affirmation of his sole deity ("you alone are God"). To the modern reader the two statements appear irreconcilably contradictory, which suggests that in some way or other we have abstracted them from their context and so misunderstood them. Israel lived in a social environment in which people believed in many deities, so the second statement in the psalm at least means that these did not exist as divine beings. If they had any existence at all, it was not as gods. Nevertheless, they were gods in the minds of their worshipers, and so the psalmist still needed to make his comparative statement.

Because these beings were all too real for those who worshiped them, it was often appropriate for the psalmists to use the language of victory rather than of negation. In one psalm the writer employs apostrophe in a striking, even startling, way, when he not only says that those who worship images are put to shame, but also commands, "worship him, all you gods!" (97:7).

Because idolatry was associated with the worship of false gods, the psalmists rejected it (96:4-5; 115:2-8). Indeed, they did more than this, for they despised it utterly, subjecting it to total ridicule. In this respect their approach is just like that found in Isaiah 40–48 and also like Elijah's in 1 Kings 18. The idols are utterly impotent and can do nothing whatever for their devotees. James Crenshaw points out that the OT's rejection of idolatry is without parallel in the ancient world,[21] so that this is a distinctive feature of OT theology.

The worship of false gods brings judgment on the worshipers. Psalm 16:4 says that the sorrows will increase of those who run after other gods. The psalmist will not be involved with their names and their libations of blood. Those who have sought after false gods are now called on to offer right sacrifice, sacrifice to Yahweh (4:2ff.), for "my glory" here is probably a title for him (cf. 106:20 and 1 Sam 4:21-22). It is he, not Baal (it is implied), who has given them grain and wine.[22]

What are we to make of the use of mythological language in some of the psalms? Its existence cannot be denied, but we need to see why it is used and

21. Crenshaw, *Psalms,* 130.
22. Cf. 4:7 and Hos 2:8.

what its theological significance is. It is a striking feature of the Psalms that has come into more and more focus in modern times, especially since the discovery of Babylonian inscriptions and literary finds from the North Canaanite Ugaritic society at Ras Shamra.[23] Broadly this language is of two kinds, one more evident than the other.

The first is the obvious use of mythological terms. For instance, there is Rahab (89:10), which is Babylonian in origin, and Leviathan (74:14), which is North Canaanite. These come from the creation stories of these peoples, and they are monstrous dragonlike deities slain in the course of creation. These terms are employed in the Psalms as symbols of the powers of evil, and this is supported by the fact that they are also used for oppressive nations such as Egypt (Rahab, 87:4) and the Mesopotamian powers (Leviathan, Isa 27:1), which the same great God overcame on behalf of his people.

This kind of feature is entirely appropriate. The OT, in many of its parts, is full of vivid imagery. Metaphor and simile abound to such an extent that a book cataloguing these exhaustively and commenting on each instance, even in the book of Psalms, would need to run to several volumes. The mythology of Israel's neighbors presented a great fund of these, and the real surprise is that this feature does not occur more often than it does.

The second kind is the psalmists' use of language from Baal's exploits (e.g., at Ugarit) that they apply to Yahweh. It is possible, but not certain, for instance, that this is a feature of 18:7-15.[24] This is less easy to see, but it can often be identified from a reading of the Canaanite literature. What are the psalmists doing in such passages? They are saying that Yahweh is so much greater than Baal that all Baal is said to have done has been wrongly attributed to him. If any victories have been achieved, any provision made, they are the work of Yahweh, not Baal. The Canaanite belief in Baal therefore appears in such passages to be a pale, threadbare copy of the psalmists' convictions about Yahweh and what he has done.[25] All this is a way of saying that no other being can possibly stand comparison with him.

Neither type implies belief in the myths, either on the part of the psalmists or of their readers, but it does imply knowledge of them. It means that everything available, whether real or mythical, could be employed to set forth and celebrate the unique power of Yahweh, God of Israel.

A feature of a somewhat different kind, which may not immediately be seen as significant by the modern reader, is the references to the heavenly

---

23. See Craigie, *Ugarit.*
24. See the exegesis of this passage.
25. For examples see the exegesis of Pss 29, 68, 74, 94, 121, 133.

bodies. When they are specifically mentioned, there is probably an antimythological reason. They were objects of worship to the Babylonians, the Egyptians, and others, and it was important to make clear that they were created by Yahweh and were fully controlled by him (e.g., 8:3; 136:7-9). Psalm 19, regarded by C. S. Lewis as the greatest poem in the Psalter,[26] with its picture of the sun as a man moving across the heavens, may seem mythological until we note that it is Yahweh who has pitched its tent. The sun therefore has no independence of movement, for it is a creature of the one true God. This is so different from the way it is viewed in the polytheistic systems of Near Eastern paganism.

The term *Elohim*, used almost exclusively of Yahweh and followed by a singular verb, is probably a plural of majesty. It is, however, employed occasionally with a plural verb and so is clearly a true plural in such passages as 82:1 and 97:7. Where it is not followed grammatically by a verb, however, its sense must be discovered from the context. In 8:5 this is not easy, although the translation "God" seemed most appropriate to the NIV translators. The LXX translators, probably influenced by the concern of Alexandrian Judaism that the transcendence of God should be in no way compromised, rendered it instead "angels."[27]

It is often suggested that angels and other heavenly beings were once beings regarded as divine, but had now been stripped of their power and reduced to subordinate status. Firm evidence for this is lacking, and it is simply an inference from passages that can be otherwise interpreted.[28] There is never any linkage of the angels or the "sons of God" to a being like Rahab. Moreover, there is no suggestion that the angels acted as a kind of decision-making body and that Yahweh was simply either the leader among equals or a monarch needing advice from others. The dependent nature of the gods of Babylon, where it was believed they needed to be fed by humans, is one thing, and Yahweh's complete independence of action quite another. While pointing to psalmic language from the world of mythology, Kraus goes on to say that these allusions "have no function of their own that would revive and employ the total myth. They are only metaphors that express the breadth and depth of Yahweh's superiority and power over all hostile powers."[29]

---

26. Lewis, *Reflections*, 56.
27. See the comment on the use of the LXX in NT quotations of the Psalms on pp. 3-4.
28. E.g., see comment on 82:1.
29. Kraus, *Theology of Psalms*, 129.

Yahweh is known by his people because he has revealed himself to them.

Yahweh is never presented as one whom human beings discover, but rather as one who reveals himself to them. This is, of course, basic to two important passages in Exodus, 3:13-15 and 34:6-7.[30] Kraus says, "God chooses to reveal himself. This shows that it is a real revelation, because it takes place in divine freedom and does not represent a possibility open to human choice."[31] He makes himself known in all kinds of phenomena, in the natural world (the voice of the Lord in Ps 29), in his acts in history, and in his interventions in the lives of individuals. Verbs of revelation and manifestation are frequent. The written word is his revelation in two senses. It gives instruction to his people as to their lifestyle but it also reveals his own qualities. Indeed, this is a principle of all biblical theology, for God is concerned for his people to represent his own character in theirs.

The תּוֹרָה, *tôrâ*, should probably be seen not only as the Decalogue or the whole Sinaitic disclosure of God or even the Pentateuch, but rather as all he has revealed, including the Psalter itself. Psalm 1, considered in itself, almost certainly relates to the Mosaic law, while, as introducing the whole book of Psalms, it was probably meant to suggest to the reader that the Psalter itself should also be approached as *tôrâ*, as message from God.

He reveals himself in his acts, and many of his qualities come into focus through them, so that, for instance, his power is seen in the acts of creation and also of redemption from Egypt, his judgment in the destruction of the Egyptians and other enemies, and his mercy and love in his many acts of salvation for his people, both communally and individually.

In 27:1 God is the psalmist's light, and the significance of this appears later (v. 11) when he asks God to teach him. This may mean that it is truth about Yahweh and not simply truth from him that gives light to his servant. In the previous psalm God's glory dwells in the house where he lives, so that his glory is himself (26:8).

Who then is this self-sufficient sole Deity? He is Yahweh. This name (LORD in the main English versions) designates him as the covenant God of Israel, and its use in the Psalms reflects his revelation to Moses in Exodus 3 and the emphasis on his character in Exod 33:18-19 and 34:5-7. It is used with great frequency in the Psalms, except for those in book 2 and part of book 3, as we have seen, and it dominates book 1. Later Jews thought it too sacred to

---

30. See the comment on Exod 34:6-7 on p. 234.
31. Kraus, *Theology of Psalms*, 32. In this book Kraus places much emphasis on Yahweh's sovereign initiative in revelation.

pronounce, but the psalmists use it constantly in speaking to and of their God. Occasionally the shorter poetic form Yah, rarely employed outside the Psalter, is used (e.g., in 68:4; 89:8; 94:7, 12; 104:35).[32]

As Yahweh dominates book 1, so Elohim does book 2 and part of book 3. It is clear, however, in both books 1 and 2, that Yahweh and Elohim apply to precisely the same being, for they so often occur together in the same psalm. A shorter form Eloah also occurs, and he is also called El seventy-five times. El was the general Semitic term for deity and was also the high god of Canaan. Moreover, it is used in various combinations for the God of Israel. This clearly shows that the revelation of Israel's God by the personal name Yahweh, special and highly significant as this was, came to a people already aware of deity in terms particularly of authority and power. Special revelation is not a denial of general revelation.

Goulder and others have seen the "Elohistic Psalter" as emanating from the northern kingdom.[33] This is in line with documentary theories of the Pentateuch that assigned the source E to the northern kingdom, although it is not dependent on acceptance of this particular theory of pentateuchal origins. As Kidner points out, it is not impossible that particular names and titles for the same God were more popular in certain parts of the country than others.[34] The rabbis viewed the distinction between Yahweh and Elohim as related to the mercy of God and the justice of God, respectively. David Mitchell accepts this and notes that the Asaph psalms, which stress God's anger and his judgment, use Elohim frequently.[35] These differing standpoints are not incompatible when we recognize that much in the northern kingdom's history must have emphasized, for its inspired poets, that God does not view sin lightly.

The term *Adonai* is employed throughout the Psalter, and simply means "lord, master," identifying the person described or addressed as having superior status. It can also be used of human beings. When used of God it is normally translated "Lord" in the main English versions.

He is also "the living God" (84:2; cf. 18:46; 36:9), constantly active or ready to act. This does not mean that there is no mystery and that there are no times when he seems hidden, even remote.[36] The Psalter contains many questions, and these show that there are things Yahweh has not disclosed, both in his dealings with Israel as a whole and with the individual psalmist, some of

---

32. Kraus, *Theology of Psalms*, 17.

33. See the discussion in Goulder, *Asaph and Pentateuch*, 17-19.

34. See Kidner, *Psalms 1-72*, 5.

35. Mitchell, *Message of Psalter*, 79-183.

36. This theme is explored in Terrien *(Elusive Presence)*, and is also the focus of a chapter in Brueggemann, *Theology of the OT*, 333-58.

which, as in Psalms 44, 77, and 89, may seem to the psalmist to be difficult to square with what he *has* revealed.[37] Even on such occasions, however, the psalmists never refrain from prayer. He may not seem to be active, but there is no doubt he is there, and that he will act in his own time and way.

There are many analogical descriptions of God. This feature is common in the OT, but instances are particularly prolific in the Psalter, perhaps because in religion as in romantic love there is always a desire to accumulate descriptions in praise of the one who is loved. They reflect the people's natural, historical, and occupational background in terms like Rock, Deliverer, and Shepherd. There is a preponderance of terms with a kingly or military flavor, and this reminds us that in ancient times the king normally led his people into battle against their foes (cf. 2 Sam 11:1, with its implied criticism of David). Both metaphor and simile are common in the Psalms, but especially metaphor. It expresses not only that the psalms are poetry but also that Hebrew has a fondness for the concrete and the picturesque. The metaphors are all meaningful as disclosures of various aspects of God's being and his relationships with his people. This is particularly the case with those in the Davidic group of psalms, with Psalm 18 as an outstanding example.

The psalms often refer to Yahweh's name, which of course means all that he has revealed about himself.[38] So it is not surprising that his name is often praised (8:1, 9; 48:10; 89:12; 115:1). In some passages a group of names and titles is used together with powerful effect (e.g., in 18:1-2; 47:1-2; 50:1; 59:9), and in such contexts the great power or the wrath of Yahweh is indicated by such an accumulation (cf. Isa 1:24).

The name Yahweh is important because it stands for what he has revealed about himself. It is possible, however, to worship Yahweh and yet to have a baalized view of him. Clearly those criticized in Psalm 50 did not have their thinking controlled by his self-revelation. In Babylon Marduk (comparable to Canaanite Baal) and the other gods depended on humans to supply them with food, and this was the function of sacrifices offered to them. This psalm pours scorn on that idea and exalts Yahweh as the Lord of all there is and as in need of nothing. Such a debased view of the true God was hardly better than the blatant paganism attacked in 115:3-8.

He is revealed both by his name and in his acts and words. He is said to speak (85:8; 95:7-11), unlike the pagan gods, who are dumb (115:5), and notably in his decrees establishing the covenants (2:7-9; 105:8-11). The prophetic psalms assume that God is speaking through the prophet, for instance, in

---

37. See Davidson, *Courage to Doubt.* Cf. the questions asked by Job in the book of Job.
38. Kraus, *Theology of Psalms,* 20-24.

Psalm 36 (cf. 2 Sam 23:1-2). Kraus quotes Grether as saying, "The revelation of the name says who it is that comes to humans in the revelation. The revelation in word says what the revealer shares with humans in the revelation."[39]

The author of Psalm 94 was clearly writing at a time when the people were governed by an evil monarch (94:20) and the wicked were oppressing the righteous. When they do this, they say, "the Lord does not see; the God of Jacob pays no heed" (v. 7). This could simply be a piece of bravado, but it grievously insulted him, viewing him as a sightless idol.

The ultimate in false views of God is, of course, that he does not exist at all. On the face of it, Psalms 14 and 53 are attacks on atheism, but this too may be practical rather than theoretical.

Yahweh's sole deity is a fixed point of faith for the psalmists.

This idea is never questioned, never even suggested for discussion. No matter what afflictions come or what problems arise, the psalmists never get near suggesting there is no God or that he is not in control. The most they ever do is to call out to him in perplexity and to ask why he is not intervening. It is an unwritten assumption that he is well able to deal with the situation. They cry to him to rise up against their enemies because once he is on the move on their behalf no power in the world can withstand him.

As sole deity Yahweh alone is worthy of praise. The psalmists call all within them to praise him ("all my inmost being, praise his holy name," 103:1). But they want everyone to worship him, so they call all God's people to join in his praise. We must not forget that "Hallelujah," so often mistakenly viewed as if it were simply an interjection, is actually an exhortation.

Yahweh Is the God of Creation

Arguments could be advanced for putting this later, as it is less prominent as a theme than some others. Not only so, but it is important to say that the religion of the OT emphasizes God's activity in history over against the nature religions that dominated Western Asia in OT days. Nevertheless, the psalmists often refer to Yahweh as creator, either explicitly or by implication. They certainly believed him to be creator of all. How could he be any less than this if he was the only God who existed? If sole deity does not imply creation of the whole cosmos, what can it mean?

39. Kraus, *Theology of Psalms*, 33.

We should not overemphasize the distinction between two points: God is the Lord of history and also the Lord of creation. Patrick Miller comments that this distinction is largely due to our tendency to systematize, and then says, "It conforms neither to our modern conceptions of the unity of the divine activity nor to the picture one receives of him from the OT, where God's activity in creation and history are parts of a whole." On this point he compares the Psalter with the hymnic sections of Isaiah 40–55 (e.g., in Isa 44:23-28), where he is presented in both these great roles.[40]

Yahweh's creation of everything is stated in a simple and straightforward way. He is the maker of heaven and earth (96:5; 104:2; 115:15). How did he accomplish this? C. H. Bullock points out that in the Psalms God is said to have created by word of command (33:6; 148:5-6), by deed (147:4), by understanding (104:24-26; 136:5-9), and by power (65:5-8).[41] His purpose was translated into action by his word.

That the world has been set firmly in place is stated twice (102:25; 104:5), and suggests the image of God as a builder. The verb יָסַד, *yāsad* ("to found"), is used of his creative work in 24:2; 78:69; 104:5, and its cognate noun in 102:25. Also God is said to stretch out the heavens like a tent (104:2). A. A. Anderson says, "The metaphor implies, in its own way, the effortlessness with which God created the world."[42]

There is no suggestion that anything preceded his creative work. If there are echoes of the Babylonian and Canaanite creation myths with their conflict motifs, this is simply to stress that his power is absolute, and therefore that no being can stand in his way. Not only did he bring everything into existence, but he is still at work in creation and providence. His continued work is seen in Psalm 139 in the creation of new human life. The psalmist says, "You created my inmost being" (v. 13). Psalm 147 says that he covers the sky with clouds and makes the grass grow (vv. 8-9), which strongly suggests present activity, and this can be seen also in 135:6-7. The link between initial creation and continual providence is especially clear in Psalm 104. Here the psalmist sees that God has provided for the needs of the various creatures of his hand as well as bringing them into being.

He is not a nature god, although he is the God of nature.

He is totally distinct from his creation and yet he is present everywhere within it. The world is in no sense part of him nor is he identified with it. His tran-

40. Miller, *Interpreting Psalms*, 74.
41. Bullock, *Psalms*, 1:126-29.
42. Anderson, *Psalms*, 2:719.

scendence does not exclude but rather is balanced by his presence within his created universe, seen especially in Psalm 139.

Human beings give some revelation of themselves by the nature and qualities of the work they do. The same is true of Yahweh: he demonstrates his attributes in the qualities to be seen in his created work. Psalm 19:1-2 expresses this, for the heavens are said to declare, to proclaim, to display, knowledge, and what they declare, proclaim, display, is the glory of God. Paul's thought in Rom 1:18-25 is completely in line with this, and so it is not surprising that Psalm 19 is also cited in Rom 10:18, where Paul's quotation of it in this context clearly implies that the God who manifested himself in creation also reveals himself in the gospel of Christ.

A multitude of images from the natural world finds employment in the Psalter, and Psalm 114, for instance, provides several vivid examples. As Bullock says of these images, "they connect the created order and the Creator in language that leaves little doubt that God is supreme over his creation."[43]

As Creator, Yahweh claims the worship of all he has made.

The divine acts of creation are not simply subjects of theological statement in the Psalter but are themes of worship, and it is particularly in the psalms of praise that the language of creation is employed. Both heaven and earth are his creations, so he is to be praised in each, which gives them beautiful harmony. In Psalm 148 the heavens and the earth are viewed in terms of their constituent elements, not exhaustively but representatively, and each is seen to be made for the praise of Yahweh. Within the earthly realm human beings, brought into being by him, and especially Yahweh's own people, are to bring him their praise.

The division of the Psalter into five books may have taken place because it was felt that the acts and words of God should not only be recorded, as in the Pentateuch, but become also causes for praise, for pentateuchal themes such as creation, the relationship of God to the patriarchs, the exodus, the law, and many others occur also in the Psalter. This does not mean, of course, that there is an exact correspondence of some sort between Genesis and book 1, Exodus and book 2, and so on, but simply that the division makes the general point that God's acts are to be themes of his people's praise.

If this is so, then the principle is well illustrated in Psalm 104, where Yahweh's creative work is celebrated, following, somewhat selectively, the pattern of Genesis 1. He is celebrated as the maker of heaven and earth especially

43. Bullock, *Psalms,* 1:107.

248

in book 4, for instance, in 90:2; 93:1; 95:4-6; 96:5; 102:25, but also in 135 and 136 and in the psalms of the Final Hallel (e.g., 148:5-6; 149:2). Miller writes of "the virtually endless list of God's creative acts in the hymns of praise."[44]

This praise of the universal Creator is to include the nations. They may be worshipers of other gods, but their worship should be directed to him, for it was he who made the heavens (96:1-9), and they too owe him allegiance as their creator. There are assertions that one day all will acknowledge him (e.g., 145:10), but they are not to wait for that day but instead to bring him their praise here and now (148:7-13). This is all the more striking when we recall that such psalms were sung by the little postexilic community, which was like a tiny island set in a great ocean of polytheistic nations.

His creative activity established order, his righteousness reestablishes and confirms it.

The root צדק, ṣdq, and words linked to it like the near synonyms צֶדֶק, ṣedeq (masculine), and צְדָקָה, ṣĕdāqâ (feminine), both translated as "righteousness" or "justice," are important in the Psalms.[45] Although they relate to the divine character, the concern in the Psalms and elsewhere is not so much with the various divine attributes considered abstractly nor with how they relate to each other within the being of God. This may be a proper interest of systematic theology, but it is not the concern of OT theology. Righteousness in the OT is a vigorously dynamic quality. Just as in human life character is shown in relationships, so it is with God. Things have gone wrong in God's world, especially in human society, and he acts in his righteousness to put them right.

M. A. Seifrid properly insists that "'righteousness' is simultaneously moral and creational, having to do with God's re-establishing 'right order' in the fallen world which he has made, an order which includes a right relationship between the world and its Creator (e.g., Isa 45:8, 24; Pss 85:4-13; 98:1-9)."[46] It is significant that in Psalm 89, the psalmist, in a context celebrating that Yahweh is God both of creation and of the covenant, declares, "Righteousness and justice are the foundation of your throne" (89:14).

Because God is the supreme judge, this righting of wrongs often uses the language of the law court. The psalmist says, for instance, "My enemies

---

44. Miller, *Interpreting Psalms*, 73.

45. "Justice" also renders מִשְׁפָּט, mišpāṭ. See comments on judgment on pp. 258-59.

46. Seifrid, "Righteousness, Justice and Justification," in *NDBT*, 741. The whole article (740-45) is a helpful exposition of these concepts. See also its bibliography.

turn back, they stumble and perish before you. For you have upheld my right and my cause; you have sat on your throne judging righteously" (9:4).

As applied to his relations with his covenant people, Yahweh's righteousness is intimately linked to his faithfulness. He is deeply concerned with situations of injustice, and can be appealed to because of his total consistency. So he can be said to save in his righteousness, for salvation in the Psalms is often from enemies who pursue unjust causes. For example, in 40:10 the psalmist says, "I do not hide your righteousness in my heart; I speak of your faithfulness and salvation" (cf. Zech 8:7-8).

Righteousness has God as its author, so that a righteous person is so because he or she has been so adjudged by God. Indeed, the righteous person in the Psalms is the godly person, and his or her godliness is shown in commitment to the Lord. As with God, then, so with his people, righteousness and faithfulness, while not identical, are closely linked. This comes across clearly in Psalm 1, which in its introductory position gives the Psalter its moral thrust.

Ultimately, God will act in righteousness to reestablish righteousness on a cosmic scale, for "he will come to judge the world in righteousness and the peoples in his truth" (96:13).

Like his sole deity, Yahweh's creatorship is a fixed point of faith.

The phrase "Maker of heaven and earth" occurs three times in the Songs of Ascents (121:2; 124:8; 134:3). It also occurs in 115:15 and 146:6, and of this phrase Crenshaw says, "The language has a ring of a confession, so it is no surprise that the brief expression found its way into the Apostles' Creed of the Early Church."[47] Magonet explores this phrase in its occurrences in Psalms 115, 121, 124, 134, 146, and shows how it has somewhat different senses in different contexts. In 121 it assures protection from natural hazards, in 124 from human enemies, in 115 it designates two realms that must be kept apart, while in 146 it is seen that God's heavenly justice is expressed in particular situations on earth.[48] The revelation that their God was the world's creator was a great cause of consolation and assurance to his people.

47. Crenshaw, *Psalms,* 139.
48. Magonet, *Rabbi,* 117-50.

Yahweh Is the God of the Exodus

This is a fact of many-sided and great theological importance. The exodus was the supreme saving act of God for his people, and it would be difficult for any reader of the OT in general or of the Psalms in particular to miss the importance given to it in this literature. It is celebrated in song in the psalm-like Song of Moses (Exod 15:1-21), sung by the people immediately after it had taken place, and there are clear references to it in Psalms 44, 68, 74, 77, 78, 80, 81, 99, 103, 105, 106, 114, 135, 136. Some of these are psalms of praise while others are laments. In the former it is often the chief cause for thanksgiving, while in the latter the psalmists call on the God of the exodus to act thus again for his people (cf. Isa 51:9-11). We will see that Israel's experience of the exodus has also colored the language of a number of other psalms. The theme is particularly featured in 78, 105, 106, 114, and 136.

The exodus is intimately linked with Yahweh's great act of creation.

This is true in more than one way. As we have seen, in a psalm like 18 the description of God calls to mind both these great acts and also that it is none other than the God of creation and of the exodus, with all the power these acts represented, who comes to the rescue of this one man.[49] He is the king, and it is as if he is reminded of all that God has already done for his people when he experiences this act of his grace and power. Yahweh comes to his aid both as the God of creation and the God of the exodus redemption.

A second feature is the use of the term "Rahab" both of God's conquest of the supernatural powers of evil (which at Ugarit was reckoned to have been accomplished at creation) and also of his victory over Egypt. It would be a mistake to assume from this that the Ugaritic model of the acts of creation was accepted, but it may reflect the belief, shown in the book of Exodus, that the group of events associated with the plagues and the exodus constituted a victory not only over the Egyptians but over their gods (Exod 12:12).

A third feature is the use of creation language to describe Yahweh's constitution of Israel as a nation and as his people. He is not only the Maker of the universe but also the Maker of Israel (Ps 95:6-7; cf., e.g., Isa 43:15). This gives his creation of them as a nation, which was achieved through the exodus, a high status.

---

49. See the exegesis of this psalm.

> *The exodus is central to both the declarative*
> *and the descriptive praise psalms.*

Claus Westermann made this distinction, stressing the priority of the declarative over the descriptive and therefore the priority of gratitude over reflection, although of course reflection serves to intensify thanksgiving.

Many psalms are purely declarative, but not many, if any, are purely descriptive. A great psalm like 145 is both, and in it the descriptions are based on the declarations. In this psalm there is no express reference to the exodus, but terms like "wonderful works" (v. 5), "awesome works" (v. 6), and "mighty acts" (v. 12) are almost certainly references to acts of God in history rather than in creation, and the exodus will certainly have featured large in this respect in the minds of the psalmists. Sometimes the evidence for a specific exodus reference is strong, for 77:12 is followed by three verses that are highly reminiscent of Exodus 15.[50] The Song of Moses recorded in that chapter has influenced psalmic language in psalms like 77 and 114.

Also the exodus and events associated with it are prominent in the historical psalms, and these often have a declarative element in them (e.g., 78:1-8; 105:1-2; 106:1-2).

> *The exodus serves as a paradigm for later acts of salvation.*

Its nature as paradigm is to be seen when its language is used for other events of national salvation, whether in terms of description, of petition, or of praise. Bullock refers to "telescoping" the past, present, and future. "The present was merely a continuation of the past, and in that sense present and future Israel participated in the benefits of God's marvelous works in the past." He refers to Deut 5:2-3.[51] Who was it that overcame the Amalekites, the Philistines, the Babylonians (through the Persians)? It was the God of the exodus.

Furthermore, the psalmists indicate that, given the right attitude on the part of the people, their God would deliver them from further dangers as he had at the exodus. This is the import of Ps 81:13-16 in the light of the exodus references earlier in the psalm. One of the earliest evidences of this was the conquest of the land of Canaan, and language is sometimes used about this that is reminiscent of that used of the exodus (e.g., in 44:3).

The stress laid by writers like Gerhard von Rad and G. E. Wright on a proclamation of Yahweh's saving deeds, a proclamation that becomes pro-

---

50. See the exegesis of this psalm.
51. Bullock, *Psalms,* 1:181.

gressively richer throughout history, can be seen in this tendency to conflate various divine acts. So J. H. Eaton describes "Yahweh reigns" or "Yahweh has become king" in Psalm 93 and elsewhere as "an event-laden proclamation."[52] The events should never be viewed in abstraction from God himself whose acts they are. It is not the events that save, but God who saves through the events.[53] We should also remember that the revelation through events was not simply a disclosure of ideas but that the people experienced actual deliverance at the same time as being taught truths about God. Both the acts and the revelation they give are important.

It cannot have been lost on those who organized the Psalter that there were similarities between the Egyptian captivity and the Babylonian exile, similarities of such a character that Psalm 107 has been interpreted of both.[54] Commenting on this psalm, Bullock notes that oppression, hard labor, cries to God, and divine deliverance all make the exile a repeat of the exodus.[55] How great is the contrast between the profound sadness of Psalm 137 and the great joy of 126! The exodus theme is especially important in book 4, which has been called "the Mosaic Psalter," and this is not surprising if this book was put together to encourage the faith of the exiles.

The exodus colors all that is said about God's relations with Israel and with individual Israelites. The many references to the mighty works of the Lord would immediately bring the exodus, the supreme OT act of salvation, to mind, and this was probably the intention. Also 136:11-12, for instance, uses language about God's outstretched arm that would recall Exod 6:6 to the reader's mind. In the Psalms Yahweh is often described as savior and sometimes as redeemer. In 26:11, for instance, the psalmist calls God to redeem him and be merciful to him. When this kind of language is employed in somewhat general terms, it is highly likely to remind the reader of the exodus.

Sometimes, of course, it is language used in the Pentateuch about the exodus that is then employed in the Psalms. As Magonet points out, this happens in all kinds of subtle ways, and he suggests it is perhaps significant that the word חָסֵר, *ḥāsēr* ("lack"), comes both in 23:1, where it is applied to an individual, and in Deut 2:7, which is communal.[56] In Psalm 18, Yahweh is David's refuge, his rock, his fortress, his deliverer, his stronghold, and so on, but the term "the Rock" appears to be the leading one, for it has pride of place

---

52. Eaton, *Psalms of the Way,* 117.
53. Bullock, *Psalms,* 1:109.
54. See the comment on this psalm.
55. Bullock, *Psalms,* 1:116.
56. Magonet, *Rabbi,* 56, 57.

and is the only one to be repeated. The locus classicus for this expression is Deuteronomy 32, the Song of Moses, where it occurs a number of times.

In 27:1 "the stronghold of my life" is used in synonymous parallelism with "my light and my salvation." Because his God is this to him, the psalmist will not fear a besieging army (v. 3). A comment by Mays is appropriate in this regard: "The motif of Yhwh's saving intervention seems to have had its definitive place in the wars of the people. This explains why the vocabulary and imagery of warfare are used so extensively in the first-person-singular prayers. It is an extended use of traditional salvation language; it can be used to describe Yahweh's saving intervention from any trouble."[57]

The term "right hand," applied to God's power, is a reminder of the frequent use of the phrase "mighty hand" in relation to the exodus in Deuteronomy (e.g., 5:15; 6:21; 7:8, 19), for it is, for most people, the right hand that is the stronger. The Psalms employ this term for God's past acts for his people (e.g., in 44:3; 77:10; 98:1), but it is also used of the salvation of individuals from their enemies (17:7; 60:5).

We see then that there was a kind of theological logic at work, as if the individual Israelite reasoned that the God who had saved the whole nation was surely willing to do the same for him. It is true that often the person concerned is a king, with a special responsibility for the defense of the nation, or a Levite holding a divine office, but there are also "orphan" psalms in which the psalmist cries out for deliverance and apparently fully expects that Yahweh will come to his rescue (91:9-16; 116:1-9).

The exodus is a major cause of the people's praise and of their faith.

Because Yahweh is the God who saves them, the hearts of his people are filled with gratitude. This is evident in both the communal hymns and the individual psalms of thanksgiving. Psalmic thanksgiving relates to specifics, to the saving deeds of God, whether these be in the life of the community or of the individual. At the human level, the chief motive behind the writing of many of them must simply have been sheer gratitude and the desire to have not only a thanksgiving sacrifice to offer but also a verbal vehicle for praise.

It is striking that salvation is by far the most frequent topic of psalms in which there are expressions of thanksgiving. Of course, the land itself provides further causes for praise, but the very possession of the land by the people was due to the exodus, for, in the words of Deuteronomy, "he brought us out . . . to bring us to this place" (Deut 26:8-9).

57. Mays, *Lord Reigns*, 29.

The exodus motif establishes trust as the basic attitude God's people should have toward him. Davidson comments that "the reliving of the past becomes the launching pad of urgent prayer for a future in which present troubles would be overcome (cf. Psalm 74)."[58] Indeed, it may well be that the exodus deliverance was in the minds of lamenting and praying psalmists even when such psalms contain no explicit use of language that evokes it.

There are two main verbs connected with faith in the Psalter, בָּטַח, *bāṭaḥ*, and חָסָה, *ḥāsâ*. The second means "to take refuge"; the refuge theme is very prominent, especially in the first two books. Here there is danger or affliction of some kind, and the psalmist as an individual or the people as a whole seek to find refuge in God. This is, of course, associated with the declarative psalms of praise, for when they find and enter this divine refuge the people express their thanksgiving to Yahweh for their safety. Mays argues for the special importance of 2:12, the first reference to the refuge theme in the Psalter, and thinks its presence in an introductory psalm was to alert readers to this feature in the subsequent psalms, beginning with Psalm 3.[59]

It is notable that the word or the idea often occurs toward the end of a psalm, as in 2:12; 3:8; 4:8; 5:11-12; 7:17. In fact, Psalms 3–7 all show the psalmist seeking refuge from his foes in God. The start and finish of particular psalms often establish their theme, whether or not they are characterized by a formal inclusio, so that they make clear the main thrust and message of a particular psalm.[60] Romans 2:6 quotes Ps 62:12, where the psalmist, assaulted, trusts God's righteous judgment, and this is at the end of the psalm.

The term *bāṭaḥ* has more the sense of resting on God, and suggests a settled attitude rather than an act in a time of trouble. It is the settled character of the psalmist's God, as revealed in a succession of his saving acts, that is the basis for a settled trust.

The word עָנִי, *'ānî*, is extensively used in the Psalms (along with its cognates), and it is often translated "poor." It indicates helplessness but without specifying its nature.[61] The word is frequently used in a context where the psalmist is casting himself, in all his need, on Yahweh.

There is a call for faith even in the way the Psalter was finally arranged, for Psalms 1 and 2, which together appear to constitute a joint introduction to the book, implicitly call for faith, the faith that the righteous are destined for happiness, the wicked for destruction, and the Davidic king for supreme hu-

---

58. Davidson, *Vitality of Worship*, 416.

59. Mays, *Psalms*, 48. Creach has explored this whole theme in *Yahweh as Refuge*; see also Sheppard, "Theology," 149-52.

60. Seybold, *Psalms*, 73-76.

61. Mays, *Lord Reigns*, 30.

man sovereignty. Mays says of Psalm 2, "The psalm is based on the faith that the LORD throned in heaven is the ultimate power. The dominion of the son must correspond to the sovereignty of the father."[62]

Faith takes its value from the strength and quality of the one trusted. On 3:3-4 Kraus makes an important point: "It is worth noting that the statements of trust begin, not with 'I,' but with 'you.' Trust has its foundation in Yahweh, not in the believing human being."[63] Such faith often banishes fear from the heart of the one exercising it, for he is confident of seeing the goodness of the Lord in the land of the living (27:2-3, 13).

The exodus encouraged the godly when they were beset by enemies.

The exodus deliverance provides something of a pattern for the imprecatory prayers of the people. Prior to the exodus, the people cried out to God because of their sufferings (Exod 2:23-25; 3:7-10; 6:5; Num 20:15-16), and he delivered them from their enemies. This pattern finds repetition in many of the psalms of lament.

The psalmists refer frequently to their enemies, and this is particularly the case in the Davidic psalms. This is understandable because we see from the books of Samuel that in at least two major periods in David's life enemies were very active against him: during his persecution by Saul and during Absalom's rebellion. Psalm 2 states the Lord's support for the king, apparently based on God's promise in 2 Samuel 7, and this is presumably the basis of the appeals to him in the Davidic psalms. There are references to the number of his enemies (Ps 3:1, 6), to their rage (7:6), to the fact that they are persecuting him (9:13), that they are liars and deceivers (12:2), and so on.

We do not always know who these enemies were. Bullock deals with six general interpretations of the enemies in the psalms. Some see them as a hostile group among the psalmist's own people, others as those who believed the psalmist was suffering divine punishment or who falsely accuse him of sin or who use sorcery against him, while others view them as foreign powers, or else think the language intentionally metaphorical and open, allowing readers to apply the psalms to their own situations.[64]

In some passages the control of God over the enemies means they can afflict the psalmist up to a point but no further. So, in John 19:36, John applies to Jesus the words, "a bone of him shall not be broken" (Ps 34:20), which

62. Mays, *Psalms*, 47.
63. Kraus, *Psalms 1–59*, 139.
64. Bullock, *Psalms*, 1:145-46.

comes from a psalm envisaging protection as complete. Clearly Christ was deeply afflicted by his enemies and brought to his death by them, but there were limits even then to the indignities they were allowed to heap on him.

There are passages where the psalmist is confident that God will deal with his enemies and punish them, removing their threat from him. He is sure of this because he knows the righteous character of God (11:5-7). At times, however, he goes further than simply stating this confidence. He prays for the defeat and even the destruction of his enemies, and he often sees their downfall as God's answer to his prayers, as in 6:8-10. If this is so, then his prayers for physical salvation and his prayers of imprecation against his enemies are not very different. The latter are the realistic extension of the former, for the downfall of the wicked is the inevitable consequence of God's act of delivering him from them.

Such prayers occur at many different points in the Psalter. Why do the psalmists pray this way? Because, probably in line with the exodus theme, they identify these people as the enemies of God and, just as he destroyed the Egyptian army in the Red Sea, so they looked to him, in connection with his later acts of salvation in response to prayer, to act in judgment on those who oppressed and persecuted them.

We should note that they do not take matters into their own hands but rather ask God to act. Had he not so acted before? They call on Yahweh as God of Israel. At the exodus and on a number of subsequent occasions, he had been the author of their salvation, and so they call on him to act again for them. If this meant safety for them, it inevitably meant ruin for their enemies. Even in Psalm 149, where the people are viewed as taking vengeance against their enemies, they do so "to carry out the sentence written against them" (v. 9), written, of course, by the Lord.

Some psalms look back not so much to the exodus as to other decisive victories of God over their enemies, as in the case of Midian (83:9-12), but this again rests on the primary victory of God for his people at the exodus.

Without doubt, such prayers raise problems for Christians. It is important that we do not play down this element but face it fairly and squarely. Zenger says quite frankly, "Hatred, enmity, violence, retaliation, and even revenge are not sub-motifs in the Psalter: they are substantive parts of it."[65] He considers that these psalms reflect an intense desire to see justice upheld in a world that is largely devoid of it. So these prayers affirm the divine integrity, which might otherwise have seemed in doubt.

One of the most striking features of these psalms is that such passages

---

65. Zenger, *God of Vengeance?* 19.

often occur in contexts where the sentiments are beautiful and not at all difficult to accept. Psalms 139 and 143 are examples of this. Both features of these
psalms seem to be the outpourings of one spirituality. The psalmist apparently did not sense the jarring discord that modern readers find in such
juxtapositioning. In line with this, we find the apostles applying to the fate of
Judas the imprecatory words of 69:25 and of the very strong 109:8 (Acts 1:20).

Crenshaw thinks these imprecatory prayers cannot be justified theologically: "the use of Psalms for daily devotion and as a model of prayer . . . runs
the risk of infecting religious people with harmful attitudes. Do the prayers
for vengeance against personal enemies sacralize violence?"[66] Surely our answer to Crenshaw must be no. There is no suggestion of the psalmist himself
taking a vengeful initiative. These passages are prayers, not programs for human action. The psalmist leaves the matter in the hands of God, calling on
him to uphold the right. In this respect, they are remarkably similar to an NT
passage, Rev 6:9-10: "I saw under the altar the souls of those who had been
slain because of the word of God and the testimony they had maintained.
They called out in a loud voice, 'How long, Sovereign Lord, holy and true, until you judge the inhabitants of the earth and avenge our blood?'"

Many readers will find Ps 137:8-9 particularly difficult, for here the
psalmist invokes a blessing on those who violently take the lives of children in
Babylon. Two points may be made. The first is that what the psalmist contemplates is what the prophet Isaiah had predicted would happen (Isa 13:16). The
second is that the OT as a whole often tends to use concrete language in contexts where modern writers are more likely to use abstract terms. This is usually helpful to us in giving vividness to the expression, but in this case the vividness is just too intense for the imagination of the modern reader, who
would be much less troubled by a simple statement that it would be good
when the evil Babylonian regime came to its divinely predicted end, for this is
what these verses mean.

Yahweh Is the God of Sinai

The Psalter shows settled convictions about God's character.

The Psalter opens by declaring the happiness of those who have a godly lifestyle and also the certain judgment of those who are wicked. As the introduction to a book of religious poems, this has important implications concerning

---

66. Crenshaw, *Psalms*, 67-68.

the character of God. The psalmists frequently appeal to him as a God of righteousness and judgment. Indeed, the psalmists were as certain of this as was Paul in a passage like Rom 3:5-8. This is quite unvarying, so these moral convictions were evidently just as much subjects of revelation as were the evidences of Yahweh's concern for his people as shown at the exodus. They too are nonnegotiable. The NIV translates several Hebrew words as "judgment," but by far the most frequent in the Psalms is מִשְׁפָּט, *mišpāṭ*, which is also sometimes rendered "justice," although this English word also translates צֶדֶק, *ṣedeq*, or צְדָקָה, *ṣĕdāqâ*, otherwise rendered as "righteousness." Occasionally *mišpāṭ* and *ṣĕdāqâ* are treated as near-synonyms, as in 99:4 and 106:3. These words inhabit the same thought world, that of the law court in which the judge acts to put right what is wrong, to transform injustice into justice, to save those who are suffering unjustly, and to punish evildoers.

In his chapter on the laments, Bullock shows how much the Psalms emphasize the character of God.[67] Crenshaw points to the use of Hebrew אַךְ, *'ak* ("surely"), in 73:1, 13, 18, saying that it functions like a credal affirmation.[68] The first of these is about a moral structure and the third is about judgment, so that their combination is somewhat like the position declared in Psalm 1. The second expresses a temptation to take a different outlook, which it is clear the author resisted, so that his negative thoughts did not win in the end.

If, as some have thought, the Psalter ended at one time with 145, it is surely significant that the moral assertions of Psalm 1 are reasserted in 145:20, "The LORD watches over all who love him, but all the wicked he will destroy." This elicits the psalmist's concluding praise (v. 21).

It is not surprising, then, to find vigorous attacks on sin. In the introductory Psalm 2, sin's irrationality is very clear and the divine laughter ridicules this. Moreover, it is seen to be fruitless (vv. 6-9). Its universality is shown very clearly in Psalm 14, and there are also appropriate references to it in Psalms 11 and 12, especially the latter. It is not only an individual matter, for there are social sins about which God is concerned. In 12:5 it is declared that the oppression of the weak and needy will be put right by God when he rises to judge.

The Sinai revelation is the chief historical basis
for these moral convictions.

One of the puzzles of the Psalter is the comparative paucity of explicit references to the giving of the law at Sinai. This paucity is particularly surprising in

67. Bullock, *Psalms*, 1:136-50.
68. Crenshaw, *Psalms*, 116-17.

passages where it would have seemed most natural, and at times almost inevitable, that it should be mentioned. Broyles comments on 78:44-55, "Particularly striking here in Psalm 78 is the omission of Mt. Sinai, of the establishment of the covenant, and of the giving of the law from the narrative sequence. . . . Sinai is similarly left out of the narrative sequence of other historical psalms."[69]

This feature of the Psalter should not be exaggerated, and it is worth an overview of the references. In book 5 the great psalm of the Law, 119, which is by far the longest in the Psalter, comes between two major groups of festival psalms. According to the Pentateuch, the festivals originated during the exodus and wilderness wanderings, so that the placing of the psalm of the Law here acted as a reminder that Sinai also belonged to this period. The element of lament in this psalm is balanced by an emphasis on the Torah as a spiritual anchor. As Sheriffs says, "we see in the juxtaposition of lament language and precept language a context for the kind of meditation that Psa 119 promulgates. . . . The content of torah is something solid, a basis for living."[70] He also says that the internalizing of torah that we see the psalmist seeking to do in 119 "counteracts the pressures on the poet's life that come from temptation and social hostility."[71]

Psalms 1 and 19 also give the Law an important place. Then there are 68, which calls Israel's God "the One of Sinai" (v. 8); 78, with its reference to the divine law (vv. 5 and 6); and 81, which alludes to the legislation establishing feast days (vv. 3-5) and where verses 8-10 clearly recall Exod 20:1-2.

There is quite a concentration of significant references in book 4, where Psalm 90 is headed, "A prayer of Moses the man of God," and is strongly moral in tone; 95 refers to events that occurred just prior to Sinai; 99:6-7 says, "Moses and Aaron were among his priests. . . . He spoke to them from the pillar of cloud; they kept his statutes and the decrees he gave them"; and 103:7 declares, "he made known his ways to Moses."

Bullock points out that it is the incidents of the manna, the quails, and the rock that are most highlighted in the narrative psalms,[72] and these of course belong to the period of the wilderness wanderings that succeeded the giving of the law. Psalm 105 focuses largely on the events associated with the exodus, referring to Moses (v. 26) and concluding, "He gave them the lands of the nations . . . that they might keep his precepts and observe his laws." Significantly Psalm 106, which follows this, focuses on the rebelliousness of the

---

69. Broyles, *Psalms,* 324.
70. Sheriffs, *Friendship of the Lord,* 121.
71. Sheriffs, *Friendship of the Lord,* 147.
72. Bullock, *Psalms,* 1:109-12.

people during their early history (cf. 78:56-58), with mention of Moses (v. 16). Referring to 106, Bullock says, "We can see that the presence of Sinai and the spirit of Israel that prevailed there are far more pervasive in the Psalms than the place itself. And most of all, it is the God of Sinai who reveals himself at every turn of history."[73]

There is much about rebellion and sin in most of the historical psalms, and this may reflect to some extent the fact that the seriousness of sin was so powerfully stressed at Sinai. Whether or not this is spelled out, the ancient reader was sure to recall that the first major manifestation of this rebellious spirit took place at Sinai itself in the worship of the golden calf, although 106:7 traces this spirit to an earlier event: the people's rebellious unbelief faced with the Red Sea ahead of them.

On a more positive note, in some passages the psalmist writes about having the law of God in the heart (37:31; 40:8) and also of the importance of the king's obedience to that law (89:30).

The comparative frequency of reference to Moses and the events of his day in book 4 is interesting. This could be due chiefly to two factors. First, the covenant with David seemed to be under threat, as we see in 89, and so the compilers of book 4, beginning it with 90, are stressing that the covenant dealings of God with his people precede by many centuries his covenant with David. Then, if this book was compiled toward the close of the exile, it was important that the rebelliousness of the people against God's law over many years should be emphasized, because it was the spiritual cause of that event.

It is evident that Yahweh's disclosure of his grace to Moses in Exodus 33 and 34 has influenced many a passage in the book of Psalms,[74] and this belongs to the Sinai revelation. Magonet shows how 145, which makes no actual reference to Sinai, meditates quite extensively on the revelation of God's grace in these two chapters of Exodus.[75] The reference to the trembling of the earth in 114:7, especially as this is associated with the mountains (vv. 4 and 6), may recall the earthquake that preceded the delivery of the law in Exodus 19 and 20. Then there is a psalm like 18, where language associated with the creation and the exodus is also blended with that of Sinai as a place where God's power was experienced by his people (vv. 7-15).

Even when all has been said, however, we might have expected more. The reasons for this comparative paucity of reference are not far to seek. The

---

73. Bullock, *Psalms*, 1:109.

74. E.g., the language of Exod 34:6-7 has clearly influenced that of Pss 86:15; 103:8; and 145:8.

75. Magonet, *Rabbi*, 42-44.

great emphasis of the Psalter is on salvation, because the laments so often plead for deliverance and the psalms of praise so often give thanks for it, that the exodus theme was bound to be more prominent than the Sinai one. Moreover, there is also an emphasis on promise, especially on the Davidic covenant promise.

It is important also to notice that the three psalms that focus particularly on the law are not simply about duty but express great delight in the law as God's revelation. Brueggemann characterizes the Psalter as moving from obedience in Psalm 1 to praise in 150, but it would be better to see it as a movement from delight to praise.[76] Paul's words in Rom 7:22, "in my inner being I delight in God's law," might almost have come straight out of the Psalter. Moreover, delight in God leads almost inevitably to praise of God, as the Westminster Shorter Catechism recognizes in saying that man's chief end is to glorify God and to enjoy him forever. Viewing Psalm 1 as a preface to the Psalter and as introducing themes culminating in praise at the end of the whole book, Konrad Schaefer has well said of the Torah here that it is "the open door to praise through which one has access to interior rooms."[77]

The Psalter also views godliness as related to God's uttered word.

The Sinai revelation has influenced the book of Psalms in quite a special way, because that revelation was verbal and obviously the Psalter too is verbal in nature. At Sinai the importance of the divine word is clear, and in the Psalter this is reflected not only in Psalm 1, where it is given emphasis at the very start of the book, but at many later points. It is true that the acts of God are very important for the OT and therefore for the Psalter, but the importance of the divine word has been too often overlooked.

Not only so, but if the final edition of the Psalter belongs to the postexilic period, it is perhaps particularly significant that a book containing so much worship material should be prefixed not with an emphasis on sacrifice but rather on the written word, although of course Yahweh's verbal revelation included the pentateuchal sacrificial regulations. We will look at the theological importance of the exile later, but meantime we should remember that during that period the people had no temple and that after their return great emphasis was placed on the written word, as the record of the solemn

---

76. This reflection owes much to a paper by Michael LeFebvre, "Psalm One and Torah-Meditation: An Invitation to 'Sound Out' Torah," which had not yet been published when this commentary was completed. Cf. Brueggemann, "Obedience and Praise."

77. Schaefer, *Psalms*, 3.

convocation in Nehemiah 8 shows. This does not imply a reduction in the importance of worship, for what is recorded in Nehemiah 8 is a worship occasion, but with the word of God in the Law taking the central place in it.

The wider and narrower connotations of tôrâ in the Psalter.

This word occurs in nine psalms (1:2; 19:8; 37:31; 40:9; 78:1, 5, 10; 89:31; 94:12; 105:45; and 25 times in 119). The wider sense of *tôrâ* is "instruction," so that it represents the verbal nature of revelation. It also has a narrower, technical sense as "law," used of specific divine commandments, the Mosaic law as a whole and also the five books of Moses. No clear case of this last meaning is to be found in the Psalter, but the wider sense and the meaning "the Mosaic law as a whole" are certainly there. The latter is most evident in Psalms 19 and 119, and the piling up of synonyms in both psalms makes this clear as most of them have a strong legal flavor. There is no passage in which these two uses of the word are either compared or contrasted. The God who had revealed his character and his moral requirements at Sinai continued to teach his people, and it was entirely appropriate for the same term to be used.

What then of Psalm 1, which opens the Psalter? Brevard Childs says, "The editorial positioning of this original Torah psalm has provided the psalm with a new interpretative function. As an introduction it designates those prayers which follow as the medium through which Israel now responds to the divine word. Because Israel continues to hear God's word through the voice of the psalmist's response, these prayers now function as the divine word itself."[78] He calls this "a hermeneutical shift." So then the practical revelatory significance of the Psalter is shown from its initial poem. If the fivefold structure of the Psalter existed prior to the positioning of Psalm 1 at its start or even was given to it at this time, the two features together may suggest that the introductory psalm is drawing attention to the Psalter as a kind of Pentateuch for worship.

We know nothing of the history of this psalm, whether it was written specially to introduce the Psalter or whether, written earlier, it was seen to be particularly apt for this purpose by the ultimate redactor. If the latter is the case, it may well be that the author has the technical sense in mind but the redactor the nontechnical, perhaps even intending the readers to understand it as an encouragement to read the book that was being put together, although we cannot be completely sure of this. There is nothing inappropriate in this kind of adaptation, for, in the history of revelation, the new is often an un-

---

78. Childs, *OT Theology,* 207.

folding of the implications of the old. Moreover, both the Mosaic law and the Psalter come within the wider understanding of *tôrâ* as instruction.

Whatever we say about the significance of Psalm 1, it is clear that much may be learned about God and his ways with his people in the Psalter. Revelation from God was not confined to the exodus period, although the fundamental truths all emerge clearly at that time. Here is further divine guidance about the way to live, no less based on the great principles of divine character seen at Sinai than are the books of the prophets.

In line with this view of it, Mays identifies Psalms 1, 37, 49, 78, and 112 as composed in a teaching style, while in others the voice of a teacher speaks in the styles of prayer, thanksgiving, and praise (e.g., in 25, 32, 92, 94, 111).[79] If there was indeed, as Westermann thought, an edition of the Psalter at one time that commenced with Psalm 1 and ended with 119, the opening and closing psalms of this constituted an inclusio. An inclusio indicates the main emphasis of a piece of literature, so that this feature here would show the importance of *tôrâ*.[80] Referring to this, Crenshaw compares the function of Hos 14:9 in the book of Hosea, which in effect makes it a wisdom book.[81]

The word of God is powerful, even effecting creation.

Psalm 29 extols the voice of the Lord that, in this context, is to be heard in the storm. Furthermore it goes out to all the world through the created universe as such, pointing to its Creator (19:1-4). His creative work is said to be by the רוּחַ, *rûaḥ* (here rendered as "breath"), of his mouth or by the power of his word (33:6, 9). At least implicitly the same idea occurs in Psalm 104, where there seems some following of the Genesis 1 structure, which highlights the function of God's word in creation.

This gives high value to the authority and power of the spoken word of God and if, as we would expect, this was shared by the psalmists as a whole, it coheres well with what they write about the authority and power of the written word.

The psalmists view Yahweh as the great teacher of his people.

R. N. Whybray points out that the concept of God as teacher, without intermediaries, is somewhat rare in the OT. He points out that the verb in 27:11 occurs with God as subject in only four psalms apart from 27, that is, in 25:8, 12;

79. Mays, *Psalms*, 15.
80. Westermann, *Praise and Lament*, 252-53.
81. Crenshaw, *Psalms*, 38-39.

32:8; 86:11; and 119:33, 102.[82] To these psalms, however, should be added at least Psalm 19, where, after referring to the many qualities and effects of the *tôrâ* and the blessings of it, the psalmist says, "By them is your servant warned" (v. 11), surely by God.

It seems from a study of such psalms that the psalmist's call to God to teach him is not so much a request for fuller understanding but rather that he should take the psalmist in hand, leading him in paths of righteousness because he needed divine enabling to walk that way. This means that just as the accusation that the prophets were Pelagians does not meet all the facts, neither could it be leveled against the psalmists. Here then law and grace are seen to go hand in hand. The great psalm of the *tôrâ* ends with a confession of failure, "I have strayed like a lost sheep. Seek your servant, for I have not forgotten your commands" (119:176).

The wilderness period, which immediately followed the Sinai revelation, comes across particularly in the historical psalms as a time when God was instructing his people, teaching them especially about his character, although they were unwilling to learn and often rebelled against him. This is a major theme in historical psalms like 78, 95, and 106.

This emphasis on Yahweh as the God of truth stands in strong contrast to what the psalmists have to say about the untrustworthiness of human utterance. Psalm 12, for instance, majors on this theme, setting human lying, deceit, and flattery over against the flawless word of God.

The psalmists in their turn became teachers of divine truth. Their experience of God in the midst of difficulties, whether of their own making or that of others, taught them much they could pass on. This is said, for instance, in Psalm 51, where the author's experience of forgiveness fits him to instruct others (vv. 12-13).

It is well known that people of the OT placed considerable emphasis on the role of memorization in learning. We can see this perhaps in the acrostic psalms if the purpose of the acrostic is to help the memory.[83]

Klaus Seybold points out that there is material in the book of Psalms that is propositional in form. He considers the alphabetical poems to have a clear theological purpose, and he says,

> In the case of Ps. 119 it is possible to detect . . . a claim to a comprehensive theology of the Word of God; however it must be seen as a weakness in

---

82. Whybray, *Reading the Psalms,* 51.

83. Soll (*Psalm 119,* 5-34) considers this feature to be primarily aesthetic, although he does acknowledge that a result of it was often to help the memory.

this theory that the chain of 22 × 8 = 176 verses achieves a systematic exploration only by "addition," the gathering of material. And yet, the massing of insights and testimonies does correspond to the general principle of the canon far more than "abstraction," analysis and evaluation.[84]

Truth learned needs to be practically expressed.

Purely uncommitted intellectualism is alien to the OT, including the book of Psalms. It is taken for granted that teaching must be implemented in practical living.

The verb הָלַךְ, *hālak* ("to walk"), is often employed to picture a person's lifestyle, especially on its moral side. Psalm 1 is the locus classicus of this. Psalm 12:8 employs the same verb, but uses it of the wicked, and the NIV translates it here vividly, in line with the context, as "strut about," which suggests their demeanor, but the closing words of the verse, "when what is vile is honored among men," suggest that it also has something of a moral flavor. It is used in the divine cry from the heart of 81:13-14, "If my people would but listen to me, if Israel would follow [*hālak*] my ways, how quickly would I subdue their enemies and turn my hand against their foes!"

The results of meditation with obedience are joy and wisdom. The linking of the *tôrâ* and joy is one of the most remarkable aspects of psalmic piety, and Eaton has brought this out well. He says of the Law in 119, "The rapturous delight it brings (14, 16 and 24) is the mystical awe and delight of contact with the Lord (120 and 131-32). It is the Lord himself who is the worshipper's shelter and shield (114), and it is the Lord he would praise (175) and the Lord he asks to seek and save him (176)."[85] This is important. Eaton also says of 1, 19, and 119 that it is remarkable that none of them gives a specification or an example of such Scripture. "No document is mentioned, no command is cited. The centre of interest thus remains the Lord himself, and the relation to him. The warm devotion centres in the fact that *he* teaches, guides, commands and promises, and therefore in mercy and faithfulness bestows life."[86]

Psalm 119, as D. N. Freedman has shown, performs a salutary function in that it contrasts the perfection of the *tôrâ* with the imperfections of human life. It does this by its structure, which combines an overall symmetry with apparently chaotic use of its key words. It does so also by its contents, which show the perfection of the divine revelation and the psalmist's life of "chaos,

84. Seybold, *Psalms*, 152-53.
85. Eaton, *Psalms of the Way*, 51.
86. Eaton, *Psalms of the Way*, 52.

trouble, and ambiguity."[87] This contrast is seen clearly when the first and last verses of the psalm are compared. For this reason, Will Soll actually classes this psalm as a lament.[88]

The category of wisdom psalms has been much disputed. Not only have quite different lists been drawn up by different scholars, but the very appropriateness of the category has been denied.[89] Nevertheless, it is unmistakable that many of the psalms show that their authors expected their readers to learn important lessons about God and about life from them, and to translate these lessons into practical living. If the whole book has a message, then that will itself communicate wisdom to those who heed it.

It is surely significant that the two introductory psalms both have a wisdom flavor. Psalm 1 is clearly a wisdom psalm, even though it does not use the term, for it shows the two ways of right and of wrong and does so in such a way as to encourage the reader to take the righteous way. Psalm 2 becomes in effect a wisdom psalm by its address to the wicked to return from their rebellion. Wisdom and warning go together in verse 10, and the whole of verses 10 to 12 are wisdom material. It ends with a beatitude, which is characteristic of wisdom psalms.

There are wisdom sections in some psalms that cannot be classified as wisdom psalms when considered as a whole. Psalm 9:17-18, for instance, seems almost like the book of Proverbs in its antithetical nature, and 11:4-7 makes assertions that are wisdom teaching. In Psalms 14 and 53 and elsewhere the fool is one who is heedless of divine counsel, and it is said that evildoers never learn. Psalm 18:25-27 seems like a wisdom psalm in its structure. Parts of 25 are particularly strong in wisdom themes and forms, and psalms of entrance, like 15 and 24, also have something of a wisdom flavor, for their concern is practical.

Such learning would give joy to the heart of the attentive reader. The emphasis on delight that is in the opening psalm (v. 2) is a keynote of the book, for there is a general sense of delight in passages where the *tôrâ* is mentioned, and especially in 19 and 119. Who can miss the depth of emotion in the heart of the psalmists when they wrote of God's ordinances, "They are more precious than gold, than much pure gold; they are sweeter than honey from the comb" (19:10) or, "Oh, how I love your law! I meditate on it all day long" (119:97)?

This forms a link between the Psalms and the book of Proverbs and also

---

87. Freedman et al., *Psalm 119*, esp. 87-94 (quotation on 93).
88. Soll, *Psalm 119*, 59-111.
89. Whybray, *Reading the Psalms*, 36-38; but see Davidson, *Wisdom and Worship*.

links the Psalter with other OT wisdom books like Ecclesiastes and Job. It perhaps vindicates the sense of appropriateness of those who decided to place it here in the ultimate arrangement of the OT canon in the LXX, the arrangement followed in our English versions. It is interesting that the church has tended to follow this arrangement rather than that favored by the Masoretes.

Yahweh Is the God of Jerusalem/Zion

Most of the historical events of high theological significance for the psalmists are associated with the beginnings of the nation, but there is one exception, the establishment of Jerusalem as its political and religious capital. "Jerusalem" refers to the city, and "Zion" was originally the name of one of the hills on which it stood, but it came to be treated as a synonym for "Jerusalem."

Establishment of king and temple at Jerusalem is most important.

In 2:6 Yahweh refers to Zion as "my holy hill," which suggests that its religious significance is most in view. Indeed, the compilers may have seen this verse to be important as setting the tone for all references to Zion/Jerusalem in the Psalter. This is not unlike the book of Isaiah, in which Zion is such an important theme and where the emphasis on it begins in chapter 1.

Though the psalmists recognize that Yahweh's throne is in heaven (11:4; 103:19), some also say that it is in Zion (9:11; 132:13-14). There is a close association between his throne and the throne of David, for the king's throne on God's holy hill was established by God himself, as Psalm 2 indicates (2:4-6).

The same duality also applies to Yahweh's temple. Sometimes it seems to be in heaven while at other times in Jerusalem. In Psalm 84 the psalmist extols the courts of the Lord as God's dwelling place and as God's house. There are also passages where throne and temple are very closely linked. In 11:4 they seem virtual synonyms. What is meant when the psalmist says that Yahweh answers prayer from his sanctuary? In 20:2 the parallelism appears to indicate that God's sanctuary is in Zion, while in verse 6 he answers his anointed from heaven. This clearly implies a close link between the two. The temple at Jerusalem was the symbol on earth of the sanctuary in heaven.

Zion is called "the city of God" in 46:4; 48:1, 8; and 87:3, and it is said to be the place where the Most High dwells (43:4; 46:4-5; 68:16; 132:13-14). It is the dwelling place of God (46:4-5), and because he is with his people there they can look to him as their refuge (46:1, 7, 11; 48:3, 8). It is this that makes the movement of the Lord's glory from the temple toward Babylon in Ezekiel

(Ezek 9:3; 10:4, 18-19; 11:23) both ominous and reassuring, ominous for those left behind and reassuring for the captives in Babylon.

John Bright refers to the centralizing significance of the ark and to its placing in the Jerusalem temple.[90] J. Gordon McConville mentions that the "Tables of the Law" were kept in the ark (Deut 10:5; cf. 31:9). Writing of Psalms 68 and 132, he says, "Jerusalem succeeds Sinai as a symbol of Israel's status as the special people of God" because the coming of the ark there meant God's election of Zion. He also points out that both the king and Zion are elected by God (2:6; 110:1ff.).[91] This means, in effect, that Jerusalem gathers up much from the past, for it was the goal of the exodus, the ark in its temple contained the law given at Sinai, and this city was the focus of covenant promises.

Psalm 68 appears to celebrate the bringing of the ark from the wilderness into Canaan and then into Jerusalem on the day of its installation there (vv. 17-18, 24-35), and it may well have been used in the temple worship on festive occasions. It is clear that the psalmist regarded this installation as a highly significant event, for, writing of Zion, he calls it "the mountain where God chooses to reign, where the LORD himself will dwell forever" (v. 16), and, in dramatic apostrophe, other mountains are rebuked because of their envy of it (vv. 15-16).[92] Psalm 132 also gives much importance to this event. The beginning of this triumphant march in Numbers 10 is recorded in a passage of leading importance for its influence on the Psalms, a passage clearly employed at the start of Psalm 68: "Rise up, O LORD! May your enemies be scattered; may your foes flee before you" (Num 10:35; cf. Ps 68:1).

There are many references to the place of worship as the temple. If the Davidic psalms were written by him, this seems anachronistic, as the temple was not built until the time of Solomon, while in David's day the ark was enclosed in a tent (2 Sam 7:2). It is possible that the use of the term "temple" is the later work of a redactor, employing a term familiar to the people of his day because of the use of these psalms in their worship, or even perhaps that David, making plans for the temple that was to come, acted as his own redactor in this respect.[93]

---

90. Bright, *History of Israel,* 161-62, 196.
91. McConville, "Jerusalem in the OT," 25-26.
92. See comments on this psalm.
93. See pp. 36-37.

> *Zion as the city of God has a special place in the people's affections.*

The Zion psalms (e.g., 46, 48, 76, 84, 87) constitute a special category; they focus on the blessings of Zion as a place of worship, as the center and symbol and focus of the community of God's people.

The attentive reader can hardly miss the emotional tone of many references to it (48:12; 87:2, 5; 126:1; 137:1-7). Levitical psalms like 42 (with 43) and 61 show the psalmist's great longing to be there worshiping the Lord, and these feelings are also evident in the Davidic 84. The very name of this city stirred deep emotions in the hearts of Jewish people. This went beyond the patriotic feelings normally associated with a capital city, for this was where the temple and its worship were located. Even the fact that it was the political capital had religious overtones, because the king was the Lord's anointed, whose reign had been undergirded by solemn covenantal promises from the Lord.

In Psalm 137 the writer pours out his passionate, anguished longing for Jerusalem, and his use of the first person plural in many of the verses shows that he is not simply writing of his own feelings but of those of the community to which he belongs, for the hearts of the people ached when they thought of the city they loved and had lost.

> *Zion is the center of a special but widening community of worshipers.*

The people's awareness that they were a divinely established community of course long preceded the capture of Jerusalem in the time of David, but undoubtedly the establishment of a capital city fosters national integration. It also gives the city a strongly religious atmosphere if it also becomes the center of its people's worship.

It is a great privilege to be born in Zion, and amazingly in one psalm (87) it is said that individuals of foreign origin would be born there. So then the community of the godly was to be expanded not by adding territory to Zion but rather by expanding Zion itself to accommodate them, much in the way that Ezekiel sees the ultimate temple to be a vastly extended reproduction of the temple at Jerusalem (Ezek 40–48), and John sees the city of God descending out of heaven from God (Rev 21:2). It almost seems at times as if Zion stands for the quintessence of Israel as the people of God.

Terms like "LORD Most High" and "Jacob" mark several of the Zion psalms (e.g., 46:4, 7, 11; 84:8; 87:2, 5). Psalm 47 shares many of the characteristics of these psalms and may be reckoned one of them, especially as the compilers placed it between 46 and 48, both Zion psalms. Zion is not mentioned in 47, but it shows some kinship with 87 when the psalmist says, "God reigns over the nations; God is seated on his holy throne. The nobles of the nations assemble *as* the people of the God of Abraham" (47:8-9). This too is a remarkable assertion.

The psalmists have a comprehensive view of praise embracing the individual, the community of the righteous, the whole of Israel, the nations, the angels, and the heavens and the earth, and such a psalm as 103 gives this expression. There is nothing narrow about the theology of worship in this book of praises.

In Zion Yahweh is offered both individual and corporate worship.

Psalmists come to the temple of God with their individual sacrifices (116:17), make their individual vows (22:25), and thankfully proclaim what God has done for them (40:9-10). They also have a real sense of individual relationship to God, for expressions like "my God" (22:1; 31:14; 38:21; etc.) and others like "my rock, my fortress, and my deliverer," and "my light and my salvation" (27:1), are by no means rare.

Their sense of corporate identity as the people of God is also very clear, and those passages where the psalmist writes of his personal relationship with God are balanced by others that speak of Yahweh as "our God" (40:3; 48:8; 50:3; etc.). So often we notice that the individual's praise is in the context of corporate worship. For instance, in 40:10 the author says, "I do not conceal your love and your truth from the great assembly" (cf. 22:22).

Childs says, "It is characteristic of the Psalter that the psalmist often suffers alone, but expresses his experience of God's salvation in the plural. It is as if God's redemptive activity cannot be fully articulated apart from the beloved community."[94] In 25:22, at the end of a highly individual psalm, the writer asks God to redeem Israel from all their troubles. This could be an editorial addition to make the psalm suitable for corporate use, but it would be quite in keeping with this individual/corporate duality that it should be an original part of the psalm.

In a later passage in the same book, Childs makes a comment that presents a different perspective than the one quoted above. Having said that the psalmist used all the means available within the cult to overcome his sense of separation from God, he goes on to say, "However, most characteristic of the Psalter are those moments when the psalmist appears to transcend the prescribed religious means and confesses to have confronted God himself directly." He then quotes 40:6-8 and 73:17, 25.[95]

94. Childs, *OT Theology,* 100.
95. Childs, *OT Theology,* 172.

The psalms make reference to sacrifices, vows, and various other ritual items (27:6), but the chief stress is on vocal praise. A great deal of work has been done on the use of the psalms in worship, especially in the wake of Gunkel's germinal work, with a focus especially on their employment at the great festivals of Israel. Although there has recently been something of a change of emphasis, with attention being given now rather more to the Psalter as a book of instruction, there is no suggestion that its use as a worship manual for Israel was unimportant.

Both praise and lament are presented to God in worship and prayer.

Most of the material in the Psalter takes the form of address to God, with wisdom and historical psalms forming the main exceptions. As Westermann's book title, *Praise and Lament in the Psalms,* indicates, such addresses may be either in a major or a minor key, although of course some psalms partake of both. Statements of doctrine about God (e.g., 9:16 and 10:16) are implicitly calls to praise, for the psalmist's thoughts about God move him to gratitude and so into the utterance of praise. We see this very clearly in a psalm like 145, a praise psalm that is full of great affirmations about the nature and the acts of God.

The people knew they could bring everything to God, that he was just as willing to hear about their sorrows, their afflictions, and their problems, and to hear their confessions, as to receive expressions of their gratitude and worship. In this way a God-centered life for the people as a whole and for individuals within it was being fostered, at least ideally.

Joy and blessing come to those engaged in heartfelt worship.

Worship fills the heart of the sincere worshiper with great joy. To be able to engage in this makes Yahweh's house very precious to psalmists (cf. Pss 42, 43, 63, 84). In 4 the psalmist says that the joy God has given him is greater than that of idolatrous revelers who bring praise to their agricultural god at the time of harvest (cf. Hos 2:8). Sometimes he writes simply of his gladness because of what Yahweh has done for him, but it is often clear in such places that he will express this joy in temple worship (5:7, 11). Great joy comes to him when he brings praise to God with a full heart (9:1-2).

Among the many beatitudes in the Psalter, some simply promise the happiness of the godly. Others use בָּרַךְ, *bārak* ("to bless"), and its cognates (as in 21:6; 37:22, etc.) to express the blessedness of God's people, but there are also passages where these words are used of what worshipers do in their praise of God. These passages are easier to identify in NASB, which uses "bless" (e.g., in 103:1; 104:1), than in NIV, which normally translates them "praise." It is uncertain how this word group came to be used in the sense of "praise," but it is quite certain that this is its meaning in this kind of context.[96]

The Psalter especially emphasizes moral qualifications for worship.

The reader who has a wide acquaintance with the OT may be surprised to find no reference in the Psalms to the genealogical qualifications required by those officiating at the temple worship, and little on ceremonial regulations,[97] but acquaintance with the prophetic attitude toward sacrifice will prepare him or her for an emphasis on right attitudes and moral qualities. This is what we find especially in Psalms 15 and 24, for the worshiper's walk should be blameless (15), and not only his hands but his heart must be pure (24). There is a considerable contrast between Psalms 14 and 15, and a strong moral emphasis in the psalms that lie between 15 and 24.[98] This is true also of 25 and 26, the second of which has been classified by some commentators as an entrance psalm, like 15 and 24.

The Covenants and the Theological Significance of the Exile

The biblical scholar does not work in isolation from the influence of other disciplines. In the nineteenth and early twentieth centuries the scholarly world in general tended to be somewhat preoccupied with origins. The growth of nationalism and the consequent interest in the historical roots of national and ethnic groups, the theory of evolution, the developing discipline of archaeology and, somewhat later, the interest of psychoanalysis in the early life of the individual human being are only some of the factors involved in this. It is not surprising therefore to find biblical scholars in this period particularly interested in origins. One aspect of this was the emphasis on the exodus and the beginnings of Israel's life as a nation.

In recent decades, however, there has been a developing interest in the exile. There are many reasons for this; for instance, many scholars have reacted against what they have felt to be the sterile nature of the Graf-

---

96. See C. W. Mitchell, *Meaning of BRK.*

97. But see 26:6 for a reference to washing at the laver (cf. 73:13), on the assumption that "wash" here is intended to be understood physically.

98. See McConville, "Who May Ascend," 36-47.

Wellhausen theory of the Pentateuch, and the emphasis being placed by Childs and others on the ultimate form of the biblical text has meant a shift of interest toward a later period of Israel's history. This does not mean that the exodus is now considered less important but that the exile has now taken its place alongside it in terms of its theological importance.

This development too has not taken place in a cultural vacuum, for it coincides with a general movement toward an interest in the future, with ends becoming as important as origins. The Second World War ended with the advent of the nuclear age, and the optimism that characterized so much nineteenth-century thinking and that, despite the advent of Freudian psychoanalysis and the horrors of the First World War, was not dead in some quarters in the 1930s, gave way to concerned anticipation of the future. There was a widespread fear that the two world wars were harbingers of greater horrors to come. As time went on, however, and the ultimate nuclear holocaust did not take place, the world community began to hope that some way could be found to avoid it in the long-term.

In this cultural setting, the exilic period could be viewed both as theologically traumatic but also as a symbol of hope, for it was followed by the restoration. God had dealt severely with his people but he had a positive purpose for them still. A glance at the subject index of many recent general works on the OT will reveal that often the references to the exile at least balance and often exceed those to the exodus.

The "Death and Resurrection" of Israel

The most difficult experiences in life are those in which people face assaults on their basic convictions and when they find themselves questioning these. This kind of experience is particularly distressing when these convictions relate to God. It is bad enough when it is just a single conviction about God that is attacked, but when it is a whole web of convictions that has undergirded the life of a person or community, then something akin to despair is not far away, and despair is very serious, for in its ultimate form it is a function of atheism.

What distinguishes the book of Psalms is that it shows not simply an individual but a whole nation facing the death of its convictions, the virtual "death" of God. Donald Gowan entitled his book *Theology of the Prophetic Books: The Death and Resurrection of Israel,* and the subtitle reference of course is to the exile and the return. Because Israel's life was so bound up with its belief in Yahweh and its special relationship with him, it might have seemed to the people that the exile was almost like a death of Yahweh himself, a much more appalling thought than anything in the Near Eastern conception of the dying (and rising) god in the world of vegetation.

Many of the psalms give the impression, at least on a first reading and out of their context in the Psalter as a whole, that the establishment of the Davidic dynasty and the worship of God at Jerusalem were just as nonnegotiable as the other matters we have been considering. George Trevelyan defined a classical age as one of "unchallenged assumptions."[99] If Judah had such a classical age, it came to an end abruptly at the exile. The exile was not only an unpleasant experience for the people concerned (nobody relishes national defeat or banishment from the land of one's birth), but an event of vast theological significance. Referring to the exodus, the establishment of the Davidic kingdom, and the Babylonian exile, John Taylor says, "The third of these seminal experiences . . . must have affected the Jewish nation as a reversal of the other two experiences and a negation of all that flowed from their reflections upon them. The Exile spelt dispersal, statelessness, victimization and the start of an age-long struggle for the survival of their identity."[100]

If book 3 of the Psalter reflects this, the concern and agonizing problems went very deeply indeed into the soul of the people. This book starts with a personal and a community lament (73–74) and finishes with another pair of the same kind (88–89).[101] Psalm 73 raises questions about the truth of the introductory Psalm 1, while 89 similarly asks agonized questions about the fulfillment of 2.[102] Many questions are put to God in 74, 77, 79, 80, 85, 88, and 89. Two psalms focus on the fall of Jerusalem (79) and (possibly) of the northern kingdom (80), and there are psalms that call on God to restore or to turn his people (80 and 85; cf. 86:16-17). Zion was no more, the temple had been utterly destroyed, with the destroyers going berserk within its sacred walls (74:4-8). The very honor of Yahweh himself seemed to be at stake (74:9-11). Some psalms elsewhere reflect the exilic trauma too, especially 137, which shows the immense sadness of the people and how impossible they felt it to sing the Lord's praises in their Babylonian environment.

Many writers have recognized the theological dimension of the trauma that the exile involved for the people of Israel. Gerald Wilson says that the exiles "underwent a painful re-identification process in order to develop a new

---

99. Trevelyan, *English Social History*, 343.

100. Taylor, *Christlike God*, 18.

101. Interestingly, book 4 opens with a communal followed by an individual psalm.

102. See Grant, "Psalms 73 and 89," 62-86.

understanding of what it meant to be a faithful follower of Yahweh."[103] Brueggemann too calls the exile "Israel's most generative theological moment," while Bright, referring to the last days of the kingdom of Judah and beyond, characterizes this as a time of "theology in crisis."[104] Gary Millar says, "The exile for Israel involved much more than their being reduced to the status of refugees; it undermined their entire theological tradition."[105]

Whether it should have undermined their theology is, of course, another matter. I will raise later the question as to whether the people's belief in the unconditional nature of this protection was based on God's promises or whether it was the result of wishful thinking on the part of the people, and also whether it was what the psalmists themselves actually believed.

The process by which the book of Psalms as we have it (including its headings) came into its final form is not yet completely clear. It is not, however, unreasonable to suppose that this took place in the postexilic period or at the very earliest in the final days of the exile. On this assumption the book embraces that period when Israel faced the greatest test of its convictions, its theological trauma — the Babylonian exile.

The Moral Nature and Requirements of Yahweh

Every one of the convictions identified above must have come into serious question at the exile. Was Yahweh, God of Israel, really the one and only God? If so, why had his chosen people been taken away by those who worshiped other gods? Moreover, these pagan deities were grandiose and all too impressive. Not only so, but the Babylonians told stories about the creation that were very different from those in the Hebrew Scriptures, and they were associated with these deities. Yahweh had delivered his people from Egyptian bondage, and his people had constantly celebrated and sung about this, but now they were captive to another great military power. He could hardly be called the God of Zion when it lay in ruins, so that there was no functioning sacrificial system or sung worship or Levitical priesthood or Davidic king.

Yes, but what of Sinai? There was a very real sense in which the revelation given there was vindicated by the exile rather than questioned by it. As the historical psalms, among others, make abundantly clear, Israel had trans-

---

103. Wilson, *Psalms*, 1:26-27.

104. Brueggemann, *Reverberations of Faith*, 39; Bright entitles ch. 6 "Theology in Crisis," in *Covenant and Promise*, 171-98.

105. Millar, "Land," 626.

gressed God's clearly expressed commandments over and over again and deserved to experience such a judgment as the exile.

What of Psalm 1? We cannot be sure whether it was written before, during, or after the exile, but its principles certainly sum up much in the OT. The people of Israel might have been inclined to understand "the righteous" (v. 6) as a reference to them, but over the years they had certainly walked in the counsel of the wicked, stood in the way of sinners, and even at times sat in the seat of mockers, as King Jehoiakim did when confronted with the word of God through Jeremiah (Jer 36). This psalm concludes, "the way of the wicked shall perish." It may be said then that the principles set forth in this psalm received marked if unexpected and unrelished illustration in the exile.

Yahweh is a God of justice, and his character revealed at Sinai differentiated him sharply from Babylon's gods. The exile taught his people more profoundly than ever before the moral nature of their God, as it was evidence that his threats against them because of their unfaithfulness to him over many centuries were not in vain, but that he meant every word. They were there in Babylon under judgment, not that of Marduk or Nebo, but of Yahweh their God, the one true and living God. In their acknowledgment of this lay their hope. So some psalms wrestle with the question of Israel's sin.

Book 3 is particularly relevant at this point. The two laments that open it are sad, but the two that close it even sadder. The two psalms that obviously relate to the fall of Jerusalem and (perhaps) Samaria (79 and 80) are both reminders of the punitive justice of God as far as his people are concerned. Some of the psalms in this book (80, 85, and 86:16-17) call on God to restore or, with an implicit acknowledgment of the habitual and ingrained nature of sin, to turn his people. Clearly they felt the need of his gracious enabling if they were to walk in his ways.

There is a strong moral emphasis in the great historical psalms, such as 106 and 78. Psalms 90 and 106, both strongly moral, have important positions at the beginning and end of book 4, and there is an emphasis on God's forgiveness in 103 (vv. 8-12).

All this shows the prime importance of Yahweh's moral character. It was this more than anything else that undergirded all his actions in his dealings with his people. The book of Psalms itself traces his activities before the exodus and the Sinai revelation, recognizing, for instance, the way he dealt with Abraham and the other patriarchs, but it is clear that in the view of the psalmists the same God was revealing himself in those days. If Yahweh was supreme, what mattered more than anything else was that he was morally consistent. The psalmists may have had problems at times in squaring events with the moral character of Yahweh, but they never gave up their belief in that character. Here ultimately, even in the midst of deep questionings, was their spiritual resting place.

The Covenantal Nature of Yahweh's Relationship with Israel

Of the Psalter's two introductory psalms, Psalm 1 certainly found fulfillment in the exile viewed as a judgment of God, but what of Psalm 2? The exile would appear to have negated that completely. What of Zion, God's holy hill? It was covered with the ruins of Jerusalem. What of the king God installed there? He was in captivity and his dynasty was in eclipse. What of the nations God had promised to make the king's inheritance? One of them had made short work of Judah and transported many of its people into captivity.

Yet it would seem on the surface of things that the covenant promises of Yahweh had to be just as firmly fixed as his moral nature. Indeed, since faithfulness is certainly a moral attribute, then the former were founded on the latter. Furthermore, Psalm 105 shows that Yahweh's covenant with his people predated the exodus, for it is called "the covenant he made with Abraham, the oath he swore to Isaac," and the psalmist then says, "He confirmed it to Jacob as a decree, to Israel as an everlasting covenant" (105:8-11). We clearly need to explore this issue further.

There has been much discussion as to the origin of the covenant concept, the extent to which it was influenced by the treaty forms of people like the Hittites and the Assyrians, and when it first began to influence the writers of the OT. These considerations, important as they are, have little concern for us here, for we are dealing with a literature in which covenant concepts are obviously important, and this importance is not tied to any of these perfectly legitimate and interesting questions.

The actual term "covenant" (בְּרִית, *běrît*) is present a significant but not a great number of times in the Psalter. In 105:8, as we have seen, it clearly relates to the patriarchal covenant, while 78:37 certainly seems to have the Mosaic covenant in view because of the reference to the law in verses 5-7. Bullock points out that the relatively long narrative of Joseph in Psalm 105 performs, like the story in Genesis, a link between the patriarchs and the exodus.[106] The relationship between these is seen in that it is a psalm of the exodus (associated of course with the Mosaic covenant) in which the faithfulness of God to Abraham is celebrated (105:42-45).

In 25:14; 44:17; 50:5; 74:20; 106:45; and 111:5, 9, the reference of the term is

---

106. Bullock, *Psalms*, 1:101.

somewhat general, so that it is impossible to tell precisely whether it is the patriarchal or Mosaic form of the covenant that is in view. This probably means that the psalmists did not make a sharp distinction between them, for the covenant nation in their day consisted of people descended both from the patriarchs and from the nation as it was at the time of Moses. A relationship based on a covenant was not simply informal or ad hoc, for it was given structure and form, just as in a formal marriage relationship.

The actual sense of relationship, however, is much wider than the use of the word. It is found in echoes of the covenant formula, "I shall be their God and they shall be my people" (Gen 17:7-9; Exod 29:45; Lev 26:9-12; Jer 31:1; etc.), to be found in passages like Ps 50:7 (cf. v. 5) and 81:8-13. It is arguable that it is implied in the very expression "God of Israel," with its clear implication of a special relationship with one people. Most widely of all, it may be thought implicit in the name Yahweh, as the revelation of this name's meaning in Exodus 3 and 6 was given to Moses and was in such close association with the establishment of the Mosaic covenant.

The word חֶסֶד, *ḥesed*, is of special covenant significance, and about half its OT occurrences are in the book of Psalms. Indeed, the frequency of its presence underlines that the divine faithful love is a major theme of this book. Furthermore, it occurs quite frequently in each of the five books of which the Psalter is composed, with frequency variations so small that they cannot be considered statistically significant. It is an attitudinal word and refers, when used strictly, to love that operates within a covenant structure. The NIV frequently translates it "enduring love," although sometimes (as in Ps 136) simply as "love."

W. H. Bellinger recognizes the importance of this word and concept, but he considers it unwise to limit it to a covenantal framework because of difficulties in dating the beginnings of covenant as a religious concept in the OT, although he refers to major scholars who do this. He then says, "the term in the lament psalms does seem to indicate a relationship between Yahweh and his people, however that is conceived, and a relationship to which Yahweh is intensely loyal."[107] The main point, in any case, is that its use underlines the deep commitment of Yahweh to those he had brought into relationship with him, and there are passages too where this is linked to definite assertions Yahweh has made (89:1-4; cf. 2:7-9; 132:11-12). It is difficult to deny the existence of the covenant concept when so many of its characteristic features are present, although the fact that the Psalter consists of items from many different periods of history makes it difficult to be definite in every case.

---

107. Bellinger, *Psalmody and Prophecy*, 60-61.

J. C. McCann observes that both the laments and the songs of praise speak of God's steadfast love.[108] In fact, *ḥesed* is found extensively in both, and they were recognized by Westermann as the two main psalm types. This is a quality in God that sets the psalmists singing in heartfelt praise. Yahweh has pledged himself to Israel, and loves them and will go on loving them come what may. It is also their source of confidence when they find themselves in trouble.

The word is also used for the people's faithful response to God, although it is less frequently applied to this. It is in Hosea that this comes forward as an important use of the word. In the Psalter, however, the people of God, at least the godly among them, are often referred to as the חֲסִידִים, *ḥăsîdîm*, frequently translated "saints" in the NIV (e.g., 30:4; 31:23) but sometimes in other ways (several times as "faithful ones" e.g., 37:28). It designates those who are characterized by faithfulness, and this too is suggestive of the love that exists within the covenant relationship. It is this that saves the whole concept of covenant from being somewhat cold and abstract, a kind of quasi-legal transaction between two parties. Just as in a good marriage, it is faithful love that imparts warmth to the relationship.

It is not surprising that psalms which show a strong community sense also often lay stress on the covenant between God and his people. This is exactly what we should expect. Peter Craigie says that this means the theology of the Psalms is popular, arising out of the people's knowledge of God, rather than abstract or philosophical, and he sums up so much when he says of the Psalms that "they respond to God in prayer, in praise, or in particular life situations because of an already existing covenant relationship which makes such response possible. . . . Because the covenant dominated all aspects of human life for the Hebrews, to a greater or lesser extent, there is no aspect of life which may not appear in the psalms."[109]

The Special Importance of the Covenant with David

This is to be expected in a book in which nearly half the contents are linked with his name. In two psalms *ḥesed* is used quite specifically of Yahweh's covenant with David (89:2, 28, 33, 49; 132:12). It is clear that this covenant is the dominant theme of both these psalms, and each of them treats the promises that established it as of great importance.

108. McCann, *Theological Introduction*, 87.
109. Craigie, *Psalms 1–50*, 40.

Psalm 2 is important, particularly because of its probable introductory function along with Psalm 1. Mays is surely right in saying that it is confessional and is more about God than about the king.[110] It rests on 2 Samuel 7, the historical narrative of the giving of the covenant promise by God. This psalm makes clear that the kingship will not be free from opposition, but that Yahweh will give it his unqualified support.

It is this that gives Psalm 89 its great poignancy. The first two-thirds of it are like an extended theological commentary on 2 Samuel 7 and Psalm 2, but then the whole tone changes and the psalmist complains that he is seeing the very opposite of divine support for the king at the present time. This psalm comes at the conclusion of book 3, much of which consists of deep laments, and in it the writer shows great concern that God's covenant with David seems to have been set aside — by God himself! He puts this concern into an anguished cry, "O Lord, where is your former great love, which in your faithfulness you swore to David?" (v. 49). It is highly probable that this psalm belongs to the time of the exile, even if, as is possible, verses 1-37 were originally penned earlier, and that the "anointed one" of verse 51 is the young king Jehoichin who was taken into captivity by the Babylonians.

It is most notable, however, that in experiencing the puzzled anguish of verses 38-52 the psalmist did not destroy his earlier verses. Clearly, even in the darkness of the exile, he still believed in the Davidic covenant. Moreover, the compilers showed great wisdom in setting Psalm 90 after 89, for it emphasizes the wrath of God against his people's sin while also encouraging the covenant petition, "satisfy us in the morning with your unfailing love" (v. 14).

The presence of Psalm 132 in book 5, as well as its reference to God's choice of Zion (v. 13) and the promise, "Here I will make a horn grow for David and set up a lamp for my anointed one," suggest that this psalmist is by no means convinced there is no future for the Davidic line of kings. As already noted, the term *hesed* occurs in many psalms ascribed to David. They may all refer to this covenant, although it is possible that some simply reflect a general recognition that what God says is true.

There has long been difference of opinion as to how many psalms should be regarded as royal. When compared with the earlier source critics, Eaton is a maximalist, for he considers thirty-seven to be clearly royal in their content, plus twenty-three less clear cases.[111] If these last are included, this would mean that well over a third of the Psalter could be thus designated. This number could be even higher, if all reference to David in the super-

---

110. Mays, *Lord Reigns*, 46.
111. Eaton, *Kingship*, esp. 1-86.

scriptions relate to authorship, although this still raises the question as to the period in David's life when they were written, and whether a psalm written when he had been anointed king but not yet established on his throne could be reckoned kingly.

The Covenant and the Individual's Experience of God

The Psalter shows us not only the traumatic experience of the people of God when they went into exile, but also such experiences at the individual level.

There can be little doubt that the faith of the individual psalmist took its origin from the covenant promises of God to his whole people. There appears to have been a sublime form of theological reasoning going on. Such psalmists appear to have reasoned thus: "If the Lord has established a covenant relationship with my people, that relationship therefore applies to me, and I can look to him for the fulfillment of promises made within that relationship."

Walter Houston says, however, that the psalms headed "of David," though often showing awareness of the community, are nearly all dominated by a sense of personal relationship with God. He then says, "most strikingly, the traditions of the community which we find gathered and developed in the narratives of the Hebrew Bible find virtually no place here. They do not form the foundation of the confidence in God which undergirds the appeal to his mercy. It is not that there is no opportunity of mentioning them." So he says that 22:4-5 and 59:5, for example, could easily have been more precise. The personal relationship is everything. "In the Davidic psalms not only does the speaker's confidence in *his* God require no undergirding by the national experience, but he is positively indifferent to it for the most part."[112]

Houston has a point, but he has expressed it too strongly. It is important for us to remember not only that David had his own covenant with God but that this was dynastic, not simply personal. It is most natural that this should often occupy his thoughts, especially in its personal application to him.

When we examine the psalms ascribed to him, we find a number in which *hesed* is used in passages where the writer at least glances at its application to the wider community of the faithful (e.g., in 17:7 and 32:10-11). In 22:3-5 he refers to the acts of deliverance God performed for the fathers. In 18:6-15, where he is crying to God to save him and receiving an answer, so much of the language recalls past acts of God. The personal reference in 103:4

---

112. Houston, "David, Asaph," 99.

precedes verse 7 with its affirmation that God made known his ways to Moses. Magonet identifies many terminological links between Psalm 25, where the word occurs in verses 6 and 10, and the great Mosaic covenant passage in Exod 34:5-7.[113] Because of this, God's *ḥesed* "from of old" (25:6) must surely relate at least to the Mosaic if not also to the Abrahamic covenant.

Craigie writes of Psalm 17, where *ḥesed* occurs in verse 7: "One of the most significant aspects of this finely proportioned psalm is the way in which it gives expression to covenant theology. The psalmist is in dire straits, pressed hard on every side, but in confidence he is able to rise above the threatening circumstances. Yet the ascent to confidence is not merely a testimony to the psalmist's stalwart faith and his ability to transcend his personal circumstances; it is primarily a testimony to the faith of the covenant community."[114]

Psalm 77, a psalm of Asaph, shows the psalmist facing not only some sort of affliction but also being tempted to doubt, but then looking to the covenant acts of God for his people and finding his faith reestablished and strengthened as a result.[115]

The Blessings of the Covenant Relationship

The blessings of the covenants are manifold. It is evident that the covenant community found great enrichment through its relationship with Yahweh. The words "blessed" and "blessing" occur fairly frequently in the Psalms, but they translate two different Hebrew words. The first, אַשְׁרֵי, *'ašrê*, simply means "happy," while the second, בָּרַךְ, *bārak*, refers to the good consequences of one party's action (in the Psalms this is God) for another. Of special importance is the blessing that consisted of the land of Canaan, which is seen as the fulfillment of a covenant promise (e.g., 44:2-3; 105:10-11). The psalmists sometimes wax eloquent about the land, as in 80:8-11 and 68:9-10, 14. The smiting of Sihon and Og, referred to in two adjoining psalms and important at least in part because of their possession of land, seems to be viewed as a continuation of the victory over Egypt, except that the means were different (135:8-12; 136:10-21).

At the start of the Davidic Psalter there is in Psalm 3 a reminder of the grace of God, for the reference to Absalom in its heading would remind the

---

113. Magonet, *Rabbi*, 75-82.

114. Craigie, *Psalms 1–50*, 165.

115. See comment on this psalm.

reader of David's sin, but also of Yahweh's forgiveness and his continued support of him. This could be seen too as a microcosmic portrayal of Israel's own situation as living in the grace of God, not to be forgotten as the reader reads further. Psalm 5:7-8 underlines this, for the psalmist there sees that his access to God's house is due to God's mercy toward him and that he can look to him for protected guidance on his path ahead. There is a concern for forgiveness (e.g., in 6:9; 19:12-14; 25:7, 18), but also a sweet consciousness of it when sincere confession has been made (32:1-5).

As we have seen already, there are frequent references to Yahweh's covenant love, and the awareness of this is strong, in both the individual and the communal psalms. It clearly had a major place in the whole outlook of the people. The awareness of a covenant relationship can form a basis for a presumptuous outlook in which sin is not felt to matter. There is, however, no clear evidence of this kind of presumption in the Psalter.

Strangely the language of love is not much used of the psalmist's attitude to God, although it does occur in 18:1, in a psalm that is acknowledged fairly widely to be authentically Davidic. Psalms 97:10 and 145:20 refer to those who love the Lord, while in Psalm 26 his awareness of God's covenant love (v. 3) finds a response in his own love for the house of the Lord (v. 8). In each case the word used of the psalmist's love is אַהֲבָה, *'ahăbâ*, the general word for love. His deep love for God is evident even when the distinctive terminology of love is not used, as in Psalms 63 and 107 and perhaps most of all in 119. There is also a deep note of joy and delight in God in many of the psalms, so many that it seems pointless to list them, but some examples may be found in 4, 16, 23, 65, 98, 126, and 132. Lest we should become too preoccupied with the laments, we should note this constant note of rejoicing in the Lord.

There is too a sense of having a life that is sovereignly controlled and guided by God as the psalmists walk in God's paths. The opening psalm indicates the prosperity of the righteous and that God watches over (lit. "knows") them. It is true that this introduces a book in which the psalmists know much trouble and grief, but their constant recourse to God at such times shows that they were looking to him to give life its shape for them. There is a strong emphasis, from Psalm 2 onward, on the fact that Yahweh is the refuge of his people.[116]

The constant sense of a relationship with God is what lies behind the many prayers contained in the book of Psalms. There is never the slightest suggestion that God is unprepared to hear the prayers of his people. They

---

116. See esp. Creach, *Yahweh as Refuge.*

know that they have acceptance with him through the covenant and this encourages them to bring all their thankfulness, all their complaints and all their petitions before him. Mays points out that the first two-thirds of the Psalter are dominated by prayer.[117]

The Responsibilities of the Covenant Relationship

Some psalms seem, at least at first sight, to suggest apparent failure on God's part to fulfill his covenant promises (e.g., Ps 44), but others make abundantly clear that the main problems arose from the sins of the people. The fact is that the covenant not only confers blessings but imposes responsibilities on those who are in covenant with Yahweh. Psalm 25:10 asserts, "All the ways of the LORD are loving and faithful for those who keep the demands of his covenant."

This can be seen at the heart of the Psalter, where, in book 3, psalms have been brought together that show not only the pain of the exile but also, in some of them, the moral and spiritual cause of it. Just as psalms with the exodus in view can be applied sometimes also to the return from exile, so psalms descriptive of earlier historical judgments on the people could be read, in the final redaction of the Psalter, in the light of the trauma of the exile. Bullock points out how strong the covenant theme is in the Asaphite psalms, and one of these psalms refers to the northern kingdom's rejection of the covenant (78:9-10, 37), although it was rather a failure to keep the terms of the covenant than a total abandonment of it.[118]

The covenant promise to David stressed the importance of the obedience of his successors and warned them of serious consequences if they disobeyed (2 Sam 7). The one consequence that lay outside these threats was the complete ending of the dynasty. In the event, the consequences were very severe and even included the ending of the reign of the Davidic kings and the destruction of their capital city. Yet, as the redactor of the Psalter was sure, the promise did not die. There would be a Davidic kingdom again.

The Unconditional/Conditional Nature of the Covenant

The apparent contradiction in the heading here is intentional, for it expresses the whole issue raised for the psalmists so acutely by the experience of exile.

---

117. Mays, *Psalms*, 51.
118. Bullock, *Encountering Psalms*, 78.

Even though Psalms 1 and 2 may not have been placed at the head of the book of Psalms until the exile was over, it was the apparent clash of the principles stated in these psalms that constituted Israel's deep theological problem. Could Yahweh at the same time be the God of both Psalms 1 and 2?

Indeed, is there a tension, even a complete contradiction, between psalms of Zion that not only extol it but seem completely confident of Yahweh's protection of it and, perhaps by implication, its king, and the traumatic experience of exile expressed in other psalms, such as 89 and 137? A careful study of what the psalms say does not support the idea of contradiction.[119]

Psalm 2 asserts that God has established his king in Zion, and there are several expressions of confidence in God's protection of this city, for instance in Psalms 46 and 48. This confidence clearly lies behind the prayers offered for the protection and peace of Jerusalem (51:18; 69:35; 129:5).

The Psalter also reflects the trauma of the exile, however, especially, as we have seen, in book 3 (in psalms like 74 and 89), and it is surely significant that 79, with its deeply distressed cry, "O God, the nations have invaded your inheritance" (v. 1), immediately follows 78, which shows the history of Israel to be one of ungrateful rebellion against their God. As a result of this rebellion, God had judged them, and the most recent judgment had fallen on "the tents of Joseph . . . the tribe of Ephraim" (78:67), an evident reference to the demise of the northern kingdom. This means that even before the destruction of Jerusalem, Israel had been deprived of much of its inheritance, at least in terms of actual occupation.

Psalm 78, however, ends on a positive note with the choice of Judah and Mount Zion and the building of the sanctuary and the choice of David. So now the limits of Israel's occupation of the land were defined by the boundaries of Judah, but the interests of little Judah were very much concentrated in its capital, as the parallelism of 78:68 ("he chose the tribe of Judah, Mount Zion, which he loved") shows us. The reference in 79:5 to God's wrath surely implies that, once more, history has repeated itself, and God's people are suffering the consequences of their rebellion against him.

In Psalm 132, which is in book 5 and therefore, in its setting at least, postexilic, God's choice of Zion is said to be forever,[120] but the actual occupation of the throne by the Davidic kings was contingent on their obedience, as

---

119. See Millar ("Land") for an exposition of the unconditional and yet conditional nature of the covenant.

120. We should remember how the concept of Jerusalem/Zion developed, even in the OT, so that, toward the close of Isaiah, it appears, although still geographically located, to be a symbol for the people of God. This is, of course, taken much further still in the NT.

in 1 Kgs 2:4 and 2 Chr 6:14-17. The relevance that their obedience has to God's protection is clear in Ps 97:8-12.

All this is in line with the revelation given to Jeremiah in the promise of a new covenant (Jer 31:31-34). As Bright says of this covenant, "It is a new covenant in that it is made anew, renewed; but it is the people who are made new. . . . The awful chasm between the demands of covenant by which the nation was judged, and the sure promises of God which faith could not surrender, is bridged from the side of divine grace."[121]

The NT, of course, provides the ultimate answer, because there the Davidic covenant receives its ultimate vindication in Christ, in whose life the ideal of Psalm 1 finds perfect fulfillment, and who in his death experienced vicariously the penalties of the broken law of God, and through whose Spirit the law is implanted in the believing heart. This is, however, to anticipate our later treatment of the fulfillment of the Psalms in Christ.

The Psalter as Means of Grace for the Traumatized People of God

As we have seen, recent research has concluded that, in the arrangement of the Psalter, book 3 reflects the trauma of the exile. It presses on the conscience of the people that its cause lay in their sin, so that penitence was needed. Book 4 builds on this, for it seeks to strengthen their faith in Yahweh, probably with the return from exile in view. This is anticipated in book 3 by Psalm 87, which gives assurance of a great and expanding hope. Whatever may be said of possible festival use of psalms in earlier books, book 5 provides many that we know for certain were employed at such times.

How do these three books figure as means of grace in the exilic situation? Book 3 is well fitted to express the people's grief and their concern and perplexity that their God allowed such events as the destruction of the temple, so poignantly pictured in Psalms 74 and 79, and the apparent ending of the Davidic dynasty, of which the psalmist complains in 89, to take place. There are calls for Yahweh to judge the nations but also a recognition of their own sin. At the same time some psalms express praise to God and trust in him.

Book 4 is a great faith-building volume, as great as anything the OT contains, and it sounds many similar notes to Isaiah 40–55. There is constant emphasis on the sovereignty of God, especially his sovereignty over the nations, and on his purpose for the whole world. We should note, however, that

---

121. Bright, *Covenant and Promise*, 196.

it opens and closes with psalms that underline the sinfulness of the people. This is implied in Psalm 90 and spelled out with crystal clarity in 106. As their faith was built up they also needed always to remember their unworthiness.

Whether book 5 was put together during the exile for use when the return had taken place or was compiled after that return, it was well fitted for renewed life in the land. Many psalms in it express the praise of the people and focus their hearts on the God who had now performed a second great act of redemption that could be placed alongside their deliverance from Egypt many centuries before.

Books 1 and 2 would also have their function, for it is highly characteristic of these that the psalmists, especially but not exclusively in the Davidic psalms, look to the Lord for deliverance from their enemies. Such psalms would be full of meaning for those who were now free once more and yet were beginning to face in the land the antagonism of those who had not been exiled.

We should note also the possibility that under the Spirit's inspiration some of the psalms we have are "second editions," constituted as such by a redactor to show their appropriateness to a new situation, especially the exile, as with the endings of Psalms 14, 51, and 69. In such cases the redactor becomes virtually a second author and the ultimate redactor the final author of the Psalter as a whole.

Yahweh as the God of the Future, the God Who Plans, the God of the Messiah and His Kingdom

A "Resurrection" Followed the Nation's "Death" in Babylon

The Psalter, even those parts evidently written before the return from exile, clearly has a hope that the history of Zion was not over. There was to be a return and a rebuilding, the basis of which was the cleansing of the people and their deep penitence. Indeed, it seems likely that the very book of Psalms itself, or as much of it as was then available (perhaps books 1-4), was to be a means of grace to this godly end.

Just as the disciples of Jesus had to see all their hopes dashed when he was taken to shame and to death, only to find renewed joy and faith when he rose from the dead, so a new Zion was to rise from the ashes of the old. It was to suffer temporary eclipse before coming to its full promise, and, as we shall see in the biblical theology section of this commentary, the fulfillment of that promise was to far outstrip the promise itself.

The Zion concept needs to be articulated with care. Was it essentially geographical? That Jerusalem/Zion is a geographical location is incontrovertible, but at its heart is the notion of God dwelling in the midst of his people. Psalm 68 sees the arrival of the ark at Jerusalem as a great moment in the history of God's people, but it is evident that he was with them in the whole journey there.

It was right for the people to rejoice in the place God gave them, for the gifts of God should always be celebrated with joyous thanksgiving, but wrong for them to view it as completely secure no matter what their attitude was. It is important to recognize that the Zion psalms were written in a spirit of praise, trust, and obedience, not of arrogant triumphalism. McConville is right: "The idea of a god who dwells on a holy hill, and thus guarantees the security of the people who worship him there within their borders, is entirely at home in Canaan, and a religious system at whose heart stands a manipulative cult."[122] It smacks of Baalism rather than of the true religion of Yahweh. The ultimate redactor would have known of Jeremiah's stinging attack on this notion in Jeremiah 7, and would have recognized in the prophet's voice the voice of God.

This does not mean, however, that there was no theological place for Zion after the exile. Books 4 and 5, both of which appear to be exilic or postexilic in redactional terms, have plenty of allusions to Zion/Jerusalem. In fact there are far more uses of these names in these books than there are in books 1-3. Does this mean that we can accuse the redactor of retrogression? No, but it does mean that such psalms need to be read in the light of the experience of the exile, so that their expressions of confidence in God's purpose for Zion cannot be understood to be so unconditional that punitive action against God's people is ruled out. They include Psalm 125, which finds geographical analogies taken from Jerusalem's location to illustrate God's protection of his people, but stresses the need not only for trust but also for uprightness in heart and conduct.

Psalm 107 has been variously understood to refer to the exodus and consequent entry into Canaan and to the return from Babylonian exile. In view of the similarity between the prayer of 106:47 and the assertion of 107:3, which the consecutive reader of the Psalter was surely intended to notice, the main reference certainly seems to be to the return from the exile, although its language was probably chosen to imply that this was a virtual repetition of the deliverance from Egypt. If the picture given in verses 4-9 is meant to be taken literally while the remainder of the psalm's main pictures present the

---

122. McConville, "Jerusalem in the OT," 29.

same event in the form of analogy, the reference to "a city where they could settle" (vv. 4 and 7; cf. also v. 36), given emphasis by repetition, could well mean Jerusalem.[123]

The Book of Psalms, as Finally Arranged, Has an Eschatological Message

In the last few paragraphs we have been considering an event that was almost certainly in the past at the time when the Psalter was finally compiled, but that was interpreted theologically by the redactor. The final edition of the book, however, was given a forward-looking thrust, and this is perhaps what we should expect, for an eschatological outlook is most appropriate in a historical faith. Israel's theology, because it was revealed in historical acts, not all of them taking place at the same time, was likely to look to the future for further divine acts, and this is particularly likely if there appear to be important issues as yet unresolved by the events that have already taken place. This we certainly see in the book of Psalms, and will now seek to demonstrate.

The Psalmists' Problems Will Find Future Resolution Involving Both the Nation and the Individual

The psalmists certainly had unresolved problems, mainly connected with issues arising out of the first two psalms. These two psalms feature theological statements of great importance, Psalm 1 declaring that the Lord watches over the way of the righteous but that the way of the ungodly will perish, and 2 that he has established his king at Zion and that the conspiracies of his enemies are bound to fail.

There is, however, another issue of a somewhat different kind, although it might be regarded as linked to the statement that the Lord watches over the way of the righteous. It concerns the destiny of the individual beyond death.

The book of Psalms refers often to Sheol, the place of the dead. Many have asserted that in the OT this is both for the righteous and for the wicked, but Philip Johnston has strongly questioned this. He draws attention to the fact that many of the references are to the wicked going into Sheol (e.g., 31:17; 55:15; 143:7-10) and that the godly's concern about it seems to be chiefly in times of depression or danger (18:4-5; 88:3; 116:3) when objectivity might well

---

123. See comments on this psalm.

have been at a discount, or when they felt themselves to be under the wrath of God (6:5). One psalmist says that a man cannot save himself from Sheol (89:48), but others say that God has himself done this (16:10-11; 18:6).

In several passages in the Psalter it looks as if an eschatological distinction is being made between the wicked and the righteous. In 9:17-18 the author says, "The wicked return to the grave [Sheol], all the nations that forget God. But the needy will not always be forgotten, nor the hope of the afflicted ever perish." More significant still is 49:12-15, where Sheol is the destiny of those who trust in themselves, "but God will redeem my life from the grave [Sheol]; he will surely take me to himself." The final line of this does not suggest simply rescue from going into death, but a destiny in fellowship with God. Psalm 143:7 says, "Do not hide your face from me, or I will be like those who go down to the pit." "Pit" is a near synonym for Sheol (cf. 30:3; 88:3-4).[124]

The reference to a destiny with God for the righteous in 49:15 finds an echo also in passages like 16:8-11; 17:15; 73:23-25, probably also in 23:6 and 139:18, and perhaps even in 11:7. It is true that we do not have, in most of these passages, the full NT doctrine of a resurrection to bliss for the righteous, but 16:8-11, with its reference to the security of the body and exemption from decay, although interpretable of rescue from the danger of dying, could also be seen, even in its OT context, as a reference to deliverance from beyond death, and so it is no surprise to find the NT applying it to the resurrection of Christ.

Many modern commentators are reluctant to understand these passages this way and, it seems to me, tend to set aside this kind of interpretation of them too easily. Dahood, on the other hand, sees many references to life after death where most commentators do not see them.[125]

The Dynastic Promise of Psalm 2 Will Be Fulfilled

What about the Davidic monarchy? Psalm 2 states that God will support the king whom he has established on Zion. Psalm 72, which closes book 2, was clearly seen by a redactor as one in which the dynastic promise was passed on to Solomon and so, presumably, to his successors, and where strong emphasis was placed on the importance of the king's character. Psalm 89, however, which brings book 3 to its close, asks why the king has not been supported and why the dynasty appears to be virtually over. There is not much doubt

---

124. See further in Johnston, "Hell"; idem, *Shades of Sheol*, 81-83.
125. See, e.g., Dahood, *Psalms*.

that a comparison of Psalm 72 with the actual record of the Davidic monarchs would have provided the answer. As the author of the books of Kings makes clear, few of them had walked in the ways of the Lord.

Wilson has argued that the purpose of the Psalter's ultimate arrangement (as distinct from a possible earlier edition, which consisted only of books 1-3) was to direct attention away from the Davidic kingship to the supreme sovereignty of Israel's God himself. If so, however, it is difficult to see why Psalm 2 was placed (or allowed to remain) as part of the general introduction to the whole Psalter. This issue finds some measure of resolution within books 4 and 5. In book 4 the emphasis is on the kingship of God, a reminder perhaps that Psalm 2 is about two kings, not just one. There is much in this book to encourage faith. The purpose of God is seen to embrace the whole human world, the nations as well as Israel, and those who had read their way through earlier books of the Psalter would perhaps recall the emphasis there on the universal sway of the king, for instance in Psalm 72.

Then in book 5 the kingly theme reemerges in messianic terms, for two psalms (110 and 132) and probably a third (148) have a messianic slant. In 110 the king portrayed is more than a king, for he is a priest as well. Then in 132, which emphasizes the Davidic covenant just as much as 89 so that it is probably placed here deliberately as a reminder, the promise is made of the raising up of a future "horn," suggesting a king of power. At the very least, as S. E. Gillingham recognizes, this is a "firm belief that God will not go back on his promises made in the past to David: he will ensure the continuation of the Davidic dynasty."[126] This last promise is repeated in 148, almost at the end of the Psalter. In this way the reader is assured that the promise of a Davidic king has not been forgotten. For full exposition of this, see David Mitchell's monograph on the Psalter's message, where he argues that the whole book was put together with the intention of highlighting the messianic hope. He cites an impressive array of other scholars who hold the same basic opinion. At the very least, he has presented a strong case.[127]

Psalm 132 combines contingency and certainty, for in verses 11 and 12 the tenure of the throne by the Davidic line of kings is contingent on their obedience, but verses 17 and 18 confidently assert that in Zion God will make a horn grow for David. Psalm 148:14 can certainly be understood as giving the same promise as 132:17-18, though by the use of the prophetic perfect.[128]

Is this all? No, for we must ask what is the role of the other kingly

---

126. Gillingham, "Messiah in Psalms," 216.
127. D. C. Mitchell, *Message of Psalter.*
128. See comments on both psalms.

psalms in the Psalter. Wilson has pointed out at what significant points important royal psalms are to be found, specifically at the seams where one book of the Psalter joins another.[129] So we find Psalm 2 at the beginning of the whole collection, 41 at the end of book 1, 72 at the close of book 2, and 89 at the end of book 3. This feature does not occur in books 4 and 5, but in book 4 there is emphasis on the kingship of God, reminding us of the divine king in Psalm 2, and then, as we have seen, some clearly messianic psalms in book 5.

It is most important for us to note that those in books 1-3 were retained in their positions by the ultimate redactor and they must have been regarded as having relevance even when there were no Davidic kings on Judah's throne.[130] This suggests that it was not only the ones in book 5 that we have already considered that must have been viewed as pointing toward a coming Messiah of David's dynasty, but the kingly psalms as a whole. Heim argues that the placing of the postscript to 89 (i.e., v. 52), which is admittedly a praise conclusion to book 3, must nevertheless have seemed most incongruous to the editors unless they believed that the Lord would answer the prayers offered in the verses that precede this.[131]

Craigie writes of the changing significance of the royal psalms. He says of Psalm 2, "Its theology pertained to the role of God in relation to the Davidic kings; that theology eventually blossomed into a fully messianic theology in one period of the history of the psalm's interpretation. The latter stage is not a new theology, but a growth and development from the initial nucleus."[132]

In this way recent scholars who have emphasized the importance of the structure of the Psalter have led to a new and wider recognition of it as a messianic book.

The Moral Affirmations of Psalm 1 Will Be Vindicated through Coming Judgment

This psalm declares that God watches over the way of the righteous while the way of the ungodly will perish, but the psalmists often complain that this principle does not seem to be operative in the world they know. We encoun-

---

129. Wilson, "Use of Royal Psalms."
130. See Mays, *Psalms*, 18; cf. Childs, *OT Theology*, 119.
131. Heim, "(God)-Forsaken King," 304-5.
132. Craigie, *Psalms 1–50*, 40-41.

ter this to a marked degree in Psalms 22 and 69, two great psalms that feature in the passion narratives in the Gospels, but it is also to be found elsewhere, and is often the unstated presupposition behind the question, "Why?" as in 10:1; 43:2; 44:23: 74:1, 11.

We should not, however, miss the fact that sometimes "How long?" is found in close association with "Why?" (e.g., 74:1, 10-11; 79:5, 10), suggesting that, despite the laments and complaints of the psalmists, they were convinced that God would ultimately act to put things right (see also 13:1-2, 5). The questions raised by the experience of the psalmists are confronted and find an answer in Psalm 73. Many scholars attach special importance to this psalm. Here, in the first psalm in the psalmic book of the exile (book 3), the issue of the prosperity of the wicked is acutely raised. The psalmist finds that the answer lies within the sanctuary of God, perhaps in the broader perspective that worship gave to him. The perspective was gained by the eschatological path. This is reinforced in 145:19-20, which could have brought the Psalter to its close at one time before the Final Hallel group was added.

This kind of issue is raised in the wisdom literature of the OT. A major wisdom psalm is 37. It would be easy to misunderstand this psalm by placing too much emphasis on the word "soon" in verse 2, and making it govern our interpretation of the whole psalm. This word is quite indeterminate, for its force will vary according to the overall timescale that is in view. The psalm contains a great many promises and threats. It is fairly clear that the fulfillment of some of these was to be in this life, but this is not true of them all. What is true is that they all promise action in the future.

So also does 1:6 as far as the wicked are concerned. If we may view Psalm 73 as a kind of exegesis of this, as 73:1 followed by an account of the psalmist's thought processes might suggest, then this reinforces the eschatological interpretation of Psalm 1. The wicked may flourish in this life, but God will deal with them in judgment eventually.

When we survey the Psalter, we note three important points. The first of these is about judgment. The judgment of God on the wicked is stated and emphasized again and again. Moreover, this is also seen as something to be greatly desired, for it is of course necessary to vindicate the character of God and his promise of blessing to his (righteous) people. Then there are the passages that we have already considered that mention Sheol, the shadowy world of the dead. Finally there is the teaching about a life with God beyond the grave in psalms like 16, 17, and 73. These too we have already considered.

When these three points are taken together, we can see that the Psalter as a whole vindicates the moral assertions of Psalm 1, when these are understood eschatologically.

Psalms 146–150 Show History Climaxing in Universal Praise

In view of what we have seen above, it is not surprising that the Psalter ends with such a paean of praise in the five great Hallel psalms, for the final redactor(s) could see that God had promised complete fulfillment of his word. This would mean that Israel's place in God's plan would be completely fulfilled, that the Gentile nations would join them in giving praise to Yahweh, their God, and that a king of the line of David would be raised up for them. The moral perfection of their God too would be completely vindicated because his judgments would be seen in all the earth. No wonder the praise in these psalms is so comprehensive and wholehearted!

THE CONTRIBUTION OF THE PSALTER TO BIBLICAL THEOLOGY

The book of Psalms makes a huge contribution to biblical theology. A major reason for this is its comprehensiveness. Mays, for instance, calls it "a virtual compendium of themes and topics found in the rest of the Old Testament."[133]

Concern to show its integration with the rest of Scripture is by no means a modern preoccupation. Athanasius, in his epistle to Marcellinus on the interpretation of the Psalms, takes great pains to show this, and his letter, often thought to have been written when he was a very young man, still has much to teach us.[134]

We can, however, speak of the Psalter's distinctiveness, largely because so much of it is devotional in nature. It is not, of course, the only devotional material in the OT, or the only literature showing people with a personal relationship with God. There are, for instance, the dialogues between God and people like the patriarchs in Genesis, Moses in Exodus and Numbers, Elijah in the books of Kings, Jeremiah, Jonah, and Habakkuk in their books. Even in Amos there is a conversation between him and God (Amos 7:1-9), and there are occasional prayers in other prophetic books (e.g., in Isa 51:9; 64:1-12). The prayer in Lamentations 5 could have come straight out of the Psalter. At the close of the book of Job, God speaks to Job and elicits response from him.

The concentration of such material in the Psalter is, however, without parallel in the OT. I will not therefore try to show that the Psalter's particular

---

133. Mays, *Psalms*, 1; cf. Dumbrell, *Faith of Israel*, 211; Murphy, *Psalms Are Yours*, 115; House, *OT Theology*, 402.

134. It occurs as an appendix to *On the Incarnation*.

emphases are peculiar to it, but rather that they are so characteristic of this book that they cannot be overlooked without serious loss. We need to give them due weight to gain a balanced grasp of biblical truth.

No doubt much of the theology in Scripture arose in the devotional lives of its writers. The great sentence immediately following the greetings in the Epistle to the Ephesians (Eph 1:3-14) does not simply state doctrine but gives praise to God. The same introductory phrase, "Blessed be the God and Father of our Lord Jesus Christ," also immediately follows the initial greetings in 2 Corinthians and 1 Peter, again introducing deeply theological passages that are devotional in tone. In the Psalter the devotional origin of the material is clear at almost every point, giving it its special character.

John Goldingay comments, "the Psalms (arguably the deepest theology in Scripture, at least in the OT), hint that an appropriate form for systematic theology in Scripture is that of adoration, thanksgiving, and lament, or at least that a context of adoration, thanksgiving, and lament ought to be a fruitful one for theological reflection on biblical narrative."[135] What he says of systematic theology is also true of biblical theology.

It is of course not simply words but the ideas they express that interest us here. Somewhat after the fashion of James Barr, Robert Davidson remarks that "theology can never be cribbed or confined within one set of words," and he illustrates this from the similarity of structure, experience, and theology (trusting in God's faithful love) that there is between Psalms 56 and 57, despite the fact that, of these two psalms, 57 alone speaks explicitly of God's faithful love.[136]

So then there is genuine theology in the Psalter. It is true that some psalms raise questions rather than give answers. Sometimes these are answered within the completed Psalter, but sometimes not even in other parts of the OT but only in the NT. Believing as Christians that God's revelation came to its fullest expression only in Christ the incarnate Word, this is what we should expect.

The nature of OT theology has been much discussed since Walther Eichrodt wrote his *Theology of the OT* (German original, 1933), and a number of writers have attempted to find a theological center for it. Eichrodt himself, for instance, thought covenant its overriding theme, while for Claus Westermann it was deliverance and blessing, and for John Bright the kingdom of God. If these suggestions apply to the OT as a whole they must fit the book of Psalms, and without doubt each is an important theme in that book.

135. Goldingay, "Biblical Narrative," 137-38.
136. Davidson, *Vitality of Worship*, 182.

Of course each could also be regarded as a subtheme of the doctrine of God, for they relate to God's covenant purpose, his acts of deliverance, and his kingdom. For this reason, as we noted earlier, some writers have concluded that the overarching OT theme is simply God, which is perhaps too obvious to be worth saying. But the OT does not speak of God abstractly but in his relationships, and the suggestions of Eichrodt, Westermann, and Bright are all about God's relations with his people.

One problem faced by OT theologians is to show the theological integration of the wisdom literature with the remainder of the OT. If the final form given to the book of Psalms establishes it as a book for meditation, this means that in a broad sense it is itself a wisdom book. It may even suggest that the wisdom material, so far from being a problem, is an important key to its theological unity. This approach to the OT seems to be suggested in the words of 2 Tim 3:15, "the holy Scriptures, which are able to make you wise to salvation through faith in Christ Jesus," an obvious purpose of the NT also.

If we pursue this wisdom connection, we note an important point of similarity between the Psalter and the books of Job, Proverbs, and Ecclesiastes. These three books are rightly classed as the wisdom books of the OT. Yet, interestingly, the LXX translators, in arranging the OT books, placed the book of Psalms between Job and Proverbs, suggesting that in their minds it too was a wisdom book. Could they have seen the significance of Psalm 1 as an introduction to the book, giving it a wisdom character, thus anticipating by hundreds of years an insight first found, among Christian writers, in Jerome?

Wisdom does not come easily to any of us. In terms of worldly wisdom, whether that of the professional philosopher or the homespun wisdom of others, it requires experience of life, deep reflection, and a clear ethical sense. Purely human wisdom, however, is bound to be inadequate, for only godly wisdom has the right starting point, the fear of the Lord that takes the godly person to the Scriptures in which practical godly wisdom is to be found (Job 28:28; Ps 111:10; Eccl 12:13). Paul quotes 94:11 in this connection (1 Cor 3:20).

I am suggesting, then, that the Psalter should be regarded as a wisdom book. After commenting on the introductory function of Psalm 1, Gerald Wilson remarks on the fact that 73, 90, and 107 (vv. 41-43), all with wisdom concerns, commence books 3, 4, and 5, respectively, and that 145, an alphabetic acrostic, and so probably intended for learning by heart, comes immediately before the Final Hallel.[137] We might add that 41, which ends book 1, and 42–43, which opens book 2, also have some wisdom characteristics.

Three of the wisdom books have a remarkable similarity in that each

---

137. Wilson, *Psalms*, 1:74.

may be viewed as an inspired search for meaning. The book of Job is largely a dialogue related to his sufferings and the perplexity they have caused him. It begins with an assurance of his righteousness, just as the Psalter starts by affirming God's blessing on the righteous life, and also with an indication of a purpose in his sufferings. The search reaches its goal at the end when God discloses himself to Job.

Ecclesiastes too records the Preacher's search for meaning in an apparently meaningless world, for "meaningless," as in NIV, is almost certainly the correct translation of הֶבֶל, *hebel,* which KJV rendered "vanity." The book's closing verses make clear to us that meaning is to be found in fearing and obeying God.

We can also regard the book of Psalms as an inspired search, with Psalms 1 and 2 giving two major theological statements, one about God's character and the other about his historical purpose. Evidence for and apparently against these statements is amassed in the psalms that follow, before a fuller understanding of their meaning emerges as the book draws to its close in great assurance and in the full-throated praise to God uttered by his people.

The book of Proverbs is somewhat different. It begins by stating that the basic principles of wisdom are to be found in listening to instruction and manifesting the fear of the Lord in a disciplined and prudent life, and it concludes with an example of such a life, picturing a wife of noble character. The wistfulness of the question, "A wife of noble character who can find?" (Prov 31:10), suggests that an ideal is being portrayed, just as Psalm 1 gives the ideal righteous person. It is also interesting to find much in the picture corresponding to the lineaments of wisdom in the book's opening chapters, especially in chapters 3 and 9. Thus we see that wisdom is practical and should be brought into personal realization.

So then we find that each of these four books has a message that is a variant of the overall wisdom theme, that true wisdom must have the fear of God as its indispensable starting point. Ultimate wisdom is found in responding trustingly to the revelation of God (Job), in fearing and obeying him (Ecclesiastes), in translating understanding of God's truth into personal character (Proverbs), and in living in circumstances both of joy and sadness with a constant orientation to him that issues in heartfelt praise (Psalms). What distinguishes the Psalter is the richness of experience that lies behind it, the many moods and emotions it expresses, and the constant movement in it toward praise.

The book of Psalms has other important theological connections within the OT. As we might expect, there are some significant ones in the Pentateuch. The song sung by the Israelites after their redemption from Egypt

(Exod 15) is not only echoed in many parts of the Psalter, but could itself be regarded as a psalm, perhaps even the first of them.[138] Yahweh's revelation to Moses recorded in Exodus 32–34 and particularly the disclosure of his character given in Exod 34:5-8 plays a big part in the Psalter. J. C. McCann Jr. highlights many points of comparison between the psalms and Exodus 32–34.[139]

Then there are two passages from Numbers, the Aaronic blessing in 6:22-27 and the invocation of Yahweh in connection with the ark's movements recorded in 10:35. The first is reflected in passages where the psalmists speak of seeing God's face (e.g., Ps 17:15), praying that his face will be turned toward them (84:9) or shine on them (31:16). There is a very clear reference to Num 10:35 at the start of Psalm 68, and in fact 67 and 68 form a contrast, for the blessing is the keynote of 67, and the ark reference, with its implied curse on the Lord's enemies, performs the same function for 68.

The links between the Psalter and Deuteronomy are manifold, and so many of the theological themes of Deuteronomy 1–11 find their echo in the Psalms. Perhaps of special importance is the Song of Moses in Deuteronomy 32, with the proclamation of Yahweh's name, his greatness, and his faithfulness with which it begins (32:3-4) and the uncompromising monotheism with which it closes (32:39-43). We note too the divinely given constitution of the king in Deut 17:14-20, with its insistence that the king should be a diligent student of the Torah, a link of thought with Psalm 1, which commences a book in which kingship is such an important theme.

Joshua 1 also has an obvious point of comparison with Psalm 1 in the way it emphasizes the importance of meditating on the book of the Law. This chapter is often seen as the first in the "Deuteronomic History" (Joshua-Judges-Samuel-Kings), a series of historical books manifesting the theology of Deuteronomy, and there is no doubt that the theology of history found in these books (perhaps most explicitly in Judg 2 and 2 Kgs 17) is identical with that in the historical psalms.

There are some psalm-like passages with similar themes to the psalms in the prophetic writings. W. H. Bellinger devotes a chapter to these and discusses especially Habakkuk and Joel.[140] David Mitchell has argued for special links between the Psalter as a whole and Zechariah 9–14.[141]

The matter could be pursued further, for there are few if any OT books without thematic links to the Psalter. Sometimes the use of similar language

---

138. G. Anderson ("Israel's Creed") calls it the earliest of all OT theologies. See esp. the comment on Ps 77.

139. McCann, *Theological Introduction*, 101-24.

140. Bellinger, *Psalmody and Prophecy*, 83-89.

141. D. C. Mitchell, *Message of Psalter*, esp. chs. 5–10.

suggests literary connections. What has already been said should encourage readers to explore these connections for themselves. Many of these connections are indicated in the exegetical section of this commentary. Indeed, the book drives us on toward an OT theology, because parts of it cannot even be properly understood without reflecting on other parts of the OT, especially Exodus.

The influence of the book of Psalms on the NT is very extensive. Others beside the Christians were interested in their contemporary relevance around NT times. For instance, the eighteen poems from a Pharisaic source and known as the *Psalms of Solomon* lament the coming of the Romans to the Holy Land and quote from the canonical Psalms. The Qumran *Thanksgiving Hymns* make much use of the psalms of lament and of thanksgiving. It is clear in both cases that their writers considered the Psalms appropriate to use in reference to the events of their own day. The NT, however, goes much further in the profound way it employs the Psalms theologically.

The Psalter is quoted more often than any other OT book, just exceeding Isaiah, and there are also frequent allusions. Some of these quotations and allusions could easily be missed by modern readers, but those used by Jesus would have been picked up by the scribes and others who knew the Scriptures well. C. H. Bullock gives the example of Ps 6:8, which is quoted in Matt 7:23 and Luke 13:27.[142] The series of beatitudes that opens the Sermon on the Mount would remind hearers of the many beatitudes in the Psalter (especially as Matt 5:5 is a virtual quotation of Ps 37:11), and the challenging illustration of the two houses that Jesus used at its end is somewhat reminiscent of the sermonette on the two ways with which the Psalter opens.

Paul's Areopagus address in Acts 17 is an outstanding example of the use of the language and ideas of the Psalms when the hearers could hardly be expected to identify it but when it has clearly molded the thought of the speaker. Here, as Bertil Gärtner has shown in *Areopagus Speech*, Paul's language is full of OT thought, much of it from the Psalms. See, for instance, points of comparison between the address and Psalm 50 (among other OT passages) in Acts 17:31 (Ps 50:4, 6), 17:25 (Ps 50:9), and 17:29-30 (Ps 50:21). In this sermon Paul kept close to the Scriptures in his theology when he was proclaiming Christ, even though he was addressing sophisticated philosophers. The same feature can be found in the address of Barnabas and Paul to the crowd at Lystra who wanted to worship them (Acts 14:14-17). Once again there is no use of any of the standard formulae used of Scripture quotations in the NT, but the description of God as "the living God, who made heaven

---

142. Bullock, *Encountering Psalms*, 89-90.

and earth and sea and everything in them," is so reminiscent of Ps 146:6 as to be a virtual quotation.

Paul undoubtedly found confirmation of the gospel in the Psalms. For instance, in his Epistle to the Romans, he quotes them in connection with God's right to judge (Ps 51:4; Rom 3:4),[143] the need of Jew and Gentile through sin (Pss 14:1-3; 53:1-3; 5:9; 140:3; 10:7; 36:1; Rom 3:10-18), justification by grace (Ps 32:1-2; Rom 4:7-8), the worldwide spread of the gospel (Ps 19:4; Rom 10:18), the rejection of the gospel by many Jews (Ps 69:22-23; Rom 11:9-10), and Gentile gratitude for the gospel (Ps 117:1; Rom 15:11).

The theological use made of the book of Psalms in the Epistle to the Hebrews is particularly interesting, and Simon Kistemaker has explored this at some length.[144] Even if he has exaggerated this, the great importance of this material for the argument of the epistle is undeniable.

The book of Revelation does not use formulae of quotation such as "it is written" or "the Scripture says," but it is saturated with the language and imagery of the OT. Not surprisingly, much of this comes from the books of the prophets, especially Isaiah, Jeremiah, Ezekiel, and also Daniel, the OT books that have the most apocalyptic material, but next to these comes the Psalter. For instance, language from Psalm 2 occurs in Rev 2:27; 11:15; 12:5; and 19:15. There are also the close verbal parallels between Rev 1:5 and Ps 89:27 and 37.[145]

What then are the book's main contributions to biblical theology?

A Warm Doctrine of God

The importance of a right doctrine of God is seen by Nahum Sarna, who says of the wicked in the Psalms, "While the wicked are motivated by base desires, the actuating cause of these evil deeds is a false theology. A fallacious understanding of the nature of God convinces these reprobates that evil can be perpetrated with impunity. . . . They believe in an otiose deity, withdrawn from the world, and morally neutral." He illustrates this from Pss 10:6, 11, and 94:4, 7.[146]

---

143. Ps 135:14 is used in the same connection in Heb 10:30.

144. Kistemaker, *Psalm Citations.* See also Bray, *Biblical Interpretation,* 71; cf. the slightly different view of Longenecker, *Biblical Exegesis,* 175.

145. See Heim, "(God-)Forsaken King," 316-22.

146. Sarna, *On Psalms,* 33.

In the OT God Is Revealed as Both Majestic and Warmly Personal

In much of the OT the majesty and closeness of God are held together in tension. H.-J. Kraus underlines that when Israel was in God's presence, the people were always aware of the distance between them and God and they viewed his steadfast love toward them with great astonishment.[147] G. C. Morgan's title for his commentary on Hosea, *The Heart and Holiness of God,* highlights the polarity. In Genesis 1 God speaks with authoritative and living power, and a whole universe is created. How different, yet beautifully complementary, is the picture that emerges in Genesis 2, where God gets his hands dirty, so to speak, in the process of creation! This intimacy of contact is continued in intimacy between God and his human creatures as he walks in the garden in the cool of the day. In chapter 1 he is Elohim, while in chapter 2 he is Yahweh Elohim, suggesting sovereignty now combined with covenant relationship. The very fact that Yahweh is a name suggests warmth and relationship.

After the fall and the loss of this intimacy, by God's gracious initiative individuals were restored to fellowship with him. As God had walked in the garden, so Enoch walked with God until he took him away (Gen 5:24), and Abraham's fellowship with God was so intimate that he could argue for the sparing of Sodom, although always with a sense that this must be by God's permission (18:22-33).

After the Abrahamic covenant came the Mosaic. Because this was with a nation, the individual's relationship to God seems less in focus, and the Sinaitic law, with its detailed regulations, makes the relationship seem at times more formal than intimate. Yet this was not true of God's dealings with Moses personally, and the whole prophetic tradition, which took its rise from his work, often demonstrates a sense of nearness between a prophet and his God, as the Confessions of Jeremiah show.

The name Yahweh or its meaning was revealed to Moses (Exod 3 and 6), and Deuteronomy frequently refers to the place where God chooses to put his name (Deut 12:5, 21; 14:23, etc.). This makes clear that worship is to be thoroughly based on God's self-disclosure. Kraus notes that this Deuteronomic name theology extends to the Psalms, and also that the ultimate manifestation of God's name is in Christ (John 17:6).[148] In him God is perfectly revealed for the trust and praise of his people.

Some of the prophets reveal autobiographical details that show their sense of closeness to God even when they passed through very difficult expe-

---

147. Kraus, *Theology of Psalms,* 12.
148. Kraus, *Theology of Psalms,* 21.

riences or, particularly in the case of Jeremiah, when beset by largely unanswerable questions about the role they were called to play (e.g., Jer 10:23-25; 12:1-17; 18:19-23; 20:7-12). It is not surprising that it was to Jeremiah that the disclosure was made of a new covenant with the nation in which the personal and inward dimension would be particularly strong (31:31-34).

Nothing in the OT surpasses the amazing passage in Hos 11:8-10, where God reveals his heart: "I will not carry out my fierce anger, nor will I turn and devastate Ephraim," followed by the deeply moving words, "For I am God, and not man — the Holy One among you. I will not come in wrath." A man would have destroyed them long before this.

The OT teaches also the hiddenness of God, and this is certainly a major theme of the book of Job, but it comes to its climax with a divine disclosure in which God addresses Job personally and even, in gently mocking irony, virtually invites him to assume the throne of the universe to perform the task of judgment. Job admits, "My ears had heard of you but now my eyes have seen you. Therefore I despise myself and repent in dust and ashes" (Job 42:5-6). It was the intimate yet awesome encounter that effected this spiritual result.

The book of Psalms goes well beyond any other OT book in its presentation of the creative tension between God's majesty and hiddenness, on the one hand, and the psalmists' sense of his accessibility, on the other. Because elsewhere this kind of feature is largely found in the divine contacts with people like patriarchs and prophets, its presence in the orphan psalms is particularly important, as showing that fellowship with this majestic God was not restricted to those with some special office or function in Israel.

In many psalms the greatness of God is set side by side with his tender concern for the weak and helpless. Psalm 8 declares the majesty of his name but shows his acceptance of praise from children. In Psalm 18 God is presented as an awesome figure, especially in verses 7-15, yet the psalmist opens by writing of his love for the Lord, whom he calls "my strength . . . my rock, my fortress . . . my deliverer . . . my shield . . . the horn of my salvation, my stronghold," and declares that God has heard his voice and reached down to pluck him from the deep waters that were about to engulf him. In Psalm 33 Yahweh is the great Creator, who made the heavens by the simple utterance of his word (v. 6), yet "the eyes of the LORD are on those who fear him, on those who hope in his unfailing love" (v. 18).

These examples, all taken from book 1, could be repeated many times over from all five books of the Psalter. What is striking is that even when the psalmists and others are aware, even smartingly aware, of God's hiddenness and apparent distance, they never feel him to be so far away that they cannot talk to him. The lines of communication between earth and heaven are still open, at least for those who are in covenant with him.

All biblical doctrine is potentially warm, but this warmth is evident at almost every point in the book of Psalms, and this special emphasis gives it distinctiveness.

The Psalter Presents a Full Doctrine of God, All of It Touched by This Warmth

Readers of the NT may be puzzled that it gives comparatively little space to teaching about God. This point should not be exaggerated, of course, for the Johannine writings in particular have much to say, but we should remember that in everything the NT assumes and builds on the OT's teaching. For the doctrine of God, no OT book is more important than the Psalter, with its fully rounded and uniformly warm and personal presentation of the God addressed in his people's prayers and exalted in their praise.

God's primary disclosure in the OT is found in the Pentateuch. Here we learn of his creatorship, his judgment, his gift of covenant relationship, his redemptive acts, his exacting standards, his patience, and so on. Deuteronomy 1–11, in particular, bring many of these themes together, and from chapter 4 almost a full summary of the OT doctrine of God may be obtained. Why was the Psalter put together in five books? Following the example of the five books of Moses, yes! But in what way and for what purpose?

Possibly the reason was that the great revealed facts and acts in the Pentateuch needed response. Yahweh had revealed himself so that his people might give him their trust and obedience and respond to his revelation in prayer and praise. This we see happening in the book of Psalms. All the great pentateuchal truths about God are now given the dimension of praise and enter the prayer life of the people. Of course this should be true of the whole biblical revelation, so that when Christians use their Bibles for personal or corporate devotion they are simply following the psalmists.

The doctrine of God in the Psalms is found in the epithets and adjectival phrases used of him, but preeminently in his great names and titles. Psalms that emphasize the attributes of God, such as 111 and 145, never do so in a cold and detached manner but always by way of praising response by the people to all that he is. Moreover, the psalmist often refers to "my God" or "our God," to "my Lord" or "our Lord." This is not without parallel elsewhere, but it is particularly full and noticeable in the Psalter. He is the God of Israel but ultimately will be praised by men and women of every nation, and this is brought out in the way 18:49 is used in Rom 15:9, Ps 117:1 in Rom 15:11, and Ps 146:6 in Acts 14:15.

The psalmists are often moved to express praise to him, with little sense of this as a duty. The overwhelming impression we get is that they praise him because they want to do so and that nothing could bring them greater joy.

A significant development in the use of the word "bless" is found in the Psalter and some other parts of the OT, in that it is applied not only to God's attitude toward his people but to theirs toward him. It suggests not only gratitude but a deep concern that not only the hearts of the worshipers but God's own heart will be warmed as he receives worship from them. As we have seen already, the Hebrew verb is בָּרַךְ, *bārak,* which is rendered "praise" in NIV, but "bless" in NRSV and NASB. It is used about two dozen times in the Psalms, and 103, 104, 135, and 145 each have it several times. Perhaps all can be summed up in the words of 103:2, "Bless the LORD, O my soul; and forget none of His benefits" (NASB). As this psalm opens, the writer calls on all he knows he has within himself to come in blessing to his God for all that he has experienced of him.

Obviously, each psalm was written by an individual, whether he wrote for himself alone or for the community of which he was a member, but the individual's sense of a personal relationship with God is a function of the community's own covenant standing. The situations out of which the psalms were written varied considerably, and sometimes, but not always, the nature of the situation is made clear; but each was brought to God with the expressed or unexpressed assumption that it was appropriate. The range of these concerns was exceedingly wide, but there is never a feeling that Yahweh may not be interested.

Heartfelt response grounded in an awareness of personal fellowship is not confined to what might be thought the Lord's gentler qualities. Even the judgment of God is touched by this warmth, for there are passages where God's judgment is anticipated with great joy (e.g., 98:7-9). This is because judgment puts things right, and therefore it is often for the blessing of those who have been oppressed and deprived of their rights. We recall the "Hallelujah!" evoked from the people of God when "Babylon" is judged in Rev 19:1-8.

The great longing for the house of God in psalms like 42, 43, 63, and 84 is really a longing for God himself and his worship. In 73:23-26 the author says, "I am always with you; you hold me by my right hand. You guide me with your counsel, and afterward you will take me into glory. Whom have I in heaven but you, and earth has nothing I desire besides you. My flesh and my heart may fail, but God is the strength of my heart and my portion forever." Clearly he had a deep sense of relationship with God that transcended anything he knew in the human realm.

The covenant promise in 2 Samuel 7 spoke of the relationship between Yahweh and the king as one of father and son, and this is confirmed in Pss 2:7 and 89:27. Although the psalms do not elsewhere use the language of filial relationship, all its ingredients are there: on the part of the Father, provision, protection, guidance, accessibility, and so much more; on the part of the son, petition, enquiry, gratitude, and so on. Of course, to the psalmists Yahweh was also the supreme authority figure, but in the cultural background of the OT, fatherhood represented authority as well as intimacy.

All this comes to its great climax in the NT, reaching wonderful new heights. Often Jesus referred to God as "my Father," strongly suggesting special intimacy, and then, in speaking to Mary Magdalene, after the resurrection, he spoke of "my Father and your Father," of "my God and your God" (John 20:17). Jesus encouraged his disciples to think of God as their heavenly Father. Paul writes of the adoption of Christians into God's family and John of their new birth, and both writers indicate that the intimacy of the Christian with Christ is based on deep spiritual union (John 17:23-26; Rom 8:9-11; 2 Cor 6:17; Eph 1:3-14). The Psalter prepares us quite significantly for this. It is no surprise that Christians, who know that fellowship with God through Christ, find that the psalmists often seem to be on the same spiritual wavelength.

This Relationship Is Shown in Yahweh's Faithfulness and His People's Faith

Human society cannot exist without trust, and the more intimate the relationship the more important is this element. It is not surprising therefore that verbs of trust and confidence are so frequent in the Psalter. Indeed, the whole of life for the psalmists was an extended exercise of trust in God. They rested on his faithfulness, even when he was working in ways they did not understand, even sometimes apparently contradicting his promises. They did not give up their confidence that he was faithful and that this would ultimately be proved true.

Arguably, the whole Bible has the faithfulness of God as its general theme. In *Toward an OT Theology* Walter Kaiser Jr. has promoted the idea that promise is the great overarching OT theme. Psalms like 105 and 106 pursue the theme through part of OT history, showing both God's faithfulness and Israel's unfaithfulness. Further, the reliability of God's word over against the frequent unreliability of human beings is often referred to in the Psalms (e.g., Ps 12).

The frequency of חֶסֶד, *ḥesed*, which occurs in the Psalter far more often than in any other OT book, is impressive. This word, often given as a synonym for faithfulness, combines faithfulness and love, love within a covenant relationship, so that it is in essence a warm word.

The NT places considerable emphasis on faith, and Paul quotes OT passages to show that the OT godly were justified by faith. He uses Psalm 32 to show God graciously blessing people with forgiveness (Rom 4:6-8) and quotes Ps 116:10, "I believed; therefore have I spoken" (2 Cor 4:13), revealing his awareness of the psalmist's faith. He goes on to say, "With that same spirit of faith we also believe and therefore speak." Much else in the Psalms could have filled out his contention that God has always responded in blessing to those who come by the way of faith.

If OT and NT faith differ, one may think that this is in terms of their object, yet this is not really true, for it is a basic truth of biblical theology that the God of both Testaments is the same God. The real difference lies in the extent to which that God has revealed himself, and he has done so with greater fullness in Christ, showing in even greater measure how utterly faithful he is.

The Psalter, as canonically arranged, exhibits the fact that problems God's people face about his faithfulness are resolved by God himself in due time and often arise because of false conclusions as to the way the promise is to find fulfillment. In the OT this is illustrated too in the story of Abraham and Isaac in Genesis 22, especially as interpreted in Romans 4 and Hebrews 11.

Several writers have noticed the close links between the Psalter and the doctrine of God to be found in Isaiah 40–55.[149] If both were written to encourage faith, such links are anything but surprising. Faith grows not by introspection but by considering its great object, and both these parts of the OT are full of great statements about the God of Israel, the object of his people's trust.

Christ is himself the ultimate vindication of God's faithfulness, so that after saying, "as surely as God is faithful" (2 Cor 1:18), Paul declares, "No matter how many promises God has made, they are 'Yes' in Christ" (v. 20). Not only so, but this vindication comes through the apparent "death" of the promises of God through the passion and death of Jesus, which went even deeper than the "death" Judah experienced at the exile, and which, unlike their experience, was not due to sin on Jesus' part. The darkness grew deeper, but beyond it the light of God's faithfulness shone in its fullest glory in his resurrection.

---

149. McCann explores these links briefly but helpfully (*Theological Introduction*, 46-47, 130).

It is no wonder then that the NT calls so confidently for faith. If God has done so much and fulfilled his promises in such an amazing way, nothing should hold us back from putting our complete trust in him.

A Firm and Confident Doctrine of Historical Revelation

Doctrine in the Psalter Is Based on Objective Revelation

In Israel the relationship to God both of the community and of the individual was based on faith and obedience. Now these are responsive attitudes and activities. In psychologically normal people they are not self-created, but clearly imply the objective existence of the person to be trusted and obeyed. They raise important questions about the nature of this person and about the grounds for confident faith and obedience.

It is clear, not only from the Psalms but also from elsewhere in the OT, that there is an objectivity about the nature and will of Israel's God. Yahweh revealed his love for his people by delivering them from Egyptian bondage, giving them grounds to trust him when other enemies came upon them. The awesome disclosure of his will in the Sinai revelation called his people to a clearly articulated obedience.

This in itself reveals how deeply theological the religious experience of the psalmists was. It could be stimulated by subjective experience, deepened by that experience, even questioned by it, but it was not based on it. Rather it rested on objective divine revelation. As we will see later, this affected every aspect of the religious life, and it is particularly important in relation to such Godward activities as prayer and worship.

The religion of the Psalter is not therefore mystical in the proper sense of that term. It is mediated by God's revelation of himself. Neither do any of the psalmists give us the impression that they are religious loners who are finding, or even seeking, a way to God not shared with the other members of their religious community. The covenant love of God was not something special to them as individuals but was shown to his people as a whole, and its great revelation was in that people's history.

This is a very important point, as it shows that a theology of the Psalter is possible, even though this is largely devotional literature consisting mostly of the words of human beings directed toward God. The literature is responsive, and the heart of the revelation consists of the great historical acts of God, in which he is revealed, and which are objective to any spiritual experience, whether of the nation or of the individual.

Special mystical experiences are not characteristic of the Bible. Paul refers to one such experience in 2 Corinthians 12 but only with great diffidence, and he says he heard inexpressible words, things that are not permissible to tell. If so, they were not part of the understanding of divine truth that his writings contain.

The pictures we are shown of the redeemed in heaven (Rev 4, 5, 7, etc.) make clear that the praise they utter is directed to the God objectively revealed in Scripture. There is a reminder of the cross in heaven, for Christ is there as the Lamb of God, slain, risen, and exalted, forever recalling for believers the decisive redemptive event of Calvary, an event in history.

This Revelation Is Given in Connection with Certain Past Events

Many psalms emphasize that the God of Israel made himself known to his people through important events. This tunes in well with what we find in the Pentateuch, the historical literature, and the books of the prophets. The emphasis of OT theology on the importance and significance of certain past events is quite unmistakable, and it appears in virtually every stratum of the OT except for the wisdom literature, although we will see that it is not completely absent even from that.

As we have seen, the events chiefly in view in the Psalms are the creation of the world, the exodus from Egypt, and a series of events closely associated with this including the revelation at Sinai, the establishment of the Davidic dynasty, and along with this Jerusalem as the religious capital of the country. In the Psalter this emphasis is most obvious in the historical psalms, but it is quite clear also in psalms of praise and even of lament.

It is better to refer here to "past events" rather than to "historical events," as "history" normally refers to the interaction of human beings and human societies, while the great facts we have in view include the creation of the universe. This is seen in the Psalms to be an event just as the exodus and other historical events were. It is unlikely that the psalmists would have made a hard and fast distinction between the events that would be regarded as historical on a strict modern interpretation of the term and the initial act of God that set everything in being and in motion. If history is "his story," then so is creation.

An examination of the apostolic preaching in the Acts of the Apostles shows clearly that the gospel proclaimed there was based on the objective event of Christ, crucified and risen, and that this was the basis of every evangelistic sermon summarized there. The hearers were not so much invited to share an experience as to put their trust in Christ as revealed in the gospel.

The Sequence of These Events Shows the Consistency of God

Sometimes these events are given separately in a recital of the deeds of God, notably in Psalm 136, but there is a distinct tendency on the part of the psalmists to merge various OT events, to use the language of one to describe another, and so on. This appears in a marked way in Psalm 18,[150] but is not by any means confined to it. Contemporary events are described in poetic language that calls these great past events to mind (e.g., 17:7; 20:6; cf. Exod 15:6), as if to say that it is the God of all this and all that who is now active for his people. There are times when it is not clear to which event or events the psalmist is referring, because the language he uses is stereotypical for great acts of God's grace and power.

This feature appears elsewhere in the OT too, especially in Isaiah 40–55, so that it is not completely unique to the Psalms. D. W. Pao finds the merging of creation and exodus themes in Psalms 74, 77, 89, 114, and he compares Exodus 15 and Isa 50:2; 51:3, 12-16. "The two are considered together when the power of God is in focus. Exodus can be understood as the historical manifestation of the divine creative power."[151] In Isa 51:9 the prophet prays that God will clothe his arm with strength as in olden days, because this kind of language is used in connection with the exodus (Exod 6:6; 15:16; Deut 5:15). His prayer receives an amazing answer, indicated in Isa 53:1, an answer so staggering that the prophet wondered whoever would believe it, for God's arm would be revealed in the sufferings of God's Servant for others.

The expression of these events in imaginative terms heightens their impact on the reader. The plenitude of similes and especially metaphors in the Psalms carries their message deep into the reader's imaginative life. Bullock is right: "In the Old Testament, metaphors not only encapsulate abstract realities in everyday language, they also transport theological truth along paths that theological abstractions cannot imitate."[152]

All this testifies to belief in divine consistency, as if certain events have paradigmatic significance for the psalmists. Certain character qualities cannot be revealed just in a moment of time or in one event, but require time and a sequence of events for their manifestation. Chief among these are faithfulness and patience, and both of these clearly meant much to the psalmists, for not only Yahweh's faithfulness but his patience too is much in evidence in the historical psalms, in which we often see Israel committing one act of sinful folly after another.

---

150. See the comments on this psalm.
151. Pao, *Thanksgiving*, 67.
152. Bullock, *Encountering Psalms*, 177.

The whole pattern of typological reference in the NT is about divine consistency. What God has done in Christ is consistent with what he did in OT days, but it goes beyond it and has an element of finality about it, because it is the supreme revelation. In this way revelation is seen to be progressive, not in the sense that what was previously viewed as revelation has to be unlearned, but rather in the sense that it is cumulative and ever-deepening.

The sovereign God may act in a variety of ways, but he always does so on the basis of consistent principles. This is shown in the way Paul handles Ps 19:4 in Rom 10:18. In this psalm the writer declares that God's word through creation has gone out to all the world. Paul uses this language in relation to the gospel, and the reason he can do so is God's consistency. It is notable that the word of God in the law becomes the main focus later in the same psalm (19:7-11), and earlier in his same chapter (Rom 10:5-10) Paul employs words from Deuteronomy (Deut 30:12-14) about the accessibility of the law and applies them to the gospel. The one God speaks in creation, in the law and in the gospel, for he is utterly consistent.

So then there is a firmness about the doctrine of revelation in the Psalter because consistency gives confidence, and every further indication of it strengthens awareness of this consistency and so strengthens this confidence.

This Consistency Features Both in the Appeals of the Laments and in the Content of Psalmic Praise

Since Westermann, it has been widely recognized that praise and lament are the two chief types of psalms, with of course considerable variety among them. When they need an intervention by Yahweh, the psalmists often look back to the great revelatory events. They return to them from the imponderables of everyday life that they bring to him in their laments. They assert their belief in them and invoke God in the character he has shown through these events and through later confirmatory events that have built up further evidence of his faithfulness. It was when they were lamenting their lot that God intervened to rescue them from Egypt (and also of course from Babylon), so it is no surprise if in other situations they look to him as the God of the exodus deliverance.

The events of Exodus 32–34 were particularly important for the psalmists. Here, after the golden calf incident and the remaking of the tablets of the law, God proclaims, "The LORD, the LORD, the compassionate and gracious God, slow to anger, abounding in love and faithfulness, maintaining love to thousands, and forgiving wickedness, rebellion, and sin" (Exod 34:6-7). Certainly he goes on to declare he will punish sin, but this declaration of his grace in such circumstances is so amazing that its influence on the Psalms is not surprising, and may be seen, for instance, in 86:15; 103:8; and 145:8.

Then there are psalms of thanksgiving, of declarative praise, asserting that God has proved his unchanging character in coming to the aid of the psalmists. Some are communal, and such acts of God for the whole people feature much. Others, a much larger number, are individual, and God's rescue of individuals often takes a paradigmatic form, especially in relation to the exodus.

Finally the psalms of descriptive praise clearly show that the divine qualities revealed in these divine acts and verbal disclosures are settled, firm, and abiding, and are integral to God's nature and character. Because of this their authors give voice to their praise.

Their Experience Sometimes Raises Major Questions for the Psalmists

Human experience confronts us with an inescapable duality. We live in a world of contingency with constant change and much uncertainty. We cannot predict what will happen in an hour's time, let alone a year's. Yet there are also fixed points, some completely and others relatively fixed. We know that in every twenty-four-hour period night will be succeeded by day and then day again by night, but we do not know what will happen during that day. We know too that the 7:30 train will run (usually!) but not how many people will be on it. Fixed points give structure to life and represent security. We also find security in the characters of people we trust, which is why parenthood is such a serious responsibility. The psalmists found this security preeminently in their God, in whom they trusted implicitly.

Yet, just as children moving into adolescence start to raise questions about their parents, there are psalms in which the writers wrestle with great questions, all ultimately questions about God. If Yahweh is the God of the exodus and so his people's savior, why is he allowing my foes to afflict me? If he is the just God of Sinai, why do the wicked often seem to prosper and the righteous to be afflicted? If he is the God who established Zion, why have Jerusalem and its temple been destroyed? If he is the God of the Davidic covenant, why is David's dynastic successor languishing in Babylon? All these questions are asked in this literature.

The two introductory psalms not only set the Psalter's tone but they also provide its main problems. Psalm 1 shows God's commitment to the righteous and to the way he has set for them, and promises them blessing.

Psalm 2 focuses on the Davidic king and is a reminder of the firm establishment of the dynasty. The experience of Israel generally and also that of individual psalmists question both.

There are huge questions too in the NT. In the Gospels the Jews constantly raise questions about Jesus. The synagogue teaching formed a fixed and, in consequence, a secure pattern they could take into everyday life. Jesus was an immensely attractive character, but his teaching and actions must have appeared, especially to the synagogue teachers themselves, a great threat to their security. Some of these questions became points of major focus in the NT, especially those about the nature of the Messiah and how people are justified before God.

Being a disciple of Jesus was both a settling and an unsettling experience. That is why so many of the questions in the Gospels are asked by the disciples themselves. Yet they stayed with him, for they had learned to trust him.

The final unsettlement came when he was taken from them and died a criminal's death. No wonder Peter refused to accept that Jesus was going to die. Yet die he did and the darkness of Easter Saturday must have been the darkest ever to descend on believers. They had heard words of reassurance about his resurrection, but had not taken these in, preoccupied as they were with the awful predictions of his death.

Such Questions Raised Issues of Interpretation, with the Convictions Purified Rather Than Abandoned

The great convictions the psalmists had were deeply rooted. There was never any question that these should be given up or found mistaken. They are part of the very fiber of their being. They could no more deny them than their own existence.

To move briefly into the NT, we may see a link here with Paul's revelation of his "religious root" (H. Dooyeweerd) when he says μὴ γένοιτο, *mē genoito*, translated "God forbid!" in KJV, but perhaps best rendered in modern parlance as "Perish the thought!"[153] There were ideas that his mind, as a Christian, could not tolerate, and they were all convictions about God, predominantly about his character.

This was true also for the psalmists even when their experience seemed to deny their convictions. This applies particularly to Yahweh's moral nature,

---

153. See Rom 3:4, 6, 31; 6:2, 15; 7:7, 13; 9:14; 11:1; 1 Cor 6:15; Gal 2:17; 3:21; 6:14.

revealed at Sinai, and his promised covenant relationship with his people, particularly with the Davidic dynasty. Psalm 89 is a striking example of this. Here the psalmist extols God's faithfulness to David in glowing words and at considerable length, only to raise deep questions about it that remain unresolved, and yet the strong statements he makes earlier in the psalm remain, suggesting that despite the agonizing questions he faced, he had not given up faith in God's promises.

There were times when clarification was needed. This appears not only in the Psalter but elsewhere in the OT, and it particularly applies to the nature of the covenants. The covenant with Israel certainly meant God committed himself to that people but not (as Paul shows in Romans) that there would be no judgments on them in which many of them would face the wrath of God and be excluded from his people. The Davidic covenant did not mean his capital city would be inviolate, nor that his line, although not obliterated, would always be reigning on the throne in that city.

Clarification comes in the course of the book as ultimately arranged. Do the wicked appear to prosper and are the righteous suffering? Yahweh is planning a great salvation in the future and his character will be vindicated in final acts of judgment. In Psalm 73, often regarded as the most important of all the psalms, even as a Psalter in miniature, the question is answered in eschatological terms. We see this eschatological perspective particularly in books 4 and 5 but not only in them.

Psalm 2 focuses on two kings, the one divine and the other human, and the one the guarantor of the other's reign. In fact, though, the history of the Davidic line had many ups and downs, with what seemed a final and decisive down at the exile. What then of the covenant and so of God's whole covenanted plan?

There was a conditional element alongside the unconditional element in the covenant, and this had to be recognized. The covenant rested on the divine word, but there was no guarantee that a Davidic king would always reign on the throne in Jerusalem. The exile and the removal from Judah's throne of the young king Jehoiachin did not invalidate the promise, not simply because he was succeeded by Zedekiah, whose miserable reign soon ended, but because of the messianic hope. Indeed, as David Mitchell argues in *Message of the Psalter,* the Psalter's eventual arrangement was intended to teach and encourage anticipation of a coming Davidic Messiah. He would be a priest-king and would be the powerful messianic horn of the future, but only after the judgment of exile.

This kind of thing also happens in Job. The book of Job raises questions, often in a most acute form, about God himself. Job could never abstract the question of suffering from the question of God, because he believed in a God who was in control. The comforters represent a system of theological security, often likened to the Deuteronomic theology but in actuality a caricature of it. Job cries out against this caricature, for his experience denied it.

All the time the reader knows that Job's experiences are a test of his faith and obedience, and despite all his doubting there is triumph in the end, for he never gives up his essential belief in a God of justice. Ernst Bloch, the somewhat unorthodox Marxist, was fascinated by the book of Job, but confessed to a measure of disappointment. He felt that at the end Job should have given up his belief in God altogether.[154] Not so, for the religious root in Job, despite his trials, was very deep. Physical pain, social ostracism, and the most agonizing questions about God himself — none of these could get him to abandon his fundamental convictions about God. What he receives is not an answer to all his questions but a new revelation of God and an assurance of the Creator's sovereign justice.

Then there is Jeremiah. He was called by God as a prophet, but life became extremely difficult, and the deep nature of the problems he faced becomes very clear when we read the passages usually referred to as his Confessions (Jer 11:18-23; 12:1-6; 15:10-21; 17:12-18; 18:19-23; 20:7-18). Like Job, he wished he had never been born, even accusing God of deceiving him, perhaps thinking of God's promises in Jeremiah 1. He was disillusioned with the monarchs of the Davidic line and saw clearly that even Josiah's reformation was not far-reaching enough.

God's covenant with Israel would survive, however, fulfilled in a perfect Davidic king and a much more intimate relationship in which individuals would know God personally (just as Jeremiah had) and have his law written on their hearts. The very passage where Jeremiah accuses God of deception contains two verses where he reaffirms his belief, despite all, in the justice of God (20:11-12). An earlier passage had also clarified the matter somewhat (15:15-21). Clearly his sufferings did not invalidate the promises but simply meant they did not guarantee him an easy life.

We find the same kind of clarification in the NT. The Pharisaic doctrine that all Israel would be saved ran counter to what the book of Psalms teaches, as did the doctrine of the merits of the patriarchs. That they are not all Israel who are descended from Israel (Rom 9:6) could have come straight out of the Psalter, and Paul sets out his case that Israel, and by extension all humanity, is rebellious largely by multiple quotations from the Psalter (Rom 3:9-20).

The NT is the ultimate expression of a new, purified perspective on the

---

154. Bloch, *Atheism in Christianity,* 84-122.

ways of God. The Christ was to suffer, for the OT preparation for him contains passages in a minor as well as those in a major key. His suffering would come first, and it would be deep beyond all plumbing; but beyond it, only just beyond it, would come his resurrection. Only at the second advent will every question be resolved, but the great nonnegotiables of the Psalter itself set out in the first two psalms were decisively reinforced by God himself in Christ.

God's People Can Go Forward into the Future with Purified and Deepened Confidence in Him

What about the future? This too rests on past events, for future salvation and judgment and the messianic hope are all based on the fact that the God of the exodus, of Sinai, and of the Davidic covenant has not changed and that divine movements then begun would surely come to their God-given consummation in due time. Each book of the Psalter makes its own contribution to this, both in terms of individual psalms but particularly when taken as a whole.

Book 1 shows God's promise recorded in 2 Samuel 7 being fulfilled. The king went through many trials and experienced much suffering, some directly attributable to his own sin (see the superscription to Ps 3), but his God supported him and did not replace him on the throne of his kingdom.

Book 2 begins to incorporate Levitical as well as Davidic psalms. Levites like Asaph and the sons of Korah faced the same kind of opposition as their king and looked to God for support, as he did. This shows it is not only the king but others in covenant with God who may trust him for the future.

Book 3 faces the great trauma of the exile, recognizing how deeply felt the destruction of the temple and the removal of the people from Judah were, and it is full of questions. The exile made the people face reality, especially the reality of their own sins. Yet at the same time there are encouragements for those who were penitent, and a psalm like 85 promises peace if there is no return to folly. So even before book 4 there was encouragement for faith and hope.

Books 4 and 5 are full of encouragements, book 4 because it presents the supremacy of the God of Israel and the fact that none can withstand his purposes and power, and book 5 in a great variety of ways, for it gave encouragement to continue to celebrate the great feasts, which not only looked to the past but implied a continued communal life. The concluding Hallel psalms present a vision of a world at worship, anticipating in some ways Revelation 4 and 5.

This feature is in marked contrast to the nature religions of many Middle Eastern people at that time. There was an element of sympathetic magic in this, for the rituals undergone by the king in the reenthronement ceremonies were thought essential if the following spring was to come and the physical needs of the people be secured.

Certainly the people of Israel needed to be obedient to their God, but his purposes were in no danger of ultimate failure, for they were secured in his promises and power.

The Psalmists See Wisdom to Be Related to the Law Given at Sinai

The OT shows the God of Israel making himself known not only in great acts but through verbal disclosures of his nature and will. For instance, 78:1-8 shows divine communication using historical analogy. It thus resembles the parables that also use analogy in the homely stories of Jesus. Interestingly, Matthew quotes this psalm (Matt 13:34-35) in connection with the parables. A major purpose of Israel's encounter with God at Sinai was the revelation of his will. If divine revelation is given for practical ends (Deut 29:29), it is appropriate to ask about its relevance to communal and individual life, and such questions are actually about wisdom.

OT theologians have often had problems with the wisdom literature because it seems bereft of the historical element. But is it? The modern writer may distinguish between creation, the bringing of the world into existence, and the acts of God in the history of his chosen people, but would the wisdom writers themselves recognize this distinction? To the OT authors, all these were acts of the one true God, Yahweh. Without doubt there is a creation theology in books like Job, Proverbs, and Ecclesiastes, and this means they are based on the self-revelation of the God of the psalmists and the prophets.

The linking of wisdom and the law, which never occurs expressly in Proverbs but which we do find in the Psalter, is therefore very important, because the law was itself given historically. Eaton remarks, "the confluence of wisdom tradition and *tôrâ* piety, especially clear in Psalm 1, is also heralded in Deuteronomy (4:5-8)."[155] It is important to note this, as so many of the great themes of OT theology occur together in Deuteronomy 1–11.

We should however note what D. N. Freedman and Andrew Welch say, after detailed study of 119:

---

155. Eaton, *Psalms of the Way*, 46.

Psalm 119, then, has no explicit reference to the following Israelite theological ideas found elsewhere throughout the Hebrew Bible: creation; patriarchal promises; covenants (patriarchal, Mosaic, or Davidic); the Temple; the Davidic dynasty, past or future; or Yahweh's mighty acts of salvation in Israel's history. Only *tôrâ* is left as the theological category of Yahweh's revelation and activity in the world.

This does not mean, however, that these other theological concepts have been rejected. Rather, "Everything else in Israelite religion — Temple, Covenant, Creation, Exodus, Messiah — is subsumed under *tôrâ*."[156] Freedman and Welch leave open the possibility that *tôrâ*, even for this psalm, is much wider than simply the Decalogue or even the Pentateuch, pointing out that Psalm 119 never specifies the contents of this *tôrâ*. It appears to be simply inexhaustible sacred literature.[157] Of course, this absence of specific content should not be overemphasized, as the very full use of legal technical terms shows that the primary reference of *tôrâ* here must be to the law, and every reader would know the nature of its contents.

Does this mean all the major convictions of the psalmists may now be reduced to one? The answer must be both yes and no. Yes, because the convictions have found literary embodiment both within the Psalter and the wider OT, and this literature is now available to us. No, because it is important in studying any literature to identify the anchor points of its thought for purposes of interpretation.

Even though the term *tôrâ* in the introductory Psalm 1 may have had the general sense of "instruction" for the ultimate redactor, so that the term "Law" is used of the Psalter even in the NT, notably by Jesus in the Gospel of John (John 10:34; 15:25), we can be sure the reader of the Psalter would be reminded particularly of Sinai by that word, and a specific Sinai reference was almost certainly in the mind of the psalmist himself. Pondering life in the light both of the Mosaic law and of the Psalter is the true path to wisdom.

The Convictions of the Psalmists Have Their Counterpart and Fulfillment in the NT

In the NT the new always has a special relationship with what is old and familiar. This applies to the new creation, the new exodus (Luke 9:31), the new

156. Freedman et al., *Psalm 119*, 91.
157. Freedman et al., *Psalm 119*, 89.

instruction given from a mountain (Matt 5–7), the new Jerusalem, and the new covenant. Thus all the great principles of the OT are gathered up and transcended in the NT, for it is one and the same God who revealed himself in both Testaments.

The book of Psalms was and still is used in worship of the one true God. Characteristically in the Psalter, this worship was carried on at the house of God in Jerusalem. The NT speaks of a new temple (John 2:21; Eph 2:21-22), but uses psalmic language about the old one to set it forth theologically, as seen, for instance, in the way Ps 118:22-23 is employed in Matt 21:42, Mark 12:11, and Luke 20:17, where Christ, the stone rejected by the builders, is the foundation of the new temple. Acts 4:11 takes up the same theme. Christ is the capstone and, although rejected, he is in fact indispensable. He is the ultimate revelation; there can be no going back. Acts 7 takes up the theme, for it shows that the Jerusalem temple was not intended as the final place of worship. Christ is the new temple, and, because they are in him, so also are Christian believers considered both collectively (1 Cor 3:16-17) and distributively (1 Cor 6:19) the temple of God.

As the people of the OT, including the psalmists, looked back to the saving act of God in the exodus from Egypt and its continuation in the entry into the land, so the people of the NT looked back to the cross and the resurrection of Jesus. These are the foundations of Christian assurance and the basis of the Christian future hope, centered in the second advent of Christ.

A Heartfelt and Expanding Sense of Community

In all normal circumstances, human life is lived in community and the society to which they belong plays a big part in shaping the characters and lifestyles of individual people. The community to which the psalmists belonged was of considerable importance in this regard.

Israel/Judah Is Yahweh's Special Richly Blessed Community

It is noticeable that a great many, probably the majority, of the psalms show a sense of community. Psalm 1 concentrates on "the man," but is aware of "the assembly of the righteous." In Psalm 2 the king's rule must logically be over subjects. His rule over the nations is a judgment of them rather than a source of blessing, although "rejoice" (v. 11) may suggest that, through their repentance, severity will give place to blessing. Psalm 3, where the psalmist faces his foes, recognizes Yahweh's personal deliverance but ends, "May your blessing be upon your people" (3:8). In 4:3 he says, "know that the LORD has set apart the godly for himself." Although "godly" is singular, it suggests a generalization and therefore membership of a community. This note is found in many of the Davidic psalms. We would expect this same feature in the Levitical psalms, for the Levites officiated for the community, and it characterizes both the Korahite (e.g., 44, 46, 47, 48) and the Asaphite psalms (e.g., 74, 75, 78, 79).

Such community involvement brings great blessing from God. In 34:8-9, for instance, after saying, "Taste and see that the LORD is good; blessed is the man who takes refuge in him," the psalmist goes on to say, "Fear the LORD, you his saints, for those who fear him lack nothing." The greatest blessing is to worship the Lord in the company of others, and in the same psalm he says, "Glorify the LORD with me; let us exalt his name together" (34:3). Such passages could be multiplied, especially in books 4 and 5.

The awareness and importance of community run right through the OT. It may seem least strong in Genesis, but even here the family is important. Indeed, many OT scholars have held that real individualism did not emerge until the time of Jeremiah and Ezekiel. This view has been questioned, but its very existence testifies to the importance of the communal perspective for the OT.

In the Psalms we see individuals supported both emotionally and theologically by their divinely established society. The psalmist shows this awareness, for instance, when finding himself somewhat isolated, as in Psalms 42–43. His great concern to be in the temple arises from his thirst for God, the living God, but also somewhat nostalgically he pictures himself there among the multitude, the festive throng (42:4).

Jeremiah too felt this alienation. In a strange union of apparently contradictory sentiments, he said, "Oh, that my head were a spring of water and my eyes a fountain of tears! I would weep day and night for the slain of my people," yet he went on immediately to say, "Oh, that I had in the desert a lodging place for travelers, so that I might leave my people and go away from them; for they are all adulterers, a crowd of unfaithful people" (Jer 9:1-2). Isolated in the loneliness of his prophetic ministry and hating the sins of his people, he nevertheless had a loving concern for them. His new covenant prophecy, although it had an important individual dimension, was with the house of Israel and the house of Judah (Jer 31:31-34). This community sense was not simply social solidarity but an awareness of belonging to God's people. Ezekiel's outlook follows that of Jeremiah in many respects.

The band of disciples Jesus gathered became the nucleus of the church established by him. In the NT the necessity for individual response and the importance of the church are found side by side. Christians tend to read the

Epistles as if they are addressed to individuals; but, except for the Pastoral Epistles and the very brief letters, this is not true, and even most of these are concerned chiefly with church matters. The book of Revelation is addressed to seven local churches and ends with a description of the final redeemed community.

This Community Concept Centers in and Is Focused on Jerusalem/Zion

The community is of course the people of Israel, variously described. The possible northern origin of some of the psalms has been much discussed, especially by M. D. Goulder in *Psalms of the Sons of Korah,* but even if this could be demonstrated, the northern kingdom was still viewed as the people of God. Normally prophets did not prophesy to foreign nations (Jonah was an exception), although they did prophesy about them. Hosea and Amos certainly addressed the northern kingdom as if its people still had a special relationship to Yahweh.

The Joseph tribes of Ephraim and Manasseh constituted the heart of the northern kingdom. Psalm 77:15 calls the redeemed from Egypt "the descendants of Jacob and Joseph," and in Gen 47:29-31 and 50:24-26 both patriarchs show their belief in God's word of promise concerning Canaan. Psalm 80 also refers to Joseph, and yet it is as "you who sit enthroned between the cherubim" that God is asked to shine forth before the northern tribes (80:1-2). This suggests the Jerusalem temple, although some have thought it may relate to a northern sanctuary. If we could be sure verse 17 refers to a Davidic king, this would show that, despite the northern references, the psalm had a focus on Jerusalem.[158] Psalm 78 traces the sad history of Israel's sin, refers to God's abandonment of the Shiloh tabernacle, and then declares his choice of Judah, Mount Zion, and David rather than Ephraim.

The names Jerusalem and Zion, virtual synonyms, are very important in the Psalter. This is understandable because of Jerusalem's association with David, who is so prominent in the book, but also because it was where the temple came to be located. For this reason many psalms show great love for the city and its place of worship. There is even an architectural interest, a pride in its appearance and in the strength of its fortifications. This could go wrong, but Psalm 48, the one in which this element is most prominent, begins and ends with God, for it is for his ends the city and its temple exist.

---

158. See the comment on this psalm.

Psalm 68 follows the ark's progress from the wilderness (68:1; cf. Num 10:35) to its installation in the sanctuary on Mount Zion (Ps 68:15-35). The Zion psalms, of course, focus completely on the city and its temple and have an unmistakable atmosphere of joy. Many of the Songs of Ascents too refer joyously to Jerusalem (122:2, 6; 125:1; 126:1; 128:5; 129:5; 132:13; 133:3; 134:3).

This harmonizes with the historical books, which show David bringing the ark to Jerusalem, his concern to build a temple there, its actual construction by Solomon, the division of the kingdom, and the apostasy of the northern tribes with their bull shrines at Dan and Bethel. There is a strong focus on Judah, Jerusalem, the temple, and the Davidic kingship in the books of Chronicles.

All this may not seem relevant to the concept of the godly community, but it is, for this community finds its unity not just in natural kinship but also in being the people of Yahweh, united in worship at his sanctuary in Jerusalem.

Jerusalem/Zion Becomes a Symbol for a Widening, Divinely Established Community

The book of Isaiah shows a development in the Jerusalem theme. In chapter 1 there is a threefold presentation of Jerusalem, ideal in the past and future and corrupt in the present (1:21-26). The chapter's introductory position suggests there may be further exposition of this theme and so there is. In chapter 4 Jerusalem is cleansed and purified. In chapters 24–27 several passages look forward to better things, and in chapters 40–66 such passages are plentiful. Zion is to become glorious (Isa 60). Gradually we gain the impression that Jerusalem, although still having a geographical dimension, has become a symbol for God's people as a community.

What about the Gentile nations? The prophecies against Moab show a spirit of grief, revealing concern for people beyond Israel (Isa 15:5; 16:11), while chapter 19, about Egypt, moves from judgment to salvation, and ends with the extraordinary declaration that Israel, Egypt, and Assyria would together constitute God's people, sharing titles that symbolize this. Isaiah 56:6-8 promises that foreigners committed to Yahweh and keeping his covenant will have the joy of worship in God's house of prayer, which should be for all nations.

The community sense of Judah's people survived the flames of Nebuchadnezzar's destruction of their capital. The Babylonian exiles needed to know they were still God's people even away from the community's normal geographical center, and Jeremiah's vision of the good and bad figs (Jer 24:1-10) assured them of this. This was confirmed in Ezekiel's vision of the

Shekinah moving from the Jerusalem temple toward Babylon (Ezek 10:4, 18-19; 11:23-24). He was still with them; they were still his people. They had no temple, but God himself would be a sanctuary to them (11:16). The essence of a worshiping community was, as it had always been, God's presence in the midst of his people.

The book of Ezekiel climaxes with his vision of an enormous temple, surely never meant literally but rather symbolizing God's great purpose for a worshiping people. It is true that Haggai and Zechariah were commissioned to encourage the building of a second temple not unlike the first in size, but immediately after the exile God's people were reduced rather than enlarged. It was necessary, as Malachi declared, to establish a purified and distinct Israel (Mal 3:1-5; 4:1-6). This must happen before enlargement would be safe, because it must be the expansion of a godly people. That expansion was, however, certain in God's purposes. Zechariah was told the Jerusalem of the future would be a city without walls because of its numerous inhabitants (Zech 2:1-13). In Zech 8:3 the Lord says, "I will return to Zion and dwell in Jerusalem," and later in the same chapter Zechariah sees great crowds coming to Jerusalem because they had heard God was there in the midst of his people (8:20-23).

The NT develops the concept still further. In Matt 16:18 Jesus speaks of building his church (cf. the use of the word again in Matt 18:17). This Gospel, with its Jewish emphasis, nevertheless sounds a universalistic note, for here Jesus speaks of his gospel going out into all the world (24:14; 26:13), and it closes with his command to go and disciple all nations (28:19), confirmed in Mark 16 and Luke 24.

In the Fourth Gospel it is the Jews (by implication) who are "his own" (John 1:11), but at the close of his ministry and just before his death "his own" have been reduced to his disciples (13:1). John 6 already shows a reduction of the disciples themselves, leaving the Twelve as the central core. Yet this Gospel displays a great concern for expansion, for its introduction would appeal to both Jew and Greek, the Logos concept there evoking for the Jewish reader the word that created the world and the powerful prophetic word, but many Gentile readers too were familiar with it from its use by philosophers. Indeed, wide concerns are unmistakable at many points in this Gospel.

Luke's two books are both highly relevant, the Gospel showing Jesus moving toward Jerusalem, where, instead of welcoming him as Messiah, the religious leaders rejected him, and Jerusalem became a place of grim destiny, both for Jesus in his crucifixion and for Israel in its rejection of him. Acts begins where the Gospel ends, and the good news goes out from Jerusalem into the whole world.

The NT has five versions of Christ's missionary commission, four in the Gospels (Matt 28:16-20; Mark 16:15-20 [in the longer ending of Mark's Gospel]; Luke 24:45-49; John 20:21-23) and one in Acts (1:8). Paul's commission, recorded in Acts and evidenced in his own awareness, was wide, and Acts shows God taking the church out of its largely Jewish exclusivism into the outside world through the encounter between Peter and Cornelius, recorded in Acts 10 but alluded to also in Acts 11 and 15 because of its relevance to the church's worldwide mission. Paul evidently saw the success of the church's Gentile mission as the way the Jews and Gentiles together would praise the name of the Lord (Ps 18:4-9; Rom 15:9). Pentecost affected Jews and proselytes from many different places, and the gift of tongues suggested a wide purpose of God embracing people of many languages, but this special divine intervention in Acts 10 was needed to get them moving.

In Acts the word "church" was first used only in the singular, with a focus on Jerusalem (5:11). It was used in the singular of the expanded church in 9:31: "Then the church throughout Judea, Galilee, and Samaria enjoyed a time of peace." Later in Acts and in the Epistles and Revelation it is in the plural (e.g., in Acts 15:41; Rom 16:4, 16; Rev 22:16), although the concept of the one church dominates the Epistle to the Ephesians.

In a most significant passage in Ephesians, the ideas both of citizenship and of temple building occur, so that Christ's church is viewed both as a spiritual city and as a temple of God, where God himself lives through the Spirit (Eph 2:19-22). In line with this, Paul says that "the Jerusalem that is above is free, and she is our mother" (Gal 4:26).

In Revelation 4 and 5 there is a great vision of people of every tribe and language, people and nation, worshiping the Lord God Almighty and the Lamb (5:9-10), and the book closes with John's vision of a new Jerusalem descending out of heaven from God and God dwelling in the midst of his people.

To what extent then can this development of the Zion concept be seen in the Psalter? The introductory Psalm 2 anticipates a worldwide empire for the Davidic king, while Psalm 72, placed at the close of book 2, shows him ruling from sea to sea and from the River to the ends of the earth (72:8). Psalm 89, closing book 3, describes him as the most exalted of the kings of the earth (89:27). Psalm 87 is at once strongly particularist and Zion-focused, yet it also has important universalist teaching, for the psalmist says of people from foreign nations, "This one was born in Zion" (87:4; cf. v. 5). To find this in book 3, probably put together during the exile, is most striking, as it was the armies of Babylon that destroyed Jerusalem. Here then we see godly faith in a wide purpose of God triumphing over natural inclinations of hatred.

Book 4 focuses more on God than on the Davidic king, but it is equally universal in its vision. In Psalm 97, for instance, there is both the big vision of verse 1, "The LORD reigns, let the earth be glad; let the distant shores rejoice," and the Jerusalem particularism of verse 8: "Zion hears and rejoices and the villages of Judah are glad." Book 5 also often calls for all the nations to worship the Lord; moreover, there are clear affirmations that one day they will do so.

In the arrangement of the Psalter, this is anticipated in another Korahite psalm. In book 2, in a context emphasizing God's kingship over all the nations, the psalmist closes by saying, "The nobles of the nations assemble *as* the people of the God of Abraham, for the kings of the earth belong to God; he is greatly exalted" (47:9). No doubt Levites, such as the writers of these psalms, must often have pondered the significance of the Court of the Gentiles, the temple's outer court, and seen in it an earnest of a fuller purpose of God for the nations.

The True Core of This Community Consists of the Godly

There is an important narrowing here. This comes out, for example, in Psalm 1, where sinners are apparently cut off from the "assembly of the righteous," so excluded from the fellowship.

The identity of the enemies in laments of the individual has been much discussed, but there is no general consensus of opinion. It seems clear, however, that in many cases their enmity is not simply against the psalmist but against his God.

The concentration of psalms like 15 and 24 on moral qualifications for worship is striking. This does not necessarily mean the psalmists were not interested in the ceremonial regulations, but it does show the great importance for them of the moral conditions of true worship. The ideal was a godly group, loving God wholeheartedly and living in the light of his holy character, coming together to praise him at his temple.

The prophets too had this concern, especially the eighth-century prophets and Jeremiah. The emphasis on sacrifice was excessive in their day, probably because fear of invasion brought people with their offerings to the temple in great numbers. This comes out in passages that attack it, like Isa 1:10-17; 29:13; Jer 7:21-26; Hos 6:4-10; Amos 4:4-5; 5:21-27; and Mic 6:6-8. It is also to be found in Psalm 50.

Sometimes a psalmist calls himself poor and needy or he extols Yahweh's concern for such, and there is here an important link with the Beatitudes. O'Donovan points out that "Blessed are the poor in spirit" (Matt 5:3) does not mean "to dissociate the idea of poverty altogether from material want, but rather to situate the experience of want within a context of a moral disposition appropriate to it." He says that spiritual poverty is not a mere analogy to material poverty; rather, "it is material poverty that has generated a spiritual orientation: dependence upon God and openness to his Kingdom."[159]

The importance of a godliness that builds on the teaching of Jesus comes out at the close of the Sermon on the Mount (Matt 7:24-27), in which the importance of a sincere walk with God is stressed. The Beatitudes include a blessing that clearly has its roots in Ps 37:11, when Jesus says, "Blessed are the meek, for they will inherit the earth" (Matt 5:5). The Acts of the Apostles records the judgment on Ananias and Sapphira and the fear this caused both within and outside the church (Acts 5:1-11). It was a clear sign from God that reality and sincerity were required of those who profess faith in Christ.

The Epistles are full of moral exhortations, and Hebrews 3 and 4 are reminders that, just as in Israel, so in the church, faith and obedience, not merely association with God's people, are the marks of real godliness (cf. Rev 22:11-19).

A Profound Doctrine of Sin

The Psalter largely concerns relationships, both with God and between people, so it is not surprising it has much to say about sin in a social context.

This doctrine's depth here is due largely to the fact that the psalmists are often surrounded by enemies, experiencing their antagonism firsthand. This antagonism is often toward them as God's servants. But more than this, some psalms (notably 51) show profound awareness of personal sin, deeper than anywhere else in the OT. We have to go to Romans 5 to find anything comparable, but while this NT passage presents the theology in the context of an argument, Psalm 51 shows it in personal experience.

Sin Is Essentially against God

If the heading of Psalm 51 guides us to its actual occasion, David has deeply offended against Uriah, both by committing adultery with his wife and by arranging for his death, and he has offended against Bathsheba by involving her in his sin. He recognizes, however, his sin's essentially Godward nature, and it is this that brings him to repentance.

159. O'Donovan, *Desire of the Nations*, 98.

The psalmists also recognize that the offenses their enemies commit against them are really against their God. This is the theological basis of their imprecations. Those who pray thus are asking for justice for themselves because the offenses are fundamentally against God. They also plead for God to vindicate his holy name when it is being put to scorn by his and their enemies, so it is clear that they have a godly concern for his glory. This theme is taken up also in Ezekiel (Ezek 36:20-23).

Helmer Ringgren is correct: "There are many gradations between the thoughtless security in days of prosperity and the open rebellion of the 'wicked,' but in both cases man tries to dethrone God — he does not let God be God, so to speak — and this is the very essence of sin."[160]

Sin Is Rebellion

Sin is characterized as rebellion in Psalm 78's historical review, where the forefathers are described as "a stubborn and rebellious generation, whose hearts were not loyal to God, whose spirits were not faithful to him" (78:8). In 106:43 the writer says, "Many times he delivered them, but they were bent on rebellion." This shows their rebellion was in the face of many acts of his merciful deliverance, and this note is heard also in Psalm 107, where both the freeing of the prisoners and the healing of the sick are completely undeserved, as they are suffering for rebelliousness (107:10-22).

Rebellion against God frequently expressed itself against his appointed representatives. The historical psalms, which often focus on the Mosaic period, give catalogues of the sins of the people. The readers would recall that Moses was often the communicator of God's word to them, and that the rebellion of Dathan and Abiram is traced to envy of Moses and Aaron (78:16-18). The emphasis is, however, on their sin against God himself.

There are many illustrations of rebellion in the Pentateuch, including rebellion against Moses, God's appointed representative. In Acts 7 Stephen highlights the initial rejection of Moses by Israel, anticipated by Joseph's rejection by his brothers, and sees this as anticipating the way many of his compatriots were in danger of rejecting the Christ of God. Psalm 95 refers to the wilderness rebellions, and Hebrews 3 and 4 show that the writer of the epistle was aware that some of his readers might unwittingly exhibit the same spirit.

In the Davidic psalms, sin against God is often seen in enmity toward the king. This is clear in the programmatic Psalm 2, where the nations revolt

160. Ringgren, *Faith of Psalmists,* 35.

against Yahweh and his anointed, whom he established. The reader, noting Psalm 3's superscription, would undoubtedly view the antagonism of the psalmist's foes there as punishment for his sins in connection with Bathsheba and Uriah (cf. 2 Sam 12:10-12), but would hardly see this as excusing Absalom's rebellious spirit and actions. There is a difference of opinion as to how many psalms are Davidic in authorship,[161] but even if the Davidic authorship is comprehensively rejected, it is evident that the ultimate redactor saw David in many and intended that the readers should.

So in the psalms, especially Psalm 2, the fact that in the NT the anti-God movement takes an anti-Christ form finds anticipation. In 41:9 the psalmist says his enemy lifted his heel against him and asks for vindication. This is applied in John 13:18 to Judas Iscariot and his betrayal of Jesus. The persecution of the church in Acts is illustrated from Psalm 2, because of its messianic bearing, and this is quoted in Acts 4:25-26. So the persecution of the church was seen as an extension of that meted out to Christ, and this is expressed in the words of the risen Christ to Saul of Tarsus, "Why do you persecute me?" (Acts 9:4).

It is sobering to find that NT epistles addressed to Christians cite psalms containing warnings against rebellious sin. In Hebrews 3 and 4 there is an exposition of Ps 95:7-11 in very solemn terms. The readers are warned not to follow the example of those who rebelled against God in the wilderness and in consequence were denied entry to the promised land.

In the temptation of Jesus, Satan tried to persuade him to be a rebel in listening to his voice rather than that of God. He quoted Ps 91:11-12 to Jesus, but did not go as far as verse 13, which promises victory over the serpent! It is clear that the psalm is addressed to the godly; moreover, in the context of the Psalter as a whole and so of Psalm 1, there is a strong emphasis on the way of the righteous, who refuse the counsel of the ungodly.

Sin Is Lying and Deceit

Surprisingly often the psalms speak of sins of the tongue, such as lying, deceit, and flattery. The psalmist often finds himself unable to trust those who surround him. Their antagonism often takes the form of covert conspiracy, where nothing is what it seems.

Perhaps it is their realization that truth is so important that causes the psalmists to say so much about lying. Because truth is a quality of God's na-

---

161. See Excursus, pp. 34-39.

ture (25:5; 40:10-11; 43:3), his word is true (119:142, 160), he does not lie (89:35). Indeed, in establishing the Davidic covenant, the Lord swore an oath to him (89:49; 132:11). Often "love and faithfulness" occur together in the Psalms (e.g., in 25:10; 57:3; 61:7; 89:14; 98:3), where "mercy" translates *ḥesed.* This links truth and faithfulness, the latter representing not simply truth of statement but commitment to promises made.

The verb כָּזַב, *kāzab,* is the one the NIV most often renders "to lie." Lying to God is very serious (78:36), even if completely useless. The wicked not only lie (58:3; 116:11) but delight in doing so (52:3; 62:4). The psalmist asks God to silence their lying lips (31:18; cf. 120:2-4), and expresses his confidence that God will do this (31:18). מִרְמָה, *mirmâ,* "to deceive," is also fairly frequent (5:6; 10:7; 35:20) and focuses on the purpose of the lie.

In Psalm 51 David says God desires truth in the inner parts, perhaps alluding to the fact that, unlike Saul (1 Sam 15:13), he immediately confessed his sin when confronted with it by the prophet Nathan (2 Sam 12:13). There is a commitment to truth that goes deeper than simply an intention not to lie or to be deceitful on any particular occasion.

Many OT passages record lying. Life in Eden was marred by a satanic lie (Gen 3), and deceit infected even the line of promise, for it is the characteristic sin of Genesis, appearing in the lives of Abraham, Isaac, Jacob, and his sons. Serious too were the lies of false prophets who were particularly active in Jeremiah's day. What is particularly distinctive of the Psalter is that here a godly man's enemies frequently used untruth in their evil cause.

This too prepares us for the NT. The Epistle of James has something of an OT flavor, and the deeply unflattering description of the tongue in James 3 reminds us of psalm passages such as 32:9 (Jas 3:3), 12:3-4, 73:8-9 (Jas 3:5), and 140:3 (Jas 3:8). In 1 Pet 3:8-12 the Christian readers are exhorted to live in harmony with one another, and Ps 34:12-16, which highlights the sinfulness of deceit, is quoted.

In the Gospels lies and deceit are employed in opposition to Christ, notably by false witnesses at his trials. The fault here lay not only with the witnesses but with those who suborned them to this evil end. Ironically, it was in the context of a series of trials in which truth was a very minor consideration that "jesting Pilate" asked, "What is truth?" (John 18:38).

Jesus confronted Satan in the wilderness temptations, where, most significantly, the evil one tried to use God's truth in Ps 91:11-12 to promote the big lie (Matt 4:6-7). Jesus identified Satan as the arch-deceiver who was active in the events leading up to the cross (John 8:44).

Satan's deceitful activity, concentrated on Jesus, is seen in the NT to be a general feature of human life, for in 2 Corinthians Paul calls him "the god of this age" who has blinded the minds of unbelievers (2 Cor 4:4), and in 1 John he is the spirit of error opposed to the Spirit of truth (1 John 4:6). In the book of Revelation his is the strategy behind the work of the beast and the false prophet. Finally he is consigned with them to the lake of fire.

Sin Is Personal Antagonism

The enemies of the psalmists are often filled with and motivated by hatred and spite. The verb שָׂנֵא, *śānēʾ* ("to hate"), with its cognates and derivatives, occurs about thirty times in the Psalter. Sometimes the NIV renders words from this root as "enemy," so that, for instance, the root occurs twice in 25:19, "See how my enemies have increased and how fiercely they hate me!" It is most common in the Davidic psalms, and we recall that Saul's frequent attempts on his life showed deep-seated and sustained antipathy. This means that sin is essentially inward, rooted in the heart. In 41:9 the psalmist writes of an intimate friend who had shown treacherous enmity.

Word study has its value in biblical theology but also its limits, as James Barr has shown in *Semantics of Biblical Language*. The terminology of hatred appears infrequently in Jeremiah, but his enemies' hatred of him and his message is very clear. The awareness that a person was a prophet probably often prevented physical assault, but the hatred felt must have been considerable. At least in terminology, the witness of the Psalms to human hatred of God's witnesses is the fullest and most significant in the OT.

In passages like Matt 10:22 (and parallels), 24:9-10, and Luke 6:22, Jesus warned his disciples that they would be hated. We find early evidence that his own ministry was stirring up a hatred that united those who were normally mutually antagonistic in antipathy to him so that they began to plot his death (Mark 3:6). His worsting of the religious leaders appears in all the Gospels, and the story moves inexorably, through their antipathy, toward his death. Such parables as the Pharisee and the tax collector (Luke 18:9-14) must have deepened their antagonism. His awareness of their hatred is clear from the parable of the ten minas: "But his subjects hated him and sent a delegation after him to say, 'We don't want this man to be our king'" (Luke 19:14). The hatred of his hearers is not explicitly mentioned when he tells the parable of the tenants (Mark 12:1-12), but its presence in their hearts is quite unmistakable.

In John 15 the world's hatred becomes a major topic. Jesus speaks first of his own love for his disciples and exhorts them to love one another (15:9-17). He then speaks of the world's hatred of them, seeing this as rooted in hatred of him (15:18-25), which in turn is hatred of his Father. Then, most significantly, he concludes with a psalm quotation, "But this is to fulfill what is written in their Law: 'They hated me without reason'" (John 15:25), equally attributable to Ps 35:19 or 69:4, both Davidic psalms. Hatred of the "typical" king has now given place to detestation of his great antitype. The ultimate manifestation of love has produced hatred, its depth soon to be revealed in the passion and death of Jesus.

The sovereignty of God is shown in the passion story. In Ps 34:11-22, which displays many of the characteristics of wisdom literature, it is acknowledged that the righteous person may have many troubles but that God will allow the adversaries to go so far and no further. "He protects all his bones, not one of them will be broken" (v. 20). This is applied to Jesus in John 19:36.

In Ps 4:4 the words, "In your anger do not sin," may have been addressed either to the psalmist's enemies or to his friends. Whichever it is, he clearly considered the angry person to be in danger of committing sin, and in Eph 4:26 this is applied to Christian readers.

Sin Is Universal and Congenital

Sin pervades human society. In the classic Christian doctrine of original sin its universality is linked to its congenital nature. In the Psalter these two facts are not found together but they do appear in different psalms,[162] which together could provide some background to Paul's teaching in Romans 5.

The psalmist is writing from the limited perspective of his own situation when he says, "Help, LORD, for the godly are no more; the faithful have vanished from among men. Everyone lies to his neighbor; their flattering lips speak with deception" (12:1-2). In Psalm 14, however, he seems to be writing in a truly general way, for "there is no one who does good" (v. 1) is not only repeated but emphasized by the addition of the words, "not even one" (v. 3). In 143:2 he clearly includes himself when he says, "Do not bring your servant into judgment, for no one living is righteous before you."

There may be a reminder of David's personal sin in the superscription to Psalm 3, for Absalom's rebellion was its punishment, and this comes at a most significant point, for this is the first psalm linked to David in its superscription. We are strongly reminded of his personal sinfulness in the final group in book 1 (Pss 38–41).[163] If Psalms 3 and 41 are in effect an inclusio, it seems we are

---

162. And so with the Psalter's overall testimony.

163. According to Wilson, the last four psalms in book 1 "reflect the uncertainty, confusion, and plotting that characterize the transition between kings" (*Psalms*, 1:90).

meant in reading the psalms between these two points to recall his personal failures. McCann is right: "Israel's story, David's story, and the psalmist's story testify to the same reality — sin pervades the human situation."[164]

Psalms 51 and 58 certainly appear to go further and to explore sin's congenital nature.[165] In 51 David's strong comment that he was sinful at his birth, indeed from his conception, is not an excuse, for he has already said that God is justified when he judges (51:3-6). His need is for a deep cleansing if he is then to have truth within (vv. 1-2 and 7), for nothing less than re-creation is required (v. 10).

Psalm 58 does not teach sin's universality, but it brings together many of the features of sin we have so far noted. In verses 3-5 the psalmist says, "Even from birth the wicked go astray; from the womb they are wayward and speak lies. Their venom is like the venom of a snake, like that of a cobra that stops its ears, that will not heed the tune of the charmer, however skillful the enchanter may be." Rebelliousness, lying, hatred, congenital sinfulness — they are all here.

All this ties in with the historical literature of the OT, where we see how pervasive sin was, even within the people of God. We have already noted the endemic nature of deceit in the godly line in Genesis from Abraham onward. The making of the golden calf, the constant complaints during the wilderness wanderings, the repeated regression during the days of the judges, all prepare us for the shocking disclosure of the profound religious and moral rottenness of those called to be God's people, which is the theme of Judges 17–21.

We find this theme particularly illustrated in the kingdom era in the conduct of the kings, which often deeply affected their people, for whom they must have served, to some degree, as role models. Saul was flagrantly disobedient; David committed adultery and murder; Solomon, who began well and himself recognized the universality of sin (1 Kgs 8:46), gave way to idolatry. Not only the northern kingdom but even Judah, which had some godly although imperfect kings, constantly fell into idolatry. The exile was a time of heart searching and purging, but things were far from perfect after the return. The books of the prophets could be opened almost at random to see evidence of their deep concern about the sinfulness of the society to which they belonged and which they undoubtedly loved. That so little of this kind of criticism is to be found in the literature of other nations, far from suggesting their

---

164. McCann, *Theological Introduction*, 103.

165. Although some writers view their language as poetic hyperbole simply stressing sin's pervasiveness; e.g., Weiser, *Psalms*, 405.

superiority, reflects instead the profound spiritual sensitivity and loving concern for their people that motivated Israel's prophets.

The story of the Passion brought together Jewish parties with very different outlooks, such as the Herodians, the Pharisees, and the Sadducees, and the individuals in the story tend to be representative characters: Annas and Caiaphas the priests, Herod the half-Jewish monarch, Pilate the Roman procurator, even Judas from the apostolic band. Peter sees this as fulfillment of Ps 2:1-2 and, after quoting it, he says, "Herod and Pontius Pilate met together with the Gentiles and the people of Israel in this city to conspire against your holy servant Jesus, whom you anointed" (Acts 4:23-28). In a kind of representative universalism in sin, Jews and Gentiles come together in the story of the cross.

In Romans 3, when Paul argues for the universality of sin, he gives a catena of references from the OT to show that Jews as well as Gentiles are there branded as sinners. Almost all of these references are from the Psalms. The verses quoted, in their order of citation, are as follows: 14:1-3; 53:1-3; 5:9; 140:3; 10:7; 36:1. He must have regarded the Psalter as a primary OT witness to the fact of universal sin. What is just as significant is that earlier in the chapter (Rom 3:4) he quotes Ps 51:4, which asserts God's right to judge, and he does so from a psalm in which David confesses his sin. If David, the man after God's own heart, was exposed as a sinner, what hope of salvation by the works of the Law did Paul's contemporaries have? He does not appear to have used the Psalter in Rom 5:12-21, the locus classicus on original sin, but this is hardly to be expected in a complex piece of reasoning based on comparison and contrast between Adam and Christ and, except for a very general statement in verse 14, with no specific reference to the OT.

Sin Merits and Receives Divine Judgment

This theme is so pervasive in the Psalter that it hardly requires illustration. It is there in Psalm 1, which concludes, "the way of the wicked shall perish" (v. 6). Psalm 2 speaks of God's wrath (v. 5) and ends with a solemn warning to submit to the Son or face destruction (v. 12), and this note is never far out of sight. As the book moves toward its close, we are reminded of 1:6 in the words of 145:20, "The LORD watches over all who love him, but all the wicked he will destroy" (cf. 146:9), while 149 sees God's people as the agents of his judgment on the nations.

Sometimes the psalmists pray for God's judgment to come, at times in very general terms, as in places where judgment and blessing are linked together, but at other times much more specifically and even personally, as in the psalms of imprecation. This element is particularly strong in some psalms, such as 109 and the closing verses of 137. We will consider later what lasting message these have for the church, but meantime we should see their consistency with the general teaching of the OT.

The psalmists are asking God to do what he said he would do, to judge those who are antagonistic to his purposes, for the psalmists' enemies are so often God's own enemies. We have noted, for instance, that even the terrible words of 137:9 are asking for the fulfillment of the divine threat in Isa 13:16.[166] It may seem less shocking in the Isaiah context than in the psalm, but its place in the psalm tunes in with Rev 19:1-3, where the great multitude in heaven cries "Hallelujah!" at Babylon's judgment. It is interesting to see that all three passages are about Babylon. In effect the psalmist was praying for a judgment to terminate an evil and oppressive empire, although the highly specific way he expresses it is difficult for us to take today.

McCann regards Psalm 109 as "the worst scenario." He points out that it is about the punishment fitting the crime and calls this psalm "theological catharsis." "The anger is expressed, but it is expressed to God and is thereby submitted to God."[167] He also points out that *hesed* (NIV "kindness" or "love") is the key word in the psalm, occurring as it does in vv. 12, 16, 21, and 26, and then says that the whole psalm "suggests that evil must be confronted, opposed, hated because God hates evil."[168] The apostles applied the words of 109:8 and also of 69:25 to Judas after his treachery and death (Acts 1:16, 20). They did not utter an imprecation themselves but rather recognized the appropriateness of the words of these psalms in reference to his death and replacement.

The language of the Psalms (102:27; 46:2) is used when God's judgment is pictured in Rev 6:14, 17.

Sin Can Be Forgiven

In a number of psalms the writer confesses his sins to God, clearly in the hope of forgiveness. There is a group of such psalms at the close of book 1 (38–41). In each of them the psalmist casts himself on the mercy of God in the obvious hope that God will forgive and accept him.

In other psalms the writer comes to a place of assurance. In 6:8-9, for instance, he says, "Away from me, all you who do evil, for the Lord has heard

166. See the comment on this psalm.
167. McCann, *Theological Introduction*, 113-14.
168. Ibid., 115.

my weeping. The LORD has heard my cry for mercy; the LORD accepts my prayer." In 51:17 he says, "The sacrifices of God are a broken spirit; a broken and contrite heart, O God, you will not despise." The psalmist (although some might suggest this is the redactor) follows his plea to God for forgiveness with an exhortation to the people as a whole, based on his deep convictions about God's purpose of redemption from sin: "O Israel, put your hope in the LORD, for with the LORD is unfailing love and with him is full redemption. He himself will redeem Israel from all their sins" (130:7-8).

Such forgiveness is blessed indeed, and David's assertion of the blessedness of a person who has known God's pardon is used by Paul as part of his evidence that the OT teaches that God credits righteousness apart from works to those who believe (Rom 4:6-8; cf. Ps 32:1-2).

A Realistic Doctrine of Suffering

Many psalms reveal the sufferings of their writers. Is it appropriate to seek for a doctrine of suffering in the Psalter? Mays believes it is, and is surely correct when he says, "The prayers for help are a theological interpretation of suffering. They place the troubles of life in a context of meaning. They provide the way to move affliction out of the realm of merely accidental, fortuitous meaninglessness into the comprehension of a view of self, world, and God."[169] The context of meaning is that group of basic convictions about God we have already identified.

In relation to the Psalms we are observers of suffering, just as we are when we watch television or read the newspapers, but because this is the Word of God, it draws Christians in. There is certainly material here for a doctrine of suffering, but we cannot study it dispassionately, for it is incarnated in the genuine sufferings of real people. They are fellow believers and we feel for them. Because it comes out of the real sufferings of real people, it expresses itself much more in entreaty than in theological statement, and this is its distinctive value.

It Is Assumed That Sin Merits Punishment and Therefore Suffering

This is both clear and important, and it is the presupposition common to two great problems facing the psalmists, the two sides of the same coin, the suffer-

---

169. Mays, *Lord Reigns*, 43.

ings of the righteous and the apparent impunity of the wicked. In Psalm 44, for instance, the psalmist complains to God concerning the defeat of the nation's armies, "All this happened to us, though we had not forgotten you or been false to your covenant. Our hearts had not turned back; our feet had not strayed from your path. But you crushed us and made us a haunt for jackals and covered us with deep darkness" (44:17-19). This is not, of course, an assertion of national sinlessness but presumably reflects a time when there were a godly king and a concern for covenant faithfulness to God.

In Psalm 73 the psalmist is deeply troubled because of the prosperity of the wicked. He then says, "Surely in vain have I kept my heart pure; in vain have I washed my hands in innocence" (73:13). He finds a new perspective when he goes into the house of God and realizes that the answer is to be found in the contrasting destinies of the righteous and the wicked (vv. 13-26). So we note that the assumption of moral justice that caused the problem was not abandoned in the solution. Sin merits punishment and will receive it in due time.

This doctrine is found widely in the OT, with the book of Deuteronomy as its classic expression, and with countless illustrations, especially in the prophetic books. Job's comforters were not wrong to believe in retributive justice, but only and tragically wrong in misapplying this doctrine. The doctrine is found in the wisdom literature as a whole, and Eccl 7:16, the apparent exception ("Do not be overrighteous"), looks like irony.[170]

The NT too assumes it, and Rom 5:12-21 finds sin to be the cause of death and of the universality of death. In line with this we find that the final state of a redeemed society involves the abolition of suffering and of death (Rev 21:4, 27).

Much Suffering Is Due to the Sins of Others

The psalmists suffer much at the hands of others, and we find this in the Davidic and Levitical psalms, but also in the orphan psalms.

In some psalms the motives or intentions of those who cause suffering are clear. In Psalm 10 the wicked persecutor of the weak is shown to be arrogant, boastful, and proud (vv. 2-6). In Psalm 22 enemies inflict social as well as physical sufferings. The poor and needy are especially vulnerable (35:10; 37:14). The exact nature of the persecution is often unclear, and it may sometimes have involved corrupt legal processes.

---

170. See Fisch, "Qohelet: A Hebrew Ironist," in *Poetry with a Purpose,* 158-78.

Psalm 69 reveals deep suffering, caused by the antipathy of enemies. Verses 4 and 5 represent a paradox, for the psalmist says, "those who hate me without reason outnumber the hairs of my head; many are my enemies without cause, those who seek to destroy me. I am forced to restore what I did not steal. You know my folly, O God; my guilt is not hidden from you." He knows he is a sinner, yet also that his enemies have no moral cause for their hatred. The same lack of an adequate cause can be seen in Psalm 35, where (in v. 19) he calls them "those . . . who are my enemies without cause," making no confession of personal sin.

This is why a psalm like 69 can be applied to Christ in the NT, because the psalmist here is innocent of what he has been accused of. In John 15:25 Jesus applies to himself either Ps 35:19 or 69:4, both of which show a believer facing enemies who hate him without adequate reason.

We do not know how their hearers treated many of the prophets, but certainly Jeremiah suffered much for his faithfulness to Yahweh, and 1 Kgs 18:4-14 mentions prophets that Obadiah hid from Jezebel's malignity. There were attempts to kill Daniel and his three Jewish companions, and in Esther the Jews were protected from the designs of their enemies. Nehemiah was pressured by Samaritan enemies while leading the project to rebuild Jerusalem's walls.

As each Gospel moves toward its climax, it increasingly concentrates on Christ's sufferings at the hands of his enemies. In Mark 8:31, 9:31, and 10:32-34 (with parallels in Matthew and Luke), Jesus warns his disciples of his destiny of rejection, and the same note is sounded in the Gospel of John (e.g., 12:23-24, 32-33).

Stephen's sermon in Acts 7 highlights the rejection of Joseph and Moses, implying that this anticipated the sufferings of Christ. He could also have employed the Psalms. In Acts the cross is seen as both a heinous act of human sin and a divine act implementing God's purpose (Acts 2:23-24). Christ (e.g., in John 16:2) predicted persecution for his followers, who, although not sinless, were given a new status with God through Christ. Luke records the martyrdoms of Stephen (Acts 6–7) and of James (12:2). It is evident from reading the Epistle to the Hebrews that its readers had endured some suffering for their faith (Heb 10:32-34).

The rhetorical questions in Rom 8:31-39 may well remind us not only of the amazing catalogue of Paul's sufferings in 2 Corinthians 11, but also of the afflictions endured by David and others for the sake of God's kingdom. They too faced antagonism (v. 31), false charges (v. 33), condemnation (v. 34), and attempts to separate them from the love of God (vv. 35-39). Paul's quotation from Ps 44:22, "For your sake we face death all day long; we are considered as sheep to be slaughtered" (v. 36), from a psalm protesting faithfulness to Yahweh, sums up much in the Psalter. This makes all the more impressive Paul's ringing assertions that God in Christ is for us and that nothing can separate us from his love. It is striking too that his comment, "For I could wish that I myself were cursed and cut off from Christ for the sake of my brothers" (Rom 9:3), a very moving and challenging echo of Christ's great cry of dereliction (Mark 15:34; Ps 22:1), follows almost immediately after this passage.

In the book of Revelation several of the churches to whom the exalted Christ writes are warned of coming persecution, while John is shown a great multitude who had come out of "the great tribulation" (7:13-14). The two witnesses in chapter 11 die because of their ministry for God (11:7), and the souls under the altar cry out to God to avenge them on those who have persecuted them (6:9-11), very much as in the Psalms (e.g., Ps 79:10).

So then, both in the Psalms and elsewhere in both Testaments, it is clear that the godly often had to undergo suffering at the hands of their enemies.

Much Suffering Is Due to the Personal Sins of the Sufferer

Without doubt the psalmists recognize that many of the trials, both of individuals and of the people as a whole, were caused by their own sin. The Psalter contains some psalms that have long been classified as "penitential," notably 6, 32, 38, 51, 102, 130, 143, all of which are psalms of the individual. We should not forget communal confessions of sin, such as 79, 80, and 85. There are also prophetic psalms like 81 and 95, which accuse the people of sin, and also the major historical psalms, some of which give a long catalogue of the offenses of the people against their God (78, 106). The great Mosaic Psalm 90 has a strong awareness of the wrath of God. In view of the fact that God's actions toward his people are determined by the moral nature of his character, references to his wrath certainly imply their consciousness of a moral cause of their sufferings (e.g., in 88:7).

It is somewhat surprising that the penitential element is not more prominent, but we must remember how varied are the themes of the psalms. The heading of Psalm 3 says it is a psalm of David, "when he fled from his son Absalom." Readers of the historical books would be well aware that the uprising of his son against him was due to David's sin but also that he had expressed genuine penitence and had been forgiven (2 Sam 12:7-13). It is perhaps significant too that the first penitential psalm (Ps 6) comes so soon after this, perhaps as a reminder, for there we read, "The LORD has heard my cry for mercy" (v. 9). These laments associated with David now focus on appeals to

God's covenant love, for, having accepted forgiveness, the sinner is able to bring petitions to the Lord with confidence.

Threats of historical judgment are frequent in the prophetic books, and the historical books furnish many examples. In each case where the cause is identified, it is the sins of those on whom the judgment falls. The NT is in harmony with this; for instance, the Acts of the Apostles records events showing the coming of judgment on particular individuals because of their conduct (Acts 5:1-11; 12:19-23).

Some Psalms of Suffering Give No Indication of Personal Sin in the Sufferer

Often a psalmist will assert his righteousness, as, for instance, in Psalm 26, where he claims he has no association with evildoers and washes his hands in innocence. If the arranging of the Psalter was purposeful, it is worth noting that in the previous psalm David asks God to forget his youthful sins and forgive his great iniquity (25:7, 11). His righteousness is not therefore sinlessness but rather, as in 26:1, consistent faithfulness to Yahweh, the one true God. Despite this commitment, he has had to face the schemes of bloodthirsty men (26:9-10). In 143:2 he says, "Do not bring your servant into judgment, for no one living is righteous before you." Not sinless, he is nevertheless God's servant and can look to God when pursued by his enemy (143:3-4). Jeremiah too never claims sinlessness, but he is aware of a call from God, and he cannot understand why it is that he is experiencing such suffering in his service. When there is no confession of wrongdoing, this does not necessarily mean the writers were unconscious of personal sin, but simply that in such psalms the focus is on the suffering caused and on the sinfulness of the enemies who caused it.

One such psalm is outstanding for the use made of it in the NT. Psalm 22 is a psalm of profound suffering, and it opens with a perplexed cry to God to come to the sufferer's aid, as God appears to have forsaken him. Here, in the early verses, it would have been appropriate to confess sin and ask for forgiveness and deliverance from enemies, but there is no such confession.

Because of this there can be no difficulty in applying the psalm to Jesus. Is it predictive or typological? Both views have been held, with the typological (Calvin's view) much the more common in modern writers. Derek Kidner says, however, "No incident recorded of David can begin to account for this."[171] It is applied to the sufferings of Jesus a number of times in the Gos-

---

171. Kidner, *Psalms 1–72*, 105.

pels, especially by Jesus in Matthew 27:46 (Mark 15:34); also in the dividing of his garments among his enemies in John 19:24 (Ps 22:18). The quotation in Heb 2:12 is from the latter part where the sufferer's vindication appears.

Wilson points out a number of phraseology links between Psalm 22 and three other psalms of suffering, 69, 70, and 71, especially the last two.[172] Psalms 69 and 70 are Davidic, and 71 is without ascription. It is possible that 71 was viewed as a continuation of 70.[173] Psalm 69 does contain a confession of guilt, but 70 and 71 do not, and 71:20 reads, "Though you have made me see troubles, many and bitter, you will restore my life again; from the depths of the earth you will again bring me up." This may be an anticipation of resurrection, although most scholars think it more likely that "depths of the earth" is metaphorical for deep trouble.

Of course, none of the prophets was without sin, but in Isaiah 40–55 a figure appears whose identity has been much discussed, the Servant of Yahweh (Isa 42, 49, 50, 52–53). The fourth Servant Song says of him, "he had done no violence, nor was any deceit in his mouth." Strictly speaking, this does not assert absolute sinlessness, but the sacrificial language used here reminds us that physical perfection was required in offerings brought for sacrifice, so that we would expect perfection of some kind in this sufferer. The use of the word "oppressed" (53:7) shows that his sufferings were wickedly inflicted. The NT applies at least the first and fourth songs to Jesus (e.g., in Matt 8:17 and 12:17-21).

Pilate confessed that Jesus was crimeless in terms of Roman law (Luke 23:4), but the NT writers go further, affirming his sinlessness (2 Cor 5:21; Heb 4:15; 7:26; 1 John 3:5), his righteousness (1 Pet 3:18), his life of goodness (Acts 10:38). Jesus said of his Father, "I do always what pleases him" (John 8:29; cf. 5:30; 6:38), and "my food is to do the will of him who sent me and to finish his work" (4:34); in relation to Satan he said, "the prince of this world is coming. He has no hold on me" (14:30); and to his enemies he said, "Can any of you prove me guilty of sin?" (8:46).

His sufferings are given vicarious meaning in the NT, as one can see in such passages as Mark 10:45; Rom 6:10-11; 2 Cor 5:14, 21; Gal 3:13; and 1 Tim 2:5-6. There have been attempts to interpret these otherwise than by substitutionary categories, but this is very difficult, as Vincent Taylor, who did not hold to substitutionary atonement, admits in a major book on the subject.[174] This important element is found clearly in Isaiah 53, but not explicitly

---

172. Wilson, *Psalms*, 1:412.
173. See comment on Ps 71.
174. Taylor, *Atonement*, 289.

in Psalm 22. There the focus is on the sufferings themselves, rather than their meaning, and they are seen to be three-dimensional, including physical pain, social ostracism, and, in the opening verse, a sense of alienation from God.

A Responsive Doctrine of Prayer and Worship

The Whole Godly Life Is a Responsive Exercise

This point is not only characteristic of the Psalter but fundamental to its whole approach. In no sense is its religion self-generated. The psalmists relate all the time to God and what he has done and said. Psalm 50 is concerned with a paganized approach on the part of many of the people in the biting words of verse 12: "If I were hungry I would not tell you." The Babylonian religious epics show the gods needing to be fed by their human devotees. What an insult to the God who creates and owns the whole world! This chimes in, of course, with the teaching of the prophets.

What makes the Psalter distinctive is that most of the psalms are expressions of prayer and praise (the prophetic and historical psalms are exceptions) and so are themselves responsive documents, and yet they became recognized as part of the divine revelation itself. They could then function in their turn as revelation that would elicit further response "from obedience to praise."[175]

This relates to the probable purpose in the minds of the Psalter's compilers. Commenting on the role of Psalms 1, 19, and 119 in the book as canonically arranged, Brevard Childs says, "Because Israel continues to hear God's word through the voice of the psalmist's response, these prayers now function as the divine word itself. . . . The study of the Psalter serves as a guidebook along the path of blessing."[176]

This means then that for the Psalter the essence of true religion is not to be found in mystical experience but in response to divine revelation. This is in tune with what we find elsewhere in the OT. God speaks and his people need to respond. God is often shown speaking to one or other of the patriarchs, and what develops is a conversation, while in Exodus–Deuteronomy God's awesome revelation at Sinai is the dominant feature. God's word to his people through the prophets clearly called for believing, penitent, and obe-

---

175. Taken from the title of an essay by Brueggemann, "Bounded by Obedience and Praise."

176. Childs, *Introduction to OT,* 513.

dient response from them. If wisdom may seem to some readers of the book of Proverbs as if it is a philosophical concept, they have misread the book, for this wisdom is grounded in the fear of the Lord (Prov 1:1-7), not in philosophical speculation, and the fear of the Lord is induced by exposure to divine revelation.

The NT is the ultimate expression of this principle. The NT writers are emphatic that the fullness of the divine revelation is to be found in Christ, the incarnate Word of God (John 1:1-18), the final Speech of God (Heb 1:1-4), and, as he indicated himself, God's final special messenger (Mark 12:6). Not surprisingly, then, all NT teaching about godliness is related to this great revelation of God in Christ.

Faith is not of saving value in itself but only as it engages with the revelation in Christ. This revelation is grounded in facts. Paul makes this clear in 1 Corinthians 15 when he underscores the great importance of the resurrection of Christ: "If Christ has not been raised our preaching is useless and so is your faith," and, a little later, "If Christ has not been raised, your faith is futile; you are still in your sins" (15:14, 17). First comes the resurrection itself, then the preaching of it, and finally the response of faith.

Paul insisted on the importance of maintaining the purity of the revelation in Christ. Having said, "I am afraid that just as Eve was deceived by the serpent's cunning, your minds may somehow be led astray from your sincere and pure devotion to Christ," he then declares, "For if someone comes to you and preaches a Jesus other than the Jesus we preached, or if you receive a different spirit from the one you received, or a different gospel from the one you accepted, you put up with it easily enough" (2 Cor 11:3-4), certainly implying criticism of them. The authenticity of the response requires authenticity in the revelation.

Authentic Worship and Prayer Are Always Responsive

This point follows from what we have already said. Godliness is trust and obedience, and these find expression in the prayers and praises of which the book of Psalms is full. Psalm 50 shows the need for worship to submit to the corrective of revelation. The material of the revelation becomes the content of the worship, so that the response is not simply theological reflection but heartfelt commitment. Because Yahweh is who he has shown himself to be, the psalmists come in worship to give and in prayer to ask.

In presenting worship and prayer as responsive activities, the psalms are consistent with the rest of the Bible. There is much about worship in the Pentateuch's legislative material, and it is clear there, from Exodus 20 onward, that Yahweh alone is to be worshiped. Moreover, the regulations for the tabernacle, the priesthood, and the sacrifices show that he was concerned that the people should worship according to his instructions.

In John 4 Jesus clearly recognized the importance of God's revelation to the Jews as the basis of their worship, yet it is important to note that he also told the Samaritan woman that the essence of true worship is spiritual as well as being based on truth (4:19-24). The nearest we get to an outline of a Christian service in the NT is in 1 Corinthians 14. Although this is a picture of human activity in worship, it seems most likely that all the elements, the hymns, the words of instruction, the messages in tongues interpreted for the church, were believed to be divinely originated, so that the worshipers were coming to God on the basis of what he had himself given them. In Col 2:23, when warning the Colossians against the beliefs and practices of the heretics, Paul refers to "self-imposed worship," the very opposite of worship generated by the divine Word.

The Epistle to the Hebrews deals with the worship system of the OT and sees it all fulfilled in Christ. In him priest, offering, and even place of worship all find their expression. John 1:14 views him as the place where God tabernacles with his people,[177] and John 2 records his comment in which he identifies his body as the temple of God (2:18-22). All that the OT worship system stood for is now focused for us in this one person: Jesus, the Son of God.

The Proper Response Is One of Trust and Praise in a Dependent Spirit

Trust and praise appear very frequently in the Psalms. The psalmists assert their trust in the Lord in passages like 20:7; 25:12; 31:6; 52:8; 55:23; 56:3; 61:4; 119:42; 143:8; and 144:2. Psalm 62 calls for trust in him and in him alone. In 116:10 the psalmist's trust in God enabled him to tell God all his troubles. Paul uses this verse in 2 Cor 4:13 in reference to the Christian's assurance that is grounded in the resurrection of Christ. Clearly he saw that faith is what unites the godly in the OT and in the Christian church. Commenting on Psalm 143, Leslie Allen notices that it is a psalm "with almost Pauline emphasis on (covenant) grace and faith," that verse 2 is echoed in Gal 2:6 and Rom 3:10, and that "the saving righteousness to which Paul turned in Rom 3:21 (cf. Rom 1:17) is the actualization of that dynamic covenant attribute of righteousness that features in Ps 143:1b and is the answer to human unrighteous-

---

177. The implication of ἐσκήνωσεν, *eskēnōsen*, rendered "made his dwelling" in NIV.

ness."[178] Praise too occurs in declarations by the psalmists that they will praise the Lord, as in Pss 22:25; 34:1; 35:28; 51:15; 71:6-8; 108:1. There are also exhortations to praise especially in the Final Hallel psalms, where this note is most dominant.

Those who pray in the psalms are often needy people deeply aware of their need who cry to God to deliver them. Mays emphasizes the frequency of such prayers and especially their relationship to psalms of thanksgiving, which are responses to God's help.[179] Those who cry out to him in this way sometimes call themselves his servants (27:9; 31:16; 86:1-2, 16; 143:2, 12), implying perhaps that because he is their master they can look to him to care for them.

Exodus 15 is of great importance, recording as it does the Song of Moses, which celebrated the great exodus deliverance. Echoes of it can be found in a number of psalms, perhaps most notably in 77.[180] Although sung by Moses and the Israelites, its opening is in the first person singular indicative. When Miriam took up the song in Exod 15:21, however, the first verb of her song is in the imperative mood, setting the tone for psalms of corporate praise.

The OT records an important historical event testing the faith both of king and people in the face of enemy assault, the attack on Jerusalem by Sennacherib, recorded in 2 Kings 18–19 and also in Isaiah 36–37 and 2 Chronicles 32. Isaiah called the king to trust in God and the king responded, leading the people in dependence on Yahweh. There are in Isaiah other calls for faith, for instance when Jerusalem was threatened in the days of Ahaz (Isa 7–8), but this time the king refused the prophet's call for faith, and the land suffered in consequence. Isaiah 12 is a kind of psalm, in which the psalmist expresses both trust in and praise toward God for all his glorious acts. Such passages are not, of course, peculiar to Isaiah among the prophets, as we see in Jer 10:6-16 and Hosea 12.

When Jesus first came preaching the good news of the kingdom, he called for belief in the gospel. Just as in the Psalms we meet needy people, so we do in the Gospels, and Jesus came to their aid in healing, in exorcism, and in giving deliverance and new hope, often calling them to faith. In a helpful passage, Mays examines the role of the needy in the Psalms and then says, "The extension of the role of the lowly to all believers is the foundation of the Beatitudes."[181] Who are the poor in spirit, the mourners, the meek, and those who

---

178. Allen, *Psalms 101–150*, 357.
179. Mays, *Lord Reigns*, 25.
180. See the comments on that psalm.
181. Mays, *Lord Reigns*, 30-31.

hunger and thirst after righteousness? They could be documented extensively from the Psalms, and Jesus obviously reckons that it is such people who are the heirs to the kingdom he came to found. Here then is an important link between the devotional literature of the OT and Christian discipleship criteria. As Mays points out in the same passage, the prayer of the Pharisee in the parable was so unlike this when he thanked God that he was not like other men.

There is a major call for faith in the NT as a whole and especially in the Gospel of John (e.g., 3:12; 5:44-47; 9:35-36). Faith and praise come together in Acts 2:43-47, when the Spirit was given. The epistles to the Galatians and the Romans have justifying faith as a major theme, and we are not surprised therefore to find Romans 11 ending in praise and also to find a distinctly praiseful tone in the great closing section of Romans 8. The importance of faith is clear in Ephesians, and Eph 1:3-14, which sets the tone for the whole epistle, is not just a statement of doctrine but a call to give praise to God. It is now widely held that the great christological passages in Philippians 2 and Colossians 1 appear to be quotations of early Christian hymns.[182] Praise too is the ultimate response of the heavenly worship of believers as we see in Revelation 4–5 and 7, where language of a psalmic type is used.

Praise Should Be Coextensive with the Character and Deeds of God

The psalmists refer to many qualities and acts of God when they utter his praise. Psalm 145 is perhaps the supreme example of this, for here there is almost a full doctrine of God. They even praise God for his judgments, because these put right what is wrong.

We may be inclined to say that it is his greatness and holiness that draw out worship and the disclosure of his love and grace that promotes prayer, but it is doubtful if the psalmists would recognize this dichotomy. Why pray if you are not coming to one great enough to answer you, and why worship if the great one you revere as God lacks the gentler qualities that are recognized as essential even to a balanced human character? Indeed, to select among the attributes of God is not worthy of the God we worship and can even be spiritually harmful. It is not surprising, however, that the gentler attributes are praised most, especially God's abiding love.

In Exod 15:21 "the model for the imperative hymn"[183] gives a reason for praising Yahweh, which is introduced by כִּי, *kî* ("for" or "because"). This

---

182. See Wilkins and Paige, eds., *Worship, Theology and Ministry.*
183. Bullock, *Encountering Psalms,* 125.

word becomes a characteristic of psalms of praise generally, for they normally give reasons for praise.

As in the book of Psalms, other passages in the OT give praise to God for particular acts of grace he has performed on behalf of his people. These include passages like the Song of Deborah (Judg 5) and Hezekiah's prayer of thanksgiving (Isa 38). There are also, however, more general songs of praise. These do not lack reasons for praise, but they are often given in general terms. For instance, the people give praise to God for his forgiveness, but not for this alone but also for the glorious things he has done, presumably largely in terms of his acts of deliverance for the nation.

Yahweh is praised as creator as well as redeemer. The placing of Psalms 103 and 104 side by side may well be significant in this regard. In other OT passages God's creative activity, even if not explicitly the subject of worship, evokes awe and wonder that is akin to worship. We encounter this, for instance, in Job 26, where, after referring to various features of God's activity in nature, Job says, "And these are but the outer fringes of his works; how faint the whisper we hear of him! Who then can understand the thunder of his power?"

NT praise centers on God's great saving intervention in Christ, as in the Benedictus (Luke 1:67-79) and Nunc Dimittis (2:29-32), although it also sometimes sets this in a wider context, as in the Magnificat (1:46-55). The passages often identified as hymns in the Pauline Epistles are strongly theological and christological, and in Colossians 1 Christ is referred to as creator as well as redeemer.

The great theological argument of Romans comes to its climax at the close of chapter 11. In chapter 1 Paul has shown how the God of creation is despised and dishonored through human sin (1:18-25). Now, having expounded the gospel of Christ in all its saving wonder and glory, he expresses his praise in as psalm-like an ascription of praise as anything to be found in his letters (11:33-36). He moves toward his conclusion with the words, "For from him and through him and to him are all things," which could refer equally to him as creator or as redeemer, perhaps with the intention of including both. In the hymnic passages in Revelation it is God's act of creation that is the focus of Revelation 4 while it is his redemptive acts in Christ that are celebrated in Revelation 5, where he is seen to be both Lion and Lamb.

Praise Should Be Wholehearted, Not Superficial

The response of the psalmists to God's revelation was not simply in terms of intellectual acceptance of what he had revealed. Often we encounter very deep emotion, for instance in psalms as diverse as 18, 84, and 98. The religion of the psalms is a religion of the heart. Moreover, there is to be no holding back, but rather a total self-giving. This comes out in the opening of Psalm 103, for instance, where the psalmist says, "Praise the LORD, O my soul; all my inmost being, praise his holy name."

This theme occurs in important passages in the prophetic books, such as Isa 1:10-17; Jer 7:21-26; Hos 6:6; Amos 5:21-24; and Mic 6:6-8. This emphasis is expressed so emphatically and with such eloquence that many scholars of an earlier generation mistakenly concluded that these prophets were totally opposed to the major outward and official forms of religion, especially the offering of sacrifice. Jeremiah declared the deceitfulness and wickedness of the human heart (Jer 17:9), but he also predicted that, in the new covenant, God would place his law in the hearts of his people (31:31-34). Such hearts would overflow with the praise of God.

There are cries from the heart of God in which he shows a divine yearning for his people to respond from the heart. For instance, when referring to their promise of obedience, he said, "Oh, that their hearts would be inclined to fear me and keep all my commands always, so that it might go well with them and their children forever" (Deut 5:29). One such cry from the heart occurs in the Psalter itself, where God says, "If my people would but listen to me, if Israel would follow my ways, how quickly would I subdue their enemies and turn my hand against their foes" (81:13-14).

It is hardly necessary to say that the NT endorses this. Christ inveighed against the hypocrisy and outwardness of Pharisaic religion (e.g., in Matt 23), and the Beatitudes place much emphasis on the heart, for poverty of spirit, meekness, and hungering and thirsting after righteousness are all concerns of the inner person. In the Apocalypse praise is unconfined.

Praise Should Be Both Personal and Corporate

There are psalms both of personal thanksgiving and of corporate praise. There are also psalms such as 42–43, 63, and 84 where the writer is clearly longing to bring praise to God in the company of others. The corporate dimension of praise was obviously important for those who engaged in worship.

The same balance is found elsewhere in the OT. The book of Genesis shows God dealing personally with each of the patriarchs, who built altars to enable them to worship him with sacrificial offerings. Yet these are all linked genealogically, and it seems highly probable that their worship was on behalf of their families as well as an expression of their personal devotion, as in Gen

8:18-20. In Exodus God calls the Israelites as a whole to go out into the wilderness to offer sacrifice to him (Exod 4:23; 5:1), which they did through Moses (24:4-8), while the sacrificial regulations in Leviticus 7 clearly have individual worship in view.

Praise Is "the Chief End" of Human Beings

Praising the Lord is what all who have breath should be occupied in doing, as the final verse of the Psalter exhorts. It is notable that in 145 and the psalms that follow it and that constitute the Final Hallel, praising God is the dominant activity of his people, so much so as almost to exclude all others.

Referring to Westermann, Bullock says: "The lament of the individual and the lament of the people incorporate words of trust and a vow to praise the Lord, both belonging in an integral way to the category of praise. Thus, even lament has an inner movement in the direction of praise."[184] Mays writes along similar lines that the facts that the Psalter's prayers are placed alongside psalms of praise in the book called *Tehillim* ("Praises"), that they are directed to the Lord, and that they so often include thanksgiving for salvation mean that they too are to be thought of as praise.[185]

Eaton writes of the psalms of God's kingdom, such as 93: "Other texts may exhort to faith, hope and patience, promising that the world's sufferings will at last be changed. But in our psalms are open gates to a celebration already begun. . . . Perhaps what these psalms offer could be called a life of realized eschatology, or of eschatology beginning to be realized — a life in this world of suffering, but suffused with resurrection light."[186]

So then the Psalter has much in common with the book of Revelation, for that is a book of praise and shows praise as the major occupation of the redeemed before the throne of God. The Psalter therefore functions in the OT as a preparation not only for the fuller revelation of God in Christ, but for the eternal praise that is the ultimate response to that ultimate revelation.

An Unshakable Doctrine of the Messiah

The adjective used in this heading may surprise the reader, but I employ it advisedly. The messianic hope was, if not built upon, nevertheless profoundly

---

184. Bullock, *Encountering Psalms*, 124.
185. Mays, *Lord Reigns*, 41-42.
186. Eaton, *Psalms of the Way*, 126.

influenced by, the great promise of God recorded in 2 Samuel 7. That this hope, although appearing at times to have been eclipsed, not only survived the failures and even apostasies of the Davidic monarchs but was stimulated to greater growth is one of the most encouraging aspects of the OT. It bears eloquent testimony not only to the faithfulness but also to the grace and patience of God.

There is an important programmatic aspect to the Bible. It is a profoundly historical and at the same time a profoundly eschatological book. This is a story that moves, that goes somewhere, that has a goal. The story reaches its goal in Christ. Stephen sought to make his hearers aware of this in Acts 7 but found them unwilling to hear it.[187] The solidity of the Jerusalem temple was not the ultimate in God's design, which was his sovereign purpose in Christ.

One significant side to this is to be found in the fact that in Scripture the future almost invariably bears the marks of the past. The new creation, for instance, is not a denial of the old but rather its fulfillment, its consummation. So in the OT the messianic future bears the marks of the Davidic past. Nowhere can this be seen more clearly than in the book of Psalms.

The Use of the Psalter in the NT

No book of the OT is more frequently quoted or alluded to in the NT than the Psalms. It is employed in several different ways. In Rom 10:17-18 the use of Psalm 19 shows that it was the one true God who revealed himself in the heavens and in Christ. Sometimes it is quoted for ethical purposes, as when 112:9 is quoted in 2 Cor 9:9 and Ps 34:12-16 in 1 Pet 3:10-12, and such use shows that the writers of the NT saw important continuity between the ethical teaching of the OT, as represented in the Psalter, and the ethics of the gospel. There can be no doubt, however, that most of the quotations are christological.

The risen Jesus referred to all that was written in the Psalms concerning him (Luke 24:44), and the NT writers explored the Psalter's witness to him. Psalm quotations and allusions occur in the sermons in Acts and in many of the NT epistles. They may also be found in Revelation without the use of quotation formulae, as is characteristic of that book's general use of the OT.

---

187. Note incidentally that 2 Sam 7 gives greater importance to David's house and so to the dynasty to which the Messiah belonged and which was underwritten by God, than to God's own house, for which God showed no concern. His purpose found its goal in a person, not an edifice.

The christological use of the Psalter is particularly important in the Epistle to the Hebrews. There are several features to this. There are fourteen quotations from the Psalms, and, as Kistemaker has shown in *Psalm Citations*, much of the theological weight of the epistle rests upon the Psalter, and certain psalms occupy key positions in the argument of the epistle. These are especially Psalms 8, 40, 95, and 110, although we may also add 2.

Two of these passages focus on the person of Christ, for Ps 2:7 (Heb 1:5; 5:5) highlights his deity and Ps 8:4-6 (Heb 2:6-8) his humanity. Two others focus on his work, for Ps 110:4 (Heb 1:13; 5:6; 7:17, 21) concerns his high priesthood and Ps 40:6-9 (Heb 10:5-7) his sacrifice. The remaining key passage, Ps 95:7-11 (Heb 3:7-11, 15, 18; 4:3, 5, 7), indicates the responsibility of the readers. These are all the main theological emphases of the epistle.

Another special feature of this epistle is the way the four key psalms identified by Kistemaker stand between the Pentateuch and Christ, for Psalm 8 is a meditation on Genesis 1, Psalm 40 on the sacrificial system the regulations for which occur in the Pentateuch, Psalm 95 on the wilderness wanderings, and Psalm 110 on the figure of Melchizedek in Genesis 14. The writer may have done this because the readers of this epistle seem to have been tempted to go back into Judaism, which was strongly Pentateuch-centered at this time.

The psalm that bears the heaviest theological weight in the epistle is 110, which occupies a special place in the NT, not only because its language has influenced its writers more than has any other OT passage, but because it was used by Jesus himself in a strongly christological fashion at the end of the day of questions shortly before his death (Mark 12:35-37).

Other psalm uses in this epistle are significant christologically, even when they are not so significant structurally as those already discussed. These are Psalm 102 (Heb 1:10-12)[188] and Ps 104:4 (Heb 1:7).

David in the Books of Samuel and Chronicles and in the Psalter

It is important to explore briefly the relationship of the Psalter to certain features of the books of Samuel and of Chronicles that present the story of David. The importance of the divine promise to David of an everlasting covenant with his house, recorded in 2 Samuel 7, hardly needs arguing and will be considered a little later.

P. E. Satterthwaite has shown that the books of Samuel, which are really

---

188. See the comment on this psalm.

one book, trace a divergence between ideal and reality in David as king, with the ideal therefore standing unfulfilled. He starts from the insight of Childs that the poetical passages in 1 Sam 2:1-10; 2 Sam 22:1-51; and 23:1-7 stand as hermeneutical brackets enabling us to interpret the whole book, and that they give it a significantly messianic emphasis. Hannah's Song introduces the promise of a God-endowed anointed one, and 2 Sam 22:51 identifies him as David, while both chapters 22 and 23 reflect on David's role as God's king. Before 2 Samuel 7 we see how the program announced in Hannah's Song is fulfilled in David's rise to power and many of his qualities, while 2 Samuel 7 promises David a stable dynasty. The remainder of the prose section plus part of the appendix shows that David fell short of the kingly ideal. The ideal therefore remained unfulfilled.[189]

Called "the last words of David," 2 Sam 23:1-7 is of special importance. In it David is seen to be a prophet uttering oracles, a singer (presumably of oracular songs), divinely exalted and anointed, and the recipient of an oracle emphasizing the importance of righteous government in the fear of God, a theme given lyric expression in Psalm 72, which appears to be the passing on of the ideal from David to Solomon and thence to his successors.[190] In David's last words, verses 5-7 are remarkable for their thematic similarity to Psalms 2 and 1, respectively, for they refer both to the covenant of God with the house of David and to the judgment of evil men. Here then the main emphases of the Psalter on the importance of righteousness and of God's support of the Davidic dynasty are remarkably summarized.

Some commentators, for instance D. R. Davis, following Keil, feel able to go further in their interpretation of 2 Sam 23:1-7. Davis gives a fairly literal translation of the passage and renders the clipped words of verse 3 as "Ruler over mankind — righteous! Ruler — fear of God!" and argues for an application to the Messiah on the grounds that the affirmation in verses 1 and 2 that this is the inspired word of God is so strong that it demands some major announcement to follow it.[191] What we can at least affirm is that only Jesus fulfills the description to the letter, and we can follow Mays in his important comment, "The idea that David's words might be the word of the LORD about the future messianic king and kingdom begins with this final poem in the narrative of Samuel."[192]

---

189. Satterthwaite, "David in the Books of Samuel: A Messianic Expectation?" in Satterthwaite et al., eds., *Lord's Anointed*, 41-65.

190. See the comment on this psalm.

191. Davis, *2 Samuel*, 244-46. The same could be said of the magnificent poem in Isa 44:24-28, which culminates in the revelation of the name and description of Cyrus.

192. Mays, *Lord Reigns*, 92.

In 1 Chr 25:1-8 the sons of Asaph, Heman and Jeduthun, all mentioned in psalm superscriptions, are said to have the ministry of prophesying, and the sons of Asaph are said to be under the supervision of Asaph, who himself is under the supervision of David. This makes an important link between the Levitical psalmists, their prophetic inspiration, and a supervision that was ultimately David's.[193]

We see then that David is important both as the first king of a dynasty underwritten by a solemn promise of God and also as producing inspired songs and supervising others who had a prophetic ministry and who themselves have psalms linked to them. These facts might even lead us to anticipate that the OT would contain what we do find: inspired songs, closely linked to David, with a kingly theme.

The Messianic Hope in the Book of Psalms

What was the overall theological purpose of the book of Psalms? If we are expected to learn this from the two introductory psalms, then it is certainly to move readers to godly conduct resulting from meditation on divine instruction, but also to encourage belief in God's special purpose for the Davidic dynasty. Psalm 72, which concludes book 2, in effect unites the two motifs, for it presents a kingly ideal both Davidic and strongly ethical. Now the OT experience of kings, even those of the Davidic line, was largely at least of failure and often of utter apostasy. The concluding chapters of 2 Samuel reveal failure in the best of them, David himself, and Isaiah's messianic prophecies occur in a historical context of imperfect kings, for even good king Hezekiah is shown warts and all in Isaiah 39.

As we have seen, Wilson promoted the view that books 1-3 focus on the Davidic dynasty but conclude by referring to its demise (Ps 89), and that books 4 and 5 seek to direct attention away from it to Yahweh, as the people's true monarch in whom they should trust. Although recognizing the value of much of Wilson's work, David Mitchell argues for an overall eschatological and messianic understanding of the Psalter. His arguments against Wilson's view are threefold. He asks why, if Wilson is right, the name of David appears in sixteen superscriptions after book 3, why passages in books 1-3 emphasizing God's apparent failure to keep his covenant promises were allowed to re-

---

193. We might compare either the ministry of men like Silas, Timothy, and Titus and their relationship with Paul or the link that existed between the Gospel writers Mark and Luke and the apostles of Christ.

main in the final redaction if the redactor was concerned to encourage faith in him, and why there is no evidence elsewhere that the postexilic Jews believed the Davidic house was finished forever.[194]

Mitchell's positive arguments for an overall eschatological and messianic structuring of the Psalter are fourfold. He points out that the Psalter's final form, after the exile, was produced in a period of eschatological expectation, as seen both in the later prophets and in the Qumranic and pseudepigraphic material; that psalm authors such as David, Asaph, Jeduthun, Heman, and Moses were all viewed as prophets, so that some future orientation in their psalms is to be expected; that certain psalms of the king use language about him that exceeds what we know of any of the historical monarchs; and that the inclusion of royal psalms by the ultimate redactor, at a time when the Davidic dynasty was in eclipse, makes sense only if they were understood eschatologically and messianically.[195]

In what respect are the Davidic psalms messianic? There are several possibilities. Perhaps they are messianic because although originally written for historical Davidic monarchs they were reapplied to the Messiah, possibly, in the case of psalms like 2, 72, and 110, with some modification of their language. The reapplication was made because the dynasty was no longer reigning. In this case the theology of the writers has become subsumed under that of the redactor. Both Childs and Mitchell view the Davidic psalms generally as intended by the redactor to point the reader to the coming Messiah.

Another possibility is that in the first two books the kingly references are historical whereas in the later books the eschatological Messiah is in view. In his more recent major work, his commentary on the psalms, Wilson sees the reference to David as the son of Jesse (with its dynastic suggestiveness) in 72:20 to imply that the "Davidic" psalms in the later books of the Psalter were meant to be understood not as references to historical Davidic monarchs, but as messianic.[196]

Roland de Vaux is prepared to go further than this. He thinks that Nathan's prophecy in 2 Samuel 7 and psalms like 2, 72, and 110 had a twofold meaning from the beginning, so that each monarch was viewed as a figure of the ultimate ideal king. "In fact, none of these kings fulfilled this ideal, but at the moment of enthronement, at each renewal of the Davidic covenant, the same hope was expressed, in the belief that one day it would be fulfilled. All

---

194. D. C. Mitchell, *Message of Psalter,* 78-81.
195. Mitchell, *Message of Psalter,* 82-87.
196. Wilson, *Psalms,* 1:76 n. 35.

these texts, then, are Messianic, for they contain a prophecy and a hope of salvation, which an individual chosen by God will bring to fulfilment."[197]

It is not easy to decide between these views, but de Vaux's, which really combines typology and prophecy, would mean that in no sense did the redactor impose a new interpretation on these psalms, and it is in keeping with the general OT recognition that the word of God has inherent authority. When they were viewed as messianic, this was simply the recognition of an important dimension they had always had. Not only so, but if these psalms were used at enthronement ceremonies, this view recognizes some merit in the form-critical approach.

De Vaux is not, of course, referring to all the Davidic psalms, but specifically to 2, 72, and 110, which have the king's royal office in view. We should distinguish these and others that have a distinctly official character (such as 45 and 132) from those that view the king largely as a human being facing human problems. Only those with a focus on the office would have been used at the enthronement and other official ceremonies. After all, it was the office that was passed on down the dynastic line, while the human experiences would vary from monarch to monarch.

Inasmuch, however, as these experiences stemmed from his office, for instance where he was loyal to the Lord but afflicted by enemies and was reposing his trust in God (who had promised to support him, as Ps 2 shows), their application to the Messiah is appropriate. Even Psalm 69, which shows an awareness of personal sin (in v. 5), is applied to him (for instance, in John 15:25; Acts 1:20;[198] Rom 11:9-10), for in verse 7 he says, "I endure scorn for your sake," and the emphasis in the psalm is much more on this than on his personal sin. When we look at specific Davidic psalms, it is remarkable that some typological element, either of royal dignity and function, or of human suffering or trust in God, appears in so many of them.

The Basis for the Messiah in the Promise of God in 2 Samuel 7

This point is evident in Psalms 89 and 132, in both of which this promise is quoted, but it appears also to be the basis of Psalm 2. All three psalms are important in themselves but also because of their placing, for this shows the way the ultimate redactor viewed them. Psalm 2's reference to the king's filial relationship to God (v. 7) is certainly reminiscent of 2 Sam 7:14. Psalm 89 closes book 3 and does so both with emphatic affirmation of the covenant promise

---

197. De Vaux, *Ancient Israel*, 1:110.
198. The quotation here is from either Ps 69 or 109:8.

and yet also with deep disappointment at the fact that God appeared to have turned against the king. Psalm 132, however, not only reaffirms the covenant promise but contemplates a future fulfillment of it. As this comes in book 5, it must indicate that, despite the exile, the redactor was convinced that a further fulfillment of the covenant promise was assured.

There are of course quotations from Psalm 2 in the NT (e.g., Acts 13:33; Heb 1:5), and Stephen appears to use phraseology from Ps 132:5 (Acts 7:46) and Paul from Ps 89:20 (Acts 13:22) when they are referring to the Davidic covenant and its fulfillment in Jesus.

Relationship to the Davidic Messianism of the Prophets

The writing prophets, well aware as they were of the many failings of the Davidic kings with whom they had contact, were nevertheless convinced that God had not finished with that line yet. Although explicit references to the Davidic covenant are rare, this note of hope in the dynasty must have had a divine, not a human, basis to it, encouraged, that is, by divine promise, not by human precedent or experience.

Some assert that messianic prophecy dates only from the Babylonian exile, in other words when there was no longer a Davidic king on the throne; but this is not true. The great prophecy of a Davidic monarch with names strongly suggestive of deity (Isa 9:2-7; cf. also 11:1-16) comes in the context of the Assyrian threat to Israel and Judah, and there is no good reason for denying it to the eighth-century prophet. We note too that in Isaiah an individual monarch rather than a dynastic succession is in view, as also in the prophecy of Mic 5:2-4. Israel did not have to wait for the prophecies of Jer 23:5-6 and 33:15-16, let alone those of Ezek 34:23 and 37:24-25, but of course these served to confirm the earlier prophecies. There are also prophecies that relate to a continued dynasty, such as Jer 33:14-22, but the chief feature of these is an affirmation that God would not break his word to David.

It may be that the eventual redaction of the Psalter was done under prophetic influence. There is certainly no disharmony between prophetic and psalmic messianism.

The Davidic Emphasis in the NT's Christological Use of the Psalter

Although the psalms are used for different purposes in the NT, with a number of them being employed for their ethical content, the most frequent use of them is for christological purposes. We should not miss the fact that when this occurs, in the great majority of cases it is Davidic psalms that are quoted or that have influenced the language of the NT. There are exceptions, with Psalm 118 particularly notable among them, but it is easy to see the aptness of this, as it occurs in the accounts of the triumphal entry at Passover time, and it was the final psalm of the Egyptian Hallel, which was always sung at Passover.

In recent years, as we have seen, there has been a major scholarly interest in the structure of the Psalter, and most Psalm scholars are now convinced that there were important theological reasons for the shape that was given to it by the ultimate redactor, and I have argued for the importance for it of the eschatological/messianic theme. But is there any evidence for this in the NT?

There is of course the statement of the risen Christ that the Psalms bore testimony to him (Luke 24:44), which certainly indicates that he viewed this book as a major part of the OT witness to him. There are also many psalms that are quoted in the course of christological passages, but it is not easy to find evidence of the recognition of a christological structural principle in the Psalter. The one possible exception, however, is the way Psalm 2 is used in various parts of the NT.

Each of the Synoptic Gospels records the baptism of Jesus that inaugurated his ministry. The divine voice from heaven that spoke on this occasion designated him as God's Son. The three accounts vary in some small details, but in each case he is called the Son of God, with whom God is well pleased. Many scholars view this as a programmatic utterance, combining Ps 2:7 and Isa 42:1, and so uniting the roles of the messianic King and the Suffering Servant, for of course Isaiah 42 introduced the Servant of God whose sufferings form the focus of the fourth Song in Isa 52:13–53:12.

This certainly fits the plan of these three Gospels, perhaps most of all the Gospel of Mark, the first half of which leads up to Peter's confession, while the second half shows Jesus instructing his disciples about his coming sufferings on the way to Jerusalem, where his passion and death occurred. In John's Gospel John the Baptist refers to the baptism of Jesus, and it is in this connection that he says, "I have seen and testify that this is the Son of God" (John 1:34).

When the church began to encounter persecution, it turned to prayer and in that prayer it quoted Ps 2:1-2, as if this psalm was to them a key passage showing the purpose of God in the events concerning Jesus (Acts 4:25-26). The Epistle to the Romans begins with a reference to the gospel, which is said to be the subject of prophecy and to concern God's Son, who was in terms of his human nature a descendant of David. As noted already, the use of the Psalms in the Epistle to the Hebrews is of great christological interest, and it is notable that after two references to Jesus as God's Son (Heb 1:2-3), the very first of the important catena of OT (mostly psalmic) passages given in chapter 1 is a quotation from Ps 2:7.

The last book of the Psalter has an outstanding messianic passage in Psalm 110. This psalm too is found in most significant places. It is widely recognized that it has had a greater influence on the language of the NT than any other OT passage. This in itself was probably due to the special place given to it by Jesus, who draws attention to its messianic significance at the end of the day of questions in all three Synoptic Gospels, and particularly to the fact that the Messiah is here seen to be David's Lord. It certainly seems the most important in the Epistle to the Hebrews, and it is the concluding psalm of the catena that started with 2 as well as providing the key OT text for the doctrine of the kingship-priesthood of the Messiah, the distinctive subject of the epistle. Eventually, in chapter 7, the writer comments on each feature of Ps 110:4, and at the end of the chapter (v. 28) he returns to his base in chapter 1 by saying that the high priest appointed was in fact God's Son.

Here then we see evidence at least of the great christological importance of Psalms 2 and 110, which were, respectively, the key introductory psalm of the Christ and the ultimate disclosure in the Psalter of his person and work. Perhaps then the NT writers did know something of the quite special messianic structure of the Psalter.

Two psalms in particular feature in the Passion narratives, 22 and 69, one from book 1 and the other from book 2. Psalm 2 had indicated that the Messiah would face opposition, but these two Davidic psalms focus on personal sufferings.

In Psalm 22 there are references both to his physical sufferings and the bitter hatred and social ostracism that he would encounter. It commences with an utterance translated, "My God, my God, why have you forsaken me? Why are you so far from saving me, so far from the words of my groaning?" The translators have made two complete sentences from the Hebrew, but in fact it consists of broken phrases, as if the sufferer finds speech very difficult. Both Matthew and Mark record the utterance of the psalm's first question by Jesus when he was hanging on the cross (Matt 27:46; Mark 15:34). It is notable that they record no other saying from those hours of suffering as if to allow this to stand on the page in all its starkness to challenge the reader to ponder its significance.

Psalm 69 focuses particularly on the sufferer's social ostracism. Both psalms indicate by a change of mood and of language that God came ultimately to the aid of the sufferer. Luke records that, just prior to his death, Jesus said, "Father, into your hands I commit my spirit" (Luke 23:46), apparently quoting Ps 31:5, a psalm in which David calls God to come quickly to his rescue (v. 2).

Psalm 16 indicates the nature of that rescue. It is quoted both by Peter and by Paul in the course of preaching and applied to the resurrection of Christ (Acts 2:25-32; 13:35-37). In fact, Peter indicates that this, rather than an experience of David, is the true meaning of the psalm. Certainly, even if it arose out of some human situation, its language clearly relates not just to rescue from mortal danger but to deliverance out of the experience of death itself, which was not known by David or any of his successors, but which was true of Jesus in his resurrection from the dead. Commenting on the whole psalm, J. A. Motyer says, "Even when David wrote this psalm he was going beyond his own personal experience: he did not, for example, always set the Lord before him, nor was he always unshaken. Both he and his contemporaries would recognize the psalm as an unrealized ideal. Rightly, therefore, the NT finds here a foreshadowing of the Lord Jesus Christ in whom its ideals and hopes were fulfilled."[199]

At other points in the gospel story psalms are quoted. Psalm 41:9, where the psalmist refers to the treachery of a close friend, is applied to Judas Iscariot in John 13:18. Psalm 118, the last of the Egyptian Hallel psalms, which were always used at the Passover, occurs prominently in each of the four accounts of the triumphal entry of Jesus.

What is the status of the messianic King? The writer to the Hebrews has no doubt that in him the divinely appointed destiny of humanity to rule, which has been grievously affected by sin, is restored (Heb 2:6-11). This is really an aspect of kingly messiahship, for in Psalm 2 the messianic King was promised universal dominion. Later in the same epistle (Heb 10:5-7), the writer quotes Ps 40:6-8, a Davidic psalm in which the psalmist confesses sin (40:12), but where he is also shown as having a great aspiration to fulfill God's will in his life, seeing this to be more important than the offering of sacrifice. The epistle applies this to Jesus, who was David's great successor, and in whom aspiration became full performance and sacrifice was done away with because of the perfection of his self-offering.

Yet his status was higher than that. The hyperbolic language of Ps 45:6-7, not a Davidic psalm but quite evidently focusing on the Davidic king, actually calls him "God."[200] This is quoted in Hebrews 1, which assembles a number of OT passages, mostly psalms, that contain exalted titles like "Son,"

199. Motyer, "Psalms," 495.
200. See the exegetical comment on this psalm and also on 102:26-28, which is also used in the same chapter.

"God," and "Lord," in order to emphasize the greatness of Jesus. In Ephesians 4, Paul applies Ps 68:18 to the exalted Jesus and the gift of the Holy Spirit, but the psalm itself is about God and the movement of the ark from the wilderness to its resting place on Mount Zion. There must have been both a conviction of the deity of Jesus and a profound typological understanding of this passage in his mind when he wrote this.

THE PSALTER'S RELEVANCE TO PRESENT-DAY THEOLOGICAL AND OTHER ISSUES

As this series is meant particularly for preachers and theological students, this part of the volume is of considerable importance, but its value will depend entirely on the extent to which the earlier parts have been done thoroughly and soundly. It will deal not only with issues in systematic theology but also those in such related departments as ethics and pastoralia. We must also look at issues arising from the interface between theology and philosophy. It may still be most convenient to structure it according to the traditional divisions of a systematic theology textbook.

In every age of the church Christian writers have applied the Psalms to contemporary experience of God and to the issues of their own day, just as the NT writers did, and as the Qumran sectaries and the Jewish authors of the Midrashim did. Martin Luther, for example, loved the Psalms and often identified personally with the experiences of the psalmists. He and Melanchthon used to sing Psalm 46 together in times of adversity, and Luther saw the doctrines of the Christian gospel in the Psalter. He produced two major commentaries on the Psalms. In the first of these he applied them to Christ and in the second also to Christians. Calvin's commentary on the Psalms shows his exceptional skill and straightforwardness as an exegete, but he discerned also the theological implications of these inspired poems.

Commentators have sometimes placed exegesis and theological or devotional exposition so close together in their comments on particular psalms that the reader does not find it easy to distinguish the one from the other. Indeed, at times there has been a tendency to neglect an exegesis showing the meaning of the text for the original reader and to replace this almost completely with contemporary exposition. It is important both to distinguish and to relate exegesis and exposition.

Some of the literature on the Psalms has useful chapters on their contemporary relevance. For instance, William Holladay devotes five chapters to "Current Theological Issues."[201]

God and Creation

In his preface to the first volume of Gerald Wilson's commentary on the Psalms, Terry C. Muck, the general editor of the NIV Application Commentary series, says, "Although the Psalms contain many 'messages' of a historical, theological, and practical nature, their primary message is that God is great and God is good. A corollary of this primary message is that we should begin all our thinking, feeling, and acting with an acknowledgement of God's primacy."[202]

In understanding any literature and particularly in seeing its contemporary relevance, the interpreter needs both a center and boundaries for his or her understanding. Psalm interpretation needs to recognize boundaries. As we have seen, some contemporary philosophies of language regard the text as lacking all objective meaning. I have argued that this will not do if the Bible (and so within it the book of Psalms) is recognized as authoritative for the Christian faith. To keep in mind the historical conditioning of the Psalms will give us boundaries for our interpretation of them. We also need an interpretive center. What should it be?

Christian Thinking Should Start with God

In the third quarter of the last century, Rudolf Bultmann and Paul Tillich had considerable influence on theology. They might appear to represent opposite theological poles. Bultmann was an extreme transcendentalist, and he viewed biblical supernaturalism as quite unacceptable to the modern concept of the universe as a closed system. This led him to a drastic program of demythologizing the NT. He did not simply reject its supernatural elements as some earlier writers had done, but instead viewed them as ways of expressing human confrontation by God in the *kerygma,* the gospel message. Tillich, on the other hand, played down the transcendence of God, at least as traditionally understood, and his theology has distinct resemblances to pantheistic systems like those of Plotinus and Spinoza.

---

201. Holladay, *Psalms,* 287-358.
202. General editor's preface to Wilson, *Psalms,* 1:12.

The two theologians were, however, at one in accepting an existentialist starting point, maintaining that our understanding of the biblical literature should take its rise from questions about human existence (Bultmann), about our ultimate concern as human beings (Tillich). It would be too much to say that their theology is simply anthropology, an understanding of human existence, but they tend to approach the doctrine of God through anthropology rather than the reverse.

The influence of these two has waned considerably, but we might imagine that their existentialist approach could be helpful for interpreting the book of Psalms, where such questions and concerns are prominent, even at times appearing to be dominant.[203] This would be a mistake.

Martin Heidegger, whose philosophy influenced both these theologians, distinguished between what he called authentic and inauthentic existence. For him the only existence that can be called authentic is one in which the individual human being faces with utter realism and commitment the challenge that arises from his or her existence in the world. He maintained that existence is never authentic until we have faced up to the fact of death. If this is so, then authenticity is a marked feature of the Psalter. In many of the psalms of lament, especially those like 22 and 69, which are often quoted in the Passion narratives of the Gospels, there is the recognition that life itself is under threat. The authenticity, the realism that existentialism calls for, is certainly present here, and is even more markedly present in the attitude of Jesus himself.[204]

Should we then turn the theological clock back and become Christian followers of existentialism? No, for we need to face a fact already noted, that the psalmists themselves go back constantly to certain great anchor points, great convictions about God. It is clear that these anchor points existed for them before the difficult experiences through which they were passing. In other words, they start off not simply with human concerns, but with an anchor in God himself. They show us we can make sense of this apparently chaotic world only when we do what they do, and begin with God.

Furthermore, these convictions were rooted in history, in events in which their God revealed himself; moreover, there was a supernatural dimension to some of these acts, for instance, the parting of the Red Sea at the exodus. So, even if we start by asking questions about the meaning of human life, we are always driven by the psalms themselves to move our

---

203. I must say, however, that Bultmann's view of the OT was largely, although not completely, negative, as may be seen in his chapter, "The Significance of the Old Testament for the Christian Faith" in Anderson, ed., *OT and Christian Faith*, 8-35.

204. For an exposition and critique of the theological standpoints of Bultmann and Tillich, see Grenz and Olson, *Twentieth-Century Theology*, 86-98 and 114-29.

main reference point to God and his deeds. These were not anticipated future deeds (although there are references to divine promises), neither were they experienced present deeds, but they were deeds that had already taken place and that were rooted in the history, the redemptive experience, of their people.

In a devastating critique of modern American evangelicalism, David Wells comments on a statistical analysis of two hundred sermons published in two leading preaching journals, which found that more than 80 percent of these sermons were anthropocentric:

> At issue here is not whether the sermons were *about* God; there are many other legitimate subjects about which a minister might want to discourse on a Sunday morning. Rather at issue is whether the reality, character, and acts of God provided an explicit foundation for what the preacher said about the life of faith, or whether the life of faith was presented as making some kind of internal sense without reference to the character, will, and acts of God.[205]

While I was writing this chapter, my wife came in to tell me she had been listening to the daily service on the BBC, a service that does not usually stray too far from historic Christianity, and that on this occasion the speaker had been extolling the outlook of the Dalai Lama, especially stressing his peaceful demeanor. But one has to say that the theology and worldview of the Buddhism of Tibet and that of the Bible, including the book of Psalms, are immensely far apart and that the former can never be used to illustrate the latter without causing serious confusion. Quite apart from anything else, there is no such stress on special historical deeds in the Buddhist outlook.

It is important for us to take our cue from the psalmists. We will therefore begin with God and moreover with God as already revealed in his acts in the history of his people. That revelation was destined to come to its great consummation in the life, death, and resurrection of Christ, and, of course, these are now the great anchor points for the Christian church. The combination of the two groups of convictions based on history can be found in the psalm-like song described as "the song of Moses the servant of God and the song of the Lamb," which closes with the words "for your righteous acts have been revealed" (Rev 15:3-4).

We have already noted that the Psalter is full of teaching about God and

---

205. Wells, *No Place for Truth*, 252.

that the NT assumes this background of teaching. In every age of the church, the nature and purposes of God have always been at the center of theological discussion, for what we believe about God affects what we believe about everything else. Theology touches everything that life touches.

Christian Thinking about God Should Be Shaped by the Biblical Revelation

Theology and philosophy overlap in their concerns. This has value, because it means that many of the questions to which theology gives an answer are questions philosophy also is asking, so providing points of interface between the two and demonstrating the relevance of the Christian faith to the world of thought. The mutual interest, however, has its negative points too, for it is all too easy to gain one's bearings in thinking about God from philosophical theology, which may be just a sophisticated version of natural theology. We then find ourselves pressing the biblical material into pigeonholes ill-fitted to take it because they were devised for philosophical purposes.

This has sometimes been a problem, not always fully recognized, for Reformed theology. To open Charles Hodge's *Systematic Theology* to consult him on Christology or soteriology is one thing and to read what he has to say on the doctrine of God quite another. The plenitude of biblical references in the former two and their paucity in the latter is very striking — and disturbing — all the more so because of the basic nature of this doctrine for all theological thinking.

God Has Revealed Himself to Be Both Transcendent and Immanent

The last century began in the heyday of liberalism, largely of the Ritschlian (neo-Kantian) and evolutionary types, but after World War I a major new theological movement arose, largely through the work of Karl Barth.[206] In place of the immanentism that had prevailed in most types of theological liberalism, Barth asserted that God is the "Wholly Other," and this conviction characterized many of the theologians influenced by him. In his later years he sought to balance this by a new stress on the immanence of God, but this was not instead of but alongside transcendentalism.

---

206. For these three movements see Grenz and Olson, *Twentieth-Century Theology*, 51-62, 65-77, and 130-34.

Not all theologians of this period, however, were transcendentalists. For all his protestations that he held to God's transcendence, Tillich's theology was difficult to distinguish from a sophisticated pantheism. Over against him, Bultmann's theology had the appearance of extreme transcendentalism, for God was so remote from his universe that there was no question of any supernatural intervention in its affairs.

The Psalms show us a God who is both transcendent and immanent, a God who is neither remote from his world nor virtually identified with it, but one sovereignly involved in it. He is very definitely the king over all, for he is the creator of everything and no other being has power in any way comparable to his. Yet in no sense is he an absentee from his universe, simply ruling it by subordinates. He is deeply concerned with the world's history, ruling the nations, overcoming them for his people's good when they trust in him, using them to punish his people when they are rebellious, and at last receiving worship from them all. A theology that plays down either his transcendence or his immanence is not true to the Psalter.

So Oliver O'Donovan, while recognizing the value of an emphasis on the theology of the poor found in liberation theology (what he calls "the Southern school"), says that this school lacks a concept of authority and that this can be recovered by development from that of the kingdom of God,[207] which itself balances transcendence and immanence, for it means that God is supreme but also that his kingship is exercised within the created universe and human society.

Indeed, both the divine kingship and a theology of the poor are found in the Psalter. Moreover, they are found together. In Psalm 140, for instance, he is the "Sovereign LORD" (v. 7) who secures justice for the poor (v. 12). It is a cause of joyful praise that "though the LORD is on high, he looks upon the lowly" (138:6). This can be a comfort to those who are ground down by oppressive regimes, giving them real hope for the future.

Because he is both transcendent and immanent, he is not only omnipotent and omniscient but also omnipresent.[208] It is true that his praises are not sung in Sheol (6:5; 88:10-12), for there is no temple there, and, if Philip Johnston is right in arguing that Sheol is intended only for the unrighteous, there are also moral reasons for the absence of praise there.[209] Whatever the reasons are, they are not ontological, for he is the one who upholds all things,

---

207. O'Donovan, *Desire of Nations*, 16.

208. See later discussion of open theism on pp. 370-74.

209. See P. S. Johnston, "Hell," *NDBT*, 542-44. He surveys the whole field of the afterlife in the OT in *Shades of Sheol*.

not just from without but also from within. This is traditional Christian theism, and the basic features of it are there in the book of Psalms (8:1; 139:7-12).

The True God Is the Creator of All

That he brought everything into existence is clearly stated over and over again. He is the Maker of heaven and earth; the gods of the nations are nonentities, and the idols that represent them are totally impotent. Mythological names such as Rahab and Leviathan appear in the Psalms, but they are symbols of evil or, in the case of Leviathan (104:26), a creature of the sea, or else their names have been transferred to major world powers like Egypt. The concept of a heavenly court makes some appearance, but we would be mistaken if we took from this that there was real consultation with its members, like a prime minister with his cabinet. They are God's subordinates, and their function is simply to carry out the dictates of his will so that there is no question of delegated powers. What he wills is translated into action in such a way that the actions are as much his as are the purposes that lie behind them.

The great creation chapter in Genesis 1 shows clear awareness of Babylonian/Canaanite religion, but in such a way as to attack it in its treatment of the sun, the moon, and the stars as creatures of the only God there is.[210] The book of Psalms too sees the heavenly bodies not as deities but as created by Yahweh, the God of Israel (e.g., in 148:1-6). Not only so, but so much that was attributed to Baal is, in the Psalter, attributed to Yahweh. It is he, not Baal, who rides upon the skies (68:4, 33); he, not Baal, who gives crops to feed his people (65:9-13).

Apologetic issues concerning the relationship between scientific views of the origins of the universe (or life) and of the human race on the one hand and the biblical doctrine of creation on the other focus largely on Genesis 1 and 2, for the Psalter says nothing about the method of creation except in the most figurative of fashions. It supplies many images of God the Creator at work, images such as the architect (24:2; 78:69; 102:25; 104:5), the tentmaker (104:2), and the storage man (33:7). Despite Walt Disney's visual portrayal of Stravinsky's *Rite of Spring* as the story of evolution in *Fantasia*, evolutionary theory supplies little to the poetic imagination, but such images as are found in the Psalms have considerable aesthetic appeal.

---

210. See, e.g., Wenham, *Genesis 1–15*, 9-10.

There Can Be No Place for Religious Pluralism
or Idolatry of Any Kind[211]

We live at a time when nature religion is finding a new lease of life in Western society under the umbrella of the New Age.[212] Gaia the earth mother is celebrated, and elements of Hindu, Buddhist, and Taoist thought are more and more in evidence in some kinds of alternative therapies. Indeed, many of the ideas being promoted seem to belong to an outlook only slightly removed from animism, although there are also strong tendencies toward pantheism.

Tom Wright highlights the neo-paganisms of the New Age movement, which has often been regarded as antiscientific and which often seems virtually to deify nature, worshiping and serving the creature rather than the Creator. Wright has Britain chiefly in view but much the same applies to Western society generally, and the pace of this paganizing movement has not diminished since he wrote *New Tasks for a Renewed Church* (1992).

Where paganism has an intellectual side, it has developed a natural theology. A psalm like 19 should warn us not to identify general revelation and natural theology. The two are clearly distinguished in Rom 1:18-32. God's revelation of his "eternal power and divine nature" (v. 20) was being clearly revealed in what he had made, but human beings "exchanged the truth of God for a lie" (v. 25). Natural theology may not always design a divine realm represented by idols, but we should learn a lesson from the fact that the highly sophisticated philosophy of Neoplatonism provided an intellectual structure in an attempt to validate all kinds of pagan religions when the Christian faith was on the ascendant in the Roman Empire. Pascal's deep conviction is still right that there is a huge gulf between the God of the philosophers and the God of the Bible.

It is abundantly clear that religious pluralism can never be squared with the theology of the Psalms.[213] As we have seen, the authors of the Psalms, with all their problems and perplexities, rest on great facts about their God. This is a far remove from the uncertainties of paganism, with its concern not only to worship (or, moving from the realm of religion to that of magic, to manipulate) the diverse and often contending gods it knows but to avoid displeasing any it does not know.[214] It is quite true, of course, that the religions

---

211. See Carson, *Gagging of God.*

212. See Bloom, *New Age;* Drane, *New Age and Church;* and Clarke and Geisler, *Apologetics in the New Age.*

213. See Newbigin, *Gospel in Pluralist Society.*

214. As in Athens, with its temple to the unknown god.

of the Near East at the time the Psalms were written were normally associated with idolatry, but the idols are intimately related to the gods they represent.

The only religion in this area that approached monotheism in OT times, apart from the abortive attempt of Akhenaton in Egypt to promote the sole worship of the sun god, was Persian Zoroastrianism, and this had a distinct bent in the direction of dualism, for it gave a large place to Angra Mainyu or Ahriman, an evil power treated as the virtual equal of God. There is, however, no sign of this in the book of Psalms. Indeed, there is not even an explicit reference to Satan there. Of course, the Bible never regards Satan as having power in any way comparable to that of the almighty God, whose sovereign rule is complete.

Some of the Psalms attack idolatry (96:5; 97:7; 115:3-8; 135:15-18); does idolatry exist in Western society? This must be answered in the affirmative, for if idolatry is defined as worshiping something in the created world rather than the Creator himself, this exists in a number of different forms in our sophisticated world.

First of all there is sociopolitical idolatry or ideological idolatry, as Walter Brueggemann calls it. He sees this as the setting up of an ideological structure, a way of viewing social and political issues, that is treated as sacrosanct, usually in support of the ruling classes.[215] This has something of a Marxist ring about it, but the important question is not its origin but its truth. Without doubt, the political and economic systems of the modern era can act as idols of an ideological kind, but this is true of systems of the political left as well as of the right, as can be seen by the way "revisionism" has often been attacked. All such ideologies are subject to the judgment of the Word of God.

Tom Wright too recognizes that paganism is alive and well in Western society, although he takes a somewhat different approach from that of Brueggemann. Referring to T. S. Eliot's insights in the 1930s, he is concerned that society has been moving toward a variety of paganism, in fact that paganism is already effectively in the driver's seat.[216] He identifies a number of paganisms, saying, for example, "science and technology are autonomous: whatever they dictate, we must do, and whatever they even suggest must at least be tried out. A society that thinks like that is a society in bondage to paganism."[217]

Closely connected with this is materialistic idolatry. Brueggemann sees this as operating in the commercial sphere, maintaining that TV advertising

---

215. Brueggemann, *Israel's Praise.* See also Smith, *Against the Stream,* esp. chs. 7 and 8.
216. Wright, *New Tasks,* xii.
217. Ibid., 36.

often mimics the thanksgiving psalm, "with a precondition of trouble and a postcondition of well-being. In between, as the transformative agent, is 'the product.' The ads propose that the product is the trustworthy agent who can transform life."[218] The extent to which such idolatries make their presence felt through the TV screens in our living rooms is considerable. Alan Storkey, writing of consumerism, goes so far as to say, "In the dynamics of our culture, consumption has now become the dominant faith and individualism, together with other subordinate commitments, serves it. Consumption is collectivist-individualist, nationalist-internationalist, the healer, the entertainer, the lover, the spiritual, the feeder and the consolation. It is the chief rival to God in our culture."[219]

Not that all the blame can be placed on the shoulders of those who produce and advertise, for there has been willing cooperation on the part of the general public. There may seem to have been of late a resurgence not of Christian faith but at least of a recognition of a spiritual dimension to life, a kind of generalized spirituality, but in those living rooms of Western society "spirituality" has often made a total surrender to the deities of materialism, or the two find themselves coexisting.

It is easy to find weaknesses in idolatry. If it has any strength, however, it is in that it represents the gods as present in the human sphere. Writing about the OT passages in which idolatry is ridiculed, James Crenshaw says, "The remarkable tenacity of idol worshipers in the face of such mockery ought to alert us to the human longing for representation of the divine."[220] We know, of course, that the NT answer to this is the incarnation, but what of the OT? In its historical literature the answer is to be found in the theophanies, but in the Psalms it is found in the metaphors, especially those that are anthropomorphic. To call God King and Shepherd, Savior and Judge, is to bring him into the human world, and to see him as performing perfectly what human beings perform imperfectly. It is significant that all these eventually became titles or descriptions of Jesus, God incarnate.

Faith Involves a Deep Conviction of the Moral Nature of God

What kind of worldview is promoted by the psalms of orientation? They show the psalmists finding a structure divinely established on which they can

---

218. Brueggemann, *Reverberations of Faith*, 212.

219. Storkey, "Postmodernism Is Consumption," 100. See also Smith, *Against the Stream*, 36-38.

220. Crenshaw, *Psalms*, 131.

rest. The most fundamental of all their convictions and one that comes to the fore constantly is the moral nature of their God. He is appealed to as the source of the moral structure of the universe. This means that this moral structure is in no way separable from the God who instituted it, but rather is a manifestation of his own nature.

Is it possible, though, that this God is the ultimate guardian of a corrupt authority structure that enables the rich to exploit the poor? I have to say that there is no real evidence for this in the Psalter, and indeed that one of the chief ethical qualities of the God of the Psalms is his justice. This is a marked feature of Psalm 9, but is evident in many other psalms (e.g., 11:4-7; 33:5; 103:6). In fact, righteousness and justice are the foundations of his throne, from which he rules the world (89:14; 97:2), so that we are not surprised to read, "I know that the LORD secures justice for the poor and upholds the cause of the needy" (140:12).

The psalms in which a kingly ideal is set forth, such as 72 and 112, show that it is important for the king to be concerned for the poor. If he is promised riches, as in 112:3, this is not simply for his own use but to enable him to give generously to the poor. Paradoxically, it may even be that his kingly absolutism, in a king of godly character, would lead to the promotion of a just society. Because of his position of authority, he could devise structures to safeguard the proper concerns of all under his rule. The message of divine warning of kingly oppression given through Samuel in 1 Sam 8:10-18 is one thing, the psalms of orientation quite another. The opening words of Psalm 72 are deeply significant, for in them the psalmist prays that the king will be endowed with God's own justice and demonstrate it in his reign. If this is a psalm written by David for Solomon, as has been suggested, it could well reflect David's own kingly concerns.[221]

Although Brueggemann's distinction between psalms of orientation (and reorientation) and those of disorientation is useful, it is important that we do not draw an absolute line between them.[222] As Brueggemann himself recognizes, in many psalms these elements occur together, not in conflict, as they appear to be in 73 (until v. 17), but side by side. Moreover, in these psalms the enemies, who are often oppressors, never appeal to the principles that lie behind the basic psalmic convictions, including the moral nature of Yahweh and his concern for justice. It is not they but the psalmists who make such appeals, and it is the psalmists, not the oppressors, whose theology has entered the NT and so has become part of the authoritative Scripture of the Christian church.

---

221. See the comment on this psalm.
222. Brueggemann, "Psalms and Life of Faith," 3-32.

Issues raised by feminist thinking are important in the modern theological world,[223] and we need to consider whether the Psalter contains anything relevant. The God of the OT is clearly personal, and the book of Psalms employs male verbal and pronominal forms in relation to him. This also applies to many of its metaphors, such as King and Shepherd. There are, however, character qualities in the God of the Psalms that are often associated in our minds, whether rightly or wrongly, more with women than with men, the tender qualities of caring and comforting. In 123:2, after the author has said, "As the eyes of slaves look to the hand of their master," he goes on to say, "as the eyes of a maid look to the hand of her mistress, so our eyes look to the LORD our God, till he shows us his mercy."

In a family children may well go to one parent (not always the father) when they need strength and to the other (not always the mother) when they need comfort. The psalmists went to Yahweh, their God, for both. In 27:10 the psalmist says, "Though my father and mother forsake me, the LORD will receive me." In this psalm we see the total adequacy of Yahweh to meet all the psalmist's needs, and so in this respect he takes the place of both parents, both of whom in a person's early years have a place of responsibility in teaching him or her God's way, which he asks God to do personally in verse 11. There is in the Lord all that human beings crave for and do not always find in their relations with both parents.

Prayer Changes Things but in No Way Changes God

Another contemporary issue concerns divine openness.[224] Some theologians are now saying that although God is unchanging in his nature and character, the shape of the future is not fixed by him except in general terms, that his knowledge of the future is incomplete, and that human prayers may effect changes in his shaping of the future. Pinnock, for instance, says, "God is unchanging in nature and essence, but not in experience, knowledge and action"; and again, "the future is a realm of possibilities not just of actualities. This is true even for God."[225] This affects even Pinnock's view of the cross, for "God only takes steps to redeem the world when it goes wrong," and the final

223. See especially the balanced treatment of the issues in James, *God's Design for Women.*

224. For an exposition and attempted defense of open theism by a major proponent of it, see Pinnock, *Most Moved Mover;* and for critical appraisal of this theology, Ware, *God's Lesser Glory.*

225. See, respectively, Pinnock, "Systematic Theology," in Pinnock et al., *Openness of God,* 118; idem, *Most Moved Mover,* 51.

state of things, for "he did not make all the decisions once and for all apart from the world but is even now making them as he works out the details of the final restoration."[226]

Changes in theology are not always due to deeper insight into Scripture, for movements in philosophy often have a large and even a determining influence. This may be denied by these theologians themselves,[227] but the outlook of a major philosopher gets into the collective intellectual consciousness at a very deep level and has long-lasting influence, as is acknowledged sometimes when Western philosophy is described as so many footnotes to Plato. One can argue that the ultimate philosophical roots of open theism are to be found in the early-nineteenth-century philosophy of Hegel. Hegel taught that the essence of reality and therefore of God is rationality. The development of human thinking throughout history and on a world scale is the process by which God, or the Absolute, comes to an increasing knowledge of his own mind, which is identical with his being.

Despite the fact that he is probably the most difficult of all major philosophers to read, Hegel's thought had considerable influence on nineteenth-century theology.[228] His outlook tuned in with the nineteenth-century interest in history, and it had points in common with evolutionary philosophy, developed later in the century. A great deal of subsequent philosophy has been either a development of or a reaction against his standpoint.

His philosophy implies that at any particular point in history — for instance, our own — there is an openness about God's future. This was taken up by process philosophy, which was largely developed by philosophers with a strong scientific interest.[229] Its influence may be seen in the Theology of Hope and, most recently, in the writings of open theists such as Pinnock and John Sanders. Kenneth Hamilton says, "The ghost of Hegel . . . is the unseen presence at the banquet to which we are invited by the theologians of hope,"[230] and he might have added, "and by the theologians of divine openness."

Without doubt the open theists have a warmer and much more attractive concept of God than Hegel had, for to them the essence of God is love, but they share with him the idea of development in God, which distinguishes

226. Pinnock, *Most Moved Mover*, 58, 59.

227. Pinnock asserts that the roots of his theology are in Scripture but agrees that his view has some points in common with the outlook of process philosophy (*Most Moved Mover*, 59).

228. Grenz and Olson, *Twentieth-Century Theology*, 31-38.

229. See Grenz and Olson, *Twentieth-Century Theology*, 130-44.

230. K. Hamilton, "Liberation Theology: An Overview," in Armerding, ed., *Evangelicals and Liberation*, 3.

their view from traditional Christian theology. They emphasize passages that speak of God repenting and deciding to set aside his threats of judgment in view of human repentance or prayer. Indeed, their theology of prayer is largely based on God's willingness to change.[231]

What do we find in the Psalms that has a bearing on this issue? Their relevance to it is due especially to the fact that the Psalter contains so much prayer, in fact more than any other part of the Bible. The open theists agree with traditional theologians that God's overall purposes are unchanging, so we will note first of all what the Psalter teaches about these before we move to the more controversial aspects of open theism.

The Psalter's arrangement clearly shows that its ultimate redactor believed that the great principles of God's dealings with his people were immutable. The first two psalms focus attention on two great divine purposes, and the remainder of the book shows these to be changeless and to be as certain at the end as at the beginning.

Psalm 1 is concerned with the moral purpose of God. He is committed to righteousness and so he blesses the righteous and judges the wicked. This is stated quite categorically. It is true that we find much in the experience of the psalmists that appears to challenge it, but Psalm 73, for instance, shows that the justice of God will be vindicated at a future time. The author came to a new understanding in the temple, but the differing ends of the wicked and the righteous were already determined before he stepped inside this place of worship. The principle enunciated in Psalm 1 is repeated in 145:20, in the very last psalm before the Final Hallel group.

Then there is God's historical purpose. This is the theme of Psalm 2, and it centers in the king on the Jerusalem throne. Just as God's moral purpose is challenged at the start of book 3 (in Ps 73), so his historical purpose is challenged at its end in Psalm 89. Whereas in 73 the vindication of God's moral purpose takes place within the same psalm, that of his historical purpose is gradually unfolded in the rest of the Psalter, and the certainty and even enrichment of the Davidic messianic hope finds expression in 110 and is asserted in 132:11-12 and 148:14.[232]

Does God's sovereign control of the future extend to matters of detail? The Final Hallel group of psalms not only indicates that the Lord is faithful forever (146:6), about which there is no dispute, but also that his understanding has no limit (147:4-6).

Does God change his mind? In Psalm 106 he is said to be intent on de-

---

231. See Rice, "Biblical Support."
232. See comments on each of these psalms.

stroying the people, but human intercession or other human action causes him to set this intent aside (vv. 23, 29-30). In verse 23, for instance, the author says, "He said he would destroy them — had not Moses, his chosen one, stood in the breach before him to keep his wrath from destroying them." What are we to make of this?

Psalms 105 and 106 are companion psalms, each tracing Israel's early history, with the covenant faithfulness of Yahweh as their uniting theme. Psalm 106 differs from its companion in stressing also the sinful unworthiness of Israel, but it links this with the covenant theme in verses 44 and 45, where the psalmist says, "But he took note of their distress, when he heard their cry; for their sake he remembered his covenant and out of his great love he relented." The intercession of Moses, for instance, was in tune with the covenant purpose of God, a purpose already established, and one that was promoted in the course of his encounter with God in prayer, while at the same time the seriousness of Israel's sin was highlighted. Although the covenant is particularly stressed by the placing of 106 after 105, it comes over clearly even in 106 considered separately.

Christian theologians have always stressed the importance of the moral factor in God's dealings with people, and that moral changes in us cause us to experience different aspects of God's character. What is the role of prayer in God's moral purposes? A threat of judgment must be perceived as real for prayer to engage the whole being of the one praying, and we should not forget that sin always merits judgment. Without the prayer the threat would be carried out, but prayer is offered and the threat is averted. Tim Chester, among others, emphasizes that we must assert two things at once: prayer does change things, but God is sovereign over all matters of detail, including the very prayer itself. Prayer is used by God to effect change, change that he himself intends, so that it is a function of his sovereignty in which we are privileged to be used in his great plan.[233]

Christian thinking about prayer often focuses on the divine activity that follows it, but it is important also to ask what divine activity precedes it and is present in it. A key passage here is Rom 8:26-27, "The Spirit helps us in our weakness. We do not know what we ought to pray for, but the Spirit himself intercedes for us with groans that words cannot express. And he who searches our hearts knows the mind of the Spirit, because the Spirit intercedes for the saints in accordance with God's will." It is God's Spirit who is active in all true prayer, that Spirit knows the mind of God, and when we pray in accordance with God's will (the only praying that is answered in the affirmative) it is be-

---

233. See Chester, *Message of Prayer*, 246-57.

cause of the activity of the Spirit within our hearts. In an amazing act of condescending grace, God communicates his will to us so that we may become involved personally in an activity that actually accomplishes his purposes. Paul's deep understanding of the theology of prayer here is difficult to square with open theism.

We may make a comparison at the deepest theological level. The Bible contains threats that God will judge sinners, and yet it reveals to us also that at the cross he dealt with sin in such a way as to vindicate his justice while at the same time manifesting his great love for sinners. There God was taking upon himself the consequences of our sins against him. In bearing our sins Christ bore our judgment (Rom 3:21-26; 2 Cor 5:21; Gal 3:13). Now although the crucifixion of Christ was at one level the act of human beings, it was, at the deepest level, the act of God eternally planned (1 Pet 1:18-21; Rev 13:8). In terms of the comparison we may say that Christ's sacrifice was his "prayer" for the forgiveness of sinners, yet at the same time it manifested the eternal plan of God.

A comment by Don Carson makes good hermeneutical sense: "From God's knowledge and sovereignty we must not justify prayerlessness; from the exhortations to pray and not give up, we must not suppose God is coerced by our much speaking (compare Matt. 6:7-8 and Luke 18:1). Precisely because God is so gloriously rich and complex a being, we must draw out the lessons the biblical writers draw out, and no others."[234]

Practical Atheism May Have Serious Ethical Consequences

Theology is not like many other subjects that may be carried on purely as intellectual exercises. There may be a difference between pure and applied science, but if such a distinction were to exist within a theology, that theology would be an abomination. Because God is who he is, we are to be what he says we are to be. To say that Christian ethics is based on Christian theology, true as this is, is not enough. We need to say that the theology necessarily implies the ethics. To treat God as simply existing to give us intellectual satisfaction is utterly remote from the theology of the Psalms; we exist for him, not vice versa.

The psalms do deal with atheism, but, like the psalmists' own theology, this is no merely abstract outlook but a practical one that affects the lives of

234. Carson, *Gagging of God*, 286. S. Williams has some shrewd comments on open theism ("More on Open Theism").

those who hold it. When we have made allowances for the fact that it has a good tune and that the composer/singer was a cult figure, the immense popularity of John Lennon's song "Imagine" shows that a theoretical atheism has some attraction for those who live as though God does not exist. Whether they think he exists or not, those against whom Psalms 14 and 53 are written reckon God irrelevant as far as everyday life is concerned. The psalmist cannot tolerate such thinking and regards it as an abomination. It certainly appears to be no surprise to him that such ungodliness leads to unrighteousness, to evil actions such as oppressing the poor.

It needs to be said, though, that present-day atheism, when it manifests itself within Western Christendom, sometimes appears to be a reaction not against the God of the Bible, the God of the psalmists, but rather against a caricature. The existence of such atheism is often an indictment of the kind of Christian attitudes and conduct that have prevailed, which ones have been observed and which ones have been rejected. Indeed, such atheists may well be unconsciously acting on moral principles derived ultimately from Scripture, even if they are unaware of this. It is interesting that Engels evidently felt the pressure of moral principle when he wrote in the *Communist Manifesto* that he felt it necessary to say that its leading ideas were conceived first of all by Marx and not by himself.[235] What was the source of this moral imperative? For a person reared in nineteenth-century Christendom there is an obvious answer. Despite his atheism, Marx, who had a partly Jewish background, had more than a touch of the OT prophet about him, and of course the prophets and psalmists shared one basic doctrine of God. As we noted earlier, Ernst Bloch, a Marxist who was much involved in dialogue with Jürgen Moltmann, the German theologian, was fascinated by the book of Job.[236]

Faith in the One True God Is a Stimulus
Both to Science and to the Arts

If the God of the Psalms is not only Israel's redeemer but the creator of the world, this has implications not only for theology for also for the arts and sciences.[237] Features of the created universe may be vehicles of the divine Word. So in Psalm 29 the voice of the Lord is heard in the storm, and in Psalm 19 the

---

235. Marx and Engels, *Communist Manifesto*, 11-12.

236. Bloch, *Atheism in Christianity*, 84-122.

237. The implications for art are explored in Rookmaaker, *Modern Art*; and for science in Polkinghorne, *Science and Belief.*

heavens declare that word. The Christian, aware of a relationship with God through grace, is able to see that same God in the created world, so that the inner work of the Holy Spirit that accompanies God's special revelation opens our eyes to see his general revelation more clearly.

Did the psalmists have a sense of beauty? It is interesting that some of the most beautiful psalms, in terms of their form and language, such as 8, 19, and 104, are poems that meditate on the natural environment. Not only so, but the sublime language used in 19 in relation to nature gives place eventually to equally beautiful, if differently structured, language about the divine *tôrâ*. Allen says of 104, "its basic view of the world as evoking numinous awe and aesthetic appreciation transcends historical barriers and has a perennial appeal."[238]

The psalmists saw the universe to be the work of a creative and ordering God, and recognition of the essential rationality of the universe has played an important part in the scientific enterprise. Science never stands still, and its history is not lacking in what Thomas Kuhn, the philosopher of science, called "paradigm shifts," when there is the emergence of a new outlook and new focus for understanding,[239] so that we must be ready for surprises. Nevertheless, the widely held conviction that the universe makes sense suggests to many that this is because it is the product of an ordering mind.

Humanity and Sin

Human Life Is Always to Be Seen as Serving the Purposes of God

All aspects of Christian theology are related to one another, but they are not all equally important and there is a proper order that should normally be adopted when they are considered. We need to recognize the crucial importance of the doctrine of God, and we should always consider humanity in its light. What human beings are, what is the purpose of our creation, what are the moral sanctions that affect us, all these issues are interrelated, but it is also necessary for us to relate them to the doctrine of God.

The Psalms constantly remind us that our proper place as human beings is to be worshipers of God and servants of his purposes. Worship not only takes us out of ourselves, but it lifts us to a higher realm in which God is at the center of everything. This can be a great blessing, giving us a more bal-

238. Allen, *Psalms 100–150*, 48.
239. Kuhn, *Scientific Revolutions*.

anced perspective on things, imparting a quiet poise, and so on, but even if it did none of these things we would still need to worship, because God deserves and ought to have our worship. Every tendency to treat worship as a human-centered activity, with such accompanying comments as, "I did not get much out of worship today," needs to be resisted.

The psalms of worship and of praise offer great variety. God is adored for his power and his wisdom, he is thanked for his provision of food and for his deliverance of his people from their foes. In a sense it matters little where the psalmist begins as long as his thought is occupied by God and he gives glory to him. Thus he fulfills his God-ordained end.

To serve such a God as the one revealed in the Psalms is a great privilege. In 119:91 the psalmist says, "Your laws endure to this day, for all things serve you." The world was created to serve God and his purposes. If this is true of the world, it is particularly true of human beings. The term "servant" is used of the writer himself in the Davidic psalms (19:11, 13; 27:9; 31:16; 86:2, 16), but also, and with a degree of emphasis, in an orphan psalm, where he says, "O LORD, truly I am your servant; I am your servant, the son of your maidservant" (116:16). Characters from the people's history, such as Abraham and Moses, are so called, particularly in 105, and the people as a whole are so described in 136:22.

Human Beings Are to Be Responsible Stewards of God's Creation

Psalm 8 is important, alongside Genesis 1, for its teaching on the place of human beings in God's universe. In Genesis 1 the sun and moon, great as they are, are created by God to give light to the earth, presumably for the benefit of humanity. In Psalm 8 the writer, contemplating the greatness of the heavens and the heavenly bodies, marvels at the concern of God with and for human beings. God's human creatures are given authority over animal life, but this is within the overall context of God's majesty as creator of all.

Does this mean that human beings can do what they will with the animals? Surely not, for in Psalm 104 God's care for all his creatures in his provision of food, drink, and shelter for them is celebrated. If humanity is to be the vicegerent of God as far as the animals are concerned, we must show the same caring attitude toward them as God does.

The use of animals for food is established in Genesis 9 and so is probably assumed by those who wrote the Psalms, but we must ask important questions about the use of animals in medical research. This is a delicate ethical issue that requires both wisdom and compassion. We must never forget that animals are constituted by God as sentient beings and that they need to be treated with the consideration that is due to such. One can argue that they may be used in pursuance of a greater good, such as the saving of human life, for this may be taken as an extension of their role as providers of food, but never in complete disregard for them as sentient creatures.[240]

Of course, larger issues are raised here. The measure of human control of the environment, which is never unlimited, must be in complete subordination to God. The cry, "We have the technology!" may be heard either as a cry of thankfulness to the giver of every skill or as an example of hubris, like the attitude of the builders of Babel's tower in Genesis 11. It also raises issues such as the responsible use of the earth's resources and issues of urgent concern for the world today such as genetic engineering, cloning, designer babies, and so on. Human beings are not God and should not act as if they are.[241] In discussions of such matters the divine purpose in creation is rarely mentioned, let alone treated as a major concern, but the Christian's outlook must be different.

Commenting on Psalm 148, William Brown asks, "Can a stream poisoned by toxic waste praise God? Can trees destined for newsprint for tabloids clap for joy? Can the heavens adequately reflect God's glory when clouded by smog?"[242] His questions are asked to provoke thought rather than introduce answers. Whatever may be said in reply, they make us realize that the interlocking of the universe and the ecological issues that stem from this show how far-reaching is human responsibility in relation to the created universe.

A positive feature of the modern media is that we are never allowed to forget world poverty for long, although of course we can get hardened to it. When we read psalms that rejoice in God's harvest provision, such as 67 and especially 65, we need to remember that the world community now has the technical ability to feed the poor in areas of famine. The resources and distribution possibilities are there, but have we the will?[243] Unhappily there are areas where civil strife makes the task very difficult, but all that can be done should be done.

Commenting on the fact that Psalm 8 begins and ends with God and his majesty in all the earth, J. C. McCann has well said, "To focus on the boundaries of Psalm 8 without an awareness of the center is escapist; human beings do have a central role in the created order. The greater danger, however, is that

---

240. See Sargent, *Animal Rights and Wrongs*.

241. See R. J. Berry, ed., *Care of Creation*; Bouma-Prediger, *For the Beauty*; Campolo, *How to Rescue the Earth*; Osborn, *Guardians of Creation*; Snyder, *Liberating the Church*.

242. Brown, *Seeing the Psalms*, 165.

243. See Sider, *Rich Christians*.

we focus on the center without an awareness of the boundaries. To put human dominion at the center of things without the context of God's sovereignty is positively dangerous."[244]

It is perhaps significant that Psalm 104, which has much to say about God's provision of food and water for his animal creation, refers to the fact that human beings must work to secure their food from what God has provided (v. 14; cf. v. 23), although the emphasis is still, as in 65:9-13, on the bounty of God's provision.[245]

Christians Should Be Concerned about Issues of Abortion and Euthanasia

Psalm 139 is remarkable for its relevance to two issues that are centers of debate today, but that were not so when the psalm was written. Verses 13-16 begin with the statement, "For you created my inmost being" (the word "you" is emphatic in the Hebrew), and they end with the words, "All the days ordained for me were written in your book before one of them came to be" (v. 16).

If we read the passage in its context, we see that it illustrates that God is all-seeing. What happens in the womb occurs out of human sight, but there a wonderful divine work is taking place and a new person is brought into being. The constant use of the first person singular is a marked feature of this psalm, and we can hardly miss the fact that the human fetus is here regarded as a living human being.

The closing statement of the passage also holds a message for today. If it is God who ordains our days, what place can there be for euthanasia? The expression "to play God" is therefore particularly apt when used in this connection.[246]

The Word of God Has an Important Place in Godly Counseling

This is a day when counseling is often offered to those who have been through traumatic experiences. People who have experienced sudden, shocking bereavement, or who have been taken hostage, or who have been threatened

244. McCann, *Theological Introduction*, 59.

245. For reflections on the theology of work, see Moltmann, "Right to Work"; idem, *God in Creation;* and Volf, *Work of the Spirit.*

246. For a Christian approach to abortion, see O'Donovan, *Begotten or Made?;* and to euthanasia, Cameron, ed., *Death without Dignity.*

with death, are assigned a counselor to whom they can talk. Often the sufferer says much more than the counselor, for one of the main concerns of this service is to get people to talk and not to bottle up their feelings about what has happened.

The Psalms can be of real help here. God is the greatest healer, and one of the ways he heals us inwardly is through his Word. Because the Psalms emphasize believing experience, they are peculiarly fitted to help us if we are Christians. A psalm like 88, which is an immensely powerful lament, shows the psalmist coming to God in the midst of his depression. At one level it may appear to offer no remedy, for the prayer seems to go unanswered. Yet the very fact that it is a prayer is an answer in itself.[247] We see that, like the psalmist, we should go to God with our problems, no matter how deep they are, and not retreat into some corner to lick our wounds. Also, its very presence in the Word of God reveals God's concern and shows that, in such experiences, the sufferer is not alone, for the psalmist has been that way too. This does not mean, of course, that there is no place for the psychiatrist or psychologist, as there are psychiatric and psychological illnesses that make the services of such a person highly desirable.

Many people would never admit to vulnerability. McCann says that many of us live in a culture where the highest virtue is autonomy. "We are taught to be self-reliant, self-made. Our goal is to be self-fulfilled, self-actualized. Wanting or needing help is a sign of weakness. The psalmist's perspective . . . helps us to understand why one of the most highly developed, healthiest, wealthiest, and most intellectually sophisticated societies in the history of the world consistently fails to produce people who are 'happy.'"[248]

Dennis Sylva seeks to combine the insights of psychology and Scripture in what he calls "theotherapy," and he focuses on the way seven psalms can help parents cope with stress in their families. He says, "The psalms are well-suited both for relieving the stress that hinders the care of children and for promoting emotional health because the psalms are literature in which the emotions of a people come to expression. What enters into the psalm is raw emotion. What emerges from the psalm is emotion guided by faith in God."[249] He has chapters on Psalm 131 and emotional security, Psalm 23 and the child's confidence in relationships, Psalm 117 and what we mean by God's steadfast love and faithfulness, Psalm 107 and how we perceive God's steadfast love, Psalm 92 and the question as to where God's steadfast love and faithful-

---

247. See Brueggemann's exposition, *Message of Psalms*, 78-81.
248. McCann, *Theological Introduction*, 40.
249. Sylva, *Psalms and Transformation*, 9.

ness are when we pass through difficult times, Psalm 62 and verbal violence, and Psalm 133 and God as the divine unifier.

God Is Lovingly Concerned with the Whole Human Race

When we consider the Psalms, it might seem most unlikely that concern with the whole human race should be seen in them. After all, it is likely that they were all written by men and that all these men were Jewish.

Do the Psalms relate at all to distinctively female concerns? On the face of it they conform to the stereotypes of a male-oriented society, but with no trace of chauvinistic demeaning of women. There are references to motherhood and especially to the physical links between mother and child (22:9-10; 71:6; 139:13), along with an allusion to labor pains (48:6). The queen is told to honor the king, who is called "your lord," but there is honor also for the women of the king's household (45:9), and the queen-elect as she comes to her wedding is described as "all glorious" (45:13).

Psalm 51:5, "Surely I was sinful at birth, sinful from the time my mother conceived me," should not be misunderstood as if it traces sin to the woman's part in procreation. The verse is in synonymous parallelism and a reference to conception following the mention of birth is quite natural. Moreover, if instead the psalmist had referred to begetting by the father, this might have suggested to the reader an illicit sexual act. The verse comes in a heartfelt confession of personal sin, and the intention is to show the psalmist's awareness that sin was part of his whole personal history from the very moment of its beginning.

In considering the strong biblical tradition that links David to the composition and encouragement of psalmody, we should note that, at least in godly circles, the society into which he was born was one where male leadership was combined with the real honoring of godly women. In the period of the judges, immediately prior to the early kingdom period, we find Deborah the prophetess and see the loving courtesy of Boaz toward Ruth and Naomi. Hannah too is most sympathetically presented in the opening chapters of 1 Samuel, and even Jael's act in assassinating Sisera is extolled. In discussions of the morality of the act, that it was a woman's act and yet it is praised (not only by Deborah but by Barak, Judg 5:1, 24-27) should not be overlooked.

The appalling treatment of a Levite's concubine recorded in Judges 19 appears in a context (Judg 17–21) where the author is exploring the deep spiritual and moral malaise affecting the people of Israel during the period of the judges. It is clear therefore that this whole event was seen by him as evidence of deep moral depravity. The opening of the book of Ruth, "In the days when the judges ruled" (Ruth 1:1), could have been intended to recall for the reader the closing chapters of Judges and to show that this was not the whole story. Joyce Baldwin writes appropriately, "In a society dominated by men it is significant that the book should have been written about two women, whose initiatives brought about the action, and whose faith was rewarded."[250]

In a volume written to view the Psalter through the lens of intertextuality, Beth Tanner seeks to show how the Psalms can minister to women when read through or in tandem with some other OT passage. Her treatment of Psalm 112 in the light of Proverbs 31 and her most moving exposition of Psalm 88 in the light of Judges 19 justifies her comment, "These songs in their final form are written by men for men. Yet despite this, because their content speaks from the heart, women have been able to transcend the language barrier and find themselves in these texts."[251]

The psalmists are sure that children are a gift of God (113:9; 127:3-4) and that when godly parents are blessed by God, their children too will enjoy that blessing (17:14; 72:4; 102:28). The strong emphasis of Deuteronomy on the importance of teaching children the word and ways of God is found here too (Pss 34:11; 78:4-8; cf. Deut 4:9; 6:4-9, etc.), and people of all ages, including children, are to join together in the praise of God (Ps 148:7-12; cf. 8:2). This shows the importance of the godly family, and has clear relevance to modern society in which in so many ways marriage and family life are under threat. It indicates too that responsible Christian parenthood means that the home has an important place in training for life. Children may be educated in the arts and sciences at their schools, but Christian parents are responsible for seeing that Christian truth and Christian values are lovingly conveyed in the context of home life, especially when these are not only ignored but both openly attacked and subtly undermined in modern society.[252]

The particularism of the OT, the selection of a particular nation for divine blessing, may appear to raise problems for modern ways of thinking. From Psalm 2 onward, the nations are often presented as being at enmity with Israel, and in a psalm like 83 the psalmist asks the Lord to deal severely with them. Is this racism?

Despite appearances to the contrary, we must answer no. Certainly the Psalter shares the general OT conviction that Yahweh has a special relationship with and purpose for Israel, but it recognizes that there are enemies of

---

250. Baldwin, "Ruth," 287.
251. Tanner, *Psalms,* 142.
252. For a discussion of the imprecation in 137:8-9, see the comment on this psalm.

God within the nation as well as outside it. Moreover, this particularism is for the larger good ultimately. Psalm 87 prophesies a time when people of many nations, including bitter enemies of Israel, will be recorded as citizens of Zion (cf. Isa 19:23-25),[253] and many psalms show concern for people of all nations to join in praise of the only true God (96:1-3; 100:1; 148:7-12), and they are sure that all will ultimately experience his just rule (67:4; 96:10-13; 98:9).

There is clearly a religious particularism in the Psalms, for the psalmists know that there is a real difference between truth and error, but that people of all nations are eventually to benefit from the blessings Israel has found in its God. The Christian gospel and the Great Commission of Christ to go into all the world and declare the good news are the ultimate expression of this.

We Need Realistically to Recognize the Sin Factor in Human Society

The Psalms recognize the presence of sin in the hearts of human beings and are convinced of God's judgment on it. This finds an important place in Psalm 1, which has an introductory function in relation to the whole book.

The absoluteness of this book and the way it often refers to "the righteous" and "the wicked" suggests clear-cut distinctions that we might see as foreign to modern ways of thinking, but would we be right? There is a tendency for the media to idolize certain people and to demonize others. What newspapers and television often seem to find difficult to handle are evidences of good traits in a person they have presented as anything but good, or the reverse. In times of war it is unacceptable to find anything good in the enemy or anything bad in ourselves. To see the world simply in terms of "the goodies" and "the baddies" might suggest the outlook of a person who has not graduated beyond the stage of childhood games.

Yet is this the way the psalmists viewed life? It might appear so at first. We need, however, to enter several riders. First of all the Psalms rightly insist that there is a real difference between right and wrong. Evil conduct is not good in the making. Then the psalmists operate with theological criteria. A righteous person is one in tune with the purpose of God, and a wicked one is a rebel against God. The enemy may be regarded as a sinner, but this is not simply because of his enmity to the psalmist but because of his enmity to God, even though this may express itself chiefly in his treatment of the psalm-

---

253. David Smith comments on the way, in this psalm, "a conventional description of the glories of Zion . . . is then suddenly and dramatically transformed" and gives place to the registering of people of many nations as citizens of that city (*Against the Stream*, 136).

ist. This theological perspective is of immense importance. Then the psalmist himself from time to time indicates his consciousness of personal sin and also that sin can be forgiven. There is a deep theology of personal sin in Psalm 51. Here the psalmist certainly does not profess to be one of the "goodies," but to have offended deeply against his God.

There is no doubt that the Psalms regard human beings as responsible for their moral defects and aberrations. We have no means of telling what the psalmists may have said about those who commit crimes because of severe mental problems or in some way because of diminished responsibility, but there is little doubt that it is for the victims that they show considerable care. A society in which much or even all crime is traced to mental problems is again a world utterly different from that of the psalmists, and they will not allow us an optimistic view of human nature. The weak doctrine of sin that characterized almost all versions of liberal theology, and against which Barth and other theologians reacted, has no place in the Psalms or in biblical teaching generally. Morally, the biblical writers call a spade a spade.

The realism of passages in the Psalms that assert the universality of sin needs to be taken into account when we think of the social and political problems of our world. An ideal society does not exist. Concepts of a utopian society, such as in James Hilton's *Lost Horizon* and J. B. Priestley's *They Came to a City,* belong to a different kind of thinking from what has prevailed since World War II. The advent of the nuclear age and the downfall of communism in country after country, a virtual domino effect, has shown clearly that human efforts at a totally egalitarian society tend to come to grief. Aldous Huxley's *Brave New World,* George Orwell's *Animal Farm* and *Nineteen Eighty Four,* and Arthur Koestler's *Darkness at Noon* were all, when they were written, eloquent pointers to a change of mood.

The psalmist refers to following "the counsel of the wicked," and sets over against this meditating on the *tôrâ* of the Lord (1:1-2). There are a large number of avenues through which the counsel of the wicked may reach us today. This may come through personal conversation, or, sadly, through influences from family or friends. It may come through the kind of advertising that appeals to low motives or that seeks to entice the viewer or reader by the implication, more or less explicit, that sexual gratification awaits the person who buys the product. It may come by stories that make no moral distinctions or promote ungodly attitudes and conduct. School teachers should not resent but should expect from parents a measure of moral scrutiny of the values they promote.

For Moltmann and other "theologians of hope," the future is open, and an important function of theology is to effect change. So, for Moltmann and

Brueggemann and other similar Christian thinkers, theology must be the basis of a social and political program of action. This is a salutary reminder that there is no area of life that can be left unaffected if we take the Word of God seriously, but we must remember too that the modern world has known oppressive regimes at both poles of the political sphere.

Do the Psalms then recognize structural sin, the organizing of society in evil, unjust ways? Perhaps 82 comes closest to this if, as I have argued, the "gods" here are human judges.[254] Their duty is to administer impartial justice and to defend the weak and defenseless. Judicial systems and their administration need to be looked at in the light of this. If there are underclasses in society, no matter whether they are the poor or immigrants or those of a minority race, language, or culture, they must receive justice equally with others. There can be no place, for example, for a police force that is biased against any particular racial or social group in a society where the God of the psalmists is honored. Psalm 94:20 asks the question, "Can a corrupt throne be allied with you — one that brings on misery by its decrees?" The answer to this question is not only self-evident but is spelled out in the psalm in terms of divine repayment of such rulers for their sins.[255]

The world of the psalmists is very much the real world. There is no attempt to anaesthetize situations where people are hurting. As we read the Psalms we are exposed to the cries of the oppressed. It is possible perhaps to get used to these, but not to the same extent as happens in modern life when some find it hard to distinguish real suffering presented on television from what may be seen in the latest film. To see this kind of thing in newsreels on occasional visits to the cinema is one thing; to encounter it every day on the television quite another.

The psalmists constantly inveigh against those who bend the truth for their own ends. Christians should demand truthfulness and an end to "spin" in government at every level. Deceit is an offense to God. We should also seek to promote the idea that a leader's character is far more important than his ability to make a good case in the nation's legislative assembly and certainly more important than the image he presents in interviews on television. Our memories must be short if we cannot recall world leaders who came over brilliantly on the media but whose characters did not bear serious investigation.

McCann gives a devastating resume of the anaesthetizing power of modern culture in the midst of a world bearing the marks of evil everywhere:

254. See comment on Ps 82.

255. For challenging studies of these issues see Gushee, ed., *Towards a Just and Caring Society*; and Nicholls and Wood, eds., *Sharing the Good News*.

"Strangely in this most brutal and frightening of eras, we have forgotten how violent and vulnerable we are, due perhaps to our vast scientific knowledge, our dazzling technology, our increasing life-spans, our abundance of possessions. We have forgotten who we are; it is an identity crisis of global proportions."[256]

God Calls Us to Penitence and Offers Forgiveness to the Truly Penitent

What about experiences of personal sin, when we become aware that we have offended God? The penitential psalms will obviously relate to us at such times. It is notable that men like Augustine and Luther, both looking back with deep penitence on past wrongdoing, found great help in Psalm 51. Bullock, however, introduces a note of caution, stressing that the Psalms do not show confession simply as in itself a form of therapy but that they couple it with divine forgiveness.[257] Diagnosis is one thing, but it is healing we need, and in this realm only God, the God of the psalmists and of Christ, can administer this. Bullock suggests we consult Psalm 32.[258] In this psalm there is a deep consciousness of sin, but also a clear awareness of forgiveness, so clearly expressed that Paul refers to the opening of this psalm when writing of justification by faith in Rom 4:7-8.

The sense of sin revealed in Psalm 51 is profound, but it is somewhat surprising that the Psalter contains comparatively few penitential psalms. A possible reason for this may be suggested. Many a preacher has found that the proclamation of the cross produces the deepest awareness of personal sin. Here we see what our sin did to the Son of God, and this gives us a devastating glimpse into our own hearts. Conviction of sin, at the deepest level, awaited the coming of Christ. His life of purity and compassion reveals our many-sided failure, but it is his death that stirs us most deeply not only to an awareness of our sin but to a deep desire to be rid of it.

The Davidic Psalms Show One Person's Humanity from the Divine Perspective

The interest in David shown in the Psalter, with psalms of David dominating book 1, having a considerable presence in book 2, being at least represented in

---

256. McCann, *Theological Introduction*, 94.
257. Bullock, *Psalms*, 1:143.
258. Ibid.

books 3 and 4, and then emerging again as a group fairly late in book 5, has significance for theological anthropology. Gerald Sheppard says that when we view the Psalms as Scripture, this feature helps us to see the humanity of one person from a divine perspective. "The Psalms, in their depiction of David's humanity, are reminiscent of wisdom literature, for they provide a 'God's eye view' of the interplay of trouble and tranquility in a particular human life."[259] Moreover, despite the fact that David was a king, there is no attempt to glorify him in any way. He is presented (or perhaps, if we see him as the author of the psalms that bear his name, we should rather say that he presents himself), as he is in the books of Samuel, warts and all. McCann points out that 2 Samuel 11 shows David breaking fully half the Ten Commandments. So we can see that "what is determinative in the story is not David's character but rather God's character," as indicated in 2 Sam 7:15. It is notable that in Psalm 51 it is to God's character that David appeals.[260]

Because Jesus is "the son of David" (Matt 1:1), we often compare and contrast David with him, which encourages us to move on from the Psalms and the books of Samuel to the NT Gospels.

Christ's Person and Work

The Psalter is quoted and alluded to more often in the NT than any other OT book, and it is evident that the NT writers considered it a major source of testimony to Christ. Some important hermeneutical questions about its use in the NT have already been addressed from a biblical theology perspective. Now we must address questions that arise for modern thinkers about this.

Typological and Predictive Witnessing to Christ
Have a Supernatural Dimension

Much of the witness of the Psalms to Christ is in terms of typology. Can typology be supported as a valid way of interpreting the Psalms in the twenty-first century? To help us to answer this question, we must analyze what typology involves. For the NT there can be little doubt that there are four factors in the relationship between an OT type and its NT antitype: similarity (e.g., Christ is like David in certain ways), difference (he is also in cer-

---

259. Sheppard, "Theology," 148.
260. McCann, *Theological Introduction*, 102.

tain ways unlike David), finality (he is the final expression of David's kind of function in God's plan), and divine intention (God intended David to fore-shadow Christ).[261]

Now most of us recognize similarity and difference between historical characters. Edmund Burke's remark after the Younger Pitt's first speech in the House of Commons, "Not merely a chip off the old block, but the old block itself," might be quoted in this respect, although of course family likeness was a factor. Of greater significance perhaps is that all kinds of identifications have been made of the antichrist, especially from Napoleon onward, while at the same time there are obvious differences between the persons so identified.

Finality is in a different category. We may of course recognize progress without finality. Was Einstein really a better scientist than Newton, or was his apparently greater quality due mostly to the fact that he was able both to build on Newton's discoveries and to modify Newton's theories? He would be a bold man who treated any human figure as final. Even in evolutionary terms, Herbert Spencer, the philosopher of evolution, believed that once evolution had reached a point of equilibrium there would be an inevitable retrogression. Hegel's assertion that in his philosophy the Absolute had finally come to full understanding of himself is not only almost unbelievable hubris, but is also denied by the fact that philosophy did not come to a dead stop with his system.

Biblical typology most fully shows its uniqueness, however, in the matter of divine intention. The NT writers evidently believed that David, for instance, was divinely intended to anticipate in his kingly office the greater kingship of Christ. This kind of thing is worked out most fully in the Epistle to the Hebrews, and it is of interest that it is in that epistle that there is particularly full use of the book of Psalms.

Here then is an aspect of typology that confronts the scholar with a theological decision, and this impinges on the question of supernaturalism, which comes still more to the fore in relation to prediction. It is true that typology is far more frequent than prediction in the NT use of the Psalms, but the latter is not altogether lacking, as we see from the interpretations of Psalms 16 and 110 in the NT, and also, perhaps in the case of Psalm 22.[262] Whether or not this great psalm should be regarded as typology or prediction, the extent of correspondence between it and the sufferings experienced by Christ is quite remarkable, and, even if it is typology, suggests a strong supernatural element in the communication of this psalm to and through its author.

261. See Grogan, "Relationship."
262. See comments on Ps 22.

There is no way in which the issue of the supernatural can be bypassed. If a theologian has experienced the grace of God as a supernatural power changing his or her inner motives and outward actions in a decisive way, this is an inner witness to the supernatural that clearly points to a supernatural dimension in the dealings of God with humanity through Christ. If the inner work of the Holy Spirit is supernatural, can we deny a supernatural dimension to that revelation in Christ to which such an inner work is a divinely induced response?

This Witness to Christ Makes Extensive Use of Analogy

The Psalms make use of many analogies in their references to God, and quite a number of these are applied in the NT to Christ. Both God and Christ are called shepherd, judge, light, redeemer, eagle, rock, and so on. What is the status of these descriptions? This issue of analogy is one that theologians have wrestled with through the ages. It was a major concern of Thomas Aquinas and in modern times has interested the neo-Thomist school.

Tillich had his own distinctive approach to this matter. He maintained that the only ontological statements we may make about God are that he is "Being" and "Ground of Being." All else is symbolic, so that this applies not only to inanimate images like rock, but to animate ones like lion and eagle, and even to human ones such as shepherd, judge, and father. These are not, he held, ultimate descriptions of God in his essential being. Tillich's thought is complex, and it is open to the charge of pantheism. It is difficult for his theology to evade this designation.

The world of the Psalms and the world of Tillich's theology are poles apart. A much deeper factor in the Psalms than any one designation of God or even of all of them put together is the psalmist's awareness that there was a definitely personal relationship between himself and God. He could praise and worship God, he could mourn and complain to God, he could even argue with God. There were times when he simply ached to be at the house of God to meet with God and worship him. An impersonal Ground of Being can hardly offer that level of relationship. Is there any suggestion that there might be a level "beyond" this personal relationship, a level where in place of fellowship there is absorption? The Psalter totally lacks this. To see such absorption as gain rather than loss is closer to Buddhism than to the faith of the psalmists.

Of course, the distinctive use of these analogical terms in the NT is in application to Christ, who, according to Christian theology, was both God and man. They serve to give vividness and important links with the OT, and therefore with the book of Psalms. In any case the kind of issues raised by Tillich have now been largely bypassed and are not in the center of theological interest today, although, as C. S. Lewis clearly saw, tendencies toward pantheistic thinking constantly resurface. The interest has now shifted to the whole matter of revelation through literature that has been raised by various types of linguistic philosophy.

Christ Is the Ideal Human Being

Some passages in the Psalter extol the ideal man or king, and they awaited the coming of Christ before these ideals were fully expressed in an actual human life. For instance, Psalm 1 sets forth the ideal of human godliness (cf. also Ps 112). Psalm 1 is not quoted or alluded to clearly in the NT, but if Christ fulfills all ideals, he fulfills this. Psalm 72 extols the virtues of the ideal king and this too can easily be applied to him. He fulfills not only all the aspirations of human beings but the standards of God, and entrance psalms like 15 and 24 too find complete realization in his character.

The Greeks had their ideals, and they sought both in their philosophy and also in their art to capture these. The philosophy of Nietzsche with its concept of the superman, the musical drama of Wagner, and the theories of *Herrenvolk* put forth by Nazi Germany, no matter how profoundly misguided some of these may have been, all sought to set forth a particular ideal of humanity. There are also physical ideals promoted in some of the popular magazines of today, and Superman and other fictional heroes meet us through the television screen. In some Western societies the ideal of the self-made man and the view that confidence is what is expected of the ideal are formative social concepts.

Alongside these "ideals," the psalmists may seem quite inadequate. What they show us is that human nature is vulnerable. It is important for us to accept this reminder, for many a human ideal has been shattered in the eyes of the observer when there has been unexpected evidence of vulnerability and of feet of clay in one who seemed to be pure gold. According to the NT, pure gold in character is to be found in Christ alone. Here was a perfectly balanced character, whose focus was on the will and purposes of the Father he loved, quite literally, more than life itself.

This Ideal Is Shown in the Roles He Fulfills

Many of the psalms reflect a society in which there is oppression and where the enemies of the psalmist often seem to be free to rove the country seeking to do him harm. There have been such times in the history of almost every nation. It would, for instance, have been no joke to live in England during the reign of Stephen or during the Wars of the Roses, and no doubt many of the English subjects of monarchs like Henry II and Henry VII would often give thanks for the coming of strong government in place of strife and, at times, near anarchy. Israel was not exempt from such times, and in David's case there was lawlessness, rebelliousness against God's law, even in the heart of Saul his kingly enemy.

Psalm 72 extols the virtues of good government, and such government depends upon the recognition of God as the supreme ruler. Whether a country is a monarchy or a republic today, there needs to be recognition of an authority above that of the state if the ruling powers in the state are themselves to rule justly. Our age knows all too well what fearful crimes can go unchecked, or even be encouraged, under governments of both the extreme right and the extreme left who forget God, the supreme governor.

Psalm 72 reveals also the character qualities of the ideal king. He is of course an authority figure who is able to overcome the oppressor, but he does this not simply as a show of sheer power but in the interests of the weak. Psalm 21 shows that the king is established by God (much as in Ps 2) and also describes the powerful way in which he will deal with the wicked. In Psalm 72 this aspect is present, but the dominant note is the king's concern for the weak and helpless.

All good and godly leadership combines a strength that is able to translate authority into power with compassion for those who are weak. This reflects the character of God. Each of the Gospels, and perhaps most of all the Gospel of Luke, show us the very incarnation of that kind of leadership, that kind of kingship, in the ministry of Christ, but the NT also makes clear that he will act in judgment in association with his second advent.

The Psalms can furnish good, challenging models for leadership at every level, whether in the state, in the courts, in business, in education, in the home, or in the church. Christians need to do some hard thinking about leadership issues when it comes not only to their personal conduct but to the kind of people for whom they vote. We can have no less a model than Christ himself.

Many of us have dictionaries of quotations on our bookshelves, and these testify to our belief in the importance of the spoken or written word. The power to utter thought in words is a great gift from God to human beings, but this gift has often been misused. The importance of truth is often highlighted in the Psalms, and the OT prophetic movement is not without its representatives among the psalmists. David is viewed in both Testaments as having a prophetic function (2 Sam 23:1-2; Acts 2:30), and there are prophetic oracles in several of the psalms (e.g., in 81:8-10; 95:7b-11). Christ's ministry too was prophetic, and, because of his perfect character, he was able to illustrate his message fully in the kind of person he was. Nothing could be more appropriate than to call him not simply "the prophet of Nazareth" (Matt 21:11) but the very Word of God incarnate (John 1:1-18). In him the truth so extolled in the Psalms is communicated in the totality of a human Life.

The priest was another important figure in Israel. Psalm 110 refers to the mysterious figure of Melchizedek who blessed Abraham (Gen 14), and, taking the concept of a valid priesthood beyond the tribe of Levi and the family of Aaron, speaks of a priest of Melchizedek's distinctive order. The Epistle to the Hebrews proclaims that he has come in Jesus and spells out the significance of this for his people. Through Christ's final sacrifice, Peter says, we are brought to God (1 Pet 3:18), and "bringing to God" certainly sounds like a reference to the work of a priest. In some of the communal psalms, such as 44, the writer utters the laments and petitions of the community to God. So in heaven itself Christ is the great intercessor (Rom 8:34; Heb 7:23-25; 1 John 2:1-2), offering prayer on behalf of all his people as their high priest.

Christ Is God's Great Redeemer Who Effects Liberty for God's People

The Psalms use the language of salvation and redemption, almost but not entirely in relation to deliverance from enemies, whether national as at the Red Sea or both national and personal as in the psalms of David. We have noted already that there are some hints of a deeper need and a profounder redemption in the Psalms,[263] but even the physical terminology itself, by the principle of typology, can point to the deeper understanding of salvation that we meet in the NT.

Is it possible, though, for this language of physical redemption to be treated as valid in its own right? Is there room for the approach of the liberation theologians in our understanding of the Psalms? The liberationists take God's attitude to Israel, captive in Egypt, as a model for God's concern for the poor and oppressed in every society. It has given birth also to such

---

263. See esp. comment on Ps 130.

movements as black theology and was also one of the sources of feminist theology.[264]

The answer to that question must be both affirmative and negative. The Psalms show a great concern for justice, and they look to God as the ultimate ground of all justice. It is true that when this is developed on a national level the concern is about the oppression of Israel by other nations, but the Psalms also indicate an extension of God's positive concern to others, so that some may be born in Zion who belong to other nations (87:1-7). It is noticeable, however, that this is through their being brought into contact with Israel/Judah.

We are therefore operating in something of a gray area. We might argue either way. Are we to interpret the Psalms through Exodus or through Romans? Both, but chiefly through Romans, for we are NT Christians and we inherit the NT writers' approach to the OT. Nevertheless, the attitude of God toward people does not change, so that we can be sure he is concerned about the oppressed.

As we have noticed already, it is surprising that there is comparatively little about sacrifice in the Psalms. This is probably because it is the personal, inward aspect of worship that is most to the fore in them. It is interesting that Psalms 50 and 51 are set side by side, for both refer to sacrifice. Psalm 50 combats the baalized idea that the Deity needs the sacrifices as food, while in 51 the psalmist recognizes that in his case it is contrition rather than sacrifice that God requires. Then in other material the concept of sacrifice is, if not exactly spiritualized, yet dealt with in such a way that the inward motivation matters more than simply the physical aspects. This is true in the quotation and comment on Psalm 40 in Heb 10:5-10. It is notable that Calvin draws attention to the fact that even in his death it is the willing obedience of Christ that is important.[265]

Christ's Work Is Necessary to Secure Full Assurance for Believers

The psalmists are somewhat ambivalent as far as their personal assurance is concerned. They have considerable assurance concerning God's great acts in the past and infer from them his consistency and his firmness, but there is

---

264. See Boff and Boff, *Introducing Liberation Theology;* Atherton, ed., *Social Christianity;* and, for evaluation, Armerding, ed., *Evangelicals and Liberation;* and Grenz and Olson, *Twentieth-Century Theology,* 200-236.

265. Calvin, *Institutes* 2.16.5.

also a lack of personal security at times, which suggests that something like the objectivity and finality of the work of Christ is necessary for the securing of this. So there is a gap here that points forward to the NT consummation of teaching. Of course, the NT itself indicates that Christ's atonement has retrospective as well as prospective effect (Rom 3:25; Heb 9:15-16), but inward assurance of forgiveness is related not only to the fullness of Christ's atonement for sin but also to our awareness of it, and in the nature of the case this in its fullness awaited the revelation given in the NT.

The Psalms May Be Viewed as the Prayers and Praises of Christ

If Christ is to be found in the Psalms, can we understand them as his prayers and praises? Many have suggested this, including Bonhoeffer: "The Psalter is the vicarious prayer of Christ for his congregation."[266] If Jesus sums up in himself the godly experience of God's people, then both the great cries of the psalmists and their fervent praises can be viewed as in a sense his, and we find him using some of them in the Gospel accounts.

This does not mean, of course, that we can apply every detail of the laments and psalms of praise to him, but we can make application of them in general principle. When we hear him giving thanks and saying, "I praise you, Father, Lord of heaven and earth, because you have hidden these things from the wise and learned, and revealed them to little children" (Luke 10:21), we are reminded of the deep thankfulness of the psalmists to God for his revelation of himself and also for the fact that he is not the God of those who are great in human estimation but has a constant concern for the poor and needy.

When too we hear him take up the words of Ps 22:1, "My God, my God, why have you forsaken me?" (Mark 15:34), we find in them all the deepest questions human beings have ever asked, questions about the nature of God, about the existence of evil, and about the meaning of suffering, questions that come to the fore in many psalms, but are all here focused in one agonized cry. Psalm 22 ends with the vindication of the sufferer and the consequent praise he offers in the midst of the worshiping congregation, but it shows us that even the darkest passages in the Psalms may shine with light when seen in relation to Christ. So Brueggemann says of Psalm 88 that it "shows us that the cross is about: *faithfulness* in scenes of *complete* abandonment."[267] George

266. Bonhoeffer, *Life Together*, 55.
267. Brueggemann, *Message of Psalms*, 81.

MacDonald wrote movingly about the experience of abandonment in the experience of the crucified Christ.[268]

The evangelists Matthew and Mark clearly saw great importance in Christ's utterance of that terrible cry in the words of the psalm. Seven utterances of the crucified Christ are recorded in the Gospels. Luke and John record three each, but Matthew and Mark have only this cry of dereliction. It looks as if they viewed it not only as evidence of the depth of suffering endured by Christ but also as having special theological importance. We recall passages like Mark 10:45, "The Son of Man did not come to be served but to serve, and to give his life as a ransom for many," and Mark 14:24, "This is my blood of the covenant, which is poured out for many," which form part of its overall literary context, and these passages have their Matthean equivalents.

Paul's theology of the cross focuses on the bearing of our penalty by Christ as God incarnate. Certainly the NT views the work of Christ on the cross from many different angles, but its penal nature is central.[269] Tom Wright also recognizes the great importance of the cross, but he "suggests" (this is his word) that we view the central category for interpreting it as "the decisive victory over the 'principalities and powers,'" and he goes on to say, "Nothing in the many other expressions of the meaning of the cross is lost if we put this in the centre."[270] To discuss this issue fully would take us beyond the limits of this commentary, but John Stott is surely right in commenting on Col 2:13-15, "Is not the payment of our debts the way in which Christ has overthrown the powers? By liberating us from these, he has liberated us from them."[271] Sin and death are dear to Satan, and in bearing our penalty in his death, Christ has dealt with both.

Patrick Miller points out the importance of deciding whether particular psalms are laments or petitions, whether the emphasis in them is on articulation of a sense of need or on the hope of divine intervention. The importance of this distinction is that in the first the sufferer seeks to share his suffering with God, to know God's fellowship in it, while in the second he looks to him to deliver him from it. He then says that the cross and resurrection suggest that "we would seem to be compelled to try to hold complaint and petition together."[272]

The cross is unique as an atoning work, but as a human experience of Christ, and especially in what the cry of dereliction tells us about this, we find

---

268. See Lewis, *George MacDonald*, 33-34.

269. See Stott, *Cross of Christ;* and Tidball, *Message of the Cross.*

270. Wright, *What Saint Paul Really Said*, 47.

271. Stott, *Cross of Christ*, 234-35.

272. Miller, *Interpreting Psalms*, 9.

him entering into and going beyond all that caused the laments of his people. Then the resurrection is the ultimate answer to the petitions in the Psalms, for in it every situation of need is forever overcome, nullified, and transcended. Here and here alone we see God's total answer to every cry of his people for rescue, which is to be the experience of believers at Christ's return.

In the NT we find Jesus Christ uttering praise to his Father (Matt 11:25), but he is also himself the object of worship, for instance in Revelation 5, so that psalm-like hymns are used to worship him.[273] There certainly seems to be some reflection not of the actual words or even phrases but of the general themes of the Psalter in the hymns to be found in the book of the Revelation. The psalm-like features in Luke's early chapters are in poems directed to God, but they have Christ as their subject.

The Grace of God, the Work of the Holy Spirit, and the Christian Life

Christian theology is an indivisible whole. Often theologians, giving thought to one aspect of it, find they are being stimulated to think about other aspects too. In this respect it is not unlike a living organism, which may be divided up by the biologist for detailed study but which cannot be properly understood except in its integrated totality. It seems best to take the themes of grace, the work of the Spirit, and the Christian life together, for they are completely intertwined.

God Has Brought His People into Covenant Relationship with Himself

Walter Eichrodt, whose *OT Theology* marked the beginning of a new era in the study of the subject, viewed covenant as the overarching theme of the OT. His work was published in 1933, soon after Hitler came to power in Germany. Was this idea of a special people in a special relationship with God a reaction against the doctrine of an Aryan *Herrenvolk*, which was a major plank in the platform of National Socialism? It would not be difficult to make out a case for this, although there is plenty of evidence that he had been thinking and working along these lines long before this. In any case what matters is not so much the intellectual forces that stimulate the development of a concept but rather its truth or falsity.

Even those who are critical of Eichrodt usually acknowledge the impor-

---

273. On the worship of Christ in the NT, see particularly Hurtado, *Lord Jesus Christ.*

tance of the covenant concept in the OT, and this was fully acknowledged at the end of the twentieth century in a major OT theology, that of Brueggemann.[274] If it is important for the OT as a whole, we would expect this to be true of the book of Psalms, and so it proves to be.

The word חֶסֶד, *ḥesed* (love within a covenant relationship), is very important in the Psalter. It is basic to the way the psalmists viewed the relationship between themselves and their God. He had given them, as a people, a special link with himself through covenant. Covenant, the new covenant, is important to the Christian, and like the OT covenants, it is based on a sacrifice, in this case the death of Christ (Luke 22:20; Heb 8:6; 9:11-15). How different this is from National Socialism, where nature (the possession of a correct natural pedigree) was the criterion for membership in the special community!

The Relationship Is the Product of God's Grace but Involves Responsibilities for His People

The idea of a special people dependent on God's grace is not always welcomed by twenty-first-century people. The whole idea of divine election and God's refusal to accept sinners on the basis of what they can offer him is abhorrent to many. Where there is belief in God there is often a conviction, difficult to shake, as many a preacher has found, that it is possible to gain acceptance with him by self-motivated actions.

Some passages in the Psalms could be so read, but it is important to realize that the righteousness there referred to is not so much legal as relational. This issue was highlighted at the Reformation, when the Protestant position was codified in the various Reformation confessions and the Roman Catholic view in the decrees of the Council of Trent. There have been attempts in modern times to bring the two theological positions closer together, but with only limited success.

There has been much recent interest in the NT polemic against Pharisaic theology. E. P. Sanders and others have presented a somewhat different picture from that which appears in the Gospels, with covenant playing a more basic part than legalism.[275] This may have been the case with the major Pharisaic teachers, but the local synagogue officials seen in the Gospels certainly seem legalistic in outlook, and Christ's parable of the Pharisee and the tax collector (Luke 18:9-14) is difficult to interpret in any other way. Craig Blom-

---

274. Brueggemann, *Theology of the OT,* 27-31.
275. Sanders, *Paul, Law.*

berg is surely right when he says that such Pauline passages as Rom 4:4-5, Gal 3:10-14, and Phil 3:7-10 still read more naturally as contrasting faith and works in the more traditional Reformation sense of those terms.[276]

John Bright in *Covenant and Promise,* in which he deals with the future in the preaching of the preexilic prophets, develops a pattern of two principles in tension, a pattern found also and quite markedly in the Psalter. Both the Mosaic and Davidic covenants were covenants of God's grace, but in the Mosaic Israel's responsibilities were highlighted, while in the Davidic there was an emphasis on an immutable purpose of God. Bright says that the church also lives under both patterns of covenant: "It is the tension between grace and obligation."[277]

The psalmists are certainly aware of a relationship in which they may pray and enter into dialogue with God, even complain to him. Deryck Sheriffs's book, *The Friendship of the Lord,* is an interpretation of OT spirituality that highlights the prayer intimacy found there and especially in the Psalms, and Tim Chester's book on the biblical theology of prayer begins, "Prayer is the conversation of friends."[278]

In Christian thought, prayer is very much a relationship matter, grounded in the work of Christ, who, in his substitutionary sacrifice for the sins of his people, bore our penalty and opened the way into the presence of God: "For Christ died for sins once for all, the righteous for the unrighteous, to bring you to God" (1 Pet 3:18). This does not mean there is no interest in the non-Christian's prayers, but the focus is very much on the prayer life of the Christian believer, with its background of acceptance by God's grace.

The Life of Faith Is Individual, Corporate, and Articulate

Faith plays an important part in the Psalms, and many psalms that begin in lament end in trust. This forms an important background to the emphasis of the NT on faith. Christians today have the benefit of the full biblical revelation to shape their faith and the final evidence in Christ of God's faithfulness. We should therefore view the psalmists with great respect, for their faith rested on an earlier stage of divine revelation. They were without the great flood of light that has come through Christ's coming and particularly through his death and resurrection.

276. Blomberg, "Critical Issues," 58.
277. Bright, *Covenant and Promise,* 198.
278. Chester, *Message of Prayer,* 27.

The life of faith to which the psalmists were called was to be exercised within the covenant community. This means then that it had a social context. Presumably the faith of the individual was stimulated within the community's general faith life. This is similar to the way the faith of Christian believers is nurtured within the life of the local church, in which we are to provoke each other to love and to good works. There is danger, of course, that in emphasizing the importance of the church we may play down the importance of personal faith, but the Psalms teach us that individual faith is important.

How much is personal faith represented in modern theology? This issue often emerges in discussions about justification. Albrecht Ritschl, the nineteenth-century Protestant theologian, held that justification is properly applicable to the church rather than to the individual Christian. Some types of Barthian theology, with their emphasis on election as related primarily to Christ and then to the church as elect in him, moved in the same direction. Miroslav Volf comments on the strange omission of faith from the soteriology and ecclesiology of Zizioulas, which is from an Orthodox perspective. In his theology faith appears to have no important role.[279]

To seek to assess the "New Perspective on Paul," introduced by E. P. Sanders, and promoted with some variations by J. D. G. Dunn and Tom Wright, would take us far beyond the proper bounds of this commentary.[280] It might seem to reduce the place of faith, but whatever we think of this outlook as a whole, such a reduction is not necessarily involved in it. It is true, for instance, that Wright, following R. B. Hays, renders "the faith of Christ" (usually understood as "faith in Christ") as "the faithfulness of Christ," but it can be seen that his translation of Rom 3:22, which he renders as "God's righteousness, through the faithfulness of Jesus the Messiah, for all who believe," still finds an important place for faith.[281]

Many modern discussions of faith within the context of religious pluralism are concerned with such issues as secret belief and anonymous Christianity. The Psalms contribute nothing to such discussions, for many of them are fully articulated confessions of faith, testimonies to the faithfulness of God. Even in those where we find the faithful puzzled, it is still to the God of the biblical revelation that the psalmists come, which means that they are

---

279. Volf, *After Our Likeness*, 98.

280. See, e.g., Sanders, *Paul and Palestinian Judaism;* Dunn, *Jesus, Paul;* and Wright, *What Saint Paul Really Said,* which includes annotated bibliography, although much has been written since its publication. For a helpful critique, see Macleod, "New Perspective"; and for a more detailed one, Kim, *Paul and New Perspective;* also Das, *Paul, the Law.*

281. Wright, *What Saint Paul Really Said,* 128.

never entirely without faith, which they declare to others by the very act of writing their psalms.

The Most Important Fact about Faith Is Its Divine Object

Some of the more radical prosperity theologians have emphasized faith so greatly that it seems almost to have been given the supreme place in the universe that belongs to God alone. Indeed, some have even maintained that God exercises faith! The governmental view of the atonement, promoted by Hugo Grotius, who was both theologian and lawyer, and discernible to some extent in the theology of R. W. Dale, seems to many theologians to give an exaggerated place to the law, as if God becomes imprisoned in his own law. This view of faith, however, is an even more serious theological aberration, for it replaces objective truth with a subjective attitude. The exhortation "Name it and claim it!" seems little concerned as to what the "it" is; if it is desirable, faith can claim it.

In these days, when Eastern types of spirituality exercise a fascination for many Western people, we should not forget that there are Eastern religions, such as Bhakti Hinduism and Amida Buddhism, that stress faith, but not faith in the God of the psalmists, the God of Israel who is also the God and Father of our Lord Jesus Christ, but rather in Krishna, Rama, or Amida. We must never forget how important it is that, like the psalmists, the object of our faith should always and exclusively be the only God there is.

The Holy Spirit Is the Only Source of Spiritual Holiness

At the Reformation, the great issue was justification, but in the seventeenth and eighteenth centuries, alongside this, attention was directed to the inner work of the Spirit in regeneration and sanctification. The perspectives of the Puritans and Methodists as to this work were somewhat different, but both were greatly interested in the Spirit's work in the heart. The Holiness movement of the nineteenth century and the Pentecostal and Charismatic movements of the twentieth and twenty-first centuries have served to keep this interest in the Spirit's work alive. Where do the Psalms stand on this?

The psalmists are much concerned with conduct, and they recognize that outward conduct is the product of inner attitudes. The law in the heart, welcomed at the very source of human conduct, is usually associated with the new covenant passage in Jer 31:31-34, but it also features in Ps 40:6-8. There is great delight in the *tôrâ* in both Psalms 19 and 119.

Does this mean that the heart of the individual is the ultimate source of godly character? Not so. Psalm 104:30 refers to the work of the Spirit in creation, and in 51:10-12 the psalmist uses the language of creation in his prayer: "Create in me a pure heart, O God, and renew a steadfast spirit within me. Do not cast me from your presence or take your Holy Spirit from me. Restore to me the joy of your salvation and grant me a willing spirit, to sustain me." His reference to the Spirit's work as creative shows his profound awareness of his moral and spiritual inability. In Psalm 143 the psalmist is beset by enemies and cries to God for guidance. This is not simply a matter of being shown a safe route for escape but has a moral dimension, for his request to be led by God's Spirit on level ground follows his prayer, "Teach me to do your will" (143:10).

For us today, this means not only that the NT gospel cannot be reduced to a mere moralism with the emphasis on humanly generated moral reformation, but that this is true also for the Psalms. Always our God is ready to supply, in grace, what he demands, so that any measure of human holiness can never be a cause of self-satisfaction or self-righteousness but only of praise to him.

The Holy Spirit Uses Scripture as a Major Means of Grace in Sanctifying Us

There is a sanctifying power in all Scripture, for it is through the Word that we are presented with Christ and the Holy Spirit seeks to conform us to his image. God's purpose is, through his Word, to move us on to Christian maturity. In Eph 5:26 the holiness of the church is by "the washing with water through the word," and in 4:11 the agents of God's work in preparing his church, the apostles, prophets, evangelists, pastors and teachers, all employ the Word of God. McCann has well pointed out that the figure of the tree in Psalm 1 is rather like that of the body in the Pauline Epistles in that both develop toward maturity, both produce fruit, and grounding in Eph 4:11-16 means that we are not driven by the wind as the chaff is in Ps 1:4.[282]

The *tôrâ* in the Psalms can be understood either narrowly of the Law or more widely, as it tends to be interpreted in much contemporary exegesis, as a reference to the divine instruction as such. For the Christian this widening includes the NT, in which the instruction of God comes to its climax in the revelation of the Word of God incarnate. If we take Ps 1:2 seriously, there can be

---

282. McCann, *Theological Introduction*, 36-37.

no escape from a Bible-centered view of Christian development. The Christian church recognizes a multiplicity of divine means of grace, but the premier one is undoubtedly Holy Scripture, for through Scripture we are reminded of all the others, of baptism and the Lord's Supper, of prayer, of worship, of fellowship, of Christian service, and so on.

The sanctifying work of the Word of God finds a place of prominence in all three main psalms of the *tôrâ*. There is a particularly close link between the openings of Psalms 1 and 119, for both concentrate not simply on the Law but on the importance of walking in the way it indicates.

In Psalm 19 the *tôrâ* gives wisdom and enlightenment (vv. 7 and 8), and the great delight of the writer in God's Word is quite unmistakable. The Word also functions to warn the reader and to instruct her or him in the way God rewards (v. 11), which is so much in tune with 1:1.

That the *tôrâ* teaches its reader the way of godliness is the great theme of Psalm 119, binding it all together. It is particularly notable, though, that despite this, and despite the obvious love the psalmist has for the way of God thus revealed, the psalm ends on a note of failure, "I have strayed like a lost sheep. Seek your servant, for I have not forgotten your commands" (v. 176). Here then is God's means of sanctifying us, but we need to be aware of our weakness and liability to failure. The walk of the Christian should be characterized not only by obedience but by humility and a realization of his or her moral frailty.

The wisdom psalms have a place in our sanctification, for wisdom in the OT is always practical. It is knowledge of God put to practical use, which implies walking in his ways.

There is an important connection between the theology of the Psalms and their devotional use, for the purpose of times of devotion is not simply to give us good feelings but to shape our lives in accordance with the deeper understanding we receive through the devotional use of God's Word.[283] The Psalms teach us the nature and purposes of God and enable us to refocus, so that every part of life is lived in awareness of him. They show us our sin, for we often find in the psalmist's confession of personal failure a reminder of our own faults.

The Psalms show us too that we are not the only ones who face problems or who pass through times of sorrow, suffering, or perplexity, but that others have been that way before us and have been able to bring such trials to God, the same God we know through Christ. That so many of the laments re-

---

283. The volume *Praying by the Book,* ed. Bartholomew and West, shows how more recent study of the theology of the Psalter, when read as a unified book, can be devotionally stimulating.

veal that they are uttered in a context of trust and that some go on to praise God for answers to prayer in such circumstances both challenge and encourage us to trust ourselves to him.

If the will of God, articulated in the words of Holy Scripture, is God's provision for the daily life of the Christian, there is a response that she or he is to make in verbal form.[284] Hosea calls Israel to repentance: "Take words with you and return to the LORD. Say to him: Forgive all our sins and receive us graciously, that we may offer the fruit of our lips" (Hos 14:2).

Christian Faith Is Focused on Christ

Is this true of the Psalter? Yes, if it is true that it was put together with the express aim of encouraging the messianic hope. The great psalms of suffering, like 22 and 69, are applied to Christ in the NT, and each of them ends on a note of praise, for God has entered the situation and vindicated his faithful servant. Moreover, the perplexity of the psalmist in 89, where it seems to him that God has forgotten his promise to uphold David's kingly line, disappears as we find the messianic hope surfacing again in 110, 132, and 148.[285]

The Psalms must have entered deeply into the devotional life of Jesus himself, for often the deepest convictions of a person are reflected in his or her approach to death, and two of his seven utterances from the cross (Matt 27:46 and Luke 23:46) were taken from the Psalter (22:1 and 31:5). The probability is that 118 was the last passage of Scripture Jesus heard read before the crucifixion (possibly read aloud by himself), for it was always sung at the close of the Passover meal. It is worth reading it and reflecting on how it would have ministered to him in the closing hours of his life. To see this is to recall that God's Word read on a regular basis often proves relevant for what particular days bring. In this way the inspiration of Scripture and the providence of God in our lives come together.

The Psalms Are of Great Value for Personal Prayer

The whole liturgical movement implies the value for purposes of worship and devotion of godly words provided by others, and these are available for personal as well as for corporate prayer. What can be better than such words

---

284. See the comment on this in Mays, *Lord Reigns,* 40-41.
285. See the comments on each of these.

coming from Scripture itself, the words of the Psalms? So many guides to private prayer over the years have emphasized the value of the Psalms for this purpose. For example, Bonhoeffer asks, "Why do I meditate? Because I am a Christian. Therefore, every day in which I do not penetrate more deeply into the knowledge of God's Word in Scripture is a lost day for me," and no part of the Bible meant more to him than the Psalter.[286] There is an intimacy about them, and many passages focus on the great attributes and acts of God, so that they form a balanced means of grace for the Christian at prayer. Sheppard sees real value in the Psalm superscriptions: "Psalm superscriptions often describe the concrete circumstances that we, the readers or hearers of scripture, must know if we want to overhear a prayer in one moment of specific, realistic profundity," and he gives Psalm 52 as an example.[287]

Tim Chester points out that the use of the Psalms in the prayer lives of Christians tends to be selective. Referring to 137:8-9, 26:1, and 109:12, he comments, "While many people love the psalms because of the range of emotions they express, we baulk at the extremes. Praying with the psalmist is not straightforward."[288] In his study of the use of Psalm 2 in prayer, Chester makes two general points: "in Psalms we understand our experience as those who are in Christ" (so, for instance, we can identify with the psalmist's "righteousness" because we are righteous in Christ and only in him), and "in Psalms we understand our experience in the context of Christ's redemptive reign."[289] This means, for instance, that in our own experiences of the kind of disorientation the psalmists experienced and that was experienced most fully by Christ himself, we can look to God's final purpose and trust every situation to him.[290]

The Psalms Encourage the Christian to Face
the Realities of Life with God

Toward the close of *Evangelicalism in Britain 1935-1995,* Oliver Barclay says, "There are two main streams emerging in the evangelical community, and this division may prove more fundamental in its long-term effects than any

---

286. Bonhoeffer, *Meditating on the Word,* 30. Bonhoeffer's whole book is of particular value to preachers.

287. Sheppard, "Theology," 145.

288. Chester, *Message of Prayer,* 138-39.

289. Chester, *Message of Prayer,* 147-48.

290. There is much more than this in Chester's christological approach to this psalm; see Chester, *Message of Prayer,* 138-51.

other. It runs right across denominational divisions and any special-interest and party groupings. It is between those who make the Bible effectively, and not only theoretically, the mainstay of their ministry, and those who do not." He says that the former will produce strong realistic Christians, while the latter "are almost certain to produce vulnerable Christians or painfully dependent people, who dare not move out from the particular congregation where they have been supported unless they can go somewhere else where they will be equally propped up."[291] If what Barclay says is true, and I am sure it is, then the profoundly realistic book of Psalms is of special importance in this respect.

Christians face problems in their walk with God. John Taylor says of the exile, which, as we have seen, appears to have greatly influenced the form at least of books 3 and 4 of the Psalter, that Christians, even when fiercely persecuted, have found it very difficult to identify themselves with the exiles, and he points out that few hymns use its imagery. He then says, "This testifies to the buoyancy we derive from our faith in the resurrection of Jesus, but also, less happily, to a facile triumphalism which has disqualified us from entering into either the spiritual insights of Judaism or the Passion of God."[292] Later on he says,

> To leave the frightening questions unasked would be a denial of love and a surrender of all claim to faith, seeing that these are the questions which multitudes of people have been asking ever since they discovered that everything is *not* right. . . . When people wonder why God does not strike tyrants dead or prosper a virtuous man's business they are actually asking for another universe with a different purpose. They resemble David Garrick who *improved* Hamlet with a happy ending![293]

McCann too expresses concern: "The really raw edges of our lives and experience are often eliminated from conversations with God. They are reserved instead for conversations with the clinical psychologist or the family therapist or the marriage counselor or the social worker or perhaps even the lawyer or the judge."[294]

---

291. Barclay, *Evangelicalism in Britain,* 139.

292. Taylor, *Christlike God,* 18.

293. Taylor, *Christlike God,* 206.

294. McCann, *Theological Introduction,* 92. A. Fernando *(I Believe),* writing from an Asian Christian perspective, challenges Western Christians to be countercultural and to return from dependence on psychology, sociology, and pragmatism to the use of Scripture as their primary source of authority.

We must not forget that those who prayed the prayers we have in the book of Psalms were sinners, but neither should we assume that they had only their own comfort in view when they cried out to God in the midst of suffering. Perhaps on more occasions than we realize their prayers were motivated by a desire to be free to carry on their service to God, in some cases in the work of government, in others in the work of the house of God, and so on. This was certainly in view when the church, facing persecution, and taking its stand on Psalm 2, prayed, "Now, Lord, consider their threats and enable your servants to speak your word with great boldness" (Acts 4:23-31). They were eager to continue their work for him, and it was this rather than their personal freedom from persecution that concerned them and motivated and shaped their praying.

How much structure should there be in the life of prayer? Is it purely a spontaneous matter, or should it have at least some rudimentary organization? Psalms 3–5 seem to suggest some kind of pattern, with 3 as a prayer for the morning, 4 for the evening, and 5 again for the morning. Perhaps they were placed here, immediately after the two introductory psalms, for that very purpose. The Word of God, which should form the basis of our meditation (Ps 1) and which focuses on Christ, who is the fulfillment of God's promise to the Davidic dynasty (Ps 2), should be taken into the place of prayer, where we meet with God at the beginning and at the end of the day (Pss 3–5).

It has been noted that a number of phrases and pictures are repeated from psalm to psalm. This is helpful when they are used in devotion, whether the devotions of the church or of the individual Christian. Mays says about the prayers in the Psalter, "the language of description is formulaic and metaphoric. It creates types of persons and predicaments. The descriptions offer roles that suit the continuing structures of neediness in human experience. It is precisely this commonality and this openness which have rendered this group of psalms so available for the uses of corporate liturgy and private devotion."[295]

The Church

This section is in some ways a continuation of its predecessor, for the work of the Spirit in the individual believer and his work in the church are obviously related, and the theme of the covenant in particular could be considered under either, as each Christian believer is the beneficiary of covenant grace and

295. Mays, *Lord Reigns*, 47.

so takes his or her place within the church as the covenant community. This new section will focus especially on the nature and functions of the church.

There Are Points Both of Discontinuity and of Continuity between Israel and the Christian Church

It may seem that Israel and the church are very different in that Israel was a nation while the church is taken from all nations; Israel was given specific and detailed regulations for its worship as part of a regulated national life in terms of the place where it was to be held, the offerings to be given, and the officials to be involved, while the church has little more than guidelines in the NT. Not only so, but all the limitations of the OT system have been removed. Sidney Greidanus quotes and translates B. Holwerda as saying,

> The Psalmist could enter the forecourts only a few times per year; he could not raise his family or have his work within the temple, and this made him jealous of the sparrows and swallows who made their nests in the temple. But this lack is fulfilled in Christ. Through him the place of worship is raised everywhere; family life and work are now permanently linked to the temple. We now have access not only to the forecourts but to the holy of holies.[296]

While accepting the general thrust of this, we note also points of real continuity. There are linguistic links, for the term ἐκκλησία, *ekklēsia*, regularly rendered "church" in the NT, is used in the LXX to translate קָהָל, *qāhāl*, meaning "assembly" or "congregation." This word is used eight times in the Psalms in connection with corporate worship. The psalmist refers, for instance, to praise in "the great assembly" (22:25; 35:18).

The people of Israel were brought together in order to worship God, and this is also true of the Christian church. In both cases there is a worshiping community, not simply worshiping individuals, and Christians worship the same God as those who wrote the Psalms, though now in his fuller revelation in Christ. Although the outward aspects of worship are different today, so that there has to be some translation in passing from the OT setting to church worship, the great principles of worship found in the Psalms are of abiding significance.

---

296. Greidanus, *Preaching Christ from the OT*, 240.

The Church's Worship of God Should Always Be Response to His Self-Revelation

The Reformers held to the "regulative principle" of worship, that is, that God is to be worshiped only in terms of his own revelation. Some take it from this that only the Psalms should be used in sung worship in the churches, because there is no absolutely clear evidence of other singing in worship within the pages of the NT. Others have maintained that the regulative principle has been honored so long as the divine revelation in Scripture controls what is sung. This point of view has perhaps been supported by the type of NT scholarship that has focused on passages that have the appearance of hymns, such as Colossians 1 and Philippians 2. Of course, it may be advanced on the other side that the evidence for this is not conclusive.

In most modern churches the Psalms are still used in worship in one way or another. In its whole history the church has employed psalms, and there are still churches that use psalms only. Some hymns are based quite fully on psalms, hymns such as "Praise, My Soul, the King of Heaven" (Ps 103), and "The King of Love My Shepherd Is" (Ps 23). The latter is not simply a metrical psalm but an interpretation of 23 in terms of Christ, for after the words "thy rod and staff my comfort still," the hymn goes on to say, "thy cross before to guide me," and it shows the influence of the NT in several other ways.

It is notable that many modern Christian songs are based on psalms. To give two examples, "From the Rising of the Sun" closely follows 113:1-3, except that the order of the verses is altered, while "Thy Loving-kindness Is Better Than Life" is based on 63:3-4. The second example gives the preacher or worship leader a good opportunity of making an important point, for it is one thing to sing these words while sitting securely in a comfortable church building, but quite another when one's life is under threat, as the psalmist's was, and yet he could still say that God's loving-kindness was better than life.

Like the temple worshipers, Christians too need to be sure they are worshiping their God in accordance with what he has shown himself to be. They may not be constructing a visible idol, and yet their conception of him may not be biblical. They may not think of him simply as just but also as harsh, not simply as loving but also as sentimental. As we have seen, Psalm 50 shows us that it is possible to call him Yahweh and yet to be thinking of him as if he is Baal. The Psalms with their God-centered theology are a most effective antidote to wrong thinking about God and so may be effective in reforming our worship.

There Is Value in a Worship Pattern That Emphasizes God's Saving Deeds

The worshiping community followed a divinely given yearly plan, with particular festivals and also a fast. Many churches today observe the Christian year, and there are similarities in that the focus is largely on events and events of saving significance at that. This stress on historical events needs to be maintained, as cutting loose from these can lead to spiritual vagueness and a kind of generalized religion and faith. The harvest festival element is somewhat muted today, however, perhaps in part at least because tins of food lack the visual impact and delicious smell of fresh fruit and vegetables, and many churches appear to have given it up. This is sad, because, even in affluent days and perhaps particularly then, we need to be aware of our dependence on the Lord for our food and also on the labors of farmers and fisherfolk.

Two great psalm sequences, the Egyptian Hallel and the Songs of Ascents, found regular use at the pilgrim feasts. They may have been chosen out of a much larger number, for other psalms refer, for instance, to the redemption from Egypt. No doubt there is a thread of consecutive meaning running through each series. If objective criteria for this understanding of them could be identified and agreed upon, such a study would be very profitable and might give some pointers to the way that Christian services, especially special celebrations, might be structured. What we can see in both series is that there was much joy in celebrating the redeeming love and redemptive acts of the God of Israel.

The church has its sacraments or ordinances, and the Lord's Supper, at least, has its counterpart in the Passover from which it emerged. There were psalms especially connected with the Passover celebrations. The church has hymns that relate to particular parts of the Christian year, as the contents page of many a hymnbook reveals.

The church too can learn from the Psalter that its newer songs should augment rather than displace the older ones, for Israel did not give up using Psalm 90 (in terms of its attribution the oldest psalm in the book) when 137, a psalm of the exile, became available. The older hymns arose out of the spiritual life of the church in earlier ages, and these have much still to give to the church for use in its worship. The psalm of Moses (90) is still used today, and not only in those churches that employ only psalms in worship, for it is the basis of the hymn "O God Our Help in Ages Past."

Worship Is a Fellowship Activity Reflecting the Unifying Grace of God

The worshiping community obviously meant much to the individual, so that there was a real sense of fellowship. Psalm 68 shows all the tribes going up, and this is referred to again in 122. The authors of psalms like 42, 43, 63, and 84 long for the house of the Lord, for fellowship with God himself and with his people. In 84 the writer pictures them going up to the temple, and he does so in a wistful manner, for he cannot go with them. Westermann points out that verbs of praise are more often found in the imperative than any other verbs in the Bible.[297] In the church it is good to encourage one another to praise the Lord.

The multinational nature of the church finds some anticipation in the Psalter, for 87 speaks of different foreigners being born in Zion. In the OT the emphasis was more on people coming to Zion than the people of Zion going out, although Isaiah 60 can be balanced by Isaiah 2. There should be no segregation within the church, between master and slave, husband and wife, and people of different social classes. Even if parents and children are divided for teaching purposes, there ought to be some common worship in which they are able to praise God together.

Some have argued that it is not always practical for Christians from two antagonistic communities to meet together. Those of us who have never found ourselves in this kind of situation need to listen sympathetically to what is being said about this. There are plenty of areas where this is a real issue. Can Jewish and Arab Christians live, work, and worship together? What about communities like those in former Yugoslavia where there is ethnic tension? We have also to face the fact that black Christians who have moved into a predominantly white area have not always found a warm welcome in white churches, and so have often tended to form their own.

It is true that cultural factors sometimes play a part in this sort of thing, and there are inevitable problems if two groups would like to worship together but do not have a common language. When all has been said, however, it is so important for strong links of fellowship to be formed. If the ideal of a local church uniting two communities seems to face insuperable difficulties, there should at least be a real sense of fellowship between them in a common love for the Savior and a common concern to reach others for him. A church in war-torn Yugoslavia where Serbs and Croats worshiped together in a spirit of love for each other in troubled times was a striking testimony to the grace of God.

297. Westermann, *Praise and Lament*, 15.

The Qualifications for Acceptable Worship Are Spiritual

The Pentateuch and the Psalter have somewhat differing emphases in their references to worship. In the Pentateuch worship regulations are laid down. Worship is to be at the sanctuary where the Lord has placed his name, the only valid priests are those of the Aaronic line of descent, and quite specific regulations for sacrifices and offerings are laid down. In the Psalter, although there are plenty of references to "the house of God" and occasional mention of sacrifices, there is a special insistence on the character of the worshiper.

Psalms like 15 and 24, known as "entrance liturgies," make no reference at all to ceremonial matters (probably these are simply assumed), while 50 inveighs against the kind of worship that would place all the emphasis on the sacrifices, with even a baalizing idea of a deity who needs the sacrifices as his food, but he says that there should be thank offerings, the paying of vows, and the offering of prayer. Psalm 51 is a profound confession of personal sin, and clearly the psalmist sees that his need is for inner cleansing. There was no sacrifice for the kind of willful sin David had committed.

Worship Should Articulate the Deep Concerns of the Worshipers

There is no doubt that the psalms of lament are neglected in the worship life of the church today, greatly to its impoverishment.[298] Brueggemann says, "It is a curious fact that the church has, by and large, continued to sing songs of orientation in a world experienced as disorientated. . . . It is my judgment that this action of the church is less an evangelical defiance guided by faith, and much more a frightened numb denial and deception that does not want to acknowledge or experience the disorientation of life."[299]

When a church is doing well there is always the danger of a triumphalism riding roughshod over the concerns of its more vulnerable members. The psalms of lament can meet the deep spiritual needs of many a beleaguered Christian who feels isolated in a family or a place of work where he or she alone is a disciple of Christ. Many of them are a standing bulwark against the prosperity theology that in its milder forms can affect the thinking of a church and be quite unrecognized. Reflecting on the troubles of the Confessing Church in Germany under Hitler, Westermann then says, "Praise out of the depths has become an argument that speaks louder than the arguments

298. See esp. Holladay, *Psalms*, 292-98.
299. Brueggemann, *Message of Psalms*, 51.

we have been accustomed to bring forth for Christendom. As such it became a sort of exegesis of Holy Scripture."[300]

Although Christian worship in every age has found a great resource for worship in the Psalter, it has too often been overly selective in the psalms that it has sung or that have influenced the language and sentiments of its hymns. Robert Davidson complains about the underuse of the laments in the third edition of the *Church Hymnary*, used in much Presbyterian worship since its publication in 1973,[301] and this will be true of other Christian hymn- and songbooks, perhaps most particularly in those published since that date.

Holladay, Tanner, and others make the point that the psalms of lament engage with the concerns of the marginalized in the community, and Holladay lists the elderly, ethnic minorities, women, children, the homeless, AIDS sufferers, victims of war, and refugees. He then says, "Any folk who are marginalized can be moved to find their voices in these psalms, and any folk who are moved to become sensitized to the marginalized can hear such voices in these psalms."[302]

What about the imprecations? Many have argued that to say that they are the Word of God and that they are suitable for public reading in Christian worship is not necessarily to say the same thing. Holladay discusses them and, while lamenting that the church has so often omitted material that seems to have a negative import and so to retreat from Christian realism, nevertheless concludes that in Christian worship it is occasionally justifiable to omit certain sequences in the Psalms.[303] It would be worth reading what he has to say and assessing it as a guide to actual practice.

Whatever decision we come to on the public reading, it is important to remember that these passages have a function in emphasizing the place of justice and in committing matters into God's hands rather than taking personal action. It is worth noting that there is no reference to any individual by name in any of the imprecations. Not only so, but only a few of them seem to be directed against one individual. Of course, enmity is not viewed in abstraction, for it was always represented by actual persons, but it is the attitude of these people rather than their identity that is in the forefront.

If a sermon is being preached on a psalm that includes imprecatory verses, it is important, even if these verses are not read aloud, not to omit these from the preacher's exposition, as Christians need to come to grips with

---

300. Westermann, *Praise and Lament*, 6.

301. Davidson, *Courage to Doubt*, 12-15.

302. Holladay, *Psalms*, 294, who then applies Ps 41 to the case of battered wives (294-96). For application of the Psalter to women as marginalized, see Tanner, *Psalms*.

303. Holladay, *Psalms*, 304-15.

their function in the psalm and so with their relevance to life. There is a moving and challenging exposition of Psalm 58 in one of Bonhoeffer's writings, all the more telling because it was written ten days after he had been placed under house arrest by the Gestapo.[304]

The Church Is Responsible to Bear Witness to God

Jesus described his people as the light of the world and as a city situated on a hill where all could see it (Matt 5:14), and this note is continued in the records of the Great Commission (Matt 28:16-20; Mark 16:15-20; Luke 24:45-49; John 20:21-23; Acts 1:8). Israel was intended to represent God to the nations but often failed, as the modern church frequently does too.

How did the OT community bear its witness in its own environment? It did so largely by meeting for worship, but also its members witnessed to one another. The psalms of descriptive praise are largely if not almost exclusively communal. It is the psalms of thanksgiving for deliverance that tend to be individual. Many of the psalms of David testify to the way God intervened in situations of distress or danger that he faced. Indeed, book 1 may be viewed as a book of testimonies. The Psalms, composed initially to express the individual's gratitude, were then employed in the context of the community's worship. Here then worship and testimony are combined.

The church's testimony to God in Christ comes largely through its preaching of the gospel, but there could be room also for some individual testimony to God's faithfulness in the context of services of worship. Many churches used to include a personal testimony in their services from time to time, but this feature is much less frequent now. There is always, of course, the danger of giving too stylized an image of Christian experience or of drawing too much attention to the individual Christians concerned, but we should take note of the extensiveness of testimony in the Psalter. Sheppard expresses concern that in our services we are likely to hear "ritualized and articulate public complaints to God," but without any testimonies to answered prayer.[305] Such testimony would certainly be in the tradition of psalmic worship.

Mays sees the great significance and value of the fact that the prayers in the Psalter occur there alongside psalms of praise, and that they do so in a book entitled *Tehillim* (Praises). Just as the praise psalms are offered to God,

---

304. Bonhoeffer, *Meditating on the Word*, 84-96.
305. Sheppard, "Theology," 145.

so are the prayers, and the element of testimony in them brings glory to him, not to those who pray them.[306] There is no reason why Christian worship should not be "worshiper-friendly," but this should never be its dominant characteristic, which must always be the giving of glory to God.

As we have seen already, many of the psalms, especially the psalms of praise, show a deep concern and in some cases a deep conviction that one day the rule of Israel's God over the whole world will be reflected in worldwide worship of him.[307] From an NT perspective, there can be no doubt that the divine means to this end is the missionary activity of the church in the power of the Holy Spirit. The church today needs to take its marching orders from Christ very seriously and address this great task as a solemn responsibility.[308] Some of the historical psalms have something to say about the bad witness Israel often gave to the nations around it, and the challenge of this too needs to be felt by the church.

The Church Has an Important Teaching Function

This is certainly anticipated in the teaching given in the Psalter. There is emphasis on the תּוֹרָה, *tôrâ*, the instruction of the Lord, and in many psalms the psalmist expresses a desire to be taught by the Lord (e.g., 25:4; 27:11; 86:11; 143:8-10). Apostolic teaching was based on instruction these men had first received from Christ. Psalm 51, in which the penitent psalmist casts himself on the mercy of God, recognizes that in his experience he is learning an inner wisdom from God (v. 6), and he goes on to say, "Then shall I teach transgressors your ways" (51:13).

The element of testimony, of declaring the Lord's name in the congregation (22:22), is also a form of teaching, for it served to reinforce the conviction of the hearers that their God was a God of deliverance. In some churches where liturgical forms are normally used, the words of 19:14, slightly adapted as "May the words of my mouth and the meditation of our hearts be acceptable in your sight, O Lord, our Strength and our Redeemer," are often used at the commencement of a sermon. In view of the emphasis of that psalm on verbal revelation, this would certainly seem to be appropriate.

---

306. Mays, *Lord Reigns*, 41.

307. Jenkins's book *Next Christendom* indicates the extent to which the church of Christ has become and still is becoming worldwide and the radical way in which its geographical center of gravity has shifted.

308. For reflections on the church's mission in the contemporary world, see D. W. Smith, *Against the Stream;* idem, *Mission after Christendom.*

Westermann says,

> Proclamation corresponds to declarative, teaching to descriptive, praise.
> As in the Psalms descriptive praise lives on declarative (or confessing)
> praise — the teaching of the church is dependent on proclamation. Just
> as descriptive praise is development and expansion of the *one* statement
> in which the one who experienced God's help confesses God's actions be-
> fore the congregation, so can all teaching, all "dogmatics" of the church
> be only development of the confession of Jesus as the Christ. . . . Theol-
> ogy, that is, speaking about God, statements about God, can exist only
> when surrounded by praise of God.[309]

There is a great need for teaching in today's church. There is often a la-
mentable lack of Bible knowledge in many who go into Bible and theological
colleges today with a view to some kind of service in the church. The courses
stress the importance of proper interpretation, and such instruction is obviously desirable, but each college needs also to address in a substantial way this
paucity of knowledge of the actual contents of the Bible. It is vital that our
churches should be well fed with God's word.

As far as the church's preaching is concerned, the Psalms should never
be neglected, for they relate very much to the experience of the individual believer as well as to those of a company of God's people gathered for worship.
A pastor dealing with a series of issues, such as depression, bereavement, and
fear, is likely to find a great deal of relevant teaching here.

Because a church possesses an institutional aspect, with regular services
and administrative structures, it is important that Christians do not forget
that its inner dynamic is the work of the Holy Spirit, which is an important
fact for the church, not simply for individual believers. Christian preaching
and teaching are not to be seen as one person's attempt to influence others,
but are spiritual activities in which one should totally depend on the Holy
Spirit. The words of 106:33, "they rebelled against the Spirit of God," remind
us of Neh 9:20, where the good Spirit of God is said to have instructed the
people on their journey from Egypt to Canaan. Church business meetings
should not be viewed as occasions for a display of human wisdom but for
seeking the guidance of the Holy Spirit, who, according to Ps 139:7, is the very
presence of God.

---

309. Westermann, *Praise and Lament*, 135.

The Church's Prayer Concerns Should Be
Both Local and Wide-ranging

The Psalter contains a great deal of prayer as well as praise, and there is considerable variety in the matters brought before God. This should encourage the church to broaden its prayer ministry, and particularly to allow individuals to raise their own prayer concerns. The Psalms also show that large issues for Israel were brought to the Lord in prayer, and this fact suggests that prayer should always include matters that go beyond those of the immediate congregation, which is in any case only a small part of the Christian church.

The concern of some psalms that the God of Israel should be worshiped by all everywhere can guide the church in its missionary praying and expectation. Preachers should meditate on such psalms. This is very much in line with the NT emphasis on the responsibility of the church to take the gospel out into all the world. Mays suggests we can use the "I" psalms as expressions of concern for others, not just for ourselves, and so identify with them in their needs. He asks, "Could the use of these prayers remind us and bind us to all those in the worldwide church who are suffering in faith and for the faith?"[310]

Some preachers in churches that have no formal liturgy have a kind of informal liturgy of their own, so that the congregation recognizes in the prayers phrases that have been used time and time again. Such an informal liturgy needs to be expanded and can be given new life through the study of psalmic Scripture.

The Church's Moral and Social Concerns
Should Be Seen as Complementary

Evangelism is of course central to the church's mission in the world, but local churches have other proper concerns too. Sometimes they have focused mostly on issues of personal morality or else on those of social justice. It would be too sweeping a generalization to say that those who emphasize the moral agenda have tended to be right of center politically while those majoring on the social agenda have tended rather to the left, yet there is a measure of truth in this. The Psalter provides an important key to a balanced union of the two, and this key can be found in summary form in its two introductory psalms.

Psalm 1 is a "moral agenda" psalm. It emphasizes the importance of the

---

310. Mays, *Lord Reigns,* 52.

moral standards to be found in Scripture, and the focus of verses 1-3 is on the individual whose thinking and lifestyle mark him or her out from the wicked (plural). Psalm 2 does not deny this, for the wicked also appear in it in opposition to the will of God just as they do in Psalm 1, but 2 is concerned also with governmental issues, and their revolt against him takes a political form. God is the supreme ruler, but the psalm shows that he has established an earthly authority in the shape of the Davidic king. This king, as Psalm 72 shows, is called to be concerned about social justice, taking pity on the weak and needy and rescuing them from oppression and violence (72:12-14). Jesus as the messianic King is the fulfillment of such psalms. This therefore shows righteousness taking a political and social as well as a personal form.

If Psalms 1 and 2 were intended to form a joint introduction to the Psalter, and if the Psalter is of abiding authority for Christ's church, then it must be concerned for both agendas. The moral destiny of the individual believer is to be a perfect likeness to Christ (1 John 3:1-3), and the social and political destiny of society is to be found in the acknowledged kingship of Christ. The emphasis of NT ethics might appear to be on the former, but a passage like Jas 5:1-6 reminds us that the concern of the OT prophets for social justice is not absent from the NT. The character of Christ shows his fulfillment of the highest divine moral standards, but at the same time he demonstrated divine compassion and grace, both in life and in death. In the perfect balance of his human character we see also the perfect balance of holiness and love in the character of God, and the church is called to be Christ's body on earth.

The Last Things

The study of eschatology has sometimes become an all-consuming pursuit for Christians, and in some cases this has meant a loss of the balance of truth. Yet at the same time we need to be aware that if we play down eschatology, we will find there are plenty who will play it up. Virtually all sects, both Christian and non-Christian, have an eschatology of some sort.

The general public are more eschatologically minded now than once they were. The fearful threats to human society through the coming of the nuclear age, the specter of dramatic environmental changes through global warming, and dire worldwide health catastrophes through the spread of medical conditions such as AIDS have made people aware that our society is much more vulnerable than we once thought. It is not surprising that people are interested in predictions of the future, although in many cases unhappily they are turning to the "prophecies" of people like Nostradamus rather than to the Bible.

At first sight the book of Psalms appears to have a somewhat thin eschatology. Its preoccupation seems to be largely with the life of the people of God in this world. There is much devotional material here, and we are used to thinking of the Christian's life of prayer as personal and private. Moreover, the impression is perhaps intensified by the fact that much of book 1 is concerned with personal experiences of affliction, especially those caused by enemies.

It is true that the Psalter does not present us with as full a doctrine of the last things as the NT does, but this is to be expected, and it is important for us not to miss what it does teach. There is more here of eschatological significance than might appear on a cursory reading.

Christian Eschatology Has Two Major Presuppositions

The first presupposition is the control of God over human history. The kingdom of God is the major context within which eschatology appears in the Bible. It is true that the phrase "the kingdom of God" appears nowhere in the OT (although "the kingdom of the LORD" occurs in 2 Chr 13:8), but the idea appears often.

This is certainly true of the book of Psalms. We can agree with Wilson that book 4 is the theological heart of the Psalter, and this book is dominated by the concept of the reign of God.[311] It is not only that the cry "Yahweh reigns!" has an important place in it but that nothing in it makes sense unless Yahweh is in control of things. This control is presupposed, for instance, when the psalmist calls on the Lord to save him from his enemies. It is not surprising that the sovereignty of God is so often a theme in songs of praise, for in a topsy-turvy world nothing can give a greater sense of security than the conviction that the sovereign God has the last word on things.

The title "father of history" is usually accorded to the Greek historian Herodotus, but this is a serious misnomer, for there are biblical writers of history whose work preceded that of the Greek by several centuries. If it be objected that their work is theologically oriented, this is surely not a valid objection, for it is now recognized that history can never be regarded simply as a record of events, since, at the very least, the historian's task involves a process of selection in which one event is preferred to another, and that implies some criteria of value. This is certainly true of the biblical historians, for they look at events from the divine perspective. The Psalms contain comments on his-

311. Wilson, *Editing*, 213.

tory, and in such psalms as 68, 78, 105, and 106 sections of the past history of the people are given theological meaning.

The second presupposition is God's ability so to control events that his servants are able to forecast the future in some way. When this second feature appears in the Psalter it is often only in fairly broad outline, but enough is given to support what is said elsewhere in Scripture. The leading motif is the conviction that God's purposes will be fulfilled on a worldwide scale so that all nations will come together to worship him, the only true God. Such a conviction is sorely needed in this war-torn, turbulent world.

The Present World Is Marked by Sin and Its Effects

We live in a far from perfect world. This is recognized everywhere in Scripture. God the Creator expressed deep satisfaction with the universe he had brought into being: "God saw all that he had made, and it was very good" (Gen 1:31), but we have only to go as far as the third chapter of the Bible to find the recognition that a principle of disorder and disharmony had been introduced through sin.

Sin and its effects can certainly be seen in the Psalter, where psalm after psalm shows the psalmist as the target of the malign designs of his foes, who so often are also the foes of God. Some of the historical psalms (notably 78 and 106) show how endemic rebellion against God was even in the people of God themselves.

Our Lord himself recognized the imperfection and instability of the present world order and spoke to his disciples about the coming of false christs and false prophets, the ever-present fact of wars and rumors of wars, and even phenomena in the natural world such as earthquakes and famines (e.g., in Mark 13:1-8).

God Has Planned and Promised That All Will Ultimately Be Put Right through Christ

The NT has both a realized and a futurist eschatology, and the two are intimately connected, so that, for instance, in the Synoptic Gospels the teaching of Christ about eternal life presents it as a future experience (Luke 18:18, 29-30), but in the Gospel of John it is entered into now through Christ (John 3:36). What is now already the experience of Christians will later be experienced in fuller manner.

The kingdom of God was a major theme in the teaching of Jesus as recorded in all the Gospels, and many now recognize that it is to be understood eschatologically. Even passages where it has a present reference are not exceptions to this, because they show that the kingdom and Christ the King are closely associated, and so, in terms of his first advent, this is a realized or inaugurated eschatology that anticipates the final manifestation of his reign in his second advent. Then the only fully stable order will be established. The writer to the Hebrews refers to God's removal of all that can be shaken, "so that what cannot be shaken may remain," for "we are receiving a kingdom that cannot be shaken" (Heb 12:27-28).

So then the future is secured by the reality of the kingdom of God. God is praised in his sovereignty in many of the psalms, especially in those of the reign of God in book 4 and in the Final Hallel of book 5, but also elsewhere. No wonder that even inanimate features of the universe, the sea, the rivers, the mountains, are represented as clapping and singing for joy when God comes to judge the world in righteousness (98:7-9; cf. 96:10-13), for judgment involves not only the punishment of rebels but also the putting right of the whole social and political order under the divine rule.

The teaching of Christ about this world's instability was given in the context of a prophecy about the final things and his second advent, and these facts are intimately linked. We are to take note of the evidence of an unstable world, because it is a world affected by sin, not simply in the interests of realism, but to induce in us a longing for and a desire to prepare for the coming of Christ and the ultimate triumph of God's great purposes to be effected through him.

Why is it that David features so much in the book of Psalms, far more than any other individual? As we have seen, many students of the book's structure have come to the conclusion that it was intended to encourage the hope of a coming Messiah, so that the answer, in the perspective of the book as a whole, must be that it is because the Messiah was to come of David's line. It is this that gives the way the Davidic superscriptions point the reader to God's protection of David not only personal but eschatological significance.

A psalm like 107, considered both in itself and also in its function as opening book 5 of the Psalter, shows the joyful thankfulness of those who had seen the exile succeeded by the return to the Holy Land, and this must, in itself, have stimulated the hope that no matter what happened God's purposes for his people would ultimately be fulfilled. The disappointment so poignantly expressed in 89 would give way to a full disclosure that the messianic hope in the Davidic dynasty would find its fulfillment.

If the book of Psalms, as finally constituted, is a forward-looking book, this gives it a special link with the NT, in which the fulfillment of the messianic hope is proclaimed, recorded, and celebrated. The peculiar blending of praise and lament, of forward-looking faith and the recognition of pain in the experience of human beings, makes the Psalter uniquely fitted to prepare the way for a Christ who was both the conquering King and the Suffering Servant. Only Isaiah, among the books of the OT, can furnish such a balanced picture to such a degree, although Gen 3:15 combines victory and suffering in one pregnant verse.

Psalm 2 presents us with a pattern of kings. God is seen as the supreme King, the rebellious monarchs are seeking to throw off the divine yoke, while God's support is given to Israel's king, whose throne is on Zion's hill. If we interpret the Davidic psalms in relation to David's life, many of them show the intention of his enemies to harass and, if possible, overthrow him. So, right from Psalm 2 onward, the threat to him is taken seriously but overshadowed by confidence in the Lord's support. Both aspects come out in 22, which is a key messianic psalm for the NT and in which deep agony is succeeded by total vindication. So there is an identification of Christ both with the sufferings of his people and with the consummating purposes of God's kingdom.

It is true that the NT points forward to the second advent, in which the note of triumph might seem completely to overshadow that of suffering, and Revelation shows all suffering being banished from the new society of the future, but it also shows that the one who is in the midst of the throne is a Lamb, and that the victory is the victory of that Lamb.

The cost of his ultimate victory to Christ is never forgotten. The future, glorious as it will be, will also bear the marks of a suffering past. It will be bliss, but not without the note of realism. The Psalter too shows that true victory comes through suffering. It has often been the suffering church that has appreciated Revelation most, and that can also identify with the sufferers in the book of Psalms.

The church today needs to preserve this balance, to be certain of ultimate victory but willing to identify itself with the suffering Lamb, and to follow him wherever he goes. In places where the church finds itself to be a small and perhaps even diminishing minority of the population, there is plenty in the Psalter to give it encouragement in its witness for Christ. God's ultimate purpose is clear, which means that the future is full of hope, and the church is called to continue with confidence to bear its witness to Christ. Where and when the church is large and growing, however, it needs to beware of an arrogant triumphalism that forgets that, as in Psalm 22, future vindication comes only after deep suffering, and that it is the church that identified with its suffering Savior, "becoming like him in his death" (Phil 3:10), that knows the power of his resurrection.

It is not easy to find a timetable of future things in the Psalter. It is true that some biblical passages have a programmatic perspective. We think, for instance, of Daniel 2 and 7, Mark 13, 1 Corinthians 15, and, at least on a premillennial understanding of Revelation 19, the closing chapters of the Apocalypse, but there is nothing to correspond to this in the Psalter. After all, however, it is the certainty of ultimate judgment and salvation and the ultimate establishment of God's kingdom and purposes that really matter, not the precise timing or order of these events, so that the book of Psalms has much to say to us.

It is beyond the scope of this volume to deal with the controversial and complex issue of the relationship of modern Israel to the promises of God. Many Christians see the return of the Jews to the promised land and the setting up of the state of Israel as heralding in some significant way the second coming of Christ, and, for this reason, they feel it important to support Israel as a modern nation. Since the 1980s a growing number of Christians have also regarded the Palestinians as having a just cause for complaint against Israel in its treatment of them. In some ways we might characterize these two groups as, respectively, Psalm 2 and Psalm 1 Christians.

From Psalm 2 onward, many psalms highlight the Davidic monarchy and some promise the reign of Israel's king over all the nations (2:8; 72:8-11). Following the NT, Christians believe these promises to be fulfilled in Jesus as the kingly Messiah, and it is clearly important for us to pray that the people of present Israel will come to accept his claims and be regrafted into the olive tree that represents the continuing people of God (Rom 11:23-24).

Psalm 1 shows the commitment of Israel's God to bless the righteous and to judge the wicked. This reveals how profoundly moral his nature is, and the messianism of Psalm 2 cannot be a denial of this but rather must be in complete harmony with it. That this is the case is clear when we see that 72:12-14 presents the worldwide reign of God's anointed king as one of concern for the weak and needy.

True penitence, whether by Israel or by the Palestinians or by any of us, will show itself in a commitment of the penitent both to justice and to compassion in dealing with others. The placing of Psalms 1 and 2 together at the start of the Psalter is a reminder that the Davidic messianism of Psalm 2 needs always to be seen as a great enterprise of the God of Psalm 1, with his commitment to bless the righteous and judge the wicked. Messianism and morality are inseparable in the heart and purposes of God.

Judgment Is Certain, with Contrasting Destinies
for the Wicked and the Righteous

The book of Revelation may present difficulties to the interpreter, but matters of crucial importance are clearly presented there. The book shows with crystal clarity both the ultimate judgment of the wicked and the ultimate bliss of those who are righteous in Christ. In this respect, it brings to final statement the ultimate principles of human destiny that one can see elsewhere in the Bible, and perhaps most notably in the teaching of Christ.

The Psalms have a great deal to say about judgment. Psalm 1 is certain that there will be a judgment of the wicked, and that certainty is carried right through the Psalter. It is true that present experience sometimes challenges this, as in Psalm 73, but there the psalmist is given a glimpse at the end of the story and that gives him reassurance. The many psalms in which the relationship of God to the nations of the world is in view are sure both of their judgment but also of the fact that they will join ultimately with the people of Israel in the praise of Yahweh. These two pictures are not at variance with each other if we interpret them through the NT, as it is clear that the world is under judgment but that, through the redeeming work of Christ, there will be people of every realm gathering to praise God in Christ (Rev 7:9-17).

What about the future of the individual? In evangelical circles over the past twenty years there has been much reexamination of the doctrine of eternal punishment with a significant number now taking the annihilationist position.[312] It would be difficult to find backing for this in the Psalter, even though it lacks the full light that came with Christ and his resurrection. The picture of Sheol that we get is gloomy and undesirable, but it does not appear to be a state of unconsciousness. It could, of course, be argued that although Sheol is presented as succeeding death, there is no indication as to whether this is the final destiny of the wicked. This means then that in our exposition of final destiny we need to move from the Psalter to the NT.

It is clear, however, in a small but significant number of psalms, that the ultimate destiny of the believing psalmist was in continued fellowship with God. He is convinced that the fellowship with God that he experienced during his lifetime would not be terminated at death but would go on and, indeed, in some way would be consummated (e.g., 17:15; 49:15; 73:24-26). The closing verses of Psalm 17, for instance, could be read most appropriately at a Christian funeral service. It may not say everything, but it expresses the glad

---

312. See esp. the discussions of this issue in Cameron, ed., *Universalism.*

assurance of awaking beyond death to see, and to be deeply satisfied in seeing, the face of God.

Holy Scripture

The God of the Psalter Is a Self-revealing God

If the Bible is our guide, the path to the knowledge of God comes to human beings through God's self-disclosure. The initiative comes always from him. This distinguishes the Bible from speculative philosophy or from any type of natural theology in which the emphasis is on human discovery rather than divine revelation. The opening chapters of the book of Exodus, where Yahweh discloses his name to Moses (Exod 3:11-15; 6:2-4), provide the locus classicus for this in the OT, just as the prologue to the Gospel of John does for the NT. The book of Psalms is in line with this. Psalm 145, for instance, affirms many of the great attributes of Israel's God, and in that psalm the intertwining of these with his acts is such that it is clear these qualities were made known in those divine acts.

His Revelation Was Given in Terms of Interpreted Deeds

Our study of the key themes of the Psalter focused attention on the great past acts of God. Clearly these had and still have value and significance, not simply for their immediate effect on God's people, but also because they reveal his nature and purposes. We see, for instance, how in 77:11-20 the psalmist encourages himself from these divine acts and in 18:7-16 how they provide language to describe his present experience of deliverance, on the assumption that God has an abiding concern to save his people.[313]

This does not mean that for the psalmists God's great acts all belonged to the past, with nothing major still to come. The messianic thrust of the Psalter considered as a whole,[314] and the emphasis, especially in books 4 and 5, on a future demonstration of God's justice in acts of judgment are important. The principle each enshrines, however, was learned from the past, from God's faithfulness to the Davidic dynasty[315] and from

---

313. See the comments on both these psalms.

314. See pp. 348-59, 429.

315. Even Ps 89, which expresses concern about the apparent nonfulfillment of them (esp. in v. 49), commences with a long celebration of those promises (vv. 1-37).

his historical judgments. The shape of the future is based on that of the past, for God is consistent.

Were these deeds *in themselves* revelatory, or did they require verbal interpretation? The traditional view is that special revelation has an important verbal dimension, and that the acts alone fall short of revelation. This conception has often been challenged in modern times. William Temple's famous dictum sums up the outlook of many: "What is offered to man's apprehension in any specific Revelation is not truth concerning God but the living God Himself."[316] For Temple, however, this encounter is not a purely mystical experience; rather it is mediated through the historical deeds of God.

The deeds are clearly indispensable to the revelation. It was, for instance, in the sequence of events connected with the exodus and Sinai that Moses encountered God, but it is difficult to deny the verbal element in the revelation. In *Old and New in Interpretation,* James Barr played down somewhat the great emphasis Gerhard von Rad and others placed on history, and stressed the verbal element in God's self-disclosure: "The acts of God are meaningful because they are set within this frame of verbal communication. God tells what he is doing, or tells what he is going to do. . . . A God who acted in history would be a mysterious and supra-personal fate if the action was not linked with this verbal communication."[317]

One might assert, of course, that the deeds are divine but that the interpretation in verbal form is human and so lacks the authority of the actual deeds, but this was clearly not the view of the biblical writers themselves.[318] The prophets, for instance, interpreted the acts of God in history, and God told them that he would give them the words to say (e.g., Exod 4:14-16; Deut 18:18; Jer 1:6-10). At least some of the psalms are prophetic in type.

At the end of his small but seminal book *According to the Scriptures,* having shown the importance of the christological interpretation of the OT for the NT writers, C. H. Dodd asserts that their unanimity needs an explanation and that the best is the one the Gospels give us, and this comes from Jesus himself.[319] There is a similar unanimity within the Psalter in relation to the great deeds of the past and how they should be understood. If this unanimity has God as its ultimate cause, then we need still to take them seriously today, although of course for Christians the NT interpretation of them will affect how they are understood.

316. Temple, *Nature, Man and God,* 322.

317. *Old and New,* 77-78.

318. It is worth noting that modern speech-act theory regards a verbal communication as itself a deed in so far as it effects change.

319. *According to the Scriptures,* 110.

Sometimes It Was Given Mainly in Words

In one of the great past acts of God, the giving of the law at Sinai, the event consists very largely in the communication of words, which certainly appear to have value as revelation in their own right. They are taken with great seriousness in Psalm 119, where the author's belief in their authoritative status cannot be missed, even though there is little reference to their content. In that the law showed God's requirements for his people, it showed his nature, for it revealed what he cared about. This is in line with the emphasis placed on words in the Pentateuch, most of all in Deuteronomy.[320]

The Psalms Are Largely Responsive Literature, but They Themselves Then Became Part of the Revelation

If *tôrâ* in Psalm 1 refers to or at least includes the Psalter,[321] this would suggest it had the same status as the earlier *tôrâ* (the Pentateuch) and so was authoritative. The fivefold structure of the Psalter may have been intended to underline this, as it was obviously based on the structure of the Pentateuch. It implies that the Lord not only wanted his people to know what he had done and said in his works and laws recorded in the Pentateuch, but that he wanted them to offer him praise for his works and words and to make them the basis of their prayers. The Reformers grasped this when they applied the regulative principle[322] to the singing of the Psalms. Those today whose sung praise includes other items beside the Psalms should still value the Psalter for its guidance as to what is proper in worship and prayer.

The Psalms are often quoted in the NT, frequently with the use of quotation formulae that were standard for Holy Scripture.[323] This shows that, even though they originated in worship and devotion and so are obviously responsive literature, they were regarded by the NT writers as divine revelation equally with other OT books. This revelation, when recorded in literary form, is treated seriously as the Word of God by later biblical writers.

---

320. This is true even of Genesis, with its reiterated "and God said" in its opening chapter.

321. See comments on Ps 1.

322. I.e., that God is concerned for his people to worship him in the way he has ordained.

323. E.g., in Matt 22:43-44 ("he says"); John 19:24 ("that the scripture might be fulfilled which said"); Acts 1:20 ("it is written").

Some Psalms Show That Their Authors
Were Under Strong Constraint to Write

Do the psalmists show any awareness of their own inspiration? Not consistently, but in some psalms at least it is clear their authors felt themselves to be under powerful and perhaps even divine constraint in their writings, somewhat like the constraint evidenced by the prophets.[324] This would certainly harmonize with David's consciousness, in 2 Sam 23:1-2, of being a channel of the inspiring Spirit, and with the fact that some of the Levites whose names are linked to psalms are described as prophets in 1 Chr 25:1.

Some of the psalms are formally somewhat like prophecies. We must be careful not to formulate a concept of prophetic inspiration that is too rigid and that imposes a uniform pattern on a somewhat diverse phenomenon. Yet it does seem likely that psalms that might be identified as prophetic should be viewed as having the same general features as those exhibited in the OT prophetic books.

We must distinguish an author's inspiration from his awareness of it. The former may be present where the latter is not. Of course, Christians take seriously the statements of the NT writers about the inspiration of the OT books, and especially the use made of them, including the psalms, by Jesus.

Any Concept of the Psalter as Scripture Should Embrace Its Redactors
as well as Its Writers, and Particularly the Final Redactor(s)

The psalms were written originally as discrete pieces of literature, and it is obviously important to view them as such and to seek to understand the message of each and its application to ourselves as Christians. The primary context therefore for any single verse or combination of verses in a psalm is that psalm as a whole.

We should not forget, however, that the form in which we have the psalms is that given to them as a complete book by their final redactor(s). This means that each psalm comes to us in a literary context. The extent to which we should take that context into account hermeneutically may be a matter of opinion, but this factor cannot be ignored, and the increased study of it since the 1980s has proved very profitable.

Are there any biblical parallels to this literary phenomenon? There are

---

324. E.g., Pss 36:1; 45:1; and perhaps 49:1-4. The relationship between the Psalter and OT prophecy is explored in Bellinger, *Psalmody and Prophecy.*

certainly some partial ones. In the Gospels the writers have recorded discourses of Jesus, such as the Sermon on the Mount (Matt 5–7) and the upper room discourse (John 14–16). There is value in seeking to understand each in itself, and yet it is just as important to relate each to its context. When we read the Acts of the Apostles we encounter the sermons of Peter, Stephen, and Paul set in the context of Luke's story of the early church. It is widely held that Paul made use of some early Christian hymns in his epistles, and there are hymns of praise to be found in the book of Revelation. In each case it is appropriate to interpret the smaller units as distinct entities but also to view them in their wider literary context.

The Psalter Is Part of a Literary Corpus in Which the Later Interprets and Builds on the Earlier

There are plenty of links between the Psalms and other parts of the OT. In many cases these passages are manifestly earlier than the psalms in question but in some they are later, while in still other cases it may not be possible to be certain. For some examples see the comments on Psalms 8; 33:6; 68:1; 77; 89; and 110.

There is evidence that earlier Scriptures became means of grace to the writers of the psalms. In Psalm 8 meditation on the Genesis creation narrative fills the psalmist with awe at the majesty of God, and he is amazed that such a God should be concerned for human beings. In 77 the troubled faith of another is rebuilt as he considers the great acts of God for his people. In 105 the record of God's dealings with his people stimulated the author's praise as he thought about God's faithfulness to his promise to Abraham.

It is clear that the NT writers, following Jesus himself, regarded the Psalter as a body of literature that bore witness to the fact and nature of his coming. In John's Gospel Jesus uses the term νόμος, *nomos* ("law"), of a psalm on two occasions (John 10:34; 15:25), and the use of this word strongly suggests authority. The Epistle to the Hebrews is quite outstanding for the way it uses OT quotations, for it often cites the OT as the word of God, of Christ, or of the Holy Spirit.[325] Moreover, much from the Psalms is used as authoritative Scripture that stands midway between the Pentateuch and Christ, furnishing a kind of hermeneutical bridge between them.

---

325. E.g., Heb 3:15-19; 7:1-22; 10:1-14.

The Psalmists Intended Their Writings to Convey
Specific Meaning to Their Readers

Poetry is often regarded as the literature of suggestion rather than of exact statement. Is this true of the poetry of the Psalms? Not altogether, for the device of parallelism tells against it. The effect of parallelism, especially the "synonymous" variety, is not only to nuance the first line of a couplet by the second, but also often to fix the sense of the whole couplet more fully than would have been possible by the use of a single line. Both lines are related to the same general meaning, for one line helps to define the other at the same time as enriching it. This suggests that NT quotation of the Psalms that attaches definite meanings to them is well founded.

If a psalmist had an urge to write, presumably this was for the understanding of the readers, although he could have had liturgical motives too. There is of course a difference between the author's intention and our understanding of it. We should therefore seek for a definite meaning, although at the same time humbly recognizing that we cannot claim infallibility for our interpretations.

The Messianic Interpretation of the Psalter as a Whole
Is in Line with the NT Understanding of It

David Mitchell, among other psalm scholars, has argued that the intention of the ultimate redactor(s) of the Psalter was to focus on Israel's future hope, including the coming of the Messiah.[326] This accords with Christ's own understanding of the Psalter, for not only did his quotation of particular psalms imply that they foreshadowed him in some way, but in Luke 24:44 he made an important general statement: "Everything must be fulfilled that is written about me in the Law of Moses, the Prophets and the Psalms."

John 1:1-18 shows that the fullness of divine revelation came in the giving of God's Son. Paul says that it was when the time had fully come that God sent forth his Son, and the context shows he meant that this time was set by God (Gal 4:1-7). One of the leading purposes of what God made known of himself earlier, according to the NT, was to testify to the Christ who was the

---

326. This is Mitchell's main concern and argument in *Message of Psalter*. In a review of the history of interpretation (his book was published in 1997), he shows that before about 1820 most scholars regarded the Psalter as foretelling eschatological events, including the coming of the Messiah, and that, although not uncontested, this type of interpretation has been resurfacing since about 1970 (*Message of Psalter*, 16-65).

ultimate revelation. Hebrews 1:1-4 affirms that both the OT revelation and the fullness of revealed truth in Christ came through God's speaking initiative. This is then followed by an annotated catena of OT quotations (Heb 1:5-14), each of which is specifically declared to be the Word of God. The sevenfoldness of this catena is probably meant to emphasize that the OT's testimony to him, though coming "at many times and in various ways," had a perfection of its own, for all of it was God's testimony to his Son. Most of these quotations come from the Psalter.

If, as Christians believe, the great purpose of the Bible is to bring Christ to us and to bring us to Christ, the book of Psalms has a major part to play in this.

Preparing a Sermon on a Psalm
(Using Psalm 8 as an Example)

This volume is intended to be of value to preachers. The following is a concrete example of the way the material in it can be used and developed. I stop short of suggesting an actual sermon, as this must depend on prayerful discernment of the situation and needs of the hearers and also on finding illustrations that will be meaningful to them. Perhaps the time available will not allow for preparation at quite such depth, but it would be good to approximate to it as nearly as possible. Some of the material here will not find its way into the sermon, but it should aid the preacher's understanding of the passage in the biblical and present-day contexts.

Basic Assumptions

1. The psalm is to be studied as a unity — because it has a simple form and in any case it is its canonical form that concerns us.
2. It is in some meaningful sense a psalm of David — the superscription refers to David, so that David is to be seen either as its author or at least as a role model for the spiritual life.
3. It occurs within a book that shows distinct signs of deliberate arrangement and chronological development. This is in book 1 with its strong Davidic concentration.
4. As part of the biblical canon it has significance for Christians today.

Psalm 8 Considered in Itself (see also the exegesis of this psalm)

1. In terms of its genre it is a descriptive praise psalm with a simple and clear structure. It starts with praise, then gives reasons for praise and

concludes with the same praise refrain. Its center (vv. 3-4) shows astonishment at the concern of such a great God for apparently insignificant humans. Verses 1b-2 and 5-8 constitute a chiastic feature (brought out well in the NRSV paragraphing), an amazed comparison between God's own glory and the glory he has bestowed on human beings.

2. It clearly rests on Genesis 1 — especially on vv. 26-28 and also on vv. 14-19. Literary dependence seems clear, with Genesis 1 as primary and Psalm 8 as dependent. If the Psalter's final editor meant the themes of the Pentateuch to be turned into praise by way of meditation (suggesting this by a fivefold structure), the reader should consider God's creative deeds (v. 3) and be led through wonder to worship. This makes reflection on revelation important.

3. It refers to a number of different orders of being:
   a. God — his glory is above the heavens, but he is also majestic in all the earth — so he is both transcendent and immanent, creating all and gloriously revealed in all.
   b. The heavenly beings — verse 5 has *Elohim,* which here could mean God or heavenly beings, that is, angels. The LXX, followed by Hebrews 7–9, takes it to be heavenly beings.
   c. Human beings — "a little lower" better fits translating *Elohim* as angels, not God.
   d. The heavenly bodies — apparently so much greater than humans, for whom nevertheless God cares.
   e. The animals — ruled over by human beings, and "made him ruler" (v. 6; cf. "crowned" in v. 5) may compare with "set in place" (v. 3), both being ordering acts of God.

So there is a hierarchical interest in this psalm. All except the heavenly beings are present in Genesis 1. N.B. Some scholars think "we" suggests a heavenly court.

4. It sees God as both great and caring — qualities implicit in Genesis 1 but here made explicit, perhaps implying that government, both divine and human, finds expression in care.

5. Genesis 1 is not interpreted in isolation — for
   a. it sees sin as present in the world, and not quiescent but aggressive (cf. the serpent and Cain, Gen 3–4);
   b. it refers to the greatness of the name Yahweh, majestic in all the earth, found in the phrase *Yhwh Elohim* in Genesis 2, its meaning then explained in Exodus 3 and 6;

c. it implies a special relationship between Yahweh and Israel, the psalmist's people, for he is Yahweh our *Adonai* (Master).

Psalm 8 as Part of the Whole Psalter

We assume that the Psalter grew as its five books were gradually brought together and will consider the significance of this psalm at three stages.

1. Within book 1 — which is strongly Davidic, focusing on his afflictions and God's protecting and rescuing care of him, promised in 2. In Psalm 8 the individual life is set in a larger perspective, always helpful when we face problems, and 19, 24, and 33 also have this perspective. Psalms 3–7 all present David as in danger from his enemies, which in Psalm 8 are shown to be God's, and, so unexpectedly, to be curbed by the praise of children, perhaps suggesting that, in the midst of his enemies, David should praise the Lord. This is what he does in Psalm 9, where God, as king (9:4), upholds him against them.

2. Within books 1-3 — where book 2 reinforces book 1's message but shows that other divinely appointed officials (i.e., Levites) were under threat from enemies and were protected and delivered. They too would be encouraged by Psalm 8's message, especially, as temple officials, the assurance that praise is a defense against foes (cf. 2 Chr 20:22ff). The majesty and glory given to the king (Ps 45) and the importance of just rule (Ps 72) apply the principles of Psalm 8 to the Davidic monarch.

   The praise hymns in book 3 certainly strongly reinforce the teaching of Psalm 8 about the majesty and glory of God and his determination to frustrate the purposes of the wicked (see, e.g., 75 and 76). Also the firm order established by God can be seen, in 87, in his establishment of Zion, which itself partakes of glory. Book 3 ends with a psalm (89) that likens the covenant with David to the establishment and order of the heavens and the earth. The laments intensify and this final psalm raises the question as to whether God has truly silenced the enemy and the avenger, as they seem to have finished off the Davidic dynasty.

3. Within books 1-5 — Yahweh's creative work and firm order are celebrated in 90, 96, 97, and, notably, in 104 (cf. also 95:4; 102:25-27). In 110 the priest-king's enemies are beneath his feet, and God's glory and care for the weak appear together in 113. In 144 the question of 8:4 is asked again, but here humanity, still experiencing God's care, is now at enmity with him. The animal creation too is here again but this time as food

and working animals. In the Final Hallel, God's provision for the animals is again celebrated (147) and God's creatures in every realm are called to praise him (148). So the psalm's teaching is reinforced over and over again in the Psalter. Israel's glorious and caring God appoints humans to rule, the king in a special way, and no enemy can stand against God's purposes for the Davidic kingship or against his people's praises. Obeying 1's injunction to meditate on God's word, these truths anchor God's people to walk in his ways, knowing he watches over (cares for) them and that he will judge the wicked.

Psalm 8 in the Context of the OT and Jewish Interpretation

In the OT its truths appear frequently, and its language appears in 144 and Job 7:17 (cf. Job 25:6), but we can neither affirm nor deny literary dependence. Hellenistic Judaism's interpretation is seen in the LXX with "perfected praise" (cf. Matt 21:16) in verse 2, and "angels" in verse 5 (cf. Heb 2:7, 9).

Psalm 8 in the Context of the NT

1. In the triumphal entry of Jesus (Matt 21) — when Jesus accepts praise from children and quotes 8:2 (LXX), suggesting his deity. Perhaps the religious leaders are seen as the foe and avenger in the psalm, although we cannot be sure.
2. In Heb 2:5-10 — where the declension due to the fall is put right by Jesus, which is a foretaste and pledge of a more general fulfillment in God's people, for many sons (an idea not present in the psalm) are brought to the glory the psalm speaks of through his death and glorification. This requires his assumption of human nature and status for this purpose (Heb 2:11-18). Note though that Jas 3:7 implies that the gift of dominion has not been removed fully from humans because they can tame the animals, but not their own tongues.
3. In the Epistles of Paul — in 1 Cor 15:24-28, which quotes Ps 8:6 (in v. 27), Paul links at least 110 and 8 and perhaps Gen 3:15. In 1 Cor 1:25-30 the weak things confounding the mighty could echo the psalm. Ephesians is dominated by Christ's exaltation, and 1:22 probably reflects both Psalms 8 and 110. Romans 16:20 recalls Gen 3:15, but possibly also Psalms 8 and 110. Paul's mind may have linked these three passages to Christ's exaltation and therefore to each other, rather in the way various OT "stone"

passages were linked in Peter's mind (see 1 Pet 2). The Palm Sunday narrative would seem to be basic both to the Pauline and Petrine passages.

Its Message for Today's Church

1. The purpose of creation is the revelation of God's glory — Kant said that the two things that impressed him most were the starry heavens above and the moral law within. Considering the heavens, or humanity, or animals, should elicit awe at God's glory and amazement at his love and grace. Also the God-given principle of order makes both science and the arts possible.

2. Human beings have been created with a dignified status — so they should not be used as mere means to an end. This has repercussions for medical ethics. God has made humans as kingly creatures, and, no matter how depraved they are, they should be respected as such.

3. God's covenant people praise him, but his enemies oppose him. Covenant should not be viewed simply in terms of privilege, for our glad responsibility is to obey him and praise him.

4. The animal creation is to be ruled and cared for as God himself rules and cares. Also conservation and the responsible use of resources are mandatory.

5. The fall has called humanity's rule into question because it has introduced disorder — this is inevitable where there is opposition to God's order.

6. Christ now fulfills God's purpose for humankind, but at much cost to himself. He came to restore proper order and to reconcile us to God, but this cost him suffering and death.

7. In Christ believers are exalted to a place of dominion, especially over evil powers. Aggressive opposition to God and his order is bound to fail ultimately.

8. God loves children and the weak and their praise of him — so instead of glorifying the humanly great we should recognize how the weak minister to God's glory (cf. 1 Cor 1–4).

9. Ultimately Christ as perfect man will hand the restored dominion back to the Father, his costly work of restoration completed, when God's "Big Story" has run its course.

10. Through this praise psalm both preacher and hearers are called to full-hearted worship of the God of creation who is also the God of our redemption through Christ.

Bibliography

Aejmelaeus, A. *The Traditional Prayer in the Psalms.* BZAW 167. Berlin: de Gruyter, 1986.

Alexander, T. D., and B. S. Rosner, eds. *New Dictionary of Biblical Theology.* Downers Grove: IL: InterVarsity Press, 2000.

Allen, L. C. "Psalm 73: An Analysis." *TB* 33 (1982): 93-118.

Allen, L. C. *Psalms 101–150.* 2nd ed. WBC 21. Nashville: Nelson, 2002.

Alter, R. *The Art of Biblical Poetry.* Edinburgh: T&T Clark, 1985.

Anderson, A. A. *The Book of Psalms.* 2 vols. New Century Bible Commentary. Repr. Grand Rapids: Eerdmans, 1981.

Anderson, B. W., ed. *The Old Testament and Christian Faith: A Theological Discussion.* New York: Harper, 1963.

Anderson, G. W. "Israel's Creed: Sung, not Signed." *SJT* 16 (1963): 277-85.

Armerding, C. E., ed. *Evangelicals and Liberation: Studies in the World Church and Mission.* Phillipsburg, NJ: Presbyterian & Reformed, 1979.

Atherton, J., ed. *Social Christianity: A Reader.* London: SPCK, 1994.

Bahnsen, G. L. *Van Til's Apologetic: Reading and Analysis.* Phillipsburg, NJ: Presbyterian & Reformed, 1998.

Baker, D. W., and B. T. Arnold, eds. *The Face of Old Testament Studies: A Survey of Contemporary Approaches.* Grand Rapids: Baker, 1999.

Baldwin, J. G. "Ruth." Pages 287-95 in *New Bible Commentary: 21st Century Edition.* Ed. D. A. Carson, R. T. France, J. A. Motyer, and G. J. Wenham. Downers Grove, IL: InterVarsity Press, 1994.

Balla, P. "Challenges to Biblical Theology." Pages 20-27 in *New Dictionary of Biblical Theology.* Ed. T. D. Alexander and B. S. Rosner. Downers Grove: IL: InterVarsity Press, 2000.

Barclay, O. *Evangelicalism in Britain 1935-1995: A Personal Sketch.* Leicester: InterVarsity Press, 1997.

Barr, J. *Old and New in Interpretation: A Study of the Two Testaments.* London: SCM, 1966.

Barr, J. *The Semantics of Biblical Language.* Oxford: Oxford University Press, 1961.

Bartholomew, C., and A. West, eds. *Praying by the Book: Reading the Psalms.* Carlisle: Paternoster, 2001.

436

Bartholomew, C., and T. Moritz, eds. *Christ and Consumerism: A Critical Analysis of the Spirit of the Age.* Carlisle: Paternoster, 2000.

Bauckham, R. J. "Biblical Theology and the Problem of Monotheism." Pages 187-232 in *Out of Egypt: Biblical Theology and Biblical Interpretation.* Ed. C. Bartholomew, M. Healy, K. Möller, and R. Parry. Scripture and Hermeneutics Series 5. Grand Rapids: Zondervan, 2004.

Bellinger, W. H., Jr. *Psalmody and Prophecy.* JSOTSup 27. Sheffield: JSOT Press, 1984.

Berry, D. K. *The Psalms and Their Readers: Interpretive Strategies for Psalm 18.* JSOTSup 153. Sheffield: Sheffield Academic Press, 1993.

Berry, R. J., ed. *Care of Creation: Focusing Concern and Action.* Leicester: InterVarsity Press, 2000.

Bloch, E. *Atheism in Christianity: The Religion of the Exodus and the Kingdom.* Trans. J. T. Swann. New York: Herder & Herder, 1972.

Blomberg, C. "Critical Issues in New Testament Studies for Evangelicals Today." Pages 51-79 in *A Pathway into the Holy Scripture.* Ed. P. E. Satterthwaite and D. F. Wright. Grand Rapids: Eerdmans, 1994.

Bloom, W., ed. *New Age: An Anthology of Essential Writings.* London: Rider, 1991.

Boff, L., and C. Boff. *Introducing Liberation Theology.* Trans. P. Burns. Maryknoll, NY: Orbis, 1987.

Bonhoeffer, D. *Life Together; Prayerbook of the Bible.* Trans. D. W. Bloesch and J. H. Burtness. Ed. G. B. Kelly. Dietrich Bonhoeffer Works 5. Minneapolis: Fortress, 1996.

Bonhoeffer, D. *Meditating on the Word.* Trans. and ed. D. Mcl. Gracie. Cambridge: Cowley, 1986.

Bouma-Preidiger, S. *For the Beauty of the Earth: A Christian Vision for Creation Care.* Grand Rapids: Baker Academic, 2001.

Bray, G. *Biblical Interpretation: Past and Present.* Downers Grove, IL: InterVarsity Press, 1996.

Bright, J. *Covenant and Promise: The Future in the Preaching of the Pre-Exilic Prophets.* Philadelphia: Westminster, 1976.

Bright, J. *A History of Israel.* 3rd ed. Philadelphia: Westminster, 1981.

Bright, J. *The Kingdom of God in Bible and Church.* London: Lutterworth, 1955.

Brown, W. P. *Seeing the Psalms: A Theology of Metaphor.* Louisville: Westminster John Knox, 2002.

Broyles, C. C. *The Conflict of Faith and Experience in the Psalms: A Form-Critical and Theological Study.* JSOTSup 52. Sheffield: JSOT Press, 1989.

Broyles, C. C. *Psalms.* New International Biblical Commentary. Peabody, MA: Hendrickson, 1999.

Brueggemann, W. "Bounded by Obedience and Praise: The Psalms as Canon." *JSOT* 50 (1991): 63-92.

Brueggemann, W. "The Costly Loss of Lament." *JSOT* 36 (1986): 57-71.

Brueggemann, W. "From Hurt to Joy, from Death to Life." *Int* 28 (1974): 3-19.

Brueggemann, W. *Israel's Praise: Doxology versus Idolatry and Ideology.* Philadelphia: Fortress, 1988.

Brueggemann, W. *The Message of the Psalms: A Theological Commentary.* Augsburg Old Testament Studies. Minneapolis: Augsburg, 1984.

Brueggemann, W. *Old Testament Theology: Essays on Structure, Theme, and Text.* Minneapolis: Fortress, 1992.

Brueggemann, W. "Psalms and the Life of Faith: A Suggested Typology of Function." *JSOT* 17 (1980): 3-32.

Brueggemann, W. *Reverberations of Faith: A Theological Handbook of Old Testament Themes.* Louisville: Westminster John Knox, 2002.

Brueggemann, W. "A Shape for Old Testament Theology." Pages 406-26 in *The Flowering of Old Testament Theology: A Reader in Twentieth-Century Old Testament Theology.* Ed. B. C. Ollenburger, E. A. Martens, and G. F. Hasel. Winona Lake, IN: Eisenbrauns, 1992.

Brueggemann, W. *Theology of the Old Testament: Testimony, Dispute, Advocacy.* Minneapolis: Fortress, 1997.

Bruner, F. D. *A Theology of the Holy Spirit.* Grand Rapids: Eerdmans, 1970.

Bullock, C. H. *Encountering the Book of Psalms: A Literary and Theological Introduction.* Grand Rapids: Baker Academic, 2001.

Bultmann, R. "The Significance of the Old Testament for the Christian Faith." Pages 8-35 in *The Old Testament and Christian Faith.* Ed. B. W. Anderson. New York: Harper, 1963.

Calvin, J. *Commentary on the Book of Psalms.* Trans. J. Anderson. Calvin's Commentaries 4. Repr. Grand Rapids: Baker Academic, 1996.

Calvin, J. *Institutes of the Christian Religion.* Trans. F. L. Battles. Ed. J. T. McNeill. 2 vols. Library of Christian Classics. Philadelphia: Westminster, 1960.

Cameron, N. M. de S., ed. *Death without Dignity: Euthanasia in Perspective.* Edinburgh: Rutherford House, 1990.

Cameron, N. M. de S., ed. *Universalism and the Doctrine of Hell.* SBET Special Study No. 5. Carlisle: Paternoster, 1993.

Campolo, T. *How to Rescue the Earth without Worshipping Nature: A Christian's Call to Save Creation.* Milton Keynes: Word (UK), 1992.

Carson, D. A. *The Gagging of God: Christianity Confronts Pluralism.* Leicester: Apollos, 1996.

Carson, D. A., R. T. France, J. A. Motyer, and G. J. Wenham, eds. *New Bible Commentary: 21st Century Edition.* Downers Grove, IL: InterVarsity Press, 1994.

Chester, T. *The Message of Prayer.* Leicester: InterVarsity Press, 2003.

Childs, B. S. *Introduction to the Old Testament as Scripture.* Philadelphia: Fortress, 1979.

Childs, B. S. *Old Testament Theology in a Canonical Context.* Philadelphia: Fortress, 1985.

Clarke, D. K., and N. L. Geisler. *Apologetics in the New Age.* Grand Rapids: Baker Academic, 1990.

Clines, D. "The Parallelism of Greater Precision." Pages 77-100 in *Directions in Biblical Hebrew Poetry.* Ed. E. R. Follis. JSOTSup 40. Sheffield: JSOT Press, 1987.

Cole, R. L. *The Shape and Message of Book III (Psalms 73–89).* JSOTSup 307. Sheffield: Sheffield Academic Press, 2000.

Cooper, A. M. "The Life and Times of King David According to the Book of Psalms." Pages 117-31 in *The Poet and Historian: Essays in Literary and Historical Biblical Criticism.* Ed. D. N. Freedman. Harvard Semitic Studies 26. Chico, CA: Scholars Press, 1983.

Craigie, P. C. *Psalms 1–50.* WBC 19. Waco: Word, 1983.

Craigie, P. C. *Ugarit and the Old Testament.* Grand Rapids: Eerdmans, 1983.

Creach, J. F. D. *Yahweh as Refuge and the Editing of the Hebrew Psalter.* JSOTSup 217. Sheffield: JSOT Press, 1996.

Crenshaw, J. L. *The Psalms: An Introduction.* Grand Rapids: Eerdmans, 2001.

Cross, F. M., Jr., and D. N. Freedman. "A Royal Song of Thanksgiving: II Samuel 22 = Psalm 18." *JBL* 72 (1953): 15-34.

Cullmann, O. *Christology of the New Testament.* Trans. S. C. Guthrie and C. A. M. Hall. Rev. ed. Philadelphia: Westminster, 1963.

Dahood, M. *Psalms.* Anchor Bible. 3 vols. Garden City, NY: Doubleday, 1966-70.

Das, P. *Paul, the Law, and the Covenant.* Peabody, MA: Hendrickson, 2001.

Davidson, R. *The Courage to Doubt.* London: SCM, 1983.

Davidson, R. *The Vitality of Worship: A Commentary on the Book of Psalms.* Grand Rapids: Eerdmans, 1998.

Davidson, R. *Wisdom and Worship.* Philadelphia: Trinity Press International, 1990.

Davis, D. R. *2 Samuel, Out of Every Adversary.* Focus on the Bible. Fearn: Christian Focus Publications.

de Vaux, R. *Ancient Israel: Its Life and Institutions.* 2 vols. Repr. New York: McGraw-Hill, 1965.

Dodd, C. H. *According to the Scriptures: The Substructure of New Testament Theology.* London: Collins, 1952.

Dooyeweerd, H. *A New Critique of Theoretical Thought.* Trans. D. H. Freeman and W. S. Young. 4 vols. in 2. Philadelphia: Presbyterian & Reformed, 1953-58.

Drane, J. *What Is the New Age Saying to the Church?* London: Marshall Pickering, 1991.

Dumbrell, W. J. *The Faith of Israel: Its Expression in the Books of the Old Testament.* Leicester: InterVarsity Press, 1989.

Dunn, J. D. G. *Jesus, Paul, and the Law: Studies in Mark and Galatians.* Louisville: Westminster John Knox, 1990.

Eaton, J. H. *Kingship and the Psalms.* 2nd ed. Sheffield: JSOT Press, 1986.

Eaton, J. H. *Psalms of the Way and the Kingdom: A Conference with the Commentators.* JSOTSup 199. Sheffield: JSOT Press, 1995.

Edwards, J. *A Treatise concerning the Religious Affections.* London: Andrew Melrose, 1998.

Eichrodt, W. *Theology of the Old Testament.* Trans. J. A. Baker. 2 vols. OTL. Philadelphia: Westminster, 1961-1967.

Fernando, A. *I Believe in the Supremacy of Christ.* London: Hodder & Stoughton, 1997.

Fisch, H. *Poetry with a Purpose: Biblical Poetics and Interpretation.* Bloomington: Indiana University Press, 1988.

Fokkelman, J. P. *Reading Biblical Poetry: An Introductory Guide.* Trans. I. Smit. Louisville: Westminster John Knox, 2001.

Fowl, S. E. "The Role of Authorial Intention in the Theological Interpretation of Scripture." Pages 71-87 in *Between Two Horizons: Spanning New Testament Studies and Systematic Theology.* Ed. J. B. Green and M. Turner. Grand Rapids: Eerdmans, 2000.

Freedman, D. N., J. C. Geoghegan, and A. Welch. *Psalm 119: The Exaltation of Torah.* Biblical and Judaic Studies 6. Winona Lake, IN: Eisenbrauns, 1999.

Gärtner, B. *The Areopagus Speech and Natural Revelation.* Trans. C. H. King. Acta seminarii neotestamentici upsaliensis 21. Uppsala: Gleerup, 1955.

Gerstenberger, E. S. *Psalms, Part 1, with an Introduction to Cultic Poetry.* FOTL 14. Grand Rapids: Eerdmans, 1988.

Gerstenberger, E. S. *Psalms, Part 2, and Lamentations.* FOTL 14. Grand Rapids: Eerdmans, 1988.

Gillingham, S. E. "The Messiah in the Psalms: A Question of Reception History and the Psalter." Pages 209-37 in *King and Messiah in Israel and the Ancient Near East: Proceedings of the Oxford Old Testament Seminar.* Ed. J. Day. JSOTSup 270. Sheffield: Sheffield Academic Press, 1998.

Gillingham, S. E. *Poems and Psalms of the Hebrew Bible.* Oxford: Oxford University Press, 1994.

Goldingay, J. "Biblical Narrative and Systematic Theology." Pages 123-42 in *Between Two Horizons: Spanning New Testament Studies and Systematic Theology.* Ed. J. B. Green and M. Turner. Grand Rapids: Eerdmans, 2000.

Goldingay, J. *Praying the Psalms.* Nottingham: Grove Books, 1993.

Goldingay, J. *Songs from a Strange Land: Psalms 42–51.* Downers Grove, IL: InterVarsity Press, 1978.

Goldingay, J. *Theological Diversity and the Authority of the Old Testament.* Grand Rapids: Eerdmans, 1987.

Goldsworthy, G. *According to Plan.* Leicester: InterVarsity Press, 1991.

Goldsworthy, G. *Gospel and Kingdom.* Exeter: Paternoster, 1984.

Gordon, R. P. *1 and 2 Samuel: A Commentary.* Grand Rapids: Zondervan, 1986.

Gottwald, N. *The Tribes of Yahweh.* Maryknoll, NY: Orbis, 1979.

Goulder, M. D. *The Prayers of David (Psalms 51–72).* JSOTSup 102. Sheffield: JSOT Press, 1990.

Goulder, M. D. *Psalms of Asaph and the Pentateuch.* JSOTSup 233. Sheffield: JSOT Press, 1996.

Goulder, M. D. *The Psalms of the Return (Book V, Psalms 107–150).* JSOTSup 258. Sheffield: JSOT Press, 1998.

Goulder, M. D. *The Psalms of the Sons of Korah.* JSOTSup 20. Sheffield: JSOT Press, 1982.

Gowan, D. E. *Theology of the Prophetic Books: The Death and Resurrection of Israel.* Louisville: Westminster John Knox, 1998.

Grant, J. "Psalms 73 and 89: The Crisis of Faith!" Pages 35-58 in *Praying by the Book: Reading the Psalms.* Ed. C. Bartholomew and A. West. Carlisle: Paternoster, 2001.

Green, J. B. "Scripture and Theology: Uniting the Two So Long Divided." Pages 23-43 in *Between Two Horizons: Spanning New Testament Studies and Systematic Theology.* Ed. J. B. Green and M. Turner. Grand Rapids: Eerdmans, 2000.

Greidanus, S. *Preaching Christ from the Old Testament: A Contemporary Hermeneutical Method.* Grand Rapids: Eerdmans, 1999.

Grenz, S. J., and R. E. Olson. *Twentieth-Century Theology: God and the World in a Transitional Age.* Downers Grove, IL: InterVarsity Press, 1992.

Grenz, S. J., and R. E. Olson. *Who Needs Theology? An Invitation to the Study of God.* Leicester: InterVarsity Press, 1996.

Grogan, G. W. "Is the Bible Hermeneutically Self-sufficient?" Pages 205-21 in *Interpreting the Bible: Historical and Theological Studies in Honour of David F. Wright.* Ed. A. N. S. Lane. Leicester: InterVarsity Press, 1997.

Grogan, G. W. "The Old Testament Concept of Solidarity in Hebrews." *TB* 49/1 (1998): 159-73.

Grogan, G. W. *Prayer, Praise and Prophecy: A Theology of the Book of Psalms.* Fearn: Christian Focus Publications, 2001.

Grogan, G. W. "The Relationship between Prophecy and Typology." *SBET* 4/1 (1986): 5-16.

Gunkel, H. *The Psalms: A Form-Critical Introduction.* Trans. M. Horner. Philadelphia: Fortress, 1967.

Gunn, G. S. *God in the Psalms.* Edinburgh: Saint Andrew Press, 1956.

Gushee, D. P., ed. *Towards a Just and Caring Society: Christian Responses to Caring in America.* Grand Rapids: Baker Academic, 1995.

Haglund, E. *Historical Motifs in the Psalms.* Coniectanea biblica: OT 23. Uppsala: Gleerup, 1984.

Hamilton, K. "Liberation Theology: An Overview." Pages 1-9 in *Evangelicals and Liberation.* Ed. C. E. Armerding. Phillipsburg, NJ: Presbyterian & Reformed, 1979.

Harman, A. *Commentary on the Psalms.* Mentor Commentary. Fearn: Christian Focus Publications, 1998.

Harris, M. J. "The Translation of Elohim in Psalm 45:7-8." *TB* 35 (1984): 65-89.

Hauge, M. R. *Between Sheol and Temple: Motif Structure and Function in the I-Psalms.* JSOTSup 178. Sheffield: Sheffield Academic Press, 1995.

Hayes, J. H. *Understanding the Psalms.* Valley Forge, PA: Judson, 1976.

Heim, K. M. "The (God-)Forsaken King of Psalm 89: A Historical and Intertextual Enquiry." Pages 296-322 in *King and Messiah in Israel and the Ancient Near East: Proceedings of the Oxford Old Testament Seminar.* Ed. J. Day. Sheffield: Sheffield Academic Press, 1998.

Hiebert, R. J. V., C. E. Cox, and P. J. Gentry, eds. *The Old Greek Psalter: Studies in Honour of Albert Pietersma.* JSOTSup 332. Sheffield: Sheffield Academic Press, 2001.

Hodge, C. *Systematic Theology.* London: Nelson, 1871.

Holladay, W. L. *The Psalms through Three Thousand Years.* Minneapolis: Fortress, 1993.

Holmes, A. *All Truth Is God's Truth.* Grand Rapids: Eerdmans, 1977.

Honeysett, M. *Meltdown: Making Sense of a Culture in Crisis.* Leicester: InterVarsity Press, 2002.

House, P. R. *Old Testament Theology.* Downers Grove, IL: InterVarsity Press, 1998.

Houston, W. "David, Asaph and the Mighty Works of God: Theme and Genre in the Psalm Collections." *JSOT* 68 (1995): 93-111.

Hurtado, L. W. *Lord Jesus Christ: Devotion to Jesus in Earliest Christianity.* Grand Rapids: Eerdmans, 2003.

James, S. *God's Design for Women.* Darlington: Evangelical Press, 2002.

Janzen, J. G. "The Root *škl* and the Soul Bereaved in Psalm 35." *JSOT* 65 (1995): 55-69.

Jenkins, P. *The Next Christendom: The Coming of Global Christianity.* Oxford: Oxford University Press, 2002.

Jinkins, M. *In the House of the Lord: Inhabiting the Psalms of Lament.* Collegeville, MN: Liturgical Press, 1998.

Johnson, A. R. *The Cultic Prophet and Israel's Psalmody.* Cardiff: University of Wales Press, 1979.

Johnston, P. S. "Hell." Pages 542-44 in *New Dictionary of Biblical Theology*. Ed. T. D. Alexander and B. S. Rosner. Downers Grove, IL: InterVarsity Press, 2000.

Johnston, P. S. *Shades of Sheol: Death and Afterlife in the Old Testament*. Leicester: Apollos, 2002.

Kaiser, W. C., Jr. *Toward an Old Testament Theology*. Grand Rapids: Zondervan, 1978.

Kidner, D. *Psalms 1–72: Introduction and Commentary on Books I and II of the Psalms*. Tyndale OT Commentary. London: InterVarsity Press, 1973.

Kidner, D. *Psalms 73–150: A Commentary on Books III-V of the Psalms*. Tyndale OT Commentary. London: InterVarsity Press, 1975.

Kim, S. *Paul and the New Perspective: Second Thoughts on the Origin of Paul's Gospel*. Grand Rapids: Eerdmans, 2002.

Kissane, E. J. *The Book of Psalms*. 2 vols. Dublin: Browne & Nolan, 1953-54.

Kistemaker, S. *The Psalm Citations in the Epistle to the Hebrews*. Amsterdam: Soest, 1961.

Kitchen, K. A. *Ancient Orient and Old Testament*. London: Tyndale, 1966.

Knapp, S., and W. B. Michaels. "Against Theory." Pages 11-30 in *Against Theory: Literary Studies and the New Pragmatism*. Ed. W. J. T. Mitchell. Chicago: University of Chicago Press, 1985.

Knapp, S., and W. B. Michaels. "Against Theory 2: Hermeneutics and Deconstruction." *Critical Inquiry* 14 (1987-88): 49-68.

Kraus, H.-J. *Psalms 1–59*. Trans. H. C. Oswald. Continental Commentary. Minneapolis: Fortress, 1988.

Kraus, H.-J. *Psalms 60–150*. Trans. H. C. Oswald. Continental Commentary. Minneapolis: Fortress, 1989.

Kraus, H.-J. *Theology of the Psalms*. Trans. K. Crim. Continental Commentary. Minneapolis: Augsburg, 1986.

Kugel, J. L. *The Idea of Biblical Poetry: Parallelism and Its History*. New Haven: Yale University Press, 1981.

Kuhn, T. *The Structure of Scientific Revolutions*. 2nd ed. Chicago: University of Chicago Press, 1970.

Lane, A. N. S. "Sola Scriptura? Making Sense of a Post-Reformation Slogan." Pages 297-327 in *A Pathway into the Holy Scripture*. Ed. P. E. Satterthwaite and D. F. Wright. Grand Rapids: Eerdmans, 1994.

Lewis, C. S. *George MacDonald: An Anthology*. London: Geoffrey Bles, 1946.

Lewis, C. S. *Reflections on the Psalms*. London: Geoffrey Bles, 1958.

Lewis, C. S. *The Screwtape Letters*. London: Geoffrey Bles, 1942.

Longenecker, R. N. *Biblical Exegesis in the Apostolic Period*. Grand Rapids: Eerdmans, 1975.

Longman, T., III. *How to Read the Psalms*. Downers Grove, IL: InterVarsity Press, 1988.

Longman, T., III. "Psalm 98." *JETS* 27 (1984): 267-74.

Macleod, D. "The New Perspective: Paul, Luther and Judaism." *SBET* 22/1 (2004): 4-31.

Magonet, J. *A Rabbi Reads the Psalms*. London: SCM, 1994.

Marx, K., and F. Engels. *The Communist Manifesto*. Repr. Moscow: Progress Publishers, 1975.

Mays, J. L. *The Lord Reigns: A Theological Handbook to the Psalms*. Louisville: Westminster John Knox, 1994.

Mays, J. L. "The Place of the Torah-Psalms in the Psalter." *JBL* 106 (1987): 3-12.

Mays, J. L. *Psalms.* Interpretation: A Bible Commentary for Teaching and Preaching. Louisville: John Knox, 1994.

McCann, J. C., Jr. "The Book of Psalms: Introduction, Commentary, and Reflections." Pages 639-1280 in vol. 4 of *New Interpreter's Bible.* Ed. L. E. Keck. Nashville: Abingdon, 1996.

McCann, J. C., Jr. "The Psalms as Instruction." *Int* 46 (1992): 117-28.

McCann, J. C., Jr., ed. *The Shape and Shaping of the Psalter.* JSOTSup 159. Sheffield: JSOT Press, 1993.

McCann, J. C., Jr. *A Theological Introduction to the Book of Psalms: The Psalms as Torah.* Nashville: Abingdon, 1993.

McConville, J. G. "Jerusalem in the Old Testament." Pages 21-51 in *Jerusalem Past and Present in the Purposes of God.* Ed. P. W. L. Walker. Cambridge: Tyndale House, 1992.

McConville, J. G. "Who May Ascend the Hill of the LORD? The Picture of the Faithful in Psalms 15–24." Pages 35-58 in *Praying by the Book: Reading the Psalms.* Ed. C. Bartholomew and A. West. Carlisle: Paternoster, 2001.

Millar, J. G. "Land." Pages 623-27 in *New Dictionary of Biblical Theology.* Ed. T. D. Alexander and B. S. Rosner. Downers Grove, IL: InterVarsity Press, 2000.

Miller, P. D. *Interpreting the Psalms.* Philadelphia: Fortress, 1986.

Mitchell, C. W. *The Meaning of BRK 'To Bless' in the Old Testament.* SBLDS 95. Atlanta: Scholars Press, 1987.

Mitchell, D. C. *The Message of the Psalter: An Eschatological Programme in the Book of Psalms.* JSOTSup 252. Sheffield: JSOT Press, 1997.

Moltmann, J. *God in Creation: A New Theology of Creation and the Spirit of God.* San Francisco: Harper & Row, 1985.

Moltmann, J. "The Right to Meaningful Work." Pages 37-58 in *On Human Dignity: Political Theology and Ethics.* Trans. M. D. Meeks. Philadelphia: Fortress, 1984.

Motyer, J. A. "The Psalms." Pages 485-583 in *New Bible Commentary: 21st Century Edition.* Ed. D. A. Carson, R. T. France, J. A. Motyer, and G. J. Wenham. Downers Grove, IL: InterVarsity Press, 1994.

Motyer, S. "Two Testaments, One Biblical Theology." Pages 143-64 in *Between Two Horizons: Spanning New Testament Studies and Systematic Theology.* Ed. J. B. Green and M. Turner. Grand Rapids: Eerdmans, 2000.

Mowinckel, S. *The Psalms in Israel's Worship.* Trans. D. R. Ap-Thomas. 2 vols. Oxford: Oxford University Press, 1962.

Muilenburg, J. "Form Criticism and Beyond." *JBL* 88 (1969): 1-18.

Mulder, J. S. M. *Studies on Psalm 45.* Oss: Witsiers, 1972.

Murphy, R. E. *The Psalms Are Yours.* New York: Paulist Press, 1993.

Nasuti, H. P. *Defining the Sacred Songs: Genre, Tradition and the Post-Critical Interpretation of the Psalms.* JSOTSup 218. Sheffield: JSOT Press, 1999.

Newbigin, L. *The Gospel in a Pluralist Society.* Grand Rapids: Eerdmans, 1989.

Newbigin, L. "Truth and Authority in Modernity." Pages 60-88 in *Faith and Modernity.* Ed. S. Sugden, P. Sampson, and V. Samuel. Oxford: Regnum Books, 1994.

Nicholls, B. J., and B. R. Wood, eds. *Sharing the Good News with the Poor: A Reader for Concerned Christians.* Grand Rapids: Baker, 1996.

O'Donovan, O. *Begotten or Made?* Oxford: Oxford University Press, 1984.

O'Donovan, O. *The Desire of the Nations: Rediscovering the Roots of the Political Theology.* Cambridge: Cambridge University Press, 1996.

Olson, D. *Deuteronomy and the Death of Moses: A Theological Reading.* Overtures to Biblical Theology. Minneapolis: Fortress, 1994.

Osborn, L. *Guardians of Creation: Nature in Theology and the Christian Life.* Leicester: Apollos, 1993.

Pao, D. W. *Thanksgiving: An Investigation of a Pauline Theme.* Downers Grove, IL: Apollos, 2002.

Pickard, S. "'Unable to see the Wood for the Trees': John Locke and the Fate of Systematic Theology." Pages 105-37 in *The Task of Theology Today: Doctrines and Dogmas.* Ed. V. C. Pfitzner and H. Regan. Grand Rapids: Eerdmans, 1999.

Pinnock, C. *Most Moved Mover: A Theology of God's Openness.* Grand Rapids: Baker Academic, 2001.

Pinnock, C., R. Rice, J. Sanders, W. Hasker, and D. Basinger. *The Openness of God: A Biblical Challenge to the Traditional Understanding of God.* Downers Grove, IL: InterVarsity Press, 1994.

Polanyi, M. *Personal Knowledge: Towards a Post-Critical Philosophy.* Chicago: University of Chicago Press, 1974.

Polkinghorne, J. *Science and Christian Belief: Theological Reflections of a Bottom-up Thinker: The Gifford Lectures for 1994.* London: SPCK, 1994.

Pritchard, J. B., ed. *Ancient Near Eastern Texts Relating to the Old Testament.* 3rd ed. Princeton: Princeton University Press, 1969.

Rendsburg, G. A. *Linguistic Evidence for the Northern Origin of Selected Psalms.* Society of Biblical Literature Monograph Series 43. Atlanta: Scholars Press, 1990.

Rice, R. "Biblical Support for a New Perspective." Pages 11-58 in C. Pinnock et al., *The Openness of God: A Biblical Challenge to the Traditional Understanding of God.* Downers Grove, IL: InterVarsity Press, 1994.

Ricoeur, P. *Freud and Philosophy: An Essay in Interpretation.* New Haven: Yale University Press, 1970.

Ringgren, H. *The Faith of the Psalmists.* Philadelphia: Fortress, 1963.

Rookmaaker, H. R. *Modern Art and the Death of a Culture.* London: InterVarsity Press, 1970.

Sailhamer, J. H. "Genesis." Pages 1-284 in vol. 2 of *Expositor's Bible Commentary.* Ed. F. E. Gaebelein. Grand Rapids: Zondervan, 1990.

St. Athanasius on the Incarnation: The Treatise De Incarnatione Verbi Dei. Trans. and ed. by a Religious of C.S.M.V. London: A. R. Mowbray, 1953.

Sampson, P., V. Samuel, and C. Sugden, eds. *Faith and Modernity.* Oxford: Regnum Books, 1994.

Sanders, E. P. *Paul and Palestinian Judaism: A Comparison of Patterns of Religion.* Philadelphia: Fortress, 1977.

Sanders, E. P. *Paul, the Law, and the Jewish People.* Philadelphia: Fortress, 1983.

Sanders, J. A. *The Dead Sea Psalms Scroll.* Ithaca, NY: Cornell University Press, 1967.

Sargent, T. *Animal Rights and Wrongs: A Biblical Perspective.* Sevenoaks: Hodder & Stoughton, 1996.

Sarna, N. M. *On the Book of Psalms: Exploring the Prayers of Ancient Israel.* New York: Schocken, 1993.

Satterthwaite, P. E., R. S. Hess, and G. J. Wenham, eds. *The Lord's Anointed: Interpretation of Old Testament Messianic Texts.* Grand Rapids: Baker Academic, 1995.

Satterthwaite, P. E., and D. F. Wright, eds. *A Pathway into the Holy Scripture.* Grand Rapids: Eerdmans, 1994.

Schaefer, K. *Psalms.* Berit Olam: Studies in Hebrew Narrative and Poetry. Collegeville, MN: Liturgical Press, 2001.

Schleiermacher, F. *The Christian Faith.* ET ed. H. R. Mackintosh. Edinburgh: T&T Clark, 1928.

Seitz, C. R. *Word without End: The Old Testament as Abiding Theological Witness.* Grand Rapids: Eerdmans, 1998.

Seybold, K. *Introducing the Psalms.* Edinburgh: T&T Clark, 1990.

Sheppard, G. "Theology and the Book of Psalms." *Int* 46 (1992): 143-55.

Sheriffs, D. *The Friendship of the Lord: An Old Testament Spirituality.* Carlisle: Paternoster, 1996.

Sider, R. J. *Rich Christians in an Age of Hunger: A Biblical Study.* Downers Grove, IL: InterVarsity Press, 1977.

Smith, D. W. *Against the Stream: Christianity and Mission in an Age of Globalization.* Leicester: InterVarsity Press, 2003.

Smith, D. W. *Mission after Christendom.* London: Darton, Longman and Todd, 2003.

Smith, G. A. *Historical Geography of the Holy Land.* 25th ed. London: Hodder & Stoughton, 1931.

Smith, M. S. *The Early History of God: Yahweh and Other Deities of Ancient Israel.* 2nd ed. Grand Rapids: Eerdmans, 2002.

Smith, M. S. "The Psalms as a Book for Pilgrims." *Int* 46 (1992): 156-66.

Smith, R. *Old Testament Theology: Its History, Method, and Message.* Nashville: Broadman & Holman, 1993.

Snyder, H. *Liberating the Church: The Ecology of Church and Kingdom.* London: Marshall Pickering, 1983.

Soll, W. *Psalm 119: Matrix, Form, and Setting.* Catholic Biblical Quarterly Monograph Series 23. Washington, D.C.: Catholic Biblical Association of America, 1991.

Spurgeon, C. H. *The Treasury of David.* 7 vols. New York: Funk, 1892-96.

Storkey, A. "Postmodernism Is Consumption." Pages 100-117 in *Christ and Consumerism: A Critical Analysis of the Spirit of the Age.* Ed. C. Bartholomew and T. Moritz. Carlisle: Paternoster, 2000.

Stott, J. R. W. *The Cross of Christ.* Leicester: InterVarsity Press, 1986.

Sylva, D. *Psalms and the Transformation of Stress: Poetic-Communal Interpretation and the Family.* Louvain: Peeters, 1996.

Tanner, B. L. *The Book of Psalms through the Lens of Intertextuality.* Studies in Biblical Literature 26. New York: Peter Lang, 2001.

Tate, M. E. *Psalms 51–100.* WBC 20. Dallas: Word, 1990.

Taylor, J. V. *The Christlike God.* London: SCM, 1990.

Taylor, V. *The Atonement in New Testament Teaching.* London: Epworth, 1940.

Temple, W. *Nature, Man and God.* London: Macmillan, 1934.

Terrien, S. *The Elusive Presence: Toward a New Biblical Theology.* New York: Harper & Row, 1978.

Thiselton, A. *New Horizons in Hermeneutics: The Theory and Practice of Transforming Biblical Reading.* Grand Rapids: Zondervan, 1992.

Thiselton, A. *The Two Horizons: New Testament Hermeneutics and Philosophical Description.* Grand Rapids: Eerdmans, 1980.

Thomas, R. L. *How to Choose a Bible Version: Making Sense of the Proliferation of Bible Translations.* Fearn: Christian Focus, 2000.

Tidball, D. *The Message of the Cross.* Leicester: InterVarsity Press, 2001.

Tournay, R. J. *Seeing and Hearing God with the Psalms: A Prophetic Liturgy of the Second Temple in Jerusalem.* Trans. J. E. Crowley. JSOTSup 118. Sheffield: JSOT Press, 1991.

Trevelyan, G. M. *English Social History.* London: Reprint Society, 1948.

Turner, M. "Scripture and Theology." Pages 23-43 in *Between Two Horizons: Spanning New Testament Studies and Systematic Theology.* Ed. J. B. Green and M. Turner. Grand Rapids: Eerdmans, 2000.

VanGemeren, W. A. "Psalms." Pages 1-880 in vol. 5 of *Expositor's Bible Commentary.* Ed. F. E. Gaebelein. Grand Rapids: Zondervan, 1991.

Vanhoozer, K. J. "Exegesis and Hermeneutics." Pages 52-64 in *New Dictionary of Biblical Theology.* Ed. T. D. Alexander and B. S. Rosner. Downers Grove, IL: InterVarsity Press, 2000.

Vanhoozer, K. J. *Is There a Meaning in This Text? The Bible, the Reader, and the Morality of Literary Knowledge.* Grand Rapids: Zondervan, 1998.

Van Til, C. *The Intellectual Challenge of the Gospel.* London: Tyndale, 1950.

Volf, M. *After Our Likeness: The Church as the Image of the Trinity.* Grand Rapids: Eerdmans, 1998.

Volf, M. *The Work of the Spirit: Toward a Theology of Work.* Eugene: Wipf and Stock, 2001.

Von Rad, G. *Old Testament Theology.* Trans. D. M. G. Stalker. 2 vols. New York: Harper & Row, 1962-1965.

Walker, W. L., ed. *Jerusalem Past and Present in the Purposes of God.* Cambridge: Tyndale House, 1992.

Ware, B. A. *God's Lesser Glory: A Critique of Open Theism.* Leicester: Apollos, 2000.

Watson, F. *Text, Church and World: Biblical Interpretation in Theological Perspective.* Edinburgh: T&T Clark, 1994.

Watts, J. W. *Psalm and Story: Inset Hymns in Hebrew Narrative.* JSOTSup 139. Sheffield: JSOT Press, 1992.

Weiser, A. *The Psalms: A Commentary.* Trans. H. Hartwell. OTL. Philadelphia: Westminster, 1962.

Wells, D. F. "Modernity and Theology: The Doctrine of God." Pages 116-35 in *Faith and Modernity.* Ed. P. Sampson, V. Samuel, and C. Sugden. Oxford: Regnum Books, 1994.

Wells, D. F. *No Place for Truth; or, Whatever Happened to Evangelical Theology?* Grand Rapids: Eerdmans, 1993.

Wenham, G. J. *Genesis 1–15.* WBC 1. Waco: Word, 1987.

Westermann, C. *The Living Psalms.* Trans. J. R. Porter. Grand Rapids: Eerdmans, 1989.

Westermann, C. *Praise and Lament in the Psalms.* Trans. K. R. Crim and R. N. Soulen. 2nd ed. Atlanta: John Knox, 1981.

Whybray, R. N. *Reading the Psalms as a Book.* JSOTSup 222. Sheffield: JSOT Press, 1996.

Widmer, M. Review of *God in the Dock: Dialogic Tension in the Psalms of Lament,* by C. Mandolfo. *Themelios* 29/2 (2004): 57-58.

Wilcock, M. *The Message of Psalms 1–72: Songs for the People of God.* Bible Speaks Today. Leicester: InterVarsity Press, 2001.

Wilcock, M. *The Message of Psalms 73–150: Songs for the People of God.* Bible Speaks Today. Leicester: InterVarsity Press, 2001.

Wilkins, M. J., and T. Paige, eds. *Worship, Theology and Ministry in the Early Church: Essays in Honour of Ralph P. Martin.* Journal for the Study of the New Testament Supplement 87. Sheffield: JSOT Press, 1992.

Williams, S. "More on Open Theism." *SBET* 22/1 (2004): 32-50.

Williams, T. F. "Towards a Date for the Old Greek Psalter." Pages 248-76 in *The Old Greek Psalter: Studies in Honour of Albert Pietersma.* Ed. R. J. V. Hiebert, C. E. Cox, and P. J. Gentry. JSOTSup 332. Sheffield: Sheffield Academic Press, 2001.

Wilson, G. H. *The Editing of the Hebrew Psalter.* SBLDS 76. Chico, CA: Scholars Press, 1985.

Wilson, G. H. "Evidence of Editorial Divisions in the Hebrew Psalter." *VT* 34 (1984): 337-52.

Wilson, G. H. *The NIV Application Commentary: Psalms Volume 1.* Grand Rapids: Zondervan, 2002.

Wilson, G. H. "The Shape of the Book of Psalms." *Int* 46 (1992): 129-42.

Wilson, G. H. "The Use of Royal Psalms at the 'Seams' of the Hebrew Psalter." *JSOT* 35 (1986): 85-94.

Wright, N. T. "The Letter to the Galatians: Exegesis and Theology." Pages 205-36 in *Between Two Horizons: Spanning New Testament Studies and Systematic Theology.* Ed. J. B. Green and M. Turner. Grand Rapids: Eerdmans, 2000.

Wright, N. T. *New Tasks for a Renewed Church.* London: Hodder & Stoughton, 1992.

Wright, N. T. *What Saint Paul Really Said: Was Paul of Tarsus the Real Founder of Christianity?* Grand Rapids: Eerdmans, 1997.

Zenger, E. "The Composition and Theology of the Fifth Book of Psalms: Psalms 107–145." *JSOT* 80 (1998): 77-102.

Zenger, E. *A God of Vengeance? Understanding the Psalms of Divine Wrath.* Trans. L. M. Maloney. Louisville: Westminster John Knox, 1996.

Index of Names

Index of Subjects

Abortion, 379

Acrostics, 19, 29, 30, 265, 297; in the exegesis, 54, 77, 86, 87, 91, 185, 187, 195, 223

Adonai, 53, 184, 244

Aesthetics of the psalms, 4-6, 365, 376

Analogy, 245, 389-90

Anthropocentrism, 361-62

Arts, 375-76

Asaph psalms, 22, 244, 283, 285, 320, 352; in exegesis, 135, 142, 143, 145, 147, 148

Atheism, 59-60, 109-10, 115, 246, 374-75

Baal, 81, 125, 200, 241, 245, 289, 365, 408

Biblical theology (contributions of the psalms to), 295-359; divine consistency, 310-12; doctrine of historical revelation, 308-19; doctrine of messianism, 348-59; doctrine of prayer and worship, 341-48; doctrine of sin, 326-35; encouragement for God's people in the future, 316-17; the psalmists' questions, 312-16; a realistic doctrine of suffering, 335-41, 403; a sense of community, 319-26; a warm doctrine of God, 301-8; wisdom linked with law, 317-18; wisdom/wisdom theme, 297-98, 317-18. *See also* New Testament theology (contributions of the psalms to)

Black theology, 393

Blessing: and the covenant relationship, 283-85; the word in psalms, 305; and worship, 272-73

Buddhism, 362, 366, 389, 400

Canonical criticism, 19, 21-28, 30

Charismatic movement, 400

Chiasm, 29, 49, 51, 77, 123, 161, 432

Children, 312, 370, 380, 382, 410

Christian life: facing the realities of life with God, 404-6; faith focused on Christ, 403; and the life of faith, 398-400, 403; personal prayer and the psalms, 403-4

Christ's person/work, 387-96; analogy and witnessing to, 389-90; as God's great redeemer, 392-93; as the ideal human being, 390; ideal shown in roles he fulfills, 391-92; NT questions about Jesus, 313, 315-16; the psalms as the prayers/praises of, 394-96; securing full assurance for believers, 393-94; sufferings of Jesus, 337-38, 339-40, 403; typological and predictive witnessing to (supernatural dimension), 387-89

Church, Christian, 406-17; bearing witness to God, 413-14; modern songs based on psalms, 408; moral/social concerns as complementary, 416-17; points of discontinuity/continuity with Israel, 407; prayer concerns both local

Hinduism, 366, 400

Historical criticism, 6-8, 32

Historical (didactic) psalms, 2, 17-18, 252, 261, 327, 376-277, 414; and the exile, 276-77; and the exodus, 252; and God's moral character, 277; and Israel's bad witness, 414; rebellion in/sin in, 261, 327

History and the psalms, 2; doctrine of historical revelation, 308-19; God's historical purpose, 372; historical (didactic) psalms, 2, 17-18, 252, 261, 327, 376-277, 414; and religious convictions of the psalmists, 234-35

Holiness movement, 400

Holy Spirit, 400-403

Humanity and sin, 376-87; the Davidic psalms and humanity from the divine perspective, 386-87; godly counseling and the word of God, 379-81; God's concern with the whole human race, 381-83; human life as serving the purposes of God, 376-77; issues of abortion and euthanasia, 379; penitence and forgiveness, 386; recognizing the sin factor in human society, 383-86; responsible stewardship, 377-79

Ideals, human, 390

Idolatry, 240, 366-68

Immanentism, 363-65

Imprecatory psalms: prayers against the psalmists' enemies, 256-58, 327; and public worship, 412-13

Inclusio, 18, 29, 255, 264, 331-32; in the exegesis, 52, 76, 92, 172, 191, 205, 224

Intertextuality, 31, 382

Jerusalem: and community concept, 321-25; establishment of king and temple at, 268-69; name of, 321; Yahweh as the God of, 268-73

Joy: and heartfelt worship, 272-73; and Jerusalem, 322; and *tôrâ*, 266

Justification, 399, 400

Kingship of God. *See* Royal psalms

Korahite psalms, 22, 153, 320, 325

Koran, 237

Lament psalms, 11, 13, 14-15, 272; and Christ, 394-96; and divine consistency, 311-12; and the exodus deliverance, 256; and God's love, 280; and marginalized people, 412; religious convictions of the writers, 233-34; and worship, 14, 272, 411-12

Last Things. *See* Eschatology, Christian

Leadership and government, 385, 391

Levitical psalms, 9, 270, 352

Liberation theology, 364, 392-93

Literary criticism, 29-31

Love. *See* God's love

Marduk, 12, 136, 245, 277

Masoretic Text (MT), 3, 4, 223, 268; superscriptions, 8

Materialism, 367-68

Messianism: and Davidic monarchy, 25, 292-93, 352-54; David's last words, 351; and NT use of the Psalter, 349-50, 355-59, 429-30; and the promise of God in 2 Samuel 7, 354-55; and the prophets, 355; as the Psalter's contribution to biblical theology, 292-93, 348-59

Moral purpose of God, 372, 373

Mosaic Psalter, 253

Mythological language of psalms, 240-42

National Socialism (Germany), 390, 396, 397

Natural theology, 68, 363, 366, 424

Neo-paganism, 366-67

Neoplatonism, 366

New Age movement, 366

New Testament: Christ's person/work, 387-96; and the Davidic covenant, 287; historical and religious truths, 234-35; references to traditional authors of OT books, 35-36, 37; sermon preparation/considering a psalm in the context of, 434-35

New Testament theology (contributions of the psalms to), 296, 300-301, 306, 387-96; Christ's person and work, 387-96; the convictions of the psalmists fulfilled in, 318-19; divine consistency, 311; doctrine of messianism, 349-50, 355-59, 429-30; doctrine of sin, 328, 329-31, 333, 334; doctrine of suffering, 336, 337-38, 339-40, 403; faithfulness of God, 307-8; a heartfelt and expanding sense of community, 320-21, 323-24, 326; the Psalter as part of a literary corpus, 428; questions about Jesus, 313, 315-16; and religious convictions of the psalmists, 235-36; responsive doctrine of prayer and worship, 342, 343, 344-45, 346, 347; warm doctrine of God, 306

North Canaanite Ugaritic society, 241

Old Testament. *See* Biblical theology (contributions of the psalms to)

Open theism, 371-72, 374

Orphan psalms, 9, 44, 122, 123, 254, 303, 336, 377

Pantheism, 360, 364, 366, 389, 390

Parallelism, 5-6, 254, 268, 286, 381, 429; in the exegesis, 44, 57, 59-60, 63, 73, 76, 81, 93, 108, 177, 209, 217, 229

Parenthood, 370, 380, 382, 384, 410

Particularism, religious, 382-83

Penitence and forgiveness, 386

Pentecostalism, 400

Pharisaic theology, 397-98

Philosophical theology, 363, 371, 424

Pluralism, religious, 366-68, 399

Poetry of the psalms, 4-6, 245, 429

Poverty, spiritual, 325-26

Praise. *See* Prayer; Worship

Praise psalms, 13, 15-16, 19, 272, 295; and Christ, 394-96; and communal worship/witness, 413-14; declarative/de-

scriptive, 13, 15, 252, 255, 312; and divine consistency, 311-12; and exodus, 252, 255; and God's love, 280; religious convictions of the writers, 233-34

Prayer: Christian life of, 404, 405-6; devotional use of the psalms, 402, 403-4; and divine openness (changing things/not God), 370-74; and God's grace, 398; and God's moral purposes, 373-74; imprecation against the psalmists' enemies, 256-58, 327; local and wide-ranging concerns of, 416; and personal/corporate praise, 347-48; praise and lament presented to God in, 272; praise as "the chief end" of human beings, 348; praise coextensive with the character and deeds of God, 345-46; the psalms as the prayers/praises of Christ, 394-96; the Psalter's contribution of a responsive doctrine of, 341-48; trust and praise, 343-45; and wholehearted (not superficial) praise, 346-47

Present-day theological issues and the Psalter's relevance, 33-34, 359-430; Christian life, 398-400, 403-6; Christ's person and work, 387-96; the Church, 406-17; feminist thinking, 31, 370, 381-82, 393; God and creation, 360-76; God's grace and the covenant, 396-98; the Holy Spirit, 400-403; humanity and sin, 376-87; the Last Things, 417-24; Scripture, 424-30; sermon preparation, 435

Process philosophy, 371

Prophets: and Davidic messianism, 355; and personal God, 302-3; relationship between psalmists and, 7-8, 299; and sacrifice, 325; and sinfulness of society, 332-33

Protestant Reformation, 397, 400

Psalm genres, 10-19

Psalms as Scripture. *See* Scripture (the psalms as)

Psalms of Solomon, 300

Index of Scripture References

460

465